SYSTEMS IN ENGLISH GRAMMAR:

AN INTRODUCTION FOR LANGUAGE TEACHERS

PETER MASTER

SAN JOSE STATE UNIVERSITY

CONTENTS

UNIT I: THE BUILDING BLOCKS OF ENGLISH

UNIT II: THE VERB

UNIT III: THE NOUN

UNIT IV: THE ADVERB

UNIT V: SENTENCE COMBINING

APPENDIXES

DEDICATION

For Amanda

ACKNOWLEDGMENTS

I am deeply grateful to Karl Lisovsky for his countless insightful comments on the logic, continuity, and usefulness of all aspects of the text. I am also indebted to Ondine Gage-Serio, Maggi Discont, and Debbie Davis for their many suggestions for improvement and their careful proofreading of the text. Finally, I would like to thank the students of my Linguistics 146 classes at California State University, Fresno, for their feedback on all phases of the manuscript.

INTRODUCTION

Systems in English Grammar: An Introduction for Language Teachers is a textbook for students and teachers who want or need to understand the basic elements of English grammar. It is primarily designed to provide present and future teachers with a clear understanding of the manner in which the systems in English grammar operate, with step-by-step instructions and plenty of exercises to consolidate what has been learned.

The guiding philosophy of the text is that students, especially the non-native speakers of English who account for a steadily increasing percentage of school populations at all levels, have the right at all times to ask their teachers why certain elements of grammar operate the way they do. When they ask such questions, they are entitled to a clear, unambiguous, and helpful explanation. For example, a student might ask, "Why do you use *do* in some questions and not in others? (e.g., *Where does he live?* vs. *Who lives here?*). Or a student might ask, "Why must I put an "s" on the verb by itself but not when it has *can* in front of it?" (e.g., *John speaks French.* vs. *John can speak French.*) Or a student might ask, "Why do I use *a* with an adjective by itself and *the* when the adjective has *most* in front of it?" (e.g., *Paris is a beautiful city in France.* vs. *Paris is the most beautiful city in France.*).

The focus of this text is grammar at the sentence level. The field is now well aware that grammatical instruction has typically neglected the role of discourse and pragmatics. However, as David Little reminds us, although discoursal and pragmatic dimensions are important in grammar, they do not dislodge sentence grammar from its central position. The goal of the text is thus to show teachers how sentences are built from the ground up, for it is only with knowledge of basic sentence structure that we can describe how sentences are assembled into discourse and how certain sentences may be used formulaically in carrying out pragmatic functions (even though pragmatic structures, e.g., lexical phrases such as *I don't know*, are thought to precede grammatical rules in language acquisition). Such knowledge is also required before teachers can begin to apply techniques for teaching grammar to nonnative speakers.

The role of grammar has undergone considerable rethinking in recent years. We now believe that it is not good teaching practice to base a class on the teaching of grammatical patterns. We want to emphasize communication first, that is, the spontaneous use of the language rather than learning about the language. Thus, there is no reason to introduce a point of grammar simply because it has been listed in the school curriculum. That is not to say that there is no role for grammar in the modern classroom. On the contrary, the need is as great as ever, especially when it comes to developing editing skills. What we have finally realized is that grammar is a tool for expressing meaning and for this reason it can have no use until there is a need for it.

What this means in the classroom is that the teacher, rather than having a preconceived idea of what elements of grammar her students need, watches for evidence of that need in classroom work. The need may become clear from a reading assignment, a composition, an oral presentation, or an argument that arises during a group task. As soon as the need is perceived, the teacher must be ready to provide just the right amount of explanation or practice to aid the student without overwhelming him or her with gratuitous information. This is where the art of teaching comes in, knowing how much is just the right amount. No textbook can tell you this.

The purpose of this text is to explain the central systems that account for the most frequently occurring grammatical structures in the language from a strictly pedagogical point of view. It does not attempt to cover all the elements of grammar, nor is it designed to be an exhaustive reference book that details every exception. Instead, it aims to describe the most common structures in a systematic way without relying on trees or formal transformational rules or other arcane linguistic devices. Every explanation is clearly linked to one or more of the sentence slots, i.e., the four roles that together create an archetypal English sentence: the subject, the verb, the object, and the adverbial.

The text is designed for teachers in general, especially those teaching in the public schools, as well as future teachers of English as a Second or Other Language (ESOL). Its purpose is not to provide engaging methods for the teaching of grammar but rather to provide a fundamental understanding of how grammar works so that a teacher is prepared to apply methods of presentation as well as provide pedagogically sound explanations, both in the classroom as questions spontaneously arise and in giving feedback on student compositions. To this end, the text utilizes a unique error correction process that requires identifying everything that is correct about the error before saying what is wrong. This process acknowledges that learning the details of grammatical structure is hard work and that students need to be encouraged to persist in their acquisition of language proficiency by receiving praise for partial correctness, thus promoting self esteem.

At the same time, it is not the intent of this text to encourage teachers to find and treat every error that a student makes. Knowing when and how much to correct is also part of the art of language teaching. The intent is rather to equip the language teacher with the means to addressing questions as they arise. One consequence of such a study is greater self assurance in one's own writing, for one begins to understand the language as a system and thus not only that "it sounds better" (which is useless advice for all but the native speaker), but why it sounds better. It should also be noted that a teacher's incomplete knowledge of an aspect of this complex system is no crime, but it is a crime to provide an inadequate, confusing, or erroneous explanation. Students respect a teacher who says, "I need to check on that. I'll tell you tomorrow," and then comes the next day with a clear explanation. They will lose respect for a teacher who is obviously guessing at an explanation or one who promises to find an answer and then never mentions it again. Knowing grammar well takes many years of teaching practice, and every question from students provides an opportunity to enlarge one's knowledge of the system.

Peter Master
1996

A Note on the Chapter Graphics

At the beginning of each chapter, there is a graphic display of the four elements of an archetypal English sentence. The gray area highlights the sentence slot that contains the focus of the chapter, while the black area indicates the specific area of focus within that sentence slot. For example, Chapter 2 focuses on the word groups in a sentence. Since such groups occur in every sentence slot, all four blocks are black. In contrast, Chapter 6 focuses on the modal auxiliary verbs. Since they occur in the verb slot, the second block in the graphic is gray. Modal auxiliary verbs always occur at the beginning of the verb slot. Therefore, the first segment of the verb slot is black.

These graphics are only a very general indication of the focus of the chapter. For example, Chapter 14 focuses on prepositions and particles. Since prepositional phrases often occur in the adverbial slot, the fourth block is gray, and since prepositions come at the beginning of the adverbial slot, the first segment of the adverbial slot is black. However, the graphic does not indicate the fact that prepositional phrases also occur as noun modifiers in the subject, object, and adverbial slots. Nor does it indicate the fact that particles belong in the verb slot. The graphics thus show the most common position of the element of grammar that the chapter describes.

TO THE TEACHER

When this text is used in a teacher training course, the following guidelines are suggested regarding the presentation of new topics in class, homework, testing, and the assignment of projects and term papers. Covering all the material in this book requires approximately two semesters.

Presenting New Topics in Class

When a new topic is presented, it should be related to earlier work whenever feasible. The following sequence of presentation is suggested:

1. Introduce the topic.
2. If there is an inductive exercise at the beginning of the chapter, have students do this exercise in pairs, and discuss the answers in class.
3. Present the first aspect of grammatical focus using examples from the book or your own examples, encouraging constant questions from the class.
4. Have students do the associated exercise(s) in class in pairs, looking up the answers themselves in the answer key when they have finished and discussing the results. Facilitate the task by wandering from pair to pair, making yourself available for questions without intruding on the activity unless specifically asked.
5. After the task has been completed, ask for questions from the class regarding the exercise or bring up problems you noticed during the pair work.
6. Present the next point and repeat the procedure, having allowed plenty of time for students to digest the material before moving on.

Homework

To be able to move through the material at a reasonable speed, homework should be assigned after every class. The following procedure is suggested:

1. Ask students to read the explanation in the text covering what has been presented in class, do the related exercises that were not completed in class, and check their answers in the answer key.
2. For topics that you think the class will be able to understand without your guidance, ask students to read the text, do the related exercises, and check their answers.
3. At the next meeting of the class, put students in groups of 4–5, assign a group leader, and ask the leader to go over the exercise by asking each member of the group to explain how the answer was obtained (not just what the answer is!). This step is especially important for the problem-solving task at the end of each section or chapter. Again, facilitate the task by wandering from group to group, making yourself available for questions without intruding on the group activity unless specifically asked.
4. Discuss with the class any problems that arose in the group work.

Testing

If the sequence presented in the text is followed, testing is a fairly easy process. A test every 2–4 weeks is suggested, with earlier tests weighted less than later ones as it takes students some time to get used to the system. The following procedure is suggested:

1. Tell students specifically what sections of the text they will be tested on.
2. Tell students that, with the exception of the first two chapters, all tests will consist of ten problems exactly like those at the end of each section in the book. They will be provided with a list of items that can be correct (e.g., correct time, correct agreement, etc.) for each grammar point. Each problem will consist of a sentence containing a single error, and they

will be expected to follow the same format they used in responding to the problem-solving items:

  a. Bracket the error.

  b. Show what is right about the error and indicate the proof of correctness in parentheses after each item, e.g., correct agreement (*boy is*)

  c. Write the correct sentence below the original erroneous sentence.

  d. Explain what the student needs to know to avoid making the error again.

3. Make up ten sentences that each contain a single error, covering the major aspects of the grammar point(s) you have discussed in class. If the test covers different aspects, it is a good idea to provide a blank before each item in which students are asked first to identify the area of focus (e.g., auxiliary, verb tense, question) to guide the student toward the selection of the appropriate list of items that can be correct. Taking such an exam with 10 items requires about an hour of class time.

4. Assign three points each to 1) a correct listing of what is right in the error, 2) the corrected sentence, and 3) the explanation. Item (1) will require adjustment depending on how many items should be correct, whether all are indicated, or whether items are erroneously deemed correct. For ten items, this amounts to 99 points, which (plus one free point) indicates the percentage correct.

5. Encourage students who do badly on the test to come a talk to you in your office so that you have a chance to see specifically what went wrong. Provide a blank copy of the test and ask them to do it again for the practice and to keep up with the rest of the class. Many subsequent items in the text are dependent on a thorough understanding of earlier material.

Projects and Term Papers

An ideal project for a class such as this is the translation of grammatical explanations into suitable lesson plans. Students might be asked to do the following in such a project:

1. Determine the area of grammar you want to focus on.

2. Describe the class for which the lesson plan is devised, including the number of students, the grade level or ages of the students, the first languages of the students, etc.

3. Provide a skeletal outline for the major phases of the lesson (e.g., greeting, linkage to earlier material, presentation, pair work, group work).

4. Create a dialog imagining every word that the teacher says in the classroom (except during pair or group work) and the kinds of questions that individual students are likely to ask in response. This section comprises the bulk of the project.

5. Provide copies of every exercise that is done in the classroom.

A term paper project for such a class could be a closer examination of a specific aspect of grammar. Students might do the following in such a term paper:

1. Research some of the questions and problems that are described in the literature regarding this point of grammar.

2. Provide a description of the exceptions to the major pattern of a particular point, how they arose, and/or how they might be accounted for.

3. Do a contrastive analysis of English and another language describing how a point of grammar is handled in each language.

OUTLINE of CONTENTS

Unit I: THE BUILDING BLOCKS OF ENGLISH

Chapter 1

WORDS

The basic unit of language that we will consider in our study of English grammar is the sentence because that is the level at which grammar primarily operates. In order to do this, we need first to consider the items that make up a sentence: the words. Words must be in a certain order for us to understand a sentence, as you can see in the following example (the star indicates that the sentence is ungrammatical):

*Woman the makes old home at bread.

The sentence illustrates the fact that if the word order is randomly altered, a speaker of English will immediately notice that something is wrong and ask for repetition or clarification.

MORPHEMES

Words in a language consist of elements called **morphemes**. You are probably familiar with the prefixes that come at the front of a word and the suffixes that come at the end of a word which can change the meaning or function of that word. Thus, the prefix *in-* can change the meaning of the word *sincere* into its opposite, *insincere*. The suffix *-ship* can change the word *friend* into the abstract notion that we know as *friendship*. In the same way, the suffix *-ed* can change the present time of a word like *rent* into the past time form *rented*. We use the term *morpheme* (*morph* means "shape" or "form") to describe the prefixes, suffixes, and other elements that make up words. There are two basic types: free morphemes and bound morphemes.

Free Morphemes

Morphemes that can stand freely by themselves as independent words are called **free morphemes**. Some examples are shown in the following list:

tiger	but
gorgeous	in
build	are
fast	these
thought	she

Free morphemes can be further divided into two groups: lexical morphemes or **content words** and grammatical morphemes or **function words**. Content words are words like those on the left side of the list: they allow us to create an image of some kind in our minds. Thus, if we hear the word *tiger*, we are able to conjure up a picture of a large striped cat; if we hear the word *gorgeous*, we imagine a person or an object with exceptionally attractive features.

Function words are words like those on the right side of the list: they show us relationships among content words, but by themselves they do not have the power to create an image in our minds. Thus, when we hear the word *but*, we must wait for further information to tell us of a contrast to some earlier information. When we hear the words *in* or *are*, we are similarly dependent on content words to give these function words a meaning. You might think that the word *she* does conjure up an image, and wonder why *she* is a function word. The answer is that the function word *she* represents a content word such as *female, mother, woman, girl-friend*, etc., and it is this content word that supplies the image.

EXERCISE 1.1

Directions: Label the following words **CW** (content word) or **FW** (function word).

train	surprise	under
every	gargle	weak
or	them	democracy
really	has	dull
antiquated	and	near
did	bee	charge
blipped	purple	the

Bound Morphemes

The elements of words that cannot stand freely and independently, like the prefixes and suffixes, are called **bound morphemes** because they are bound or connected to free morphemes. A few examples are shown in the following list:

re-	-s
co-	-ing
-ness	-er
-ous	-ed

We see immediately that bound morphemes have no meaning until they are attached to free morphemes, specifically content words:

restate	pencils
coexist	talking
quietness	smaller
mysterious	helped

Bound morphemes can be further divided into two groups: derivational morphemes and inflectional morphemes. **Derivational morphemes** are like those on the left side of the list. They allow us to make new words in the language and to change one grammatical category into another. Thus, *restate* is a new word built from *state* and *coexist* a new word built from *exist*, while the noun *quietness* is derived from the adjective *quiet* and the adjective *mysterious* is derived from the noun *mystery*.

Inflectional morphemes are like those on the right side of the list. Their purpose is not to create new words or grammatical categories but rather to show the grammatical function of a word. In other words, they have a job or a function in the sentence: they show us how many things we are talking about (e.g., *pencils*), the time at which something happens (e.g., *They are talking right now; They helped me yesterday*), a comparison to another adjective (e.g., *This box is smaller than that one*), and so on. Inflectional morphemes are always suffixes (i.e., they always come at the end of a word), and there are exactly eight of them in English: four attached to verbs, two attached to nouns, and two attached to adjectives.

VERBS	NOUNS	ADJECTIVES
-s (walk<u>s</u>)	-s (river<u>s</u>)	-er (great<u>er</u>)
-ing (teach<u>ing</u>)	-'s (the boy<u>'s</u>)	-est (brav<u>est</u>)
-ed$_1$ (jump<u>ed</u>)		
-ed$_2$ (giv<u>en</u>[1])		

We will soon be discussing the names of these functions, the meaning of the terms *verb*, *noun*, and *adjective*, and the difference between *-ed$_1$* and *-ed$_2$*, as they are very important in understanding grammar. For now, you should simply be able to recognize bound morphemes.

EXERCISE 1.2

Directions: Label the underlined portions (the bound morphemes) of the following words derivational (**DM**) or inflectional (**IM**).

fast<u>est</u>	John<u>'s</u>	violin<u>ist</u>
<u>co</u>operate	hugg<u>ing</u>	attract<u>ive</u>
friendli<u>er</u>	prov<u>en</u>	<u>pro</u>long
king<u>dom</u>	<u>tri</u>athalon	develop<u>ed</u>
tremendous<u>ly</u>	provoke<u>s</u>	train<u>ee</u>
watermelon<u>s</u>	<u>sub</u>category	rac<u>ist</u>
<u>anti</u>biotic	fanci<u>ful</u>	<u>ir</u>relevant

EXERCISE 1.3

Directions: Underline the bound morphemes in the following sentences. Write **CW** (content word) or **FW** (function word) below each word in the sentence and **DM** (derivational morpheme) or **IM** (inflectional morpheme) above each morpheme.

<pre>
            IM   IM   DM
 Example: The cats meowed into the darkness.
            FW CW   CW   FW FW   CW
</pre>

1. Numerous satellites in the night sky are busily sending data to the Earth.

2. Even the industry's strongest warnings were not taken seriously by the government.

3. If the plane landed on water, the fuselage is probably recoverable.

4. A shorter description appears on the next page of this official document.

5. Magellan circled the globe between 1519 and 1522.

EXERCISE 1.4

Directions: Copy five sentences from the newspaper, leaving sufficient room to label the bound and free morphemes in each sentence in the same way as you did in Exercise 1.3.

---

[1] *-Ed$_2$* is often referred to as *-en* since several *-ed$_2$* forms end with these letters. *Ed$_2$*-forms also include *-ed*, *-n*, and other forms. See Irregular Verbs, p. 470.

WORD CLASSES

Now that we have an understanding of how words are created from bound and free mor-phemes, we are ready to learn the classes that these words fall into. The word classes are also known as *parts of speech*. We have already seen that all words can be divided into two major types, content words and function words, and we know that content words typically create an image in the mind whereas function words serve only to show a relationship to or between content words and thus create many more meanings than we could with content words alone. The word classes also reflect the division into content words and function words, as shown in the box below:

CONTENT WORDS	FUNCTION WORDS
nouns	pronouns
verbs	auxiliary verbs
adjectives	determiners
adverbs	prepositions
	conjunctions

Nouns

You have no doubt heard the traditional description of a noun as a person, place or thing. It is actually easier to identify nouns by the bound morphemes that are attached to them, specifically the inflectional morpheme *-s* , which shows whether the noun is **singular** or **plural,** and *-'s*, which shows whether the noun is possessive or not. However, the most reliable way to identify a noun is by its position in a sentence. This is especially important for nouns that have the same form as verbs. For example, *paint* is a noun in the sentence *Paint is expensive,* but it is a verb in the sentence *Artists paint pictures*.

Nouns can be divided into **proper nouns** and **common nouns**. Proper nouns are the formal names or titles of people, countries, days and months, languages, businesses, and so on, which are almost always identified in English by beginning with a capital letter. All other nouns are common nouns. The following list shows proper nouns with their equivalent com-mon noun forms:

PROPER NOUNS	COMMON NOUNS
Doctor Suarez	doctor
Indonesia	country
Monday	day
IBM	computer company

Nouns can also be divided into **concrete nouns** and **abstract nouns**. Concrete nouns describe things we can touch or sense in some way. Abstract nouns are nouns that have no substance and can only be imagined or thought about. The following list shows some examples:

CONCRETE NOUNS	ABSTRACT NOUNS
garden	idea
air	voyage
spider	hope
molecule	function
wine	socialism
Mrs. Chen	The North Atlantic Treaty Organization (NATO)

EXERCISE 1.5

Directions: Underline the nouns in the following sentences. Write **P** (proper noun) or **C** (common noun) above the noun and **con** (concrete noun) or **abs** (abstract noun) below the noun. Some nouns (e.g., countries) can be both abstract and concrete. If the noun is concrete, you must be able to answer "Yes" to questions such as "Can you touch it?" or "Can you see it under a microscope?" If the noun is abstract, the answer to such questions must be "No."

> P   C   P
> *Example:* <u>Sally</u> reviews <u>drama</u> in <u>New York</u>.
> con   abs   con

1. The annual growth of a <u>tree</u> is shown in <u>its</u> rings.

2. The brown <u>bear</u>, which is native to <u>Tibet</u>, is an endangered <u>species</u>.

3. Alexander Fleming discovered penicillin before the Second World War.

4. The government of Italy is speaking for a new openness in public affairs.

5. The idea that Neptune has several moons was confirmed by Voyager 2 on September 2.

Nouns may also be labeled **count nouns** and **noncount nouns**. Count nouns are those forms of a noun that may be counted. If a noun can be counted, then it must also have a plural form. For example, the word *apple* is usually a count noun because it is possible to say *I bought <u>three</u> apples* but not *I bought *apple*. Noncount nouns are those forms of a noun that cannot be counted. If a noun cannot be counted, then it can only have a singular form. For example, the word *water* is usually a noncount noun because it is possible to say *We need water* but not *We need *waters* or *There are two *waters on the floor*. The following list shows examples of count and noncount nouns:

COUNT NOUNS	NONCOUNT NOUNS
pencil	milk
teaspoon	plastic
planet	gold
error	incompetence
equation	dynamism

Most nouns have both count and noncount forms. For example, the noun *stone* has the count form in the sentence *The investigators found several <u>stones</u> in the bird's stomach.* However, the same noun has the noncount form in the sentence *This axe is made of <u>stone</u>.* Count nouns always indicate a more specific form of the noun, while noncount nouns always indicate a more general form. In the example sentences, a stone as a discreet object in a bird's stomach is specific, whereas stone as a material for making axes is general. In some cases, the more specific count noun has a completely different meaning from the noncount equivalent. The box below shows examples of specific (count) and general (noncount) pairs:

SPECIFIC (COUNT)	GENERAL (NONCOUNT)
a chicken (a bird)	chicken (food)
an onion (a vegetable)	onion (an ingredient)
a wood (a forest)	wood (a material)
a baseball (equipment)	baseball (a game)
a medicine (a remedy)	medicine (a field of study)
democracies (governments)	democracy (a principle)
a wire (a segment)	wiring (a system)
a table (a single piece)	furniture (a mass noun)
a dollar (a single bill)	money (a mass noun)

EXERCISE 1.6

Directions: Underline the nouns in the following sentences. Write **C** (count) or **NC** (noncount) above each noun. If the noun is count, it can be counted and made plural. If the noun is noncount, it cannot be counted or made plural.

1. An iron is made of iron, a glass is made of glass, but a light is not made of light.

2. That guy is not very careful with his money. He gave me two dollars, three nickels, and a penny in change.

3. Don't buy a paper; it uses too much paper.

4. In space, the spaces between galaxies are almost inconceivable distances.

5. The students found a lot of literature about air pollution but only a single article on noise pollution in American cities.

Verbs

Verbs are typically said to describe an action or a state of being. This is true, but, like nouns, verbs can more easily be identified by their position in a sentence and by the inflectional morphemes that are attached to them. For example, verbs usually come after a noun in an English sentence, and they are usually marked by the inflectional morphemes -s, -ing, -ed₁, and -ed₂, as we saw earlier. Verbs that describe an action are called **dynamic verbs**; they typically show activities, processes, and transitional and momentary events. Verbs that describe a state of being are called **stative verbs**; they typically show cognition, perception, emotion, and relation. Some examples are shown in the box below:

DYNAMIC VERBS	STATIVE VERBS
drink [activity]	understand [cognition]
rain [activity]	hear [perception]
change [process]	love [emotion]
arrive [transitional event]	be [relation]
jump [momentary event]	own [relation]

There are other classifications of verbs (e.g., active/passive, transitive/intransitive), which we will study in later chapters.

EXERCISE 1.7

Directions: Underline the verbs in the following sentences. Put a second line under the inflectional morpheme if one is present. Above the verb, write **dyn** (dynamic) or **stat** (stative).

dyn
Example: The mongoose killed the snake.

1. The students are working in pairs.

2. My uncle dislikes his neighbors.

3. The spaghetti sauce smelled wonderful.

4. The sunflowers had grown to a height of six feet.

5. The pelican died from contamination by pesticides.

Adjectives

Adjectives **modify** the nouns with which they occur, that is, they tell us the qualities of a noun such as its size, shape, condition, age, color, and origin. Most adjectives in English come directly before the noun. These are known as **attributive adjectives**. However, adjectives can also be disconnected from the noun they modify, in which case they typically come after a verb like *be* (e.g., *That woman is beautiful*). These are known as **predicate adjectives**. Adjectives cannot usually be identified by their inflectional morphemes because the morphemes that bind to adjectives, namely *-er* and *-est*, are specialized forms that are only applied when we need to compare one noun to another. In other words, adjectives usually have no inflectional morphemes bound to them, though they may have derivational ones, e.g., *-ful, -ive, -ed, -ing, -like,* and *-ly*.

Some examples of adjectives with appropriate nouns are shown in the box below with inflectional morphemes in boldface:

ADJECTIVE and NOUN	ADJECTIVE + INFLECTIONAL MORPHEME and NOUN
wonderful news	larger population
grotesque statue	quieter moments
pink noses	friendlier official
basic fact	darkest room
undivided attention	prettiest expression

EXERCISE 1.8

Directions: Underline the adjectives in the following sentences.

1. The little old lady raced to her favorite supermarket in her maroon Cadillac.

2. It was a tempestuous day, a day of racing clouds and roaring wind.

3. It was impossible to imagine that a simple peasant could be so beautiful.

4. The woolly mammoth, a hairy, elephant-like creature, roamed the earth until 10,000 B.C.

5. A waiter should be attentive, cordial, careful, and unobtrusive.

Adverbs

Adverbs tell us something about the verbs with which they occur, i.e., they modify those verbs. What they tell us about verbs is how frequently they take place, how they take place, to what degree they take place, where and when they take place, and so on. Adverbs can also modify adjectives and other adverbs in similar ways. Some examples are shown in the following sentences in which the adverb is underlined:

ADV + **VERB**	Regina <u>often</u> **travels** to Paris.	[how frequently]
VERB + ADV	The man **talked** <u>slowly</u> when he was with his mother.	[how]
ADV + **ADJ**	The waitress was <u>very</u> **beautiful**.	[degree]
ADV + **ADV**	Her son learned French <u>amazingly</u> **quickly**.	[degree]

Adverbs are the most mobile word class in a sentence. They can occur directly before or after a verb, and they can occur at the end or at the beginning of a sentence. When an adverb is not directly adjacent to a verb, it tends to modify the whole sentence rather than the verb alone.

SENTENCE + ADV	**The bus cannot meet you** <u>here</u>.	[where]
ADV + SENTENCE	<u>Tomorrow</u> **I'll buy the ticket**.	[when]

EXERCISE 1. 9

Directions: Underline the adverbs in the following sentences.

1. Gracefully, the ballerina leaped across the stage.

2. The secretary wasn't very happy yesterday.

3. Ducks seldom take new mates.

4. Nobody can exchange any money there.

5. Pharmacists must work fast to fill their prescriptions.

Pronouns

The function of a pronoun is to take the place of a noun that has been clearly identified in a text or by a situation. We use pronouns so as not to have to repeat a noun. Look at the following sentences:

a) Jason lives in Piraeus but <u>Jason</u> works in Athens.

b) Jason lives in Piraeus but *he* works in Athens.

In this example, we do not need to repeat the proper noun *Jason* in Sentence (a) because it is already clear who we are talking about. In Sentence (b), the noun that the pronoun *he* refers to or replaces, in this case *Jason*, is called the **antecedent** of that pronoun. There are several different types of pronouns (e.g., subject, object, possessive, reflexive, and demonstrative pronouns), which we will discuss in detail later. Some examples are shown in the following list.

I	me	myself	mine
he	him	himself	his
they	them	themselves	theirs
everyone	each	some	that

EXERCISE 1.10

Directions: Underline the pronouns in the following sentences.

1. We met him at the airport in my station wagon.

2. She didn't give herself enough time to get the name of everybody in the room.

3. Some countries are developed, some are not. This is the basis of the north-south dialog.

4. *To each his own* means that each person has the right to decide what he or she likes.

5. Has anyone seen the coffee? It must be somewhere in these cupboards.

Auxiliary Verbs

The purpose of the auxiliary verbs is to help main verbs to accomplish certain functions. For this reason, they are also known as helping verbs. The auxiliary verbs include the words *be*, *have*, and *do*. These words also function as main verbs. We can distinguish the auxiliary verbs from the main verbs because we know that only main verbs occur by themselves in a sentence.

In other words, an auxiliary verb needs a partner, whereas a main verb does not. Look at the following examples:

AUX	MAIN VERB	AUXILIARY VERB + MAIN VERB
be	John **is** a carpenter.	John **is working** at home.
have	Mary **has** a cold.	Mary **has felt** weak all morning.
do	The maid **does** the dishes.	The maid **does** not **clean** windows.

The auxiliary verbs also include a group of words and phrases called **modals**. Unlike *be*, *have*, and *do*, modals can never function as main verbs. Their function is to show possibilities and obligations, which we will study in detail in Chapter 6. Examples are shown below:

will	is going to
must	has to
should	ought to
can	is able to
might	is likely to

Like the other auxiliaries, the modals cannot occur by themselves. They must occur with a main verb. Examples are shown below with the main verb *follow*:

The man **will** follow the rules.	The man **is going to** follow the rules.
The man **must** follow the rules.	The man **has to** follow the rules.
The man **should** follow the rules.	The man **ought to** follow the rules.
The man **can** follow the rules.	The man **is able to** follow the rules.
The man **might** follow the rules.	The man **is likely to** follow the rules.

EXERCISE 1.11

Directions: Underline the auxiliary verbs in the following sentences.

1. Water is coming under the door.

2. That actor has starred in many films.

3. People should help the children in poor countries.

4. The fine is one hundred dollars.

5. My brother has an old Chevrolet.

6. The government will free the hostages next month.

7. The records ought to reveal the mistake.

8. Her grandparents do odd jobs for the community.

9. The students were showing the photographs to their friends when the teacher came in.

10. His father had to have an operation last year.

Prepositions

The function of a preposition is to show a particular relationship between two or more nouns. This relationship most commonly indicates either place or time.[2] Other prepositions show accompaniment (*with*, *without*), comparison (*like*, *as*), possession or relation (*of*), means (*by*, *by means of*), and several other functions. Some examples of prepositions are shown in the box below:

PREPOSITIONS OF PLACE		PREPOSITIONS OF TIME		OTHER PREPOSITIONS	
at	to	at	on	with	of
in	from	since	for	without	as
on	up	in	by	like	
around	through	before	after	by	
towards	away	until	during	by means of	

EXERCISE 1.12

Directions: Underline the prepositions in the following sentences.

1. After class, Alice has a cup of tea in a restaurant before she goes to the library so that she can study for the evening.

2. An ape is like a monkey with no tail.

3. Frogs covered the highway from one side to the other.

4. The ambulance arrived in five minutes by traveling through the park.

5. The ship sailed out of the harbor, under the bridge, around a small island, and then out into the open ocean.

Determiners

The function of a determiner is to establish or determine certain features of a noun that are different from the qualitative features described by adjectives. These features primarily indicate quantity (e.g., *many*, *all*, *five*), but they can also show definiteness (e.g., *the*), possession (e.g., *my*, *John's*), and sequence (e.g., *first*, *second*). Determiners always come before the noun or its modifiers, and the principle characteristic of a determiner is that it cannot occur without a noun. Many determiners have the same form as a pronoun; for example:

Each apple costs fifty cents.   [determiner]

Each costs fifty cents.   [pronoun]

The difference is that the pronoun, *each* in this case, can stand alone but the determiner cannot. It is thus impossible to say *That is *my* or *Please give me *the* as a complete sentence because a determiner always requires a noun to be present. Some examples are shown below:

---

[2] Adverbs also show place and time, but they are content words with their own meanings, whereas prepositions are function words which only have meaning once a relationship has been established. For example, the adverb *now* can be defined, but the preposition *at* has no meaning until it is attached to a noun, e.g., *at school*.

<u>a few</u> books	<u>a</u> cat	<u>two</u> people
<u>all of the</u> profits	<u>the</u> door	<u>the seventh</u> chapter
<u>a lot of</u> money	<u>every</u> student	<u>another</u> beer
<u>both</u> parties	<u>her</u> mother	<u>the other</u> day

EXERCISE 1.13

Directions: Underline the determiners in the following sentences.

1. Jupiter is the largest planet in the solar system.

2. Every story has a good guy and a few bad guys.

3. Sally's parents asked her sister to take her and her brother to another doctor.

4. A lot of time was spent on revising three chapters in the second edition.

5. Almost all of the people in this country have a little trouble with their income taxes.

Conjunctions

The function of a conjunction is to conjoin or connect two or more grammatical elements (words, phrases, or clauses). They usually appear either between two grammatical elements, or just before the end of a list of such elements. There are several types of conjunctions, but those that will concern us here are called **coordinating conjunctions** because they conjoin things of coordinate or equal value. The most common coordinating conjunctions are *and*, *but*, *or*, and *so*. *And* shows additional information, *but* shows contrary information, *or* shows alternative information, and *so* shows consequential information. Some examples are shown below:

Ants <u>and</u> spiders represent different species.

The repairman cannot come today, <u>but</u> he can come tomorrow.

The CPU, <u>or</u> central processing unit, controls the computer.

Sharon needed a job, <u>so</u> she moved to New York.

EXERCISE 1.14

Directions: Underline the coordinating conjunctions in the following sentences.

1. The king and the queen are not at home, so please come back on Tuesday.

2. A bacteria, but not a virus, can be killed by antibiotics.

3. You must pay the fee or face the consequences.

4. Those boys have lived and worked in Calcutta all their lives.

5. Whether beautiful or disfigured, intelligent or retarded, every human being has the right to a happy life.

CONCLUSION

The purpose of this chapter has been to introduce you briefly to the content words and function words that comprise the word classes in English. You have also been introduced to the bound derivational morphemes or endings that are attached to and characterize certain word classes. It is ultimately more important to recognize that a word class is determined more by the position or function of a word in a sentence than by any definition of the word class, as we shall see in Chapter 2. This is particularly true in English, where word order determines meaning and where the same word can often perform the function of different word classes, as shown in the following examples:

A large <u>record</u> company <u>records</u> several types of <u>records</u>.   [adjective, verb, noun]

<u>Dark</u> objects cannot be seen in the <u>dark</u>.   [adjective, noun]

They <u>fast</u> once a month with their <u>fast</u> friends, and time   [verb, adjective]
goes <u>fast</u> when they have begun the <u>fast</u>.   [adverb, noun]

EXERCISE 1.15

Directions: Copy the following sentences onto a piece of paper, leaving three lines above each sentence labelled (a), (b), and (c). Lines (b) and (c) will be completed as part of a later exercise; just leave them blank for now. On line (a) above each sentence, indicate the class of each word using the following abbreviations:

N = noun   PRO = pronoun
V = verb   AUX = auxiliary verb
ADJ = adjective   PREP = preposition
ADV = adverb   DET = determiner
CONJ = coordinating conjunction

Example:

        (a)   DET   N   V   DET   N   PREP   N
        (b)
        (c)
            The   rabbit   changes   its   color   in winter.

1. A small bomb killed several people at the airport yesterday.

2. Several young women milk the cows in the evening.

3. Most of the students can speak another language.

4. Jonathan needed a new pencil so he bought one at the supermarket.

5. The insects have attacked every tree on my block.

6. Leave this house now!

7. In the fall, the leaves on the trees fall to the ground.

8. The engineer carefully removed all the accumulated oil from the gear box.

9. The children are visiting the old man and they are watering his garden.

10. Elsie doesn't take cream in her coffee.

SUMMARY

This chapter has introduced a number of grammatical terms that apply to words. These terms are summarized in the charts below.

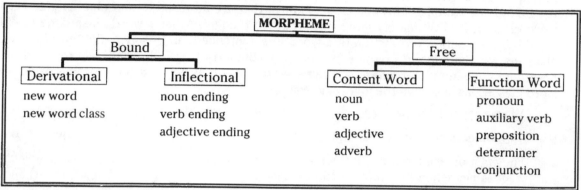

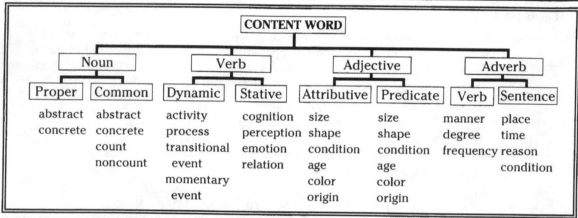

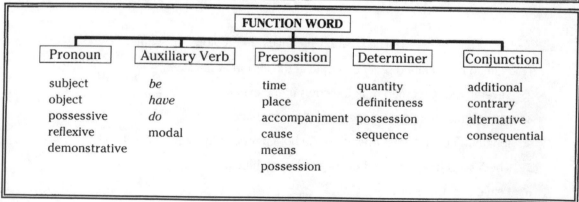

Chapter 2

GROUPS OF WORDS

In Chapter 1, we studied the names given to the various word classes. Now we turn to the names given to various patterns of groups of words, specifically phrases, clauses, and sentence roles. At this point in our study of the systems in English grammar, we are interested primarily in being able to identify and name these groups. A detailed explanation of their structure and use will come in later chapters.

PHRASES

When we write or speak English, we seldom use individual words alone. We are much more likely to use groups of words called **phrases**. A phrase consists of a main word plus words closely associated with it, and the name of the phrase is based on the main word. Thus, we have noun phrases based on a noun, prepositional phrases based on a preposition, verb phrases based on a verb, adjective phrases based on an adjective, and adverb phrases based on an adverb.

Noun Phrase (NP)

A noun phrase consists of a determiner, an optional adjective phrasep, a noun, and optional prepositional phrases. We can write this structure as a formula:

$$NP \rightarrow DET \ (AdjP) \ N \ (PP)_n \quad \text{or} \quad NP \rightarrow PRO$$

The formula reads as follows: a noun phrase [NP] consists of a determiner [DET], an optional adjective phrase [AdjP] (the parentheses indicate optionality), a noun [N], and any number of optional prepositional phrases [PP] (the small n indicates any number). From this formula, we can see that a determiner is always part of a noun phrase and that a noun phrase always contains a determiner. Since a pronoun refers to an earlier noun phrase, a pronoun is a noun phrase, too, but it has no determiner. Below are some examples of noun phrases:

a large black **chicken**	DET + ADJ + ADJ + **N**
two healthy **girls**	DET + ADJ + **N**
the **sound** of a train in the night	DET + **N** + PP + PP
cold **water**	DET [Ø] + ADJ + **N**
they	Pronoun

It is important to mention that the most frequently occurring determiner in English is the zero determiner, which we indicate with the symbol Ø. The zero determiner occurs with a plural noun, with a **noncount noun**, or with a **proper noun**. A noncount noun (or mass noun) is one that cannot be counted or made plural and typically refers to substances or abstract notions. Examples are shown below:

<u>Elephants</u> never forget.   [Ø determiner + the plural noun *elephants*]
<u>Water</u> is essential.   [Ø determiner + the noncount noun *water*]
<u>John</u> lives here.   [Ø determiner + the proper noun *John*]

EXERCISE 2.1

Directions: Underline all the noun phrases [NP] in the following sentences. Above them, write the word classes contained in the noun phrase.

       PRON   DET ADJ   N
Example: <u>We</u> sat and watched <u>the stormy sea</u>.

1. A long green snake slithered across my foot.

2. Hot coffee is great on a cold morning.

3. Kennedy wanted to send a man to the moon by the end of the sixties.

4. Life without water is impossible for most creatures on this planet.

5. Two policemen examined the fingerprints on the broken window.

Prepositional Phrase (PP)

A **prepositional phrase** consists of a preposition and a noun phrase. In fact, the name *preposition* (meaning "before position") describes the fact that prepositions always come before the other words in a prepositional phrase. The formula for this structure is:

     PP ➜ **PREP** NP

The formula reads as follows: A prepositional phrase [PP] consists of a preposition [PREP] plus a noun phrase [NP]. But we have already seen that a prepositional phrase can be part of a larger noun phrase. Below are some examples of prepositional phrases alone and of prepositional phrases that contain prepositional phrases within their noun phrases:

under a log	**PREP** + NP [DET + N]
in the morning	**PREP** + NP [DET + N]
in the corner **of** the room	**PREP** + NP [DET +N + PP]
at her house **in** the country	**PREP** + NP [DET (*her*) + N + PP]

EXERCISE 2.2

Directions: Underline the prepositional phrases in the following sentences. Above them, indicate the word classes contained in the prepositional phrase.

       PREP DET ADJ   N
Example: We swam <u>in   the cold river</u>.

1. The Pacific Ocean is the largest ocean in the world.

2. The fluid in the brain cavity must be removed.

3. The starship came from the Pleiades with a message for mankind.

4. The apartment on the top floor has a fantastic view over the city.

5. The inmates dug a tunnel under the wall and escaped to freedom.

Verb Phrase (VP)

A **verb phrase** consists of a verb plus all the words that follow it in a simple sentence. Since it includes everything in the sentence except the subject, another term for *verb phrase* in English is **predicate** (the term *subject* will be described in the next section of this chapter). A verb phrase consists of a verb with an optional noun phrase and optional prepositional phrases. There are two major types of verb phrase that we are interested in and we will call them "Type I" and "Type II." The formula for the **Type I verb phrase** is:

$$\text{VPI} \rightarrow \textbf{V} \text{ (NP) (PP)}_n$$

The formula reads as follows: a Type I verb phrase [VPI] consists of a verb [V], an optional NP, and any number of optional prepositional phrases [PP]. Below are some examples of Type I verb phrases preceded by a subject (*Mary)* in brackets:

[Mary] **teaches**.	V
[Mary] **teaches two classes**.	V + NP
[Mary] **teaches in the summer**.	V + PP
[Mary] **teaches two classes in the summer**.	V + NP + PP
[Mary] **teaches two classes at Harvard in the summer**.	V + NP + PP + PP

EXERCISE 2.3

Directions: Underline the verb phrase [VP, or predicate] in the following sentences.

1. We drove along the river to the county fair.

2. The doctor cured the patient with an herbal tea.

3. Light travels at 186,000 miles per second.

4. The hungry, growling beast in the dungeon clawed at the damp walls.

5. Snowflakes drifted gently to the ground.

The **Type II verb phrase** always contains the verb *be* or some other linking verb (e.g., *appear, become, look, remain, seem*). When such a verb is present, the verb is followed by a noun phrase or an adjective phrase and optional prepositional phrases. The formula for the Type II verb phrase is:

$$\text{VPII} \rightarrow \textbf{be} \begin{bmatrix} \text{NP (PP)}_n \\ \text{PP}_n \\ \text{AdjP (PP)}_n \end{bmatrix}$$

The formula reads as follows: a Type II verb phrase [VPII] consists of a linking verb (here represented by the most common linking verb *be*) plus either a) a noun phrase [NP] with any number of optional prepositional phrases [PP], b) at least one nonoptional prepositional phrase [PP], or a nonoptional adjective phrase [AdjP] with any number of optional prepositional phrases [PP] (the large brackets indicate either/or). Below are some Type II verb phrases preceded by a subject (*John)* in brackets:

[John] **is a lawyer**.	V + NP
[John] **is a lawyer for a large firm**.	V + NP + PP

[John] **is in the courtroom**.	V + PP
[John] **is brilliant**.	V + AdjP
[John] **is really brilliant in the courtroom**.	V + AdjP + PP
[John] **is a brilliant lawyer for poor people in the courtroom**.	V+ NP+PP+PP

EXERCISE 2.4

Directions: Underline the verb phrases in the following sentences.

1. The capital of the largest country in the world is the city of Moscow.

2. Stars are gigantic balls of superheated gas.

3. My sister has been successful in her chosen profession of nursing.

4. The mouse was at the bottom of the cookie jar in a state of restful repose.

5. Tuesday is the day of the week with the best conditions for working at home.

Adjective Phrase (AdjP)

An **adjective phrase** consists of any number of adjectives plus any of their adverb modifiers. There are two types of adjective phrases: attributive and predicate. **Attributive adjective phrases** are part of a noun phrase, where they fill the optional adjective position between the determiner and the noun. **Predicate adjective phrases** occur after the verb *be* (or another linking verb) in Type II verb phrases. The formula for an adjective phrase is:

$$AdjP \rightarrow (ADV)_n \; ADJ_n$$

The formula reads as follows: An adjective phrase [AdjP] consists of any number of optional adverbs [ADV] (in truth, there is sometimes one, rarely two, and almost never three) and any number of adjectives [ADJ], although the number is rarely more than three. Some examples are shown below. The entire adjective phrase is shown in boldface while the adjective (or adjectives) around which the adjective phrase is built, always at the right end of the phrase, is underlined:

That **scratched old yellow** bus belongs to my aunt.	[attributive AdjP]
A cactus is an **amazingly vigorous** plant.	[attributive AdjP]
Marilyn Monroe was **gorgeous, sexy, and blonde**.	[predicate AdjP]
The man's face was **deeply, painfully scarred**.	[predicate AdjP]

EXERCISE 2.5

Directions: Underline the adjective phrases in the following sentences.

1. Sophia is a dark, spirited Italian horse.

2. The new manager is intelligent, extremely organized, and diplomatic.

3. The entire deciduous forest was red-yellow-orange brown in its autumnal dress.

4. The mechanic removed the small egg-shaped device near the fuel pump.

5. Tired, hungry, thirsty, and weak, the soldier limped into the completely deserted village.

Adverb Phrase (AdvP)

An **adverb phrase** consists of an adverb plus any number of its adverb modifiers. Adverb phrases usually come at the end (or the beginning) of a sentence, where they show time, place, manner, degree, etc., as adverbs typically do. In fact, we really only need the term *adverb phrase* to account for the use of more than one adverb together. The formula for an adverb phrase is:

$$AdvP \rightarrow (ADV)_n \; ADV$$

The formula reads as follows: an adverb phrase [AdvP] consists of optional modifying adverbs [ADV] (usually one, but sometimes two) followed by an adverb [ADV]. Some examples are shown below. The entire adverb phrase is shown in boldface while the "head" adverb is underlined:

> The train is leaving **right <u>now</u>**.
>
> Sheila finished the exam **extremely <u>quickly</u>**.
>
> **Very <u>gently</u>**, the nurse turned out the light.
>
> Joseph wrote, **much too <u>angrily</u>**, a letter to his ex-wife.

EXERCISE 2.6

Directions: Underline the adverb phrases in the following sentences.

1. The gun was found precisely here.

2. Too often, the rich get richer while the poor get poorer.

3. The teacher patiently and thoroughly corrected her students' essays.

4. I want an answer now.

5. The bolt must be tightened very carefully.

EXERCISE 2.7

Directions: Above the following sentences, identify the type of phrase that is used. Starting with the smallest (NP, AdjP, or AdvP, then PP, then VP), indicate the phrases within phrases by using brackets as shown in the example below.

>   [NP [AdjP]   ] [VP [PP [NP   ]]]
> *Example:* An injured bird flew into the house.

1. This building uses heat too inefficiently.

2. The story in that magazine is very well written.

3. The river flows very quickly at this spot.

4. Unfortunately, the baseball team will move to another city.

5. The old monk's skin was yellow and darkened with age.

EXERCISE 2.8

Directions: Continue EXERCISE 1.15 from the previous chapter, in which you copied the following sentences onto a piece of paper, leaving three lines above each sentence labelled (a), (b), and (c). On line (b) above each sentence, indicate the type of phrase using the following abbreviations:

NP = noun phrase
PP = prepositional phrase
VP = verb phrase
AdjP = adjective phrase
AdvP = adverb phrase

Example: (a) DET   N   V   DET   N PREP N
(b) [NP   ] [VP   [NP   ] [PP [NP]]]
(c)

The rabbit changes its color in winter.

1. A small bomb killed several people at the airport yesterday.

2. Several young women milk the cows in the evening.

3. Most of the students can speak another language.

4. Jonathan needed a new pencil so he bought one at the supermarket.

5. The insects have attacked every tree on my block.

6. Leave this house now!

7. In the fall, the leaves on the trees fall to the ground.

8. The engineer carefully removed all the accumulated oil from the gear box.

9. The children are visiting the old man and they are watering his garden.

10. Elsie doesn't take cream in her coffee.

EXERCISE 2.9

Directions: Bracket and label the phrases in the following passage.

David lived in the country in his childhood. He was very happy there. His grandfather had an organic vegetable farm. In the morning, he helped his grandfather in the garden and fed the chickens. He played in the fields and woods every afternoon until dinner time. The closest village was six miles away. Sometimes, David rode his bicycle to the village, but he usually took the bus. David's grandfather is dead now and David owns the farm.

CLAUSES

As we have seen, a phrase is simply a word class with its associated modifiers. But English has another type of word group called a **clause**. A clause is different from a phrase in that it always shows a subject-verb relationship and is thus more sophisticated than a phrase. Some examples are shown below:

SUBJECT NP	VP
The elephant	roared.
The doctor	lives in North Africa.
My boss	understands.

These examples each show a subject NP and a VP, which are the minimal requirements for a clause. They are called **independent clauses** because they are complete in themselves and can stand alone.

A **dependent clause**, on the other hand, also shows a subject-verb relationship (in boldface below), but it is dependent on the presence of an independent clause. The dependent and independent portions of three example sentences are shown in the box below:

INDEPENDENT	DEPENDENT CLAUSE	INDEPENDENT
The elephant roared	when **the hunter appeared**.	
The doctor	whom **we saw** last Christmas	lives in North Africa.
My boss understands	why **Mary wants** a raise.	

The dependent clauses in the box above are dependent because the word that introduces them (i.e., *when*, *whom*, and *why*) establishes a dependence on another idea, making them unable to stand alone as complete sentences. In fact, if we were to use a dependent clause alone in an essay, it would be marked as a **fragment**, or incomplete sentence.

The first word of a dependent clause is called a **clause marker**. Without the clause marker, the dependent clauses in the box above would become independent (i.e., *The hunter appeared*; *We saw the doctor last Christmas*; *Mary wants a raise*). Dependent clauses can be identified by the type of clause marker that is present. There are three types of dependent clauses: adverb clauses, adjective clauses, and noun clauses.

Adverb Clauses

The first type of dependent clause is called an **adverb clause** because, like the word class called an adverb, its purpose is to tell us when, why, how, to what degree, etc., the verb takes place.

The elephant roared <u>when the hunter appeared</u>.   [when]
The elephant is protected <u>because it is an endangered species</u>.   [why]

Some adverb clause markers are listed below:

when	because	although (even though)	if
while	as	despite the fact that	whether

EXERCISE 2.10

Directions: Underline the adverb clauses in the following sentences.

1. Bruce eats cereal in the morning because it energizes him.

2. Although I never wear a watch, I am rarely late.

3. Monica had a haircut while she was waiting for her boyfriend.

4. The tree grew despite the fact that nobody ever watered it.

5. As the plane was landing, a bird flew into one of the jet engines.

Adjective Clauses

The second type of dependent clause is called an **adjective clause** (traditionally known as a relative clause) because its purpose is to modify a noun. Unlike adjective phrases, which usually occur before a noun (except predicate adjectives, which are rarely adjacent to a noun), adjective clauses always come after a noun. Nevertheless, they are still part of the noun phrase in which the noun occurs. We are used to the idea of phrases within phrases. Clauses can occur within phrases, too. Examples are shown below with the complete noun phrase underlined and the dependent adjective clause in boldface:

The doctor **whom we saw last Christmas** lives in North Africa.

The class **that I want** is Biology 110.

We can see that the structures *whom we saw last Christmas* and *that I want* are clauses because they contain a subject-verb relationship (i.e., *we saw, I want*). They are preceded by a clause marker for an adjective clause. The clause markers for adjective clauses are listed below.

who
whom
whose + noun
which
that

EXERCISE 2.11

Directions: Underline the adjective clauses in the following sentences.

1. The stream which we followed came from a small cave.

2. The man whose leg is broken is in Room 242.

3. My dog refuses to eat food that comes from a can.

4. A person who is rich is not necessarily happy.

5. The official whom we spoke with could not give us any details.

Noun Clauses

The third type of dependent clause is called a **noun clause** because, like a noun phrase, it can function as the subject or object of a sentence. A noun clause is different from a noun phrase, however, in that it shows a subject-verb relationship. Examples are shown below:

My boss understands **why Mary wants a raise**.

Where John lives depends on his work.

They could see **that Joan was unhappy**.

We can see that the structures in boldface are clauses because they contain a clause marker and a subject-verb relationship (*Mary wants, John lives,* and *Joan was*). Some of the clause markers for noun clauses are listed below:

that	how
where	how far
when	how long
why	how much
what	what color, what language, etc.

EXERCISE 2.12

Directions: Underline the noun clauses in the following sentences.

1. She didn't know why he was angry.

2. How much it costs is of little importance.

3. Can you see what time it is?

4. I understand that you are looking for an apartment.

5. What the university requires is a complete transcript of all the courses that you have taken.

The different types of phrases and clauses are summarized in Table 2.1.

Table 2.1 Summary of Phrase and Clause Types

PHRASE TYPE & SYMBOL	EXAMPLE	CLAUSE TYPE & SYMBOL	EXAMPLE
Noun Phrase (NP)	the large dog	Noun Clause (NCl)	what the dog eats
Prep. Phrase (PP)	in the yard	————	————
Verb Phrase (VP)	bit three people	————	————
Adjective Phrase (AdjP)	awfully large	Adjective Clause (AdjCl)	which the cat teases
Adverb Phrase (AdvP)	very quickly	Adverb Clause (AdvCl)	when she is hungry

[Note: There is no such thing as a prepositional clause or a verb clause.]

EXERCISE 2.13

Directions: Underline and identify the adverb clauses (**AdvCl**), adjective clauses (**AdjCl**), and noun clauses (**NCl**) in the following sentences.

                     AdjCl   AdvCl
    Example: The plant <u>that we bought</u> died <u>because we ignored it</u>.

1. What I want to know is the name of the person who told you about the meeting.

2. The forest that they knew when they were children has disappeared.

3. She doesn't care how long it takes; she just wants a portrait that she can be proud of.

4. Because most of the gold is in the river, prospectors are always present.

5. The earthquake did not frighten us although it did wake us up.

SENTENCE ROLES

We have looked at the parts of speech, the phrases, and the clauses which together constitute English sentences. Now we will look at the way these words and groups of words function within sentences. We call these functions **sentence roles**. When we looked at verb phrases, we saw that there are two basic types, which we called Type I and Type II. In a sentence with a Type I verb phrase, the sentence roles are usually in this order:

SUBJECT	VERB	OBJECT	ADVERBIAL
John	drinks	coffee	in the morning.

In a sentence with a Type II verb phrase, which has two possible forms, the sentence roles are usually in this order:

SUBJECT	LINKING VERB	PREDICATE NOUN	ADVERBIAL
John	is	a student	at the university.

SUBJECT	LINKING VERB	PREDICATE ADJECTIVE	ADVERBIAL
John	is	happy	at the university.

The minimal requirement for an English sentence is that the role taken by the verb, the verb slot, must be filled. The subject slot is usually filled, but not always. The object (or predicate noun or adjective) and adverbial slots are filled under certain conditions, but they are often empty.

The Subject Slot

The **subject** usually comes at the beginning of a sentence. It usually shows who or what initiates the action or state shown by the verb. It always consists of a noun phrase (or clause) and when it is linked to a predicate it creates a complete sentence. When we speak of the subject of a sentence, we are referring to the entire noun phrase. The core of the subject is called the **bare subject** (shown in boldface in the boxes below), and it is this noun that must agree with the verb.

SUBJECT	VERB	OBJECT	ADVERBIAL
The **cat**	catches	a mouse	every morning.
The **shop** on the corner	is selling	plants	this year.
The **man** who bought my 1969 Jaguar	works		in a garage on weekends.

SUBJECT	VERB	PRED ADJ	ADVERBIAL
The **policy** of the United States government in regard to nuclear arms proliferation	is	uncertain	at present.

To show a change of emphasis, the adverbial slot can be moved to the front of the sentence. A comma is often added to show where the subject begins. For this reason, the subject (shown in boldface below) may not always be the first element that you see in a sentence.

Every morning, **the cat** catches a mouse.

This year, **the shop on the corner** is selling plants.

On weekends, **the man who bought my 1969 Jaguar** works in a garage.

At present, **the policy of the United States government in regard to nuclear arms proliferation** is uncertain.

EXERCISE 2.14

Directions: Underline the subjects in the following sentences. Then draw a second line under the bare subject.

Example: A tiny green frog jumped into the swimming pool.

1. The largest city in Turkey is Istanbul.

2. Before he came to the United States, Van's father had had many horrifying experiences.

3. The weather for the northern part of the Central Valley will be cloudy and cool tomorrow.

4. The new bridge that connects the two islands has improved business opportunities.

5. Unfortunately, the damaged space probe is not sending data back to the earth.

The Verb Slot

The **verb** usually follows the subject of a sentence. It shows the action that the subject performs or the state that the subject is in. Every English sentence must have a verb; otherwise, it is just a fragment, a part of a sentence. It is possible to have a verb with no subject, as shown in the examples below:

SUBJECT	VERB	OBJECT	ADVERBIAL
(You)	**Go!**		
(You)	**Go**		to your room!
(You)	**Put**	the book	on the table.

These subjectless sentences are called **commands**. The subject is understood to be *you*. However, it is generally not possible to have a complete sentence containing a subject with no verb.

The verb slot in a sentence extends from the end of the subject to the beginning of the object (or predicate noun/adjective). It includes the **core verb** of the sentence plus any auxiliary verbs or adverbs that occur before the object or, if the object slot is empty, before the adverbial slot. Examples are shown below with the core verb in boldface:

SUBJECT	VERB	OBJECT	ADVERBIAL
The train	eventually **left**	the station.	
Steven	has **lived**		in Hawaii for six years.
The ministers	are very carefully **suggesting**	changes in policy	this week.

EXERCISE 2.15

Directions: Underline the entire verb slot in the following sentences.

1. Marianne lives in Scandinavia.

2. We usually take our dog when we go into the mountains.

3. The cliff suddenly and violently collapsed after the rainstorm.

4. During the operation, the doctor will carefully remove the appendix.

5. Antibiotics are only effective for the treatment of bacterial infections.

The Object Slot

The **object** of a sentence shows who or what receives the action that was initiated by the subject. It only occurs with Type I verb phrases. Like the subject, it always consists of a noun phrase or clause. Although objects are not always required to make a complete sentence, they are often present. Some examples are shown below:

SUBJECT	VERB	OBJECT	ADVERBIAL
Roger	pulled	the car	out of the mud.
Sylvia	left	the city of her childhood	at midnight.
Many people	drink	orange juice	in the morning.

Verbs that can have objects after them, like those in the sentences above, are called **transitive** verbs because they can *transfer* the action of the verb onto a noun phrase. Dictionaries identify transitive verbs with the abbreviation *v.t.* for "verb transitive." Not all verbs in English can have objects after them. We call such verbs **intransitive** because it is not possible to transfer the action initiated by the subject onto a noun phrase. Dictionaries identify intransitive verbs with the abbreviation *v.i.* for "verb intransitive." Some examples of sentences with intransitive verbs are shown below:

SUBJECT	VERB	OBJECT	ADVERBIAL
Norman	sleeps		until noon.
We	talked		every evening.
This fish	always goes		to the bottom of the pond.

Remember that transitive verbs always have an object after them. In the set of transitive example sentences, you can see that it is possible to pull, leave, or drink something. Intransitive verbs, on the other hand, cannot have an object after them. In the set of intransitive example sentences, you can see that it is not possible to sleep, talk, or go something. Certain verbs have both a transitive and an intransitive form, which can have different meanings, e.g., drink, push, take.

EXERCISE 2.16

Directions: Underline the words that fill the object slot in the following sentences. Then indicate if the main verb is **vt** (transitive) or **vi** (intransitive).

    Example: The dog **bit** the cat. **vt**

1. The hurricane devastated the city in a few hours. _____

2. Adele's father works for the government in Belo Horizonte, Brazil. _____

3. Few animals kill for no reason. _____

4. This thermometer measures temperature in degrees Centigrade. _____

5. The artist painted until he could paint no more. _____

6. Her aunt died in Toronto. _____

7. My office needs a person who can type 100 words per minute. _____

8. The plumber complained about his assistant's work. _____

9. The stapler fell into the wastebasket. _____

10. Help that poor child! _____

The Predicate Noun and Predicate Adjective Slot

A predicate noun or predicate adjective can only occur after a linking verb (a Type II verb phrase). They take the same position as the object of a Type I verb phrase.

A **predicate noun** is always a noun phrase (or clause) and always follows a linking verb (usually *be*), but it is not always a required element of a sentence. If the predicate noun phrase slot is empty, however, an adverbial is required. The reason that a predicate noun must follow a linking verb is that the function of a **linking verb** is to equate the subject with whatever follows the verb rather than to show who or what receives the action of a verb as in Type 1 verb phrases. In the case of a predicate noun, the linking verb shows that the subject NP and the predicate noun NP are identical. Examples are shown below:

SUBJECT	LINKING VERB	PREDICATE NOUN	ADVERBIAL
A leopard	is	a type of cat.	
Albert Schweitzer	was	a doctor	in Africa.
A bee	is	an insect that makes honey.	
The girls	were		on the telephone.

Notice that in the examples above the subjects are identical to the predicate nouns:

> a leopard = a type of cat
> Albert Schweitzer = a doctor
> a bee = an insect that makes honey

A **predicate adjective**, on the other hand, is always an adjective phrase and always follows a linking verb (usually *be*), but unlike the predicate noun, it is a required element of the sentence. The function of the linking verb is to associate the adjective phrase with the subject NP. Examples are shown below:

SUBJECT	LINKING VERB	PREDICATE ADJECTIVE	ADVERBIAL
The girl	is	terribly unhappy	at work.
The film	was	incredibly superficial.	
Wind damage	was	minimal	in the cities.

Notice that it is possible to invert the adjective phrase to create a noun phrase:

> the terribly unhappy girl
>
> the incredibly superficial film
>
> minimal wind damage

However, some adjective phrases may only take the predicate adjective position and not the attributive position, e.g., *The girl is asleep* ≠ **the asleep girl.*

EXERCISE 2.17

Directions: Underline and identify the predicate noun or adjective phrase in the following sentences.

P ADJ
Example: The dog is <u>tired</u>.

1. Trains are always late in this country.

2. The chairman was really a remarkably gifted man in many ways.

3. An analysis of the characters in this novel would be quite interesting.

4. The sari is a dress that is worn by many Indian women.

5. The opera is a tale of revenge and a commentary on the mores of the time.

The Adverbial Slot

The **adverbial** is the part of the sentence that shows us the time (when), the place (where), the manner (how), the reason (why), the degree (how much), etc., that an action or state took place. Although the adverbial is usually at the end of the sentence, it can move quite freely to the front of the sentence, in which case it is often followed by a comma. There are several different types of phrases and clauses that can occur in the adverbial slot. The most common adverbial is one or more prepositional phrases, but it can also be an adverb phrase or an adverb clause. Examples are shown below:

SUBJECT	VERB	OBJECT	ADVERBIAL
The taxi	drove	the minister	up the hill to the church.
Her health	deteriorated		very quickly.
The man	left	the country	because he wanted a job in Spain.

The subject-verb-object-adverbial or subject-verb-predicate noun/adjective-adverbial structure of sentences also occurs in adverb clauses. The only difference is that an adverb clause is always preceded by a **clause marker**. The last example above contains a dependent adverb clause, which is shown in boldface below:

SUBJECT	VERB	OBJECT	ADVERBIAL				
			Clause Marker	Clause SUBJECT	Clause VERB	Clause OBJECT	Clause ADVERBIAL
The man	left	the country	**because**	**he**	**wanted**	**a job**	**in Spain.**

EXERCISE 2.18

Directions: Underline the adverbial in the following sentences. Above the adverbial, indicate the dependent clause sentence roles.

	Clause Marker	Clause SUBJECT	Clause VERB	Clause ADVERBIAL
Example: Janet bought a dog	when	she	moved	to Atlanta.

1. Vincent taught English when he lived in Bangkok.

2. Although she was only a girl, Sarah was the mother of the house.

3. The patient went to the beach even though his doctor warned against it.

4. If there is a major earthquake in Los Angeles, many people will die.

5. Since he is an actor, he will probably be a good politician.

EXERCISE 2.19

Directions: Continue EXERCISE 2.8, in which you copied the following sentences onto a piece of paper, leaving three lines above each sentence labelled (a), (b), and (c). On line (c) above each sentence, indicate the sentence roles: SUBJECT, VERB, OBJECT (or PREDICATE NOUN/ADJECTIVE), and ADVERBIAL.

Example:

Word Classes	(a)	DET	N	V	DET	N	PREP	N
Phrases	(b)	[NP	]	[VP	[NP	]	[PP [NP]]]	
Sentence Roles	(c)	SUBJECT		VERB	OBJECT		ADVERBIAL	
		The rabbit	changes	its color	in winter.			

1. A small bomb killed several people at the airport yesterday.

2. Several young women milk the cows in the evening.

3. Most of the students can speak another language.

4. Jonathan needed a new pencil so he bought one at the supermarket.

5. The insects have attacked every tree on my block.

6. Leave this house now!

7. In the fall, the leaves on the trees fall to the ground.

8. The engineer carefully removed all the accumulated oil from the gear box.

9. The children are visiting the old man and they are watering his garden.

10. Elsie doesn't take cream in her coffee.

EXERCISE 2.20

Directions: Copy the following sentences onto a piece of paper, leaving four lines above each sentence labelled (a), (b), (c), and (d). In (a), indicate the **type of phrase** using brackets; in (b), indicate the **type of clause** using brackets; in (c) indicate the **nature** (dependent or independent) **of the clause** using brackets, and in (d) indicate the **sentence roles**.

Example:

Type of Phrase	(a)	[NP] [VP [AdjP]	[NP]	[VP [AdjP]
Type of Clause	(b)		[AdvCl	]
Nature of Clause	(c)	[Independent Clause	[Dependent Clause	]]
Sentence Role	(d)	SUBJECT VERB PRED ADJ	ADVERBIAL	
		The train is always late	if the weather is bad.	

1. President Lincoln is famous because he freed the slaves.

2. As the flight attendant was walking to the plane, she slipped on an oil spot.

3. The children who live in Managua must return to the bus at five o'clock.

4. The dinner was delicious even though it was cold.

5. A spy was hiding in the cupboard when Yoli came into the room.

6. The class which they took last year is not available this semester.

7. The volcano erupted since pressure had accumulated in the magma chamber below it.

8. Where a person works usually determines where he or she lives.

9. By tomorrow morning, a bulldozer will have removed the soil that is blocking the stream.

10. The chemistry instructor cannot explain why forty-five students failed the exam.

CONCLUSION

We have discussed the building blocks of English sentences, starting with the word classes in Chapter 1 and moving on to the phrases, clauses, and sentence roles in Chapter 2. These have been presented as a hierarchy of structures, each with increasing numbers of words. You undoubtedly have many questions about how these various patterns are formed. At this stage, however, we only want to be able to recognize some of the patterns that we will find in our more detailed explorations in coming chapters. We also want to be familiar with some of the grammatical terminology that is used to describe sentences. The terms that we have encountered up to this point are summarized in the list below.

TERM	DEFINITION	EXAMPLE
adjective [ADJ]	a word that modifies and usually precedes a noun	*pretty, green, big*
adjective clause	a clause that postmodifies the noun in a noun phrase	*the class that I am taking*
adjective phrase	the group of adjectives and adverbs that modify a noun	*the <u>very old</u> train*
adverb [ADV]	a word that modifies a verb or adjective and that may occur before a verb or at the end or beginning of a sentence	*usually, very, fast*
adverbial	the usually optional final slot in a typical sentence that contains adverbs, prepositional phrases, and/or dependent clauses	*in the morning, now, when I left Ohio*
adverb clause	a clause that shows time, place, manner, condition, etc.	*where she lives; if I succeed*
adverb phrase	a group of adverbs that modify a verb or a sentence	*She ran <u>extremely fast</u>.*
antecedent	the word that a pronoun replaces or points back to	*John ← he; a book ← it*
attributive adjective	an adjective that comes before a noun in a noun phrase	*a <u>curious</u> phenomenon*
auxilliary verb [AUX]	a verb that always occurs with another verb, which it is said to help (synonym: helping verb)	*be, do, have,* and the modals
bare subject	the core noun of a subject noun phrase	*the old <u>man</u> who lives nearby*
clause	a structure that contains a subject-verb relationship	*the man bought a house; because the sun shines*
clause marker	a grammatical word that comes at the beginning of a clause	*when, why, if, because, who*
command	a sentence whose subject is understood to be "you"	*(You) Close the door, please!*
conjunction [CONJ]	a word that joins two phrases or clauses	*and, but, or, so, yet, for*
content word	a word (N, V, ADJ, ADV) that creates a picture in the mind	*dog, run, big, slowly*
count noun	a noun form that may be counted and therefore has a singular and plural form	*table, star, idea, problem*

dependent clause	a clause that must be attached to an independent clause in order to be a full sentence and not a fragment	*when I was in LA; if you saw a cat; that I like*
determiner [DET]	the first word(s) of a noun phrase (e.g., an article)	*a, all, the, my, this, Ann's*
function word	a word (DET, PREP, CONJ, AUX, PRO) that shows a grammatical relationship between content words	*a, in, and, have, they*
helping verb	[see "auxiliary verb"]	
independent clause	a clause that can stand by itself (synonym: sentence)	*Horses love chocolate.*
intransitive verb	a verb (v.i.) that does not allow an object to follow it	*go, sleep, live*
linking verb	a verb that establishes equality between the subject and a predicate noun or adjective	*be, seem, look, get, become, appear*
mass noun	a singular noun that refers to a liquid, material, or category	*milk, wood, furniture, fruit*
modal	an auxiliary verb that shows obligation, possibility, ability, future, necessity, etc.	*can, will, should, must, ought to, could, would*
noun [N]	a content word that forms the core of a noun phrase	*house, uncle, idea, tree*
noun phrase [NP]	a phrase consisting of a DET, optional ADJ, N, and optional postmodification or a lone PRON that serves as the subject and/or object of a sentence or a PP	*the big door; a pretty dress; I; them; men in the class*
noun clause	a clause that takes the place of a noun phrase	*where they live; what it cost*
noncount noun	a noun form that cannot be counted and therefore has only a singular form [see "mass noun"]	*water, chalk, furniture,*
object	the third slot in a sentence that shows who or what receives the action of the subject	*Jill kicked <u>the ball</u>; the man killed <u>the bear</u>.*
phrase	a structure containing a key word and its close associates that forms a natural group	*in the morning* (PP); *the old man* (NP)
plural	a form that indicates more than one entity	*rooms, women, are*

postmodification	modifying words/phrases/clauses occur after a noun in an NP	*the girl <u>in the window</u>*
predicate	all of a sentence except the subject NP (synonym: VP)	*lives in a tree; works now*
predicate adjective	an adjective that occurs after a linking verb in the VP	*She is <u>cool</u>; he seems <u>smart</u>*
predicate noun	a noun that occurs after a linking verb in the VP	*He is <u>a student</u>; they're <u>dogs</u>*
preposition [PREP]	a function word that shows a relationship between nouns	*at, on, in, under, before, of*
prepositional phrase	a phrase consisting of a PREP plus an NP (acronym: PP)	*in a room, at the top, of mine*
pronoun [PRO]	a function word that represents an earlier noun which it is unnecessary to repeat	*he, she, her, they, this, many*
proper noun	a noun in the form of a name which is usually capitalized	*John, Mrs. West, Dr. Smith*
referent	[see "antecedent"]	
sentence	an independent clause containing at least a verb	*I like salad; Shut up!*
singular	a form that indicates a single entity	*room, woman, is*
subject	the first slot in a sentence consisting usually of an NP	*<u>John</u> likes dogs; <u>She</u> paints.*
transitive verb	a verb (v.t.) that allows an object to follow it	*kill, drink, drive, read*
verb [V]	a word showing action/state or the second slot in a sentence	*go, taken, living; He <u>left</u>.*
verb phrase [VP]	[see "predicate"]	
zero [Ø] determiner	the empty determiner slot (zero article) in a noun phrase	*[Ø] Aristocrats drink [Ø] tea.*

Unit II: The Verb

Chapter 3

THE AUXILIARY SYSTEM

The English auxiliary system consists of the auxiliary verbs, which are also known as *helping verbs* because they can only help another verb to carry out its function; they can never stand alone. The auxiliary verbs have four categories: *be*, *have*, *do*, and a whole class of words called the modal auxiliaries, or **modals**. The first three categories can pose a problem in English because the three words have a dual role. When they occur with another verb, they are auxiliaries. When they stand alone, they are no longer auxiliaries, but rather **main verbs**. The modals, on the other hand, can never stand alone and therefore can never be main verbs.

THE AUXILIARY VERB *BE*

The auxiliary verb *be* is the most frequently occurring auxiliary in English. It is used as a function word to construct both the continuous tenses in English and the passive voice, both of which will be discussed in the next chapter. In the following examples, the auxiliary verb is in boldface and the main verb (the one that is being "helped") is underlined.

> The cat **is** <u>sitting</u> in the window.   [continuous tense]
> This poem **is** <u>taken</u> from Hamlet.   [passive voice]

It is also possible for the verb *be* to be the main verb in a sentence and thus become a content word.

> Cairo **is** the capital of Egypt.   [NP *be* NP]
> This problem **is** impossible.   [NP *be* AdjP]

The verb *be* as a content word is known as a linking verb because it shows that the elements on either side of it should be considered as one (e.g., *Cairo = the capital of Egypt*; *this problem = impossible*, i.e., this impossible problem). It can only occur in a Type II verb phrase.

Agreement and Time

One of the considerations in using the auxiliary verb *be* is the **agreement** of the subject of the sentence with its auxiliary. If the subject is **singular** (i.e., there is only one), then the auxiliary must be singular: *is*, e.g., <u>The cat is</u> *eating a mouse*. In other words, the subject and the auxiliary must "agree" that they both concern a single entity. Likewise, if the subject is **plural** (i.e., there is more than one), then the auxiliary must be plural: *are*, e.g., <u>The cats are</u> *eating mice*. However, if the subject is "I" then the auxiliary verb *be* has its own special form in the present tense: *am*, e.g., <u>I am</u> *eating a mouse.*[1]

Another consideration is the time that the auxiliary shows. The present time is concerned with things that are happening or of interest now. The past time is concerned with things that

---

[1] *You* refers to either a single person or to more than one. However, for historical reasons, the agreement is always plural (e.g., *are* for both singular and plural forms of *you*).

happened or were of interest at some time in the past. The forms of *be* for these two times are shown in Table 3.1.

Table 3.1 Forms of the Auxiliary *Be*

SUBJECT	PRESENT	PAST
Singular	is	was
Plural	are	were
"I"	am	was

In the following exercise, work out the correct form (agreement and time) of *be* from the information contained in the rest of the sentence.

EXERCISE 3.1

Directions: First, identify the bare subject by drawing a line under it. Identify the nature of the subject (singular, plural, or "I") and the time when the sentence takes place (past or present). Then choose the correct form of *be* from Table 3.1.

Example: Jack _____ getting some water right now.

Solution: Subject: _Sing._ Time: _Pres._ _Jack_ is getting some water right now.

1. Subject:____ Time:_____ The Cantors _____ living in Madison when I saw them.

2. Subject:____ Time:_____ I _____ taking several classes this semester.

3. Subject:____ Time:_____ The hostage slipped the reporter a note, which said, "Help us! We _____ being tortured."

4. Subject:____ Time:_____ After the terrible fire, the little boy _____ told never to play with matches again.

5. Subject:____ Time:_____ The passengers on the plane _____ asked to remain calm after the pilot described the storm ahead.

THE AUXILIARY VERB *HAVE*

The auxiliary verb *have* is used as a function word to construct the perfect tenses in English, which will also be discussed in the next chapter. In the following examples, the auxiliary verb is shown in boldface and the main verb (the one that is being "helped") is underlined:

The president **has** <u>signed</u> an agreement with China.	[perfect tense]
Researchers **have** <u>discovered</u> a new form of the HIV virus.	[perfect tense]

It is also possible for the verb *have* to be the main verb in a sentence and thus become a content word.

Marianne **has** a black Porsche.	[NP *have* NP]
We **have** ten minutes to get to the airport.	[NP *have* NP]

The verb *have* as a content word generally means "to possess" but has several other meanings in different contexts (e.g., "limit of duration" in the second example sentence). Unlike *be* when it stands alone, *have* only occurs as a Type I verb phrase. The forms of the auxiliary verb *have* are shown in Table 3.2.

Table 3.2 Forms of the Auxiliary *Have*

SUBJECT	PRESENT	PAST
Singular	has	had
Plural	have	had
"I"	have	had

The problems with agreement and time that we noted for the use of the auxiliary *be* also apply to the auxiliary *have*. In the following exercise, work out the correct form of *have* from the information contained in the rest of the sentence.

EXERCISE 3.2

Directions: First, identify the bare subject by drawing a line under it. Identify the nature of the subject (singular, plural, or "I") and the time when the sentence takes place (past or present). Then choose the correct form of *have* from Table 3.2.

   Example: The owner _____ already received the new tax forms.

   Solution: Subject: _Sing._ Time: _Pres._   The <u>owner</u> has already received the new tax forms.

1.   Subject:____ Time:_____   The Ajax Company _____ employed over 200 new workers in the last three weeks.

2.   Subject:____ Time:_____   Before coming back to the U.S., Brian _____ taught English in Spain for many years.

3.   Subject:____ Time:_____   I _____ increased my knowledge of the Solar System.

4.   Subject:____ Time:_____   The lifeboats sank when they _____ taken on too much water.

5.   Subject:____ Time:_____   Tiny hearing aids with no visible wires or batteries _____ done much to improve the lives of the hearing impaired.

THE AUXILIARY VERB *DO*

The auxiliary verb *do* has two basic functions in English: to show negation, and to construct questions[2]. In the following examples, the auxiliary verb is shown in boldface and the main verb (the one that is being "helped") is underlined:

---

[2] Auxiliary *do* is occasionally used to show emphasis. Emphatic use of the auxiliary verb requires that *do* receive the main stress in the sentence and that the sentence show a situation involving a disagreement, an argument or a response to an expression of disbelief (e.g., I *did* return the key!).

Riding a bicycle **does** not <u>require</u> a license.   [negation]
Do bats <u>fly</u> in the daytime?   [question]

It is also possible for the verb *do* to be the main verb in a sentence and thus become a content word.

John **does** his homework at the library.   [NP *do* NP]
The captain **did** his duty in abandoning the ship.   [NP *do* NP]

The verb *do* generally means "the performance or carrying out of something." Like *have*, *do* only occurs as a Type I verb phrase. The forms of the auxiliary verb *do* are shown in Table 3.3.

Table 3.3 Forms of the Auxiliary *Do*

SUBJECT	PRESENT	PAST
Singular	does	did
Plural	do	did
"I"	do	did

The problems with agreement and time that we noted for the use of the auxiliaries *be* and *have* also apply to the auxiliary *do*. In the following exercise, work out the correct form of *do* from the information contained in the rest of the sentence. Note that in certain question forms the subject comes directly after the auxiliary rather than before it.

EXERCISE 3.3

Directions: First, identify the bare subject by drawing a line under it. Identify the nature of the subject (singular, plural, or "I") and the time when the sentence takes place (past or present). Then choose the correct form of *do* from the list above.

Example: A tiger _____ not usually have spots.
Solution: Subject: <u>Sing.</u> Time: <u>Pres.</u> A <u>tiger</u> does not usually have spots.

1. Subject:____ Time:_____ Where _____ mosquitoes come from?

2. Subject:____ Time:_____ _____ Eleanor pay the rent yesterday?

3. Subject:____ Time:_____ I _____ have a master's degree! If you think I'm lying, ask my mother.

4. Subject:____ Time:_____ Many people in the southern hemisphere _____ not have enough to eat.

5. Subject:____ Time:_____ _____ *inflammable* mean "burns easily" or "does not burn easily"?

THE MODAL AUXILIARY VERBS *WILL* AND *CAN*

The modal auxiliary verbs (modals) constitute the fourth and final category of auxiliary verbs. Since they will be discussed in detail in Chapter 5, we will be concerned only with the modals *will* and *can* here. Unlike the auxiliary verbs *be, have,* and *do,* the modals *will* and *can* have no singular and plural forms. In the following examples, the auxiliary verb is shown in boldface and the main verb (the one that is being "helped") is underlined:

> A plant **will** die if you fail to water it.
>
> He **can** run faster than a dog.

The problems with agreement that we noted for the use of the auxiliary verbs *be, have* and *do* do not apply to the modals *will* and *can*. However, some students will attempt to apply the rules of agreement they have learned for the other auxiliaries and make sentences such as *Jan *cans speak Dutch*. In the following exercise we will be concerned not with the correct form of *will* and *can* but with the choice of *will* or *can* that is most appropriate for the sentence. *Will* indicates "high probability" while *can* indicates "ability".

EXERCISE 3.4

Directions: Fill the blanks with *will* or *can*.

1. When _____ you finish your master's degree?

2. Our office needs a person who _____ speak fluent Brazilian Portuguese.

3. _____ you please help me to move this piano?

4. Our office needs a person who _____ not be late.

5. _____ paper burn in a weightless environment?

USING AUXILIARY VERBS WITHOUT A MAIN VERB

In all the examples we have looked at so far, an auxiliary verb has occurred with a verb that it "helps." Every auxiliary verb must be attached to a verb. However, there are certain situations in English in which this verb is "understood", just as the subject in a command sentence is understood to be *you*. The verb following an auxiliary is only understood if that verb has already appeared, either in the same sentence or the sentence before. This often occurs in making comparisons and contrasts. Look at the following example:

> CONTRAST: Mary cannot swim but John **can**.

The verb *swim* in the first part of the sentence is understood to be the verb after *can*, but it is not necessary to restate that verb. In fact, it sounds rather odd to do so. Here are some other examples:

> COMPARISON: Mr. Ghoti has finished his dinner and Mr. Iram **has**, too.
>
> CONTRAST: Mario doesn't like pasta but Guido **does**.
>
> CONTRAST: Sylvia is not living at home but her sister **is**.

Notice in these examples that it is not only the verb that is understood but the entire predicate or verb phrase. Of course, we could say "Mr. Ghoti has finished his dinner and Mr. Iram has finished his dinner, too," but it would sound wordy and repetitious.

EXERCISE 3.5

Directions: Draw a line through the "understood" predicates that are not necessary in the sentence.

     Example: Elvira will not swim in a river, but Elvis will ~~swim in a river~~.

1. The important papers were not taken from the safe but the jewelry was taken from the safe.

2. The women are singing in the fall concert and some of the men are singing in the fall concert, too.

3. Jaqueline does not like eggplant, and neither does Jack like eggplant.

4. My brother had never seen a badger, but I had seen a badger.

5. Some people cannot eat food prepared with MSG. Can you eat food prepared with MSG?

PROBLEM SOLVING WITH THE AUXILIARY SYSTEM

It was noted earlier in this chapter that students often have certain problems with the auxiliaries. However, we know that second language learning is a complex and delicate process. The motivation to persist in acquiring a language can be easily damaged by negative emotional experiences. For this reason, we want to praise a language student for his or her accomplishments before we begin to suggest that that student has made a mistake because he or she failed to use a rule of grammar. The greatest problems with auxiliaries are agreement and time. However, it is also possible to get one or the other of these elements correct. Throughout this book, it will be our practice to praise for what is right about an error before we indicate what is wrong. In the case of auxiliaries (AUX), it is possible to get the following right:

    a. correct SUBJECT-AUX AGREEMENT (singular or plural)
    b. correct TIME (past, present, or future)
    c. correct CATEGORY OF AUX (*be, have, do* or a modal)

These aspects reflect what students are likely to do wrong in using an auxiliary: a) fail to make the subject agree with the AUX, b) use the wrong time of AUX, or c) use the incorrect category of AUX.

EXERCISE 3.6

Directions: In the following sentences, a student made a single error in using an auxiliary verb. Your job is to address the error in three stages:

    a) bracket the error to focus your attention
    b) list what the student got right about the bracketed error (in this case, the error is the form of the auxiliary) and show this in parentheses
    c) compare the original erroneous sentence to the correct sentence and explain what mistake the student made

    Example: *The boy are living with his mother now.
          [The star (*) indicates that the sentence contains an error.]

Solution: a) Bracket the error (the auxiliary verb or verbs):
*The boy [are] living with his mother now.

b) Show what is right about the auxiliary:

correct time of AUX (present) [Note: *are* is one of the forms that *be* can take to show present time]

correct category of AUX (*be*) [Note: the student correctly chose a form of *be* rather than *have*, *do*, or a modal]

c) Compare the erroneous sentence to the correct form and explain the mistake:

*The boy [are] living with his mother now.

The boy   is   living with his mother now.

Explanation: The subject (*the boy*) is singular so the auxiliary should also be singular (*is*), not plural (*are*), to make the subject and AUX agree.

1. *The marathon runner have won two gold medals so far.

2. *What had your girlfriend say to you last night?

3. *I was working for a computer company at present.

4. *The prime minister wills speak to the parliament tomorrow afternoon.

5. *When the thieves entered the bank, they did already disconnected the alarm system.

6. *Will you prefer chicken or fish for dinner, sir?

7. *A bouquet of flowers are delivered every Friday morning.

8. *When does Alexander Graham Bell invent the telephone?

9. *Susan had been very involved with this case since she joined the law firm earlier this month.

10. *Every other day, I is taken to the hospital for a dialysis treatment.

REVIEW

EXERCISE 3.7

Directions: Using the ten corrected sentences from Exercise 3.6 as a data base, answer the following questions:

1. How many NPs are there in Sentence 5?

2. Which sentences, if any, have NPs that contain PPs?

3. Is the verb in Sentence 3 transitive or intransitive? What about the verb *prefer* in Sentence 6?

4. Which sentences contain adverbials that have been moved in front of the subject?

5. Which sentences contain dependent clauses? Are they adverbial, adjective, or noun clauses?

Chapter 4a

THE VERB TENSE SYSTEM

No sentence in English can exist without a verb. This is because the verb is "the central component of a clause, and [it] determines a significant amount of the sentence structure. Sentence grammar is to a large degree *verb* grammar."[1] The verb tense system consists of the various forms that verbs can take in the verb slot of a sentence, i.e., the slot that comes directly after the subject noun phrase.

TENSE

The term *tense* is used in this book to refer to the full name of the verb form, which always consists of two elements: a time and an aspect.

Time

There are three times that are expressed by English grammar: **past**, **present** and **future**. The present time is concerned with things that are happening or of interest at the moment of speaking. The past time is concerned with things that happened or were of interest at some time in the past. The future time is concerned with things that will happen or will be of interest at some time in the future. Strictly speaking, English only has two times, past and present, because the future is expressed with a modal (e.g., *She will go*) rather than a different verb form as in some other languages. However, to make the tense system easier for students to understand, we will follow tradition in using a future time as well.

Aspect

Aspect describes certain characteristics of the activity or state represented by a verb. There are two aspects in English: continuous and perfect. When neither of these aspects is used, we say the aspect is simple. So there are really three aspects: **simple**, **continuous**, and **perfect**. The simple aspect indicates an activity that is completed (e.g., *The war ended in 1945*) or habitual (e.g., *It rains in winter*). The continuous aspect indicates an activity that continues through time (e.g., *I am writing a letter*). The perfect aspect indicates an activity that began prior to the moment of speaking but has relevance only at that moment (e.g., *She has lived in many places...and therefore would be a good travel agent*).

The Inflectional Morphemes Attached to Verbs

We saw in Chapter 1 that there are four inflectional morphemes or endings that are attached to verbs: *-s*, *-ing*, *-ed₁*, and *-ed₂*. To these we must add a fifth possible ending, the invisible form *-Ø*. These are summarized in Table 4.1.

---

[1] P. L. Hubbard, "Non-transformational theories of grammar: implications for language teaching." In T. Odlin (Ed.), *Perspectives in Pedagogical Grammar* (Cambridge: Cambridge University Press, 1994), 69.

Table 4.1 Verb Endings

ENDING	EXAMPLE
–s	John walks to school every day.
- ing	Mary Lou is teaching biology today.
- ed$_1$	The frog jumped into the stream.
- ed$_2$	Dr. Esparza has delivered two babies this week.
- Ø	Cats hunt [Ø] at night.

These endings can also be attached to the auxiliary verbs *be, have,* and *do* (but not to the modals). A verb, either main or auxiliary, can have only one ending. Once it has an ending, no other may be attached. A verb can be compared to a one-car garage and a verb ending to a car. Once a single car occupies the garage, no others will fit.

EXERCISE 4.1

Directions: Underline the verb endings (or add Ø) in the following passage.

> *Example:* Although the patients are walking now, some use [Ø] canes and others have complained of back aches.

Watching the Rain

I watch quietly as the rain comes down. It has flooded the depressions in the field that the tractor carved as it was coming home last night. When the rain stops, those tiny lakes reflect the light of the evening clouds like television screens that are recording the passage of the day. Now the sky is darkening again, and the light in the puddles disappears. Great torrents of rain strike my window. The thunder roars. The lightning flashes. And I am happy to be safe and warm in my Navajo blanket.

THE VERB TENSES

Each verb tense in English is constructed from one of the three times and one or more of the three aspects. English structure is very efficient: it uses every possible combination of times and aspects to produce the twelve tenses in English, as shown in Table 4.2.

Table 4.2 The Twelve Tenses in English

ASPECT	TIME		
	PAST	PRESENT	FUTURE
SIMPLE	Simple Past	Simple Present	Simple Future
CONTINUOUS	Past Continuous	Present Continuous	Future Continuous
PERFECT	Past Perfect	Present Perfect	Future Perfect
PERFECT CONTINUOUS	Past Perfect Continuous	Present Perfect Continuous	Future Perfect Continuous

[Note: We traditionally reverse the order of time and aspect in the simple tenses.]

Seven of the twelve tenses are used much more frequently than the remaining five. These are shown in boldface in Table 4.2; they include the three simple tenses and the past and present forms of the continuous and perfect tenses. Although all twelve tenses are described in detail below, you may decide to concentrate on these seven and ignore the remaining five until you have specific questions about or reasons for using them.

The Simple Tenses

The simple tenses include the simple present tense, the simple past tense, and the simple future tense. The simple aspect means that neither the continuous nor the perfect aspect applies.

THE SIMPLE PRESENT TENSE

Before we take a closer look at the simple present tense, try the following exercise.

EXERCISE 4.2

Directions: Underline all the verbs in the following passage with a single line. Underline the time expressions (expressions that indicate when the action takes place) with a double line.

The Canine Teeth

The canine teeth lie on either side of the front teeth, the incisors. They have two main duties: they guide the teeth in chewing and they generally maintain the proper shape of the face. The canines are the strongest teeth in the mouth, and dentists often use them as anchors for partial dentures or bridges. The canine tooth has the longest roots of all the teeth and it decays more slowly than the others. For this reason, a person tends to keep the canines longer, especially if he or she is careful to clean them every day.

The word *canine* comes from the Latin word for *dog*. In animals, the canines cut food, tear flesh, and defend territory. They also sometimes function as a whetstone, i.e., they sharpen the teeth every time they mesh together.

Form

Let's make a list of the verbs you underlined with a single line:

lie	decays	tear
have	tends	defend
guide	to keep	function
maintain	is	sharpen
are	to clean	mesh
use	comes	
has	cut	

We will ignore the infinitive structures (*to keep, to clean*), which we will discuss in Chapter 15, and the word *chewing*, which is a noun, not a verb, in this passage. The remaining verbs can be classified into two categories: 1) those with the *s*-ending and 2) those with the Ø-ending. In Chapter 3, we saw that the irregular verb *be* has special forms of its own: *be* + *s* = **is** and *be* + Ø = **are**.

VERB + **s**	VERB + **Ø**	
has	lie	tear
decays	have	defend
tends	guide	function
is [*be* + *s*]	maintain	sharpen
comes	cut	mesh

What is it that tells you whether or not a verb requires the *s*-ending or the Ø-ending? Let's look back at the passage on the canine teeth and make a list of the subjects of all the verbs under the "VERB + **s**" column.

Subject	Verb
the canine tooth	has
it (the canine tooth)	decays
a person	tends
he or she	is
the word *canine*	comes

What do all these subjects have in common? They are all **singular**. If we made a list of the subjects of all the verbs under the "VERB + Ø " column, we would find that they are all **plural**.

We can generalize this information into a formula for the simple present tense:

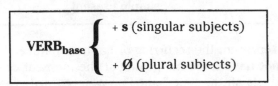

This formula indicates that the **base form** of the verb (the dictionary form) requires the *s*-ending if the subject is singular and the Ø-ending if the subject is plural. The exceptions are *I* and *you*, singular subjects that always require Ø.

Time Expressions

Now let's make a list of the time expressions you underlined in the passage with a double line:

Time Expressions

+generally
+often
+every day
+sometimes
+every time

[Note: The "+" sign in front of a time expression indicates that it also occurs with other tenses.]

What do these expressions have in common? They all indicate habitual or recurring actions, which are typically used in reporting facts about the world. Notice the location of these time expressions. Three of them occur in the verb slot, before the verbs *maintain*, *use*, and *function*. These time expressions are known as **adverbs of frequency**, and they often occur with the simple tenses (though not exclusively with the simple present tense, which is why there is a "+" in front of each time expression in the list above). The adverbs of frequency also include words such as *normally*, *usually*, *frequently*, *occasionally*, *seldom*, *rarely*, and *never*. They show habitual actions that occur over the full range of possibilities, from constantly to not at all.

Every day and *every time* occur in the adverbial slot. This is the most common location of time expressions linked to verb tenses. Other adverbial time expressions linked to the simple present tense include expressions such as *all the time*, *on Sundays*, *every week*, *every month*, *every year*, *on occasion*, *once in a while*, and *now and then*. They show habitual actions of varying frequency.

Generalization

The simple present verb has two forms: $VERB_s$ for singular subjects and $VERB_{\emptyset}$ for plural subjects. The simple present tense shows habitual or recurring actions, especially facts. It can be represented on a time line as follows:

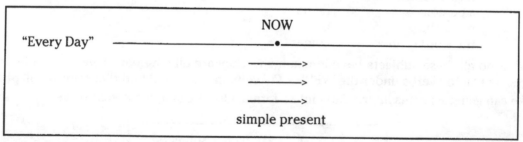

The repeated arrows represent the recurring or habitual nature of the simple present tense. A habitual action does not have to be happening at the moment of speaking. If you say, "My sister reads Victorian novels all the time," she is not necessarily reading a novel at this very minute. The same can be said of the statement, "The sun shines every day," which is true even at night.

Work on the following exercise with a partner. If you are a native speaker of English, you know these forms unconsciously so you will have no trouble getting them correct. Imagine that you are trying to explain the answer to a nonnative speaker, who has no intuitive knowledge of what "sounds right." First identify the time expression, which usually tells you which tense to use. Then identify the bare subject to determine if it is singular or plural. This should enable you to explain why you selected the form you did. One exception to the use of time expressions to indicate tense is general facts about the world, which are often reported in the simple present tense without a time expression of any kind, as you will see in the following exercise.

EXERCISE 4.3

Directions: Draw a double line under the time expression in the following sentences, if there is one. Draw a single line under the bare subject. Then fill the blank with the correct form of the verb in parentheses.

    Example: John (work) _____ in a factory on weekends.

    Solution: John works in a factory on weekends.

1. Uncle Ralph (go) _____ to church every Sunday.

2. Lionesses usually (defend) _____ their cubs from predators.

3. The moon (circle) _____ the Earth every twenty-eight days.

4. My friends and I (like) _____ to go dancing once in a while.

5. The capital city of Malaysia (be) _____ Kuala Lumpur.

6. During the winter season, Doris usually (rent) _____ an apartment on the Côte d'Azur.

7. Two hundred and thirty-one cubic inches of water (equal) _____ one gallon.

8. Bats (be) _____ rarely visible in the daytime.

9. Winds in a low-pressure area (whirl) _____ counterclockwise in the northern hemisphere, clockwise in the southern.

10. The government (announce) _____ the unemployment statistics once a month.

THE SIMPLE PAST TENSE

Before we look at the simple past tense, try the following preliminary exercise.

EXERCISE 4.4

Directions: Underline all the verbs in the following passage with a single line. Underline the time expressions with a double line.

Abraham Lincoln

Abraham Lincoln came into the world on February 12, 1809, almost two hundred years ago. When he was a small boy, he and his family moved to the frontier of Indiana. At that time, his mother taught him to read and write. Although he had very little formal education, he became one of the best-educated men in the Great West. When Lincoln was a young man, his family moved to Illinois. He earned a living at an early age, but in his leisure time, he studied law. He soon became one of the best-known lawyers in the state capital at Springfield, Illinois. In 1860, Lincoln was elected President of the United States. Soon after his election, some of the Southern states withdrew from the Union and set up the Confederate States of America. This action triggered the Civil War, which lasted from 1861 to 1865. During the war, Lincoln issued his famous Emancipation Proclamation. After the war ended, the Thirteenth Amendment, which outlawed slavery, was added to the Constitution of the United States. A few days later, an actor named John Wilkes Booth shot the President, who died on April 14, 1865.

Form

Let's make a list of the verbs you underlined with a single line:

came	became	became	lasted	shot
was	was	was elected	issued	died
moved	moved	withdrew	ended	
taught	earned	set up	outlawed	
had	studied	triggered	was added	

We will ignore the passive structures (*was elected, was added*). The phrase *to read and write* functions as a noun in this passage. The remaining verbs can be classified into two categories: those ending with *ed* and those with other forms. The verbs ending with *ed* are called **regular** verbs because they consistently have this form. The other verbs are called **irregular** verbs because their forms are not predictable. Nevertheless, all of the verbs in this list are formed with the ed_1 morpheme described in Chapter 1, with the stipulation that if an *e* is already present in the base form of a regular verb, it is dropped before -ed_1 is added. For example, the $VERB_{base}$ *move* + ed_1 produces the regular verb *moved*, whereas the $VERB_{base}$ *come* + ed_1 produces the irregular verb *came*. The combination will be referred to as $VERB_{ed_1}$.

Regular Verbs ($VERB_{ed_1}$)	Irregular Verbs ($VERB_{ed_1}$)
moved	came
earned	was
studied	taught
triggered	had
lasted	became
issued	withdrew
ended	set up
outlawed	shot
died	

Whether or not a verb is regular or irregular has nothing to do with subject-verb agreement. In fact, in the second sentence of the passage about Lincoln, we see that the plural subject *he and his family* is followed by the simple past verb *moved*. Then in the fifth sentence, we see that the singular subject *his family* is also followed by the simple past verb *moved*. In other words, subject-verb agreement is not required in the simple past tense.

Regular and irregular verbs are a product of the history and development of the English language. We do know that irregular verbs tend to become regular over time. The verb *help* had the irregular past form *holp* in the seventeenth century and there are several irregular past verbs that are being challenged by current usage. Do you say *hung* or *hanged? lit* or *lighted? dove* or *dived?* Or are there perhaps situations in which you would use one form but not the other?

We can generalize this information into a formula for the simple past tense:

$$\text{VERB}_{ed_1} \left(\text{VERB}_{base} + ed_1 \right)$$

This formula indicates that the base form of the verb requires the $-ed_1$ ending in all cases, though this ending will only manifest itself as *ed* for regular verbs.

Time Expressions

Now let's make a list of the time expressions you underlined in the passage with a double line:

Time Expressions

> on February 12, 1809
> almost two hundred years ago
> when he was a small boy
> at that time
> +when Lincoln was a young man
> +at an early age
> in 1860
> soon after his election
> from 1861 to 1865
> during the war
> after the war ended
> +a few days later
> on April 14, 1865

What do these expressions have in common? The expressions marked with a "+" could take place at any time (i.e., they can also occur with present and future tenses, e.g., *Children* **learn** *to communicate* <u>*at an early age*</u>; *We* **will fly** *to Scotland* <u>*a few days later*</u>). All the rest indicate a time in the past that is not connected to the present. Notice that all the time expressions occur in the adverbial slot, sometimes at the beginning of the sentence, sometimes at the end.

Generalization

The simple past verb has one form, VERB_{ed_1}, though the *ed*-ending is only visible in regular verbs. The simple past tense shows actions or states that occurred at a time in the past that has no connection to the present. It can be represented on a time line as follows:

```
                                              NOW
"Back Then" ————•——————//———————•——————
            simple past
```

Work on the following exercise with a partner. Remember that you are trying to explain the answer to a nonnative speaker. First identify the time expression. Then determine whether the verb is regular or irregular.

EXERCISE 4.5

Directions: Draw a double line under the time expression in the following sentences, if there is one. Then fill the blank with the correct form of the verb in parentheses.

   Example: John (live) _____ in Norway from 1978 to 1980.
   Solution: John lived in Norway <u>from 1978 to 1980</u>.

1. The Second World War (begin) _____ in 1939.

2. The handle of the cup (break) _____ when it fell on the floor.

3. In the old days, his grandmother (collect) _____ the harvest by herself.

4. Dinosaurs (roam) _____ the earth until the end of the Cretaceous period.

5. The Minoan civilization on the Greek island of Crete (invent) _____ the flush toilet in about 2000 B.C.

6. The principal (call) you _____ less than two minutes ago.

7. As the surgeon was performing the operation, he (cut) _____ his thumb.

8. When she was a girl, Iliana (take) _____ ballet lessons from a famous teacher.

9. In 1893, Edison (show) _____ the first motion picture.

10. David (lose) _____ his home in the hurricane of 1992.

THE SIMPLE FUTURE TENSE

Before we take a closer look at the simple future tense, try the following exercise.

EXERCISE 4.6

Directions: Underline all the verbs (the entire verb slot, i.e., everything between the subject and the object or adverbial, but not the entire verb phrase) in the following passage with a single line. Underline the time expressions with a double line.

A Trip to Switzerland

Roger Greenbaum is going to travel to Switzerland next year. He and his brother Joseph will fly from New York to Geneva on June 3 on Swiss Air. They'll arrive at about seven o'clock at night. The next day, they are going to walk around the city. A few days later, Roger will drive to Zürich by himself. The trip will take about three hours. After that, he'll probably visit the sights in and around Zürich. At the end of the week, he will return to New York. His brother will stay in Europe for another two weeks before he returns. They're going to have a great time, and I am going to pick them up at the airport when they get home.

Form

Let's make a list of the verbs you underlined with a single line:

is going to travel	will take	're (are) going to have
will fly	'll (will)...visit	am going to pick...up
'll (will) arrive	will return	get
are going to walk	will stay	
will drive	returns	

We will ignore the contractions (*'ll = will; 're = are*) and the simple present forms *returns* and *get*. The remaining verbs can be classified into two categories: those beginning with the modal *will* and those beginning with the auxiliary modal equivalent *be going to*.

Verbs with the Modal **will**	Verbs with the Modal Equivalent **be going to**
will fly	is going to travel
will arrive	are going to walk
will drive	are going to have
will take	am going to pick...up
will visit	
will return	
will stay	

What is it that controls whether the verb structure begins with *will* or *be going to*? *Be going to* generally serves to introduce a narrative in the future, whereas *will* tends to continue that narrative.

What is it that controls the choice of *is* or *are* before *going to*? You can probably guess by now, but if not, look back at the passage about the boys' trip to Europe. The subject of *is going to travel* is *Roger Greenbaum*. The subject of *are going to walk* and of *are going to have* is *they*. The subject of *am going to pick [them] up* is *I*. The first subject is singular, the second two are plural (i.e., *they* = Roger and Joseph), and the third is *I*. We discussed the forms of auxiliary *be* in Chapter 3 (singular subject + *is*; plural subject + *are*; "I" + *am*).

The simple future tense is the first tense we have looked at that requires an auxiliary verb. That is why the verbs in the list above all have two elements: the auxiliary and the main verb that it helps. The main verb must always be the base form ($VERB_{base}$) when a modal auxiliary is used.

We can generalize this information into a formula for the simple future tense:

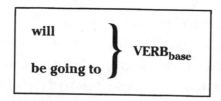

This formula indicates that the modal auxiliary *will* or *be going to* is always followed by the base form of the verb. The form of *be* in *be going to* must agree with its subject.

Time Expressions

Now let's make a list of the time expressions you underlined in the passage with a double line:

Time Expressions

   next year
+on June 3
+at about seven o'clock at night
+the next day
+a few days later
+about three hours
+after that
+at the end of the week
  before he returns
  when they get home

What do these expressions have in common? The expressions with a "+" could take place at any time (they can also occur with past and present tenses, e.g., *The children **left** on June 3*; *She always **flies** home the next day*). All the rest indicate a time in the future that is not connected to the present. Notice that the time expressions occur in the adverbial slot, sometimes at the beginning of the sentence, sometimes at the end.

Generalization

The simple future verb has two forms, *will* + VERB$_{base}$ or *be going to* + VERB$_{base}$. *Will* has only one form and therefore does not require agreement with the subject; *be going to* begins with *be*, which must always agree with the subject. The simple future tense shows actions or states that occurred at a time in the future that has no connection to the present. It can be represented on a time line as follows:

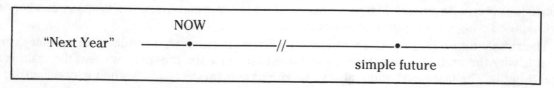

Work on the following exercise with a partner. Remember that you are trying to explain the answer to a nonnative speaker. First identify the time expression. Then determine which "sounds better," *will* or *be going to*. Finally, determine whether the auxiliary must agree with the subject.

There is another form of the simple future tense that simply attaches a future time expression to the simple present or the present continuous tense, as shown in the following examples:

John leaves tomorrow.   [simple present + future time expression]
Jane is flying home tonight.   [present continuous + future time expression]

You may prefer one of these forms in completing the following exercise.

EXERCISE 4.7

Directions: Draw a double line under the time expression in the following sentences. Then fill the blank with the correct form of the verb in parentheses.

Example: Mary (study) _____ in Portugal next year.

Solution: Mary will study in Portugal <u>next year</u>.

1. The meeting (begin) _____ at eight o'clock tonight.

2. The Simpsons (return) _____ from their vacation a week from tomorrow.

3. I (remind) _____ my sister of her appointment with you this afternoon.

4. In a few minutes, Rhonda's husband (jump) _____ from the top of a cliff wearing a parachute.

5. The cook and her staff (need) _____ ten gallons of milk per day when the students return to school.

6. The free trade agreement (open) _____ the borders between the participant countries three years from now.

7. The school (pay) _____ for the drinks at the party at the end of the semester.

8. Control of the island (revert) _____ to the native inhabitants in five years.

9. On August 11, 1999, a solar eclipse (be) _____ visible from Europe.

10. After you take this medicine, you (feel) _____ somewhat sleepy.

REVIEW OF THE SIMPLE TENSES

Most of the exercises you have done so far have had time expressions in them that allowed you to quickly determine the appropriate tense. However, most sentences in English do not have a time expression. They depend on the context of the story to establish the time (see "The Elementary Classroom" in Exercise 4.9). In sentences with no time expression, it is the verb tense itself that indicates the time.

EXERCISE 4.8

Directions: Write the full name of the tense of the underlined verb in the blank.

> *Example:* Monkeys <u>live</u> in trees. _____simple present_____

1. My father <u>fought</u> in World War II. *simple past* _____
2. I'<u>m going to buy</u> you a mockingbird. *simple future* _____
3. The U.S. space shuttle Challenger <u>exploded</u> *simple past*
   with seven people on board. _____
4. The sea urchin <u>has</u> a mouth with five teeth on *simple present*
   the underside of its body. _____
5. A new bridge over San Francisco Bay <u>will cost</u> *simple future*
   several million dollars. _____
6. Thirty pounds <u>was</u> just too much for the child to carry. *simple past* _____
7. The butcher <u>cut</u> the steak in half. *simple present & past* _____
8. Women <u>marry</u> at younger ages than men. *simple present* _____
9. A snake with two heads <u>is</u> a rare sight. *simple present* _____
10. The children <u>are going to take</u> their mother out to dinner. *simple present & future* _____

The Continuous Tenses

The continuous tenses include the present continuous tense, the past continuous tense, and the future continuous tense. Each tense consists of a time (past, present, or future) plus an aspect (continuous). The continuous aspect indicates that the action continues over time, usually without interruption. For this reason, the continuous aspect is also called the *progressive* aspect.

THE PRESENT CONTINUOUS TENSE

Before we look at the present continuous tense, try the following exercise.

EXERCISE 4.9

Directions: Underline all the verbs in the following passage with a single line. Underline the time expressions with a double line.

An Elementary Classroom

We are inside an elementary teacher's classroom. At this moment, Mrs. White is standing in front of the class. She's holding a large colored picture of a forest scene. The children are watching intently. Now she is pointing to the deer in the picture, and she asks what the deer is doing. "It's looking at the weasel," say a few of the students. "It's smoking a cigarette," says the class clown. "And the rabbits?" asks the teacher? "They're eating berries," says a young girl. "They're holding their noses because of the skunk," says the clown. "This skunk lives in this hole in the tree, right?" the teacher continues. "Well," replies a boy at the back of the room, "for the time being he's living in that tree, but normally, he lives in the ground." "Tell me what the skunk is doing right now," concludes the teacher. "It's watching the frogs," say the students. "Good," says the teacher. "And right now I am closing the book for today so that we can play an animal game."

Form

Let's make a list of the verbs you underlined with a single line:

are	say	lives	's (is) watching
is standing	's (is) smoking	continues	say
's (is) holding	says	replies	says
are watching	asks	's (is) living	am closing
is pointing	're (are) eating	lives	can play
asks	says	tell	
is doing	're (are) holding	is doing	
's (is) looking	says	concludes	

We will ignore the structure made with the modal *can* (*can play*) and we will also not be concerned with the simple present forms (*are, asks, say, says, continues, replies, tell,* and *concludes*), all of which represent a special use of the simple present tense called the **narrative present** (the job of verbs in the narrative present is simply to move the story along no matter whether the story takes place in the past, present, or future). Finally, we will not be concerned with the verb *lives*, which occurs in sentences that are facts about the world and must therefore be in the simple present tense. The remaining verbs can be classified into one category: all consist of *be* plus a verb with the *ing*-ending, or VERB$_{ing}$(traditionally known as a present participle). These we will divide into three groups depending on the form of *be*.

is + VERB$_{ing}$	**are + VERB$_{ing}$**	**am + VERB$_{ing}$**
is standing	are watching	am closing
is holding	are eating	
is pointing	are holding	
is doing		
is looking		
is smoking		
is living		
is watching		

You know now what controls the choice of *is, are* or *am* because the auxiliary *be* must always agree with its subject.

We can generalize this information into a formula for the present continuous tense:

$$\textbf{be } (\textit{am, is or are}) \textbf{ VERB}_{\text{ing}}$$

This formula indicates that the auxiliary verb *be* must have a form that agrees with its subject (singular, plural, or "I") followed by a verb with the *ing*-ending. We said earlier that a verb can only have one ending, and we can see now that the continuous aspect is indicated by VERB$_{\text{ing}}$. But a verb tense must also show the time, and since it is not possible to add a second ending to a verb, e.g., **lookings* (VERB + *ing* + present -*s*) or **lookinged* (VERB + *ing* + past -*ed$_1$*), we need an auxiliary verb to act as a carrier for the second verb ending. In other words, the main verb (VERB$_{\text{ing}}$ in this case) shows the aspect, while the auxiliary verb (*be* in this case) shows the time and, when necessary, the agreement.

Time Expressions

Now let's make a list of the time expressions you underlined in the passage with a double line:

Time Expressions

at this moment
now
for the time being
+normally (associated with the simple present tense form *live*)
right now

With the exception of *normally,* these expressions all indicate the present moment and, in the case of *for the time being*, a present moment that is only temporary. Notice the location of these time expressions. They occur in the adverbial slots, which, in this passage, all happen to come before the subjects.

Generalization

The present continuous verb has one form: *be* + VERB$_{\text{ing}}$. *Be* must always agree with the subject. The present continuous tense shows actions that are occurring at the present moment which may be of temporary duration. It can be represented on a time line as follows:

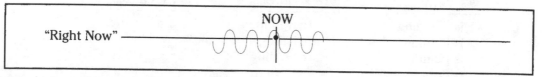

Work on the following exercise with a partner. Remember that you are trying to explain the answer to a nonnative speaker. First identify the time expression. Then determine whether the auxiliary *be* agrees with the subject.

EXERCISE 4.10

Directions: Draw a single line inder the bare subject and a double line under the time expression in the following sentences. Then fill the blank with the correct form of the verb in parentheses.

Example: My secretary (talk) _____ on the telephone right now.

Solution: My <u>secretary</u> is talking on the telephone <u>right now</u>.

1. The plane (move) _____ down the runway at this very moment.

2. All the members of the basketball team (play) _____ very well right now.

3. Now, I (descend) _____ into the mouth of the volcano.

4. We (live) _____ in Baltimore for the time being, but we soon hope to move to Washington, D.C.

5. At present, the company (have) _____ a very difficult time because of the recession.

6. My son (be) _____ silly right now because you are here, but he's not normally like this.

7. Right at this precise second, the comet (pass) _____ closest to the sun.

8. For the time being, I (use) _____ a rental car, but I will be happy to have my own car again when it's repaired.

9. The woman with the sunglasses (now tell) _____ the tourists to meet back at the hotel.

10. At the moment, I (work) _____ for a software company.

THE PAST CONTINUOUS TENSE

We will follow the same procedure as we have done before in finding verbs in context.

EXERCISE 4.11

Directions: Underline all the verbs in the following passage with a single line. Underline the time expressions with a double line.

Coming to America

I came to the United States on March 15, 1988, and I remember my first day here very clearly. My friend was waiting for me when my plane landed at Los Angeles Airport. It was raining when I arrived, but I was too excited to mind. I was terribly hungry, so we went to a restaurant near the airport. While I was ordering, my friend called her parents to let them know that I was here. The food was strange but nourishing. As we were leaving the restaurant, I saw an old friend from my home country go by in a taxi, but he didn't see me. The rain decreased while we were driving to my friend's house, but I was too tired to notice. I slept like a log.

Form

Let's make a list of the verbs you underlined with a single line:

came	was	to let	go by
remember	to mind	know	didn't see
was waiting	was	was	decreased
landed	went	was	were driving
was raining	was ordering	were leaving	was
arrived	called	saw	slept

We will not be concerned with the infinitive verb forms (*to mind, to let, know,* and *go by*), with the narrative present form (*remember*), nor with the negative verb forms (*didn't see*), which we will discuss in Chapter 6. The remaining verbs can be classified into two categories: 1) verbs in the simple past tense ($VERB_{ed_1}$) and 2) verbs consisting of *be* + $VERB_{ing}$.

Simple Past Tense ($VERB_{ed1}$)	*be* + $VERB_{ing}$
came	was waiting
landed	was raining
arrived	was ordering
was (*be* + ed_1)	were leaving
went	were driving
called	
saw	
decreased	
slept	

We have learned that the simple past tense indicates an action or state that occurred at some time in the past. We have also learned that *be* followed by a verb with the *ing*-ending is a continuous tense, which indicates an action that continues over time. In the list above, however, you see that the forms of *be* that come before $VERB_{ing}$ are different from those we saw in the present continuous tense. In fact, they are past forms of auxiliary *be*, which is why this is called the past continuous tense. If you look in the passage for the subjects of *was waiting, was raining,* and *was ordering,* you will find that they are all singular (*my friend was waiting, it was raining, I was ordering*). Notice, too, that "I" no longer has its own special form of *be* in the past tense; it is simply treated as a singular subject. The subjects of *were leaving* and *were driving* are both plural (*we were leaving, we were driving*). In other words, the past continuous tense requires agreement with the subject, just as the present continuous tense did.

We can generalize this information into a formula for the past continuous tense:

---

be (*was* or *were*) **$VERB_{ing}$**

This formula indicates that the auxiliary verb *be* must have a form that agrees with its subject (singular or plural) followed by a verb with the *ing*-ending.

Time Expressions

Now let's make a list of the time expressions you underlined in the passage with a double line:

<u>Time Expressions</u>

+on March 15, 1988
when my plane landed at the Los Angeles Airport
when I arrived
while I was ordering
as we were leaving the restaurant
while we were driving to my friend's house

With the exception of the one with a "+", these expressions all indicate a time in the past at which something else was taking place, and they all consist of clauses rather than phrases, i.e., they all contain a subject and a verb. Sometimes the clause contains a past continuous verb, sometimes a simple past verb. Notice the location of these clauses: they occur in the adverbial slot, which occurs either at the end or at the beginning of the sentence. The past continuous tense is generally not used in English unless there are two verbs present (or implied), one showing a continuous action, the other showing an event that intersects with that continuous action.

Generalization

The past continuous verb has one form: *be* + VERB$_{ing}$. *Be* must always agree with the subject. The past continuous tense shows an action that was occurring at the moment that another action took place, acting as a backdrop in front of which the simple past tense is spotlighted. In the present continuous tense, there was always a single reference time: the present moment, or "right now." In the past continuous tense, there is no readily identifiable reference time; "right then" (the opposite of "right now") could be at any time. Therefore, we use a simple past verb to identify the reference time so that we have a situation parallel to the present continuous tense in which a continuous verb intersects with the reference time.

This can be represented on a time line as follows:

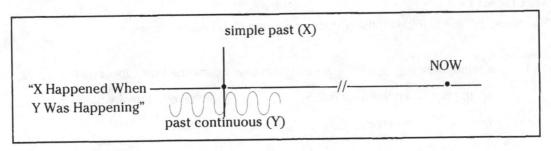

Work on the following exercise with a partner. Remember that you are trying to explain the answer to a nonnative speaker. First identify the time expression. Then determine whether the auxiliary *be* agrees with the subject. This should enable you to explain why you selected the form you did.

EXERCISE 4.12

Directions: Draw a line under the verb in the following sentences. Then fill the blank with the correct form of the second verb in parentheses.

      Example: I (take) _____ a shower when the phone rang.
      Solution: I was taking a shower when the phone rang.

1. When we left home, it (snow) _____ .

2. The war began when David (work) _____ in Zagreb.

3. As the children (cross) _____ the street, a drunk driver missed them by an inch.

4. My dog (walk) _____ through the park when a giant Siamese cat ambushed him.

5. When the guitarists (travel) _____ in Mexico, one of them lost his instrument.

6. I saw them when they (eat) _____ at the neighborhood Chinese restaurant.

7. Julio's uncle got sick when he (drive) _____ to Alaska.

8. The young woman slipped as she (get) _____ into a taxi.

9. While we (have) _____ lunch, there was a bomb scare.

10. The moon (shine) _____ brightly as we rowed across the lake.

Remember that there is no need for the past continuous tense if there is no simple past reference time stated (or implied). Keep this in mind as you try the next exercise.

EXERCISE 4.13

Directions: Fill the blank with the correct form of the verb in parentheses.

1. The wind (blow) _____ several trees over during the hurricane. I (get)_____ off the bus when the wind (blow) _____ my hat off. It (really blow) _____ hard by the time I (get) _____ home.

2. Mr. Laroche (drive) _____ from Paris to Frankfurt last year. He (drive) _____ through Reims when he (get) _____ a flat tire. He finally (drive) _____ into Frankfurt as the sun (go) _____ down.

3. Jane (read) _____ an entire issue of *The New York Times* yesterday. She (read) _____ the last page when her friend Steve (come) _____ over. Then he (read) _____ the paper while she (prepare) _____ dinner.

4.   The children (play) _____ a lot of games yesterday because it (rain) _____ all

day. When they (play) _____ Scrabble, Sally, the youngest, (spill) _____ her

lemonade all over the game board. While Sally (clean) _____ up the sticky mess,

the children (play) _____ another game. Then they all (play) _____ together

for the rest of the day.

5.   When World War II (start) _____, Jaime (live) _____ and (work) _____

in Japan. He (live) _____ there for a total of six years and then he

(return)_____ to Argentina. He (work) _____ at a language school while his

wife Anna (study) _____ Japanese at the university, but as soon as she (get)

_____ her certificate, he (begin) _____ his own studies. The war (change)

_____ all that.

THE FUTURE CONTINUOUS TENSE

We will follow the same procedure as we have done before in finding verbs in context.

EXERCISE 4.14

Directions: Underline all the verbs in the following passage with a single line. Underline the
time expressions with a double line.

Working for the Peace Corps

Kevin is very excited because next year he is going to be working for the Peace Corps in the Sudan. The plan is as follows: When he arrives, he will be living in Khartoum for a short while until he becomes accustomed to the life and culture of this desert nation. After two weeks, he will be moving into a house with other volunteers in a small village far in the south, near Juba. There, they will be helping the local population to learn new techniques of growing cotton. He will also be teaching an English class in the village school because he has an MA degree in teaching English. Later he will be training young adults to work in a food processing plant. Of course, while he is there he will be learning Arabic and a dialect of Sudanese. It will be a difficult assignment, but he knows that he and his colleagues are going to be experiencing a completely different culture, and he knows the rewards will be tremendous.

Form

Let's make a list of the verbs you underlined:

is	will be moving	is
is going to be working	will be helping	will be learning
is	to learn	will be
arrives	will...be teaching	knows
will be living	has	are going to be experiencing
becomes	will be training	knows
	to work	will be

Since it is unusual to have only one tense in a paragraph, we will focus on the verb forms that concern us. It should not surprise you that there are two categories, just as there were in the last section on the past continuous tense: 1) verbs in the simple present tense (VERB$_s$ or VERB$_\emptyset$) and 2) verbs consisting of modal + *be* + V$_{ing}$.

Simple Present Tense (**VERB$_s$ or VERB$_\emptyset$**)	Modal + *be* + VERB$_{ing}$
is	is going to be working
arrives	will be living
becomes	will be moving
has	will be helping
knows	will be teaching
	will be training
	will be learning
	are going to be experiencing

We have learned that the simple present tense indicates a habitual event or a fact. In this case, however, the simple present tense merely functions as a reference time, so it loses the sense of regularity and habit that it has when there is only a single verb present. We have also learned that VERB$_{ing}$ indicates a continuous aspect and that *will* and *be going to* signal future time, which is why this is called the future continuous tense. The future forms of *be* are *will be* and *is going to be, are going to be,* or *am going to be.*

We can generalize this information into a formula for the future continuous tense:

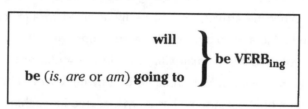

This formula indicates that the auxiliary modal *will* (or its equivalent *be going to*) plus the base form of *be* is followed by a verb with the *ing*-ending.

Time Expressions

Now let's make a list of the time expressions you underlined in the passage with a double line:

> <u>Time Expressions</u>
>
> next year
> when he arrives
> +for a short while
> until he becomes accustomed to the life and
>   culture of this desert nation
> +after two weeks
> +later
> while he is there

The expressions with a "+" can take place at any time. With the exception of *next year*, all the rest indicate a time at which something else will be taking place, and all consist of clauses rather than phrases, i.e., they all contain a subject and a verb. Notice the location of these clauses: they occur in the adverbial slots, either at the beginning or at the end of the sentence. Like the past continuous tense, the future continuous tense is generally not used in English unless there are two verbs present (or implied by the context), one showing a continuous action, the other showing an event that intersects with the continuous action.

Generalization

The future continuous verb has two forms: *will be* + VERB$_{ing}$ or *be going to be* + VERB$_{ing}$. The future continuous tense shows an action that will be occurring at the moment that another action takes place. In the present continuous tense, there was always a single reference time: the present moment, or "right now." In the future continuous tense, there is no readily identifiable reference time; "right then" (the opposite of "right now") could be at any time. Therefore, we use a simple present verb to identify the reference time so that we have a situation parallel to the present continuous tense in which a continuous verb intersects with the reference time. This can be represented on a time line as follows:

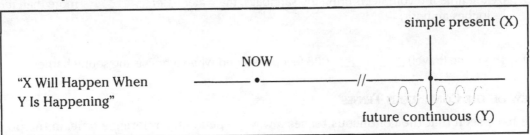

Work on the following exercise with a partner. First identify the time expression. Then select the appropriate form of the verb and explain why you selected the form you did.

EXERCISE 4.15

Directions: Draw a line under the verb in the following sentences. Then fill the blank with the correct form of the second verb in parentheses.

  Example: The whole family (wait) _____ for you when your plane lands.
  Solution: The whole family will be waiting for you when your plane <u>lands</u>.

1. By the time the letter gets here, Joan (fly) _____ over the Atlantic Ocean.

2. My neighbors (live) _____ in Honolulu when the baby comes.

3. When the emergency plan takes effect, the dockers (work) _____ twelve-hour shifts until the situation changes.

4. If he gets the night job, Sarah (usually sleep) _____ when her husband goes to work.

5. Her mother (probably hope) _____ for a grandchild until the day she dies.

6   I (water) _____ the garden when you arrive, so please come around to the back.

7. At the time the merger is complete, the companies (still produce) _____ films separately, but they are planning a joint venture for early next year.

8. Please don't come over on Saturday because I (paint) _____ the floor.

9. By the time the volunteers bring the sandbags, the water (rise) _____ more than three inches an hour.

10. The plane (travel) _____ 1088 feet per second when it breaks the sound barrier.

REVIEW OF THE CONTINUOUS TENSES

We have seen that the continuous tenses always depend on a reference time. In the present continuous tense, that reference time is a stated (or implied) time expression that indicates the present moment. In the past and future continuous tenses, the reference time is indicated by a stated (or implied) verb in the simple past tense or the simple present tense, respectively.

Verbs That Cannot be Continuous

There is a class of verbs in English that rarely occurs in the continuous tenses. These are the stative verbs. Stative verbs typically show cognition, perception, emotion, and relation. For these verbs, even if a time expression such as *right now* is present, the verb remains in the simple tense. Look at the following examples:

COGNITION: The chef forgets (*is forgetting) the recipe right now, so you'd better come back next week.

PERCEPTION: We saw (*were seeing) our cousin when we went to the beach.

EMOTION: The conservatives will hate (*will be hating) the new regulation when it becomes law.

RELATION: At present, Sheila's parents own (*are owning) several properties in the Sydney area.

EXERCISE 4.16

Directions: Draw a double line under the time expression in the following sentences, if there is one. Then fill the blank with the correct form of the verb in parentheses. Write the full name of the tense of that verb in the blank on the right.

> *Example:* My sister (live) _____ at home
> for the time being.   _____
> *Solution:* My sister is living at home <u>for the time being</u>.   present
>   <u>continuous</u>

1. The squirrel (run) _____ across the road when a car hit it.   *past continuous*

2. Right now, everybody (love) _____ that actress. Let's see what happens in a couple of months.   *simple pres.*

3. The moment they discover the loss, the thief (carry) _____ the jewels into Luxembourg.   *future continuous*

4. The vice president of that company (presently take) _____ a leave without pay because of the budget crunch.   *present cont.*

5. Mrs. Gompias (have) _____ four horses when she lived in Ireland.   *simple past*

6. No one (watch) _____ the dial when the reactor began to overheat.   *past continuous*

7. By the time you get this letter, I (cut) _____ timber in the pine forests of the Northwest.   *future cont.*

8. The children (sleep) _____ just now. Can you come back later?   *present cont.*

9. The coach yelled, "You (sit) _____ on the bench during the entire football season unless you work that fat off!"   *fut. cont.*

10. At the moment, Barbara (think) _____ she likes her neighbor, but tomorrow, she may not.   *simple present*

The Perfect Tenses

The perfect tenses include the present perfect tense, the past perfect tense, and the future perfect tense. The perfect aspect indicates an activity or state that began before the moment of speaking but has relevance only at that moment.

THE PRESENT PERFECT TENSE

We will follow the same procedure as we have done before in finding verbs in context.

EXERCISE 4.17

Directions: Underline all the verbs in the following passage with a single line. Underline the time expressions with a double line.

A Letter from School

Dear Alicia,

I am sorry I haven't written to you for such a long time, but it has been a busy semester for me. Despite my heavy work schedule, however, I have had a lot of fun. Since I arrived, I have gone on a tour of this city and have visited some famous landmarks and tourist spots. I have taken some pictures to prove it, too. I have spent a huge amount of money on magazines, books, and art reproductions.

My cousin lives about ten miles away, and he has experienced much more than I. He has tried river rafting. He has climbed the highest mountain in this area. He has even jumped off a high bridge attached to a bungee cord. We have also done a few things together. For instance, we've swum in the Kanawha River several times.

I still haven't done everything I'd like to do this year. I haven't been to a symphony concert or to a ballet performance yet. So far, I haven't seen any art galleries or museums, either. I also haven't made any new friends up to now, but I hope to meet some soon. Write soon.

Love,

Helena

Form

Let's make a list of the verbs you underlined with a single line:

am	have taken	has...jumped	haven't seen
haven't written	to prove	have...done	haven't made
has been	have spent	've [have] swum	hope
have had	lives	haven't done	to meet
arrived	has experienced	'd [would] like	write
have gone	has tried	to do	love
have visited	has climbed	haven't been	

We will ignore the simple present verb forms (*am, lives, hope, write, love*), the simple past form (*arrived*), the infinitive forms (*to do, to meet, to prove*), the reduced passive form *attached*, and the modal structure (*would like*). We will also ignore the negative elements attached to the auxiliaries as we will not be studying these until Chapter 6. The remaining verbs can be classified into two categories: 1) those consisting of the auxiliary *have* and a **regular** VERB$_{ed2}$ form of the verb and 2) those consisting of *have* plus an **irregular** form of VERB$_{ed2}$.

have + Regular **VERB**$_{ed_2}$	**have** + Irregular **VERB**$_{ed_2}$	
have visited	have written	have swum
has experienced	has been	have seen
has tried	have had	have made
has climbed	have gone	
has jumped	have taken	
	have spent	
	have done	

We know from our study of the simple past tense that irregular verb forms are a product of the history and development of the English language. But what is it that controls the use of *have* or *has*? Once again, a brief look at the subjects of the verbs in the passage will tell you that agreement is required for the present forms of auxiliary *have*. Singular subjects require *has*; plural subjects require *have*. Singular *I* and *you* also require *have*.

We can generalize this information into a formula for the present perfect tense:

$$\boxed{\textbf{have } (\textit{has or have}) \textbf{ VERB}_{ed_2}}$$

This formula indicates that the appropriate form of auxiliary *have* is followed by a verb with the *ed*$_2$-ending (traditionally known as a past participle), though this ending will only manifest itself as *ed* for regular verbs.

Time Expressions

Now let's make a list of the time expressions you underlined in the passage with a double line:

<u>Time Expressions</u> (expressions with "+" can occur with other tenses)

+for such a long time
since I arrived
+still (associated with negative structures)
+several times
+this year
yet (associated with negative stuctures)
so far
up to now

With the exception of the ones marked with "+", these expressions all indicate that something occurred in the past that has relevance to the present. Notice that most of the time expressions occur in the adverbial slot, sometimes at the beginning of the sentence, sometimes at the end. Even though the time expression *still* can occur with other tenses, it is the only one that occurs in the verb slot (like the adverbs of frequency) rather than the adverbial slot.

Generalization

The present perfect verb has one form, *have* + VERB$_{ed_2}$, though the *ed*-ending is only visible in the regular forms. The present perfect tense shows actions or states that occurred at some time in the past but that have relevance in the present. This is why it is called the present perfect tense in English. A good example of the present relevance of past events is in a job interview. The prospective employer, seeking to determine whether the applicant's past experience will enable him or her to do the job, is likely to ask questions such as "How long have you been a teacher?" or "Have you ever worked with caustic chemicals?"

The same structure appears in several European languages, but in all cases the parallel usage indicates a time in the past, not the present. For example, a German or French speaker might say, *I *have lived in the country when I was a child*, but this is not correct in English (it should be *I lived in the country when I was a child*) because *when I was a child* indicates a time in the past that is not considered to have present relevance.

The present perfect tense can be represented on a time line as follows:

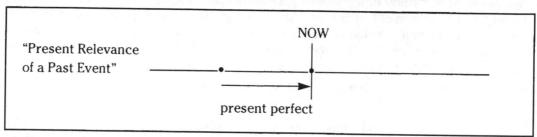

Work on the following exercise with a partner. Remember that you are trying to explain the answer to a nonnative speaker. First identify the time expression. Then determine if the subject is singular or plural/"I". Then determine whether the verb is regular or irregular.

EXERCISE 4.18

Directions: Draw a double line under the time expression in the following sentences, if there is one. Then fill the blank with the correct form of the verb in parentheses.

> *Example:* The athletes (live) _____ in the capital city since 1980.
> *Solution:* The athletes have lived in the capital city <u>since 1980</u>.

1. Mrs. Bumphries (be) _____ the mayor of this town for six years.

2. The boys (visit) _____ Mexico City many times.

3. Nancy (read) _____ five Victorian novels this year.

4. The Svensons (smoke) _____ salmon for many generations. It's the best.

5. Rats and mice (exist) _____ on this planet since the Oligocene period forty million years ago.

6. So far, the soccer team (lose) _____ three times and won four.

7. George (learn) _____ to conjugate ten Russian verbs since he started studying.

8. That heart patient and his wife (have) _____ very bad luck up to now.

9. We (try) _____ that seafood restaurant several times, but the fish is always too greasy.

10. My father (work) _____ hard all of his life, so he's ready to retire now.

THE PAST PERFECT TENSE

We will follow the same procedure as we have done before in finding verbs in context.

EXERCISE 4.19

Directions: Underline all the verbs in the following passage with a single line. Underline the time expressions with a double line.

On the Professor's Time

When the professor finally showed up, the students had waited for more than twenty minutes. He apologized and told them that he had lost his watch. He asked one of the students for the time, but the student replied that he had misplaced his watch, too. Another student announced that she had seen Big Ben the summer before if that was any help. By the time the students had really settled down, it was almost a quarter to four. The professor proceeded to ask the students some questions which he had prepared for them. When he had finished, he asked them to turn in a composition which he had assigned two weeks earlier. After he had given another homework assignment for the next week, he dismissed the class, right on time. Most of the students were used to this because they had had the same professor the previous semester.

Form

Let's make a list of the verbs you underlined with a single line:

showed up	replied	was	to turn in
had waited	had misplaced	proceeded	had assigned
apologized	announced	to ask	had given
told	had seen	had prepared	dismissed
had lost	was	had finished	were
asked	had...settled down	asked	had had

We will ignore the infinitive forms (*to ask, to turn in*). The remaining verbs can be classified into two categories: 1) those consisting of auxiliary *had* and a regular or irregular form of $VERB_{ed_2}$ and 2) those consisting of the simple past tense ($VERB_{ed_1}$).

had + $VERB_{ed_2}$	Simple Past Tense ($VERB_{ed_1}$)
had waited	showed up
had lost	apologized
had misplaced	told
had seen	asked
had settled down	replied
had prepared	announced
had finished	was
had assigned	proceeded
had given	dismissed
had had	were

Notice that the auxiliary *had* requires no agreement. Like the simple past verbs (and the modal *will*), it has only one form for either singular, plural, or "I" subjects.

We can generalize this information into a formula for the past perfect tense:

$$\boxed{\text{had } VERB_{ed_2}}$$

This formula indicates that auxiliary *had* is followed by a verb with the ed_2-ending, though this ending will only actually be spelled *ed* for regular verbs.

Time Expressions

Now let's make a list of the time expressions you underlined in the passage with a double line:

<u>Time Expressions</u> (expressions with "+" can occur with other tenses)

> when the professor finally showed up
> +for more than twenty minutes
> by the time the students had really settled down
> when he had finished
> after he had given another homework assignment
> +right on time

With the exception of the ones marked with a "+", these expressions all indicate something that occurred in the past in particular relation to another event that happened in the past. Look back at the first sentence in the passage. Two actions are indicated: showing up (*showed up*) and waiting (*had waited*). Which happened first? Well, the students had to wait before the professor showed up, right? So the waiting came before the showing up. How is the waiting expressed? In the past perfect form *had waited*. How is the showing up expressed? In the simple past form *showed up*. If you look at the rest of the passage, you will see that the action expressed by the past perfect verb always comes before the action expressed by the simple past verb. This is the function of the past perfect: to show that one action preceded another in the past.

Generalization

The past perfect verb has one form, *had* + VERB$_{ed_2}$. The past perfect tense shows actions or states that occurred at some time in the past before another event or state in the past. This is exactly analogous to the relationship between the present and past continuous tenses. The present continuous is dependent on the present moment as a reference time and therefore needs no second verb, whereas the past continuous needs a simple past verb to establish the reference time. Likewise, the present perfect is dependent on the present moment as a reference time and therefore needs no second verb, whereas the past perfect needs a simple past verb to establish the reference time. The present perfect is only concerned with the present relevance of a past event, while the past perfect is only concerned with the relevance of a preceding event at the past reference time in one way: that it came before it in real time. The past perfect tense can be represented on a time line as follows:

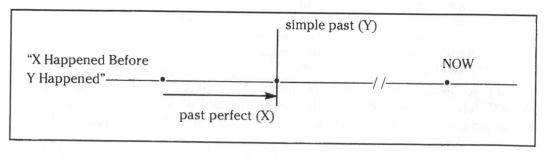

Work on the following exercise with a partner. Remember that you are trying to explain the answer to a nonnative speaker. First identify the time expression. Then determine whether the verb is regular or irregular.

EXERCISE 4.20

Directions: Draw a line under the verb in the following sentences. Then fill the blank with the correct form of the second verb in parentheses.

> *Example:* By the time we got to Memphis, we (drink) _____ all our water.
>
> *Solution:* By the time we <u>got</u> to Memphis, we had drunk all our water.

1. When Mrs. Gooch (do) _____ the dishes, she went to bed.

2. The candidate gave a rousing speech, but we suspect that someone (write) _____ it for him.

3. The bus driver suddenly realized that he (take) _____ the wrong road.

4. The miners said they (search) _____ for years before they found any gold.

5. After Mary (sign) _____ the back of the check, the bank cashed it for her.

6. When she got home, Linda found that a thief (broke into) _____ her house.

7. Farmer Brown sowed his fields with alfalfa after his eldest son (plow) _____ them up.

8. When I invited him to lunch, he said that he (have) _____ lunch, thank you.

9. The children had permission to watch television after they (finish) _____ their homework.

10. George Eliot wrote *Middlemarch* in 1872. She (write)_____ several other novels in earlier years.

EXERCISE 4.21

Directions: Use the appropriate past perfect and simple past verb forms in the following sentences.

> *Example:* The orphans (arrive) _____ at 9 p.m. The adoptive parents (get) _____ there two hours earlier.
>
> *Solution:* The orphans arrived at 9 p.m. The adoptive parents had gotten there two hours earlier.

1. The victim (be) _____ sure that she (see) _____ the man before.

2. At the trial, the lawyer (ask) _____ the oil company executive whom he (tell) _____ about the Alaska oil spill.

3. The professor's assistant (correct) _____ the papers that the students (write) _____ in class the hour before.

4. It (be) _____ quite clear that the telephone operator (give) _____ us the wrong number.

5. The anguished mother (want) _____ to know what (happen) _____ to her daughter during the hurricane.

6. The host (ask) _____ his wife why the Johnsons (leave) _____ so early.

7. As soon as the painter (apply) _____ the first coat of paint, it (be) _____ obvious that the color (clash) _____ with the wallpaper.

8. The Coast Guard (capture) _____ the smugglers long before the FBI (hear) _____ about the case.

9. When the musician (compose) _____ four symphonies, she (send) _____ one to a famous conductor for evaluation.

10. In 1553, after he (divorce) _____ Catherine of Aragon, Henry VIII (marry) _____ Anne Boleyn, who (give) _____ birth to Queen Elizabeth I.

THE FUTURE PERFECT TENSE

We will follow the same procedure as we have done before in finding verbs in context.

EXERCISE 4.22

Directions: Underline all the verbs in the following passage with a single line. Underline the time expressions with a double line.

Getting to a Conference in Japan

By the time they get to Tokyo, the doctors will have flown for more than 14 hours. They will have crossed six thousand miles of ocean and have eaten at least four meals. They will not have taken a shower since they left Chicago, so they are bound to make their presence known. Hopefully, before they attend the conference, they will have had time to bathe, to rest, and to recover from jet lag. They will also have met the hosts that were assigned to them and will no doubt have introduced themselves to the other members of the international panel, which is the highlight of the conference and their principal reason for coming to Japan. The leader of this group says that, when it is over, this will have been the third conference he has participated in this year, although it is the first one at which he will have presented a paper. The Japanese hosts say that, at the conclusion of this meeting, it will have been the second conference in as many years that has taken place in Tokyo, and they hope to host many more such meetings in the future.

Form

Let's make a list of the verb forms you have underlined:

get	will have had	will have been
will have flown	to bathe	has participated in
will have crossed	to rest	is
[will] have eaten	to recover	will have presented
will [not] have taken	will...have met	say
left	were assigned	will have been
are bound to	will...have introduced	has taken place
to make	is	hope
[be] known	says	to host
attend	is	

As usual, we will ignore the infinitive verb forms (*to make, to bathe, to rest, to recover, to host*), the simple past form (*left*), the passive form (*[be] known*), the modal-like form (*are bound to*), the passive-like form (*are bound to*), and the present perfect forms (*has participated in, has taken place*). *Coming* is a noun in this passage. The remaining verbs can be classified into two categories: 1) those consisting of *will have* + the VERB$_{ed_2}$ form of the verb and 2) those consisting of the simple present tense (VERB$_s$ and VERB$_\emptyset$).

will have + VERB$_{ed_2}$	Simple Present Tense (**VERB$_s$ and VERB$_\emptyset$**)
will have flown	get
will have crossed	attend
will have eaten	is
will have taken	says
will have had	say
will have met	hope
will have introduced	
will have been	
will have presented	
will have been	

Notice that the auxiliary *will have* requires no agreement. Like the simple past verbs, it has only one form for singular, plural, or "I" subjects. We can generalize this information into a formula for the future perfect tense:

$$\boxed{\textbf{will have VERB}_{ed_2}}$$

This formula indicates that auxiliary *will have* is followed by a verb with the *ed$_2$*-ending, though this ending will only actually be spelled *ed* for regular verbs.

Time Expressions

Now let's make a list of the time expressions you underlined in the passage with a double line:

Time Expressions (expressions with "+" can occur with other tenses)

by the time they get to Tokyo
+for more than fourteen hours
+since they left Chicago
before they attend the conference
when it is over
+at the conclusion of this meeting
+in as many years
+in the future

With the exception of the ones marked with a "+", these expressions all indicate something that will occur in the future prior to another event that will happen in the future (indicated in the simple present tense). Look back at the first sentence in the passage. Two actions are indicated: getting to Tokyo (*get to Tokyo*) and flying (*will have flown*). Which will happen first? Well, the doctors will have to fly to Tokyo before they can get there, right? So the flying will take place before the getting to Tokyo. How is the flying expressed? In the future perfect form *will have flown*. How is the getting to Tokyo expressed? In the simple present form *get*. If you look back at the rest of the passage, you will see that the action expressed by the future perfect verb always comes before the action expressed by the simple present verb. This is the function of the future perfect: to show that one action came before another in the future.

Generalization

The future perfect verb has one form, *will have* + VERB$_{ed_2}$. The future perfect tense shows actions or states that will occur at some time in the future before another action or state in the future. Like the past perfect tense, which needed a simple past verb to establish the reference time, the future perfect tense requires a simple present verb to establish the reference time. The past perfect tense was only concerned with the past reference time in one way: that it came before it in real time. Likewise, the future perfect tense is only concerned with the present reference time in one way: that it comes before it in real time. The future perfect tense can be represented on a time line as follows:

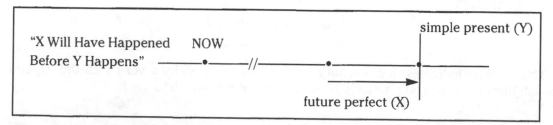

Work on the following exercise with a partner. Remember that you are trying to explain the answer to a nonnative speaker. First identify the time expression. Then determine whether the verb is regular or irregular. This should enable you to explain why you selected the form you did.

EXERCISE 4.23

Directions: Draw a line under the verb in the following sentences. Then fill the blank with the correct form of the second verb in parentheses.

    Example: By the time Anne arrives in Lisbon, she (fly) _____ half way around the world.

    Solution: By the time Anne <u>arrives</u> in Lisbon, she will have flown half way around the world.

1. If Shirley passes Anatomy 1, she (take)_____ all the courses necessary to graduate.

2. By the time this building is complete, it (cost) _____ the taxpayers ten million dollars.

3. When he retires, my grandfather says he (accomplish) _____ everything he set out to do.

4. If our top salesman gets his brother to buy a car at this dealership, he (sell) _____ over one hundred automobiles this year.

5. The logging company (remove) _____ every old-growth redwood in this region by the time the court-ordered injunction to cease arrives.

6. The firefighters (cross) _____ every mountain range in the state when the fire season ends in October.

7. When she finishes *Mr. Noon*, Heather (read) _____ every novel that D.H. Lawrence wrote.

8. If the gymnastics team from China gets a bronze medal for the next floor exercise, it (win) _____ medals in every category.

9. If Ram has the opportunity to speak with the representative from the old Soviet Union, he (meet) _____ every member of the U.N. Security Council.

10. By this time tomorrow morning, the hot-air balloon (cross) _____ the Atlantic Ocean.

REVIEW OF THE PERFECT TENSES

We have seen that, like the continuous tenses, the perfect tenses always depend on a reference time. In the present perfect tense, that reference time is a stated (or implied) time expression that indicates the present moment. In the past and future perfect tenses, the reference time is indicated by a stated (or implied) verb in the simple past tense or the simple present tense, respectively.

EXERCISE 4.24

Directions: Draw a double line under the time expression in the following sentences, if there is one. Then fill the blank with the correct form of the verb in parentheses. Write the full name of the tense of that verb in the blank on the right.

> *Example:* Roger (study) _____ medicine for ten years.
> *Solution* Roger <u>has been studying</u> medicine <u>for ten years</u>.

_____
<u>present perfect
continuous</u>

1. When the bicyclists finally arrived in Vienna, they (travel) _____ over 1000 kilometers.

   Past Perf

2. By the time the boat docks at Southampton, the passengers (be) _____ at sea for nearly a week.

   future perf

3. Chanel No. 5 is the only perfume that Roberta (wear) _____ _____ so far this season.

   Prest perf

4. Since 1066, over ten thousand words of French (enter) _____ the English language.

   Prest perf

5. When I started to get pains in my chest, I knew that I (have) _____ enough exercise.

   Past perf

6. Tom did not believe the story until he (see) _____ the evidence for himself.

   Past perf

7. Senator Ross (deliver) _____ more speeches on this subject than anyone in the Senate when he finishes this talk on the economy.

   fut perf

8. After he (conquer) _____ Austria, Napoleon moved on to Italy.

   Past perf

9. After she (prepare) _____ her lesson plans, Sally usually reads for the rest of the evening.

   prest. perf

10. My grandmother (do) _____ many exciting and wonderful things in her life.

    Prest. perf

The Perfect Continuous Tenses

The perfect continuous tenses include the present perfect continuous tense, the past perfect continuous tense, and the future perfect continuous tense. These tenses make use of both the perfect and the continuous aspects.

THE PRESENT PERFECT CONTINUOUS TENSE

We will follow the same procedure as we have done before in finding verbs in context.

EXERCISE 4.25

Directions: Underline all the verbs in the following passage with a single line. Underline the time expressions with a double line.

Mr. Groats Goes to the Doctor

Old Mr. Groats has been living in southern Iowa for a very long time, and he has no intention of living anywhere else. He has been working on the land all his life and he sees no reason to stop now. However, recently his legs have been bothering him, and the joints in his hands have been hurting, so his wife has been urging him to get some help. He resisted for a good many years, but now he is willing to consult a doctor. He's been seeing old Doctor McCarthy since he was a boy, so of course he trusts him. But it's one thing to trust a doctor, another to actually go and see him. Finally, he allows his wife to take him into town.

"You have been having problems with your legs for how long, Mr. Groats? Three years! And your hands? They've been causing you pain for a few years, too, you say. Well, a kind of flu has been going around in these parts, but I think you might have a touch of arthritis. Keep yourself warm and, even though you've been taking care of your farm by yourself all these years, try and get a little help now and again. And come and see me again in two months. Goodbye, Mr. Groats."

Form

Let's make a list of the verb forms you have underlined:

has been living	resisted	to take
has	is	have been having
has been working	to consult	've [have] been causing
sees	's [has] been seeing	say
to stop	was	has been going
have been bothering	trusts	might have
have been hurting	's [is]	keep
has been urging	to trust	've [have] been taking
to get	to. . . go and see	try and get
	allows	come and see

As usual, we will ignore the infinitive forms (*to stop, to get, to consult, to trust, to go and see, to take*), the simple past form (*was*), and the modal structure (*might have*). *Living* is a noun in this passage. The remaining verbs can be classified into two categories: 1) those consisting of *have been* + VERB$_{ing}$ and 2) those consisting of the simple present tense (VERB$_s$ and VERB$_\emptyset$).

have been + VERB$_{ing}$	Simple Present Tense (**VERB**$_s$ and **VERB**$_\emptyset$)
has been living	has
has been working	sees
have been bothering	is
have been hurting	was
has been urging	trusts
has been seeing	allows
have been having	say
have been causing	keep
has been going	try and get
have been taking	come and see

Notice that the form of auxiliary *have*, as we have seen in other perfect tenses, must agree with the subject in the present forms: singular subjects + *has*, plural subjects and "I" + *have*.

We can generalize this information into a formula for the present perfect continuous tense:

> **have** (*has* or *have*) **been VERB**$_{ing}$

This formula indicates that auxiliary *have been* (the present perfect form of *be*) is followed by a verb with the *ing*-ending.

Time Expressions

Now let's make a list of the time expressions you underlined in the passage with a double line:

Time Expressions (expressions with "+" can occur with other tenses)

+for a very long time
all his life
+now
recently
+for a good many years
+now
since he was a boy
+finally
three years
all these years
+in two months

With the exception of the ones marked with a "+", these expressions all indicate that something has been happening continuously for some time and that it is likely to continue beyond the present.

Generalization

The present perfect continuous has two forms, *have been* + VERB$_{ing}$ and *has been* + VERB$_{ing}$. The present perfect continuous tense shows actions or states that began occurring in the past and will continue occurring in the same unbroken fashion. It differs from the present perfect tense in that the present perfect tense is more concerned with the result or effect of the past event in the present whereas the present perfect continuous is concerned with the duration of that event into the present. In addition to indicating the unbroken continuity of the action, the present perfect continuous suggests that the action will continue as it has. For this reason, it is often used to express irritation (e.g., *He's been bugging me for months!*) or emphasis (e.g., *He's always been living here!*). The present perfect is ambiguous in this regard: maybe the action will continue, maybe it won't. Furthermore, verbs that indicate processes (e.g., *live, work*) show very little difference in meaning between the present perfect and the present perfect continuous. The present perfect continuous can be represented on a time line as follows:

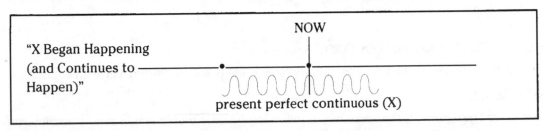

Work on the following exercise with a partner. Remember that you are trying to explain the answer to a nonnative speaker. First identify the time expression. Then determine if the subject is singular or plural/"I".

EXERCISE 4.26

Directions: Draw a double line under the time expression in the following sentences, if there is one. Then fill the blank with the correct form of the verb in parentheses. Indicate whether the sentence could be interpreted to show irritation or emphasis.

> *Example:* Those cats (live) _____ in the basement since last winter and they are still living there now.
>
> *Solution:* Those cats have been living in the basement <u>since last winter</u> and they are still living there now. (irritation)

1. The faucet (leak) _____ continuously for twenty-four hours. Don't you think we should call a plumber?

2. It (rain) _____ steadily since we arrived here, and all my clothes are damp and sticky.

3. Mr. and Mrs. Walton-Smith (contribute) _____ to the AIDS hospice on a regular basis since their son died two years ago.

4. The artist (work) _____ on the portrait without interruption for two weeks, but it still doesn't look very much like his model.

5. The telephone (ring) _____ continuously since you left! I am not your secretary!

6. Julia (study) _____ philosophy for six years now and she hopes to complete her doctoral degree by next June.

7. Your brother (talk) _____ non-stop since he got back from India. He used to be such a shy fellow.

8. David (have) _____ problems with his car this week, but that's nothing new. He insists on buying old cars.

9. The children (swim) _____ since 3 o'clock. Don't you think they should come out of the pool for a little while?

10. John (play) _____ the piano since he was a boy, but he's never taken any lessons.

THE PAST PERFECT CONTINUOUS TENSE

We will follow the same procedure as we have done before in finding verbs in context.

EXERCISE 4.27

Directions: Underline all the verbs in the following passage with a single line. Underline the time expressions with a double line.

Tragedy at Sea

The men had been working on the oil rig for only three hours when the deadly storm came out of the North Sea. The helicopter that had been trying to get the men to safety on the Shetland Islands flew into the side of the ten-story platform, killing all six men on board. There was now no way of getting off the rig. Gale force winds had been blowing steadily since the night before, and the waves were often 30 feet high. No ship could maneuver in such seas. The radio communications station through which the platform had been keeping in contact with the mainland had been hit by a blade from the falling helicopter. The men had now been waiting over fifteen hours for help from the coast guard. Their only fear was that the rig itself might collapse. The foreman of the rig had been writing a letter to his wife just before the storm struck, but that letter, like the men on the rig, would never reach land.

Form

Let's make a list of the verbs you underlined with a single line:

had been working	getting	was
came	had been blowing	might collapse
had been trying	were	had been writing
to get	could maneuver	struck
flew	had been keeping	would...reach
killing	had been hit	
was	had...been waiting	

We will ignore the infinitive form (*to get*), the passive form (*had been hit*), the VERB$_{ing}$ form with no AUX (*killing, getting*), and the past modal forms (*could maneuver, might collapse, would reach*). The remaining verbs can be classified into two categories: 1) those consisting of auxiliary *had* + the $VERB_{ed_2}$ form of *be* (*been*) + the $VERB_{ing}$ form of the verb, and 2) those consisting of the simple past tense ($VERB_{ed_1}$).

had + been + $VERB_{ing}$	Simple Past Tense ($VERB_{ed_1}$)
had been working	came
had been trying	flew
had been blowing	was
had been keeping	were
had been waiting	struck
had been writing	

Notice that the auxiliary *had* requires no agreement. Like the simple past verbs (and the modal *will*), it has only one form for either singular, plural, or "I" subjects.

We can generalize this information into a formula for the past perfect continuous tense:

$$\boxed{\text{had been } VERB_{ing}}$$

This formula indicates that auxiliary verb *had been* (the past perfect form of *be*) is followed by a verb with the *ing*-ending.

Time Expressions

Now let's make a list of the time expressions you underlined in the passage with a double line:

Time Expressions (expressions with "+" can occur with other tenses)

+for only three hours
+now
  since the night before
+often
+over fifteen hours
  just before the storm struck

With the exception of the ones marked with a "+", these expressions indicate that something had been happening continuously up to and beyond a time in the past.

Generalization

The past perfect continuous has one form, *had been* + $VERB_{ing}$. The past perfect continuous tense shows actions or states that began occurring in the past and continued occurring in the same unbroken fashion up to and beyond a time in the past. It differs from the past perfect tense in emphasizing the duration of an event prior to another event in the past rather than the simple sequence of events shown by the past perfect tense.

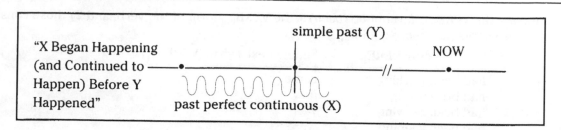

Work on the following exercise with a partner. Remember that you are trying to explain the answer to a nonnative speaker. First identify the time expression. Then determine if the subject is singular or plural/"I". Then determine whether the verb is regular or irregular.

EXERCISE 4.28

Directions: Draw a line under the verb in the following sentences. Then fill the blank with the correct form of the second verb in parentheses.

> *Example:* Robinson Crusoe (wait) _____ for more than two years before the rescue ship finally arrived.
>
> *Solution:* Robinson Crusoe had been waiting for more than two years before the rescue ship finally <u>arrived</u>.

1. The prospectors (look) _____ for the gold mine without pause since they found the old claim map in an attic.

2. It was easy to see that Fiona (cry) _____, because her eyes were all red.

3. The hurricane victims (live) _____ on bottled water for several days as they could not trust the water supply.

4. It became clear that the witness (lie) _____ the whole time when the attorney confronted him with the new evidence.

5. The victim (bleed) _____ for more than thirty minutes by the time the rescue team got to her.

6. You could tell that the boys (swim) _____ because their hair was still wet.

7. Julia (drive) _____ for eight hours straight when the deer ran in front of her and she drove off the road.

8. The dam (generate) _____ 1807 megawatts of electricity per day until the turbine malfunctioned.

9. The nurse (help) _____ hundreds of people each week until she became sick herself.

10. It turned out that the bank clerk (take) _____ money from the first moment he began working at the new branch.

THE FUTURE PERFECT CONTINUOUS TENSE

We will follow the same procedure as we have done before in finding verbs in context.

EXERCISE 4.29

Directions: Underline all the verbs in the following passage with a single line. Underline the time expressions with a double line.

Probing Mars in 2021

When the unmanned space vehicle lands on Mars, it will have been traveling for seven months at a speed of 2000 miles per hour. It will have been recording every moment of its passage through space and through the Martian atmosphere. The land probe will then leave the space vehicle and head for the south pole. When it reaches the pole, it will have been taking photographs every five minutes so that a complete picture of the terrain is available to future researchers. It will also have been making a continuous analysis of the soil and the lower atmosphere in an effort to determine once and for all if there are any signs of organic life. In 2021, the projected date of arrival of the land probe at the south pole, scientists will have been concentrating on the Martian topography for 50 years, ever since the Russians sent the first probe to the red planet in 1971. The findings of the probe will be essential for the next step in the human colonization of Mars, a small space port somewhere near the equator, where the temperatures hover around 39°F.

Form

Let's make a list of the verb forms you have underlined:

lands	will...have been making
will have been traveling	to determine
will have been recording	are
will...leave	will have been concentrating
[will] head	sent
reaches	will be
will have been taking	hover
is	

As has been our custom, we will ignore the infinitive verb form (*to determine*), the simple future verbs forms (*will leave, will head, will be*), which naturally occur in descriptions of future events, and the simple past form (*sent*), which accompanies the time expression *in 1971*. The remaining verbs can be classified into two categories: those consisting of *will have been* + the VERB$_{ing}$ form of the verb and 2) those consisting of the simple present tense (VERB$_s$ and VERB$_\emptyset$).

will have been + VERB_{ing}	Simple Present Tense (**VERB_s** and **VERB_ø**)
will have been traveling	lands
will have been recording	reaches
will have been taking	is
will have been making	are
will have been concentrating	hover

Notice once again that the auxiliary *will have been* requires no agreement. Like the simple past verbs, it has only one form for singular, plural, or "I" subjects.

We can generalize this information into a formula for the future perfect continuous tense:

$$\boxed{\textbf{will have been VERB}_{\textbf{ing}}}$$

This formula indicates that auxiliary *will have been* is followed by a verb with the *ing*–ending. As in all continuous tenses, the main verb, i.e., the last word in the verb structure, is a VERB_{ing} form.

Time Expressions

Now let's make a list of the time expressions you underlined in the passage with a double line:

Time Expressions (expressions with "+" can occur with other tenses)

    when the unmanned space vehicle lands on Mars
+then
    when it reaches the pole
+every five minutes
+in 2021
+for fifty years
+ever since the Russians sent the first probe to the red planet in 1971

With the exception of the ones marked with a "+", these expressions indicate something that will be occurring in the future prior to another event that will happen (indicated in the simple present tense). This is exactly the same relationship shown in the future perfect tense except that the future perfect suggests the result of the prior action, whereas the future perfect continuous indicates the duration or the continuing or uninterrupted nature of the prior event. Look back at the first sentence in the passage. Two actions are shown: landing on Mars (*lands on Mars*) and traveling (*will have been traveling*) to Mars at 2000 miles per hour. Which happens first? The space probe has to travel before it can reach Mars. Notice that the first event is expressed in the perfect tense, as is always the case in English, whereas the second event is expressed in a simple tense, as is likewise always the case in English. The aspect of the first event is not only perfect but also continuous, showing that the traveling at 2000 miles per hour also happens continuously, without interruption, thereby indicating the duration of that action rather than its result.

Generalization

The future perfect continuous tense has one form, *will have been* + VERB$_{ing}$. The future perfect continuous tense shows actions or states that will occur in a continuous fashion at some time in the future before another action or state in the future occurs. It is exactly analagous to the future perfect tense except that the duration or continuity of the first event is emphasized. The future perfect continuous tense can be represented on a time line as follows:

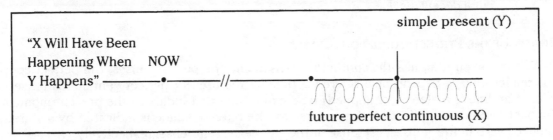

Work on the following exercise with a partner. Remember that you are trying to explain the answer to a nonnative speaker. First identify the time expression. Then determine whether the verb is regular or irregular.

EXERCISE 4.30

Directions: Draw a double line under the time expressions in the following sentences. Then fill the blank with the correct form of the verb in parentheses.

> *Example:* When the patient wakes up tomorrow, his body (function) _____ with a baboon heart for fifteen hours.

> *Solution:* When the patient wakes up tomorrow, his body will have been functioning with a baboon heart <u>for fifteen hours</u>.

1. When Ms. Dahl retires next year, she (teach) _____ science for forty years without a sabbatical leave.

2. If the couple from Georgia can last until midnight, they (dance) _____ for a total of sixty-five hours non-stop, a new world record.

3. The top female marathon runner (average) _____ a speed of twelve miles per hour if she passes this point within the next thirty-five seconds.

4. By the time he finishes his PhD, Bruce (study) _____ without interruption for twenty-four years.

5. The mountaineers (climb) _____ for ten hours straight by the time they reach the summit.

6. If my old Volkswagen can survive until next month, it (run) _____ without major repairs for two decades.

7. By the time the tunnel construction crews meet each other deep beneath the Gotthard Pass, they (dig) _____ continuously for ten years.

8. When the boy finally has the first operation to remove the tumor in his brain, he (suffer) _____ from intense nighttime headaches for nearly two solid years.

9. Senator Jarelewski (serve) _____ in the Senate for eight years when he comes up for re-election next fall.

10. If we do indeed reach Teheran by nightfall, we (drive) _____ for six hours without a decent meal.

REVIEW OF THE PERFECT CONTINUOUS TENSES

We have seen that, like the continuous tenses and the perfect tenses, the perfect continuous tenses always depend on a reference time. In the present perfect continuous tense, that reference time is a stated (or implied) time expression that indicates the present moment. In the past and future perfect continuous tenses, the reference time is indicated by a stated (or implied) verb in the simple past tense or the simple present tense, respectively.

EXERCISE 4.31

Directions: Draw a double line under the time expression in the following sentences, if there is one. Then fill the blank with the correct form of the verb in parentheses. Write the full name of the tense of that verb in the blank on the right.

Example: The dogs (bark) _____ continuously since yesterday.

Solution: The dogs have been barking continuously
<u>since yesterday</u>   present perfect
                                                                      continuous

1. When we got to the ranch, the cowboys (round up) _____ the cattle since six o'clock that morning. *[Past per. cont.]*

2. My grandparents (live) _____ in this house continuously for fifty years. *[Pres. Per. cont.]*

3. By the time they reach the Whitehouse, the marchers (sing) _____ peace songs one after the other for three hours. *[fut. Per. cont.]*

4. My father (water) _____ his vegetable garden since this afternoon. *[Pre. Pert. cont.]*

5. Humans (inhabit) _____ this planet for more than five million years by the time the sun expands into a red giant. *[fut. Pert. cont.]*

6. When Jane received the letter, her boyfriend (date) _____ the other woman for three months. *[Past Perf. cont.]*

7. If Roger keeps it up <u>past next payday</u>, he (work) _____ longer than any other person in his family.

8. Julia (take) _____ photographs for many years when she was asked to participate in an exposition of her work.

9. <u>By nine o'clock tonight</u>, my wife (have) _____ _____ contractions for <u>three hours</u>.

10. The government (print) _____ that magazine <u>every month since the war started in 1983</u>.

Handwritten margin notes:
- fut. Perf. Con.
- Past Perf. cond.
- fut. Perf
- Pres. Perf. cond.

PROBLEM SOLVING WITH THE TENSE SYSTEM

The philosophy of this text is that we want to praise a language student for his or her accomplishments before we begin to suggest that that student has made a mistake because he or she failed to use a rule of grammar. The greatest problems with the English tenses are agreement, time, and aspect. However, it is also possible to get one or the other of these elements correct. In the case of the tenses, it is possible to get the following right:

> a. correct SUBJECT-VERB/AUX AGREEMENT (singular or plural)
> b. correct TIME (past, present, or future)
> c. correct ASPECT (simple, continuous, perfect, or perfect continuous)
> d. correct POSSIBLE FORM (the form exists in English but it is not
>   correct here)

These elements reflect what students are likely to do wrong in using a tense: a) fail to make the subject agree with the VERB or AUX, b) use the wrong time, c) use the wrong aspect, or d) use a possible form in the wrong place. In several tenses, agreement between the subject and its verb or auxiliary is not always required, as shown in the following list:

<u>Agreement Required</u>	<u>Agreement Not Required</u>
1. simple present	1. simple past (all verbs but *be*)
2. simple future with *be going to*	2. simple future with *will*
3. present continuous	3. future continuous with *will*
4. past continuous	4. past perfect
5. future continuous with *be going to*	5. future perfect with *will*
6. present perfect	6. past perfect continuous
7. future perfect with b*e going to*	
8. present perfect continuous	
9. future perfect continuous with *be going to*	

In the problem solving exercises below, it is not correct to say that agreement is correct when it is not required. In such cases, agreement is simply ignored.

Problem Solving with the Seven Most Commonly Used Tenses

EXERCISE 4.32

Directions: In the following sentences, a student made a single error in using a verb tense. Your job is to address the error in three stages:

   a) bracket the error to focus your attention
   b) list what the student got right about the bracketed error (in this case, the error is the form of the verb tense) and show this in parentheses
   c) compare the original erroneous sentence to the correct sentence and explain what mistake the student made

Example: *George studies at the library right now.
            [The star (*) indicates that the sentence contains an error.]

Solution: a) Bracket the error (the verb):
                *George [studies] at the library right now.

             b) Show what is right about the verb:
                correct subject-verb/AUX agreement (*George studies*)
                correct time (present)
                correct possible form (*studies*)

             c) Compare the erroneous sentence to the correct form and explain the mistake:
                *George [studies]   at the library right now.
                George is studying at the library right now.

Explanation: The time expression *right now* requires the present continuous tense. The present continuous form of *study* is *is studying*, not *studies*.

1. *Sally [took] a shower when the phone rang. *was taking*

2. *John [works] for IBM since 1982, so he knows a lot about computers. *has worked*

3. *My aunt are [waiting] for me in the parking lot right now. *was waiting*

4. *Janet was [crossing] the bridge last night when the earthquake strikes. *crossed*

5. *When Steven [had complete] his term paper, he put it in the instructor's mailbox. *completed*

6. *The university have [helped] migrant students for many years. *has helped*

7. *My grandmother [is knowing a lot] about English grammar. *knows*

8. *The plane [arrived] at 2 o'clock tomorrow morning. *will arrive*

9. *The tree [falled] on the roof of the house last night. *fell*

10. *Susan [writes] three letters so far this morning. *has written*

Problem Solving with the Twelve Tenses

EXERCISE 4.33

Directions: Using the same procedure described in the introduction to Exercise 4.32, find and explain the single error in each of the following sentences:

1. *The patient's arm bled for three hours without stopping when he finally arrived at the emergency room.

2. *By the time the shuttle returns to the launching pad, it will circle the earth twenty-one times.

3. *Up to now, only one of the students have received a scholarship.

4. *Every evening, the cat is chasing the dog around the garden.

5. *My family has been living in this house for 100 years at this time next autumn.

6. *That old drunk has been given his money away for the last fifteen minutes. [Do you think we should call the police?]

7. *The carpenter was stepping on a nail when he was walking across the lumber yard.

8. *By this time next year, Celia is going to sailing across the Atlantic by herself.

9. *After the banker has written the check, he sent it to his lawyer.

10. * [What can you see through the telescope?] I am seeing the rings of Saturn at the moment.

THE ENGLISH TENSE SYSTEM IN DISCOURSE

Knowing how to use the tense system within a sentence (tense use at the sentence level), which has been the focus of this chapter, is only part of the problem that students have with the tense system. It is just as important to know which tense should be used in the sentences comprising a paragraph (tense use at the discourse level). In this regard, it is helpful to know that there are really only two "times" in English, namely the past time and the present time, as the future time is only a special form of what is known as the modal present (e.g., *will* signals future, whereas *must* only implies it). The generalization that can be made is that, within a paragraph, with certain exceptions, all the tenses should be either present (simple or modal present, present or modal continuous, present or modal perfect, or present or modal perfect continuous) or past (simple past, past continuous, past perfect, or past perfect continuous). Crossing over the "line" between these two major time categories within a paragraph is generally not good practice. Look at the following example:[2]

---

[2] From *The World We Live In* (Young Readers Edition) by the Editorial Staff of *LIFE* and Lincoln Barnett. Text especially adapted by Jane Werner Watson from the Original Version. ©1956 Time-Life Books Inc.

The last ice ages <u>began</u> about a million years ago. Glaciers <u>covered </u>more than one fourth of the earth's land surface. As they <u>moved</u> southward, the ice sheets <u>stripped</u> soil from eastern Canada and <u>carried</u> it down over the midwestern area of the United States. At least four times the glaciers <u>moved</u> down and <u>retreated</u> again. The last advance <u>ended</u> about 10,000 years ago.

The ice caps <u>have</u> now <u>melted</u> back as far as Greenland and the Antarctic continent, which <u>are</u> still <u>capped</u> by five million cubic miles of ice. The mountains of Alaska, New Zealand, and Scandinavia <u>are</u> still <u>topped</u> with glaciers. So are the higher Himalayas, Andes, and Alps. But the ice <u>is retreating</u>. In the Rockies and the Alps some glaciers <u>have</u> almost <u>disappeared</u> within the memory of living men. The ice packs of the Arctic and Antarctic <u>are melting</u> year by year.

The earth's climate <u>may continue</u> to grow warmer for several thousand years. As the polar ice caps <u>melt</u>, the seas <u>will rise</u>. If the caps <u>melt</u> away entirely, the ocean levels <u>will rise</u> by more than 100 feet—enough to cover New York, London, Paris, and many other coastal cities.

Notice that all the verbs in the first paragraph are in the past tense (all are simple past verbs), whereas all the verbs in the second and third paragraphs are in the present tense (present perfect, simple present passive [to be discussed in the next section], present continuous, and modal present). The author never crosses over from the past to the present or vice versa within the paragraph.

Aspect and Discourse

The perfect tenses all signal an event before the moment of interest, suggesting a **sequence** of activities. The continuous tenses all signal an activity that is in progress at the moment of interest, suggesting the **simultaneous** occurrence of activities. The simple tenses signal neither sequential nor simultaneous activities because the event is the moment of interest.

Specific Tenses and Discourse

The individual tenses also have larger functions in discourse. The simple present tense is the principal means of **expressing facts**, which is why it is the most frequently occurring tense in scientific writing. The simple past tense is the principal tense for **telling stories**. The present continuous tense can indicate that the action is **temporary** rather than permanent (e.g., *I'm living at home for the time being*). The past perfect is the principal means of **correcting a past narrative** (e.g., *I left home at 4 p.m. I had already said goodbye to my parents before I left home*). The present perfect is the principal means of **expressing the experience** of the speaker (e.g., *Why should we give you this job? Well, I have studied computer engineering for four years, I have worked in two different computer plants assembling components, and I have always been interested in computers*). The simple future modal *be going to* **begins a narrative in the future**, whereas the future modal *will* **expands the narrative** (e.g., *We are going to visit France next summer. We'll rent a car and visit Paris. Then we'll visit the Loire. Finally, we will spend a week in Marseilles*).

The discourse requirements of the tenses are particularly important in the teaching of writing.

EXERCISE 4.34

Directions: Make a copy of three paragraphs in a book or a magazine and underline every verb structure that shows tense, ignoring passive stuctures (*be* + VERB$_{ed_2}$) for the time being. First, label the tense of each verb in the margin. Then, analyze the nature of these verbs. Are they consistently past **or** present within a single paragraph or do you sometimes see a past verb among a sea of present verbs, or vice versa? If the intrusion doesn't bother you, what makes it acceptable? Analyze the discourse intent of the different tenses. Can you identify a simple present tense that reports a fact? a present perfect tense that reports the experience of the subject? a past perfect tense that repairs a past narrative? or any other example of a tense used with a specific discourse intent?

Example[3]:

1 "Arthur Burdon and Dr. Porhoët <u>walked</u> [s. past] in silence. They <u>had lunched</u> [past perfect] at a restaurant in the

2 Boulevard Saint Michel, and <u>were sauntering</u> [past continuous] now in the gardens of the Luxembourg. Dr. Porhoët

3 <u>walked</u> [s. past] with stooping shoulders,his hands behind him. He <u>beheld</u> [s. past] the scene with the eyes of the

4 many painters who <u>have sought</u> [pres. perfect] by means of the most charming garden in Paris to express their

5 sense of beauty. The grass was scattered with the fallen leaves, but their wan decay little <u>served</u> [s. past]

6 to give a touch of nature to the artifice of all besides. The formal garden <u>reminded</u> [s. past] one of a light

7 woman, no longer young, who <u>sought</u> [s. past], with faded finery, with powder and paint, to make a brave

8 show of despair. It <u>had</u> [s. past] those false, difficult smiles of uneasy gaiety, and the pitiful graces which

9 <u>attempt</u> [s. present] a fascination that the hurrying years <u>have rendered</u> [pres. perfect] vain."

[Note: An analysis of this paragraph is shown in the answer key.]

---

[3] Excerpted from W.S. Maugham, *The Magician* (1908), 11. Used with permission of A.P. Watt on behalf of The Royal Literary Fund.

SUBJECT	VERB	OBJECT	ADVERBIAL

THE VOICE SYSTEM

The English voice system consists of two voices: the active voice and the passive voice. The active voice is the grammatical structure that places the subject in the subject slot of a sentence, where we have come to expect the subject to occur. The passive voice is a grammatical structure that allows the object of a verb to be placed in the subject slot. The active voice is used much more frequently in English than the passive voice. This is not to suggest that the passive voice is unnecessary; on the contrary, it plays a vital role in English grammar despite many injunctions against its use (e.g., it makes your writing weak, it avoids responsibility).

When we speak of voice as being active or passive, we are considering only one part of a sentence, namely, the subject. In English, we need to know 1) whether the subject in a sentence is acting or causing something to happen or 2) whether it is being acted upon or bearing the result of something that happened. Subjects that act are called active; subjects that are acted upon are called passive.

THE ACTIVE VOICE

Although it is the subject that must be considered in determining whether the voice is active or passive, it is the verb that conveys this information to the listener or reader. Practically every verb we looked at in Chapter 4a was in the active voice. Let's look at a few examples:

SUBJECT	VERB	OBJECT	ADVERBIAL
Lionesses	defend	their cubs	from predators.
His grandmother	collected	the harvest	by herself in the old days.
The free trade agreement	will open	the borders	three years from now.

The subjects are all acting upon the objects in the sentences: *lionesses* act upon *their cubs*; *his grandmother* acts upon *the harvest*; *the free trade agreement* acts upon *the borders*. The recipients of this action are the objects: *the cubs* receive defense; *the harvest* "receives" collection; *the borders* "receive" opening. The verbs *defend*, *collect*, and *open* are all in the active voice: they indicate that the subjects did something, initiated an action, or caused something to happen.

EXERCISE 4.35

Directions: Make the following subjects act upon or do something to their objects by choosing an active verb.

>   *Example:* the dog - the man
>   [Note: Ask yourself, "What did the dog do to the man?"]
>   *Solution:* The dog bit/chased/scared the man.

1.   the truck - a deer

2.   the doctor - a patient

3.   the professor - a book

4.   a thermometer - temperature

5.   Shakespeare - Hamlet

6.   poison - the ants

7.   the arrow - the target

8.   the astronomer - the moons of Saturn

9.   a thief - the woman who lives next door

10.   an earthquake with a magnitude of 7.0 on the Richter scale - a small village in Columbia

Because they all contain a subject which acts upon or does something to the object, all of the verbs in Exercise 4.35 are called active verbs, and all of the sentences you have generated are said to be in the active voice.

THE PASSIVE VOICE

There are some occasions in English when the noun phrase that occupies the subject slot in an active sentence is a redundant or inconsequential word. Look at the following example:

SUBJECT	VERB	OBJECT	ADVERBIAL
People	speak	English	in London.

The reason that *people* is redundant is that it is obvious from our knowledge of the world that it is only people who speak. The word *people* is essentially unnecessary and is only present because the subject slot must always be filled in an English sentence (notwithstanding apparent exceptions such as the command form, e.g., "Go home!" where the subject is understood to be *you*).

In this situation, the passive voice becomes very useful because it allows us to replace the redundant subject with a more consequential noun phrase, namely, the object of the sentence. Let's see how this works:

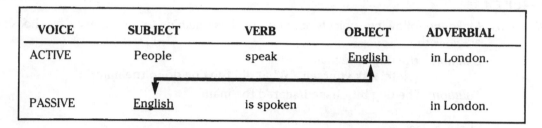

VOICE	SUBJECT	VERB	OBJECT	ADVERBIAL
ACTIVE	People	speak	English	in London.
PASSIVE	English	is spoken		in London.

To change the active into the passive voice, we remove the active subject, move the object to the subject position, and change the verb to a form of *be* plus the VERB$_{ed_2}$ form of the verb. This use of *be* + VERB$_{ed_2}$ is a new combination of auxiliary and main verb. In Chapter 4a, we learned that *be* occurs with VERB$_{ing}$ to show a continuous tense and that *have* occurs with VERB$_{ed_2}$ to show a perfect tense.[1]

ACTIVE VOICE	PASSIVE VOICE
be + VERB$_{ing}$ (*is speaking*)	*be* + VERB$_{ed_2}$ (*is spoken*)
have + VERB$_{ed_2}$ (*has spoken*)	

Two processes are involved in transforming an active verb into a passive verb: 1) selecting the correct form of *be* and 2) changing the active verb into its corresponding VERB$_{ed_2}$ form. The first process is more difficult because it involves transferring the active tense (time *and* aspect) to the auxiliary *be* and then making sure that the form of *be* agrees with the new subject of the sentence. The second process is relatively easy; you just have to remember the VERB$_{ed_2}$ form for each verb (e.g., *help→helped*; *take→taken*; *fight→fought*; *drink→drunk*). These forms are shown in the appendix under Irregular Verbs. The two processes can be explained as a series of steps for transforming an active into a passive sentence.

Steps for Changing an Active into a Passive Sentence

We will transform the following active sentence into its passive form:

> *People speak English in London.*

1. Remove all material in the adverbial slot because it is not involved in the process:
   > *People speak English*

2. Remove the active subject:
   > _____ *speak English*

3. Move the object into the subject position:
   > *English speak*

4. Determine the tense (time and aspect) of the active verb:
   > tense of *speak* = simple (aspect) present (time)

5. Determine the form(s) of *be* that have the same tense as the active verb:
   > simple present form of *be* = *am*, *is* or *are*

---

[1] A form of *have* + VERB$_{ing}$ (the fourth possible combination of auxiliary + verb) is discussed under sequential VERB$_{ing}$ complements in Chapter 15. No combination is wasted.

6. Determine the number (singular, plural or "I") of the passive subject:
   English = singular
7. Choose the form of *be* that agrees with the passive subject and place it after
   that subject: *English is*
8. Transform the active verb into the VERB$_{ed_2}$ form and place it after *be*:
   English is spoken
9. Re-attach the adverbial that was removed at the beginning:
   English is spoken in London.

EXERCISE 4.36

Directions: Using the nine steps above, transform the following active sentences with redundant or inconsequential subjects into passive sentences with strong subjects:

1. Someone built the bridges in 1945.

2. Somebody produces aluminum from bauxite.

3. Something formed the planet billions of years ago.

4. People grow peanuts in Georgia.

5. Something hit me in the eye.

The Twelve Tenses of *Be*

Step 5 in the above procedure requires knowing the name of the tense of the active verb in the sentence and determining what form of *be* has the same tense. The meaning of the verb is contained in the VERB$_{ed_2}$ form in the passive voice, but the time, aspect, and number are not. This information must all be carried by the auxiliary *be*. The forms of *be* in the simple tenses are as follows:

Simple Present	is/are/am	English **is** spoken in London.
Simple Past	was/were	English **was** spoken in London.
Simple Future	will be	English **will be** spoken in London.

The forms of *be* in the continuous tenses are a little more complicated. In Chapter 4a, we made a comparison between verbs (including auxiliary verbs) and a one-car garage: as soon as the garage (i.e., the verb) has one car in it (i.e., a verb ending), no others can fit. What do we do, then, if we need to attach not only the continuous ending (*-ing*) but also the present ending (*-s*) to the auxiliary? We cannot say **ising* because that would be equivalent to having two cars in a one-car garage. The solution: use a second auxiliary *be*. The forms of *be* in the continuous tenses are as follows:

Present Continuous	is/are/am being	English **is being** spoken in London.
Past Continuous	was/were being	English **was being** spoken in London.
Future Continuous	will be being	English **will be being** spoken in London.

The forms of *be* in the perfect tenses are complicated in a different way. We know that perfect forms require the auxiliary verb *have*. Therefore, *be* in the perfect tenses is constructed with auxiliary *have* and the VERB$_{ed_2}$ form of *be*, which is *been*. *Be* in the perfect tenses therefore takes the following forms:

Present Perfect	has/have been	English **has been** spoken in London.
Past Perfect	had been	English **had been** spoken in London.
Future Perfect	will have been	English **will have been** spoken in London.

The forms of *be* in the perfect continuous tenses combine the perfect form with the continuous form. They are as follows:

Present Perfect Continuous	has/have been being	English **has been being** spoken in London.
Past Perfect Continuous	had been being	English **had been being** spoken in London.
Future Perfect Continuous	will have been being	English **will have been being** spoken in London.

However, since the sound of *been being* in the perfect continuous tenses is generally an unpleasant one to the native ear, these structures are very seldom used.

EXERCISE 4.37

Directions: Choose the correct form of *be* in the following passive sentences.

1. Steel _____ produced from iron, carbon, and other trace elements.

2. The first locomotives _____ powered by steam.

3. Hundreds of people _____ killed because of storms this year.

4. A lot of coffee _____ grown in South America.

5. The solar system _____ formed approximately 4.5 billion years ago.

6. My street _____ repaired at the moment. There's dust everywhere.

7. The next space module _____ sent to Venus.

8. The pores in a leaf _____ called stomata.

9. Microcomputers _____ used more and more in the future.

10. A pound of potatoes _____ needed for this experiment.

11. The brain chemical that regulates growth _____ recently synthesized.

12. The dissidents were sure the house _____ watched night and day.

13. The check _____ signed by a clever forger when it was deposited in the account.

14. At that very moment, the people of the nation _____ told to prepare for a missile attack.

15. The national debt _____ calculated to be over three hundred billion dollars.

Choosing the Correct Voice

In Exercise 4.36, we changed active verbs with redundant or inconsequential subjects into their equivalent passive forms. In fact, changing from active to passive and passive to active is not an operation that one is normally required to do in speaking or writing the language. A far more useful skill is choosing the correct voice of the verb in a given situation. Look at the following example:

The Golden Gate Bridge (build) _____ in 1937.

The most important thing we have to decide is whether the subject of the sentence is performing or carrying out the action (i.e., voice = active) or whether the subject is receiving the action or being acted upon (i.e., voice = passive). The subject of the sentence is *the Golden Gate Bridge* and we are told that the verb is some form of *build*. We must ask ourselves, "Is it possible for a bridge to build something or somebody?" (i.e., verb = active). Our knowledge of the world tells us that this is not a possibility: bridges don't build things. The only other option is that the bridge was being acted upon (i.e., verb = passive). The verb must therefore consist of *be* + VERB$_{ed_2}$. The VERB$_{ed_2}$ form of *build* is *built*, so we know that the form will be some form of *be* + *built*. How do we determine the correct form of *be*? Remember that the auxiliary *be* in a passive verb form must show both tense (time and aspect) and number. We work out the tense of a verb by looking first to see if there is a time expression. The time expression in the sentence is *in 1937*. This shows that the tense must be the simple past. The simple past form of *be* is *was built* or *were built* and thus requires agreement with the subject. Since the subject is singular, we choose *was built*. The correct answer is therefore:

The Golden Gate Bridge *was built* in 1937.

Let's review the steps we followed to solve this kind of problem.

1. Determine if the subject of the sentence is active or passive by asking yourself if it is possible for the subject to perform the action described by the verb.

2. If the subject is active, follow the procedures in Chapter 4a for determining the correct form of the verb. If the subject is passive, the verb will be some form of *be* + VERB$_{ed_2}$.

3. Determine the tense (time and aspect) of the verb by:
   a. looking for a time expression (for all simple tenses and the present perfect and present continuous tenses)
   b. looking to see if a reference verb is present (past and future continuous, perfect, and perfect continuous tenses), or
   c. looking to see if the sentence represents a fact (simple present) or whether some other knowledge of the world is implied that would tell you what the tense is likely to be (e.g., a sentence about the dinosaurs is likely to be in the simple past)
4. Determine the number of the subject (singular, plural, or "I") so that you can choose the correct form (singular, plural, or "I") of the auxiliary in order to make them agree. Remember: modals such as the future *will* do not require agreement.

EXERCISE 4.38

Directions: Choose the correct form of the verb in parentheses following the described steps.

1. The letters (mail) _____ yesterday morning.

2. Relief supplies (distribute) _____ at this very moment.

3. The doctor (examine) _____ hundreds of patients so far.

4. When the treaty (sign) _____ , trade increased significantly between the two countries.

5. By 2020, electric automobiles (require) _____ in all major cities.

6. The treatment of Gandhi in his early life (dismay) _____ the school children.

7. The ship was attacked while it (load) _____ with hidden weapons.

8. By the time we reach Lisbon, this plane (fly) _____ eighteen hours nonstop.

9. Every day I (carry) _____ to the palace in my rickshaw.

10. Your husband (operate) _____ on at the time you arrive, so you will have to wait in the lounge until the procedure is finished.

An overview of the active and passive verb structures is shown in Table 4.3.

Transitivity and the Passive Voice

There are certain verbs in English for which it is difficult to determine whether the subject is performing the action or receiving the action. Look at the following examples:
   a) The accident <u>happened</u> last night.
   b) The error <u>occurs</u> in the second paragraph.
   c) The party <u>will take place</u> at the Chancellor's house.

In Sentence (a), it is hard to imagine the accident as performing the action of happening. In Sentence (b), the error doesn't really perform the action of occurring. In Sentence (c), the party doesn't perform the action of taking place. Yet these are all active verbs. The problem lies in the nature of the verb. We have seen how a passive subject is derived from the object of

Table 4.3 Overview of the English Verb Tenses (Model Verb: TAKE, took, taken)

TENSE		ACTIVE VOICE					PASSIVE VOICE				
Time	Aspect	*will*	*have*	*be*	*be*	**VERB**	*will*	*have*	*be*	*be*	**VERB**
Present	Simple	—	—	—	—	takes	—	—	is	—	taken
Past	Simple	—	—	—	—	took	—	—	was	—	taken
Future	Simple	will	—	—	—	take	will	—	be	—	taken
Present	Continuous	—	—	is	—	taking	—	—	is	being	taken
Past	Continuous	—	—	was	—	taking	—	—	was	being	taken
Future	Continuous	will	—	be	—	taking	will	—	be	being	taken
Present	Perfect	—	has	—	—	taken	—	has	been	—	taken
Past	Perfect	—	had	—	—	taken	—	had	been	—	taken
Future	Perfect	will	have	—	—	taken	will	have	been	—	taken
Present	Perfect Continuous	—	has	been	—	taking	—	has	been	being	taken
Past	Perfect Continuous	—	had	been	—	taking	—	had	been	being	taken
Future	Perfect Continous	will	have	been	—	taking	will	have	been	being	taken

an active verb: *Somebody ate the cake→The cake was eaten.* It follows that if there is no active object, then there is no NP to take the role of passive subject. The verbs in Sentences (a–c) above cannot have objects because they are all intransitive (i.e., you cannot happen, occur, or take place something or someone[2]). In other words, only transitive verbs can have a passive form while intransitive verbs can never occur in the passive voice.

What this means for the steps outlined for choosing the correct voice is that we need one additional step before we begin: Determine whether the verb is transitive or intransitive. If it is intransitive, it simply cannot be passive, and active is the only option. If it is transitive, then you are ready to determine if the subject is active or passive by asking if the subject performs or receives the action of the subject. This step removes the need to ask in the sentences above whether an accident performs or receives the action of "happening" and so on. Since the verbs are all intransitive, the voice must be active and cannot be passive.

EXERCISE 4.39

Directions: Which of the following sentences could only be in the active voice because the verb is intransitive?

1. The hunter shot the deer.

2. The girl fell asleep.

---

[2] Many learners of English understand "be happened" to mean "be caused to happen," which leads them to make statements like *The accident was happened last night.* "Students who make this common error are thus overgeneralizing from statements like *That store is located on Elm Street* rather than misapplying the passive." P.L. Hubbard, Nontransformational theories of grammar: implications for language teaching. In T. Odlin (Ed.), *Perspectives in Pedagogical Grammar* (Cambridge: Cambridge University Press, 1994), 56.

3. Maria is catching a butterfly.

4. Albert Einstein died in 1955.

5. Moscow is the capital of Russia.

6. The mailman has delivered the package.

7. The children cannot go to school today.

8. Uncle Harry drove to Miami.

9. Some birds built a nest in the attic.

10. The crowd roared with laughter.

PROBLEM SOLVING WITH THE VOICE SYSTEM

The active voice with its twelve possible forms was discussed in Chapter 4a, where we analyzed errors in terms of agreement, time, aspect, and "possible form," the possibility that the form existed in English even if it was not correct in the sentence being considered. With the passive voice, we must also consider agreement, time, aspect, and "possible form," but to these we will add a fifth consideration: voice. We want to praise a language student for his or her accomplishments before we point out a mistake in the use of a rule of grammar. Thus, in the problems below, it is possible to get the following right:

a. correct SUBJECT-VERB/AUX AGREEMENT (singular or plural)
b. correct TIME (past, present or future)
c. correct ASPECT (simple, continuous, perfect, or perfect continuous)
d. correct POSSIBLE FORM (the form exists in English but it is not correct here)
e. correct VOICE (active or passive)

These elements reflect what students are likely to do wrong in using a verb: a) fail to make the subject agree with the VERB or AUX, b) use the wrong time, c) use the wrong aspect, d) use a correct tense form in the wrong situation, or e) use the wrong voice. In the problem solving exercises below, remember that it is not correct to say that agreement is correct when it is not required. In such cases, agreement is simply ignored.

Problem Solving with the Seven Most Commonly Used Tenses

EXERCISE 4.40

Directions: In the following sentences, a student made a single error in using a verb. Your job is to address the error in three stages:

   a) bracket the error to focus your attention
   b) list what the student got right about the bracketed error (in this case, the error is the form of the tense) and show this in parentheses
   c) compare the original erroneous sentence to the correct sentence and explain what mistake the student made

Example: *A famous painting took from the museum yesterday.
[The star (*) indicates that the sentence contains an error.]

Solution:

a) Bracket the error (the verb slot):
*A famous painting [took] from the museum yesterday.

b) Show what is right about the verb:
correct aspect (simple)
correct time (past)
correct possible form (*took*)

c) Compare the erroneous sentence to the correct form and explain the mistake:
*A famous painting [took]   from the museum yesterday.
A famous painting was taken from the museum yesterday.

Explanation: Since it is not possible for a painting to take something (active), the voice must be passive. The simple past passive form of *take* is *was taken.*

1. *Many snakes are lived in dry desert regions.

2. *When she had been finished the dishes, Sarah went to bed.

3. *A box of old photographs were found in the attic.

4. *Mahler's Fourth Symphony will be perform on campus tomorrow night.

5. *My grandfather has been grown a long white beard this year.

6. *The school cafeteria is renovated right now.

7. *I came home and found that my apartment has been robbed.

8. *Ralph's brother had an accident when the road was been repaired.

9. *Thousands of people were died during the Black Death.

10. *Next year, the automobile company introduced an electric car.

Problem Solving with the Twelve Tenses

Exercise 4.41

Directions: Using the same procedure described in the introduction to Exercise 4.40, find and explain the single error in each of the following sentences:

1. *We are being bombarding with cosmic rays even at this very moment.

2. *English taught in many countries in the world.

3. *Herbal remedies have used by the Chinese for thousands of years.

4. *As the cake has been being taken out of the oven, the cook slipped and dropped it on the floor.

5. *By the time we get home, the sun will have been gone down.

6. *In 1492, Columbus discover America.

7. *A tree will be planting in his honor at a ceremony next week.

8. *My young son is been being grouchy all day.

9. *When the end of the next century arrives, perhaps spaceships will be being send through black holes.

10. *The students were not allowed to leave until they will have paid their phone bills.

THE ENGLISH VOICE SYSTEM IN DISCOURSE

The focus of this chapter has been the use of the passive voice within a sentence. It is also important to know the larger discourse considerations that may dictate the use of the passive voice. There are definite reasons for using the passive voice in certain situations, one of which is related to the use of *by*-phrases.

Passive Sentences with *By*-Phrases

Passive sentences with *by*-phrases are used when the active subject of the passive verb is not a redundant or inconsequential word like *somebody* but rather a noun phrase of some significance. Look at the following examples:

a) The thief was caught <u>by a 10-year-old boy</u>.

b) *Hamlet* was written <u>by Shakespeare</u>.

It is clear that the information in the *by*-phrases is important and cannot be deleted (this occurs in about 20% of all passive sentences in English). The logical question that arises from these examples is: How do you know when to use the passive form shown in the example and when to use the active forms (i.e., A 10-year-old boy caught the thief/Shakespeare wrote *Hamlet*)? The answer depends upon the topic of the paragraph in which such a sentence occurs.

Sentence (a) above might be found in a paragraph in the newspaper in which a crime was described and the actions of the thief delineated. The subject of the sentence is the topic of the paragraph. If, on the other hand, the paragraph described the adventures of a group of street children and someone asked, "Who caught him?", then the active form, *A 10-year-old boy caught the thief*, would be preferable. Similarly, Sentence (b) would occur in a passage about *Hamlet*, perhaps including the plot, the characters, and the language of that play. If, on the other hand, the passage concerned the life of Shakespeare, then the active form, *Shakespeare wrote Hamlet*, would be preferable. Generally speaking, the topic of a passage is encoded as the subject of the sentence. The passive construction thus provides the flexibility to allow either the subject or the object of an active sentence to be in "topic position", that is to say, to take the role of subject in the sentence. If the active subject is more closely related to the topic, the verb will be active. If the active object is more closely related to the topic, the verb will be passive.

EXERCISE 4.42

Directions: Underline the complete subject of each sentence in the following paragraph. If the subject is different from the topic, analyze the object to see if it is allied to the topic. If so, move the object to the subject position. Rewrite the paragraph, using pronouns to avoid redundancy where possible, and delete any unnecessary *by*-phrases.

Some Uses of Plants[3]

A plant is a living organism. Different parts, each with particular purposes or functions, make up the plant. Some parts of the plant may be removed without harming it. Food is stored in the roots of plants such as beets, carrots, and potatoes. Other plants are able to take nitrogen from the air and add it to the soil. Scientists call these plants legumes. If they are plowed under, they make the soil more fertile.

EXERCISE 4.43

Directions: Describe a doctor's consulation chronologically, using the following information:
  greet patient
  ask patient for details about the problem
  examine patient
  prescribe treatment or medication for the patient
  arrange follow-up visit for the patient

A Doctor's Consulation

Dr. Smith is a general practitioner in a small town in Kentucky. This morning, his first patient is Mrs. Green. First, he greets the patient. Then... [continue to describe the sequence]

Directions: Now describe the consultation from the point of view of the patient using the same information:

A Medical Student's First Patient

Mr. Singh is a new medical student at a large urban hospital. He will be meeting his first patient in a few minutes, so he reviews what he has learned. First, the patient is greeted by the doctor. Then... [continue to describe the sequence]

Directions: Now write a brief paragraph in your own words on the following pair of topics (or another pair of topics of your own choice) using the same model: The Life of a Lumberjack versus The Life of a Tree.

Special Cases of the Passive Voice

There are two special cases of the passive voice which need to be mentioned because they occur fairly frequently. One is the *get*-passive. The other is the quasi-passive. The *get*-passive replaces the auxiliary *be* in a passive construction with the word *get*. The result is rather informal in tone and would therefore be inappropriate in formal academic writing. It can only occur with dynamic (never with stative) verbs and often implies a greater emotional involvement on the part of the speaker. Look at the following examples:

---

[3] Adapted from Alan Mountford, *English in Agriculture* (Oxford University Press, 1977),1. Used with permission.

My brother <u>was</u> bumped from the flight to Dallas because it had been overbooked.

My brother <u>got</u> bumped from the flight to Dallas because it had been overbooked.

The first example is a simple statement of fact. The second example suggests the anger of the speaker.

The quasi-passive looks like a passive structure because it contains auxiliary *be* + VERB$_{ed2}$. Look at the following examples:

John <u>was born</u> in England.

When I returned to the accident, the policeman <u>was gone</u>.

Quasi-passives have no active counterpart like true passive structures. You might consider the active counterpart of *John was born in England* to be *John's mother bore him in England* but the meaning of *bore* (present: *bear*) is "to carry" while the meaning of *born* is "to stop carrying" or "to bring into the world." Such a change in meaning would not occur with a true passive. The quasi-passives are actually a remnant of the Germanic origin of the English language (German generally uses *be* with verbs that denote an action or motion).

Chapter 5

THE NEGATION SYSTEM

Negation in English grammar concerns the manner in which the meaning of a statement is reversed such that a positive statement becomes a negative one. The negation can be absolute, as in *George is not here,* or it can indicate a tendency, as in *George is seldom here.* We will be concerned with four types of negation: 1) auxiliary negation, 2) adverbial negation, 3) noun phrase negation, and 4) morphological negation.

AUXILIARY NEGATION

Auxiliary negation is the most frequently occurring type of negation in English. It is dependent on the auxiliary verb forms (and the main verb *be*) that we studied in Chapter 3. Auxiliary negation occurs with and without an overt (i.e., visible) auxiliary verb.

Auxiliary Negation with an Overt Auxiliary Verb

Auxiliary negation simply places the negative adverb *not* after the auxiliary verb. Look at the following example:

      a) John is singing.

      b) John is <u>not</u> singing.

The steps for performing this operation are as follows:

      1) Find the AUX (the auxiliary verb).

      2) Place the word *not* directly after the AUX.

It is very common in English to make the AUX + *not* structure into a **contraction** (although contracted forms are commonly avoided in formal academic writing). This we do by placing the word *not* adjacent to the AUX, removing the letter *o* from *not*, and adding an apostrophe to show that a letter has been removed. This procedure works for contracting the negative forms of *have*, *do*, most of the modals, and all forms of *be* except *am* and the future forms with *will*.[1] There is no contracted form of *am not* (we cannot say **amn't* in standard English) and the contracted form of *will not* is *won't*, which is based on phonology rather than syntax (i.e., it is easier to say *won't* than **willn't*). The third step in the process is thus:

      3) Contract AUX + *not* when appropriate.

Negating a statement with an overt auxiliary thus requires the following steps:

---

[1] The auxiliary verbs *had* and *would* are unusual in that they both contract to *'d* (e.g., *I'd, he'd*) and the original form must be determined from the context of the sentence.

••*Steps for Negating a Statement with an Overt AUX*••	*Example:* John is singing.
1. Identify the AUX.	John <u>is</u> singing.
2. Place the word *not* directly after the AUX.	John <u>is not</u> singing.
3. Contract AUX + *not* when appropriate.	John <u>isn't</u> singing.

EXERCISE 5.1

Directions: Make the following sentences negative by using auxiliary negation. Use contractions where appropriate.

1. The children are feeling well today.

2. Roger has visited Prague since he was a teenager.

3. John can speak Swahili.

4. I am putting that chair in the living room.

5. You should tell her what you think.

6. The tourists will have a very good time with Henry.

7. I had seen the Blue Grotto before.

8. The earth is flat, as many people once thought.

9. Bill was angry when his wife left him.

10. The Simpsons were very pleased with their new car.

Auxiliary Negation with No Overt Auxiliary Verb

The procedure for negation becomes more complicated when there is no auxiliary verb present in the sentence. There are three possible sentence forms in which this can happen: a sentence containing a singular subject with a verb in the simple present tense, a plural subject with a verb in the simple present tense, or any subject with a verb in the simple past tense.

SINGULAR SUBJECT WITH THE MAIN VERB IN THE SIMPLE PRESENT TENSE

The following sentence contains a singular subject (*the boy*) with the main verb in the simple present tense (*lives*):

The boy lives in Santiago.

In this case, if we were to follow the first of our steps for negating a statement (find AUX), we could not continue the transformation because no AUX is present. If we cannot find the AUX in a sentence, then we must "dig up" the AUX, which is said to be "buried." When we do this, the AUX is **always** a form of *do* (i.e., only the AUX *do* can be buried). Like the auxiliaries *be* and *have*, the auxiliary *do* is required to agree with the subject in the simple present tense.

In the example sentence, the verb *lives* agrees with the singular subject *the boy* because *live* has the *s*-ending. In order to maintain agreement between the subject and the unburied AUX, we transfer the *-s* from the main verb to *do*, leaving the main verb in its base form. The conventions of English spelling require us to add an *e* to the *-s* before we connect it to *do*, making it *does* (just as we do with *go* in the simple present form *goes*).

The boy lives in Santiago.

(do)

The boy lives in Santiago.

do + -s = does

*The boy live in Santiago.

Now that we have determined the AUX, we follow the steps for negating a statement.

1. Find AUX. (Dig it up if it's buried.)   *The boy (<u>does</u> live) in Santiago
2. Place the word *not* directly after the AUX.   The boy does <u>not</u> live in Santiago.
3. Contract AUX + *not* when appropriate.   The boy <u>doesn't</u> live in Santiago.

PLURAL SUBJECT WITH THE MAIN VERB IN THE SIMPLE PRESENT TENSE

The following sentence contains a plural subject (*the girls*) with the main verb in the simple present tense (*like*)[2]:

The girls like punk hairstyles.

If the statement has no AUX and contains a verb with the zero ending (*like* + Ø), that zero ending is transferred to *do*, leaving the verb in the base form.

The girls like punk hairstyles.

(do)

The girls like(Ø) punk hairstyles.

do + Ø = do

The girls like punk hairstyles.

Now that we have determined the AUX, we follow the steps for negating a statement.

1. Identify the AUX. (Dig it up if it's buried.)   *The girls (<u>do</u> like) punk hairstyles
2. Place the word *not* directly after the AUX.   The girls do <u>not</u> like punk hairstyles.
3. Contract AUX + *not* when appropriate.   The girls <u>don't</u> like punk hairstyles.

---

[2] Notice that if the *s*-ending is on the subject (*the girls like*), then it does not occur on the verb. If the *-s* is on the verb (*the girl likes*), then it does not occur on the subject. Students often fail to put the *s*-ending in either place (or else they put an *-s* in both places), and they will continue to do this even when they know English quite well. The reason for this error is that forgetting to put the *-s* (or using *-s* in both places) never causes a native speaker to misunderstand the sentence, and no language learner wants to waste time (until he or she is quite advanced) on rules that do not cause misunderstanding. You might point out the fact that the *-s* can only be in one place—either on the subject **or** on the verb—but don't get upset if your students continue to make errors with this. All learners do it. It's part of the natural process of language acquisition.

ANY SUBJECT WITH THE MAIN VERB IN THE SIMPLE PAST TENSE

The following sentence contains a subject (*the children*) with the main verb in the simple past tense (*wanted*):

The children wanted a dog.

If the statement has no AUX and contains a verb marked with the *ed*-ending, that ending is transferred to *do*, leaving the verb in the base form. English spelling doesn't allow **doed* but substitutes the irregular form *did* instead. The auxiliary *do* takes the same forms as the main verb *do*, which is not regular (it has the forms *do/did/done*).

The children wanted a dog.

(do)

The children want**ed** a dog.

do + *-ed* = **did**

The children want a dog.

Now that we have determined the AUX, we follow the steps for negating a statement.

1. Identify the AUX. (Dig it up if it's buried.)   *The children (<u>did</u> want) a dog
2. Place the word *not* directly after the AUX.   The children did <u>not</u> want a dog.
3. Contract AUX + *not* when appropriate.   The children <u>didn't</u> want a dog.

Notice that, as is the case for all verbs and auxiliaries except *be*, no agreement is required with *do* in the simple past tense. If we made the subject singular (*the child*), the auxiliary verb form would still require *did*, not **dids*, because we know that the base form of a verb can only take one ending, i.e., only one car can fit into the garage at a time.

The three cases described above can be consolidated into the following steps:

••*Steps for Negating a Statement with No Overt AUX*••	*Example:* The children wanted a dog.
1. Identify the AUX. (Dig it up if it's buried.)	*The children (<u>did</u> want) a dog
2. Place the word *not* directly after the AUX.	The children <u>did not</u> want a dog.
3. Contract AUX + *not* when appropriate.	The children <u>didn't</u> want a dog.

EXERCISE 5.2

Directions: Make the following sentences negative using auxiliary negation. Use contractions where appropriate.

1. Lions mate for life.

2. The eucalyptus tree grows in colder climates.

3. Astronauts got to the moon in the first half of the twentieth century.

4. Rats are welcome in the basement.

5. I like the sweater that Janet is wearing.

6. The house had been taken care of.

7. The professor who helped me most in my studies retired when he was 65.

8. A computer always knows how to solve problems.

9. We were wearing our seat belts when the accident occurred.

10. Please do your homework on the kitchen table.

ADVERBIAL NEGATION

A second way to negate a sentence is by means of adverbial negation. Adverbial negation negates a sentence by inserting an adverb of frequency. The adverbs of frequency occur primarily in the verb slot, directly before the verb. The absolute negative adverb of frequency is *never*, while the adverbs *seldom*, *rarely*, and *hardly ever* indicate a negative tendency. Look at the following examples:

    a) Tom sleeps with the window open.

    b) Joan <u>never</u> sleeps with the window open.

Sentence (a) is a positive sentence. In Sentence (b), the adverb *never* occurs before the verb and is quite similar in meaning to *Joan doesn't sleep with the window open*. If auxiliary verbs are present, the adverb of frequency always occurs after the **first** auxiliary. Look at the following examples, in which the adverb of negation is shown in boldface:

    a) A child <u>will</u> **seldom** cry without reason.

    b) The lowland gorilla <u>had</u> **rarely** <u>been</u> seen in the wild.

In Sentence (a), the adverb of frequency *seldom* comes after the auxiliary *will*. In Sentence (b), the adverb of frequency *rarely* comes after the first auxiliary *had*, not after the second auxiliary *been*.

EXERCISE 5.3

Directions: Make the following sentences negative by inserting an appropriate negative adverb of frequency.

1. Trees grow well in low light.

2. Letters without ZIP codes reach their destination on time.

3. In California, it rains in the summertime.

4. A black hole emits visible light.

5. Early intertribal battles took prisoners of war.

NEGATION WITH *NO*

Negation with *no* is primarily concerned with the negation of a noun phrase. However, *no* is also used to negate comparative adjectives and adverbs.

Noun Phrase Negation

So far, we have looked at two ways to negate a sentence by working within the verb slot. Another way to negate a sentence is to negate a noun. This can only be done with the determiner *no*. Look at the following examples:

    a) The money was found at the bottom of the river.

    b) <u>No</u> money was found at the bottom of the river.

Sentence (a) is positive. Sentence (b) has been negated by the use of a negative noun phrase in the subject slot of the sentence. Negative noun phrases can occur in any sentence slot that allows an NP, as you see in the following examples:

He will drink <u>no</u> wine before its time.	[object]
You are <u>no</u> Jack Kennedy!	[predicate NP]
They got help from <u>no</u> government organization.	[adverbial]

In conjunction with auxiliary negation, a noun phrase may also be negated with the pronoun or determiner *any*, as will be discussed in Chapter 10.

EXERCISE 5.4

Directions: Make the following sentences negative by negating an appropriate noun phrase.

1. A senator has a higher salary than the president.

2. The striking mine workers got help from their colleagues.

3. The richer children will get preferential treatment under all circumstances.

4. Visitors are allowed beyond this point.

5. There is a chance that it will rain tomorrow.

6. A candidate with an education will have a hard time winning the election.

7. An African team has won the Americas Cup sailing competition. [add "ever"]

8. The geologist said that a land plant was older than moss or algae.

9. A planet in the solar system has a greater equatorial diameter than the gas giant Jupiter.

10. When the trekkers reached the Dead Sea, they were told that a place on earth was lower in elevation.

Negation of Comparative Adjectives and Adverbs

No is also used to negate adjectives and adverbs of comparison. Look at the following examples:

    a) The central processor is <u>no</u> bigger than a postage stamp.

b) Mr. Wortleburg can <u>no</u> longer teach in this district.

c) The old man knew that he would see his daughter <u>no</u> more.

There is seldom a simple relationship between the positive and negative forms of a comparative adjective or adverb. In Sentence (a), the positive equivalent of *no bigger than* (which means "the same size as") would be *bigger than* or *smaller than*. In Sentence (b), the positive equivalent of *can no longer teach* would be *can teach*. In Sentence (c), the positive equivalent of *no more* would be *again*.

EXERCISE 5.5

Directions: Negate the following sentences using a comparative adjective or adverb with *no* such that they reflect the statement in brackets.

1. The star Beta Centauri is brighter than Betelgeuse. [False. They are equally bright.]

2. Miss Hinkle works for IBM. [False. She quit her job two weeks ago.]

3. Mars has fewer satellites than Neptune. [False. They have the same number.]

4. The Union of Soviet Socialist Republics (USSR) exists. [False. The union dissolved in 1991.]

5. Mt. Kunyang Kish in India is taller than Mt. Dakum in Nepal. [False. They are equally tall.]

MORPHOLOGICAL NEGATION

Morphological negation is the attachment of a negative prefix to an adjective or adverb. The most common negative prefixes are *il-*, *im-*, *in-*, *ir-*, *non-*, and *un-*. The following pairs of words illustrate the negating effect of these prefixes:

Positive	Negative
legal	**il**legal
proper	**im**proper
sufficient	**in**sufficient
relevant	**ir**relevant
parallel	**non**parallel
likely	**un**likely

EXERCISE 5.6

Directions: Change the following negative sentences so that they make use of a negative prefix in place of the negation type used. This will sometimes require changing the word class.

Example: That elephant is not happy.

Solution: That elephant is unhappy.

1. Harry's reasoning isn't very logical.

2. In my view, that painter has no imagination.

3. A-type personalities are never very patient.

4. Some government officials have no (sense of) responsibility.

5. The methods that the committee suggested were hardly ever practical.

6. Aunt Hilda is not capable of keeping a houseplant alive.

7. The Vermeer painting that was stolen last night is simply not replaceable.

8. The Christmas holidays weren't very pleasant this year.

9. Medical supplies were not existent.

10. No students in this class are literate in their first languages.

MULTIPLE NEGATORS

Unlike languages that require two elements in the negation process (e.g., French), English is very mathematical in regard to negation; that is to say, two negatives make a positive, three negatives a negative, etc. Since we have the option of using multiple negatives or not, the speaker who chooses to do so usually has a specific intention. Look at the following examples:

   a) John is <u>not</u> <u>un</u>happy with his work.
   b) <u>No</u>body is <u>in</u>capable of <u>ir</u>rationality.

In Sentence (a), the two negatives (*not* and *un-*) make the sentence ultimately positive, suggesting that John is happy with his work. The difference between *being happy with* and *being not unhappy with* is a question of degree, the latter implying that perhaps things could be a little better than they are. Incidentally, the use of the double negative in many varieties of nonstandard English (e.g., *He *ain't never home*) is often used to make the negative more emphatic.

In Sentence (b), the three negatives (*no, in-* and *ir-*) make the sentence ultimately negative, suggesting that all people are capable of irrationality. However, triple negatives begin to tax the comprehension even of native speakers, so they are rarely used.

EXERCISE 5.7

Directions: In the following letter (taken from Chapter 4a), there are both positive and negative structures. Rewrite the letter such that all the positive and negative statements are reversed, but keep the letter logical. The purpose of this exercise is to help you see that negating a sentence can affect other grammatical structures in unexpected ways (e.g., *some* becomes *any*; *still* becomes *already*).

A Letter from School

Dear Alicia,

I am sorry I haven't written to you for such a long time, but it has been a busy semester for me. Despite my heavy work schedule, however, I have had a lot of fun. Since I arrived, I have gone on a tour of this city and have visited some famous landmarks and tourist spots. I have taken some pictures to prove it, too. I have spent a huge amount of money on magazines, books, and art reproductions.

My cousin lives about ten miles away, and he has experienced much more than I. He has tried river rafting. He has climbed the highest mountain in this area. He has even jumped off a high bridge attached to a bungee cord. We have also done a few things together. For instance, we've swum in the Kanawha River several times.

I still haven't done everything I'd like to do this year. I haven't been to a symphony concert or to a ballet performance yet. So far, I haven't seen any art galleries or museums, either. I also haven't made any new friends up to now, but I hope to meet some soon. Write soon.

Love,

Helena

PROBLEM SOLVING WITH THE NEGATION SYSTEM

In the process of providing feedback on grammatical errors, we want to be able to praise a student before we begin to point out problems. In the problems below, it is possible to get the following correct:

      a. correct NEGATION TYPE (auxiliary, adverbial, NP, or morphological)

      b correct FORM OF NEGATOR (choice or spelling of negator or negative prefix)

      c. correct POSITION OF NEGATOR (after the first AUX (or before the main verb), as part of an NP, as an adjective or adverb prefix)

      d. correct CONTRACTION (the apostrophe is in the right place and the correct letter, or sometimes letters, have been removed)

These elements reflect what students are likely to do wrong in using negation: a) fail to use the correct type of negation, b) use the incorrect form of negator, c) put the negator in the wrong position, or d) form the contraction incorrectly.

EXERCISE 5.8

Directions: In the following sentences, a student made a single error in using negation. Your job is to address the error in three stages:

      a) bracket the error to focus your attention

      b) list what the student got right about the bracketed error (in this case, the error is the form of the negation) and show this in parentheses

      c) compare the original erroneous sentence to the correct sentence and explain what mistake the student made

    Example: *She can no speak English.

        [The star (*) indicates that the sentence contains an error.]

    Solution: a) Bracket the error (the negator and the auxiliary, noun, adjective or verb with which it is associated):

        *She [can no] speak English.

      b) Show what is right about the negation:

        correct negation type (auxiliary negation)

        correct position of negator (after first AUX)

      c) Compare the erroneous sentence to the correct form and explain the mistake:

        *She [can no] speak English.

        She can not   speak English.[3]

  Explanation: Auxiliary negation requires the negator *not*, not *no*.

1. *Many wild animals do'nt like fire.

2. *Mary says never "Hello!"

3. *People with low self-esteem are often undecisive.

4. *I amn't satisfied with my test results.

---

3 *Can not* is usually written *cannot*, although no other auxiliary negation may be written in this way. It is also possible to contract *can not* to *can't*, especially in spoken English.

5. *The photography team spoke with the native peoples hardly ever.

6. *The children haven't sleeping at the moment.

7. *My older sister will eat absolutely not red meat.

8. *Computer hard disk drives are sometimes irreliable.

9. *The astronomers couldn't see no rings around Saturn last night.

10. *Bonn is not longer the capital of Germany.

Chapter 6

THE MODAL SYSTEM

Modality in English concerns "the area of meaning that lies between yes and no — the intermediate ground between positive and negative polarity."[1] It is expressed primarily through the modal system but also through clauses such as *It is neccessary that...., You are required to...,* and *We insist that....* .

The modal system makes up one of the four classes of auxiliary verbs, as we saw in Chapter 3. The word *modal* comes from the word *mood*, specifically the moods that languages tend to grammaticize, such as certainty, wish, command, emphasis, or hesitancy. The word *modal* was originally used as an adjective for the type of auxiliary (i.e., modal auxiliaries), but now we commonly use the word *modal* as a noun to refer to this type of auxiliary verb.

All modals require that the verb being helped must be in the base (or dictionary) form, $VERB_{base}$. In this respect, modals are similar to the inflectional endings that we applied in Chapter 4a. We said that the verb was like a one-car garage, the ending like a car. As soon as one car occupies the garage, no other can fit. The modals also count as cars, only they come before and are not attached to the verb, whereas the inflectional endings come after the verb and are attached to it. The point is that when a modal is present, no endings may be attached to the verb that follows. Look at the following example:

    a) The boy <u>drinks</u> milk in the morning.

    b) The boy **should** <u>drink</u> milk in the morning.

In Sentence (a), the verb *drink* has the *s*-ending to make it agree with the bare subject *boy*. In Sentence (b), the modal *should* removes the need for the *s*-ending. Many ESL students will continue to add the *-s* to the verb, producing *The boy should *drink<u>s</u> milk in the morning,* or even to the modal, *The boy *should<u>s</u> drink milk in the morning.* This shows that they have learned the rules for agreement with the subject but that they haven't learned yet that modals do not require agreement. In this way, modals are different from most of the other forms of auxiliary verbs, which do require agreement.

EXERCISE 6.1

Directions: Add the modal in parentheses to the sentence that follows, making any other changes that are necessary.

    1. (should)   Aluminum melts at 660°C.

    2. (can)   Some toys are lethal for children.

    3. (will)   The best student in the department gets the Dean's Medal.

---

[1] M.A.K. Halliday, *Introduction to Functional Grammar* (London: Edward Arnold, 1985), 335.

4.   (would)   The government announced that it allowed AIDS victims to enter the country.

5.   (must)   The United Nations has financial support from many countries.

6.   (may)   Sunlight relieves depression in a surprising number of people.

7.   (could)   Windows shatter in an earthquake and injure people in the streets below.

8.   (might)   Daphne is bringing her boyfriend to the party.

9.   (had better) Dog owners clean up after their pets or they will be fined.

10. (used to)   I lived with my uncle when I was a child.

THE MEANINGS OF THE MODALS

There are two major categories of modals, those which show social obligation and those which show logical possibility (these are also known as *root* and *epistemic* modals, respectively).

Social Obligation vs. Logical Possibility

A modal usually has one meaning that shows social obligation and another meaning that shows logical possibility, although the modal itself doesn't change. Look at the following examples:

a) The driver <u>must</u> pay the parking ticket.   [social obligation]
b) The woman <u>must</u> be tired.   [logical possibility]

In Sentence (a), the word *must* signifies that the driver has a social obligation to pay the parking ticket or face the consequences. In Sentence (b), the word *must* signifies that there is a logical possibility that the woman is tired, judging from criteria that are not stated (e.g., she looks haggard, she has been up all night, she has six children). These meanings are more clearly distinct than they might sound: there is a social obligation to pay a parking ticket but not to be tired; similarly, it is logically possible to conclude that someone is tired but not that someone pays a parking ticket.

The reason that there are so many modals is not that there are so many moods but rather that there are varying degrees of social obligation and logical possibility, and we use different modals to signify different degrees. Look at the following examples:

a) The driver <u>must</u> pay the parking ticket.   [high degree of social obligation]
b) The listener <u>could</u> help the radio station.   [low degree of social obligation]

c) The woman <u>must</u> be tired.   [high degree of logical possibility]
d) The creature <u>could</u> be an extraterrestrial.   [low degree of logical possibility]

Several modals are presented in Table 6.1 to show the degrees of social obligation and logical possibility. Each of these degrees will be given a name, which you will need to know to complete the problem solving section at the end of the chapter.

Table 6.1. The English Modal System[2]

DEGREE OF OBLIGATION	SOCIAL OBLIGATION	MODAL	LOGICAL POSSIBILITY	DEGREE OF CERTAINTY
HIGH	FACT The man leaves tomorrow.	Ø	FACT Water boils at 100°C.	HIGH
	1 COMMAND All citizens <u>will</u> pay taxes.	will	CERTAINTY Gas <u>will</u> burn when ignited.	
	2 REQUIREMENT Drivers <u>must</u> have licenses.	must	CONCLUSION The child <u>must</u> be upset.	
	3 OBLIGATION Sisters <u>should</u> help each other.	should	PROBABILITY Aspirin <u>should</u> help you.	
	4 OPPORTUNITY Tourists <u>can</u> visit the ruins.	can	CAPABILITY This car <u>can</u> do 150 m.p.h.	
	5 OPPORTUNITY Tourists <u>may</u> visit the ruins.	may	POSSIBILITY Lead <u>may</u> cause illness.	
	6 SUGGESTION The boy <u>could</u> take geometry.	could	CHANCE The disease <u>could</u> be fatal.	
LOW	7 SUGGESTION The officers <u>might</u> try next door.	might	CHANCE It <u>might</u> rain tomorrow.	LOW

Degree of obligation can also be understood as the degree of subject control: the higher the degree of social obligation, the lower the degree of control that the subject of the sentence has. In other words, the subject of the COMMAND sentence above (i.e., *all citizens*) is allowed much less control than the subjects of the SUGGESTION sentences (i.e., *the boy, the officers*) in terms of the power to decide what to do.

EXERCISE 6.2

Directions: Circle the word that best describes the meaning of the modal in the sentence.

1.	command	certainty	Female lions will defend their cubs from males.
2.	requirement	conclusion	The plane must have mechanical problems.
3.	obligation	probability	Doctors should have a pleasant bedside manner.
4.	opportunity	possibility	Aluminum may be the cause of Alzheimer's disease.
5.	suggestion	chance	Alice's mother could increase her daily exercise.

[2] The modal charts are provided to help native English speakers understand the modal system. They are not designed for use in the ESOL classroom (except perhaps for advanced students) because the information is too compact. ESOL students should work with one pair of modals at a time, e.g., social obligation *must* vs. social obligation *should*, or social obligation *must* vs. logical possibility *must*.

6.	requirement	conclusion	Students must pass English 1 in order to graduate.
7.	opportunity	possibility	Students at the university can take courses in the evening.
8.	command	certainty	The soldiers will report to headquarters on Monday at 7 A.M.
9.	suggestion	chance	The volcano might errupt at any time in the next few days.
10.	obligation	probability	An electron microscope should reveal the structure of the virus.

EXERCISE 6.3

Directions: Make the following letter more forceful by replacing the high-subject control modals with low subject-control modals.

Dear College Applicant:

In order to be admitted to this program, you could submit an example of your written work. You might send it by certified mail. You may be informed about our decision in four weeks.

We wish you success in your endeavors.

> Yours sincerely,
> Admissions Office

EXERCISE 6.4

Directions: Make the following letter more polite by replacing the low-subject control modals with high subject-control modals.

Dear Employer:

I am writing to ask if you will consider my application for a teaching position in your institution. Since I'll be in Arizona next week, I should stop by your office to meet the director. I must visit your school on Tuesday morning. I will appreciate your letting me know if this is possible.

> Yours sincerely,
> Applicant

MODAL EQUIVALENTS

Almost every modal has an equivalent phrase that signifies nearly the same mood. These phrases are called **modal equivalents**. Most of the modal equivalents end with the particle *to*.[3] In addition, modal equivalents, unlike modals, are usually required to agree with the subject. Look at the following examples:

   a) The ambassador <u>will</u> visit Rome next week.
   b) The ambassador <u>is going to</u> visit Rome next week.

---

[3] When a preposition following a verb (e.g., *pick **up**, throw **away**, look forward **to***) changes the meaning of that verb, it is called a particle rather than a preposition.

Sentence (b) shows agreement between *ambassador* and *is*. It also shows that the meaning of the modal equivalent *is going to* is not substantially different from the modal *will* in Sentence (a). However, if two words or phrases had an absolutely identical meaning, there would be no reason for both to exist. The subtle difference between *will* and *be going to* was discussed in Chapter 4a.

Modal equivalents for the modals in Table 6.1 are shown in Table 6.2.

Table 6.2. Modal Equivalents for the Modals in Table 6.1

NO.	MODAL	SOCIAL OBLIGATION	LOGICAL POSSIBILITY
1	will	be to	be going to
2	must	be required to	have to
3	should	be supposed to	ought to
4	can	have the opportunity to	be able to
5	may	have the opportunity to	be likely to
6	could	be advised to	have the possibility to
7	might	be recommended to	have the chance to

EXERCISE 6.5

Directions: Rewrite the sentences in Exercise 6.2, substituting a modal equivalent for the modal.

　　　　Example: The ambassador will visit Rome next week.

　　　　Solution: The ambassador is going to visit Rome next week.

1. Female lions will defend their cubs from males.

2. The plane must have mechanical problems.

3. Doctors should have a pleasant bedside manner.

4. Aluminum may be the cause of Alzheimer's disease.

5. Alice's mother could increase her daily exercise.

6. Students must pass English 1 in order to graduate.

7. Students at the university can take courses in the evening.

8. The soldiers will report to headquarters on Monday at 7 A.M.

9. The volcano might errupt at any time in the next few days.

10. An electron microscope should reveal the structure of the virus.

OTHER MODALS

Most of the modals fit into the social obligation/logical possibility schema shown in Table 6.1. However, there are a few that do not. These include the modals that show hypothetical situations, permission, polite requests, preference, repeated actions in the past, and threat or emergency response.

Hypothetical Situations

Hypothetical situations are indicated with the modals *would* and *could*, which are often accompanied by an adverb clause starting with *if*. Look at the following examples:

a) The smog <u>would</u> increase if the volcano erupted **right now**.

b) Many endangered species <u>could</u> survive **today** if we stopped polluting the environment.

Notice that the past forms *erupted* in Sentence (a) and *stopped* in Sentence (b) occur with the present time expressions *right now* and *today*. This juxtaposition of a past tense verb form with a present time expression automatically signals a hypothetical situation in English. Historically, *would* and *could* were also past forms of the modals *will* and *can,* even though in modern English modals are considered to have no tense. A modal equivalent for *would* is *would be certain to* or *would be sure to*. A modal equivalent for *could* is *would have the chance to*.

Permission

Permission is indicated with the modals *may* and *can*. *May* is more formal in tone, *can* less formal. Look at the following examples:

a) Students <u>may</u> park in the faculty parking lot after 4 P.M.

b) Students <u>are allowed</u> to park in the faculty parking lot after 4 P.M.

c) You <u>can</u> take the car as long as you're home by midnight.

d) You <u>have permission to</u> take the car as long as you're home by midnight.

The modal equivalent for *can* and *may* is *be allowed to* (or *have permission to*).

Polite Requests

Polite requests are formed with the modals *may, would* and *could*. *May* is a request for permission. *Would* and *could*, the hypothetical modals, are polite because politeness requires that the addressee have a hypothetical choice. However, *could* has a slightly less insistent and formal tone than *would*. Look at the following examples:

a) <u>May</u> I have a word with you?

b) <u>Would</u> you put these books back on the shelf?

c) <u>Could</u> you put these books back on the shelf?

Sentence (a) could be paraphrased as "Do I have your permission to have a word with you?" since the modal equivalent for *may* in polite requests is *be allowed to* or *have permission to*. Sentence (b) could be paraphrased as, "If I asked you to put these books back on the shelf, would you do it for me?" The use of *will* in this context is more direct and less polite because no hypothetical situation is implied. Sentence (c) could be paraphrased as, "If I asked you to help me out by putting these books back on the shelf, would you do it?" The use of *can* in this context, which would be less polite because no hypothetical situation is implied, is only appropriate in casual requests among peers. There are no modal equivalents for the modals *would* and *could* in polite requests.

Preference

Preference is indicated with the modal *would* together with the adverb *rather*. In the following examples, the modal and modal equivalents are underlined, while the comparative forms they require have dotted underlines:

    a) Harold <u>would rather</u> go to college <u>than</u> join the military.

    b) Harold <u>prefers to</u> go to college <u>rather than</u> join the military.

The modal equivalent for *would rather* (with *than*) is *prefer to* (with *rather than*).

Repeated Actions in the Past

Repeated actions in the past are also indicated with the modals *used to* and *would*. Look at the following examples:

    a) When she was a girl, Marilyn Monroe <u>used to</u> go to the cinema every day.

    b) When she was a girl, Marilyn Monroe <u>would</u> go to the cinema every day.

The modal equivalent for *would* is *used to*. The relationship between *used to* and *would* parallels the relationship between *be going to* and *will*. *Used to* generally serves to introduce a narrative, whereas *would* tends to continue that narrative.

Threat and Emergency Response

Threat and emergency response are indicated with the modal-like structure *had better*. The past tense (*had*) suggests that this form is also a variation of the hypothetical situations discussed above. Look at the following example:

    a) You <u>had better</u> move your car or I'll call the police.

    b) We <u>had better</u> take Alice to the hospital.

Sentence (a) could be paraphased as "It would be better for you if you moved your car. If you don't, I will call the police." Sentence (b) could be paraphrased as "It would be better for Alice if we took her to the hospital." Many nonnative speakers of English confuse the meaning of *had better* with *be better to*, making sentences like "You had better take ESL before English 1." What they should have said is, "It is better to take ESL before English 1" because the sentence is not meant to be a threat or an emergency response. There is no modal equivalent for *had better*.

EXERCISE 6.6

Directions: Circle the word that best describes the meaning of the modal in the sentence.

1.	permission	capability	Bamboo plants can grow several inches a day.
2.	hypothetical situation	repeated past action	If it rained right now, there would be an avalanche.
3.	polite request	possibility	May women ask for a divorce in your country?
4.	command	threat/ emergency response	Small dogs had better stay away from mountain lions.

5.	hypothetical situation	polite request	Would you mail this letter for me?
6.	permission	opportunity	Passengers with children may board the plane now.
7.	hypothetical situation	repeated past action	Susan's father would read her a story in the evening.
8.	polite request	possibility	May I have another cup of tea?
9	capability	permission	Can the children go to the beach this afternoon?
10.	suggestion	polite request	Could you live in a quieter neighborhood?

NEGATIVE MODALS

Most of the English modals do not change their basic meanings when they are negated, with a few important exceptions. First we look at the negated modals of social obligation and their equivalents. Then we look at the negated modals of logical possibility and their equivalents.

Negated Modals of Social Obligation

The following sentences exemplify the degrees of social obligation:

	FACT	Pilgrims visit Jerusalem.
1	COMMAND	Pilgrims **will** visit Jerusalem.
2	REQUIREMENT	Pilgrims **must** visit Jerusalem.
3	OBLIGATION	Pilgrims **should** visit Jerusalem.
4	OPPORTUNITY	Pilgrims **can** visit Jerusalem.
5	OPPORTUNITY	Pilgrims **may** visit Jerusalem.
6	SUGGESTION	Pilgrims **could** visit Jerusalem.
7	SUGGESTION	Pilgrims **might** visit Jerusalem.

In the example sentences above, the decreasing social obligation (or increasing ability to choose) to visit Jerusalem is clear.

The following sentences show what happens when we negate these modals. Notice that in 5, 6, and 7, negation changes the meaning of the modal (meaning changes are shown in boldface capitals). In 5, OPPORTUNITY becomes PERMISSION; in 6, SUGGESTION becomes OPPORTUNITY; and in 7, SUGGESTION becomes CHANCE.

	FACT	Pilgrims do not visit Jerusalem.
1	COMMAND not to	Pilgrims **will not** visit Jerusalem.
2	REQUIREMENT not to	Pilgrims **must not** visit Jerusalem.
3	OBLIGATION not to	Pilgrims **should not** visit Jerusalem.
4	no OPPORTUNITY	Pilgrims **cannot visit** Jerusalem (on this trip).
5	**no PERMISSION**	Pilgrims **may not** visit Jerusalem.
6	**no OPPORTUNITY**	Pilgrims **could not** visit Jerusalem (because of the war).
7	**CHANCE not to**	Pilgrims **might not** visit Jerusalem.

In the sentences above, we see that the modals at the low end of the social obligation continuum sometimes change their meanings when they are negated. The following examples show what happens when we negate the modal equivalents of social obligation:

	FACT	Pilgrims do not visit Jerusalem (in the heat of summer).
1	COMMAND not to	Pilgrims **are not to** visit Jerusalem.
2	REQUIREMENT not to	Pilgrims **are required not to** visit Jerusalem.
3	OBLIGATION not to	Pilgrims **are not supposed to** visit Jerusalem.
4, 5	no OPPORTUNITY	Pilgrims **do not have the opportunity to** visit Jerusalem.
6, 7	**SUGGESTION** not to	Pilgrims **are advised not to** visit Jerusalem.

Cannot and *may not* share the same modal equivalents as *could not* and *might not*. For this reason, only a single sentence occurs under OPPORTUNITY and SUGGESTION. These sentences show that most of the negative modal equivalents retain the meaning of the original positive modals and it is only the modal equivalents at the low end of the social obligation continuum that tend to change meaning.

EXERCISE 6.7

Directions: Negate the following sentences a) using the modal provided and b) using a modal equivalent. Indicate whether the result changes the basic meaning of the modal in the original sentence.

1. Students must put their feet on the furniture.

2. Subjects will sit in the presence of the king.

3. Passengers might watch the in-flight movie.

4. Patients may be visited after 8 P.M.

5. Guests can swim in the canal.

6. You could take your dog on the ship with you.

7. Hikers should feed the animals in the forest.

8. The children must be left alone.

9. The priest might have a large congregation.

10. Oil should be dumped in the garbage.

Negated Modals of Logical Possibility

The following sentences exemplify the degrees of logical possibility:

		FACT	Plutonium causes cancer.
1	CERTAINTY		Plutonium **will** cause cancer (if it is ingested).
2	CONCLUSION		Plutonium **must** cause cancer.
3	PROBABILITY		Plutonium **should** cause cancer (if it is ingested).
4	CAPABILITY		Plutonium **can** cause cancer.
5	POSSIBILITY		Plutonium **may** cause cancer.
6	CHANCE		Plutonium **could** cause cancer.
7	CHANCE		Plutonium **might** cause cancer.

In the sentences above, the decreasing possibility that plutonium causes cancer is clear. The following sentences show what happens when we negate the sentences above:

		FACT	Plutonium does not cause cancer.
1	CERTAINTY not to		Plutonium **will not** cause cancer.
2	CONCLUSION		Plutonium **must not** cause cancer.
3	PROBABILITY not to		Plutonium **should not** cause cancer.
4	no CAPABILITY		Plutonium **cannot** cause cancer.
5	POSSIBILITY not to		Plutonium **may not** cause cancer.
6	**CERTAINTY not to**		Plutonium **could not** cause cancer
7	CHANCE not to		Plutonium **might not** cause cancer.

In the sentences above, we see that one of the modals at the low end of the logical possibility continuum (the word in boldface capitals) changes its meaning when it is negated.

The following sentences show what happens when we negate the modal equivalents of logical possibility:

	FACT	Plutonium causes cancer.
1	CERTAINTY not to	Plutonium **is not going to** cause cancer.
2	**CHANCE not to**	Plutonium **does not have to** cause cancer.
3	**POSSIBILITY not to**	Plutonium **ought not to** cause cancer.
4	no CAPABILITY	Plutonium **is not able to** cause cancer.
5	**PROBABILITY** not to	Plutonium **is not likely** to cause cancer.
6	**CERTAINTY** not to	Plutonium **does not have the possibility to** cause cancer.
7	**CERTAINTY** not to	Plutonium **does not have the chance to** cause cancer.

These sentences show that negating the modal equivalents of logical possibility causes substantial changes in meaning, especially towards the lower end of the continuum. In some ways, the continuum becomes reversed, with certainty at the lower end, chance at the upper. These meanings stem primarily from the sometimes absolute nature of negation, e.g., *does not have the possibility to* does not lower the degree of possibility but rather implies its opposite, impossibility.

EXERCISE 6.8

Directions: Negate the following sentences a) using the modal provided and b) using a modal equivalent. Indicate whether the result changes the basic meaning of the modal in the original sentence.

1. A small amount of ultraviolet light will harm the skin.

2. Chemotherapy may halt the spread of breast cancer.

3. Cold temperatures must affect aquatic mammals.

4. Daffodil bulbs might bloom every year.

5. Air bags could harm the driver or the passengers.

6. This medication should decrease your blood pressure.

7. A motorcycle helmet can protect the rider from serious back injuries.

8. The United Nations will send troops to this troubled region.

9. Gold may be found in the sunken galleon.

10. Divorce must end in bitterness between the husband and wife.

PAST MODALS

Most of the English modals have past forms. First we look at the past modals of social obligation and their negated forms. Then we look at the past modals of logical possibility and their negated forms.

Past Modals of Social Obligation

The following sentences exemplify decreasing degrees of social obligation:

	FACT	Automobile drivers are insured.
1	COMMAND	Automobile drivers **will** be insured.
2	REQUIREMENT	Automobile drivers **must** be insured.
3	OBLIGATION	Automobile drivers **should** be insured.
4	OPPORTUNITY	Automobile drivers **can** be insured.
5	OPPORTUNITY	Automobile drivers **may** be insured.
6	SUGGESTION	Automobile drivers **could** be insured.
7	SUGGESTION	Automobile drivers **might** be insured.

The past modals of social obligation are usually formed with the past form of the modal equivalent. This is demonstrated in the following sentences:

	FACT	Automobile drivers were insured.
1	COMMAND	Automobile drivers **were to** be insured.
2	REQUIREMENT	Automobile drivers **had to** be insured.
3	OBLIGATION	Automobile drivers **were obliged to** be insured.
4, 5	OPPORTUNITY	Automobile drivers **had the opportunity to** be insured.
6, 7	SUGGESTION	Automobile drivers **were advised to** be insured.

Can and *may* share the same past modal equivalents as *could* and *might*. For this reason, only a single sentence occurs under OPPORTUNITY and SUGGESTION.

When the past modals of social obligation are negated, they generally retain their original basic meanings:

	FACT	Automobile drivers were not insured.
1	COMMAND not to	Automobile drivers **were not to** be insured.
2	no REQUIREMENT	Automobile drivers **did not have to** be insured.
3	no OBLIGATION	Automobile drivers **were not obliged to** be insured.
4, 5	no OPPORTUNITY	Automobile drivers **did not have the opportunity to** be insured.
6, 7	no SUGGESTION	Automobile drivers **were not advised to** be insured.

EXERCISE 6.9

Directions: Put the modals in the following sentences into the past form using the time expression in parentheses. Indicate whether there is any change in meaning.

1. All bicycles must be registered. (last year)

2. Whale watchers can observe migrations of gray whales from Point Reyes. (three weeks ago)

3. The gang members will not return to that neighborhood. (until two years had passed)

4. Farmers could spray their crops to avoid fruit fly infestation. (last summer)

5. Children should take care of their parents in their old age. (in the nineteenth century)

6. We may visit the Statue of Liberty or the Empire State Building. (on our trip last year)

7. Mothers might disguise bad-tasting medications in a teaspoonful of jam. (at the meeting yesterday)

8. The heirs to the family fortune will share the money equally. (after the old man died)

9. Tulip bulbs must not be planted until late fall. (last season)

10. The doctors should not operate on the accident victim now. (at that moment)

Past Modals of Logical Possibility

The following sentences exemplify decreasing degrees of logical possibility:

	FACT	Metal fatigue causes airplane crashes.
1	CERTAINTY	Metal fatigue **will** cause airplane crashes.
2	CONCLUSION	Metal fatigue **must** cause airplane crashes.
3	PROBABILITY	Metal fatigue **should** cause airplane crashes.
4	CAPABILITY	Metal fatigue **can** cause airplane crashes.
5	POSSIBILITY	Metal fatigue **may** cause airplane crashes.
6	CHANCE	Metal fatigue **could** cause airplane crashes.
7	CHANCE	Metal fatigue **might** cause airplane crashes.

The past modals of logical possibility are always formed with the modal followed by the present perfect form of the verb (*have* + VERB$_{ed_2}$). This is demonstrated in the following sentences (the underlined modals are different from their present forms):

	FACT	Metal fatigue caused the airplane crash.
1	CERTAINTY	Metal fatigue <u>**would**</u> **have** caused the airplane crash.
2	CONCLUSION	Metal fatigue **must have** caused the airplane crash.
3	**UNREALIZED PROBABILITY**	Metal fatigue **should have** caused the airplane crash (but didn't).
4	CAPABILITY	Metal fatigue <u>**could**</u> **have** caused the airplane crash.
5	POSSIBILITY	Metal fatigue **may have** caused the airplane crash.
6	CHANCE	Metal fatigue **could have** caused the airplane crash.
7	CHANCE	Metal fatigue **might have** caused the airplane crash.

Notice that the past form of *should* (*should have*) has the characteristic of being contrary to fact, i.e., there was a probability that an event would occur but in fact it did **not** occur. Notice also that the past form of *will* is *would have*, not *will have*. Furthermore, the form *can have* does not exist in English as a modal form; it is replaced with *could have*, leaving an ambiguity between capability and chance.

When the past modals are negated, they generally retain their original basic meanings (the underlined modals are different from their present forms):

		FACT	Metal fatigue did not cause the airplane crash.
1		CERTAINTY not to	Metal fatigue **would** not have caused the airplane crash.
2		CONCLUSION	Metal fatigue **must not have** caused the airplane crash.
3		**REALIZED LOW PROBABILITY**	Metal fatigue **should not have** caused the airplane crash (but did).
4		no CAPABILITY	Metal fatigue **could** not have caused the airplane crash.
5		POSSIBILITY not to	Metal fatigue **may not have** caused the airplane crash.
6		**CERTAINTY not to**	Metal fatigue **could not have** caused the airplane crash.
7		**POSSIBILITY not to**	Metal fatigue **might not have** caused the airplane crash.

Again, we see that negation has a differential effect on the meanings of the past modals, with those at the low end of the logical possibility scale showing the greatest changes (indicated in boldface capitals). The "contrary to fact" effect of *should have* is also present in the negative *should not have*. However, since two negatives make a positive, the "contrary to fact" effect is cancelled, leaving a fact (i.e., the airplane did indeed crash).

EXERCISE 6.10

Directions: Put the modals in the following sentences into the past form using the time phrase in parentheses. Indicate whether there is any change in meaning.

1. Elizabeth will finish her medical training. (by that time)

2. The bomb could explode at any minute. (after it was dropped down the hospital chimney)

3. The passengers must not know that the ship is on fire. (because nobody jumped into the water)

4. Barbiturates can cause the rashes on his hands and feet. (in regard to the patient released last week)

5. A disaster might be avoided with the installation of a safety net. (last year)

6. Ice on the wings should be reason enough to ground the plane. (in the last major accident)

7. Engineers may not open the valves in time. (during the first emergency drill)

8. The students will not be ready for such a difficult examination. (two months ago)

9. The starving women must not be aware of international relief efforts. (in the last famine)

10. The unsatisfied tenants should not pay the rent. (last month)

PROBLEM SOLVING WITH THE MODAL SYSTEM

In the process of providing feedback on grammatical errors, remember to praise a student before you begin to point out errors. In the problems below, it is possible to get the following right:

a. correct MODAL OR EQUIVALENT MEANING (modal or modal equivalent)

b. correct MODAL FEATURES (present/past; positive/negative)

c. correct VERB FORM AFTER MODAL (VERB$_{base}$ or VERB$_{ed_2}$)

d. correct CONTRACTION (the apostrophe is in the right place and the correct letter, or sometimes letters, have been removed)

These elements reflect what students are likely to do wrong in using a modal: a) use the incorrect modal or modal equivalent for the meaning shown in brackets at the beginning of the problem sentence, b) fail to apply the features of tense and polarity (i.e., positive or negative) to the modal, c) use the incorrect verb form after the modal, or d) form the contraction incorrectly.

EXERCISE 6.11

Directions: In the following sentences, a student made a single error in using a modal. Your job is to address the error in three stages:

a) bracket the error to focus your attention

b) list what the student got right about the bracketed error (in this case, the error is the form of the modal) and show this in parentheses

c) compare the original erroneous sentence to the correct sentence and explain what mistake the student made

Example: *[CONCLUSION] The weather should be cold this year.
[The star (*) indicates that the sentence contains an error.]

Solution: a) Bracket the error (include the modal and the verb that follows):
*[CONCLUSION] The weather [should be] cold this year.

b) Show what is right about the modal:
correct modal features (present; positive)
correct verb form after modal (*be*)

c) Compare the erroneous sentence to the correct form and explain the mistake:

*[CONCLUSION] The weather [should be] cold this year.
[CONCLUSION] The weather must be   cold this year.

Explanation: The present modal for conclusion is *must*, not *should*.

1. *[OPPORTUNITY] Teachers can influencing their students in many ways.

2. *[POSSIBILITY] People with bone problems may not get enough calcium in their youth.

3. *[POLITE REQUEST] Will you help me with my homework?

4. *[CONCLUSION] You must have like chocolate when you were a child.

5. *[SUGGESTION] The pharaoh's wife was to remain in the pyramid with her husband.

6. *[THREAT] He'd better left me alone!

7. *[PERMISSION] The children ca'nt swim anymore because it's getting late.

8. *[HYPOTHETICAL SITUATION] A fire wouldn't burns if there was no oxygen.

9. *[OBLIGATION] A government would protect its citizens from harm.

10. *[REPEATED PAST ACTION] In his youth, Martin Luther King use to be a first-class wrestler.

11. *[CAPABILITY] Acid rain could of reduced the fish population in the early 1980s.

12. *[CERTAINTY] Tax rates willn't be lowered this year because of the budget crisis.

13. *[CHANCE] The AIDS virus might could infect certain monkey species.

14. *[COMMAND] The sailors were not leave the ship until 7 o'clock that night.

15. *[REQUIREMENT] Scientists must to protect the ozone layer that shields the earth from ultraviolet rays.

REVIEW

EXERCISE 6.12

Directions: Using the fifteen corrected sentences from Exercise 6.11 as a data base, answer the following questions:

1. What is the complete subject in Sentence 2? What is the bare subject? What is the complete object in Sentence 15?

2. Which sentences contain dependent clauses? Which are adverbial clauses? Which are adjective clauses?

3. Which sentences contain passive verb forms?

4. Which sentences have a pronoun as the independent clause subject? Which sentences have a pronoun as a dependent clause subject?

5. Which sentences contain intransitive verbs?

Chapter 7

THE QUESTION SYSTEM

The question system allows us to transform statements into their corresponding question forms. There are four different types of questions in English: 1) yes/no questions, 2) information questions, 3) tag questions, and 4) echo questions. All but one of these question types require the movement of some part of the sentence to another position. It is a good idea to show this movement by using colored rods (known as Cuisenaire rods) to represent the different parts of the sentence so that students can clearly see which parts of the sentence must be moved. For younger or beginning-level students, the sentence parts can be written on different colored pieces of construction paper. For an even more engaging activity, the sentence parts can be spoken by students standing in a line, who change places to show the transformation.

YES/NO QUESTIONS

Yes/no questions are questions that request a simple yes or no answer. Before we discuss the actual steps in their formation, try Exercise 7.1.

EXERCISE 7.1

Directions: In each sentence below, move one word in the sentence to form a question that requires a simple yes or no answer.

1. Maria can speak Swedish.

2. The alligator is a reptile.

3. Motorists should pay a road tax.

4. My sister has seen the Eiffel Tower.

5. George doesn't like vegetables.

Yes/No Questions from Statements with an Overt Auxiliary

You probably found it quite easy to make a yes/no question from these sentences. You simply moved the word that follows the subject NP, which happens to be an auxiliary verb or the main verb *be*, to the front of the sentence (actually, in front of the subject of the sentence) and added a question mark. Let's look at the operation in terms of steps, which your students will always be glad to see. We'll use the first sentence in Exercise 7.1 as an example.

••*Steps for Making a Yes/No Question with an Overt AUX*••	*Example:* Maria can speak Swedish.
1. Find AUX.	Maria <u>can</u> speak Swedish
2. Move AUX in front of the subject.	*<u>Can</u> Maria speak Swedish
3. Add a question mark.	Can Maria speak Swedish<u>?</u>

INTONATION PATTERN

You have probably already noticed another difference between the simple statement and the yes/no question: your voice rises at the end of the question instead of falling as it does in the statement. **Statement intonation** in English usually rises and falls within the last content word in the sentence. For example, the last content word in our example sentence is *Swedish*. The word *Swedish* happens to have its word stress on the first rather than the second syllable (each word has its own word stress). For this reason, in a statement the voice rises on the first (stressed) syllable and falls on the second (unstressed) syllable.

Maria can speak ⌐Swe⌐dish.

Yes/no question intonation rises sharply on the vowel in the stressed syllable and then continues to rise slightly on the second syllable instead of falling.

Can Maria speak Sw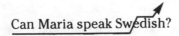édish?

EXERCISE 7.2

Directions: Transform the following statements into yes/no questions <u>by following the steps</u>. Remember, the purpose of the exercise is not only to test your knowledge of yes/no question formation but also to give you a chance to explain it to someone who does not speak English. Notice how the intonation pattern changes in the yes/no question form.

1. This disease is contagious.

2. The children were well-behaved.

3. Evelyn should take the train.

4. The university has applied for a patent.

5. John can use the car tonight.

6. The ambassador could be appointed to a new post.

7. The new program was installed in the computer.

8. The money doesn't reach the people who need it.

9. Your parents shouldn't be concerned about the children's health.

10. Pierre hasn't told the immigration office that he wants to stay.

Yes/No Questions from Statements with No Overt Auxiliary

All the sentences we have looked at so far have contained an auxiliary verb (AUX) and it is important to begin the teaching of yes/no questions in this way. Now we will consider what happens when the statement does not contain an auxiliary verb. Look at the following example:

> The boy lives in Santiago.

You may recognize this example from our discussion of negation in Chapter 5. When there is no AUX present, we must "dig up" *do* and transfer the ending from the main verb on to the AUX. Now that we have found an AUX, we follow the steps for making a yes/no question.

• *Steps for Making a Yes/No Question with No Overt AUX*••	*Example:* The boy lives in Santiago.
1. Find AUX. (Dig it up if it's buried.)	*The boy (<u>does</u> live) in Santiago
2. Move the AUX in front of the subject.	*<u>Does </u>the boy live in Santiago
3. Add a question mark.	Does the boy live in Santiago<u>?</u>

EXERCISE 7.3

Directions: Transform the following statements into yes/no questions by following the steps. Notice how the intonation pattern changes in the yes/no question form.

1. The plane makes a stopover in New York.

2. The book costs more than two hundred dollars.

3. The president of the company works on Fridays.

4. This tomato plant needs more direct sunlight.

5. Mary wants to get a master's degree.

The following exercise reviews both forms of yes/no questions.

EXERCISE 7.4

Directions: Transform the following statements into yes/no questions by following the steps. Remember, your purpose is to explain what you are doing, by means of the steps, to nonnative speakers of English. As a native speaker, you are able to make this transformation unconsciously, so it should come as no surprise that you are able to get the form correct without thinking about what you are doing. Notice how the intonation pattern changes in the yes/no question form.

1. The janitor came to work last night.

2. Whales migrate south during the winter.

3. The people are unhappy with the government.

4. The drinking water contains impurities.

5. The pilot could have saved the plane.

6. The person who committed the crime went to jail.

7. Sales of tropical hardwoods have increased this year.

8. The lawyer for the defense is being overly cautious.

9. Women with young children have problems with their careers.

10. The heiress has a yacht in Piraeus.

Problem Solving with Yes/No Questions

We turn now to the kinds of errors that students are likely to make with yes/no questions. As stated in earlier chapters, we want to be careful not only to tell a student that he or she has made a mistake and to explain the rule but to praise the student for what he or she got right about the structure. In the case of yes/no questions, it is possible to get the following right:

    a. correct POSITION OF AUX (before the subject)
    b. correct CATEGORY OF AUX (*be, have, do,* or modal)
    c. correct SUBJECT-AUX AGREEMENT (singular or plural)
    d. correct TENSE OF AUX (past or present)
    e. correct PUNCTUATION (question mark)

These aspects reflect what students are likely to do wrong in making a yes/no question: a) put the AUX in the wrong place, b) use the incorrect category of AUX, c) fail to make the subject agree with the AUX, d) put the wrong tense on the AUX, or e) use the wrong punctuation.

EXERCISE 7.5

Directions: In the following sentences, a student made a single error in yes/no question formation. Address the error in three stages:

    a) bracket the error to focus your attention

    b) list what the student got right about the bracketed error (in this case, the error is the form of the yes/no question) and show this in parentheses
        OPTIONAL: Derive the yes/no question from its statement form

    c) compare the original erroneous sentence to the correct sentence and explain what mistake the student made

Example: *Do she live in Los Angeles now?

Solution: a) Bracket the error (the AUX, main verb, and/or punctuation):
          *[Do] she live in Los Angeles now?

        b) Show what is right about the yes/no question:
          correct position of the AUX for a yes/no question (before the subject)
          correct category of AUX (*do*)
          correct tense of AUX (simple present)
          correct punctuation (?)

Derivation:	She lives in Los Angeles now.
1. Find AUX. (Dig it up if it's buried.)	*She (<u>does</u> live) in Los Angeles now
2. Move the AUX to the front.	*<u>Does</u> she live in Los Angeles now
3. Add a question mark.	Does she live in Los Angeles now<u>?</u>

        c) Compare the erroneous sentence to the correct form and explain the mistake:
          *[Do] she live in Los Angeles now?
          Does she live in Los Angeles now?

Explanation: The student forgot to transfer the *-s* from *lives* to the AUX *do* when she "dug up" the buried AUX. In other words, she failed to make AUX agree with the singular subject *she*.

1.   *Richard does work in the evenings?

2.   *Was the dog eat your dinner last night?

3.   *Has your parents received their passports yet?

4.   *Do you visit Scotland last year?

5.   *Did the plane arrive safely.

INFORMATION (WH-) QUESTIONS

Information questions are used when we require more than a simple yes or no answer. These are the questions that start with the words *who, what, where, when, why,* and *how*. Because most of these questions begin with the letters *wh*, they are commonly referred to as WH-questions.

The WH-Question Words

Before we look at the operations required to make WH-questions, we need to take a closer look at the WH-question words. The WH-question words listed above have a **broad** questioning role. English also makes use of question words with a **narrow** questioning role. Table 7.1 shows the WH-question words and what they question about. The underlined words may be replaced with the words in parentheses or with similar words.

Table 7.1. Broad and Narrow WH-Question Words

QUESTION ABOUT	BROAD	NARROW
a person	WHO(M)	WHAT person (man, woman, child, etc.)
a thing	WHAT	WHAT color (language, flavor, class, time, etc.)
a place	WHERE	(in) WHAT city (country, room, place, etc.)
a time	WHEN	(at/on/in) WHAT time (day, date, year, age, etc.)
a reason	WHY	for WHAT reason (purpose)
a manner	HOW	in WHAT manner (way, form)
a degree	——	HOW long (often, old, far, hot, etc.)
a quantity	——	HOW many books (people, ideas, etc.)
	——	HOW much water (cloth, hope, etc.)
a particular one	——	WHICH book (room, plane, woman, etc.)
a possessor	——	WHOSE hat (purse, hand, watch, car, etc.)

Before we are able to construct WH-questions, we need to know what the various WH-question words represent. The broad WH-question words are single words. The narrow WH-question words consist of a WH-word plus a noun or noun phrase. They also sometimes require a preposition in front of the WH-word. The narrow WH-question words always act together as a unit, and when they have to move, they move together. This is because they are specialized noun phrases (or prepositional phrases in the case of *for what reason* or *in what manner*) with a WH-word as the determiner. *How long* is a specialized adjective phrase with the question word *how* acting as an adverb modifying the adjective *long*.

Your students may have some difficulty with the pronunciation of the WH-words. Notice that all of the WH-words begin with the sound [w] except *who(m)* and *how*, which begin with the sound [h].

EXERCISE 7.6

Directions: Determine appropriate broad and narrow WH-question words (when possible) for the following words and phrases.

	Broad	Narrow
Example: the red dress	what	what dress/which dress

1. Michael Gorbachev
2. the University of California
3. your briefcase
4. on Tuesday
5. fifty floors
6. a hundred kilometers
7. a girl on a horse
8. Beijing
9. since he has no money
10. a mosquito
11. because he wants a better job
12. once a month
13. in Paris
14. nineteen years old
15. green
16. 20,000 dollars
17. two and a half years
18. the planet's surface
19. the man wearing sunglasses
20. at home

All WH-questions are constructed to ask about an unknown element in a statement. If the unknown element is a person, we use the WH-word *who*. If it is about a place, we use the WH-word *where*, and so on. This is what the "Question About" column shown in Table 7.1 indicates.

EXERCISE 7.7

Directions: Make a WH-question about the underlined phrase in the following sentences.

> *Example:* <u>John</u> lost his wallet.
> *Solution:* Who lost his wallet?

1. <u>Someone</u> is knocking at the door.
2. <u>The faulty signal</u> caused the accident.
3. John lost <u>a ring</u>.
4. Mary shrank <u>her husband's sweater</u>.
5. The suit cost <u>three hundred dollars</u>.
6. <u>The lack of water and the summer heat</u> caused the fire to spread quickly.
7. That's <u>the mayor of Cincinnati</u>.
8. Doctors must have <u>adequate insurance</u>.

9. The government closed the old people's home.

10. The teacher left her job because she wanted to travel.

Why is it that some of the questions you have formed require an AUX and others do not? Your students will want to know the answer to this question, too. The answer is explained in the next section.

S-form WH-Questions

In Chapter 1, we learned that all sentences can be divided into a SUBJECT and a PREDICATE (or a noun phrase and a verb phrase). This distinction is important for WH-questions in which the unknown element is in the subject, not in the predicate. Look at the following statement:

Angela cleaned the apartment.

If we divided the sentence into its subject and predicate, the sentence would be split like this:

SUBJECT	PREDICATE
Angela	cleaned the apartment.

Now let's imagine that we really don't know who cleaned the apartment. In other words, let's make the subject the unknown element that we want to ask a WH-question about. You have perhaps already guessed that we simply substitute the appropriate WH-question word, *who*, in place of the subject, *Angela*, and add a question mark.

Who cleaned the apartment?

A WH-question like this in which the subject is the unknown element is called an S-form (subject-form) WH-question. The steps for making an S-form WH-question are as follows:

••Steps for Making an S-form WH-Question••	Example: Angela cleaned the apartment.
1. Determine the unknown element of the statement.	Angela cleaned the apartment
2. Replace the unknown element with an appropriate WH-question word.	*Who cleaned the apartment
3. Add a question mark.	Who cleaned the apartment?

INTONATION PATTERN

We said before that statement intonation in English usually rises and falls within the last content word in the sentence.

Angela cleaned the a | part | ment.

WH-question intonation is exactly the same: it rises and falls within the last content word. WH-question intonation does not rise at the end as it does in yes/no question intonation.

Who cleaned the a⌐part⌐ment?

EXERCISE 7.8

Directions: Make a WH-question about the underlined phrase in the following sentences. Be sure to use the correct intonation pattern.

1. <u>Thomas Hardy</u> wrote *The Return of the Native*.

2. <u>Pink</u> usually causes people to relax.

3. <u>John and Cindy's classes</u> are in the morning.

4. <u>Fifteen students</u> passed the exam.

5. <u>The assassination of Archduke Ferdinand</u> triggered the First World War.

P-form WH-Questions

A WH-question in which the unknown element is in the predicate is called a **P-form** (predicate-form) WH-question. P-form WH-questions are formed from statements with or without an overt auxiliary.

P-FORM WH-QUESTIONS FROM STATEMENTS WITH AN OVERT AUXILIARY

In the last section, we divided a sentence into its subject and predicate.

SUBJECT	PREDICATE
Brian	is painting the house.

We then asked a question about the subject. Now let's imagine that we know who is doing the painting (*Brian*) but we don't know what he is painting. In other words, we'll let something in the predicate (in this case, the object) be the unknown element.

    Brian is painting <u>the house</u>.

You will notice right away that if we followed the same steps for making an S-form WH-question, we would produce an ungrammatical sentence.

    *Brian is painting what?

You may recognize that this form is acceptable if we stress the word *what*, but it is not a WH-question since the WH-word(s) in a WH-question are always at the front of the sentence (i.e., in front of the subject) and are usually not stressed. In fact, it's a different type of question called an echo question, which we shall discuss shortly. This ungrammatical sentence is therefore only partially complete as a WH-question because the WH-question word must be moved in front of the subject.

    *What Brian is painting?

However, this is still only partially complete because when we move an element in a WH-question, we must let the listener (or reader) know that we have done so by putting the AUX right after the WH-question word.

    What is Brian painting?

The steps for making a P-form WH-question are as follows:

••*Steps for Making a P-form WH-Question*••	*Example:* Brian is painting the house.
1. Determine the unknown element of the statement.	Brian is painting <u>the house</u>
2. Replace the unknown element with an appropriate WH-question word.	*Brian is painting <u>what</u>
3. Move the WH-question word in front of the subject.	*<u>What</u> Brian is painting
4. Find AUX.	*What Brian <u>is</u> painting
5. Move AUX directly after the WH-question word.	*What <u>is</u> Brian painting
6. Add a question mark.	What is Brian painting<u>?</u>

P-FORM WH-QUESTIONS FROM STATEMENTS WITH NO OVERT AUXILIARY

If the AUX is buried, then we must follow the same procedure for digging it up that we used in yes/no questions. (You may have noticed that if we remove the WH-question word from our sentence above, what remains is a yes/no question: *Is Brian painting?*) Let's apply the steps to such a sentence:

••*Steps for Making a P-form WH-Question with A Hidden AUX*••	*Example:* The doctor works in Iran.
1. Determine the unknown element of the statement.	The doctor works <u>in Iran</u>
2. Replace the unknown element with an appropriate WH-question word.	*The doctor works <u>where</u>
3. Move the WH-question word in front of the subject.	*<u>Where</u> the doctor works
4. Find AUX. (Dig it up if it's buried.)	*Where the doctor (<u>does</u>) work
5. Move AUX directly after the WH-question word.	*Where <u>does</u> the doctor work
6. Add a question mark.	Where does the doctor work<u>?</u>

Intonation Pattern

WH-question intonation always applies in the same way whether we ask about something in the subject (S-form) or in the predicate (P-form). It rises and falls within the last content word.

Where does the doctor work?

EXERCISE 7.9

Directions: Make a WH-question about the underlined phrase in the following sentences. Be sure to use the correct intonation pattern.

1. D. H. Lawrence wrote *Sons and Lovers*.

2. The movie star has called her agent three times.

3. John and Cindy's classes are in the morning.

4. Nancy usually orders two dozen roses for the church.

5. Birds fly south in the winter because the north is too cold.

The following exercise requires you to note where the unknown element is in the sentence (i.e., decide whether it is an S-form or P-form situation) before making the WH-question.

EXERCISE 7.10

Directions: Determine whether the question will be S-form or P-form and write "S" or "P" in the blank. Then make a WH-question about the underlined phrase. Be sure to use the correct intonation pattern.

1. _____ Your nephew will be on the corner next to the bus station.

2. _____ Alice left because she was bored.

3. _____ The computers are doing most of the calculations.

4. _____ That was the governor's house.

5. _____ The bride wants ten cases of champagne for the reception.

6. _____ You should take the medicine at night.

7. _____ It's 150 miles to San Francisco.

8. _____ The people who live in the northernmost area of Alaska travel by dogsled.

9. _____ The soldiers prefer Turkish cigarettes.

10. _____ This word means boredom.

Note in sentences 3 and 8 that when the unknown element is the subject, we always use the singular ending on the verb or AUX with a broad WH-question word. For example, when we hear a knock on the door, we say, "Who is there?", not "Who are there?" The general rule is that if the number (singular or plural) is not known, then we assume it to be singular, not plural.

Problem Solving with WH-Questions

We turn now to the kinds of errors that students are likely to make with WH-questions. Once again, we want to be careful not only to tell a student that he or she has made a mistake and to explain the rule but also to praise the student for what he or she got right about the structure. In the case of WH-questions, it is possible to get the following right:

a. correct CHOICE OF WH-QUESTION WORD(S)
b. correct POSITION OF THE WH-QUESTION WORD (at the front of the main clause)
c. correct POSITION OF THE AUX FOR A WH-QUESTION (after the WH-question word)
d. correct CATEGORY OF AUX (*be, have, do,* or modal)
e. correct SUBJECT-AUX or SUBJECT-VERB AGREEMENT (singular or plural)
f. correct TENSE OF AUX (past or present)
g. correct PUNCTUATION (question mark)

These aspects reflect what students are likely to do wrong in making a WH-question: a) use the wrong WH-question word(s), b) put the WH-question word(s) in the wrong place, c) put the AUX in the wrong place or not use one at all, d) use the incorrect AUX, e) fail to make the subject agree with the AUX or verb, f) put the wrong tense on the AUX, or g) use the wrong punctuation.

EXERCISE 7.11

Directions: In the following sentences, a student made a single error in WH-question formation. Address the error in three stages:

a) bracket the error to focus your attention
b) list what the student got right about the bracketed error (in this case, the error is the form of the WH-question) and show this in parentheses
   OPTIONAL: Derive the WH-question from its statement form
c) compare the original erroneous sentence to the correct sentence and explain what mistake the student made

Example: *What time it is?

Solution:　a) Bracket the error (the WH-question word, AUX, main verb, and/or punctuation):

　　　*What time [it is]?

　　b) Show what is right about the WH-question:
　　correct choice of WH-question word (*what*)
　　correct position of the WH-question word
　　　(at front of main clause)
　　correct category of AUX (*be*)
　　correct agreement between the subject and the AUX (*it is*)
　　correct tense of AUX (present)
　　correct punctuation (?)

Derivation: It is 4 o'clock.

1. Determine the unknown element of the statement.   It is <u>4 o'clock</u>
2. Substitute the unknown element with an appropriate
   WH-question word.   *It is <u>what time</u>
3. Move the WH-question word in front of the subject. *<u>What time</u> it is
4. Find AUX.   *What time it <u>is</u>
5. Move AUX directly after the WH-question word.   *What time <u>is</u> it
6. Add a question mark.   What time is it<u>?</u>

     c) Compare the erroneous sentence to the correct form and explain the
       mistake:

       *What time [it is]?
       What time is it?

Explanation: The student forgot to move the AUX (*is*) into the position after the
WH-question word(s), which is always required when the unknown
element is in the predicate.

1.   *What did they get a divorce?

2.   *Can you buy where this book?

3.   *When you did arrive in Madrid?

4.   *How much is this book cost?

5.   *Whose story does the police believe?

6.   *How is President Kennedy killed?

7.   *Who wrote that story.

8.   *Who are coming with me?

9.   *How many water will you need?

10.   *What did kill the sheep?

TAG QUESTIONS

The third type of question that we will consider is the tag question. A tag question is a statement plus a short question (the question tag) that is "tagged" on to the end of the statement
after a comma. Look at this example:

     It's hot, <u>isn't it</u>?

The question tag is underlined. Question tags are much more complicated in English than
they are in most European languages, which usually have a single phrase that accomplishes
the same function. In French, one would say, *n'est ce pas?*; in German, *nicht wahr?* or *gel?*; in
Spanish, *no?* And even in colloquial English, we often use *right?* or *don't you think?* Before we
begin our discussion of tag questions, try Exercise 7.12.

EXERCISE 7.12

Directions: Make the following statements into tag questions.

1. You are a teacher.

2. Edward isn't home today.

3. Those children live in Austria.

4. Susan has taken her medicine.

5. The newspaper didn't tell the whole story.

Tag Questions from Statements with an Overt Auxiliary

We have now gotten used to the fact that the AUX plays a very important role in question formation, so we will begin our discussion of tag questions with a simple statement that contains an overt AUX.

> Takeshi can speak Russian.

The first step is to find the AUX.

> Takeshi <u>can</u> speak Russian.

We make a copy of this AUX, change its polarity (i.e., make a positive AUX into its corresponding contracted negative or a negative AUX into its corresponding positive form), and put the changed AUX at the end of the sentence preceded by a comma.

> ┌─can {+/-} can't ─┐
> *Takeshi <u>can</u> speak Russian, <u>can't</u>

Finally, we make a copy of the subject of the sentence, transform it into its corresponding **subject pronoun** form, and put the pronoun at the end of the sentence. Pronouns are covered in detail in Chapter 9, so for now we will refer to the list of subject pronouns in Table 7.2.

Table 7.2 Subject Pronouns

PERSON	SINGULAR	PLURAL
First Person (speaker/s)	I	we
Second Person (addressee/s)	you	you
Third Person (other/s)		
male	he	they
female	she	they
non-human	it	they
existential	there	there

*<u>Takeshi</u> can speak Russian, can't *<u>he</u>*
└─ Takeshi {NP→PRO} he ─↗

We add a question mark at the end, and the tag question is complete.

Takeshi can speak Russian, can't he?

Let's look at the steps required to transform a statement into a tag question:

•• Steps for Making a Tag Question with an Overt AUX••	Example: John is working.
1. Find AUX.	John <u>is</u> working
2. Copy AUX.	<u>is</u>
3. Change polarity of AUX. Contract if negative.	<u>isn't</u>
4. Place AUX after a comma at the end of the sentence.	*John is working, <u>isn't</u>
5. Find SUBJECT.	*<u>John</u> is working, isn't
6. Copy SUBJECT.	<u>John</u>
7. Transform into corresponding subject pronoun.	<u>he</u>
8. Place pronoun at the end of the sentence.	*John is working, isn't <u>he</u>
9. Add a question mark.	John is working, isn't he<u>?</u>

Intonation Pattern

There are two possible intonation patterns for tag questions. The first and most common is rising intonation, which is the same as the pattern for yes/no question intonation except that the intonation rises through the contracted negative and continues to rise on the subject pronoun, both of which are function words (remember that in yes/no questions, the intonation rose and fell within the final content word). A tag question with rising intonation is a true question: the answer is not known or presumed.

John is a student, isn't he? ↗

The second pattern is falling intonation, which is the same as statement and WH-question intonation except that it rises on the AUX and falls within the contracted negative and subject pronoun, both of which are function words. A tag question with falling intonation is not a true question: it presumes that the listener or reader agrees with the statement or at least should agree with it. For this reason, it is common to use this intonation pattern when arguing or showing off (e.g. "I'm always wrong, aren't I? [Note: We use *aren't* in place of *amn't*]). The usage often has a condescending tone (e.g.,"We don't do that here, do we?").

John is a student, is n't he?

EXERCISE 7.13

Directions: Make the following statements into tag questions. Note which intonation pattern sounds
better with the tag question: rising, falling, or either one.

1. Acid rain is hurting the forest.

2. Simon would never drink and drive.

3. The insects are terrible there.

4. There hasn't been much rain this year.

5. The rabbits won't be harmed.

Notice in number 5 that the adverb *never* is sufficient to make the environment negative. All
the negative adverbs (e.g., *seldom, rarely, hardly ever*) discussed in Chapter 6 have the same
effect.

Tag Questions from Statements with No Overt Auxiliary

When the statement that we want to transform into a tag question contains no AUX, we
must use the same process that we used in making yes/no questions and WH-questions about
the predicate: dig one up.

•• *Steps for Making a Tag Question with No Overt AUX* ••	*Example:* John lives in Ohio.
1. Find AUX. (Dig it up if it's buried.)	*John (<u>does</u> live) in Ohio
2. Copy AUX, then rebury AUX in original statement.	<u>does</u> (John <u>lives</u> in Ohio)
3. Change polarity of AUX. Contract if negative.	<u>doesn't</u>
4. Place AUX after a comma at the end of the sentence.	*John lives in Ohio, <u>doesn't</u>
5. Find SUBJECT.	*<u>John</u> lives in Ohio, doesn't
6. Copy SUBJECT.	<u>John</u>
7. Transform into corresponding subject pronoun.	<u>he</u>
8. Place pronoun at the end of the sentence.	*John lives in Ohio, doesn't <u>he</u>
9. Add a question mark.	John lives in Ohio, doesn't he<u>?</u>

INTONATION PATTERN

Either the rising or the falling intonation pattern can be applied to this sentence. However,
notice that the question mark remains no matter what the intention of the speaker is. This is
because it is the grammatical structure that dictates the punctuation in a tag question, not the
intended sense of the sentence.

EXERCISE 7.14

Directions: Make the following statements into tag questions. Note which intonation pattern sounds better with the tag question: rising, falling, or either one.

1. Your uncle writes novels.

2. It isn't raining now.

3. The plane arrived at 8 P.M.

4. There weren't many people at the concert.

5. This exam has been given before.

6. The guests had to leave early.

7. Those houses cost quite a lot.

8. His girlfriend had a headache.

9. You shouldn't be such a snob.

10. The book will be returned next week.

Notice in number 6 that the modal equivalent *had to* is treated as a main verb with a buried AUX. This is because *had to* is not a true modal but a modal equivalent in American English and thus *had* cannot be separated from it. As a result, we would make the yes/no question *Did the guests have to leave early?* (not **Had the guests to leave early?*) and the tag question *The guests had to leave early, didn't they* (not *The guests had to leave early, *hadn't they?*).

Problem Solving with Tag Questions

Now we consider the kinds of errors that students are likely to make with tag questions. Once again, we want to be careful not only to tell a student that he or she has made a mistake and to explain the rule but to praise the student for what he or she got right about the structure. In the case of tag questions, it is possible to get the following right:

    a. correct CATEGORY OF AUX (*be, have, do,* or modal)

    b. correct SUBJECT-AUX AGREEMENT (singular or plural)

    c. correct TENSE OF AUX (past or present)

    d. correct POLARITY OF AUX (positive or negative)

    e. correct POSITION OF AUX FOR A TAG QUESTION (before tag pronoun)

    f. correct CATEGORY OF PRONOUN (subject, not object or possessive pronoun)

    g. correct TYPE OF PRONOUN (human versus non-human)

    h. correct GENDER OF PRONOUN (male or female)

    i. correct AGREEMENT OF PRONOUN (singular or plural)

    j. correct POSITION OF PRONOUN FOR A TAG QUESTION (after the tag AUX)

    k. correct PUNCTUATION (question mark)

These aspects reflect what students are likely to do wrong in making a tag question. In selecting the correct form of AUX, a student could a) chose the wrong category (*be, have, do,* or modal) of AUX, b) fail to make the AUX agree with the subject, c) use the wrong tense of AUX, d) use the wrong polarity of AUX, or e) put the AUX in the wrong place. In selecting the correct pronoun, the student could f) use the wrong category of pronoun, g) use the wrong type (human versus non-human) of pronoun, h) use the wrong gender (male or female) of pronoun, i) fail to make the pronoun agree in number with the subject, j) put the pronoun in the wrong position, or k) not use a question mark at the end of the tag question.

EXERCISE 7.15

Directions: In the following sentences, a student made a single error in tag question formation. Address the error in three stages:

    a) bracket the error to focus your attention

    b) list what the student got right about the bracketed error (in this case, the error is the form of the tag question) and show this in parentheses
    OPTIONAL: Derive the tag question from its statement form

    c) compare the original erroneous sentence to the correct sentence and explain what mistake the student made

Example: *The book costs $2.50, isn't it?

Solution: a) Bracket the error (the AUX, pronoun and/or punctuation in the question tag):

        *The book costs $2.50, [isn't] it?

    b) Show what is right about the tag question:
        correct subject-AUX agreement (*it is*)
        correct tense of AUX (present)
        correct polarity of AUX (negative)
        correct position of AUX for a tag question
           (before tag pronoun)
        correct category of pronoun (subject)
        correct type of pronoun (non-human)
        correct agreement of pronoun (singular)
        correct position of pronoun for a tag question
           (after tag AUX)
        correct punctuation (?)

Derivation:	The book costs $2.50.
1. Find AUX. (Dig it up if it's buried.)	*The book (<u>does</u> cost) $2.50
2. Copy AUX, then rebury AUX in original statement.	<u>does</u> (The book <u>costs</u> $2.50)
3. Change polarity of AUX. Contract if negative.	<u>doesn't</u>
4. Place AUX after a comma at the end of the sentence.	*The book costs $2.50, <u>doesn't</u>
5. Find SUBJECT.	*<u>The book</u> costs $2.50, doesn't
6. Copy SUBJECT.	<u>the book</u>
7. Transform into a subject pronoun.	<u>it</u>
8. Place pronoun at the end of the sentence.	*The book costs $2.50, doesn't <u>it</u>
9. Add a question mark.	The book costs $2.50, doesn't it<u>?</u>

c) Compare the erroneous sentence to the correct form and explain the mistake

*The book costs $2.50, [isn't] it?
The book costs $2.50, doesn't it?

Explanation: The correct category of AUX to use when there is a hidden AUX is *do*, not *be*. The student was probably trying to use one form (*isn't it?*) for all question tags.

1. *The boy works in a factory, can't he?

2. *Mice live underground, doesn't they?

3. *The dinner was expensive, isn't it?

4. *You can't park here, can't you?

5. *Norma hasn't finished her work, she has?

6. *John likes to swim, doesn't John?

7. *Mr. Gomez is a physician, isn't him?

8. *The policeman drove to the accident, didn't it?

9. *The actress has lost a lot of weight, hasn't he?

10. *The men hadn't received a paycheck, had he?

11. *Sally knows the rules, she doesn't?

12. *There is a flag on the moon, isn't there.

ECHO QUESTIONS

The fourth type of question we will consider is the echo question. This is perhaps the easiest type of question to make. We have not considered it before this point, however, because there are important restrictions on its use and we wouldn't want our students to mistakenly use this form in place of the far more frequent yes/no, WH-, and tag questions. There are two types of echo questions. The first we shall call a regular echo question. The second is the WH-echo question.

Regular Echo Questions

Just as there can be no echo without an initial sound, so there can be no echo question without an initial sentence that is repeated or "echoed" in the echo question. Once a statement has been made, the corresponding regular echo question simply repeats that statement verbatim and adds a question mark.

Statement: Heidi has green hair.
Echo Question: Heidi has green hair?

Regular echo questions have an implication that the other question types do not have: they imply **disbelief**. In other words, the only reason one could have for making the regular echo question above is that the speaker could not believe that Heidi had green hair. It would therefore be silly to make a regular echo question concerning something about which there is unlikely to be disbelief, e.g., *A horse has four legs? We need water to survive?*

••*Steps for Making a Regular Echo Question*••	*Example:* Heidi has green hair.
1. Copy the statement.	*Heidi has green hair
2. Add a question mark.	Heidi has green hair?

Intonation Pattern

A regular echo question must have rising intonation, just as if it were a yes/no question.

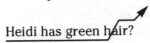

The pattern differs from the yes/no question, however, in that it rises on the **focus** of the disbelief. In the example above, the speaker could imagine that Heidi might have green shoes or even green eyes, but not green hair. It follows that if the speaker knew of several people who had green hair but could not believe that Heidi would have joined this group, then she would have said:

Heidi has green hair?

By the same token, if the speaker knew that Heidi planned to dye her hair purple for the parade and couldn't believe that she had changed the color, she would have said:

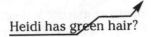

EXERCISE 7.16

Directions: Make the following sentences regular echo questions when appropriate. Notice where the intonation pattern would rise.

1. Columbus discovered America in 1942.

2. The Hawaiian Islands are the tallest mountains in the world.

3. Bats usually sleep at night.

4. The computer costs twenty-five dollars.

5. Cows are meat-eaters.

6. The United Nations Building is located in New York City.

7. Shakespeare wrote "Ode on a Grecian Urn."

8. The government has doubled the taxes for next year.

9. Big fish eat little fish.

10. Fleming invented the telephone.

WH-Echo Questions

WH-echo questions also require an initial sentence that is "echoed" in the WH-echo question. The difference is that once a statement has been made, the corresponding WH-echo question repeats that statement but substitutes a WH-question word for a single element of the sentence and adds a question mark.

>Statement: The doctor broke her lip.
>WH-Echo Question: The doctor broke her what?

WH-echo questions have an implication that regular echo questions do not have: they imply **misperception**. In other words, the primary reason one would have for making the WH-echo question above is that the speaker did not correctly hear, or thought she misheard, what the doctor broke.[1] For this reason, echo questions occur primarily in spoken English.

••*Steps for Making a WH-Echo Question*••	*Example:* The doctor broke her lip.
1. Identify the misperceived element.	*The doctor broke her <u>lip</u>
2. Replace the misperceived element with an appropriate WH-question word.	*The doctor broke her <u>what</u>
3. Add a question mark.	The doctor broke her what<u>?</u>

It is very useful for nonnative speakers of English to know how to construct WH-echo questions because students learning English often understand everything in a sentence except a single word. Students then typically say, "What?" or "Excuse me?" because they haven't caught that single word. This response is an ambiguous one for a native speaker as it can suggest that the student is challenging the native speaker, and it is sometimes perceived as being rude. A WH-echo question, on the other hand, indicates that the listener heard and understood everything in the sentence except precisely what was not heard, and this is exactly what the nonnative speaker wants to have repeated.

Intonation Pattern

A WH-echo question must have rising intonation, just as if it were a yes/no question. Unlike the regular echo question, which can rise within different words depending on the focus of disbelief, the WH-echo question intonation pattern always rises within the WH-question word.

<u>The doctor broke her what?</u>

---

[1] Native speakers sometimes use the WH-echo question to register disbelief as well, but for the sake of clarity, we'll restrict the function of WH-echo questions to misperception.

EXERCISE 7.17

Directions: Make the following sentences WH-echo questions, assuming that the underlined portion is the misperceived element. Notice where the intonation pattern rises.

1. A <u>XXXXXXX</u> landed in our back yard.

2. My sister married <u>XXXXXXXXX</u>.

3. The surgeon removed the <u>XXXXXX XXXXXXXXXX XXXXX</u>.

4. We had to make an emergency landing <u>in XXXXXXXXXXXX</u>.

5. A movie ticket costs <u>XXX XXXX</u>.

6. I'll be in Europe <u>for XXXXXXXXXXXX</u>.

7. This is <u>XXXXXXXXX's</u> book.

8. They can't eat pasta because <u>XXXXXXXXXXXXXXXXXXXXXXXXXXXXXX</u>.

9. <u>XXXXX XXXXX</u> are clogging the drain.

10. You can remove the stain <u>by XXXXXXX XX XXXXX XXXXX</u>.

Notice in number 9 that the WH-question word requires singular agreement even in a WH-echo question.

Problem Solving with Echo Questions

We turn now to the kinds of errors that students are likely to make with echo questions. In the case of echo questions, it is possible to get the following right:

      a. correct CHOICE OF WH-QUESTION WORD (*what, where, how,* etc.)

      b. correct POSITION OF WH-QUESTION WORD (sentence position)

      c. correct AGREEMENT BETWEEN SUBJECT WH-QUESTION WORD AND AUX OR THE MAIN VERB (singular or plural)

      d. correct PUNCTUATION (question mark)

These aspects reflect what students are likely to do wrong in making an echo question: a) choose the wrong WH-question word, b) put the WH-question word in the wrong place, c) fail to make the WH-question word agree with the AUX or the main verb, or d) use the wrong punctuation.

EXERCISE 7.18

Directions: In the following sentences, a student made a single error in echo-question formation. Address the error in three stages:

a) bracket the error to focus your attention

b) list what the student got right about the bracketed error (in this case, the error is the form of the echo question) and show this in parentheses
OPTIONAL: Derive the echo question from its statement form

c) compare the original erroneous sentence to the correct sentence and explain what mistake the student made

Example: *She met what at the party?

Solution: a) Bracket the error (the WH-question word, AUX, main verb, and/or punctuation):
*She met [what] at the party?

b) Show what is right about the echo question:
correct position of WH-question word (object)
correct punctuation (?)

Derivation:

1. Identify the misperceived element.   She met XXX at the party.
2. Replace the misperceived element with an appropriate WH-question word.   She met <u>XXX</u> at the party
   *She met <u>who</u> at the party
3. Add a question mark.   She met who at the party<u>?</u>

c) Compare the erroneous sentence to the correct form and explain the mistake:
*She met [what] at the party?
She met who(m) at the party?

Explanation: The student replaced the misperceived element with the WH-question word for a thing rather than a person. You don't usually meet a "thing" at a party.

1. [WH-echo] *Your suitcase weighs how long?

2. [regular echo] *The frog turned into a carriage.

3. [WH-echo] *Who kept you out all night.

4. [WH-echo] *You flew to when?

5. [regular echo] *Did the lawyer worked for free?

6. [WH-echo] *She said what.

7. [WH-echo] *The general is leaving when the country?

8. [WH-echo] *Who are going to help you?

9. [regular echo] *What he failed the course?

10. [WH-echo] *Who Diane met at the party?

REVIEW OF THE FOUR QUESTION FORMS

EXERCISE 7.19

Directions: Make the following statements into the indicated question form. The unknown
element is underlined.

1. The train left the station <u>at 8 o'clock</u>.
2. English is taught <u>all over the world</u>.
3. The children will be living in Paris <u>for a year</u>.
4. Sally cleans the motel rooms <u>thoroughly with soap and water</u>.
5. <u>These computers</u> have been tested by the quality control department.
6. <u>Therese</u> was jilted by her lover several times.
7. Before he came to California, John had never seen <u>Yosemite National Park</u>.
8. Students are afraid of grammar <u>because they feel inadequate</u>.
9. Ants usually live <u>in colonies</u>.
10. <u>A foreign language</u> cannot be mastered in a few weeks.

1. a. Yes/No _____

   b. WH _____

   c. Tag_____

   d. WH-Echo _____

2. a. Yes/No _____

   b. WH _____

   c. Tag_____

   d. Reg. Echo _____

3. a. Yes/No _____

   b. WH _____

   c. Tag_____

   d. WH-Echo _____

4. a. Yes/No _____

   b. WH _____

   c. Tag_____

   d. Reg. Echo _____

5. a. Yes/No _____

    b. WH _____

    c. Tag_____

    d. WH-Echo _____

6. a. Yes/No _____

    b. WH _____

    c. Tag_____

    d. Reg. Echo _____

7. a. Yes/No _____

    b. WH _____

    c. Tag_____

    d. WH-Echo _____

8. a. Yes/No _____

    b. WH _____

    c. Tag_____

    d. Reg Echo _____

9. a. Yes/No _____

    b. WH _____

    c. Tag_____

    d. WH-Echo _____

10. a. Yes/No _____

    b. WH _____

    c. Tag_____

    d. Reg. Echo _____

Unit III: THE NOUN

Chapter 8

SUBJECTS AND OBJECTS

The subject and object slots in an English sentence are filled with the same type of constituent, either a noun phrase or a noun clause, as we have seen in earlier chapters. In this chapter, we first review noun phrases, then look at noun clauses in greater detail, and finally discuss three kinds of objects: direct objects, the objects of prepositions, and indirect objects.

NOUN PHRASES

Noun phrases should be quite familiar to you by now as they are the most frequent occupiers of the subject and object slots in a sentence. The following are examples of noun phrases:

a.	wine	[Ø determiner + common noun]
b.	Paul	[Ø determiner + proper noun]
c.	the old woman's dog	[possessive determiner + common noun]
d.	the small boy	[determiner + adjective + noun]
e.	a girl with a balloon	[determiner + noun + prepositional phrase]
f.	the pill that cured me	[determiner + noun + adjective clause]
g.	men in suits who lie	[Ø determiner + noun + prepositional phrase + adjective clause]
h.	they/them	[pronoun]

A noun phrase can occur as either the subject, the object, or the object of a preposition in a sentence. Pronouns replace noun phrases that are already familiar to the listener or reader and therefore count as noun phrases as well. However, pronouns have different forms depending on whether they occur in the subject or object slot, as we shall see in Chapter 9.

NOUN CLAUSES

Like noun phrases, noun clauses fill the subject and object slots in a sentence. Unlike noun phrases, however, noun clauses always contain a clause subject and a clause verb because they are derived from complete statements or questions. There are two types of noun clauses: embedded statements and embedded questions. Examples are shown below with the noun clause underlined:

TYPE	SUBJECT	VERB	OBJECT/PRED NP or PRED ADJ
Embedded Statements	a) Sheila	said	that she was tired.
	b) That nurses work hard	is	common knowledge.
Embedded Questions (WH)	c) Ellen	knows	what her mother wants.
	d) Where the boy found the gun	was	a mystery.
Embedded Questions (Yes/No)	e) The visitor	asked	whether (or not) the guide knew the name of the church.
	f) Whether (or not) the student is an immigrant	is	irrelevant.

In these examples, Sentence (a) shows an embedded statement in the object position and Sentence (b) an embedded statement in the subject position. Sentence (c) shows an embedded WH-question in the object position and Sentence (d) an embedded WH-question in the subject position. Sentence (e) shows an embedded yes/no question in the object position and Sentence (f) an embedded yes/no question in the subject position. The six different types of noun clauses are discussed in detail below.

Embedded Statements

An embedded statement is a noun clause derived from a statement that is contained or embedded in the subject or object slot of a sentence. An embedded statement usually begins with the clause marker *that*, which is why it is also known as a *that*-clause.

EMBEDDED STATEMENTS AS THE OBJECT OF THE MAIN CLAUSE

Embedded statements most commonly occupy the object slot in a sentence. Look at the following examples:

SUBJECT	VERB	OBJECT
a) Paul	knows	Mrs. Thatcher.
b) Paul	knows	economics.
c) Paul	knows	New Delhi.
d) Paul	knows	that the trip will cost $15,000. [embedded statement]

In Sentence (d), the original (independent) statement *The trip will cost $15,000* can be embedded in the main sentence because the addition of the clause marker *that* signals the beginning of a (dependent) noun clause.[1]

---

[1] The noun clause marker *that* is often deleted in short noun clauses functioning as objects, especially in spoken English. For teaching purposes, however, it is a good idea to retain it. In this way, every dependent clause has a clause marker.

••Steps for Embedding a Statement as the Object of the Main Clause••	**Example:** Paul knows X. X = The trip will cost $15,000.
1. Add the clause marker *that* to the beginning of the statement.	X$_1$ = <u>that the trip will cost $15,000</u>
2. Embed the clause in the main sentence.	Paul knows <u>that the trip will cost $15,000</u>.

EXERCISE 8.1

Directions: Complete the following sentences with the correct embedded form of the statement in brackets.

1. [She will get the job.] Susan believes...

2. [The class had been cancelled.] The dean told the angry students...

3. [The patient will live for several years.] The doctors hope...

4. [The storm would continue for another three days.] The weatherman said...

5. [The witness had been lying.] The detectives discovered...

EMBEDDED STATEMENTS AS THE SUBJECT OF THE MAIN CLAUSE

Embedded statements can also occupy the subject slot in a sentence. Look at the following examples:

SUBJECT	**VERB**	**PREDICATE NOUN PHRASE**
a) The rain	is not	her fault.
b) Roger's mood	is not	her fault.
c) The spoiled egg salad	is not	her fault.
d) <u>That he dislikes opera</u> [embedded statement]	is not	her fault.

In Sentence (d), the original (independent) statement *He dislikes opera* can be embedded in the main sentence because the addition of the clause marker *that* makes it a (dependent) noun clause.

••Steps for Embedding a Statement as the Subject of the Main Clause••	**Example:** X is not her fault. X = He dislikes opera.
1. Add the clause marker *that* to the beginning of the statement.	X$_1$ = <u>that</u> he dislikes opera
2. Embed the clause in the main sentence.	<u>That he dislikes opera</u> is not her fault.

Embedded statements in the subject slot often sound better if they are preceded with the noun phrase *the fact* or *the idea*:

> The fact that he dislikes opera is not her fault.

> The idea that man must conquer nature is no longer acceptable.

EXERCISE 8.2

Directions: Using the steps, complete the following sentences with the correct embedded form of the statement in brackets.

1. [The famine would not end soon.] X was of no interest to him.

2. [He has had too much to drink.] X is patently obvious.

3. [Money is the root of all evil.] X has been known since the dawn of economics.

4. [Dentists do not like to cause pain.] X is rarely what patients think about in the dentist's chair.

5. [You'd rather be alone.] X is written all over your face.

Embedded Questions

An embedded question is a noun clause that is derived from a question and embedded in the subject or object slot of the sentence. There are two types of embedded questions: **embedded WH-questions** and **embedded yes/no questions**. Before we begin, try exercise 8.3.

EXERCISE 8.3

Directions: Complete the sentence with the question in brackets.

> *Example:* [What does Joseph think?] I don't really know...
> *Solution:* I don't really know what Joseph thinks.

1. [Who made this mess?] Would somebody please tell me...

2. [Did her mother buy the house?] Ask Susan...

3. [Why hasn't Paul finished his dinner?] I have no idea...

4. [Is the moon made of cheese?] They wonder...

5. [How far is it to New Delhi?] The map shows...

EMBEDDED WH-QUESTIONS

An embedded WH-question is a noun clause that is derived from a WH-question. The clause marker is always a WH-question word.

Intonation Pattern

Since many students are confused about the difference between WH-questions and embedded WH-questions, the intonation pattern is discussed here as it was in Chapter 7. In that chapter, we learned the pattern for yes/no and WH-questions: the voice rises or falls, respectively, within the last content word. The presence of an embedded WH-question does not affect this pattern since it is simply a noun clause in the main sentence into which it was embedded. The main sentence can be a statement, a yes/no question, or a WH-question, and the intonation pattern (as well as the punctuation) is governed by the nature of that sentence, as shown in the examples below:

STATEMENT: Susan explained why she was upset.

YES/NO QUESTION: Did Susan explain why she was upset?

WH-QUESTION: Who explained why she was upset?

Types of Embedded WH-Questions

We learned in Chapter 7 that there are two types of WH-questions: P-form, in which the unknown element is in the predicate, and S-form, in which the unknown element is the subject. Since embedded WH-questions are derived from WH-questions, they also reflect this basic distinction. The first type is called a **P-form embedded WH-question** and the second an **S-form embedded WH-question**. Look at the following examples, in which the embedded WH-questions are underlined and the WH-question word is in boldface:

a) The zoo keeper knows **what** the alligator ate.   [P-form embedded WH-question]
b) The zoo keeper knows **what** ate the alligator.   [S-form embedded WH-question]

In Sentence (a), the unknown element, now replaced by the WH-question word *what*, would have indicated something that the alligator ate. In the mind of the zoo keeper, the answer to a WH-question about this could have been something like *The alligator ate a fish*. The transformation of the WH-question into this statement and then into a noun clause is shown below:

P-Form WH-QUESTION	STATEMENT	P-Form NOUN CLAUSE
What did the alligator eat? →	The alligator ate **a fish**. →	**what** the alligator ate

In the P-form WH-question, *fish* is replaced by *what* and moved in front of the subject. Since it is a P-form WH-question, an AUX (*did*) must follow the WH-word. In the statement, *a fish* is the object, and objects always occur in the predicate of a sentence (this is why both the WH-question and the noun clause are called P-form). In the P-form noun clause, *a fish* is replaced by *what* and moved to the front of the clause. We call this type of noun clause an embedded WH-question to distinguish it from other types of noun clauses, i.e., embedded statements and embedded yes/no questions.

In Sentence (b), the unknown element, now replaced by the WH-question word *what*, would have indicated something that ate the alligator. In the mind of the zoo keeper, the answer to a WH-question about this could have been something like *A lion ate the alligator*. The transformation of the WH-question into this statement and then into a noun clause is shown below:

S-Form WH-QUESTION	STATEMENT	S-Form Noun Clause
What ate the alligator? →	A lion ate the alligator. →	what ate the alligator

In the S-form WH-question, *a lion* is replaced by *what* and stays in front of the verb. Since it is an S-form WH-question, no hidden AUX follows the WH-word. In the statement, *a lion* is the subject (this is why both the WH-question and the noun clause are called S-form). In the S-form noun clause, *a lion* is replaced by *what* and remains at the front of the clause. Again, we call this type of noun clause an embedded WH-question to distinguish it from other types of noun clauses, i.e., embedded statements and embedded yes/no questions.

EXERCISE 8.4

Directions: Classify the underlined portion of the sentence as an S-form embedded WH-question or a P-form embedded WH-question by circling the appropriate description.

Embedded WH-Question Type

1. I don't really know <u>what Joseph thinks</u>.   S-form   P-form

2. Would somebody please tell me <u>who made this mess?</u>   S-form   P-form

3. I have no idea <u>why Paul hasn't finished his dinner</u>.   S-form   P-form

4. The police would not reveal <u>what caused the explosion</u>.   S-form   P-form

5. The map shows <u>how far it is to New Delhi</u>.   S-form   P-form

EMBEDDED WH-QUESTIONS AS THE OBJECT OF THE MAIN CLAUSE

Embedded WH-questions occur as the object of a main clause in either the P-form or the S-form, as you saw in Exercise 8.4.

P-FORM EMBEDDED WH-QUESTIONS AS THE OBJECT OF THE MAIN CLAUSE: OVERT AUXILIARY

An embedded WH-question with an overt auxiliary contains a visible auxiliary verb in the statement form of the question. Look at the following examples:

SUBJECT	VERB	OBJECT
a) John	knows	Mr. Rampal.
b) John	knows	mathematics.
c) John	knows	Montreal.
d) John	knows	<u>how much the car **will** cost</u>. [embedded question]

In Sentence (d), the embedded WH-question occurs in the object slot and the overt auxiliary verb is in boldface. The clause marker for an embedded WH-question is always a WH-question word. Notice that the WH-question *How much will the car cost?* cannot be directly embedded into a statement.

*John knows <u>how much will the car cost</u>.

It must first be transformed into an embedded WH-question. To make this transformation, we begin with the sentence in this form:

John knows X.

X = How much will the car cost?

The transformation applies only to the WH-question (X). The first step is to invent an answer to the question.

X_1 = the car will cost <u>$10,000</u>

Since the invented part of the sentence is actually the unknown element, we replace it with an appropriate WH-question word.

X_2 = the car will cost <u>how much</u>

Finally, since we are now accustomed to the fact that clause markers always occur at the beginning of a clause, we move the WH-question word to that position.

X_3 = <u>how much</u> the car will cost

The structure is now ready to be embedded in the original statement.

John knows X.

John knows <u>how much the car will cost</u>.

••Steps for Embedding a P-form WH-Question with an Overt AUX as the Object of the Main Clause••	**Example:** John knows X. X = How much will the car cost?
1. Make the WH-question into a statement by inventing an answer.	X_1 = the car will cost <u>$10,000</u>
2. Replace the unknown element with an appropriate WH-question word.	X_2 = the car will cost <u>how much</u>
3. Move the WH-question word(s) to the front of the clause.	X_3 = <u>how much</u> the car will cost
4. Embed the clause in the main sentence.	*John knows <u>how much the car will cost</u>
5. Add the appropriate punctuation.	John knows how much the car will cost.

You may have noticed that the steps for transforming a WH-question into an embedded WH-question are the exact opposite from those we used in transforming a statement into a WH-question in Chapter 7. That is why we must remove the question mark.

EXERCISE 8.5

Directions: Using the steps, complete the following sentences with the correct embedded form of the P-form WH-question in brackets.

1. [When can father leave the hospital?] Tomorrow they'll tell us...

2. [Why doesn't Pierre like American coffee?] You know perfectly well...

3.   [What color should she dye her hair?] She wants to know…

4.   [Where was the library?] Mrs. Fong had forgotten…

5.   [How long is the Mississippi River?] I can never remember…

P-FORM EMBEDDED WH-QUESTIONS AS THE OBJECT OF THE MAIN CLAUSE: NO OVERT AUXILIARY

We now look at P-form embedded WH-questions with no overt auxiliary. When we begin with a P-form WH-question, the non-overt AUX is, of course, visible. *Non-overt* means that the AUX is not visible in the **statement** form of the question, in which case the AUX *do* is used rather than any other auxiliary verb. The transformation of a P-form WH-question into a parallel P-form embedded WH-question again requires the reversal of the procedure for making a WH-question from a statement. Look at the following example:

John knows X.

X = Where does Mary live?

The first step is to invent an answer to the question (this is where the reversal really takes place for it requires that the AUX be reburied).

X_1 = Mary lives <u>in New Zealand</u>

Since the invented part of the sentence is the unknown element, we replace it with an appropriate WH-question word.

X_2 = Mary lives <u>where</u>

Finally, we move the WH-question word or clause marker to the front of the clause.

X_3 = <u>where</u> Mary lives

The structure is now ready to be embedded in the original statement.

John knows X.

John knows <u>where Mary lives</u>.

••Steps for Embedding a P-form Embedded WH-Question with No Overt AUX as the Object of the Main Clause••	**Example:** John knows X. X = Where does Mary live?
1. Make the WH-question into a statement by inventing an answer.	X_1 = Mary lives <u>in New Zealand</u>
2. Replace the unknown element with an appropriate WH-question word.	X_2 = Mary lives <u>where</u>
3. Move the WH-question word(s) to the front of the clause.	X_3 = <u>where</u> Mary lives
4. Embed the clause in the main sentence.	*John knows <u>where Mary lives</u>
5. Add the appropriate punctuation.	John knows where Mary lives.

EXERCISE 8.6

Directions: Using the steps, complete the following sentences with the correct embedded form of the P-form WH-question in brackets.

1. [Why did the building collapse?] Everyone is afraid to ask...

2. [When does the next train arrive?] The timetable shows...

3. [How often do dogs attack their masters?] The veterinarian wasn't sure...

4. [Where did Columbus land?] The old map indicated...

5. [What does *tardy* mean?] Students always conveniently forget...

S-FORM EMBEDDED WH-QUESTIONS AS THE OBJECT OF THE MAIN CLAUSE

In the examples above, the unknown element in the embedded question is in the predicate, e.g., the car will cost ___ (*how much*); Mary lives ___ (*where*); her boyfriend left ___ (*why*). We know from our experience with WH-questions that the form is different when the unknown element is the subject. Look at this example:

> I can't remember X.
>
> X = Who takes sugar?

The first step is to answer the question by inventing an answer.

> X$_1$ = <u>Helene</u> takes sugar

We replace the invented portion with a WH-question word.

> X$_2$ = <u>who</u> takes sugar

The next step is normally to move the WH-word to the front of the clause, but in S-form embedded WH-questions it is already there. So we can skip this step and embed X$_2$ directly into the main sentence.

> I can't remember <u>who takes sugar</u>

We add a period because the main sentence is a statement, not a question, and the process is complete.

> I can't remember who takes sugar.

••*Steps for Embedding an S-form Embedded WH-Question as the Object of the Main Clause*••	*Example:* I can't remember X. X = Who takes sugar?
1. Make the WH-question into a statement by inventing an answer.	X$_1$ = <u>Helene</u> takes sugar
2. Replace the unknown element with an appropriate WH-question word.	X$_2$ = <u>who</u> takes sugar
3. Embed the clause in the main sentence.	*I can't remember <u>who takes sugar</u>
4. Add the appropriate punctuation.	I can't remember <u>who takes sugar</u>.

EXERCISE 8.7

Directions: Using the steps, complete the following sentences with the correct embedded form of the S-form WH-question in brackets.

1. [Who stole the car?] The police discovered...

2. [How much wine was left in the bottle?] It was easy to see...

3. [What had killed the trees?] No one knew...

4. [Which government official ordered the massacre?] People are afraid to say...

5. [Whose wallet contains a fifty-dollar bill?] The guests have to guess...

EMBEDDED WH-QUESTIONS AS THE SUBJECT OF THE MAIN CLAUSE

In the examples we have been looking at, the embedded WH-question, or noun clause, has occupied the object slot in the sentence. An embedded question can also fill the subject slot, and it can occur in either the P-form or the S-form.

P-FORM EMBEDDED WH-QUESTIONS AS THE SUBJECT OF THE MAIN CLAUSE: OVERT AUXILIARY

We are now accustomed to the fact that an embedded WH-question with an overt auxiliary contains a visible auxiliary verb in the statement form of the question. Another way to think of it is that, unlike a non-overt auxiliary (i.e., *do*), an overt auxiliary (e.g., *must*) can never be buried. Look at this example:

SUBJECT	VERB	OBJECT
How long the drought **might** last	deeply concerns	her.

In the example, the embedded question is derived from the P-form WH-question *How long might the drought last?* containing the overt auxiliary *might*.

••*Steps for Embedding a P-form WH-Question with an Overt AUX as the Subject of the Main Clause*••	*Example:* X deeply concerns her. X = How long might the drought last?
1. Make the WH-question into a statement by inventing an answer.	X_1 = the drought might last <u>six years</u>
2. Replace the unknown element with an appropriate WH-question word.	X_2 = the drought might last <u>how long</u>
3. Move the WH-question word(s) to the front of the clause.	X_3 = <u>how long</u> the drought might last
4. Embed the clause in the main sentence.	*<u>How long the drought might last</u> deeply concerns her
5. Add the appropriate punctuation.	How long the drought might last deeply concerns her.

P-FORM EMBEDDED WH-QUESTIONS AS THE SUBJECT OF THE MAIN CLAUSE: NO OVERT AUXILIARY

P-form embedded questions that fill the subject slot also occur with no overt auxiliary. Noun clauses of this type often appear alone as newspaper headlines (e.g., Why the Dollar Fell) or as essay or book titles (e.g., How San Francisco Survived the Earthquake). Look at this example:

SUBJECT	VERB	OBJECT
When the train leaves	doesn't interest	her

In the example, the embedded question is derived from the P-form WH-question *When does the train leave?*

••*Steps for Embedding a P-form WH-Question with No Overt AUX as the Subject of the Main Clause*••	*Example:* X doesn't interest her. X = When does the train leave?
1. Make the WH-question into a statement by inventing an answer.	X_1 = The train leaves <u>at six o'clock</u>
2. Replace the unknown element with an appropriate WH-question word.	X_2 = the train leaves <u>when</u>
3. Move the WH-question word(s) to the front of the clause.	X_3 = <u>when</u> the train leaves
4. Embed the clause in the main sentence.	*<u>When the train leaves</u> doesn't interest her
5. Add the appropriate punctuation.	When the train leaves doesn't interest her.

EXERCISE 8.8

Directions: Using the steps, complete the following sentences with the correct embedded form of the P-form WH-question in brackets.

1. [Where do swans go in winter?] X is a mystery to me.

2. [What will the Queen wear to the dinner?] X is of vital importance to the fashion world.

3. [Why did Houdini die?] X is the subject of a new book.

4. [How does John do on this test?] X will determine his course grade.

5. [Whom should she choose as a husband?] X has completely preoccupied the media.

S-FORM EMBEDDED WH-QUESTIONS AS THE SUBJECT OF THE MAIN CLAUSE

The final category of embedded WH-questions is S-form embedded WH-questions that function as the subject of the main clause. Look at this example:

SUBJECT	VERB	PREDICATE NOUN PHRASE
Who killed the horse	is still	a mystery.

In the example, the embedded question is derived from the S-form WH-question *Who killed the horse?*

••*Steps for Embedding an S-form WH-Question as the Subject of the Main Clause*••	*Example:* X is still a mystery. X = Who killed the horse?
1. Make the WH-question into a statement by inventing an answer.	X_1 = <u>a madman</u> killed the horse
2. Replace the unknown element with an appropriate WH-question word.	X_2 = <u>who</u> killed the horse
3. Embed the clause in the main sentence.	*<u>Who killed the horse</u> is still a mystery
4. Add the appropriate punctuation.	Who killed the horse is still a mystery.

EXERCISE 8.9

Directions: Using the steps, complete the following sentences with the correct embedded form of the S-form WH-question in brackets.

1. [What causes the disease?] X is the most troubling health question of the century.

2. [Who should sound the alarm?] X is explained in the handbook.

3. [Whose work generated the most criticism?] X will not be addressed in this lecture.

4. [What color reduces violence?] X has been the subject of continuous debate.

5. [Whoever can find work?] X deserves the nicest bedroom.

The following exercise contains examples of all four types of embedded WH-questions:
- P-form embedded WH-questions as the object of a main clause (overt and non-overt AUX)
- P-form embedded WH-questions as the subject of a main clause (overt and non-overt AUX)
- S-form embedded WH-questions as the object of a main clause
- S-form embedded WH-questions as the subject of a main clause

However, instead of starting with a WH-question, the problems in this exercise begin with a statement. This means that you can go directly to the second step (X_2) of the "Steps for Making Embedded Questions."

EXERCISE 8.10

Directions: Make the underlined portion in the following sentences into an embedded WH-question and embed it in the sentence provided. Notice the intonation pattern.

      Example: [The man studied English_at night school.] I don't know...

      Solution: I don't know where the man studied English.

1. [The tiger ate the hunter.] Does anyone know...?

2. [The hurricane had destroyed several coastal villages.] The newspaper described...

3. [The moths come around in the evening.] The insect collector wants to know...

4. [The fire started because some boys were playing with matches.] The city has no idea...

5. [John learned about the surprise party by finding an invitation.] We can't work out...

6. [A friend told him to cheat on the test.] It makes no difference...

7. [I live in Miami.] Why does the newspaper want to know...?

8. [Electrical storms cause the lightning to flash.] ...is still a mystery to the researchers.

9. [This is Heinrich's notebook.] Can someone please tell me...?

10. [She will buy the house with the blue roof.] Joan has decided...

Other Features of Embedded Noun Clauses

Now that we have had some practice with embedding, we are ready to consider two grammatical processes that apply to embedded noun clauses: **sequence of tenses** and **the use of infinitive verb forms**. Sequence of tenses only applies when the main verb is in a past tense, whereas the use of infinitive verb forms only applies when the main subject and the noun clause subject are identical.

SEQUENCE OF TENSES

Sequence of tenses describes a grammatical process in which the main verb in a sentence exerts a kind of magnetic effect on the verb in a noun clause, "pulling" it into a time that matches the time of the main verb.[2] This "pulling" effect only works in one direction, however: past time main verbs "pull" present time clause verbs into a past tense. The aspect of the clause verb remains the same as it was in the original clause (what we have been calling "X"). Exceptions occur only when the verb is in the simple or continuous past tense, in which case it is pulled into the past perfect or the past perfect continuous tense, respectively. The effect of sequence of tenses is summarized in Table 8.1.

---

[2] Sequence of tenses may be ignored if the clause is supposed to represent a fact or a truth about the world, as shown in the following examples:

      Columbus knew that the world is not flat.

      The tabloid reported that extraterrestrials are living in Los Angeles.

In this case, the clause verb remains in the present time even though the main verb is in the past.

Table 8.1. Sequence of Tenses

VERB	PRESENT TIME	PAST TIME
Main Clause	The doctor **says** (present) that . . .	The doctor **said** (past) that . . .
Embedded Clause	the patient <u>will improve</u>. (present modal)	the patient <u>would improve.</u> (past modal)
	the patient <u>must rest</u>. (present modal)	the patient <u>had to rest.</u> (past modal)
	the patient <u>sleeps</u> well. (simple present)	the patient <u>slept</u> well. (simple past)
	the patient <u>is eating</u>. (present continuous)	the patient <u>was eating.</u> (past continuous)
	the patient <u>has lost</u> weight. (pres. perfect)	the patient <u>had lost</u> weight. (past perfect)
	the patient <u>went</u> home. (simple past)	the patient <u>had gone</u> home. (past perfect)
	the patient <u>was getting</u> stronger. (past continuous)	the patient <u>had been getting</u> stronger. (past perfect continuous)

[Note: The examples in Table 8.1 are embedded statements, which were discussed on p. 166]

The effect of sequence of tenses in embedded WH-questions is shown in the following example:

> John knew X.
>
> X = When does the boss go to the bank?

By following the steps for making an embedded question, we get the incorrect embedded form:

> *John knew when the boss <u>goes</u> to the bank.

This sentence is not correct because the time of the main verb *knew* (past) "pulls" the tense of the clause verb *go* (simple present) into *went* (simple past), while the aspect (simple) remains unchanged. This requires the addition of another step to the steps for making an embedded question, but only with past main verbs: Adjust for sequence of tenses. The correct final form is:

> John knew when the boss went to the bank.

EXERCISE 8.11

Directions: Make the underlined portions in the following sentences into embedded questions and embed them in the sentence provided. Use the correct sequence of tenses.

> *Example:* She was asleep <u>for two hours</u>. The nurse didn't say...
>
> *Solution:* The nurse didn't say how long she had been asleep.

1. [She has left the keys <u>at home</u>.] Mary suddenly remembered...

2. [The plane will land <u>at 10 P.M.</u>] Did they say...?

3.   [Mother Theresa helps the poor in India.] I cannot forget...

4.   [Sally is angry because Richard insulted her.] Who told you...?

5.   [It is Virginia's handerkerchief.] The police didn't know...

THE USE OF INFINITIVE VERB FORMS

When the subject of the verb in an embedded noun clause is either the same as the subject of the main verb or is a generalized subject (e.g., *one* or *people*), the subject may be deleted if a general situation is implied. Once the subject is deleted, the verb is no longer finite, so it automatically reverts to the infinitive form. Look at the following example of this grammatical process at work in an embedded WH-question:

Mary remembered X.

X = Where did Mary find the key?

By following the steps for making an embedded WH-question, we get the incorrect embedded form:

*Mary remembered where Mary had found the key.

Since the main subject (*Mary*) is the same as the clause subject (*Mary*), we have two options. We can show a particular situation in which only the clause subject performs the action, or we can show a general situation in which any subject could perform the action. To show the particular situation, we simply replace the identical clause subject with a subject pronoun. To show the general situation, we remove the identical clause subject, which forces the clause verb into the infinitive form.

a) Mary remembered where she had found the key.   [particular situation]

b) Mary remembered where to find the key.   [general situation]

In Sentence (a), the use of a pronoun (*she*) shows a particular situation. In Sentence (b), the presence of an infinitive (*to find*) as a clause verb shows a general situation. This grammatical process requires the addition of another step to the steps for making an embedded question, but only when the main and clause subjects are identical: Adjust the clause verb to show a general or particular situation. Let's try another example:

The new nurse doesn't know X.

X = How does one take blood from a patient?

By following the steps for making an embedded question, we get:

The new nurse doesn't know how one takes blood from a patient.

This sentence uses the pronoun *one* in the particular-situation format, which sounds rather formal in American English. However, since the clause describes the regular duties of **any** nurse, a general condition is implied, which allows the use of an infinitive clause verb.

The new nurse doesn't know how to take blood from a patient.

In this example, *the new nurse* is the subject of the main verb, but the subject of the clause verb *take* is generalized (*one*). The clause subject is therefore deleted and the clause verb reverts to the infinitive form.

EXERCISE 8.12

Directions: Make the underlined portions in the following sentences into embedded questions and embed them in the sentence provided. Use the correct infinitive verb form.

> *Example:* [The woman painted her living room <u>blue</u>.] Last week, the woman didn't know...
>
> *Solution:* Last week, the woman didn't know what color to paint her living room.

1. [The engineer eventually found a job <u>in Atlanta</u>.] At first, the engineer wasn't sure...

2. [People usually trust <u>their parents</u>.] The abandoned child didn't know...

3. [Employees do <u>a variety of service jobs</u>.] The new employee had no idea...

4. [The laundry charged <u>seven dollars</u> for cleaning a sweater.] The laundry knows exactly...

5. [The older boys never stop teasing <u>until the children cry</u>.] The older boys don't know...

EMBEDDED YES/NO QUESTIONS

An embedded yes/no-question is a noun clause derived from a yes/no question. Just as in embedded WH-questions, the noun clause can be embedded either in the object or in the subject slot of the main sentence, although subject embedding is less common than object embedding.

Intonation Pattern

The intonation pattern for embedded yes/no questions is exactly the same as the pattern for embedded WH-questions: the pattern usually rises or falls within the last content word. The main sentence can be a statement, a yes/no question, or a WH-question, and the intonation pattern (as well as the punctuation) is always governed by the nature of the main sentence, as shown in the examples below:

STATEMENT: Jay asked if he should leave.

YES/NO QUESTION: Did Jay ask if he should leave?

WH-QUESTION: Who asked if he should leave?

Embedded Yes/No Questions as the Object of the Main Clause: Overt Auxiliary

An embedded yes/no-question functioning as the object of a main clause can occur with either an overt or a non-overt auxiliary verb. Look at the following examples:

SUBJECT	VERB	OBJECT
John	asked	a question.
John	asked	if the parrot **could** talk. [embedded yes/no question]

In this example, the embedded yes/no question occurs in the object slot and the overt auxiliary is in boldface. Notice that the yes/no question *Can the parrot talk?* cannot be directly embedded into a statement.

*John asked can the parrot talk.

It must first be transformed into an embedded yes/no question. To make this transformation, we begin with the sentence in this form:

John asked X.

X = Can the parrot talk?

The transformation applies only to the yes/no question. The first step is to answer the question.

X_1 = The parrot can talk

In order to show the listener (or reader) that the yes/no question has been embedded, we insert the clause marker *if* at the front of the noun clause.

X_2 = if the parrot can talk

The structure is now ready to be embedded in the original statement.

John asked X.

*John asked if the parrot can talk

Sequence of tenses, the effect in which a past main verb "pulls" a clause verb into the past time, applies to embedded yes/no questions in the same way as it does to embedded WH-questions. Therefore, since the main verb *asked* is in the past time, sequence of tenses forces the clause verb to be in the past time, too. The past time of the modal *can* is *could* (see Table 8.1).

John asked if the parrot could talk

Finally, we add the appropriate punctuation to get the correct sentence:

John asked if the parrot could talk.

••*Steps for Embedding a Yes/No Question with an Overt AUX as the Object of the Main Clause:* ••	*Example:* John asked X. •• X = Can the parrot talk?
1. Make the yes/no question into a statement by answering the question.	X_1 = The parrot can talk.
2. Insert the word *if* at the front of the clause.	X_2 = if the parrot can talk
3. Embed the clause in the main sentence.	*John asked if the parrot can talk
4. Adjust for sequence of tenses.	*John asked if the parrot could talk
5. Add the appropriate punctuation.	John asked if the parrot could talk.

EXERCISE 8.13

Directions: Using the steps, complete the following sentences with the correct embedded form of the yes/no question in brackets. Remember sequence of tenses. Use the correct intonation pattern.

1. [Is there blood on the knife?] The policewoman asked...

2. [Can she have a room with a bath?] She wants to know...

3. [Has there been much rain this summer?] Can you tell us...

4. [Must the interpretation be so dramatic?] The critic wondered...

5. [Are the passes open?] The skiers need to find out...

Embedded Yes/No Questions as the Object of the Main Clause: No Overt Auxiliary

The transformation of a yes/no question with no overt auxiliary into its embedded yes/no question form requires a reversal of the procedure for making a yes/no question from a statement. Look at the following example:

> The girl asked me X.
>
> X = Did the dog die?

The first step is to answer the question.

> X_1 = The dog died

In order to show the listener (or reader) that this clause has been embedded, we insert the clause marker *if* at the front of the noun clause.

> X_2 = if the dog died

The structure is now ready to be embedded in the original statement.

> The girl asked me X.
>
> *The girl asked me if the dog died

The final step is to adjust for sequence of tenses (see Table 8.1) and add the correct punctuation.

> The girls asked me if the dog had died.

••*Steps for Embedding a Yes/No Question with No Overt AUX as the Object of the Main Clause*••	*Example:* The girl asked me X. X = Did the dog die?
1. Make the yes/no question into a statement by answering the question (rebury the AUX).	X_1= <u>The dog died</u>
2. Insert the word *if* at the front of the clause.	X_2 = <u>if</u> the dog died
3. Embed the clause in the main sentence.	*The girl asked me <u>if the dog died</u>
4. Adjust for sequence of tenses.	*The girl asked me if the dog <u>had died</u>
5. Add the appropriate punctuation.	The girl asked me if the dog had died.

EXERCISE 8.14

Directions: Using the steps, complete the following sentences with the correct embedded form of the Yes/No-question in brackets.

1. [Does the "M" bus go downtown?] The tourist asked the guide...

2. [Do the children cry at night?] She wants to know...

3. [Does Harriet want a divorce?] Can you tell me...

4. [Did you like the play?] The director wondered...

5. [Does the conductor sell tickets?] The passengers wanted to find out...

Embedded Yes/No Questions as the Subject of the Main Clause

Like all the embedded noun clauses that we have looked at, embedded yes/no questions can also function as the subject of the main clause. Look at the following examples:

SUBJECT	VERB	PREDICATE NOUN PHRASE
Mary's life	is	nobody's business.
<u>Whether Mary has found a boyfriend</u> [embedded yes/no question]	is	nobody's business.

In this example, the underlined embedded yes/no question occurs in the subject slot. The yes/no question *Has Mary found a boyfriend?* cannot be directly embedded in a statement.

　　　*Has Mary found a boyfriend is nobody's business.

It must first be transformed into an embedded yes/no question. To make this transformation, we begin with the sentence in this form:

　　　X is nobody's business.

　　　X = Has Mary found a boyfriend?

The transformation applies only to the yes/no question. The first step is to answer the question.

X_1 = <u>Mary has found a boyfriend</u>

In order to show the listener (or reader) that the yes/no question has been embedded, we add the clause marker *whether* (or *whether or not*) to the front of the noun clause.

X_2 = <u>whether (or not)</u> Mary has found a boyfriend

The structure is now ready to be embedded in the original statement.

<u>Whether (or not) Mary has found a boyfriend</u> is nobody's business.

EXERCISE 8.15

Directions: Using the steps, complete the following sentences with the correct embedded form of the yes/no-question in brackets.

1. [Can Jorge speak French?] X is not important for this job.

2. [Do all bears sleep in winter?] X is not precisely known.

3. [Should new medical students see patients?] X is the focus of a Harvard study.

4. [Did Hitler keep a diary?] X is the subject of a new television "docudrama."

5. [Will I go to Europe this summer?] X has still not been decided.

PROBLEM SOLVING WITH NOUN CLAUSES

We turn now to the kinds of errors that students are likely to make with noun clauses. In noun clauses, it is possible to get the following right:

    a. correct CHOICE OF NOUN CLAUSE MARKER (*that, if, whether*, or a WH-word)

    b. correct POSITION OF NOUN CLAUSE MARKER (at the beginning of the noun clause)

    c. correct AGREEMENT BETWEEN SUBJECT WH-QUESTION WORD AND AUX OR VERB (singular or plural)

    d. correct REBURYING OF AUX (if the starting point of X is a question with no overt AUX)

    e. correct SEQUENCE OF TENSES

    f. correct DELETION OF IDENTICAL OR GENERALIZED SUBJECT

    g. correct USE OF INFINITIVE FORM OF VERB (usually *to* + VERB$_{base}$)

    h. correct PUNCTUATION (period or question mark)

These aspects reflect what students are likely to do wrong in making a noun clause: a) fail to rebury the AUX, b) choose the wrong clause marker, c) put the clause marker in the wrong place, d) fail to make the subject WH-question word agree with the AUX or the main verb, e) not apply sequence of tenses, f) forget to delete an identical or generalized subject, g) fail to revert the clause verb to the correct infinitive form, or h) use the wrong punctuation.

EXERCISE 8.16

Directions: In the following sentences, a student made a single error in noun clause formation. Address the error in three stages:

a) bracket the error to focus your attention

b) list what the student got right about the bracketed error (in this case, the error is the form of the noun clause) and show this in parentheses
OPTIONAL: Derive the noun clause from its unembedded form

c) compare the original erroneous sentence to the correct sentence and explain what mistake the student made

Example: *He knows where does Mary live.

Solution: a) Bracket the error (the WH-question word, AUX, main verb, and/or punctuation):
*He knows where [does Mary live].

b) Show what is right about the noun clause:
correct choice of clause marker (*where*)
correct position of clause marker (at the beginning of the noun clause)
correct punctuation (period)

Derivation: He knows X.
X = Where does Mary live?

1. Make the WH-question into a statement by inventing an answer.	X_1 = Mary lives <u>in Geneva</u>
2. Replace the unknown element with an appropriate WH-question word.	X_2 = Mary lives <u>where</u>
3. Move the WH-question word(s) in front of the subject.	X_3 = <u>where</u> Mary lives
4. Embed the clause in the main sentence.	*He knows <u>where Mary lives</u>
5. Add the appropriate punctuation.	He knows where Mary lives.

c) Compare the erroneous sentence to the correct form and explain the mistake:
*He knows where [does Mary live].
He knows where Mary lives.

Explanation: In transforming a WH-question into a predicate embedded WH-question, a non-overt AUX must be reburied before it can be embedded.

1. *I can't remember when does the plane arrive.

2. *Does your mother know who to make bread?

3. *We're not sure it is how far to Sacramento.

4. *Please tell me who are in my office.

5. *Leandre knew how much beer his cousin drinks that night.

6. *Satoko always knows what Satoko says at a job interview.

7.   *I am going to get the job is still not sure.

8.   *The cook never forgets add a little salt.

9.   *I can never remember what day it is?

10.   *She asked me that I spoke Finnish.

OBJECTS

Up to this point, we have discussed the object as a sentence role or a slot. We will have to become more precise from now on because there are actually three different types of objects: **the direct object**, **the object of a preposition**, and **the indirect object**.

The Direct Object

The object slot is actually known as the direct object because it directly receives the action of the verb. Of course, only a transitive verb can be followed by a direct object for it is the direct object that the action of the verb is transferred to. A direct object can be either a noun phrase or a noun clause. It can usually be identified by asking *WHAT?* or *WHOM?* after a verb. For example, in the sentence *Sally loves roses*, the answer to the question *Sally loves WHAT?* is *Roses*. *Roses* is therefore the direct object.

EXERCISE 8.17

Directions: Write a direct object for the subject and verb in the following sentences:

1.   The car hit _____.

2.   A van loaded with dynamite destroyed _____.

3.   Ultraviolet rays from the sun can cause _____.

4.   Picasso created _____.

5.   Pigs eat _____.

The Object of a Preposition

While the direct object always follows a verb, the object of a preposition always follows a preposition. As is the case for all objects, the object of a preposition can be either a noun phrase or a noun clause. However, a noun clause as the object of a preposition is comparatively rare and only occurs in embedded question form. Look at the following examples:

a)   The thief escaped **with** <u>the jewels</u>.   [noun phrase]

b)   The thief escaped **with** <u>what he had grabbed from the safe</u>.   [noun clause]

c)   Mary immersed herself **in** <u>her new role</u>.   [noun phrase]

d)   Mary immersed herself **in** <u>who she had become</u>.   [noun clause]

EXERCISE 8.18

Directions: Make the information in parentheses into the object of an appropriate preposition and insert the resulting prepositional phrase in the correct place in the sentence that follows.

 Example: (the old metal bucket) The water leaked all over the floor.

 Solution: The water in the old metal bucket leaked all over the floor.

1. (the university) The daughter of the ambassador is studying engineering.

2. (the corner of the garden) The children buried the dog.

3. (a cliff at the beach) The geologists found a perfectly preserved fossil.

4. (the United States) The President has signed a new treaty.

5 (the top shelf) The cheese is in the refrigerator behind the milk.

6. (Whoever was passing by?) The dog barked.

7. (What had his son accomplished?) Joseph's father had little awareness.

8. (Where was the target located?) The missile was guided.

9. (How well could his fiancee cook?) Ralph was impressed.

10. (Why did the accused want another lawyer?) The defense counsel wasn't happy.

The Indirect Object

Indirect objects indicate the recipient or the beneficiary of an object rather than the receiver of the action (which we now know as the direct object). This is why they are said to be "indirect." Indirect objects are usually animate, i.e., people or animals, and they can only occur after a limited group of verbs. Look at the following example:

SUBJECT	VERB	DIRECT OBJECT	ADVERBIAL
1) The nurse	gave	some flowers	to the patient.

In this sentence, the direct object (*some flowers*) receives the action (*the nurse gave WHAT?*). *The patient* is the object of the preposition *to*, and the prepositional phrase *to the patient* occupies the adverbial slot of the sentence. However, since *the patient* is also the recipient of *some flowers*, the patient is also an indirect object. Indirect objects that come after the direct object and a preposition (*to* or *for*) in this way are **external indirect objects**.

Most indirect objects have a unique option: they can also be placed directly in front of the direct object, as in the following example:

SUBJECT	VERB	INDIRECT OBJECT	DIRECT OBJECT
2) The nurse	gave	the patient	some flowers.

When indirect objects are placed in this position, they become **internal indirect objects** and the preposition (*to* or *for*) is always deleted. Indirect objects cannot occur unless a direct object is present in the sentence. We could not say, "The nurse gave the patient after lunch" as a complete sentence because the response would be, "Gave what?" which is a demand to know the direct object.

INDIRECT OBJECTS WITH *To*

An indirect object (I.O.) with *to* indicates the recipient of the direct object (D.O.). Verbs like *give* allow both the external form of the indirect object (D.O. + Preposition + I.O.), as in (1) above, and the internal form (I.O. + D.O.), as in (2). Other verbs that function like *give* include the following:

bring	lend	read	tell
deny	offer	send	throw
do	owe	serve	write
grant	pass	show	
hand	pay	take	
leave	promise	teach	

EXERCISE 8.19

Directions: Make the object of the preposition in the following sentences into an indirect object.

1. Jerry threw the ball to his teammate.

2. Could you pass the salt to me?

3. The angry father denied his rightful inheritance to his son.

4. The Tax Office sent the rebate check to the wrong person.

5. The government owed a lot of money to a Caribbean bank.

6. Have we shown the slides from our last vacation to our neighbors yet?

7. The gallant suitor promised the earth to his lady love.

8. The policeman offered some coffee to the young prisoner.

9. Some reseachers have taught a sign system to dolphins.

10. Would you read a story to the children?

Verbs like *ask* do not allow the two possible forms of the indirect object. Look at the following examples:

      a) *He asked a question <u>to Mary</u>.

      b) He asked <u>Mary</u> a question.

In Sentence (a), the indirect object cannot function as the object of a preposition (the external form). It can only occur in the internal form before the direct object. Other verbs like *ask* include the following:

allow	cost	wish (desire that a
bill	fine (to pay a penalty)	person receive)
charge	refuse	

EXERCISE 8.20

Directions: Repair the following sentences:

1. The coast guard refused any assistance to the boat people.

2. The judge fined $500 to the drunk driver.

3. The investigation cost a lot of prestige to the senator.

4. June's fortune cookie wished good fortune to her.

5. Should parents allow greater freedom to their teenage offspring?

6. The carpenter billed $250 to the roofing company.

7. The school charged $5000 to the boy's parents for the damage from the pipe bomb.

8. A washing machine will cost a year's salary for a poor family.

9. The captain allowed one evening's shore leave to the crew.

10. The wicked stepmother wished harm to her husband's daughter.

Verbs like *explain* allow the indirect object to be in the external form but not in the internal form. Look at the following examples:

      a) She explained the rules <u>to the team</u>.

      b) *She explained <u>the team</u> the rules.

Other verbs like *explain* include the following:

acknowledge	introduce	say
address	mention	sentence (e.g., to prison)
admit	point out	signal
announce	propose	speak
communicate	prove	state
confess	refer	subject
declare	repeat	suggest
describe	report	treat

EXERCISE 8.21

Directions: Repair the following sentences:

1. Alice repeated the professor the question.

2. Sally introduced the family her boyfriend.

3. The doctor never said his patients "Good morning!"

4. The senator announced his supporters his candidacy for re-election.

5. The veteran treated a hot meal his old comrade.

6. Don't mention me that man's name!

7. The young nun confessed the Mother Superior her sins.

8. The discovery proved the anthropologists the existence of a high Indian culture.

9. The docent pointed out the interested museum-goers the details of the painting.

10. How soon after her husband's death is it polite to propose a widowed acquaintance marriage?

INDIRECT OBJECTS WITH *TO* AND *FOR*

An indirect object with *to* indicates who or what receives the direct object. An indirect object with *for* indicates who or what benefits from the action. Look at the following examples:

      a) I mailed the letter <u>to</u> my brother.

      b) I mailed the letter <u>for</u> my brother.

In Sentence (a), the indirect object (*my brother*) is the recipient of the direct object (*the letter*). Whether he will benefit from the letter, pass it on to someone else, or destroy the letter is not indicated or even suggested. In Sentence (b), the indirect object (*my brother*) does not even receive the letter. However, he clearly benefits from the mailing because presumably he was too busy or too ill to do it himself. A verb like *mail* can therefore take indirect objects with either *to* or *for*. Other verbs like *mail* are shown below:

bring	read
do	send
get	take
leave	teach
pay	write

EXERCISE 8.22

Directions: Choose the correct preposition (*to* or *for*) in the following sentences:

1. John's grandfather left his entire estate _____ him and his sister.

2. Mr. Porridge paid the rent _____ his poor and troubled friend.

3. Did you bring some magazines _____ her to read?

4. You should take this sweater _____ the dry cleaner.

5. When the professor was ill, a graduate student taught his seminar _____ him.

6. Alice read the speech _____ her brother, who could not be present at the ceremony.

7. Will the post office get this letter _____ the income tax office in time?

8. Could you please write down the address _____ me?

9. Ellen did the dishes _____ her sister while she was away.

10. The engineer sent the schematic diagram _____ the manufacturer.

INDIRECT OBJECTS WITH *FOR*

An indirect object with *for* indicates who or what benefits from the direct object. Verbs like *buy* allow both the external and the internal form of the indirect object.

       a) John bought a book <u>for Mary</u>.
       b) John bought <u>Mary</u> a book.

Other verbs that function like *buy* include the following:

bring	paint (a picture)
find	play (a record, a song)
get	prepare (a meal)
leave	reserve
make	save
order	spare

EXERCISE 8.23

Directions: Make the object of the preposition in the following sentences into an internal indirect object.

1. The students brought an apple for the teacher.

2. I'll leave a key in the mailbox for your mother.

3. The maid prepared a light dinner for the exhausted cook.

4. The disc jockey has never played a record on the air for his girlfriend.

5. The employment office was unable to find a job for the distraught waitress.

6. The secretary reserved a seat on the midnight flight to Chicago for his boss.

7. Please save a piece of cake for the birthday girl.

8. The fashion designer made an evening gown for the president's wife.

9. Could you get some milk for me?

10. The boys ordered milkshakes for their girlfriends while they were in the ladies' room.

Verbs like *open* allow the indirect object to be in the external form but not in the internal form. Look at the following examples:

a) He opened the door _for Mary_.

b) *He opened _Mary_ the door.

Other verbs like *open* include the following:

answer	paint (a house)	pronounce
cash	pay (a bill)	repair
change	play (the piano)	supply
close	prepare (a room)	thank
do (the dishes)	prescribe	watch (the luggage)
drive (a car)	provide	write (a letter)

EXERCISE 8.24

Directions: Repair the following sentences:

1. Could you please watch me my luggage?

2. We have prepared your mother-in-law a nice room over the garage.

3. I must thank the beautiful present you gave me you.

4. The doctor prescribed the child an antibiotic.

5. Gary refused to do his brother the yardwork.

6. The TV shop repaired the customer the faulty stereo free of charge.

7. I could not close him the garage door because my hands were full.

8. The doctor wrote down the dying patient the last will and testament.

9. Uncle Joe played the wedding party the accordion.

10. The bank will only cash people with accounts in that bank checks.

CHOOSING THE INTERNAL VS. THE EXTERNAL FORM OF THE INDIRECT OBJECT

For verbs like *give* and *buy*, which allow both the internal and external (prepositional phrase) forms of the indirect object, how do we know which form to choose? This depends on how new the information in the noun phrase is perceived to be. New information tends to come last in a sentence. Look at the following examples:

a) Give the book _to David_ (not to Nina).

b) Give David _the book_ (not the bracelet).

In Sentence (a), the focus is on **who** should receive the book. The new information (*David*, the recipient) comes later in the sentence and therefore requires the prepositional phrase form of the indirect object. In Sentence (b), the focus is on **what** each person should receive. The new information (*the book*) comes later in the sentence and therefore requires that the recipient (*David*, the indirect object) be placed in the earlier (internal) sentence position.

This discourse-based choice is, of course, only available for verbs like *give* and *buy*, which allow either form of the indirect object. It is not available for verbs like *ask*, *explain* or *open*, which only allow one or the other form of indirect object.

EXERCISE 8. 25

Directions: Rewrite the following paragraph using the correct form and position of the direct and indirect objects between the vertical lines.

Yesterday, Sarah took | Betty and Harriet get-well presents | , her good friends who had both been hurt in an

auto accident. She brought | Betty a murder mystery | and | Harriet an embroidery kit | . However, when Sarah

gave | Betty the book | , she didn't seem terribly interested. Sarah wondered to herself if she should

perhaps have given | Harriet the book | and | Betty the embroidery kit |. But Harriet was delighted with

the embroidery kit. The dilemma was resolved when Harriet suggested that they each share the

wonderful presents that Sarah had brought. Later, Betty wrote | Sarah a note | thanking her for her

thoughtfulness.

Indirect Objects with Direct Object Pronouns

The choice of the internal or the prepositional phrase form of the indirect object is also not available when the direct object in the sentence is a pronoun. Look at the following examples:

 a) John gave the book to Mary.
 b) John gave it to Mary.
 c) John gave Mary the book.
 d) *John gave Mary <u>it</u>.

 e) Sally bought a book for Susan.
 f) Sally bought it for Susan.
 g) Sally bought Susan a book.
 h) *Sally bought Susan <u>it</u>.

In Sentences (d) and (h), the presence of the direct object pronoun *it* does not allow the internal form of the indirect object under any circumstances in American English. Thus, if the direct object is a pronoun (usually *it* or *them*), the only form of indirect object allowed is the external form.

EXERCISE 8.26

Directions: Replace the direct object (underlined) with the appropriate pronoun and make the necessary changes.

       Example: John gave Mary the book.

       Solution: John gave it to Mary.

1. Grandmother will read the children a story.

2. Could you please hand Larry the scissors?

3. The agency was unable to find Mr. Lin the perfect job.

4. We sold our neighbors the car.

5. Mrs. Grant always tells her friends the latest news.

6. The priest made the visitor a sandwich.

7. That company has sold the government faulty computer chips.

8. The politician sent the reporter a threatening letter.

9. Would you order me a soda while I make a quick phone call?

10. The artist is painting his friend a portrait of his youngest daughter.

The use of indirect objects is summarized in Table 8.2.

Table 8.2. The Use of Indirect Objects

PREP	TYPE	POSITION	EXAMPLE	EXAMPLE WITH PRONOUN D.O.
to	"give"	External Internal	John gave a book to Mary. John gave Mary a book.	John gave it to Mary. *John gave Mary it.
to	"ask"	External Internal	*John asked a question to Mary. John asked Mary a question.	*John asked it to Mary. *John asked Mary it.
to	"explain"	External Internal	John explained the map to Mary. *John explained Mary the map.	John explained it to Mary. *John explained Mary it.
to	"mail"	External Internal	John mailed a letter to Mary. John mailed Mary a letter.	John mailed it to Mary. *John mailed Mary it.
for	"mail"	External Internal	John mailed a letter for Mary. *John mailed Mary a letter.	John mailed it for Mary. *John mailed Mary it.
for	"buy"	External Internal	John bought a book for Mary. John bought Mary a book.	John bought it for Mary. *John bought Mary it.
for	"open"	External Internal	John opened the door for Mary. *John opened Mary the door.	John opened it for Mary. *John opened Mary it.

Problem Solving with Indirect Objects

In the process of providing feedback on grammatical errors, we want to be able to praise a student before we begin to point out mistakes. In the problems below, it is possible to get the following right:

  a. correct POSITION OF INDIRECT OBJECT (internal or external)

  b. correct PREPOSITION (*to* or *for*)

  c. correct POSSIBLE SEQUENCE (I.O. + D.O. or D.O. + Prep + I.O.)

These elements reflect what students are likely to do wrong in using an indirect object: a) put the indirect object in the incorrect position in the sentence, b) use the incorrect preposition, or c) use a correct possible sequence of indirect object (I.O.) and direct object (D.O.) even though it may not be allowed with the verb in the present sentence.

EXERCISE 8.27

Directions: In the following sentences, a student made a single error in using an indirect object. Your job is to address the error in three stages:

  a) bracket the error to focus your attention

  b) list what the student got right about the bracketed error (in this case, the error is the form of the indirect object) and show this in parentheses

  c) compare the original erroneous sentence to the correct sentence and explain what mistake the student made

Example: *John bought a book to Mary.
          [The star (*) indicates that the sentence contains an error.]

Solution: a) Bracket the error (the indirect object and/or the preposition):
              *John bought a book [to] Mary.

            b) Show what is right about the indirect object:
              correct position of indirect object (external)
              correct possible sequence (D.O + Prep. + I.O.)

            c) Compare the erroneous sentence to the correct form and explain the mistake:
              *John bought a book [to] Mary.
              John bought a book for   Mary.

Explanation: Verbs like *buy* require *for* if the indirect object is external, not *to*.

1. *The bank cashed Jimmy the check.

2. *My brother owed ten dollars for me.

3. *The boy drove the farmer the tractor.

4. *The personnel manager refused an interview to the applicant.

5. *The drunk driver didn't report the police the accident.

6. *[The dictionary is on the table next to you.] Could you pass me it, please?

7. *The pilot has saved a seat to his girlfriend.

8. *[There is a list of rules on the box.] John will read the class them.

9. *The thief is confessing the priest her crime.

10. *A local restaurant supplied the picnic the food.

Chapter 9

THE PRONOUN SYSTEM

The pronoun system includes all the words that may be substituted for noun phrases (and occasionally noun clauses) in English. The noun phrase that is replaced by a pronoun is called the **antecedent** of that pronoun. Look at the following example:

The doctor called the hospital, but she was immediately put on hold.

In this example, the pronoun is *she* and the antecedent of *she* is the underlined noun phrase *the doctor*.

There are nine categories of pronouns in English: subject pronouns, object pronouns, possessive pronouns, reflexive pronouns, demonstrative pronouns, universal pronouns, indefinite pronouns, reciprocal pronouns, and WH-pronouns.

PRONOUNS THAT SHOW PERSON, GENDER, AND NUMBER

The first four categories of pronouns have different forms depending on the person, gender, and number of the antecedent. **Person** refers to the speaker and his or her relationship to the conversation partner. **First person** refers to the speaker (*I*). **Second person** refers to the listener (*you*). **Third person** refers to a human or humanized being (*he* or *she*) or a non-human entity (*it*) outside the conversation. Humanized beings include pets, countries, ships, cars or any other non-human entity with which a human being might claim to have a personal relationship.

Gender refers to the masculine or feminine sex of a human or humanized entity or the neutral gender of non-human entities. It only applies to third person singular pronouns.

Number refers to the singular or plural nature of the noun phrase. When the number of the pronoun matches the number indicated by the verb, the pronoun and verb are said to agree. First, second and third person each have singular and plural forms: *I/we, you/you* and *he, she, it/they*, respectively. Remember that we use the same form (*you*) for singular and plural pronouns in the second person.

Subject Pronouns

The most common type of pronoun is the subject pronoun. Subject pronouns replace the subject of a sentence or a dependent clause. The full set of subject pronouns is displayed in Table 9.1.

Table 9.1 Person, Gender, and Number in the Subject Pronoun System

PERSON	FIRST	SECOND	THIRD		
GENDER	—	—	Masculine	Feminine	Neuter
NUMBER Singular	I	you	he	she	it
Plural	we	you	they		

EXERCISE 9.1

Directions: Determine the person (1st, 2nd or 3rd), gender (masc., fem., or neut.), and number (sing. or plur.) of the underlined antecedent in the first sentence and supply a corresponding subject pronoun in the blank. If a category is not discernible, write "n/a" ("not applicable").

1. <u>Joan</u> (person:_____; gender: _____; number: _____) has lived in Hong Kong for many years. _____ works at the University in the English Department.

2. Somebody stole <u>my computer</u> (person:_____; gender: _____; number: _____) last night._____ was worth over $4000.

3. Good morning, <u>Mr. Robecon</u> (person:_____; gender: _____; number: _____). How are _____ feeling today?

4. <u>The children</u> (person:_____; gender: _____; number: _____) are sleeping at the moment. _____ should be awake in about fifteen minutes.

5. <u>I</u> (person:_____; gender: _____; number: _____) have a wide range of experience in the business world. _____ am therefore fully qualified for this position.

6. Welcome home, <u>students</u> (person:_____; gender: _____; number: _____)! I hope _____ had an enjoyable flight.

7. <u>Mediterranean fruit flies</u> (person:_____; gender: _____; number: _____) are a serious threat to fruit farmers. For this reason, _____ have been subjected to an eradication program.

8. <u>An emaciated old man with a long white beard</u> (person:_____; gender: _____; number: _____) came hobbling towards the bus. _____ looked amazingly peaceful.

9. <u>My wife and I</u> (person:_____; gender: _____; number: _____) are planning to have a baby in the next year or so. _____ are hoping for a little girl.

10. I had to take <u>my poodle Rogér</u> (person:_____; gender: _____ ; number: _____) to the veterinary clinic last week. _____ needed to have a rabies shot.

Object Pronouns

The object pronouns occur as direct objects, indirect objects, or objects of a preposition in a sentence. Look at the following examples:

DIRECT OBJECT: Per is a student from Norway. I met <u>him</u> at school.

INDIRECT OBJECT: Per is a student from Norway. We gave <u>him</u> a ride last summer.

OBJECT OF PREPOSITION: Per is a student from Norway. My sister wants to travel with <u>him</u>.

Like the subject pronouns, object pronouns also differ according to the person, gender, and number of the antecedent, as shown in Table 9.2.

Table 9.2 Person, Gender, and Number in the Object Pronoun System

PERSON	FIRST	SECOND	THIRD		
GENDER	—	—	Masculine	Feminine	Neuter
NUMBER Singular	me	you	him	her	it
Plural	us	you	them		

Notice that three of the object pronouns have the letter *m* in them: **me**, **him**, and **them**. Notice also that the second person pronouns (*you* singular and *you* plural) as well as the third person neuter pronoun (*it*) are exactly the same as the corresponding subject pronouns in Table 9.1.

EXERCISE 9.2

Directions: Determine the person (1st, 2nd, or 3rd), gender (masc., fem., or neut.), and number (sing. or plur.) of the underlined antecedent in the first sentence and supply a corresponding subject pronoun in the blank. If a category is not discernible, write "n/a" ("not applicable").

1. There were <u>some interesting people</u> (person:_____; gender: _____; number: _____) at the jazz concert last night. After the show, we had a drink with _____ at a local night spot.

2. Is this <u>Dr. Watanabe</u> (person:_____; gender: _____; number: _____)? I would like to see _____ this afternoon if you have time.

3. <u>I</u> (person:_____; gender: _____; number: _____) got a ticket for running a red light. The policeman told _____ I needed to be more careful in future.

4. After <u>Mrs. White</u> (person:_____; gender: _____; number: _____) gave me the injection, I spoke to _____ about the dangers of re-using needles.

5. When you are finished with <u>the lawn mower</u> (person:_____; gender: _____; number: ___), please put _____ back in the garage.

6. My brother and I (person:_____; gender: _____; number: _____) are planning to fly up to Lake Tahoe together next weekend. Would you like to come with _____?

7. The Titanic (person:_____; gender: _____; number: _____) hit an iceberg and sank off the coast of Greenland in 1912. The ship took 1513 passengers with _____ to a watery grave.

8. If you see Robert (person:_____; gender: _____; number: _____), could you tell _____ I'll be over later?

9. Good afternoon, ladies and gentlemen (person:_____; gender: _____; number: _____). Today, I would like to talk to _____ about alcohol abuse.

10. After you have put these plants (person:_____; gender: _____; number: _____) in the ground, be sure to give _____ plenty of water for the next few days.

Possessive Pronouns

The possessive pronouns replace a noun phrase that indicates a possessive relationship. Look at the following example:

    a) After you have read your letter, you can read mine.

    b) The boys went to their room and Susie went to hers.

In Sentence (a), mine refers to *my letter*, but since the word *letter* has been stated earlier in the sentence in the noun phrase *your letter* (the reason for the dotted underline is that *your letter* is not the true antecedent but a parallel one), there is no need to say *letter* again; the possessive pronoun is sufficient. Sentence (b) shows a similar situation with the word *room*. We must be careful not to confuse the possessive pronouns with the possessive determiners. The difference is that possessive pronouns always stand alone (e.g., *mine*), whereas possessive determiners (e.g., *my*) must always be attached to a noun (e.g., *my letter*). Like the subject and object pronouns, the possessive pronoun also differs according to the person, gender, and number of the noun phrase it replaces, as shown in Table 9.3.

Table 9.3 Person, Gender, and Number in the Possessive Pronoun System

PERSON	FIRST	SECOND	THIRD		
GENDER	—	—	Masculine	Feminine	Neuter
NUMBER Singular	mine	yours	his	hers	*its
Plural	ours	yours	theirs		

[Note: The asterisk (*) indicates that the pronoun *its* does not occur in English.]

Notice that, with the exception of *mine*, all the possessive pronouns are created from a parallel possessive determiner by adding an *s* with no apostrophe (e.g., *your* [DET] → *yours* [PRON]). Since the masculine possessive determiner *his* already ends with an *s*, an additional *s* (i.e., **hiss*) would be confusing. For this reason, the masculine possessive pronoun has the same form as the masculine possessive determiner *his*. *Its* does not occur as a possessive pronoun, however, but only as a possessive determiner, e.g., *its weight*. We must be careful not to confuse *its* with *it's*, a contracted form of *it is* and not a possessive pronoun. Many learners make mistakes with these two forms.

EXERCISE 9.3

Directions: Fill the blank with an appropriate possessive pronoun.

1. We will eat our junk food in the living room. The children can eat _____ in the kitchen.

2. My book has a picture on the front, my friend, but I can see that _____ doesn't.

3. Our neighbors' house has four bedrooms, but _____ has only three.

4. I have never lost my passport, but my uncle has lost _____ twice.

5. The older manufacturers check their safety devices once a year, but the newer manufacturers check _____ at least three times a year.

6. Students, I have an announcement. The tour guide is taking **his** luggage on the plane but _____ has already been checked.

7. Rita's house is in the country while _____ is in the city near where I work.

8. My story is silly enough, but _____ is utterly ridiculous, at least the way **you** tell it!

9. Joseph's grandfather lost all his money in building speculation while my grandfather lost _____ in gambling casinos.

10. Aunt Joan spends her holidays in Tenerife while Aunt Dorothy spends _____ at home.

Reflexive Pronouns

The function of reflexive pronouns in English is to "reflect" the same NP that occurs in another sentence position, usually, the subject. For this reason, reflexive pronouns always function as objects (direct, indirect, or object of preposition), never as subjects.[1] Look at the following examples:

      a) The policeman shot <u>him</u>.
      b) The policeman shot <u>himself</u>.

In Sentence (a), the object pronoun *him* cannot refer to the subject (*the policeman*) and is therefore interpreted to mean some other male human. In Sentence (b), however, the reflexive pronoun *himself* refers to the subject (*the policeman*) and no other person. Reflexive pronouns allow the same individual(s) to be both the subject and the object of a sentence. No other pronoun allows such an antecedent.

Reflexive pronouns consist of two elements: a determiner or a pronoun plus the word *self* or *selves*, which are written as a single word. Like the subject, object and possessive pronouns, reflexive pronouns also differ according to the person, gender, and number of the antecedent, as shown in Table 9.4.

---

[1] This is not true of the emphatic use of reflexive pronouns (e.g., I *myself* would never do such a thing), which is not discussed in this book.

Table 9.4 Person, Gender, and Number in the Reflexive Pronoun System

PERSON	FIRST	SECOND	THIRD		
GENDER	—	—	Masculine	Feminine	Neuter
NUMBER Singular	myself	yourself	himself	herself	itself
Plural	ourselves	yourselves	themselves		

Notice that first and second person reflexives are different from third person reflexives. First and second person reflexives are formed from **a possessive determiner** plus *self* whereas third person reflexives are formed from **an object pronoun** plus *self*. This inconsistency leads to errors such as *He hurt *hisself* and *They helped *theirselves*, in which the first and second person rule is applied to the third person. Notice also that *self* occurs with singular forms, *selves* with plurals.

EXERCISE 9.4

Directions: Fill the blank with a reflexive pronoun based on the underlined noun phrase.

1. The oven turns _____ off when the food is cooked.

2. The common conviction of minority rights activists is the statement, " If we don't help _____, nobody will."

3. I cut _____ with a knife when I was making the salad.

4. The young actress found _____ to be the object of intense media attention.

5. Several Buddhist monks have burned _____ as a protest against their governments' policies.

6. Even though he smiled at his colleagues, the man in his midlife crisis thought to _____, "What am I doing here? I don't even like these people."

7. "Driver, **you** are responsible. It is not enough to tell _____ that you are perfectly capable of driving after a few drinks. You put other people in danger."

8. Computer programs are now being designed that can teach _____ how to deal with unexpected events.

9. "Young people of the nation, you must educate _____ . The government will do its best to help you, but ultimately, you have to take charge of your own lives."

10. The flea-ridden dog scratched _____ to the point of bleeding.

The four types of pronouns that we have looked at so far are subject pronouns, object pronouns, possessive pronouns, and reflexive pronouns. These four types are summarized in Table 9.5. The possessive determiners are included in boldface for comparison.

Table 9.5 Person, Gender, and Number in the Pronoun System

PERSON	FIRST		SECOND		THIRD			
NUMBER	Sing.	Plural	Sing.	Plural	Singular			Plural
GENDER					Masc.	Fem.	Neut.	——
TYPE								
Subject	I	we	you	you	he	she	it	they
Object	me	us	you	you	him	her	it	them
Possessive	mine	ours	yours	yours	his	hers	*its	theirs
Possessive determiner	my	our	your	your	his	her	its	their
Reflexive	myself	ourselves	yourself	yourselves	himself	herself	itself	themselves

[Note: The asterisk signifies that the possessive pronoun *its* does not occur in English.]

EXERCISE 9.5

Directions: Fill the blanks with an appropriate form of the pronoun or possessive determiner indicated by the pronoun or pronoun category in parentheses.

1. The photograph of (he) _____ and (he) _____brothers was taken while (they) _____ were having a beer.

2. My grandmother and (I) _____ are leaving for Rome tomorrow.

3. He doesn't trust (reflexive) _____ to make the right decision.

4. Just between (you) _____ and (I) _____ , this project is a waste of time.

5. Jane was freezing, so (we)_____ lent (she) _____ (you) _____ coat. Hope (you) _____ don't mind.

6. We like to congratulate (reflexive) _____ for being compassionate human beings.

7. (I) _____ am not sure whether the fault is (she) _____ or (they) _____, but (it) _____ must be addressed.

8. Every company has (it) _____ own special interests.

9. If Steve doesn't have a bicycle, (he) _____ can take (I) _____.

10. The Smiths built (reflexive) _____ a new garage last spring.

11. The Americans are responsible for (they) _____ problems and (we) _____ are responsible for (we) _____.

12. Sally is a good friend of (I) _____.

13. Those children of (you) _____ are wonderfully behaved.

14. A snake cannot protect (reflexive) _____ if (it) _____ head is trapped.

15. If a student does not speak English as a native language, is it fair to put (he or she)_____ into a class with native English speakers right from the beginning?

PRONOUNS THAT SHOW NUMBER

The pronouns that show number include the demonstrative, the universal, the indefinite, and the reciprocal pronouns. The demonstrative pronouns have singular and plural forms while the universal and indefinite pronouns show either singular or plural number but not both. The reciprocal pronouns show only plural number.

Demonstrative Pronouns

The demonstrative pronouns are the "pointing" (or deictic) pronouns. In addition to showing the singular or plural number of the antecedent, demonstrative pronouns indicate whether the antecedent is near the speaker in place (here) and time (now) or not near to the speaker in place (there) and time (then). The demonstrative pronouns are shown in Table 9.6.

Table 9.6 The Demonstrative Pronoun System

LOCATION	HERE/NOW	THERE/THEN
NUMBER **Singular**	this	that
Plural	these	those

EXERCISE 9.6

Directions: Fill the blanks with the correct form of the demonstrative pronoun.

1. We like that painting at the back of the store. Is _____ the only landscape you have?

2. The lawyer holds up the knife that was found in the defendant's pocket. "Does _____ look familiar to you?" asks the lawyer coldly.

3. This afternoon, the women are playing in the symphony. After_____ , they plan to do a little sightseeing.

4. "What are you going to do with the chairs in the basement?" "_____ are for my nephew. He'll come and pick them up tomorrow afternoon."

5. "What beautiful jewels you are wearing! What are they?" "Well, _____ are diamonds, while _____ around the edge are emeralds."

6. Columbus discovered America in 1492. _____ was a pivotal year in the history of both Europe and the Americas.

7. "Remember how we used to go dancing every Friday night?" "Ah, yes, _____ were the days!"

8. "How are you going to divide the marbles your uncle gave you?" "Easy! _____ next to you are nothing special; they're for my brother. _____ here are neat; they're for me."

9. Once upon a time there was a princess who was going to be married. _____ was a big day for her because she would be leaving the house of her father.

10. You shouldn't put bleach in the water when you wash your tennis shoes because _____ will ruin the rubber.

Universal, Indefinite, and Reciprocal Pronouns

The majority of the universal, indefinite, and reciprocal pronouns require singular agreement. The exceptions are the universal pronoun *all*, which may be plural, and the indefinite pronouns *many* and *few*, which must be plural.

UNIVERSAL PRONOUNS

The universal pronouns apply either to an entire group or concept or to every member in a group, which is why they are called "universal". They include the pronouns *all*, *each*, and *everybody* or *everyone*.

The pronoun *all* refers to an entire group or concept. It can be singular or plural depending on the nature of the antecedent, as shown in the following examples:

a) Nobody wanted to take a part in the play, but <u>all</u> were eager to see it.
b) We were a happy village before the war, but now <u>all</u> is lost.

In Sentence (a), *all* refers to the people who were asked to take a part in the play and therefore has plural agreement. In Sentence (b), *all* refers to something like the happiness of the village before the war and therefore has singular agreement.

The pronoun *each* is always singular. It refers to every member of a restricted group, human or nonhuman, which must thus consist of at least two members, as shown in the following examples:

a) Those watermelons cost a dollar <u>each</u>.
b) After the church service, <u>each</u> was left alone to make peace with the departed.

In Sentence (a), *each* refers to every single watermelon, not to the group of watermelons. For this reason, *each* commonly appears on price tags. In Sentence (b), *each* refers to every participant in the church service and therefore has singular agreement (*was*).

The pronoun *everybody* (or *everyone*) is also always singular, as the singular form of the combining word *-body* or *-one* makes clear. The pronoun *everybody* refers to each member of an unrestricted human group and therefore implies at least three, though the number is normally much higher.

a) <u>Everybody</u> dies alone in this world.
b) <u>Everyone</u> had a great time at the party last night.

In Sentence (a), *everybody* refers to every human being in the world. In Sentence (b), *everyone* refers to every person who attended the party. The two pronouns are more or less interchangeable.

EXERCISE 9.7

Directions: Fill the blank with the appropriate universal pronoun: *all, each,* or *everybody/ everyone.*

1. These houses are _____ different. _____ has its own unique floor plan.

2. The boss wants _____ on the job at 8 A.M. sharp, so don't be late!

3. After the fire, _____ was confusion and disarray.

4. After the storm, _____ was running around trying to find food for the starving cattle.

5. The pewter figurines show magical figures: dwarves, wizards, and dragons.
    _____ has a price tag glued discreetly to the bottom.

INDEFINITE PRONOUNS

The indefinite pronouns refer to individuals without regard for their membership in a group (which distinguishes the universal pronouns) or whether they are known or identified in any way, which is why they are called "indefinite." They include 1) *some* and its relatives, and 2) *many* and its relatives.

Some and Its Relatives

Some and its relatives include *some* (and the combined forms *somebody, someone, something*), *any* (and the combined forms *anybody, anyone, anything*), and *none* (and the combined forms *nobody, no one, nothing*).

The pronoun *some* occurs in a positive grammatical environment, whereas the pronoun *any* occurs in a negative or interrogative environment. For this reason, *some* is more likely to occur in a positive statement whereas *any* is more likely to occur in a negative statement or a question.[2] Look at the following examples:

> a) Some people like coffee; <u>some</u> don't.
> b) I know my brother needs some money, but I don't have <u>any</u>.
> c) We're collecting old newspapers. Do you have <u>any</u>?

In Sentence (a), *some* occurs in the positive environment of a statement (the first use of *some* is a determiner). In Sentence (b), *any* occurs in the negative environment of a sentence with auxiliary negation. In Sentence (c), *any* occurs in the interrogative environment of a yes/no question. The use of *some* and *any* is described in terms of grammatical environment rather than grammatical structure because there are times when either pronoun may be used, as in the following example:

> a) There's a little bit of pie left. Do you want <u>any</u>?
> b) There's a little bit of pie left. Do you want <u>some</u>?

---

[2] The same positive versus negative/question distinction occurs in the use of *do* in statements versus negative statements or questions. In a statement, no form of *do* is required (e.g., Ken works in Portland), whereas in a negative statement (e.g., Julia **doesn't** work in Portland) or in a yes/no question (e.g., **Does** Ken work in Portland?), a form of *do* is required.

In Sentence (a), *any* in an interrogative environment is normal, but in Sentence (b), the use of *some* in a question does not adhere to the rules described above but in fact is perfectly acceptable, even preferable to (a). The reason is that the positive environment of *some* in (b) makes the question more polite as it invites a positive response, whereas the purely interrogative environment of *any* in (a) may consciously or unconsciously convey the speaker's desire for a negative response.

When *any* and *some* are combined with *-body, -one,* or *-thing,* the same general rules apply. However, the pronouns with *any* have an unrestricted sense, whereas the pronouns with *some* have a restricted sense, as shown in the following examples:

    a) UNRESTRICTED: She'll talk to <u>anyone</u>.
    b) RESTRICTED: She needs to talk to <u>someone</u>.

Sentence (a) suggests that the subject is an uninhibited (even unbalanced) talker, whereas Sentence (b) suggests that the help of an unspecified individual (e.g., a counselor) is required.

The pronoun *none* (and the combined forms *nobody, no one, nothing*) is the negative equivalent of *some* and *any,* as shown in the following examples:

    a) The boys have some/don't have any.
       The boys have <u>none</u>.
    b) The prisoner wants to see somebody/doesn't want to see anybody.
       The prisoner wants to see <u>nobody</u>.
    c) The cat ate something/didn't eat anything.
       The cat ate <u>nothing</u>.

EXERCISE 9.8

Directions: Fill the blanks with *some, any, none* or one of their combined forms with *-body, -one,* or *-thing.*

1. The mother seal refused to let _____ touch her offspring.

2. There's plenty of wine. Would you like _____?

3. Susan called the insurance office but _____ answered.

4. Don't get so upset! _____ can make a mistake!

5. _____ makes her husband angrier than a bicycle in the driveway.

6. _____ broke into the warehouse and stole a few tools.

7. The police examined the freshly dug grave, but they didn't find _____ .

8. There used to be three or four cafes in this neighborhood, but now there is _____ .

9. Is there _____ on TV tonight that you'd like to watch?

10. There were lots of dinosaurs in North America. Were there _____ in Africa?

Many and Its Relatives

Many and its relatives include *many/much*, *a lot/lots*, *a few/few*, and *a little/little* . The pronouns *many*, *a few*, and *few* occur only with plural count nouns. *Many* and *a few* refer to large groups and small groups, respectively, in a positive (or neutral) environment. *Few* refers to small groups in a negative environment, usually suggesting that the small number is unsatisfactory in some way. Look at the following examples:

> a) While many people are appalled at the carnage, <u>many</u> support the government.
>
> b) A few trees were already in bloom; <u>a few</u> still had no leaves at all.
>
> c) Few books remained undamaged by the fire, and <u>few</u> were salvageable.

In Sentence (a), *many* occurs in the positive environment of a statement (the initial uses of *many*, *a few*, and *few* are determiners) and is interpreted to mean *a large number* . In Sentence (b), *a few* also occurs in the positive environment of a statement and is interpreted to mean *a small number*. In Sentence (c), *few* occurs in a negative semantic environment (i.e., damage) and is interpreted to mean *not many*.

The pronouns *much*, *a little*, and *little* occur with noncount nouns. *Much* and *a little* refer to a large amount and a small amount, respectively, in a positive environment. *Little* refers to a small amount in a negative environment, usually suggesting that the small amount is unsatisfactory in some way. Look at the following examples:

> a) While much work has been completed, <u>much</u> remains to be done.
>
> b) The painter spilled a little paint on the floor and got <u>a little</u> on his nose.
>
> c) The people have little food for themselves and <u>little</u> for their families.

In Sentence (a), *much* occurs in the positive environment of a statement (the initial uses of *much*, *a little*, and *little* are determiners) and is interpreted to mean *a large amount*. In Sentence (b), *a little* also occurs in the positive environment of a statement and interpreted to mean *a small amount*. In Sentence (c), *little* occurs in a negative semantic environment (i.e., having little food) and is interpreted to mean *not much* or *not enough*.

The pronouns *much* and *many* are usually replaced with *a lot* or *lots* in positive environments, while *much* and *many* remain dominant in negative and interrogative environments (thus paralleling the use of *some* and *any*). Although *a lot* and *lots* may be used interchangeably, *lots* is much less formal. Interestingly, agreement with the verb is controlled by the antecedent of *a lot* and *lots* (shown in boldface below) and not by the pronoun *lot* or *lots*, as shown in the following examples:

> a) While a lot of **people** were appalled at the carnage, <u>a lot</u> support the government.
>
> b) While lots of **work** has been completed, <u>lots</u> remains to be done.

In Sentence (a), the main clause verb *support* has the plural ending (∅), agreeing with *people* rather than *lot*, which is otherwise singular. In Sentence (b), the main clause verb *remains* has the singular ending (*-s*), agreeing with *work* rather than *lots*, which is otherwise plural.

EXERCISE 9. 9

Directions: Draw a line through the **incorrect** choice of indefinite pronoun.

1. After the accident, the bridge was covered with oil. Did (much/many) spill into the river?

2. The economy is bad for small businesses, but the mayor is happy that (a few/few) were able to open earlier this month.

3. The doctors could do (much/little) to help the terminal cancer patient.

4. Sandra has a lot of friends, but she was sad when so (many/few) came to her graduation ceremony.

5. The water should be purified with chlorine bleach. Add (a little/little) to the container and let it sit for 15 minutes.

6. The candidate was besieged with telegrams, and (a lot/lots) came from the South.

RECIPROCAL PRONOUNS

The reciprocal pronouns show a mutual relationship between two or more (usually animate) entities. There are only two: *each other* and *one another*. They can best be explained with examples:

> a) Betty looked at Sarah. Sarah looked at Betty. The girls looked at <u>each other</u>.
> b) Each elephant looked at all the other elephants. The elephants looked at <u>one another</u>.

Sentence (a) suggests that *each other* describes two reciprocal individual actions while Sentence (b) suggests that *one another* refers to three or more reciprocal individual actions. However, the substitution of either reciprocal pronoun is acceptable to most native speakers.

PRONOUNS THAT SHOW NEITHER PERSON, GENDER, NOR NUMBER

The only pronouns that show neither person, number, nor gender are the WH-pronouns.

WH-Pronouns

The WH-pronouns include the interrogative pronouns and the relative pronouns. *Interrogative pronoun* is another name for a WH-question word. *Relative pronoun* is another name for an adjective clause marker.

INTERROGATIVE PRONOUNS

The interrogative pronouns include the words *what, when, where, who, whom, whose, why,* and *how*. Since these words were described in Chapter 7, no further explanation will be provided. Do you remember in that chapter how we substituted a WH-question word for the unknown element in a sentence in order to create a WH-question? That procedure used a pronoun in place of its earlier antecedent, which explains why the broad WH-question words (i.e., the WH-words by themselves) are pronouns whereas the narrow WH-question words are WH-determiners with attached nouns. In Chapter 8, we used interrogative pronouns as noun clause markers in creating embedded WH-questions.

RELATIVE PRONOUNS

The relative pronouns include the words *which, who, whom, whose,* and *that.* In Chapter 11, we will see how a relative pronoun replaces a repeated noun phrase in an earlier sentence and becomes the clause marker for an adjective clause. Replacement usually involves pronouns of one kind or another, which explains why adjective clause markers are also pronouns.

EXERCISE 9.10

Directions: Fill the blanks with an appropriate form of WH-pronoun.

1. Swahili and Urdu are both fascinating languages. I don't know _____ I should learn first.

2. *Hamlet* is a play _____ is known around the world.

3. There are two glasses here. _____ is this? It's Fredericka's!

4. _____ could the alchemists make lead into gold?

5. With _____ do you wish to speak?

6. The woman _____ works in the office next to mine is the boss's wife.

7. Do you have any idea _____ the plane will arrive?

8. The people cannot understand _____ the government failed to act.

9. _____ was supposed to take out the garbage?

10. I can't hear _____ the guide is saying.

REVIEW EXERCISES

Table 9.7 summarizes the pronoun system presented in this chapter.

Table 9.7 Summary of the English Pronoun System

CONTROLLING FACTORS	PRONOUN CATEGORY	PRONOUN FORMS
Person, Gender, and Number	Subject Pronouns	I, we, you, he, she, it, they
	Object Pronouns	me, us, you, him, her, it, them
	Possessive Pronouns	mine, ours, yours, his, hers, theirs
	Reflexive Pronouns	myself, ourselves, yourself, yourselves, himself, herself, itself, themselves
Number only	Demonstrative Pronouns	this, these, that, those
	Universal Pronouns	all, each, everybody (everyone)
	Indefinite Pronouns	some, somebody, something, any, anybody, anything, none, nobody, nothing, much, many, a lot, lots, a few, few, a little, little
	Reciprocal Pronouns	each other, one another
(None)	WH-Pronouns	what, where, when, which, who, whom, whose, why, how, that

EXERCISE 9.11

Directions: Fill the blank with the appropriate pronoun form or pronoun category indicated in parentheses.

1. (demonstrative) _____ boxers over there really dislike (reciprocal) _____, don't (they) _____?

2. (indefinite) _____ is cosier than a warm fire on a stormy night.

3. Don't worry! (indefinite) _____ will harm (we) _____.

4. A thing like (demonstrative) _____ can happen to (indefinite) _____.

5. (indefinite) _____ should ever lose sight of (he or she) _____ cultural roots.

6. These apples cost fifty cents (universal) _____. Should (we) _____ buy (universal) _____ of (they) _____?

7. Hello? Is (indefinite) _____ there? (WH)_____ 's there?!

EXERCISE 9.12

Directions: Name the category of the underlined pronoun using the following list:

subject	possessive	demonstrative	universal	interrogative
object	reflexive	indefinite	reciprocal	relative

Example: He is a saint.

Solution: He is a saint.   ___subject___

1. Everybody felt the earthquake.   _____

2. Tell her she's late.   _____

3. I don't know what I want.   _____

4. He blames himself for the accident.   _____

5. Shelly ate some bread but Bill didn't have any.   _____

6. The story that you heard is completely false.   _____

7. They love to swim at night.   _____

8. You went to school looking like that?   _____

9. Those guys hate one another.   _____

10. I don't take from your plate, so please don't take from mine.   _____

EXERCISE 9.13

Directions: Add an appropriate pronoun or determiner to the following passage.

The Ex-President's Daughter[3]

Interviewer: Since _____ father is no longer President, _____ would _____ say in retrospect is the most difficult part of being the President's daughter?

Davis: _____ was seeing _____ father make policies with _____ _____ disagreed so strongly and yet could do _____ about. Like Nicaragua. _____ would make statements about the war there _____ _____ knew were simply not true, and yet _____ could persuade the American people to accept _____ . For example, to place a trade embargo on a particular country, the President has to state that such a country poses a clear and present danger to the United States. Well, Nicaragua is a country of 3.5 million people, a large percentage of _____ are children. To say that such people pose a danger to the United States is stretching the truth just a bit.

Interviewer: _____ know that _____ disagreed with _____ father on the Vietnam war, that _____ were very much against _____ and _____ was not. _____'ve also supported the Equal

---

[3] Adapted from Lloyd Shearer, "The Ex-President's Daughter," *Parade*, 12 November, 1989, 22-23. Used with permission.

Rights Amendment, gun control and _____ of other issues _____ opposes. But at _____ point did _____ decide _____ could no longer discuss politics with _____?

Davis:_____ memory for dates is awful, but _____ think _____ was in 1982. _____ took Helen Caldicott [the Australian physician _____ then led the antinuclear coalition Physicians for Social Responsibility] to the White House, and the three of _____ met for over an hour. And after _____ meeting, _____ decided that _____'d never again discuss politics with _____ father because _____ was just too futile and too painful. _____ mean, _____ were so far apart. There were no grounds even for discussion. _____ felt like _____'d been beating _____ head against the same wall for years, and _____ couldn't do _____ anymore.

Patti Davis is recognized as a professional author, currently busy plotting _____ third novel. Among _____ contemporaries, _____ is respected as a writer-activist of integrity, unafraid to disagree publicly with _____ conservative parents on the important problems of the day.

PROBLEM SOLVING WITH THE PRONOUN SYSTEM

In the process of providing feedback on grammatical errors, we want to be able to praise a student before we begin to point out mistakes. In the problems below, it is possible to get the following right:

- a. correct PRONOUN CATEGORY (subject, object, possessive, reflexive, etc.)
- b. correct PERSON (first, second, or third)
- c. correct NUMBER (singular or plural)
- d. correct GENDER (masculine, feminine, neuter)
- e. correct WH-PRONOUN (human, non-human, place, time, reason, manner)
- f. correct recognition of GRAMMATICAL ENVIRONMENT (positive, negative or interrogative; nearby or not nearby)
- g. correct POSSIBLE FORM (the pronoun that has been used exists in English but is not correct in this sentence)

These elements reflect what students are likely to do wrong in using a pronoun: a) use the incorrect pronoun category, b) use the incorrect person, c) use the incorrect number, d) use the incorrect gender, e) use the incorrect WH-pronoun, f) fail to recognize the grammatical environment controlling the pronoun, or g) use an existing English pronoun but in the wrong grammatical context.

EXERCISE 9.14

Directions: In the following sentences, a student made a single error in using a pronoun. Your job is to address the error in three stages:

- a) bracket the error to focus your attention
- b) list what the student got right about the bracketed error (in this case, the error is the form of the pronoun) and show this in parentheses
- c) compare the original erroneous sentence to the correct sentence and explain what mistake the student made

Example: *[Magda is Joachim's girlfriend.] Joachim met she at a party.
[The bracketed information provides background information for the next sentence. The star (*) indicates that the sentence contains an error.]

Solution: a) Bracket the error (the pronoun):
  *Joachim met [she] at a party.
  b) Show what is right about the pronoun:
  correct person (third)   correct number (singular)
  correct gender (feminine)
  correct possible form (*she*)
  c) Compare the erroneous sentence to the correct form and explain the mistake:
  *Joachim met [she] at a party.
  Joachim met her   at a party.

Explanation: A pronoun in the object slot must be an object pronoun, not a subject pronoun.

1. *[Sandra bought a new car.] She wants to keep him in the garage.

2. *All animals need to protect theirselves from the cold.

3. *The prince and the servant girl truly loved each another.

4. *Jennifer wants to sit between you and I during the horror film.

5. *[Where did the flowers come from?] That? They are for Hilda's birthday.

6. *We made the last payment on our house today, so the house is really theirs now.

7. *[The actress accepted the Oscar.] He thanked the Academy with a few well-chosen words.

8. *The police rang the doorbell but anybody was home.

9. *The house is full of guests, but all is leaving tomorrow.

10. *The doctor which operated on my father is quite famous.

11. *[The United Nations consists of 159 members]. Each desire peace in the world.

12. *[Mrs. Swambo lives in Berlin now]. What did she live before she moved to Berlin?

13. *[At a dinner party] Would you like any bread with your mock turtle soup?

14. *Those silver bracelets did not cost more than $100 any.

15. *[How do you do, sir?] I am very happy to meet me.

Chapter 10

THE DETERMINER SYSTEM

The determiner system includes the words and phrases that come at the beginning of a noun phrase. A noun phrase must contain at the very minimum one determiner and one noun. Since every noun phrase has at least one determiner, the determiners constitute some of the most frequently used words in the language.

What a determiner determines is the grammatical reality of the noun to which it is attached. For example, the noun *book* by itself represents the abstract notion of pages that are printed and bound in a certain manner. However, it has no concrete reality in this form. This is where the determiners come in. They allow us to specify a real book, e.g., *that book, his book, a book, any book, the book, each book, neither book, all books, some books, no books, a hundred books,* etc. Traditionally, the determiners were called adjectives, but it is clear from this list that determiners describe not the characteristics of the book but rather the quantity or size of the set of books that is intended. Thus, determiners quantify the noun in a noun phrase whereas adjectives qualify it.

There are three categories of determiners: predeterminers, central determiners, and postdeterminers. In the few cases where all three categories occur in one noun phrase, they occur in this order (e.g., <u>*all the other*</u> *candidates*). However, since the central determiners comprise the largest and most important category, the discussion will begin with the central determiners.

THE CENTRAL DETERMINERS

The most important characteristic of the central determiners is that they are mutually exclusive, meaning that only one can be present at a time. For example, we can say *the book* or *my book* but not **the my book*; we can say *no method* or *any method*, but not **no any method*. The central determiners can be classified into eight categories, but in terms of frequency, the first category, the articles, is by far the most important. The eight categories are listed below:

1) articles (*a, the,* Ø)
2) possessive (e.g., *my, John's*)
3) demonstrative (*this, that, these,* and *those*)
4) assertive/nonassertive (*some* and *any*)
5) negative (*no*)
6) universal (*each* and *every*)
7) dual (*either* and *neither*)
8) WH-determiners (*what, which,* and *whose*)

You will perhaps recognize some of the words that we called pronouns in the last chapter (e.g., *this, some, each, which*). The important distinction between pronouns and determiners is that pronouns can stand alone in a sentence because they represent full noun phrases whereas determiners must be attached to a noun because they constitute only part of a noun phrase.

EXERCISE 10.1

Directions: Indicate whether the underlined word is a pronoun (PRO) or a determiner (DET).

1. Get <u>that</u> cat off <u>the</u> table!
   1   2   _____ _____

2. Will <u>they</u> print <u>this</u>?
   1   2   _____ _____

3. <u>These</u> apples cost a dollar <u>each</u>.
   1   2   _____ _____

4. <u>Every</u> house should have <u>one</u>.
   1   2   _____ _____

5. <u>Some</u> people don't have <u>any</u>.
   1   2   _____ _____

6. She can't tell <u>which</u> boy is <u>which</u>.
   1   2   _____ _____

7. There are <u>no</u> fleas on <u>theirs</u>.
   1   2   _____ _____

8. I want <u>all</u> power or <u>none</u>.
   1   2   _____ _____

9. <u>Neither</u> person is <u>my</u> candidate.
   1   2   _____ _____

10. <u>What</u> are <u>you</u> talking about?
    1   2   _____ _____

The article system is first discussed in detail by itself. Then we will consider the other central determiners as a group.

The Article System

The article system contains the words *a(n)* and *the* and the zero article (or zero determiner), represented by the symbol Ø. *A(n)* and *Ø* are a natural pair in opposition to *the*. *A* is used before a consonant **sound**, as in *a horse, a university,* or *a one-hour program. A* takes the form *an* before a vowel **sound**, as in *an apple, an umbrella,* or *an hour. A(n)* can only occur with singular count nouns, meaning those nouns that can be counted and made plural, such as *house, star, idea,* and *mistake. Ø* generally occurs with plural count nouns such as *books, rocks,* and *slogans* or noncount nouns, meaning those nouns that cannot usually be counted or made plural, such as *oil, air, love,* and *food. The* can be used with singular, plural, count, and noncount nouns. These uses are summarized in Table 10.1.

Table 10.1 Uses of The Article System

ARTICLE	NUMBER	COUNTABILITY	EXAMPLES
a	singular	count	a dog, an honor, a unicorn, an idea, a man
Ø	plural	count	Ø magazines, Ø whales, Ø stories, Ø sheep
	singular	noncount	Ø coffee, Ø gold, Ø wisdom, Ø life, Ø power
the	singular	count	the pen, the planet the thought, the number
	plural	count	the cats, the trees, the rubies, the women
	singular	noncount	the air, the wine, the cement, the furniture

[Note: Since *an* is simply a phonetic variant of *a*, *a* is used to refer to both *a* and *an*.]

The difference between the use of *a/Ø* and *the* is that *a* and *Ø* classify nouns whereas *the* identifies them.

CLASSIFICATION VERSUS IDENTIFICATION

The articles have two primary functions: 1) to classify a noun, that is, to indicate whether the noun is a member of a group or class of like others, or 2) to identify a noun, that is, to show that the noun has been singled out in some way. The articles *a* and *Ø* classify, the choice determined by the features described in Table 10.1, whereas the article *the* identifies. Asking the question *What is this?* usually prompts a classifying response: e.g., *It's a book, It's [Ø] salt.* Asking the question *Which X is this?* usually prompts an identifying response: e.g., *It's the red one, It's the one I bought yesterday.*

One way to visualize the difference between classification and identification is to imagine that you are at the airport watching the passengers come out of a plane. If you are not expecting anyone in particular, you simply see Ø passengers, Ø flight attendants, perhaps **a** woman with **a** baby (notice the articles used: Ø and *a*). However, if you are expecting a particular person to arrive, you ignore the other passengers as you try to identify **the** person you are waiting for, perhaps **the** special person in your life (notice the article used: *the*). Another way to see the difference is to compare the effect of the identifying and classifying articles on the meaning of a sentence:

Christina has a twelve-year-old son and an eleven-year-old daughter.

    a) Every morning, she drives <u>the children</u> to school.

    b) Every morning, she drives <u>Ø children</u> to school.

In Sentence (a), we understand *the children* to mean Christina's own children and thus interpret Christina to be the children's mother or guardian. In Sentence (b), we understand *Ø children* to mean an unspecified group and thus interpret Christina to be, perhaps, a school bus driver.

EXERCISE 10.2

Directions: Indicate whether the underlined noun phrases in the following passage are classified (class) or identified (iden) by circling **class** or **iden** below each one.

Inertia[1]

               1   2   3

There was once <u>a little boy</u> who had <u>a red wagon</u>. He liked to carry <u>a ball</u> around in
         class iden   class iden   class iden

   4   5

<u>the wagon</u>. As he trotted about with it, he noticed <u>an interesting thing</u>. Whenever he started
class iden   class iden

     6   7   8   9

up, <u>the ball</u> in <u>the wagon</u> rolled to <u>the back</u>. Whenever he stopped, <u>the ball</u> rolled to
  class iden   class iden   class iden   class iden

  10   11   12   13   14

<u>the front</u> of <u>the wagon</u>. <u>The boy</u> went to his father. "What makes <u>the ball</u> roll to <u>the back</u>
class iden   class iden class iden   class iden   class iden

            15   16   17

when I start up and to <u>the front</u> when I stop?" he asked. "<u>People</u> call it <u>inertia</u>," said his
                class iden   class iden   class iden

      18   19

father. "<u>The rule</u> is that anything at rest tends to remain at rest, and <u>a thing</u> in motion tends
   class iden   class iden

              20   21

to keep on moving in <u>the same direction</u> at <u>the same speed</u>. If you look closely, you will
                class iden   class iden

           22   23   24

see that when you start <u>the wagon</u>, <u>the ball</u> doesn't really roll backward. <u>The back</u> of
               class iden class iden   class iden

  25   26   27   28

<u>the wagon</u> just catches up with <u>the ball</u>. When you stop <u>the wagon</u>, <u>the ball</u> keeps on
 class iden   class iden   class idenclass iden

           29   30   31   32   33

moving. It catches up to <u>the front</u> of <u>the wagon</u>. That is <u>the result</u> of <u>the inertia</u> in <u>the ball</u>."
                class iden class iden   class iden class iden   class iden

Classified Noun Phrases

    Classification, the use of Ø and *a*, is expressed in several ways. These include first mention, general characteristics with *have* and *be*, generic nouns, and after existential *there*.

---

[1] From, *The World of Science* by Jane Werner Watson. © 1958 Western Publishing Company, Inc. Used by permission.

FIRST MENTION

One of the easiest types of classification to understand is first mention. The first time we introduce a new noun into a story, we usually mark it with *a* or *Ø*. Look at the following example:

> a) Once upon a time, a king lived in a stone castle. b) The king was
> lonely in the castle because he didn't have a wife or children.

In Sentence (a), the king and the castle are mentioned for the first time (first mention) and, without further information, we interpret the king to be simply someone classified as a king and the castle to be something classified as a castle. In Sentence (b), the second sentence in the story, the king and the castle are now identified with *the* (we know now that not just any king and castle is meant but the king and the castle in this particular story). However, since the wife and the children are mentioned for the first time, they are still classified. In many cases, the classified noun can be interpreted to mean "any" or "no particular" since classification indicates membership in a group or class of like others.

If we ask the questions *what* and *which* as described earlier, we see that in Sentence (a), we could ask "What is this?" (Response: "It's a king; it's a castle."), but not "Which king is this?" or "Which castle is this?" (Response: "How should I know?"). In Sentence (b), however, we could ask "Which king is this? (Response: "It's the king who lives in the castle.") or "Which castle is this?" (Response: "It's the castle which the king lives in.") but not "Which wife?" or "Which children?" (Response: "How should I know?"). Thus, we see that the answer to the question *what* often indicates first mention, while the answer to the question *which* often indicates subsequent mention.

EXERCISE 10.3

Directions: Fill the blanks with *a(n)*, *Ø*, or *the*.

Once upon a time, __1__ entrepreneurial mouse owned __2__ cheese shop in __3__ small western prairie town. __4__ mouse had risen to prominence due to his success, so he was ready to take on __5__ political position. Since __6__ town was fundamentally democratic, there had to be __7__ election, but each candidate had to supply his or her own ballots. In order to improve his chances, __8__ mouse had ballots printed on thin slices of cheese from __9__ cheese shop. On the day of __10__ election, __11__ mouse was quite confident of winning the post of Rodentia Prima. But when the ballot box was opened, not a single cheese ballot had been deposited. As a result, __12__ election went to __13__ hitherto unknown prairie dog, who had had his ballots printed on __14__ dried oleander leaves.

GENERAL CHARACTERISTICS WITH *HAVE* AND *BE*

When describing a class or group, it is natural that we describe general characteristics. These are often presented with the main verbs *have* and *be*. Look at the following examples:

> a) Marsupials have <u>a pouch/Ø pouches</u> for their young.
> b) Venus is <u>a planet</u> that is covered with <u>Ø clouds</u> of <u>Ø carbon dioxide</u>.

In Sentence (a), the class of marsupials can be described as having a pouch for their young as a general characteristic. Thus, we use classifying *a* or *Ø* with *pouch/pouches* since we are not referring to a unique, known, or identified pouch, which would be something like *Look at the pouch on that kangaroo!* In Sentence (b), Venus is classified as a planet, which thus requires classifying *a* since it presumes that there are other planets. It is then further classifed as having Ø clouds of Ø carbon dioxide, which require classifying Ø.

Sentence (b) is an example of the classic Aristotelian definition formula "An A is a B that C" in which the term to be defined (A) is placed in a larger classification (B) but is distinguished from others in that class by certain characteristics (C). If we identify *the planet* in (B), we shift from a definition to a description. (Imagine that you have been teaching students about the planets Mars and Venus. Having limited the set of planets to these two, you could now say, "Venus is the planet that is covered with clouds of carbon dioxide" or ask, "Which is the planet that is covered with clouds of carbon dioxide?" These sentences describe rather than define Venus.)

EXERCISE 10.4

Directions: Fill the blanks in these "general characteristic" sentences with *a(n)* or Ø.

1. Do _____ leopards have _____ stripes or _____ spots?

2. Dolores's car had _____ green hood with _____ purple fenders.

3. _____ thermometer is _____ instrument that measures _____ temperature.

4. _____ dinosaurs were not _____ lizards but rather _____ gigantic bird-like creatures.

5   _____ isotope is _____ unstable variant of _____ chemical element.

GENERIC NOUNS

The term *generic* applies to most classified terms, many of which have been used in the preceding exercise. In truth, generic nouns can take all three forms of the article: *a*, Ø and *the*. However, the three forms can only be used interchangeably in formal or abridged definitions. Other types of noun phrases (i.e., agents of change, generalized instances) restrict the use of generic articles, as shown in the following examples:

DEFINITIONS: a) A musk ox [is an animal that] survives well on the tundra.
                b) Ø Musk oxen [are animals that] survive well on the tundra.
                c) The musk ox [is an animal that] survives well on the tundra.

NONDEFINITIONS:

Agent of Change a) *A computer is changing the business world.
                b) Ø Computers are changing the business world.
                c) The computer is changing the business world.

Generalized   d) Every family should own a car.
Instance   e) All families should own Ø cars.
                f) *Every family should own the car.

Agents of change may not occur with generic *a*, while generalized instances may not occur with generic *the*. Only generic Ø can be used in all circumstances. Generic *the*, which is discussed under "Identification," identifies a class and thus cannot occur with a generalized instance.

If a noun is not generic, then it is said to be specific. Look at the following examples:

a) GENERIC: <u>A teacher</u> can have a strong influence on a young student.

b) SPECIFIC: <u>The teacher</u> motivated her students to do well on the exam.

The subject of Sentence (a) is generic because it speaks about the effect that any teacher can have on a student. The subject of Sentence (b) is specific because it speaks about the effect of a particular teacher on a particular group of students. Generic statements are often made with *have* and *be*, but they also occur with other verbs, as in *Ø Elephants <u>live</u> in Ø wooded areas*. Generic nouns, with the exception of generic *the*, take the classifying articles *a* and *Ø*. Specific nouns take identifying *the*.[2]

EXERCISE 10.5

Directions: Write (G) generic or (S) specific above the incomplete noun phrases underlined. Then insert the appropriate article in the blank before the noun.

1. _____ <u>lawnmower</u> is _____ <u>device</u> for cutting _____ <u>grass</u>.

2. Did_____ <u>surgeon</u> remove _____ <u>appendix</u> from _____ <u>patient</u>?

3. _____ <u>recipe</u> calls for _____ <u>wine</u> but you can use _____ <u>mixture</u> of _____ <u>vinegar</u> and _____ <u>apple juice</u> instead.

4. _____ <u>car that gets forty miles per gallon</u> would be fine for _____ <u>needs of your family</u>.

5. We hiked in _____ <u>mountains</u> last weekend. We learned that, when camping at _____ <u>high elevations</u>, _____ <u>hikers</u> should be sure to carry _____ <u>food and water</u>, _____ <u>warm clothing</u>, _____ <u>suitable tent</u>, and _____ <u>reliable stove</u>, not to mention _____ <u>compass</u>.

AFTER EXISTENTIAL *THERE*

Another situation in which we usually use classifying rather than identifying articles is after existential *there*.[3] Existential *there* is commonly used to introduce a new topic of discussion. It is never stressed and always occurs at the beginning of a clause. In contrast, locative *there* typically occurs in a brief response to a *where*-question (e.g., *Where is it?*). It is always stressed and can occur in several positions in a sentence. These are compared in the following examples:

a) <u>There</u> is a book on the counter.   [existential there]

b) The book is <u>there</u> on the counter.   [locative there]

In Sentence (a), *there* is unstressed and followed by *be* and a noun phrase with classifying *a* (*a book*). It shows the existence of a book on the counter, which is why we call it "existential" *there* and suggests that a discussion will now ensue about that book. In Sentence (b), *there* is stressed. It shows the location of the book, which is why we call it "locative" *there*. There are

---

[2] Linguists make a distinction between generic indefinite *a* and specific indefinite *a*, as in the following examples:

    a) <u>A</u> book makes a great gift.   [generic indefinite]
    b) Joseph bought <u>a</u> book for his girlfriend. [specific indefinite]

This distinction is too subtle for all but the most advanced students and is really not pedagogically relevant since the same article is used in each case. *Classification* covers both situations.

[3] An exception occurs when the nouns following *be* are identified for the speaker but not for the listener:
    What needs to be done?
    Well, there's <u>the car</u> to wash, <u>the lawn</u> to mow, <u>the dog</u> to feed, and <u>the garbage</u> to be emptied.

no limitations as to the verbs or articles that locative *there* occurs with or the positions it can take (e.g., *There's the book* or *A book is on the counter <u>there</u>*). With locative *there*, no further discussion is required or expected.

EXERCISE 10.6

Directions: Indicate whether "existential" *there* or "locative" *there* is being used in the following sentences.

1. There has never been a deeper crisis in the world. _____

2. There he is! Throw him a rope! _____

3. Whenever there's an earthquake, the horses go crazy. _____

4. The Waltons go to Sardinia every year. They love it there. _____

5. Gertrude Stein is famous for having said about Oakland, California: "There's no **there** there." _____

Identified Noun Phrases

Identification, the use of *the*, is also expressed in several ways. These include subsequent mention, ranking adjectives, shared knowledge, and generic *the*.

SUBSEQUENT MENTION

Subsequent mention refers to the second, third or subsequent time that the same noun is referred to in a text. First mention requires a classifying article (*a* or Ø), whereas subsequent mention requires the identifying article (*the*) because the noun has become identified through prior mention. In Exercise 10.3, the same subsequent mention nouns occurred earlier in the story. However, the noun does not have to be the same as long as it refers to the same referent. Look at the following examples:

1   2

a) First, mix <u>butter, sugar, and an egg</u> and then add flour to <u>the mixture</u>.

1   2

b) Uncle Jim bought <u>a Mercedes</u>, but <u>the car</u> had an oil leak.

In Sentence (a), the first mention of *butter, sugar, and an egg* creates a mixture. Subsequent mention uses *the mixture* to avoid repeating the original words, but it clearly refers to the same thing. Likewise, in Sentence (b), *the car* refers to *a Mercedes* and not to some other car.

EXERCISE 10.7

Directions: Draw a single line under every case of first mention, a double line under every case of subsequent mention, and an arrow connecting the same referents.

1. When mud is placed into a glass of water, the sediment sinks to the bottom of the liquid.

2. Huge undersea ranges divide the ocean floor. The mountains are sometimes high enough to break the surface and become islands.

3. Adequate water is crucial to local growers of vegetables. The farmers depend on the moisture to nourish the plants that are their only source of income.

4. Last summer, we visited a spectacular cave in a limestone quarry. Water had dissolved the rock to create the underground cavern.

5. The entomologists watched two praying mantisses mate just before dawn. The early morning light prevented the females from devouring the males for breakfast because they couldn't see them.

RANKING ADJECTIVES

Ranking adjectives are adjectives that identify nouns by relating them to others in a fixed pattern. Since they are identified, they always require *the*. There are three types of ranking adjectives: superlative, sequence, and unique adjectives.

SUPERLATIVE ADJECTIVES

Superlative adjectives show the most extreme member of a group, identifying the noun through its unique position at the top (or bottom) of a hierarchy. Superlative adjectives thus rank on a **vertical** scale, as shown in the following examples:

a) Greenland is the largest island in the world.
b) Paris is the most beautiful city in Europe.
c) The lowest prime number is 1.

SEQUENCE ADJECTIVES

Sequence adjectives show an object's place in a sequence, identifying the noun through its position relative to those that come before or after it. Sequence adjectives rank on a **horizontal** scale, as shown in the following examples:

a) The Suez Canal was the first modern man-made shipping lane.
b) Aluminum is number 13 on the periodic table. The next[4] element is silicon.
c) The final stage of a small star is called a white dwarf.

Other sequence adjectives include *the second, the third, the following, the penultimate, the last*, etc.

UNIQUE ADJECTIVES

Unique adjectives do not rank on a scale. Rather, they identify nouns of which there is only one example, as shown in the following examples:

a) The people of Serbia speak the same language as the people of Croatia.
b) The only[5] survivor of the Seven Wonders of the World is the Egyptian pyramids.
c) The Earth is the one planet in the Solar System that sustains life.

---

[4] An exception occurs when referring to points in time from the present moment. In this case we use *next* or *last* with the zero article, e.g.:

Cindy hiked in Mexico last year and she plans to climb Mt. Whitney next week.

[5] The adjective *only* in *an only child* means a child with no siblings. Both meanings of only may occur in the same sentence:

Bobby is the only only child in the class.

Other unique adjectives include *main* (e.g., *the main* event), *principal* (e.g., *the principal investigator*), *chief* (e.g., *the chief* problem), *whole* (e.g., *the whole* town), *entire* (e.g., *the entire planet*), *complete* (*the complete* works), and *original* (e.g., *the original* cast).

Several of the words in this list can take *a* rather than *the*, e.g., *a principal export, a whole loaf of bread, an entire carton, a complete idiot, an original composition*. The reason for this is that some unique adjectives can have alternative meanings. For example, *a principal export* can suggest "one of many important exports" rather than "the most important export"; *a whole loaf* and *an entire carton* can represent "all of one example" rather than "the entire example"; *a complete idiot* means "a thorough idiot" not "the entire idiot"; and *an original composition* means "a new composition" rather than "the first composition."

EXERCISE 10.8

Directions: Underline the article plus the ranking adjectives in the following passage and label them "SUP" (superlative), "SEQ" (sequence), or "UN" (unique).

Mount St. Helens began to issue steam and ash on March 27, 1980 in preparation for the largest eruption in Washington in 123 years. The last time the same mountain had erupted was in 1827. The first indication that something was going to happen was a series of earthquakes that lasted almost a week. Then, on May 18 at 8:32 A.M., 1,300 feet of the previously 9,677-foot tall mountain, the entire north side, was blasted into the air leaving a huge, bowl-shaped depression. In the next few minutes, a cloud of ash and steam rose 11 to 15 miles, spreading fine ash up to 500 miles away. One hundred and fifty square miles of forest were laid flat. The principal dangers on the mountain were forest fires and flash floods, and over 400 loggers, forest rangers, and others were evacuated. The only reason that there were not catastrophic floods is that Spirit Lake, at the base of the mountain, became plugged at the outlet by a slide of dirt and volcanic rock. Government officials set the lowest damage estimate at 1.5 billion dollars.

SHARED KNOWLEDGE

Shared knowledge describes nouns that are automatically identified because we know from previous experience exactly which noun is meant. There are three levels of shared knowledge: universal, regional/local, and immediate.

UNIVERSAL SHARED KNOWLEDGE

Universal shared knowledge describes those aspects of the universe that every person on the planet can automatically identify, including *the universe, the sun, the moon, the earth, the sky*, and *the ground*. We would be very surprised if someone were to say, "Which sun?" or "Which moon?" for it would suggest that person was from another planet.

REGIONAL/LOCAL SHARED KNOWLEDGE

Regional/local shared knowledge describes the geographical aspects that every person in a certain region or location can identify. For example, *I'm going to the city* means something quite different for residents of northern California than it does for residents of southern England. Other words describing regional geography are *the river, the beach, the mountains, the capital*, and *the desert*, while words describing local features might include *the lake, the park*, *the post office, the store, the university,* and *the airport.* In all cases, we would expect only local residents to share knowledge of what these features refer to and so would not be surprised to hear a stranger ask, "Which river?" or "Which park?"

IMMEDIATE SHARED KNOWLEDGE

Immediate shared knowledge describes the features that every person in a room would be able to identify, including *the ceiling, the floor, the door, the window, the light switch, the blackboard, the telephone,* and *the refrigerator.* In a car, the same would apply to *the heater, the headlights, the radio, the radiator, the water pump,* and *the muffler.* Having purchased a new camera, for example, we would not be surprised to see, in the instruction manual, reference to *the lens, the shutter,* and *the flash.* All of these items are identified because they are known or presumed to be in the immediate environment of the listener or reader. Hence, they all take *the.*

EXERCISE 10. 9

Directions: The following directions were written down during a telephone conversation. Orally reconstruct the directions using complete sentences as the speaker on the telephone originally gave them.

1. Take Franklin Freeway to bridge
2. Cross bridge
3. Left at Court House
4. Right at university
5. Left at gas station
6. Drive around park
7. Right at library
8. Stop at second green house
9. Open door (it's unlocked)
10. Turn on light
11. Go through living room
12. Take stairs down to back garden
13. Simon working in garage

GENERIC *THE*

Generic nouns normally occur with the classifying articles *a* and Ø. The only exception is when we want to identify a class rather than a specific individual or group. Then we use generic *the.* Generic *the* only occurs with a singular countable noun that names the class, which is most commonly an invention (e.g., *the clock, the computer, the particle accelerator*), a plant (*the maple tree, the prickly pear cactus, the royal palm*), or an animal, body part or infectious agent (*the lion, the stomach, the AIDS virus*), although it can be applied to any item when its history is discussed (e.g., *the fork, the ball-point pen, the hoop skirt*). Generic *the* thus tends to appear most often in scholarly works and literature.

Generic statements are more likely to occur in the simple tenses unless the subject is an agent of change, in which case continuous tenses can be used, as shown in the following examples:

a) The elephant eats (*is eating) leaves and tree bark.   [definition]

b) The telephone affects/is affecting the way we live.   [agent of change]

In Sentence (a), the continuous verb form would cause *the elephant* to be interpreted as a specific rather than a generic noun. In Sentence (b), both the simple and continuous tenses are allowed because the subject is acting as an agent of change.

EXERCISE 10.10

Directions: Underline the uses of generic *the* in the following sentences.

1. The giraffe is the tallest living quadruped mammal.

2. Diseases of the heart are the number-one killer in the United States.

3. Frogs and turtles bury themselves in the mud below frozen streams, while snakes and toads sleep through the winter under logs and leaves.

4. The bomb that was dropped on Nagasaki was based on the principle of nuclear fission (division), whereas the hydrogen bomb is based on the principle of fusion.

5. The paper clip is one of the most widely used paper fasteners in the world.

PROBLEM SOLVING WITH THE ARTICLE SYSTEM

In the process of providing feedback on grammatical errors, we praise a student before we begin to point out mistakes. In the problems below, it is possible to get the following right:

  a. correct CLASS/IDEN (*a(n)/Ø* for classification; *the* for identification)
  b. correct COUNTABILITY (count or noncount for classified nouns only)
  c. correct NUMBER (singular or plural for classified count nouns only)
  d. correct INITIAL SOUND (vowel or consonant sound for classified singular count nouns only)
  e. correct POSSIBLE FORM (NP structure exists but is not correct)

These elements reflect what students are likely to do wrong in using an article: a) use *a(n)* or *Ø* with an identified noun or *the* with a classified one, b) label a classified singular count noun with *Ø* or a classified noncount noun with *a(n)*, c) use *Ø* with a singular classified noun or *a(n)* with a plural classified noun, (d) use *a* before a vowel sound or *an* before a consonant sound, or e) use a possible article + noun structure but in the wrong grammatical context.

EXERCISE 10.11

Directions: In the following sentences, a student made a single error in using an article. Your job is to address the error in three stages:

  a) bracket the error to focus your attention
  b) list what the student got right about the bracketed error (in this case, the error concerns an article) and show this in parentheses
  c) compare the original erroneous sentence to the correct sentence and explain what mistake the student made

  Example: *Steve had a orange for breakfast.
    [The star (*) indicates that the sentence contains an error.]

Solution:
   a) Bracket the error (the article): *Steve had [a] orange for breakfast.
   b) Show what is right about the article:
       correct class/iden (classification)
       correct countability (count)
       correct number (singular)
   c) Compare the erroneous sentence to the correct form and explain the mistake:
       *Steve had [a] orange for breakfast.
       Steve had an orange for breakfast.

Explanation: An is required when the noun begins with a vowel sound.

1. *Joe has a same hairstyle as Margaret.

2. *A car that I bought from you last week is a piece of junk!

3. *A moon affects the ocean tides on our planet.

4. *The Sears Tower in Chicago is a tallest building in the United States.

5. *[Definition] A plumber is the person who fixes leaking pipes and clogged drains.

6. *This castle has a tower that is made completely of a stone.

7. *[Ring! Ring!] Could you answer a telephone for me?

8. *I don't think there is the bookshop in this town.

9. *Would you like to go to an ocean with us this weekend?

10. *[An old man was walking down a dusty road with a boy.] The man was tired, the road
     was long, and a boy was hungry.

ARTICLES WITH PROPER NOUNS

The rules for articles with proper nouns, which include Ø and *the* but not *a*, are different from the rules for articles with common nouns. Some generalizations can be made but many uses of articles with proper nouns appear to be arbitrary. Table 10.2 shows examples of the use of Ø and *the* with proper nouns (generalizations are underlined).

Table 10.2 Articles with Proper Nouns

CATEGORY	EXAMPLES WITH Ø	EXAMPLES WITH *THE*
POLITICAL ENTITIES	**Names**	**Titles**
Continents	Africa	the continent of South America
Countries	Somalia	the People's Republic of China
States	Idaho	the state of California
Cities	Taipei	the city of Paris
Departments	Chemistry	the Department of Applied Linguistics
Officials	President Clinton	the President of the U.S.
GEOGRAPHICAL FEATURES	**Singular**	**Plural**
Islands	Wake Island	the Aleutian Islands
Mountains	Mt. Fuji	the Andes
Lakes	Lake Titicaca	the Great Lakes
Other Geographical Features	(no generalization)	
Oceans	—	the Arctic Ocean
Seas	—	the Black Sea
Rivers	—	the Mississippi River
Canals	—	the Panama Canal
Deserts	—	the Kalahari Desert
Forests	Sherwood Forest	the Black Forest
Valleys	Desolation Valley	the Shenandoah Valley
ASTRONOMICAL FEATURES	**Distant**	**Local**
Galaxies	Andromeda	the Milky Way
Stars	Sirius	the North Star, the Sun
Planets	Saturn	the Earth
Moons	Ganymede	the Moon
Comets	—	
CULTURAL FEATURES	**Without *of***	**With *of***
Holidays	Christmas	the Fourth of July
Schools	Harvard University	the University of Hawaii
Streets	Market Street	the Avenue of the Americas
	Language	**People**
Ethnicity	Italian	the Italians
Other Cultural Features	(no generalization)	
Wars	World War II	the Boer War, the Second World War
Parks	Central Park	—
Museums	—	the British Museum
Businesses	Hewlitt-Packard	the Xerox Corporation
Buildings	Carnegie Hall	the World Trade Center

EXERCISE 10.12

Directions: Fill the blanks with *the* or Ø.

   Example: ___ Amazon River empties into ___ Atlantic Ocean.
   Solution: The Amazon River empties into the Atlantic Ocean.

1. ___ Sears Tower in ___ city of Chicago is one of the tallest buildings in ___ North America.

2. ___ Suez Canal connects ___ Port Said on ___ Mediterranean Sea and ___ Port Taufiq on ___ Gulf of Suez in ___ Red Sea.

3. ___ Little Colorado River begins at ___ Zuni Reservoir in ___ Arizona, just south of ___ Petrified Forest, an extensive exhibit of petrified wood. It flows north of ___ city of Flagstaff and empties into ___ Colorado River, which passes through ___ Grand Canyon National Park.

4. ___ Mt. Kilimanjaro (19,340 ft.) is situated in ___ north Tanzania between ___ Lake Victoria and ___ Indian Ocean. ___ Serengeti National Park lies to the west of it, ___ Masai Steppe to the south, and ___ Yatta Plateau to the northeast.

5. ___ LeConte Hall houses ___ Physics Department at ___ University of California at ___ Berkeley.

6. Bones from the largest known mammal, the baluchitherium, were found in ___ Gobi Desert in ___ People's Republic of Mongolia. This desert is southeast of ___ Khangai Mountains.

7. ___ Library of Congress, ___ Air and Space Museum, ___NASA (___ National Air and Space Administration) and ___ Department of Agriculture are all located on ___Independence Avenue in ___ Washington D.C.

8. The largest of ___ Hawaiian Islands is ___ Hawaii. ___ Kilauea, one of ___ world's most active volcanoes, is located there.

9. When sailing from ___ city of Vancouver, one passes through ___ San Juan Islands to ___ Victoria, the capital of ___ British Columbia on___ Vancouver Island. ___ Pacific Ocean lies to the west.

10. ___ Apple Computer Company, situated in ___ "Silicon Valley" near ___ Stanford University, competes with ___ IBM and other companies concerned with microelectronics.

The Other Central Determiners

The other central determiners include the following :

   2) possessive (e.g., *my*, *John's*)
   3) demonstrative (*this*, *that*, *these*, and *those*)
   4) assertive/nonassertive (*some* and *any*)
   5) negative (*no*)
   6) universal (*each* and *every*)
   7) dual (*either* and *neither*)
   8) WH-determiners (*what*, *which*, and *whose*)

THE POSSESSIVE DETERMINERS

The possessive determiners show that the scope of a noun is limited by being the property (in both the literal and figurative sense) of someone or something. There are first, second, and third person forms that parallel the possessive pronouns, as shown in the following examples:

PERSON	POSSESSIVE PRONOUN	POSSESSIVE DETERMINER
First	This book is <u>mine</u>.	It's <u>my</u> book.
Second	They found <u>yours</u>.	They found <u>your</u> wallet.
Third	Are these <u>hers</u>?	Are they <u>her</u> earrings?

Any noun phrase can be made into a possessive determiner by the addition of an apostrophe plus *s* (*'s*) for singular nouns and *s* plus an apostrophe (s') for plural nouns, as shown in the following examples:

a) <u>The man who lives on the corner's</u> girlfriend paid the bill.   [singular]

b) <u>The students'</u> visas will expire on December 31.   [plural]

The possessive determiners are summarized in Table 10.3.

Table 10.3 Person, Gender, and Number in the Possessive Determiner System

PERSON	FIRST	SECOND	THIRD		
GENDER	—	—	Masculine	Feminine	Neuter
NUMBER					
Singular ('s)	my —	your —	his a man's	her Jane's	its the dog's
Plural (s')	our —	your —	their the doctors'		

EXERCISE 10.13

Directions: Fill the blank with a possessive determiner derived from the underlined word plus a noun from the first sentence.

    Example: [<u>He</u> possesses a valuable ring.] _____ is made of gold.

    Solution: His ring is made of gold.

1. [<u>He</u> owns a fishing boat.] _____ is docked at a marina on the Columbia River.

2. [<u>Saturn</u> has over 1000 rings.] _____ are made mostly of ice.

3. [<u>I</u> possess a stainless steel watch.] _____ is powered by a battery.

4. [<u>They</u> have fences everywhere.] _____ are all electrified.

5. [You own a boa constrictor.] _____ is over 10 feet long.

6. [The schools have problems.] _____ concern drugs, gangs, and firearms.

7. [We possess a gold mine.] _____ is in Amazonia.

8. [She had a beautiful daughter.] _____ was only sixteen when she died.

9. [It has a varnished surface.] _____ has been badly scratched.

10. [This model has a 68000 central processor.] _____ is not as fast as newer versions.

THE DEMONSTRATIVE DETERMINERS

The demonstrative determiners show that the scope of a noun is limited by being located either near the speaker or away from the speaker in space or time. They have singular and plural forms, as shown in the following examples:

a) Jamie went skiing <u>this weekend</u>.   [singular]
b) Who made <u>these cookies</u>?   [plural]

c) What did you do <u>that summer</u>?   [singular]
d) I love <u>those earrings</u> you're wearing.   [plural]

The demonstrative determiners, which have the same form as the demonstrative pronouns, are shown in Table 10.4.

Table 10.4 The Demonstrative Determiners

NUMBER	HERE/NOW	THERE/THEN
Singular	this	that
Plural	these	those

EXERCISE 10.14

Directions: Add *this*, *that*, *these*, or *those* to the blanks.

1. In _____ days, people used to throw garbage into the street!

2. If you want to stay in _____ house, you will follow the house rules.

3. Do you see _____ building in the distance? I used to live there.

4. Do _____ glasses suit my personality, do you think?

5. Sheila has worked over fifty hours _____ week.

The Assertive/Nonassertive Determiners

The assertive determiner is *some* and the nonassertive determiner is *any*. *Some* in its **stressed** form shows that the scope of a noun is limited to part of a larger group, as in the following examples:

a) <u>Some</u> meat is tough; <u>some</u> meat is tender. [singular]

b) <u>Some</u> people like dogs; <u>some</u> people like cats. [plural]

Some in its **unstressed** form (pronounced /sm/ and written *s'm* for grammatical reference only) indicates a portion or small group, as in the following examples:

a) Could I have <u>s'm</u> bread? [singular]

b) <u>S'm</u> men came to see you. [plural]

Like the pronoun *some*, the determiner *s'm* usually occurs in a positive environment. Since *s'm* often takes the place of the zero article, some grammarians believe it should be considered part of the article system.

Any in its stressed form shows that the scope of a noun is unlimited. It can occur with singular or plural nouns, as shown in the following examples:

a) <u>Any</u> weapon carried on a commercial plane is illegal. [singular]

b) <u>Any</u> individuals found with weapons will be arrested. [plural]

Like the pronoun *any*, the determiner *any* in its unstressed form (pronounced /ni/ and written *'ny* for grammatical reference) only occurs in a negative or interrogative environment and, like Ø, only with a noncount or plural count noun, as shown in the following examples:

a) NEGATIVE: We never have <u>'ny</u> problems in our neighborhood.

b) INTERROGATIVE: Is there <u>'ny</u> water left?

EXERCISE 10.15

Directions: Fill the blanks with *some* or *any* **where appropriate**. Place an accent mark (´) over the word when the stressed form is needed.

1. There are _____ apples in the refrigerator.

2. Would you like _____ tea?

3. The earth was inhabited by _____ dinosaurs in the Jurassic period.

4. _____ snakes bear live young while others lay eggs.

5. The voting material should be readable by _____ person with a high-school education.

6. We haven't had _____ tornadoes, hurricanes, or tropical storms this year.

7. _____ aspirin is a common pain-reliever.

8. Did _____ insects survive the atomic bomb tests that took place in the South Pacific?

9. No human being has the right to hurt _____ other human being.

10. _____ people called to see if you wanted to buy a condo in Florida.

THE NEGATIVE DETERMINER

The negative determiner is *no*. It limits the scope of the noun so completely that nothing remains. *No* occurs without limitation as to countability or number, as shown in the following examples:

a) He drinks <u>no wine</u> before its time.	[noncount]
b) <u>No gun</u> was found at the scene of the crime.	[singular count]
c) There were <u>no people</u> on the beach.	[plural count]

EXERCISE 10.16

Directions: Rewrite the following sentences using the negative determiner.

1. The advisor didn't have any further comments.

2. Not a tree was standing after the forest fire.

3. What would you do if you were stranded in a foreign country without money?

4. Julia's grandfather will not allow cats in the house.

5. I didn't have the slightest idea that you were in town!

THE UNIVERSAL DETERMINERS

The universal determiners *each* and *every* are used to describe the members of a group. However, although the members must be part of a group, the universal determiners describe the individual members, not the collective membership, which is why *each* and *every* can only occur with singular count nouns. *Each* describes the individuals in a limited group, as shown in the following examples:

LIMITED GROUP: a) <u>Each</u> participant in the conference was selected by a committee.
b) <u>Each</u> book on this table costs fifty cents.

Every describes the individuals in an unlimited group, as shown in the following examples:

UNLIMITED GROUP: a) <u>Every</u> child should have a pet.
b) <u>Every</u> dog has its day.

THE DUAL DETERMINERS

The dual determiners are used to describe the members of a pair. However, although the members must belong to a pair, the dual determiners describe the individual members, which is why *either* and *neither* can only occur with singular count nouns. There are two types of dual determiners: the nonassertive and the negative.

The nonassertive dual determiner is *either*. *Either* limits the noun set to two members but does not assert the supremacy of one over the other. Examples are shown below:

a) <u>Either</u> method works equally well.

b) The injection can be taken in <u>either</u> arm.

The negative dual determiner is *neither*. *Neither* completely limits the two members of the noun set so that none remains. Examples are shown below:

a) <u>Neither</u> eye has 20/20 vision.

b) <u>Neither</u> polar region is safe from environmental pollution.

THE WH-DETERMINERS

The WH-determiners are *what*, *which*, and *whose*. They limit the scope of the set to the noun or nouns suggested in prior discourse or through shared knowledge. The nouns with WH-determiners can be singular or plural. In WH-questions and noun clauses, a WH-determiner with an associated noun constitutes what we called a *narrow WH-question word* in Chapter 7. The WH-determiner *whose* with its associated noun can also play the role of relative pronoun. Examples are shown below:

  a) <u>What</u> language do you speak?

  b) Paul forgot <u>which</u> street Alina lived on.

  c) A mother <u>whose</u> son is killed is also a casualty of war.

EXERCISE 10.17

Directions: Fill the blanks with *each, every, either, neither, what, which,* or *whose*.

1. _____ color would you like your house to be painted?

2. Astronomers know the position and magnitude of _____ star in the night sky.

3. Janet has been to Malawi and Joel has been to Zimbabwe, but stay-at-home Paula has been to _____ country.

4   _____ dishes are those in the sink? They certainly aren't mine!

5. The two parties each nominate one person, but many voters don't care for _____ candidate.

6. The hospital orderlies bathe _____ patient on the ward on a daily basis.

7. The starving people didn't care _____ food they received as long as they got something to eat.

8. Jack's mother likes old houses but his father likes new ones. _____ kind does your wife prefer?

9. _____ book that is published has an ISBN number.

10. The thieves didn't know _____ car they had stolen, but they knew that the owner would try to find them.

PROBLEM SOLVING WITH THE OTHER CENTRAL DETERMINERS

In the process of providing feedback on grammatical errors, we praise a student before we begin to point out mistakes. In the problems below, which cover all the central determiners except the articles, it is possible to get the following right:

  a. correct DETERMINER CATEGORY (possessive, negative, WH, etc.)

  b. correct NUMBER (singular or plural)

c. correct ENVIRONMENT (nearby or not nearby for demonstratives; positive, negative or interrogative for assertive/nonassertive; limited or unlimited group for universal; pair for dual)

d. correct POSSIBLE FORM (NP structure exists but is not correct in this case)

These elements reflect what students are likely to do wrong in using a central determiner: a) use the wrong category of determiner, b) use the wrong singular or plural form with a certain determiner, c) identify the incorrect environment for the limitations of determiner use, and (d) use a possible determiner + noun structure but in the wrong grammatical context.

EXERCISE 10.18

Directions: In the following sentences, a student made a single error in using a central determiner. Your job is to address the error in three stages:

  a) bracket the error to focus your attention

  b) list what the student got right about the bracketed error (in this case, the error concerns a central determiner) and show this in parentheses

  c) compare the original erroneous sentence to the correct sentence and explain what mistake the student made

Example: *Sorry, the bank has any money left.
  [The star (*) indicates that the sentence contains an error.]

Solution:

  a) Bracket the error (the determiner):
     *Sorry, the bank has [any] money left.

  b) Show what is right about the central determiner:
     correct environment (negative)
     correct possible form (*any money*)

  c) Compare the erroneous sentence to the correct form and explain the mistake:
     *Sorry, the bank has [any] money left.
      Sorry, the bank has no   money left.

Explanation: To use the determiner *any* in a negative environment, either auxiliary or adverbial negation must also be present in the sentence. Otherwise, as in this case, the negative determiner *no* must be used.

1. *[There is a book on the table in the kitchen.] Bring me this book, please.

2. *Mr. Smith, don't forget yours credit card.

3. *All child deserves a good education.

4. *[This soldier will have to be carried.] She cannot use neither leg.

5. *Which time does the plane arrive?

6. *Last semester, students couldn't get some money, not even a student loan.

7. *We have had absolutely not problem with this machine.

8. *[One company wants to reduce worker salaries. The other wants to move to a developing country.] Either company is being very fair to its workers.

9. *How many stereos have you sold that week?

10. *Every person could have contaminated the milk container.

THE NONCENTRAL DETERMINERS

The noncentral determiners include the predeterminers and the postdeterminers. They are not nearly so varied and complex as the central determiners. However, they provide important refinements of the mechanism of determination which are primarily concerned with quantity.

The Predeterminers

The predeterminers are words that precede the required central determiner in a noun phrase. They consist of the quantifiers (*all* and *both*), the fractions (e.g., *half, one-third*), and the intensifiers (*what* and *such*). Like the central determiners, the predeterminers are mutually exclusive. The categories of predeterminers have different restrictions as to which central determiners they can occur with.

THE QUANTIFYING PREDETERMINERS

The quantifying predeterminers include the words *all* and *both*. *All* includes an entire mass (e.g., *all petroleum*) or group (e.g., *all snakes*), whereas both includes an entire pair (e.g., *both eyes*). These predeterminers freely co-occur with the articles *the* and *Ø*, the possessive, and the demonstrative determiners (with optional *of*). They may generally not occur with the article *a* or the other central determiners because they have number restrictions of their own. Look at the following examples:

all (of) the milk	both (of) the recipes
all (of) his problems	both (of) his sisters
all (of) these people	both (of) those districts
*all (of) a story	*both (of) a hill
*all (of) some cake	*both (of) any numbers
*all (of) no money	*both (of) no doctors
*all (of) every book	*both (of) each chapter
*all (of) either party	*both (of) neither accusation
*all (of) which rooms	*both (of) what seasons

All occurs with plural count nouns, e.g., *all plants, all (of) the plants*, and noncount nouns, e.g., *all garbage, all (of) the garbage. Both* occurs only with plural count nouns, e.g., *both restaurants, both (of) the restaurants.*

EXERCISE 10.19

Directions: Fill the blanks with *all (of)* or *both (of)* **where possible**.

1. _____ my relatives came to the family reunion.

2. Sally should have _____ some food before she leaves.

3. The patient had fluid in _____ his lungs.

4. How can you throw away _____ those old love letters?

5. Customers may use _____ either elevator.

THE FRACTIONAL PREDETERMINERS

The fractional determiners include the fraction *half (of)*, *a quarter of*, *a tenth of*, etc. *Half* (without *a*) can freely co-occur with all the articles and the possessive and demonstrative central determiners. *Of* may be used except when it co-occurs with Ø, as shown in the following examples:

      a) He consumed <u>half (of) a watermelon</u>.

      b) The bomb destroyed <u>half (of) the city</u>.

      c) <u>Half (of) their property</u> was sold.

      d) You ate <u>half (of) this box of strawberries</u>?

      e) A centaur is <u>half Ø man</u> and <u>half Ø horse</u>.

Sentence (e) is a special descriptive use of *half* that can only occur with Ø (never with *a* or *the*) and must appear twice. The remaining fractions (always with *a* or *one*) also freely co-occur with all of the articles and the possessive and demonstrative central determiners. *Of* must be used except in the special descriptive use of a fraction with Ø (see Sentence e), as in the following examples:

      a) Each person was given <u>an eighth of</u> a chicken.

      b) The disease killed nearly <u>a fifth of</u> the inhabitants.

      c) <u>A quarter of</u> my schoolmates are out of work.

      d) You can't read <u>a third of</u> these numbers.

      e) Your grandfather was <u>one third</u> genius, <u>one third</u> bandit, and <u>one third</u> fool.

EXERCISE 10.20

Directions: Write out the following numerical fractions in their correct form.

1. (1/2) _____ the trees were knocked down in the hurricane.

2. More than (3/4) _____ your native peoples died of influenza.

3. That guy would eat (1/4) _____ a sheep if you let him.

4. His latest text is (1/3) _____ story book and (2/3)_____ style manual.

5. The Concorde will allow you to get to Paris in (1/2) _____ the time.

THE INTENSIFYING PREDETERMINERS

The intensifying predeterminers are *such* and *what*. They co-occur only with the classifying articles *a* and Ø. *Such* and *what* both start out as noun phrases in the direct object or predicate noun slots. However, *such*-phrases cannot be fronted (moved to the front of the clause), whereas *what*-phrases must be fronted. Look at the following examples:

a) That is <u>such a</u> great idea! <u>What a</u> great idea that is!

b) You bring <u>such Ø</u> terrible news! <u>What Ø</u> terrible news you bring!

Negative statements cannot be fronted and therefore only occur with *such*:

a) He's not <u>such a</u> wonderful cook. *<u>What a</u> wonderful cook he isn't.

b) Susie never had <u>such Ø</u> problems! *<u>What Ø</u> problems Susie never had!

EXERCISE 10.21

Directions: Fill the blanks with *what* or *such* and the appropriate article.

1. The Prime Minister was always _____ gentleman.

2. "_____ nonsense!" screamed the witness.

3. San Francisco isn't _____ large city.

4. The team only realized _____ wonderful athlete Billie Jean was after she had left.

5. The audience had never heard _____ beautiful music.

The Postdeterminers

The postdeterminers are words that follow the required central determiner in a noun phrase. They include the numerals, *many* and its relatives, and the forms of *other*. Unlike the other determiner types we have seen, the postdeterminers are not mutually exclusive, as shown in the following examples:

a) Alice's <u>three</u> <u>other</u> dogs are spaniels.

b) My <u>two</u> <u>second</u> favorite cars are a Mercedes and a BMW.

c) <u>Many</u> <u>other</u> issues were discussed at the conference.

Postdeterminers co-occur with the articles and the possessive and demonstrative central determiners.

THE NUMERALS

The numerals include the cardinal and ordinal numerals. The cardinal numerals are the ordinary numbers, such as *one, two, seventy-eight, three million*. The ordinal numerals are the numbers in their descriptive form (*first, second, seventy-eighth, three millionth*). These occasionally co-occur with predeterminers, as shown in the following examples:

a) <u>All of her eighth</u> chapter was eaten by the family dog.

b) <u>Both of those two</u> white powders are quite harmless.

However, it is more common that, when determiners co-occur at all, predeterminers occur with central determiners and central determiners with postdeterminers.

EXERCISE 10.22

Directions: Write out the correct form of the numbers in parentheses.

1. Stockholm was (1) _____ city to ban traffic in the city center.

2. There were over (200) _____ guests at the wedding.

3. Oxygen is (8) _____ element on the periodic table.

4. (16) _____ moons of Jupiter include Ganymede, the largest moon in the Solar System.

5. Mars is (4) _____ planet from the sun.

MANY AND ITS RELATIVES

Many and its relatives are members of a small group of frequently occurring post-determiners whose selection is dependent on 1) the countability of the noun they precede, 2) the magnitude of the quantity (large or small), and 3) the positive/neutral or negative environment in which the noun occurs. They include *many, much, a lot of, lots of, a few, few, a little,* and *little*.

For plural count nouns, the choice is limited to *many, a lot of, lots of, a few,* and *few,* as shown in the following examples:

 a) <u>Many</u> people have an aversion to snakes.

 b) <u>A lot of</u> people have an aversion to snakes.

 c) <u>Lots of</u> people have an aversion to snakes.

 d) Richard bought <u>a few</u> shirts to take to Australia.

 e) <u>Few</u> plants can tolerate constant wind.

In Sentence (a), the plural count noun *people* is modified by *many,* which can be paraphrased as *a large number of.* However, the use of *many* usually sounds better in negative and interrogative environments. *Many* is normally replaced with *a lot of* in positive environments, as in Sentence (b). In informal contexts, *many* can be replaced with *lots of,* as in Sentence (c). In Sentence (d), the plural count noun *shirts* is modified by *a few,* which shows a small number in a positive environment, i.e., there is a positive (or neutral) response to the small number. *A few* can be paraphrased as *a small number of.* In Sentence (e), the plural count noun *plants* is modified by *few,* which shows a small number in a negative environment, i.e., there is a negative response to the small number. *Few* can be paraphrased as *not many*.

For noncount nouns, the choice is limited to *much, a lot of, lots of, a little,* and *little,* as shown in the following examples:

 a) <u>Much</u> concern has been expressed about the depleted ozone layer.

 b) <u>A lot of</u> concern has been expressed about the depleted ozone layer.

 c) <u>Lots of</u> concern has been expressed about the depleted ozone layer.

 d) The doctor said she should drink <u>a little</u> wine with her dinner.

 e) There is <u>little</u> hope that the baby will survive.

In Sentence (a), the noncount noun *concern* is modified by *much,* which can be paraphrased as *a large amount of.* However, as is the case for *many,* the use of *much* in a positive environment sounds unnatural in most contexts. Normally, *much* is replaced with *a lot of,* as in

Sentence (b), and in informal contexts with *lots of*, as in Sentence (c). *A lot of* and *lots of* thus occur with both count and noncount nouns. In Sentence (d), the noncount noun *wine* is modified by *a little*, which shows a small amount in a positive environment, i.e., there is a positive (or neutral) response to the small amount. *A little* can be paraphrased as *a small amount of*. In Sentence (e), the noncount noun *hope* is modified by *little*, which shows *a small amount* in a negative environment (i.e., there is a negative response to the small number). *Little* can be paraphrased as *not much*.

There is not yet complete agreement as to where the dividing line between quantifiers and adjectives should occur, i.e., whether words such as *abundant, ample, numerous, plenteous, prolific, profuse,* and *sundry*, which also express non-specific quantities, function as postdeterminers or whether they function as adjectives.

EXERCISE 10.23

Directions: Fill the blanks with *many, much, a lot of, lots of, few, a few, little,* or *a little*.

1. The old woman kept _____ cows to supply her family with milk.

2. _____ children send letters to Santa Claus at Christmas time.

3. There are _____ problems that can't be solved with _____ patience.

4. Not _____ water is left in the local reservoir.

5. The mother wept with joy when the jury found _____ evidence that her boy was guilty.

THE POSTDETERMINER *OTHER*

The postdeterminer *other* co-occurs with the articles and the central determiners *some* and *any* to indicate a variety of meanings. Forms with the classifying articles *a* and *Ø* show an unlimited relationship to similar nouns, whereas forms with identifying *the* show a limited relationship. Examples are shown in Table 10.5.

Table 10.5 Combinations with the Postdeterminer *Other*

NUMBER	UNLIMITED (*an*, Ø) MEANING		LIMITED (the)	MEANING

Singular	another
	any other
	some other
		one more
		one but not this
		not this but
		  one from a
		  defined group
			the other
			———
			———
				not this but that one
				———
				———

Plural	Ø other
	any other
	
	some other
		not these
		all except these
		
		a few but
		  not these
			the other
			any of the other
			
			some of the other
				not these but those
				all the members of a
				  defined group but
				  not these
				a few from a defined
				  group but not these

EXERCISE 10.24

Directions: Use the correct form of *other* (from Table 10.5) in the blanks.

1. Ralph would like _____ beer, please.

2. Pluto with one moon has fewer satellites than _____ outer planets.

3. Some animals sleep in the daytime while _____ animals sleep at night.

4. If one side of the brain is damaged, _____ side can compensate to some degree.

5. I'm terribly busy at the moment. Could you call _____ day next week?

Problem Solving with the Noncentral Determiners

In the process of providing feedback on grammatical errors, we praise a student before we begin to point out mistakes. In the problems below, which cover only the predeterminers and postdeterminers, it is possible to get the following right:

  a. correct NONCENTRAL DETERMINER CATEGORY (quantifying and intensifying predeterminers, fractions, numerals, *many* and its relatives, and forms of *other*)
  b. correct CO-OCCURRING CENTRAL DETERMINER (article, possessive, or demonstrative central determiner)
  c. correct CLASS/IDEN OF CO-OCCURRING CENTRAL DETERMINER (*a(n)*/Ø for classification; *the* for identification)
  d. correct COUNTABILITY (count or noncount)
  e. correct NUMBER (singular or plural)
  f. correct POSSIBLE FORM (NP structure exists but is not correct)

These elements reflect what students are likely to do wrong in using a noncentral determiner: a) use the wrong category of noncentral determiner, b) use the wrong co-occurring central determiner, c) use classifying in place of an identifying co-occurring article, or vice versa, (d) use incorrect countability, e) use the wrong number, or (f) use a possible determiner + noun structure but in the wrong grammatical context.

EXERCISE 10.25

Directions: In the following sentences, a student made a single error in using a noncentral determiner. Your job is to address the error in three stages:

> a) bracket the error to focus your attention
> b) list what the student got right about the bracketed error (in this case, the error concerns a noncentral determiner) and show this in parentheses
> c) compare the original erroneous sentence to the correct sentence and explain what mistake the student made

Example: *John has a scar on one leg and a bruise on another leg.
[The star (*) indicates that the sentence contains an error.]

Solution:

> a) Bracket the error (the determiner):
> *John has a scar on one leg and a bruise on [another] leg.
> b) Show what is right about the noncentral determiner:
> correct noncentral determiner category (form of *other*)
> correct countability (count: <u>*ano*</u>*ther* leg)
> correct number (singular: *another* leg)
> correct possible form (*another* leg)
> c) Compare the erroneous sentence to the correct form and explain the mistake:
> *John has a scar on one leg and a bruise on [another] leg.
> John has a scar on one leg and a bruise on the other leg.

Explanation: Since the number of legs a person has is limited, the identifying article *the* plus *other* must be used.

1. *It was what a hot day yesterday.

2. *A chicken's top speed (9 mph) is the quarter of a rabbit's top speed (35 mph).

3. *Humans often do not hear equally well with both ear.

4. *Sean is writing the six revision of his term paper.

5. *Half the fish in this lake died; other half got sick.

6. *In this house, all of children go to bed at 9:00 P.M. sharp.

7. *Daphne always goes dancing with few friends on Saturday night.

8. *Both of that regions were harmed by the 1987 drought.

9. *There is more acid rain today than at some other time in history.

10. *It will take them several days to climb such high mountain.

Chapter 11

THE ADJECTIVE SYSTEM

The adjective system includes all the words and phrases that modify a noun. In general, modifiers show the quality of a noun whereas determiners show quantity. There are two different types of adjective structures: adjective phrases and adjective clauses.

ADJECTIVE PHRASES

Adjective phrases consist of attributive adjectives and predicate adjectives.

Attributive Adjectives

Attributive adjectives are the words that come between the determiner and the noun in a noun phrase. They can only premodify a noun. There are several ways to change other parts of speech into attributive adjectives. In addition, when more than one is present, attributive adjectives tend to come in a particular order.

ADJECTIVE SUFFIXES

There are several derivational morphemes that allow us to change nouns and verbs into adjectives.

Changing Nouns into Adjectives

Nouns can be transformed into adjectives by means of derivational suffixes. The most common suffixes for doing this are shown in Table 11.1.

Table 11.1 Suffixes that Change Nouns into Adjectives

SUFFIX	*NOUN*	*ADJECTIVE*	*SUFFIX*	*NOUN*	*ADJECTIVE*
-al	person	personal	**-less**	child	childless
	brute	brutal		home	homeless
-ary	revolution	revolutionary	**-like**	child	childlike
	custom	customary		life	lifelike
-ful	faith	faithful	**-ly**	friend	friendly
	beauty	beautiful		time	timely
-ic	artist	artistic	**-ous**	mystery	mysterious
	base	basic		nerve	nervous
-ish	self	selfish	**-y**	cloud	cloudy
	fool	foolish		wealth	wealthy

Changing Verbs into Adjectives

Verbs may also be changed into adjectives by means of derivational suffixes. In addition, certain verb forms function directly as adjectives without the need for suffixes.

SUFFIXES

The most common suffixes for changing verbs into adjectives are shown in Table 11.2.

Table 11.2 Suffixes that Change Verbs into Adjectives

SUFFIX	VERB	ADJECTIVE
-able	agree	agreeable
	remark	remarkable
-ent	depend	dependent
	urge	urgent
-ible	eat	edible
	sense	sensible
-ive	attract	attractive
	create	creative

EXERCISE 11.1

Directions: Using Tables 11.1 and 11.2, put the noun or verb in parentheses into the correct adjective form in the blank.

1. Paris is a very (beauty) _____ city.

2. The cancer patient made a (remark) _____ recovery.

3. The (base) _____ problem with nuclear power is disposing of nuclear waste.

4. How Marilyn Monroe died is still very (mystery) _____.

5. Young mammals are (depend) _____ on their parents during their early years.

6. The people in the midwestern section of the U.S. are often very (friend) _____.

7. The (child) _____ couple were anxious to adopt a baby.

8. People who suffer from manic depression are often extremely (create) _____ .

9. It is (custom) _____ in Japanese houses to remove your shoes at the door.

10. Brightly colored mushrooms are usually not (eat) _____ .

VERB FORMS AS ADJECTIVES

Many VERB$_{ing}$ and VERB$_{ed2}$ forms function as adjectives without changing their form. These forms are called ING-adjectives and ED$_2$-adjectives. Look at the following examples:

SUBJECT	VERB	OBJECT	ING–ADJECTIVE	ED$_2$–ADJECTIVE
A story	**fascinates**	the children.	a **fascinating** story	the **fascinated** children
That ride	**thrilled**	the adults.	that **thrilling** ride	the **thrilled** adults
Your film	**is boring**	the audience.	your **boring** film	the **bored** audience
The weather	**has frozen**	the river.	the **freezing** weather	the **frozen** river

Notice that the ING-adjectives always modify the subject noun phrase (e.g., *a fascinating story*) whereas the ED$_2$-adjectives always modify the object noun phrase (e.g., *the fascinated children*).

Most adjectives of this sort do not have acceptable ING **and** ED$_2$ forms like those shown in the examples. ING-adjectives typically occur with objects or materials that are either designed to perform an activity (e.g., *cleaning agents, a drying rack*) or act or produce an action by themselves (e.g., *a spinning top, a bleeding ulcer*). ED$_2$-adjectives typically describe a person, animal, object, or material to which something has been done (e.g., *a paid assassin, endangered species, a lost letter, powdered sugar*). The ING– and ED$_2$–adjectives thus parallel the active and passive voices, respectively.[1]

EXERCISE 11.2

Directions: Change the verb in parentheses into an appropriate ING- or ED$_2$-adjective. Then describe why the alternative form could not be used.

1. (interest) The professor gave a really _____ lecture yesterday.

2. (inherit) Sickle cell anemia is an _____ condition.

3. (polish) The dancers slipped on the _____ floor.

4. (exhaust) Many students complained about the _____ registration process.

5. (steal) The _____ jewelry was found in a garbage can.

6. (demand) A _____ career can have a negative effect on personal relationships.

7. (damage) The _____ buildings would have to be rebuilt within a year.

8. (neglect) The animal pound is full of _____ pets.

9. (work) Roger built a _____ model of a steam locomotive.

10. (rule) The _____ classes make up the aristocracy.

---

[1] ING/ED$_2$ adjectives formed from process verbs emphasize actions in process (e.g., *melting snow*) and completed actions (e.g., *melted snow*), respectively, rather than the active/passive sense.

SEQUENCE OF ADJECTIVES

When more than one attributive adjective is present, they usually have a preferred sequence. Look at the following pairs of noun phrases and determine which sound better to you.

1. a) a white big house
   b) a big white house

2. a) an old rickety chair
   b) a rickety old chair

3. a) a spectacular French design
   b) a French spectacular design

4. a) a spherical large object
   b) a large spherical object

You probably chose 1b, 2b, 3a, and 4b. The reason for this is that there is an order of adjectives that most native speakers of English prefer. Praninskas[2] describes seven categories of adjectives in their preferred (though not absolute) sequence:

1. opinion (usually an emotional response such as
   beautiful, disgusting, etc.)

2. size

3. shape

4. condition

5. age

6. color

7. origin

Looking back at the examples, we can see in (1a), for example, that color precedes size in the NP *a white big house.* You probably chose (1b) as the better sounding phrase because the sequence is size followed by color. Analyze your responses to the remaining phrases in the same way.

Although several attributive adjectives before a noun are theoretically possible, native speakers typically use one or two, and in rare instances three. Four or more adjectives sound awkward in most cases unless one is gushing with praise or heaping invective upon an opponent.

EXERCISE 11.3

Directions: Place the adjectives in parentheses in the blank in the appropriate order.

1. Greg bought a (Russian, heavy) _____ coat for the winter.

2. Margaret said that her neighbor was a (silly, old) _____ bat.

3. The valve stem is a (cylindrical, thin) _____ metal rod.

4. That couple found a (burgundy, flawless) _____ prayer rug at a small bazaar.

5. The (square, ugly) _____ room began to feel like a prison.

---

[2] J. Praninskas, *Rapid Review of English Grammar* (Englewood Cliffs, NJ: Prentice-Hall, 1975), 262.

Predicate Adjectives

Predicate adjectives are adjectives that occur without a noun in the predicate of a sentence. They only occur in Type II verb phrases, most commonly after the verb *be*, where they have their own special sentence slot. Look at the following examples:

a) Paris is a <u>beautiful</u> city.   [attributive adjective]

b) The city of Paris is <u>beautiful</u>.   [predicate adjective]

In Sentence (a), *beautiful* functions as an attributive adjective. In Sentence (b), *beautiful* functions as a predicate adjective. Since *be* is a linking verb, the predicate adjective is associated with the subject (*the city of Paris*), which it thus modifies. Although the meaning of *beautiful* in these two sentences is essentially interchangeable, many predicate adjectives either cannot take the role of attributive adjective (or vice versa) or else have a different meaning if they do. Look at the following examples:

a) The children are <u>asleep</u>.   [predicate adjective]

b) *The <u>asleep</u> children lay on the floor.   [attributive adjective]

c) *A child is <u>only</u>.   [predicate adjective]

d) An <u>only</u> child is often spoiled.   [attributive adjective]

e) The Mafia is <u>responsible</u>.   [predicate adjective]

f) A <u>responsible</u> employee delivered the money.   [attributive adjective]

The reason that Sentences (b) and (c) are starred is that predicate adjectives tend to refer to temporary or occasional features of a noun, whereas attributive adjectives tend to describe permanent or characteristic attributes.[3] In Sentences (a) and (b), the adjective *asleep* functions as a predicate adjective but not as an attributive adjective (the attributive form of *asleep* is *sleeping*) because *asleep* describes a temporary condition. In Sentences (c) and (d), the adjective *only* (meaning "without siblings") functions as an attributive adjective but not as a predicate adjective because being an only child is a permanent condition. In Sentences (e) and (f), the adjective *responsible* means "to blame in this instance" (a temporary condition) as a predicate adjective but "trustworthy" (a permanent condition) as an attributive adjective.

EXERCISE 11.4

Directions: If it is possible, change the noun phrase into a sentence with a predicate adjective (1–5) and the sentence with a predicate adjective into a noun phrase (6–10). Indicate whether there is a change in the meaning of the adjective.

1. invisible ink
2. the angry sea
3. an L-shaped room
4. the whole world
5. a complete idiot

6. The baby is awake.
7. The movie was repulsive.
8. The thief is sorry.
9. The whale was dead.
10. The thugs were responsible.

---

[3] This distinction was described by D. Bolinger (1967), Adjectives in English: Attribution and Predication, *Lingua* 18,1-34 and expanded by M. Celce-Murcia and D. Larsen-Freeman, *The Grammar Book* (Cambridge, MA: Newbury House Publishers, 1983), 390-395.

Problem Solving with Adjectives

In the problems below it is possible to get the following right:

    a. correct POSSIBLE ADJECTIVE FORM (e.g., *fool* + *ish*)

    b. correct SEQUENCE OF ADJECTIVES (e.g., size before color)

    c. correct PLACEMENT OF ADJECTIVE (in front of noun being modified; after a linking verb)

These elements reflect what students are likely to do wrong in using an adjective: a) fail to select the appropriate adjective suffix, b) put adjectives in the wrong order, or c) put an adjective in the wrong place.

EXERCISE 11.5 ◉

Directions: In the following sentences, a student made a single error in using an adjective. Your job is to address the error in three stages:

    a) bracket the error to focus your attention

    b) list what the student got right about the bracketed error (in this case, the error concerns the adjective) and show this in parentheses

    c) compare the original erroneous sentence to the correct sentence and explain what mistake the student made

Example: *We saw a very interested film last night.
    [The star (*) indicates that the sentence contains an error.]

Solution:

    a) Bracket the error (one or more of the adjectives):
    *We saw a very [interested] film last night.

    b) Show what is right about the adjective:
    correct possible adjective suffix (*interest* + *ed*)
    correct placement of adjective (in front of *film*)

    c) Compare the erroneous sentence to the correct form and explain the mistake:
    *We saw a very [interested] film last night.
    We saw a very interesting   film last night.

Explanation: Since the head noun (*film*) arouses interest instead of receiving interest, the ING–adjective is required.

1.   *This water is not [drinkible.]
    drinkable

2.   *My grandmother really misses her [little gray faithful] dog.
    faithful little   gray

3.   *A [stream narrow glacial] meandered across the alpine meadow.
    narrow glacial stream

4.   *Hilda thought that her boyfriend's embarrassment was quite [amused.]
    amusing

5.   *Nathan had heard that the local people were warm and [friendish.]
    friendly

6.   *The snake ingested several [alive] mice.
    live

7.   *Sheila bought a [Persian antique priceless] carpet.
    priceless antique persian

8.   *The night sky was filled with [fireworks colorful.]
    colorful fireworks

9.   *The frightening kitten hid beneath the bed.
          frightened

10. *This friend of mine is very old [*old* = "friends for a long time"].
          This is a very old...

THE ADJECTIVE CLAUSE SYSTEM

The adjective clause[4] system allows us to describe a noun (e.g., *book*) by adding information in a clause that follows that noun (e.g., *the book which the student bought*). This noun (which we call the head noun to distinguish it from other nouns that may be in the adjective clause) together with its modifiers make up a noun phrase. Thus, adjective clauses do not generally occur outside a noun phrase. Modifiers that come before the head noun, such as attributive adjectives (e.g., *the red book*), are called **premodifiers**. Modifiers that come after the head noun, such as adjective clauses (e.g., *the book which we lost*), are called **postmodifiers**. The only other type of noun postmodification we have discussed is a prepositional phrase within a noun phrase (e.g., *the book on the table*).

EXERCISE 11.6

Directions: Insert each of the modifiers at an appropriate position in the sentence.

1. A man stole the bicycle.
    a. who was wearing a gray jogging suit
    b. that I just bought
    c. young
    d. beautiful new

2. The train went through a tunnel.
    a. long dark
    b. which Germany has just developed
    c. that comes out on the Italian side of the Alps
    d. modern electric

3. The cat caught a mouse.
    a. that we have had for many years
    b. tiny frightened
    c. old Persian
    d. with beady red eyes

4. George had forgotten the wallet.
    a. black leather
    b. ,who is very careful with his money,
    c. which his mother had given him for his birthday
    d. my friend

---

[4] Adjective clauses have traditionally been called *relative clauses*. However, since the term *relative* does little to remind students of the modifying nature of such clauses, the more descriptive term *adjective clause* has been used throughout.

5. The President has signed a treaty.
   a. ,who is very popular now,
   b. that will improve the economic relations between our two countries
   c. new
   d. of the U.S.

6. That man looks like my father.
   a. folded
   b. with the newspaper
   c. tall
   d. who is walking up the stairs

7. The film is about a guy.
   a. crazy
   b. who falls in love with a girl
   c. fascinating
   d. who used to be his secretary
   e. at the Paramount Theater

8. The thing is a watch.
   a. gold
   b. that I want most
   c. with a calendar

9. Experts disagree with the scientist.
   a. who invented the compound
   b. pharmaceutical
   c. Polish
   d. at various medical schools

10. Mohammad is studying engineering.
    a. my classmate
    b. ,who comes from Saudi Arabia,
    c. ,an important subject,
    d. electrical

In order to understand adjective clauses, we need to consider the relative pronouns, th construction of adjective clauses, and the reduction of adjective clauses.

Relative Pronouns

Like all clauses, adjective clauses are identified by the clause markers that come at the beginning of the clause. The clause markers for adjective clauses are usually called relative pronouns[5], even though, strictly speaking, *whose* is a possessive determiner. For this reason, *whose* must always be attached to a noun in an adjective clause and, like all determiners, can never occur by itself.

---

[5] The traditional term *relative pronoun* is used for the clause marker of an adjective clause, since a term such as "adjective pronoun" would be confusing rather than descriptive.

Who and *whom* are the relative pronouns for persons. *Which* and *that* are the relative pronouns for things. However, *that* can be used for persons in impersonal contexts such as definitions (e.g., *A geologist is a person that studies the composition of the earth*). *Whose* is the possessive relative pronoun for persons as well as things. The five relative pronouns are shown in Table 11.3.

Table 11.3 Relative Pronouns

PRONOUN	REFERENT	PRONOUN ROLE	EXAMPLE
who	person	subject	The woman **who** helped me is a nurse.
whom	person	object	The man **whom** I met had a wooden leg.
which	thing	subject/object	The book **which** he bought cost ten dollars.
that	thing/person	subectj/object	The disease **that** we are studying is called AIDS.
whose + N	person/thing	poss. subject/obect	The boy **whose** leg is broken is in Room 137.

EXERCISE 11.7

Directions: Fill the blank with *who, whom, which, that,* or *whose.*

1. The actor _____ played Dracula has had trouble finding other roles.

2. The thing _____ I like about June is her sense of humor.

3. The person with _____ you should talk is the vice president.

4. The state _____ economy was most affected by the storm was Florida.

5. The city _____ we really enjoyed was Sarajevo.

6. My uncle works with a woman _____ spent seven years in Zimbabwe.

7. It would be impossible to live on a planet _____ atmosphere had no oxygen.

8. This wine was prepared by a method _____ has been used for centuries.

9. That doctor is not a man in _____ I have a great deal of confidence.

10. Heloise had to sell the ring _____ her mother had given her.

The Construction of Adjective Clauses

One way to understand the construction of adjective clauses is by deriving them through the process known as sentence combining (we used a similar process to generate noun clauses). In this process, two sentences that share a common NP are combined into a single sentence containing an adjective clause. In other words, one of the sentences is transformed into a dependent clause, which thus becomes subordinate to the other sentence (the independent clause). The shared NP in the subordinate clause is replaced with a relative pronoun, which becomes the clause marker for the adjective clause. The adjective clause is then inserted into the original sentence directly after the common NP.

FORMS OF ADJECTIVE CLAUSES

The construction of an adjective clause depends on whether it has the subject form (S-form) or the predicate form (P-form).

S-Form Adjective Clauses

An S-form (or subject form) adjective clause is one in which the relative pronoun replaces a noun phrase that is the **subject** of the clause. Look at the following example:

a) The man is a doctor.   [main clause]

+b) **The man** lives next door.   [subordinate clause]

c) The man <u>who lives next door</u> is a doctor.

In this example, Sentence (a) is the main clause while Sentence (b) is the subordinate clause that will be inserted into Sentence (a) after being transformed into an adjective clause. The result is Sentence (c). This is possible only because the two sentences share a common NP, *the man*. The shared NP (in boldface) in the subordinate clause is replaced with the relative pronoun *who* because the NP is a person rather than a thing and because it replaces a subject NP rather than an object NP (see Table 11.3).

An adjective clause is usually less important or relevant (hence, subordinate) to the topic of discussion than the main clause, often because the information it contains is already known to the listener. In Sentence (c), we can imagine that the topic of discussion is the qualities of the man (who happens to live next door) and that the speaker is providing new information about this man, namely, that he is a doctor. If the topic of discussion were the houses of the people living in the neighborhood, the man's profession would be less important (perhaps already known) than where he lives, and the resulting sentence combination might be: *The man who is a doctor lives next door.* Thus, the decision as to which sentence should be the main clause and which the subordinate clause depends on the topic of discussion.

The procedure for making an S-form adjective clause can be expressed as a series of steps:

••Steps for Making an S-Form Adjective Clause by Sentence Combining••	*Example:* The man is a doctor. + The man lives next door.
1. Decide which of the two sentences is the subordinate clause.	*the man lives next door*
2. Identify the common NP.	*the man*
3. Determine whether the NP is a person, thing, or possessive.	*the man* = <u>person</u>
4. Determine the role of the NP in the subordinate clause.	*the man* = <u>subject</u>
5. Select the appropriate relative pronoun.	person + subject → <u>*who*</u>
6. Replace the NP in the subordinate clause with the relative pronoun to make the adjective clause.	<u>who</u> lives next door
7. Insert the adjective clause after the common NP in the main clause.	The man <u>who lives next door</u> is a doctor.

EXERCISE 11.8

Directions: Using the steps above, combine the following pairs of sentences into a single sentence containing an adjective clause. Let (a) be the main clause and (b) the subordinate clause.

1. (a) The boy is only ten years old.
    (b) The boy delivers the paper.

2. (a) The dog was taken to the pound.
    (b) The dog bit the mailman.

3. (a) The plane was trying to land at JFK Airport.
    (b) The plane crashed.

4. (a) The bank was robbed last night.
    (b) The bank gave us a loan.

5. (a) The girl will live with her older sister.
    (b) The girl lost her mother last week.

Since noun phrases occur as the subject, the object, the indirect object, and the object of a preposition and since an adjective clause must be part of a noun phrase, it follows that adjective clauses can also occur in these sentence positions. All of the S-form examples that we have looked at so far have been S-form adjective clauses that modify the subject NP. However, S-form adjective clauses can occur in any sentence position that allows an NP.[6] Look at the following examples:

---

[6] S-form adjective clauses parallel other S-form structures in which a WH-pronoun replaces the subject NP of the clause:
  a) WH-QUESTIONS: <u>Who</u> stole the pies?
  b) NOUN CLAUSES (Embedded WH-Question): We don't know <u>what</u> caused the fire.
  c) ADJECTIVE CLAUSES: The man <u>who</u> helps us is a male nurse.
Notice that the WH-pronoun is always followed by a verb, which is what we expect if the pronoun is the subject.

   a) DIRECT OBJECT: The police found <u>the boy **who took the money**</u>.
   b) INDIRECT OBJECT: An old lady gave <u>the boy **who took the money**</u> a lecture.
   c) OBJECT OF PREPOSITION: A counselor talked with <u>the boy **who took the**</u>
              <u>money</u>.

EXERCISE 11.9

Directions: Underline the nouns in the following sentences. Then insert the S-form relative clause
          in brackets after the appropriate noun.

1.   The airline offered the passengers a free ticket. [that had waited the longest]

2.   People can cause nonsmokers to get cancer. [who smoke cigarettes]

3.   The hotel gave the irate guests a room. [which had no bathroom]

4.   The dog was lying next to a bird. [whose feathers were saturated with oil]

5.   The play was about a man and his father in a prison camp. [that disturbed me the most]

S-FORM ADJECTIVE CLAUSES WITH *WHOSE*

   S-form adjective clauses with *whose* follow the procedure for the construction of S-form
adjective clauses. The only difference is that the common NP in the main clause must be in the
possessive form in the subordinate clause. Look at the following example:

   a) The man was taken to the hospital.   [main clause]
 + b) **The man's** <u>lung collapsed.</u>   [subordinate clause]
   c) The man <u>whose lung collapsed</u> was taken to the hospital.

   The common noun phrase in the two sentences is *the man*. However, in the subordinate
clause *the man* has been made into a possessive determiner by the addition of *'s*. It is this situation that requires the use of *whose* as it is also a possessive determiner. Since no determiner
can stand alone, *whose* must always be accompanied by the noun to which it is attached,
which in this case is *lung*.

EXERCISE 11.10 ⊘

Directions: Combine the following pairs of sentences into an S-form adjective clause with *whose*.
          Let (a) be the main clause and (b) the subordinate clause.

1.   (a) The student will win a trip to Disneyland.
     (b) The student's grades improve the most.
              whose grades improve the most
2.   (a) The trees will not suffer during the drought.
     (b) The trees' roots have reached the water table.
              whose roots have reached the water table
3.   (a) The woman ran to the next village for help.
     (b) The woman's friend was bitten by a poisonous snake.
              whose friend was bitten by a poisonous snake
4.   (a) A truck should use the runaway truck ramp.
     (b) A truck's brakes fail on this hill.
              whose brakes fail on this hill

5.   (a) A neighbor is not a good neighbor.
     (b) A neighbor's dog barks all night.

whose dog barks all night.

P-Form Adjective Clauses

A P-form (or predicate form) adjective clause is one in which the relative pronoun replaces a noun phrase that occurs in the **predicate** of the clause. Look at the following example:

a) The man is a doctor.   [main clause]

+b) I met **the man**. _____   [subordinate clause]

c) The man <u>whom I met</u> is a doctor.

In this example, Sentence (a) is the main clause while Sentence (b) is the subordinate clause that is inserted into Sentence (a) after being transformed into an adjective clause. The result is Sentence (c). This is possible only because the two sentences share a common NP, *the man*. The shared NP in the subordinate clause (in boldface) is replaced with the relative pronoun *whom*[7] because the head noun represents a person rather than a thing and because it replaces an NP in the predicate (the object) rather than a subject NP. However, since *whom* is the clause marker for the adjective clause and we know that all clause markers must come at the beginning of the clause, we must move the relative pronoun to the front of the clause to get *whom I met*. The adjective clause is then inserted into the original sentence directly after the common NP. This movement of the relative pronoun is the difference between S-form and P-form adjective clauses. The difference is shown in the following examples:

a) P-FORM: This is the dog <u>that Mary bit</u>.

b) S-FORM: This is the dog <u>that bit Mary</u>.

The marked difference in meaning between the two otherwise identical sentences shows the effect of using one adjective clause form over the other. The P-form adjective clause in Sentence (a) is derived from the sentence *Mary bit the dog*. The S-form adjective clause in Sentence (b) is derived from the sentence *The dog bit Mary*.

P-FORM ADJECTIVE CLAUSES WITH *WHOSE*

P-form adjective clauses with *whose* follow the procedure for the construction of P-form adjective clauses, except that the common NP in the main sentence must be in the possessive form in the subordinate clause. Look at the following example:

a) The woman gave me a reward.   [main clause]

+b) I found **the woman's** wallet. _____   [subordinate clause]

c) The woman <u>whose wallet I found</u> gave me a reward.

The common noun phrase in the two sentences is *the woman*. In the subordinate clause (b), *the woman* has the form of a possessive determiner (*the woman's*). It must therefore be replaced with the relative pronoun *whose* accompanied by the noun to which it is attached, which in this case is *wallet*.

EXERCISE 11.11

Directions: Combine the following pairs of sentences into a single sentence containing a P-f adjective clause with *whose*. Let (a) be the main clause and (b) the subordinate cla

_____

[7] The relative pronoun *who* is also grammatically correct in this sentence. However, for the sake of consist
  ~ause *whom* is required in P-form adjective clauses with fronted prepositions, all uses of *who* in P-forr
   are shown with *whom*. The *m* in *whom* is consistent with the *m* in the object pronouns *him* and *t*

1. (a) The lady was not satisfied.
   (b) Betty made the lady's dress.

2. (a) The planet is the moon.
   (b) Mankind first landed on the moon's surface.

3. (a) A fawn has little chance of survival.
   (b) A hunter has killed a fawn's mother.

4. (a) The virus continued to destroy programs.
   (b) The computer engineers were searching for the virus's structure.

5. (a) People deserve a new government.
   (b) A government cannot protect people's lives.

The procedure for making P-form adjective clauses is shown below.

••**Steps for Making a P-Form Adjective Clause by Sentence Combining**••	**Example:** The man is a doctor. + <u>I met the man.</u>
1. Decide which of the two sentences is the subordinate clause.	<u>I met the man</u>
2. Identify the common NP.	*the man*
3. Determine whether the NP is a person, thing, or possessive.	*the man* = <u>person</u>
4. Determine the role of the NP in the subordinate clause.	*the man* = <u>object</u>
5. Select the appropriate relative pronoun.	person + object → <u>*whom*</u>
6. Replace the NP in the subordinate clause with the relative pronoun.	*I met <u>whom</u>
7. Move the relative pronoun to the front of the clause.	<u>whom</u> I met
8. Insert the adjective clause after the common NP in the main clause.	The man <u>whom I met</u> is a doctor.

EXERCISE 11.12 ◉

Directions: Using the steps above, combine the following pairs of sentences into a single sentence containing a P-form adjective clause. Let (a) be the main clause and (b) the subordinate clause.

1. (a) The classes were really interesting.
   (b) We took the classes last semester.
   which we took last semester

2. (a) Some of the astronauts became public figures.
   (b) The U.S. sent the astronauts to the moon.
   whom the U.S. sent to the moon.

3. (a) The film is *Europa, Europa*.   *which helen most enjoyed*
   (b) Helen most enjoyed the film.

4. (a) The villagers can hardly be expected to support the government.
   (b) The army tortured the villagers.   *that the army tortured*

5. (a) The volcano spewed hot ashes up to 25 miles away.
   (b) Scientists had predicted the volcano's erruption.   *whose erruption scientists predicted*

Like S-form adjective clauses, P-form adjective clauses can occur in any sentence position that allows an NP.[8] Look at the following examples:

   a) DIRECT OBJECT: The couple saw the baby **which they had adopted**.
   b) INDIRECT OBJECT: The woman gave the baby **which she had adopted** a bath.
   c) OBJECT OF PREPOSITION: The man played with the baby **which he had adopted**.

EXERCISE 11.13

Directions: Underline the nouns in the following sentences. Then insert the P-form relative c l a u s e in brackets after the appropriate noun.

1. The agreement allowed loaded trucks to be carried on trains. [which the government made]

2. The babysitter told the children a story. [whom she was preparing for bed]

3. The president nominated a woman. [whose accomplishments the nation admired]

4. The journalist found several errors in the article. [that the editor had rejected]

5. The bicycle should only be ridden on smooth roads. [whose tires we replaced]

P-FORM ADJECTIVE CLAUSES WITH PREPOSITIONS

When a P-form adjective clause contains a preposition in the predicate, we have the option of choosing the degree of formality of the sentence. Look at the following example:

   a) The subject is mathematics.
   +b) Paula does well in mathematics.
   c) The subject which Paula does well **in** is mathematics.   [less formal]
   d) The subject **in** which Paula does well is mathematics.   [more formal]

Sentence (c) is produced using the steps for making a P-form adjective clause. However, with the preposition in this position, the sentence is less formal, i.e., more likely to be used in colloquial spoken and written language. In Sentence (d), the preposition has been moved in

---

[8] P-form adjective clauses parallel other P-form structures in which a WH-pronoun replaces an NP in the predicate of the clause:

   a) WH-QUESTIONS: Where does Sarah live?
   b) NOUN CLAUSES (Embedded WH-Question): We don't know why the bees left.
   c) ADJECTIVE CLAUSES: The man whom she loves is a rock star.

Notice that the WH-pronoun is followed either by an auxiliary or an NP, never by a verb.

front of the relative pronoun. This makes the sentence more formal, i.e., more likely to occur in formal spoken or written language.

The more formal P-form adjective clause, unlike the less formal form, does not allow the use of the relative pronoun *that*. We can readily see this if we replace the relative pronoun *which* in Sentences (c) and (d) above with the relative pronoun *that*.

a) The subject <u>that</u> Paula does well **in** is mathematics.   [less formal]

b) *The subject **in** <u>that</u> Paula does well is mathematics.   [more formal]

Sentence (a) is grammatical with *that*, but Sentence (b) is not.

The steps for making a sentence with a formal P-form adjective clause are shown below:

••*Steps for Making a Formal P-Form Adjective Clause with a Preposition by Sentence Combining*••	*Example:* The subject is mathematics. + <u>Paula does well in mathematics.</u>
1. Decide which of the two sentences is the subordinate clause.	<u>Paula does well in mathematics</u>
2. Identify the common NP.	<u>*mathematics*</u>
3. Determine whether the NP is a person or a thing.	*mathematics* = <u>thing</u>
4. Determine the role of the NP in the subordinate clause.	*mathematics* = <u>object of prep.</u>
5 Select the appropriate relative pronoun.	thing + object of prep. → <u>*which*</u>
6. Replace the NP in the subordinate clause with the relative pronoun.	*Paula does well in <u>which</u>
7. Move the relative pronoun to the front of the clause.	<u>which</u> Paula does well in
8. Move the preposition in front of the relative pronoun.	<u>in</u> which Paula does well
9. Insert the adjective clause after the common NP in the main clause.	The subject <u>in which Paula does well</u> is mathematics.

EXERCISE 11.14

Directions: Using the steps above, combine the following pairs of sentences into a single sentence containing a formal P-form adjective clause. Let (a) be the main clause and (b) the subordinate clause.

1. (a) The country is the United States.
   (b) The UN depends on the United States for the largest proportion of its operating expenses.

2. (a) Midnight was the time.
   (b) Cinderella's carriage turned back into a pumpkin at the time.

3. (a) This is a situation.
   (b) You should not interfere in a situation.

4. (a) The printer is the device.
    (b) The company has had the most problems with the device.

5. (a) Romania is the central European nation.
    (b) Monica knows a great deal about the central European nation.

TYPES OF ADJECTIVE CLAUSES

There are two basic types of adjective clauses: defining and nondefining. The only visible difference between them is the absence or presence of commas around the adjective clause. However, the two types of clauses have different functions.

Defining Adjective Clauses

Defining[9] adjective clauses define a noun so as to differentiate it from other similar nouns. Imagine that someone told you that there was a poisonous spider in a small box in front of you and asked you to put your hand inside it. Naturally, you would refuse because you wouldn't want to be bitten. Then imagine that the same person brought out an identical box and told you that there was a $100 bill in it which you could have if you would reach in the box to get it, but then mixed up the boxes. You might be tempted to take the risk, but the chances are you would refuse to put your hand in either box. Now imagine that a trusted friend of yours is allowed to look into both of the boxes and then makes the following statement:

The box that is on your left contains the spider.

Now, without much hesitation, you could reach into the box on the right and take out the $100 bill. The reason is that by defining the box with the spider as being the one on your left, your friend has told you the contents of each box. The sentence that your friend uttered contained the defining adjective clause *that is on your left*, and it is this clause that allowed you to make the right decision.

This little story makes an important point about defining adjective clauses: the only time that we need to use a defining adjective clause is when there are at least two entities that need to be differentiated. Just as it would have been silly to say, "The box that is on your left contains the spider" if there had been only one box present, there is no reason to use a defining adjective clause when there is only one noun (or one group of nouns) that is being discussed.

Defining adjective clauses are commonly found in formal **definitions** (note the similarity of the words *defining* and *definition*) such as the following:

A thermometer is an instrument <u>that measures temperature</u>.

In this sentence, the defining adjective clause *that measures temperature* serves to differentiate the instrument called a thermometer from other instruments, such as a clock (an instrument that measures time), a speedometer (an instrument that measures speed), and so on. Definitions that contain adjective clauses are written without commas, and defining adjective clauses never have commas either. In fact, the most obvious indicator of a defining adjective clause (assuming it has been written correctly, which it often isn't) is the fact that it has **no commas**. Another indicator is the presence of the relative pronoun *that*, which may occur in defining but never in nondefining adjective clauses.

---

[9] Adjective clauses without commas have traditionally been called *restrictive* to show that the set indicated by the head noun is restricted to a limited group (whereas adjective clauses with commas indicate an unlimited set and are therefore *nonrestrictive*). Since many students apply the term *restrictive* in unintended ways, the more descriptive term *defining* is used throughout.

EXERCISE 11.15

Directions: Add a defining adjective clause after the underlined noun.

> *Example:* The carpenter was a <u>student</u>.
>
> *Solution:* The carpenter was a student who was working his way through college.

1. The <u>woman</u> had very little money.

2. A stranger bought the <u>person</u> a loaf of bread.

3. Some boys torture <u>insects</u>.

4. Joy's grandfather left her a cottage in a <u>village</u>.

5. The doctor was taking a nap when the <u>nurse</u> called him.

Nondefining Adjective Clauses

Nondefining adjective clauses are best understood by contrasting them with defining adjective clauses. Look at the following examples:

> a) My aunt who lives in New York is an actress.   [defining]
>
> b) My aunt, who lives in New York, is an actress.   [nondefining]

Sentence (a) implies that the speaker has at least two aunts, one of whom lives in New York. Sentence (b), on the other hand, implies that the speaker has only one aunt, who happens to live in New York.

The next example shows the effect on the actual number of entities implied by a defining adjective clause in contrast to a nondefining adjective clause:

> a) The cars which were painted have already begun to rust.   [defining]
>
> b) The cars, which were painted, have already begun to rust.   [nondefining]

Imagine that the speaker is a used-car salesperson with 100 cars on his lot. How many cars is the salesperson speaking about? Sentence (a) implies a number between 2 and 99. The minimum must be 2 because the head noun, *cars*, is plural. The maximum is 99 because a defining relative clause indicates that there is at least one member of the set that is not under consideration; otherwise, there would be no need to define it. Sentence (b), on the other hand, implies 100 cars because a nondefining adjective clause indicates that the entire set (i.e., all of the cars) is meant.

Another way to understand the difference between defining and nondefining relative clauses is to analyze the noun that is modified by the adjective clause (the head noun). The following examples show defining relative clauses that are not correct in the nondefining form (with the head noun in boldface):

> a)   Think of a **tree** that begins with *c*.
>
> b) *Think of a **tree**, which begins with *c*.
>
> c)   Can you name three **animals** that live underground?
>
> d) *Can you name three **animals**, which live underground?

In Sentence (a), the singular head noun *tree* represents **one of many** trees that begin with *c*. Sentence (b) is incorrect because it suggests that the word *tree* begins with *c*. In Sentence (c), the plural head noun *animals* represents **some** of the animals that live underground (there are many more than three). Sentence (d) is incorrect, except perhaps as an informal spoken afterthought.[10]

For comparison, the following examples (with the head noun in boldface) show nondefining relative clauses that are not correct in the defining form:

   a)   The **Eiffel Tower**, which is the pride of Paris, was constructed in 1889.

   b)   *The **Eiffel Tower** that is the pride of Paris was constructed in 1889.

   c)   The **Himalayas**, which include Mt. Everest, are the highest mountains in the world.

   d)   *The **Himalayas** that include Mt. Everest are the highest mountains in the world.

In Sentence (a), the singular head noun *Eiffel Tower* represents the only one that exists. Sentence (b) is incorrect because it implies that there are other Eiffel Towers, which we know is not the case. In Sentence (c), the plural head noun *Himalayas* represents all of the mountains in the Himalaya range. Sentence (d) is incorrect because it suggests that there are other ranges of Himalayas, which we also know is not the case.

The different features of defining and nondefining adjective clauses are compared in Table 11.4.

Table 11.4 Comparison of Defining and Nondefining Adjective Clauses

FEATURE	DEFINING ADJECTIVE CLAUSES	NONDEFINING ADJECTIVE CLAUSES
Information supplied:	essential	nonessential
Implies head noun is **when singular:** **when plural:**	 one of many some members of a set	 the only one all members of a set.
Use of commas:	not allowed	required
Relative pronouns **used with:**	*who, whom, which, whose,* and *that*	*who, whom, which, whose* (but not *that*)

A logical way to introduce the differences between defining and nondefining adjective clauses is to provide sample sentences using common nouns with defining adjective clauses and proper nouns with nondefining adjective clauses. Proper nouns are good candidates for nondefining adjective clauses because it is usually common knowledge that there is only one of them. Later, potentially ambiguous sentences can be introduced.

EXERCISE 11.16

Directions: Add commas to the following sentences where necessary. State the implications of the sentence if the commas are not present.

---

[10] Informal English allows nondefining adjective clauses that comment on the clause they follow rather than modifying a particular noun in it. In this case, the adjective clause is not part of an overt NP.

   a) The woman told Joe to hide behind the store, which saved him from the angry mob.

   b) Susan gave me a lot of useful advice, which was very kind of her.

1. The person whom my cousin married was from a poor family.
   other relatives married from a richer family

2. Margaret Thatcher, who used to be the Prime Minister of Great Britain, was the first woman to hold that office. *sentence is okay*

3. Buses, which usually have no dining facilities, are an uncomfortable way to travel long distances.

4. The planets which have rings orbit in the outer Solar System.
   have some rings

5. Few creatures are stronger than the ant, which can carry many times its body weight.

6. The European Common Market, which unites most of the countries of Europe into a single economic block, has had a variety of difficulties to overcome.

7. Flying saucers, for which there has never been any material evidence, still excite the imaginations of modern earthlings.

8. Many people do not eat sufficient dietary fiber, which is thought to reduce the risk of colon cancer.

9. The Maya, whose settlements date back to 9000 B.C., first appeared on the shores of Belize.

10. The energy which fires the Sun is being harnessed in the laboratory as fusion power.
    only the sun's energy

The Reduction of Adjective Clauses

Reduction is the removal of words from a sentence that do not affect the meaning in any way. Function words are removed in this process, but not content words. In the reduction of adjective clauses, only the relative pronouns and certain forms of *be* may be removed. The two major types of reduction are dependent on the form of the adjective clause. We will begin with P-form reduction, as it is the simplest form, and then look at S-form reduction.

P-FORM REDUCTION

P-form reduction is only possible with defining adjective clauses. Nondefining P-form adjective clauses must retain their full, nonreduced form.

The Reduction of P-Form Defining Adjective Clauses

The reduction of defining P-form adjective clauses requires the removal of the relative pronoun. Look at the following example:

a) The man <u>whom I met</u> is a doctor.   [nonreduced form]
b) The man <u>I met</u> is a doctor.   [reduced form]

The example shows the reduction of the adjective clause *whom I met* in Sentence (a) to *I met* in Sentence (b). *Whom* is the relative pronoun that occurs only in P-form adjective clauses. Since reduction is applied in all but the most formal academic contexts, the relative pronoun *whom* is usually absent, which explains why many native speakers feel unsure about the correct use of *whom* in English. The relative pronouns *which* and *that* are also typically removed when they occur in P-form adjective clauses. However, *whose + NOUN* can never be reduced because the clause marker (*whose*) is attached to a content word whose removal would affect the meaning of the sentence, as shown in the following example:

    a)   The man <u>whose leg was broken</u> is in Room 107.

    b) *The man <u>was broken</u> in Room 107.

Formal defining adjective clauses with fronted propositions may also not be reduced, as shown in the following example:

    a)   The city <u>in which Einstein was born</u> is Ulm, Germany.

    b) *The city <u>in Einstein was born</u> is Ulm, Germany.

EXERCISE 11.17

Directions: Reduce the following adjective clauses. If reduction is not possible, explain why.

1. The magazine that Jacob is reading contains a story about his sister.

2. A vegetable that has seeds is technically a fruit.

3. The young couple did not like the house which the realtors showed them.

4. The political appointees to whom the President referred are becoming increasingly nervous.

5. One species whose existence is seriously threatened is the cheetah.

6. The ferry, which is always on time, runs between Naples and Palermo.

7. A television station gave a man whom I work with a free ticket to Hawaii.

8. Some men are intimidated by a woman who knows her own strength.

9. The room that the guest complained about was directly above the kitchen.

10. John's grandmother, whom he loved with all his heart, came from an aristocratic family.

S-FORM REDUCTION

S-form reduction is possible with both defining and nondefining adjective clauses.

Reduction of S-Form Defining Adjective Clauses

S-form defining adjective clauses can be reduced when the main or auxiliary verb *be* is present. To reduce the clause, we take out both the relative pronoun and the auxiliary. Look at the following examples:

    a) The money ~~which was~~ **stolen** from the bank was never recovered.

    b) The money stolen from the bank was never recovered.

    c) The man ~~who is~~ **sitting** on that bench is Sally's teacher.

    d) The man sitting on that bench is Sally's teacher.

    e) The apples ~~that are~~ **on** the table are mine.

    f) The apples on the table are mine.

These examples show that when *be* is followed by VERB$_{ed2}$, VERB$_{ing}$, or a preposition (in boldface) in an adjective clause, it may be reduced. On the other hand, when *be* is followed by an adjective[11] or a noun phrase in an adjective clause, it may not be reduced. Look at the following examples:

a)   Women <u>who are beautiful</u> are often unhappy.

b)   *Women beautiful are often unhappy.

c)   A teacher <u>who is a parent</u> is not necessarily a better teacher.

d)   *A teacher a parent is not necessarily a better teacher.

EXERCISE 11.18

Directions: Reduce the following S-form defining adjective clauses. If reduction is not possible, explain why.

1.   The person who is teaching this ESL class is a graduate student in Applied Linguistics.

2.   We have learned more about the planets which are in the Solar System than in any other decade in history.

3.   Children who are overweight are often ostracized.

4.   Cats that are spayed at six months of age appear to be least harmed by the process.

5.   Type A personalities are associated with men and women who are very competitive.

S-form defining adjective clause reduction can result in what appears to be the postmodification of a noun with an attributive adjective (which is possible in some languages but not in English). Look at the following examples:

a)   In the script you are performing, the <u>underlined</u> *words* require special emphasis.

b)   In this first draft of your paper, the *words* <u>underlined</u> need to be changed.

In Sentence (a), *underlined* is an attributive adjective. Like most attributive adjectives, it describes a permanent or characteristic feature, i.e., that the script is printed with underlined words to aid the actor. In Sentence (b), *underlined* is the reduced form of *that are underlined.* Like most predicate adjectives, it describes a temporary or occasional feature, i.e., that the words have been underlined in a draft of a paper which will soon be revised and written again without such markings. However, the permanent/temporary distinction is not a rigid one for many native speakers of English.

---

[11] A few adjectives ending in *-ble* do allow S-form reduction, e.g., *capable, possible, responsible,* and *visible).*

EXERCISE 11.19

Directions: Decide if the the underlined noun requires a permanent or a temporary form of the adjective in parentheses and insert it in the appropriate place.

1. (ruined) a. He was a <u>man</u>, an individual whose life would be forever changed.
   b. Yesterday, he was a <u>man</u>. Today, he's on top of the world.

2. (expelled) a. After the explosion, the <u>gas</u> will be collected and analyzed.
   b. <u>Students</u> are not allowed to register for new classes.

3. (listed) a. The <u>courses</u> in the Spring schedule are subject to change.
   b. The <u>ingredients</u> in this can of peaches include sugar and water.

4. (visible) a. Venus is one of the <u>planets</u> in the night sky.
   b. Venus was the only <u>planet</u> that cloudy night.

5. (given) a. All substances melt at a <u>temperature</u>.
   b. The only <u>information</u> was that a tornado might touch down sometime during the night.

Reduction of S-Form Nondefining Adjective Clauses

When the auxiliary *be* is present, an S-form nondefining adjective clause can also be reduced. We remove the relative pronoun along with the auxiliary if it is followed by VERB$_{ed2}$, VERB$_{ing}$ or a preposition (shown in boldface below). Look at the following examples:

a) Sylvia, ~~who was~~ **married** at eighteen, was still happy with her husband 45 years later.

b) Sylvia, married at eighteen, was still happy with her husband 45 years later.

c) Sargeant Crow, ~~who was~~ **standing** by the door, had seen no one enter the house.

d) Sargeant Crow, standing by the door, had seen no one enter the house.

e) The king, ~~who was~~ **under** pressure from his government, allowed tourists to enter his palace.

f) The king, under pressure from his government, allowed tourists to enter his palace.

This type of reduction is usually only possible when some form of postmodification is also present (i.e., *at eighteen*, *by the door*, and *from his government*).

APPOSITIVE CLAUSES

If the main (or linking) verb *be* is present, a nondefining adjective clause may be reduced when it is followed by a predicate noun phrase. Look at the following example:

a) Dr. Oporto, ~~who is~~ a physician at the UCLA Medical Center, has an international reputation.

b) Dr. Oporto, a physician at the UCLA Medical Center, has an international reputation.

The reduced nondefining S-form adjective clause in Sentence (b) is an **appositive clause**. Its primary function is to provide identifying information about the head noun it modifies. If that noun is a person, it often indicates rank or position.

EXERCISE 11.20

Directions: Add the appositive clause in brackets at the appropriate place in the sentence.

1. Dr. R.D. Smith introduced his new graduate assistant. [an Associate Professor of Biology]

2. Berlin is 1078 air miles from Istanbul. [the new capital of Germany]

3. The magma is forced up through the vent to the volcanic crater. [a body of molten rock]

4. Rudolf Nureyev never danced with Mikhail Baryshnikov. [the first Russian ballet dancer to defect to the West]

5. Ruth Bader Ginsburg has joined Sandra Day O'Connor on the bench. [the second woman on the U.S. Supreme Court]

EXERCISE 11.21

Directions: Reduce the following S-form nondefining adjective clauses. If reduction is not possible, explain why.

1. Gerald cannot stand his uncle, who is well-meaning but selfish.

2. The clouds, which are moving in from the west, will bring us much-needed rain.

3. The shaman, whose advice was taken very seriously by every member of the community, could not prevent the oil companies from drilling on tribal land.

4. The old bull, who is in a field by himself, is not particularly friendly to humans.

5. Deciduous trees, which require abundant water, lose their autumn leaves early in times of drought.

EXERCISE 11.22 ●

Directions: Reduce the following adjective clauses. If reduction is not possible, explain why.

1. The book which I am currently reading takes place in South Africa.

2. Dr. Smith, who is a physician at Valley Medical Center, was nominated for a Nobel Prize.

3. A house which is painted is more valuable than one which is not.

4. Tomatoes that are grown in Fresno are larger than those grown in Oakland.

5. The box which is in the garage needs to be taken to the dump.

6. The physics professor, whom Michael cannot stand, required a thirty-page research report.

7. The high density of stars in the Milky Way, which can be seen as a faint path across the sky, results from looking along the plane of the galaxy.

8. The telephone, which was invented by Alexander Graham Bell, has brought the world together.

9. Stars which are red are older than stars which are blue.

10. A turtle, which was found dead on the beach, was covered with sticky oil.

Problem Solving with the Adjective Clause System

In the problems below it is possible to get the following right:

   a. correct CATEGORY OF RELATIVE PRONOUN (*who/whom/that* for a person, *which/that* for a thing, no *that* after prepositions or in nondefining adjective clauses)

   b. correct GRAMMATICAL FORM OF RELATIVE PRONOUN (S-form, P-form)

   c. correct PLACEMENT OF ADJECTIVE CLAUSE (directly after the head noun it modifies)

   d. correct PLACEMENT OF PREPOSITION (in front of WH-relative pronouns in formal contexts, after verb in informal contexts)

   e. correct REDUCTION FORM (remove relative pronoun in P-form reduction, remove relative pronoun + *be* in S-form reduction)

   f. correct DEFINING/NONDEFINING PUNCTUATION (defining + no commas, nondefining + commas)

These elements reflect what students are likely to do wrong in using an adjective clause: a) fail to select the appropriate relative pronoun, b) use the incorrect form of a relative pronoun (applies only to *who* versus *whom*), c) put the adjective clause in the wrong position, (d) put a preposition in the wrong place, e) use an incorrect or impossible form of adjective clause reduction, or f), use the incorrect punctuation with an adjective clause.

EXERCISE 11.23 ⊘

Directions: In the following sentences, a student made a single error in using an adjective clause. Your job is to address the error in three stages:

   a) bracket the error to focus your attention

   b) list what the student got right about the bracketed error (in this case, the error concerns the adjective clause) and show this in parentheses OPTIONAL: Derive the adjective clause from its uncombined form

   c) compare the original erroneous sentence to the correct sentence and explain what mistake the student made

Example: *The woman which applied for the job was from India.
         [The star (*) indicates that the sentence contains an error.]

Solution:

   a) Bracket the error (some aspect of the adjective clause):
      *The woman [which] applied for the job was from India.

   b) Show what is right about the adjective clause:
      correct placement of adjective clause (directly after the head noun *woman*)
      correct defining/nondefining punctuation (defining + no commas)

Derivation: The woman is from India.
                  + The woman applied for the job.

1. Decide which of the two sentences is the   the woman applied for the job
    subordinate clause.
2. Identify the common NP.   *the woman*
3. Determine whether the NP is a person, thing,   *the woman* = person
    or possessive
4. Determine the role of the NP in the .   *the woman* = subject
    clause sentence
5. Select the appropriate relative pronoun.   person + subject→*who*
6. Replace the NP in the clause sentence   who applied for the job
    with the relative pronoun to make
    the adjective clause.
7. Insert the adjective clause after the   The woman who applied for
    common NP in the main sentence.   the job is from India.

    c) Compare the erroneous sentence to the correct form and explain
    the mistake:
        *The woman [which] applied for the job was from India.
        The woman   who   applied for the job was from India.

Explanation: Since the head noun *(woman)* is a person, a form of *who* is required.
            Which is only used for things.

1. *John doesn't like the [whom he met girl.]
2. *The man (whom) told you that story is a liar.
3. *John rides a motorcycle, who lives in Los Angeles.]
4. *Mary can't find the room in that she stayed.
5. *The books, they bought at a library sale, are all paperbacks.
6. *The CIA, that has its headquarters in Washington D.C., is feared by many people.
7. *The man with who I travelled to Atlanta was an old friend.
8. *Jan's mother who was born in Detroit came to California in 1941.
9. *The student is sitting in your office wants to talk to you.
10. *John's girlfriend, he plans to marry someday, has a Mercedes.
11. *The computer George wants it costs over $2000.
12. *A man, who is wealthy, is not neccessarily happy.
13. *The class Alice really likes which is philosophy.
14. *The student helped me to correct the exams receives financial aid.
15. *The boy stole a sandwich who lives next door.

UNIT IV: THE ADVERB

Chapter 12

THE ADVERBIAL SYSTEM

The adverbial system includes the words, phrases, and clauses that modify a verb. Adverbials are the most mobile elements in English grammar, and most can take more than one sentence position: sentence-initial (before the subject), sentence-medial I (after the first auxiliary), sentence medial II (after the subject), and sentence-final (at the end of the sentence), as shown in the following examples:

SENTENCE-INITIAL POSITION: <u>Generally</u>, the weather has been quite good this year.

SENTENCE-MEDIAL POSITION I: The weather has <u>generally</u> been quite good this year.

SENTENCE-MEDIAL POSITION II: The weather, <u>generally</u>, has been quite good this year.

SENTENCE-FINAL POSITION: The weather has been quite good this year <u>generally</u>.

Sentence-final position is the position that almost all adverbials can take. It is also where we have become accustomed to finding the adverbial slot. Many adverbials can also take sentence-initial position. However, sentence-medial position I is generally restricted to adverbs, while sentence-medial position II is likely to be used only with very short phrases or in "repairing" conversations (e.g., *Timothy, although he hates piano lessons, agreed to practice for six months.*)

The adverbial system includes adverbs, prepositional phrases, adverb clauses, and prepositional noun phrases (i.e., prepositional phrases without a preposition), as shown in the following examples:

a) ADVERB: Lawrence drove his bus <u>carefully</u>.

b) PREPOSITIONAL PHRASE: Lawrence drove his bus <u>without a license</u>.

c) ADVERB CLAUSE: Lawrence drove his bus <u>even though he was sick</u>.

d) PREPOSITIONAL NOUN PHRASE: Lawrence drove his bus <u>last night</u>.

The following sections treat the four kinds of adverbials separately, even though they all share the same function of showing manner, place, and time. If more than one adverbial is present and they are of equal length, they tend to order themselves in the manner-place-time sequence, as shown in the following example, though many native speakers would also find place-manner-time an acceptable sequence:

MANNER   PLACE   TIME

The old man worked <u>tirelessly</u> <u>in his workshop</u> <u>every night</u>.

However, it is rare to have three structures in the adverbial slot in a single sentence. The example sentence sounds better when one of the structures is fronted:

<u>Every night</u>, the old man worked <u>tirelessly</u> <u>in his workshop</u>.

ADVERBS

The adverbs are perhaps the most difficult word class to grasp because they have many different functions and because they can take different positions in a sentence. Certain adverbs also serve to modify other word classes. The generalization, "If you're not sure which class a word belongs to, it's probably an adverb" indicates the difficulty that people often have in identifying them. Many adverbs can be identified by the presence of the derivational morpheme -*ly* at the end of the word, though there are several exceptions (e.g., *fast*, *often*, *well*, *too*).

Adverb Suffixes

There is one derivational morpheme for changing adjectives into adverbs, one for changing nouns into adverbs, and one for changing prepositions and prepositional noun phrases into adverbs. The first morpheme (-*ly*) occurs much more frequently than the others. The adverb suffixes are shown in Table 12.1.

Table 12.1 Suffixes that Change Adjectives, Nouns, and Prepositions into Adverbs

PART OF SPEECH	SUFFIX	EXAMPLE	ADVERB
Adjective	-ly	quick	quickly
		sad	sadly
		usual	usually
Noun	-wise	clock	clockwise
		weather	weatherwise
Preposition **Prepositional NP**	-ward(s)	back	backwards
		home	homeward(s)
		west	westward(s)

EXERCISE 12.1

Directions: Put the adjective, noun, preposition, or prepositional noun phrase in parentheses into the correct adverb form in the blank.

1. Leontyne Price sang the part of Aida (beautiful) _____ .

2. The satellite signal was finally directed (earth) _____ by the computers at Mission Control.

3. Ralph doesn't have much experience (education) _____, but he's a wizard at fixing electronic instruments.

4. Rosetta answered the telephone somewhat (guarded) _____ for several weeks after the man who had been harassing her was apprehended.

5. The trend has always been for people to move to the west, but now they seem to be heading (east) _____ again.

The Functions of Adverbs

Adverbs have many different functions but the most frequent is to show manner, place, and time.

MANNER ADVERBS

The manner adverbs generally answer the question *How*? They show ways and means (in answer to the questions *In what way?* or *By what means?*), intensification (in answer to the questions *To what extent?* or *How intensely?* with either a positive or negative effect), and point of view (in answer to the questions *From what point of view?* or *From whose point of view?*). Look at the following examples:

Function	Example
Ways and Means In what way? By what means?	a) He spoke to her <u>courteously</u> b) The Siamese twins were separated <u>surgically</u>. c) The evidence was examined <u>microscopically</u>.
Intensification To what extent? How intensely?	a) They <u>certainly</u> were impolite! b) Eric <u>absolutely</u> refuses to leave. c) Sylvia <u>barely</u> caught the train.
Point of View From what/whose point of view?	a) <u>Financially</u>, it's a very sound proposition. b) The coup d'etat was disastrous <u>politically</u>. c) <u>Weatherwise</u>, temperatures should drop later tonight.

EXERCISE 12.2

Directions: In the blank, indicate the function of the underlined adverbs (ways and means, intensification, or point of view).

1. _____ Jake was treated <u>abusively</u> as a child.

2. _____ <u>Technically</u>, Washburn won the match.

3. _____ The room must be cleaned <u>thoroughly</u> before you leave.

4. _____ The stage can be raised <u>hydraulically</u>.

5. _____ The army <u>nearly</u> forced me to quit.

6. _____ The parachute opens <u>automatically</u>.

7. _____ <u>Frankly</u>, I don't care where you go.

8. _____ The northern part of the city is <u>ethnically</u> quite varied.

9. _____ Robin has always dressed rather <u>carelessly</u>.

10. _____ These two plays differ <u>stylistically</u>.

PLACE ADVERBS

The place adverbs answer the question *Where?*, indicating either location (answering the question *In what location?*) or direction (answering the question *In which direction?*). There are comparatively few adverbs that show place as this function is dominated by prepositional phrases. Look at the following examples:

Function	Example
Location In what location?	a) These tomatoes are grown <u>locally</u>.
Direction In which direction?	a) The swallows fly <u>southward</u> in the winter. b) The soldiers marched <u>homeward</u>.

TIME ADVERBS

The time adverbs answer the question *When?* They generally indicate a point in time (answering the questions *At what time?* or *At what point?*), duration (answering the question *For how long?*), or frequency (answering the question *How often?*). Look at the following examples:

Function	Example

Point in time
  At what time?
  At what point?
	a) The reporters spoke <u>simultaneously</u>.
	b) The actress <u>eventually</u> won the Oscar.
	c) <u>Subsequently</u>, the city center was closed to traffic.

Duration For how long?	a) We haven't seen any good movies <u>lately</u>. b) John is <u>temporarily</u> out of work. c) The school was closed <u>indefinitely</u>.
Frequency How often?	a) The principal is paid <u>monthly</u>. b) <u>Ordinarily</u>, the church is not open on Tuesdays. c) Falcons are <u>rarely</u> seen here anymore.

EXERCISE 12.3

Directions: In the blank, indicate the function of the underlined adverbs (point in time, duration, or frequency).

1. _____ The hospital was ordered to close <u>immediately</u>.

2. _____ The bridge has been closed <u>permanently</u>.

3. _____ We watch the news <u>nightly</u>.

4. _____ <u>Previously</u>, Alice had been married to a lawyer.

5. _____ The children are hungry <u>constantly</u>.

6. _____ The wine cellar is <u>presently</u> taking orders for next year's vintage.

7. _____ The President spoke <u>briefly</u> with reporters.

8. _____ This bus is <u>invariably</u> late.

9. _____ My uncle comes to visit us <u>occasionally</u>.

10. _____ Alfreda <u>recently</u> lost her glasses.

Adverbs that Modify Other Word Classes

Adverbs can modify adjectives and other adverbs, determiners, prepositions, and noun phrases. Such modification usually has the function of intensification.

ADVERBS THAT MODIFY ADJECTIVES AND OTHER ADVERBS

Most of the adverbs that modify adjectives and other adverbs come before (i.e., premodify) the word being modified. Look at the following examples:

    a) That coat is **expensive**.

    b) That coat is <u>very</u> **expensive**.

    c) John drinks **heavily**.

    d) John drinks <u>very</u> **heavily**.

Sentence (b) with an adjective (*expensive*) and Sentence (d) with an adverb (*heavily*) show the intensifying effect of the modifier *very*, the most common adverb used for this function. Other premodifying adverbs include *extremely, quite, rather, really, so, somewhat, surprisingly, terribly, unusually*, etc. In informal speech, *pretty* is used in positive environments while *that* is used in negative environments to intensify an adjective or adverb, as shown in the following examples:

    a) This beer is <u>pretty</u> tasteless.

    b) He's not <u>that</u> good-looking.

The one adverb that comes after (i.e., postmodifies) an adjective or other adverb is *enough*, as shown in the following examples:

    a) Ralph wasn't strong <u>enough</u> to lift the piano.

    b) The women didn't dress warmly <u>enough</u>.

Sentence (a) with an adjective (*strong*) and Sentence (b) with an adverb (*warmly*) show the intensifying effect of the modifier *enough*, meaning "sufficiently".

EXERCISE 12.4

Directions: Add the intensifying adverb in brackets to the sentence that follows.

1. [very] Although the storm was frightening, the house was not harmed.

2. [enough] The satellite failed to communicate because the signal wasn't strong.

3. [quite] The Charleston was popular in the 1920s.

4. [amazingly] Dr. Evans is calm under pressure, isn't he?

5. [that] Algebra isn't difficult if you put your mind to it.

ADVERBS THAT MODIFY DETERMINERS

The adverbs that modify determiners affect certain predeterminers, central determiners, and postdeterminers. These include *about, almost, approximately, nearly, over, roughly, virtually,* etc. Look at the following examples, in which the determiner is shown in boldface:

PREDETERMINER: a) <u>Almost</u> **all** the children were undernourished.

CENTRAL DETERMINER: b) <u>Nearly</u> **every** nuclear plant had had some kind of malfunction.

POSTDETERMINER: c) <u>Over</u> **20,000** people were killed in the Indian earthquake.

ADVERBS THAT MODIFY PREPOSITIONS AND NOUN PHRASES

The adverbs that modify prepositions and noun phrases are quite restricted. Prepositions can be modified by the words *just, right* and *well.*

     a) The plumber arrived <u>just</u> **in** time.

     b) The plane flew <u>right</u> **into** the mountain.

     c) The athlete jumped <u>well</u> **over** seven feet.

The most common adverb to modify a noun phrase is *quite.* Since it modifies the noun phrase, not just the noun, it precedes the determiner, as in the following examples:

     a) That's <u>quite</u> **a hat** you're wearing!

     b) Justin can be <u>quite</u> **the diplomat** when he wants to be.

EXERCISE 12.5

Directions: Add the intensifying adverb in brackets to the sentence that follows.

1. [almost] Three quarters of the planet's fresh water lies in the Antarctic Icecap.
   Almost three quarters of the planet's...
2. [well] The weight was within the tolerance limit of the elevator.
   The weight was (well) within...
3. [quite] The Riyadh Airport is a piece of architecture.
   The Riyadh Airport is a (quite) piece...
4. [over] The rent on the coast is twice the rent in the interior.
   The rent on the coast is (over) twice...
5. [just] Ruth lives outside the city limits.
   Ruth live (just) outside...

PREPOSITIONAL PHRASES

Prepositional phrases always have an adverbial function when they are not a constituent of a noun phrase. Like the adverbs, prepositional phrases occur in several positions, but they occur more often in sentence-final and sentence-initial than in sentence-medial positions.

The Functions of Prepositional Phrases

Prepositional phrases have the same general function as the adverbs. They show manner, place, and time.

MANNER PREPOSITIONAL PHRASES

Like the manner adverbs, the manner prepositional phrases generally answer the question *How?* to show ways and means, intensification, and point of view. Look at the following examples:

Function	Example
Ways and Means	a) The actor often spoke <u>in an irritating manner</u>.
In what way?	b) The rope had been cut <u>with a knife</u>.
By what means?	c) The climbers were rescued <u>by helicopter</u>.
Intensification	a) He knew <u>for certain</u> that he had won.
To what extent?	b) Erin is <u>by far</u> the best cook I know.
How intensely?	c) She is not <u>in the least</u> interested in his problems.
Point of View	a) <u>From an ecological point of view</u>, it's a disaster.
From what/whose point of view?	b) Danny never had much sense <u>with respect to money</u>.
	c) <u>From the children's perspective</u>, food means survival.

EXERCISE 12.6

Directions: In the blank, indicate the function of the underlined prepositional phrases (ways and means, intensification, or point of view).

1. _____*ways & means*_____ The sidewinder rattlesnake moves <u>in a curious fashion</u>.

2. _____*Point of view*_____ The ending of the film is unconvincing <u>from a psychological point of view</u>.

3. _____*intensification*_____ <u>Of course</u>, the boy will be expelled from school.

4. _____*ways and means*_____ It's over twenty miles <u>by road</u> to the next hostel.

5. _____*ways and means*_____ The thieves broke into the bank <u>by means of a laser gun</u>.

6. _____*intensification*_____ The sister is better than the brother <u>in all respects</u>.

7. _____*Point of view*_____ The family has little influence <u>with respect to education</u>.

8. _____*ways and means*_____ Susan wrote <u>like a Victorian novelist</u>.

9. _____*Point of view*_____ <u>As to politics</u>, my husband never tells me a thing.

10. _____*intensification*_____ The two countries still disagree <u>to some extent</u>.

PLACE PREPOSITIONAL PHRASES

The place prepositional phrases answer the question *Where?*, indicating location or direction, although most prepositional phrases can indicate both functions. Location and direction are much more likely to be indicated with a prepositional phrase than with any other kind of adverbial. Look at the following examples:

Function	Example
Location In what location?	a) The explosion occurred <u>in the basement</u>. b) <u>Underneath the landscape</u>, an exquisite portrait was discovered.
Direction In which direction?	a) The children ran <u>along the canal</u>. b) The nomads had to move <u>across the mountains</u> before the winter.

EXERCISE 12.7

Directions: In the blank, indicate the function of the underlined prepositional phrases (location or direction).

1a. _location_ The patio is <u>behind the house</u>.

  b. _direction_ The sun moved <u>behind a cloud</u>.

2a. _direction_ The little girl wandered <u>through the park</u>.

  b. _location_ The tunnel was built <u>through the mountains</u>.

3a. _location_ There's a hole <u>in your sweater</u>.

  b. _direction_ Put the cat <u>in the garage</u>.

4a. _direction_ The pelican flew <u>above the water</u>.

  b. _location_ The Jimsons live in the apartment <u>above the manager</u>.

5a. _location_ The oil derrick is situated <u>off the coast</u>.

  b. _direction_ The boat drifted <u>off course</u>.

TIME PREPOSITIONAL PHRASES

The time prepositional phrases answer the question *When?*, indicating a point in time, duration, or frequency. Look at the following examples:

Function	Example
Point in time	a) She wasn't living in Alabama <u>at that time</u>.
At what time?	b) The class begins <u>in January</u>.
At what point?	c) The boys went home <u>after the concert</u>.
Duration	a) The bear was hibernating <u>for the winter</u>.
For how long?	b) The meteorites will be visibile <u>until Tuesday</u>.
	c) <u>Since 1992</u>, the weather has been distinctly different.
Frequency	a) <u>From time to time</u>, we visit my mother-in-law.
How often?	b) <u>On Thursdays</u>, Bob cleans house.
	c) I have only been to Asia <u>on two occasions</u>.

EXERCISE 12.8

Directions: In the blank, indicate the function of the underlined prepositional phrases (point in time, duration, or frequency).

1. _Point of time_ A juggler can keep several rings, clubs, and hoops in the air <u>at the same time</u>.

2. _Frequency_ I like a pizza <u>from time to time</u>.

3. _duration_ Karen's grandfather slept <u>during the performance</u>.

4. _Frequency_ The mail is only delivered <u>on Fridays</u>.

5. _Point in time_ World War II ended <u>in 1945</u>.

6. _duration_ The strange stones had been there <u>since time immemorial</u>.

7. _Point of time_ Rita didn't like the novel very much <u>at the beginning</u>.

8. _duration_ The storm lasted <u>for several hours</u>.

9. _Frequency_ The rent is to be paid <u>by the week</u>.

10. _Point in time_ <u>Before you move in</u>, we have to establish a few ground rules.

ADVERB CLAUSES

Adverbial clauses are the most common kind of dependent clause. Like all clauses, they contain a clause marker and a subject-verb relationship. Adverb clauses occur primarily in sentence-final and sentence-initial positions.

The Functions of Adverb Clauses

Adverb clauses also show manner, place, and time.

MANNER ADVERB CLAUSES

There are very few adverb clauses that express manner as this function is usually performed by adverbs and prepositional phrases. The primary clause marker associated with manner is *as*, although *if* can occur with certain expressions, as shown in the following examples with the clause marker in boldface:

Function	Example
Ways and Means In what way?	a) She dressed **as** he wanted her to dress. b) Do **as** I say, not **as** I do.
Intensification	[not possible]
Point of View From what/whose point of view?	a) **As** far as Lydia is concerned, the wedding is off. b) **If** you ask me, I think the whole idea is absurd.

PLACE ADVERB CLAUSES

There are very few adverb clauses that express place as this function is usually performed by prepositional phrases. The primary clause markers associated with place are *where* and *wherever*, as shown in the following examples with the clause marker in boldface:

Function	Example
Location In what location?	a) John's father is buried **where** he was born. b) The animals forage **wherever** they can.
Direction In which direction?	a) I will not go **where** I am not wanted. b) The compass points **wherever** the magnet lies.

EXERCISE 12.9

Directions: Insert the appropriate clause marker of manner or place (*as, if, where,* or *wherever*) in the blanks.

1. Nancy prefers to vacation ___where___ the rich and famous congregate.

2. The young chess player wasn't very clever ___as___ far as psychology was concerned.

3. The people in this religious order live ___wherever___ the archbishop tells them to live.

4. ___if___ you ask the local residents, there'll be no peace until that dam is removed.

5. The Red Cross goes ___wherever___ people are suffering.

TIME ADVERB CLAUSES

There are several adverb clauses that express time. The primary clause markers associated with time are *after*, *as*, *before*, *once*, *since*, *until*, *when*, *whenever*, and *while*. The specific function of each clause marker (in boldface) is shown in the following examples:

Function	Example
Point in time At what time? At what point?	a) It was already past midnight **when** the plane arrived, b) **Once** we get a cat, the rats will leave. c) **After** she had left the house, Betty's headache disappeared. d) The grass needs to be cut **before** the rains come. e) **As** she was walking to her car, a man pulled up beside her.
Duration For how long?	a) Shirley hasn't seen her cousin **since** she was in school. b) **While** their parents are looking for food, the cubs are in considerable danger. c) Rodney refused to leave the burning house **until** he was sure there were no more people inside.
Frequency How often?	a) Heather's aunt goes gambling **whenever** she has the chance. b) The bell chimes **when** the clock strikes the hour.

Adverb clauses of time are generally ordered chronologically. In other words, the adverb clause is fronted if the event it describes occurs before the event in the main clause. This is exemplified in the point-in-time clauses above. In Sentence (a), being past midnight occurs before the plane arrived. In Sentence (b), getting a cat occurs before the rats will leave. In Sentence (c), Betty's leaving the house occurred before her headache disappeared.

EXERCISE 12.10

Directions: Insert the appropriate clause marker of time (*after*, *as*, *before*, *once*, *since*, *until*, *when*, *whenever*, and *while*) in the blanks.

1. __Before__ the flag was raised into the air, the fireworks lit the sky behind it.

2. The shuttle will not be launched __until__ all the safety systems are in good working order.

3. Steven lived in Los Angeles __when__ he was a boy.

4. Dimitri hasn't been back to Russia __since__ his parents left in 1948.

5. Ants come into the house __whenever__ there is too little water outside.

6. President Kennedy was shot __before__ he completed his Dallas motorcade.

7. __once__ the pipeline was repaired, the danger of explosion diminished.

8.   The second earthquake occurred ___While___ the people were clearing the rubble from the first.

9.   The hostilities began ___after___ the nations had declared independence.

10.   Jill's father works ___until___ 10 or 11 P.M. every night.

PREPOSITIONAL NOUN PHRASES

Prepositional noun phrases always have an adverbial function when they occur in the adverbial slot of a sentence. Prepositional noun phrases are essentially prepositional phrases that have lost their prepositions over time. A classic example is the prepositional NP *tomorrow*. This word is derived from the prepositional phrase *on the morrow* with the preposition *on* used as it is with all other days (e.g., *on Friday*, *on September 28*, on *New Year's Day*), but it has evolved into its present form for phonological reasons. Prepositional noun phrases occur primarily in sentence-final position, though a few can occur sentence-initially.

The Functions of Prepositional Noun Phrases

Prepositional noun phrases have the same general functions as the other adverbials. They show manner, place, and time.

MANNER PREPOSITIONAL NOUN PHRASES

Like the other manner adverbials, the manner prepositional noun phrases answer the question *How?* to show ways and means, intensification, and point of view. Look at the following examples:

Function	*Example*
Ways and Means	a) The pastry should be folded <u>this way</u>.
In what way?	b) We have to walk through the passage <u>single file</u>.
By what means?	c) Send the letter <u>first class</u>.
Intensification	a) His wife always spoke <u>a great deal.</u>
To what extent?	b) When he was nervous, Stan drank <u>a lot</u>.
How intensely?	c) The baby cries <u>a bit</u> when she is tired.
Point of View	a) <u>The way Iraq saw it</u>, Kuwait was just another province.
From what/whose point of view?	

EXERCISE 12.11

Directions: In the blank, indicate the function of the underlined prepositional noun phrases (ways and means, intensification, or point of view).

1. _____*means*_____ Cynthia would like to cook <u>the way her mother did</u>.

[handwritten above: ways]

2. _____*intensification*_____ It is a good idea to walk <u>a little bit</u> after a meal.

3. _____*Point of view*_____ <u>The way the workers see it</u>, this is only a temporary abode.

4. _____*intensification*_____ Tina used to date <u>a great deal</u> before she met her husband.

5. _____*ways and means*_____ If you don't send the package <u>air mail</u>, it will never get there in time.

PLACE PREPOSITIONAL NOUN PHRASES

The place prepositional noun phrases answer the question *Where?*, indicating location or direction. Location and direction are primarily indicated with prepositional phrases, but there are a few prepositional noun phrases that serve this function.

Function	Example
Location In what location?	a) Jacinta was born <u>a long way from here</u>. b) The hikers heard the thunder <u>a good distance away</u>. c) The bulbs are located <u>six inches below the surface</u>.
Direction In which direction?	a) The messenger has traveled <u>a long way</u> to tell you this. b) The grenade threw shrapnel <u>a good distance</u> away. c) A cow flew <u>ten feet into the air</u> before it landed.

TIME PREPOSITIONAL NOUN PHRASES

The time prepositional noun phrases answer the question *When?*, indicating a point in time, duration, or frequency. Look at the following examples:

Function	Example
Point in time At what time? At what point?	a) Whitney arrived <u>last night</u>. b) The parade takes place <u>next month</u>. c) The attack occurred <u>a year ago</u>.
Duration For how long?	a) We froze <u>the whole winter</u>. b) The truckers had been on the road <u>a long time</u>. c) The store is not open <u>weekends</u>.
Frequency How often?	a) Tom gets his hair cut <u>four times a year</u>. b) <u>Every Tuesday</u>, they have lunch with the Dean. c) Virginia has only been to Los Angeles <u>a few times</u>.

EXERCISE 12.12

Directions: In the blank, indicate the function of the underlined prepositional noun phrases (point in   time, duration, or frequency).

1. _frequency_ The moon is full <u>twelve times a year</u>.
2. _duration_ Jackie's father was miserable <u>the whole evening</u>.
3. _duration_ The lumber mill is open <u>Monday to Friday</u>.
4. _point in time_ Charlie's birthday will be celebrated <u>tomorrow</u>.
5. _frequency_ The restaurant is closed <u>every other Monday</u>.
6. _point in time_ Oil was discovered <u>the following year</u>.
7. _duration_ The pilot has only been flying <u>a short time</u>.
8. _point in time_ There have been two robberies on my block <u>this week</u>.
9. _frequency_ Sam has climbed this rock face <u>many times</u>.
10. _point in time_ The taxi was here just <u>a minute ago</u>.

REVIEW OF THE ADVERBIAL SYSTEM

The purpose of this chapter has been to show that the four types of adverbials express the same functions in different grammatical forms. This information is summarized in Table 12.2.

There are certain adverbials that have functions other than showing manner, place, and time. The most important of these are the adverbials that show cause, effect, and purpose. These will be covered in Chapter 14 when we discuss coordination and subordination.

Table 12.2 Summary of Adverbial Functions and Types

Function	Subcategory	Adverbial Type	Example	Sentence Position
manner	ways and means	adverb	carefully	initial, medial I, final
		prep. phrase	with care	initial, final
		adverb clause	as she wanted to	final
		prep. NP	this way	initial, final
	intensification	adverb	certainly	initial, medial I, final
		prep. phrase	for certain	initial, final
		adverb clause	———	———
		prep. NP	a great deal	final
	point of view	adverb	politically	initial, final
		prep. phrase	from my point of view	initial, final
		adverb clause	as far as I'm concerned	initial, final
		prep. NP	the way I see it	initial, final
place	location	adverb	locally	initial, final
		prep. phrase	near the house	initial, final
		adverb clause	where the money is	initial, final
		prep. NP	two miles from here	initial, final
	direction	adverb	westward	initial, final
		prep. phrase	into the lake	initial, final
		adverb clause	where the sun sets	initial, final
		prep. NP	a long way	final
time	point in time	adverb	simultaneously	initial, medial I, final
		prep. phrase	at two o'clock	initial, final
		adverb clause	when the cat died	initial, final
		prep. NP	last night	initial, final
	duration	adverb	indefinitely	initial, final
		prep. phrase	for an hour	initial, final
		adverb clause	since he was a boy	initial, final
		prep. NP	a long time	final
	frequency	adverb	weekly	final
		prep. phrase	on Sundays	initial, final
		adverb clause	whenever they can	initial, final
		prep. NP	every year	initial, final

PROBLEM SOLVING WITH THE ADVERBIAL SYSTEM

In the problems below it is possible to get the following right:

  a. correct ADVERBIAL TYPE (adverb, prepositional phrase, adverbial clause, or prepositional noun phrase)

  b. correct FUNCTION (manner, place, or time)

  c. correct SENTENCE POSITION (initial, medial, or final)

  d. correct POSSIBLE FORM (the structure exists in English but is not correct in this instance)

These elements reflect what students are likely to do wrong in using an adverbial: a) fail to select the correct type of adverbial, b) choose an inappropriate function for a given sentence, c) put the adverbial in the wrong sentence position, or (d) use a form that exists in English but is not correct in this sentence.

EXERCISE 12.13

Directions: In the following sentences, a student made a single error in using an adverbial. Your job is to address the error in three stages:

  a) bracket the error to focus your attention

  b) list what the student got right about the bracketed error (in this case, the error is the adverbial) and show this in parentheses

  c) compare the original erroneous sentence to the correct sentence and explain what mistake the student made

Example: *John has since he came to the United States lived in New York.
  [The star (*) indicates that the sentence contains an error.]

  Solution:

  a) Bracket the error (some aspect of the adverbial):
    *John has [since he came to the United States] lived in New York.

  b) Show what is right about the adverbial:
    correct adverbial type (adverbial clause)
    correct function (time: duration)
    correct possible form (*since he came to the United States*)

  c) Compare the erroneous sentence to the correct form and explain the mistake:
    *John has [since he came to the United States] lived in New York.
    Since he came to the United States, John has   lived in New York.

  Explanation: An adverbial clause can only occur in sentence-final or sentence-initial position. Since John's coming to the U.S. precedes his living in New York, the adverbial clause should be in sentence-initial position.

1. [On occasionally] the ladies like to play bingo at the local church.

  occasionally,

2. *The students put the puppy [at 3 o'clock.]

  put is a place prep

3. *This country needs really an ocean port.

  switch to really needs

4. *Weather[wards] the temperatures will drop by tomorrow evening.

  wards changs to weatherwise

5. *In the summertime, the sheep are allowed (to) wander to wherever they like.
    to can be deleted

6. (*Monthly) the magazine is delivered to his doorstep.
    monthly goes to the end

7   *The children didn't sleep very well (at) last night.
    delete at → no need for a prep.

8. (*A great deal) the keeper has a tendency to tease the animals.
    put after animals

9. *The beaver cut down with its teeth a few trees.
    after a few trees

10. *Hortensia likes to dress (an aristocratic manner.)
    add in

Chapter 13

THE PREPOSITION AND PARTICLE SYSTEMS

The preposition and particle systems are comprised of an array of small but important function words. The prepositions come at the beginning of a prepositional phrase. The particles come after a verb. The two word classes look very similar but their functions are quite different.

PREPOSITIONS

The general function of a preposition is to show a precise relationship between two units in a sentence. The second unit lies within a prepositional phrase and its function is to modify the first unit. When prepositions modify a noun, they follow (postmodify) that noun and become a part of a noun phrase, taking on an adjectival function. When prepositions modify a verb, they postmodify that verb, taking on an adverbial function.

Prepositions range from simple prepositions, small single words that occur frequently (e.g., *at*, *by*, *for*, *from*, *in*, *of*, *on*, *to*, *with*) to complex prepositions, a maximum of four words that occur infrequently (e.g., *up to*, *in comparison with*, *for the sake of*). Prepositions have several specific functions, but by far the most common is to show time and place. Other functions of prepositions are to show accompaniment, destination, means, possession, and relation.[1] However, before looking at these functions in detail, we begin with a discussion of *at*, *on*, and *in*, three common prepositions that have a variety of uses.

At, On and In

The prepositions *at*, *on*, and *in* cause learners of English difficulty because they are used for so many different functions, because they are difficult to translate, and because they are rarely stressed and are thus difficult to hear.

THE PREPOSITION AT

The preposition *at* refers to 1) a location that implies a function or 2) a point in time, place or measure.

Location That Implies a Function

The preposition *at* indicates that the subject of the sentence is doing those things which we associate with the object of the preposition. It is therefore common to use *at* with objects

---

[1] The additional prepositional functions of addition, contrast, and cause are discussed under subordination in Chapter 14.

such as *the butcher, the post office, the supermarket, the dentist,* etc., because they all have clearly defined associations. Look at the following examples:

    a) The tourist group is still <u>at the airport</u>.

    b) Ann's mother is <u>at the beauty shop</u>.

    c) Henry is <u>at school</u> today.

In Sentence (a), the tourist group is at the airport. Whether the group is inside the terminal, on the tarmac, or outside in the parking lot is irrelevant. The preposition *at* merely indicates that the group is doing those things which we associate with airports: taking or picking up a passenger, buying a ticket, looking for lost luggage, etc. The same is true in Sentence (b). Ann's mother is doing things that one associates with a beauty shop, i.e., having one's hair done, etc. In Sentence (c), Henry is doing things one associates with school, i.e., sitting in class, listening to lectures, going to the library, playing sports, etc. It is not the physical location that is important but rather the reason one is there.

Point in Time, Place, or Measurement

The preposition *at* also indicates a specific point in time, place, or measurement, as shown in the following examples:

    a) The film will begin <u>at 7:30 p.m</u>.

    b) He is standing <u>at the exact spot</u> from which Archduke Ferdinand was shot.

    c) Water boils <u>at a temperature of 100° C</u>.

Sentence (a) indicates a specific time, Sentence (b) a specific place, and Sentence (c) a specific measurement (it could have been weight, voltage, magnitude, etc.).

THE PREPOSITION ON

The preposition *on* refers to an object's place on a surface or a line.

Surface

"Surface" in the physical world suggests either a two-dimensional plane or the surface layer of a sphere or other non-planar shape. It also has metaphorical associations. Look at the following examples:

    a) You should only write <u>on</u> one side of the paper.

    b) There were many boats <u>on</u> the river that summer.

    c) We saw a wonderful program <u>on</u> television last night.

    d) It's the most beautiful place <u>on</u> Earth.

    e) What's <u>on</u> your mind?

    f) Most children love to ride <u>on</u> trains.

    g) She left her coat <u>on</u> the couch and her hat <u>on</u> the chair.

    h) The policeman was standing <u>on</u> the corner.

    i) Mrs. Winter is <u>on</u> the education committee.

Sentences (a), (b), (c), and (d) represent surfaces. Sentence (e) represents a metaphorical surface and suggests that something is pressing on that surface, inducing worry, fear, disagreement, or other (usually negative) emotions. Sentence (f) shows that public transportation is considered a surface when it doesn't enclose a person the way a car, van, truck, or other individual carrier does. Similarly, in Sentence (g), a couch is considered a surface, as is a chair, unless it is the enclosing armchair variety. In Sentence (h), the policeman is standing on an external corner, not in an enclosed, internal one as would be the case in a room. Finally, in Sentence (i), Mrs. Winter is on the list (a metaphorical surface) of people who comprise the committee.

Line

A line represents a one-dimensional feature or its metaphorical extensions. Look at the following examples:

- a) How could anyone build a house <u>on</u> a known fault line?
- b) We were standing <u>on</u> the border of Bulgaria and Yugoslavia.
- c) How would you rate that film <u>on</u> a scale of one to ten?
- d) Check the reading <u>on</u> the thermometer.
- e) When you stood <u>on</u> the edge, you could see all the way to the bottom of the cliff.
- f) Some of the teachers are <u>on</u> the verge of a nervous breakdown.

Sentence (a) represents a physical line, Sentence (b) an abstract one. Sentences (c) and (d) indicate a line that has been graded into degrees of measurement. Sentence (e) represents the physical line formed from planes at right angles, and Sentence (f) is a metaphorical extension of that edge to a psychological limit.

THE PREPOSITION IN

The preposition *in* refers to containment or mode.

Containment

"Containment" suggests enclosure in a physical (i.e., three-dimensional) or metaphorical space. Look at the following examples:

- a) The cake is <u>in</u> a white cardboard box.
- b) Put the flowers <u>in</u> a vase.
- c) The dog is asleep <u>in</u> the car.
- d) What have you got <u>in</u> your hand?
- e) People were dancing <u>in</u> the streets.
- f) Did you notice the rip <u>in</u> the carpet?
- g) The people <u>in</u> his division are all faceless bureaucrats.
- h) Susan was born <u>in</u> January.
- i) I don't know what I would do <u>in</u> his situation.
- j) Claudia is <u>in</u> love.
- k) What does he have <u>in</u> mind?

Sentences (a) and (b) represent containers. Sentence (c) represents a mode of transportation that encloses an individual. In Sentence (d), a hand holding something is a container (whereas a piece of chalk on the back of the hand can only be a surface). In (e), dancing requires a three-dimensional, not just a two-dimensional space, so *streets* represents an area rather than a surface. In (f), the rip goes beyond the surface into the three-dimensional thickness of the carpet, no matter how thin it may be. In (g), a division is a group to which people belong (we also say <u>in</u> the family, <u>in</u> the tribe, <u>in</u> the community) and one is therefore "contained" by the group. In (h), January "contains" all the days of the month. In (i), a situation (like a case or a position) is something that one is metaphorically contained by. Similarly, in (j), we are immersed in emotions which surround and thus contain us. In (k), which can be expressed as "What preconceived ideas does he have?", the ideas are already "contained" in the person's mind.

Mode

"Mode" refers to an action or a measurement category. Look at the following examples:

    a) The sea is always <u>in</u> motion.
    b) The cats were <u>in</u> a fight last night.
    c) Rory's girlfriend was <u>in</u> a motorcycle accident.
    d) The politician was wrong <u>in</u> taking that money.
    e) The suitcase was 30 inches <u>in</u> length.
    f) A long-playing record is 12 inches <u>in</u> diameter.
    g) One gram of water is one cubic centimeter <u>in</u> volume.

Sentences (a), (b), (c), and (d) show actions (*in* + VERB$_{ing}$ is a common form). Sentences (e), (f), and (g) show measurement categories.

Table 13.1 may help you to link the uses of *at*, *on*, and *in* with calendar time and place of address:

Table 13.1 The Prepositions *At*, *On*, and *In* with Calendar Time and Place of Address

CALENDAR TIME		PLACE OF ADDRESS
Time: The party is <u>at 8 o'clock</u>.	**AT**	House: John lives <u>at 210 Bay St</u>.
Day: The class begins <u>on Monday</u>. Date: They met <u>on June 2, 1964</u>.	**ON**	Street: He lives <u>on Bay Street</u>.
Month: It rains here <u>in May</u>. Season: It's hot <u>in the summer</u>. Year: Kennedy was shot <u>in 1963</u>. Decade: Music changed <u>in the '60s</u>. Century: The story began <u>in the 9th century</u>.	**IN**	City: He lives <u>in Berkeley</u>. County: He lives <u>in Alameda County</u> State: He lives <u>in California</u>. Country: He lives <u>in the U.S.A</u>. Continent: He lives <u>in North America</u>.

EXERCISE 13.1

Directions: Fill the blanks with *at*, *on*, or *in*.

    1. The plane leaves _____ 2:45 P.M.

    2. What street does the President live _____?

    3. The pot-bellied pig is asleep _____ father's favorite armchair.

    4. I want you to finish every drop of soup _____ your bowl.

5. When you said you wanted to try a new manufacturing process, did you have anything specific _____ mind?

6. Cinderella's carriage turned back into a pumpkin _____ midnight.

7. World War II ended _____ 1945.

8. There was a strange woman _____ the bus yesterday.

9. The Robertson family is going to have a picnic _____ July 4.

10. Cathy's purse was stolen while she was _____ the post office.

11. What does your baby have _____ his mouth?

12. Who spilled coffee _____ the couch?

13. This restaurant is closed _____ Mondays.

14. Two million gallons of crude oil is now floating _____ the Indian Ocean.

15. Who left a bicycle _____ the driveway?

16. Don't ask me now! I have a lot of things _____ my mind!

17. Please look up these words _____ the dictionary.

18. What did you do _____ school on Friday?

19. Travelers can rent a car _____ the airport.

20. How many professors are there _____ the faculty _____ your department?

21. We have a beautiful house _____ the country.

22. It rarely snows here _____ winter.

23. Her husband always goes to Italy _____ September.

24. Since it will be very cold tonight, you should put an extra blanket _____ your bed.

25. Susie couldn't have any dessert until she had finished everything _____ her plate.

26. There's a hole _____ his sweater!

27. A bird _____ the hand is worth two _____ the bush.

28. How many people live _____ Calcutta?

29. We met a really interesting woman _____ the plane from Paris.

30. My brother lives _____ 450 Sutter Street in San Francisco.

31. He doesn't know how many countries there are _____ the Western Hemisphere.

32. The service station is _____ the corner of Main Street and Columbus Avenue.

33. Do cats get lonely _____ night?

34. That plant would look pretty _____ the corner of the dining room.

35. The words _____ this page are a little difficult to read.

36. She's an expert _____ biochemistry.

37. Alex always rides _____ the roller coasters _____ amusement parks.

38. The bookseller took great joy _____ leafing through ancient volumes.

39. There was a lot of blood _____ the road after the accident.

40. How many people are living _____ your house now?

41. The teacher never let the students write _____ the blackboard.

42. The old shaman lived _____ the top of the hill.

43. What's _____ the menu today?

44. What's _____ T.V. tonight?

45. Why are you _____ such a bad mood?

46. Cuba is slightly larger than New Zealand _____ area.

47. She planted a lot of daffodils _____ her garden.

48. If you don't want it, throw it _____ the fire.

49. The duchess is leaving _____ midnight.

50. He was a good leader _____ many ways.

Prepositions of Time

The prepositions of time include those that describe range, starting point, duration, and end point.

RANGE: □ ◄—► □ FROM, TO, UNTIL, BETWEEN...AND, THROUGH

Range indicates a time that begins with the object of the preposition *from* and ends with the object of the preposition *to*, *until*, or *through*. Range can also begin with the object of *between* and end at the time indicated by a noun phrase after the conjunction *and*. To and *until* occur with all tenses, while *through* and *between* occur with all tenses except the present perfect. *To*, through, and *between* occur only in prepositional phrases, while *until* occurs in both prepositional phrases and adverbial clauses. Look at the following examples (the dotted line indicates a word that is associated with a certain preposition):

   a) The exhibition **took place** <u>from</u> September <u>to</u> December.
   b) The exhibition **takes place** <u>from</u> September <u>until</u> December.
   c) The exhibition **is taking place** <u>between</u> September <u>and</u> December.
   d) The exhibition **will take place** <u>from</u> September <u>through</u> December.

Sentences (a), (b) and (c) are ambiguous as to when in December the exhibition will end, though they are commonly interpreted to mean the beginning. Sentence (d) indicates that the exhibition will last until the end of December.

STARTING POINT: □ ➞ SINCE, NOT...UNTIL

The preposition *since* indicates the point at which something begins. It must be used with a present perfect or past perfect tense (or their continuous forms) and occurs in either a prepositional phrase or an adverbial clause. Look at the following examples:

   a) California **has been** a state <u>since</u> 1850.
   b) Sheila **has been working** at the hospital <u>since</u> February.
   c) David **had loved** animals <u>since</u> he was a boy.

Sentence (a) shows that the starting point of *being a state* is indicated by *since* in a prepositional phrase. Sentence (b) shows that the starting point of *working at the hospital* is also indicated by *since* in a prepositional phrase. In both sentences, the object of the preposition *since* is the "name" of a time rather than units of time. Sentence (c) shows that the starting point of *loving animals* is indicated by *since*, which here functions as the clause marker for an adverbial clause.

The preposition *until* in conjunction with a negated verb also indicates the point at which something begins. It is used with all tenses except the present perfect and occurs in both prepositional phrases and adverbial clauses. Look at the following examples:

   a) The leaf colors do <u>not</u> change <u>until</u> autumn.
   b) The captain would <u>not</u> leave his ship <u>until</u> all his passengers and crew were safe.

Sentence (a) shows that the verb (*change*) does not take effect before the starting point indicated by *until* in a prepositional phrase. Sentence (b) shows that the verb (*leave*) is not actuated before the starting point indicated by *until*, the clause marker of an adverbial clause.

DURATION: □ ➞ □ FOR, WITHIN, DURING, THROUGHOUT

Duration may be indicated either as units of time or as a single event (or events).

Duration as Units of Time

The preposition *for* shows duration in units of time such as hours, days, and months. *For* has no tense restrictions and occurs only in a prepositional phrase. Look at the following examples, which show the verb in boldface:

   a) Janie **has studied** medicine <u>for</u> six years.
   b) Kamal **visited** Cairo <u>for</u> three weeks.
   c) The children **had been** in the pool <u>for</u> 45 minutes.
   d) Her uncle **will not be** in Naples <u>for</u> several months.

Because Sentence (a) is in the present perfect tense, it can also be stated in terms of a starting point with *since*, e.g., *Janie has studied medicine since 1990*. The same is true for Sentence (c) in the past perfect, e.g., *The children had been in the pool since 2:15 P.M.* However, restatement as a starting point is not possible for Sentences (b) and (d) because the verbs are not in the present or past perfect tense. This distinction is understandably a source of error for learners. Finally, Sentence (d) shows a *not...for* usage that is parallel to *not...until*, i.e., the verb (*will be*) does not come into effect before the object of *for* (*several months*) has elapsed.

The preposition *within* also shows duration in time units such as hours, days, or months. It differs from *for* in that it emphasizes what will happen before the end of the duration. *Within* has no tense restrictions and occurs only in a prepositional phrase. However, it often occurs in a sentence containing a modal auxiliary as it usually implies a time beyond the moment of speaking. Look at the following examples:

    a) The project **had to be finished** <u>within</u> a week.
    b) Joe Green **has opened** four restaurants <u>within</u> four years.
    c) The mall **will be completed** <u>within</u> two months.
    d) The rocket **exploded** <u>within</u> seconds of liftoff.

In Sentences (a), (b), and (c), *within* is commonly shortened to *in*, which is different from the preposition *in* that signals containment or mode. The *within X of* structure in Sentence (d) is the only use of *within* that may not be so shortened.

The shortened form of *within* may also be used with a single event in certain time phrases. Look at the following examples:

    a) I'll see you <u>in</u> the morning.
    b) The linguistics classes were all <u>in</u> the evening.
    c) She wants to get there <u>in</u> time for the hors d'oeuvres.

Sentence (a) is understood to mean "I'll see you before the end of the time period we know as morning, i.e., before noon." The same applies to Sentence (b). Sentence (c) is interpreted as, "She wants to get there within the time that remains before the hors d'oeuvres are eaten."

Duration as a Single Event

Duration as a single event is shown by *during* and *thoughout*. The preposition *during* indicates "at some point within a given time period." *During* occurs with all tenses except the present perfect and only occurs in a prepositional phrase. Look at the following examples:

    a) Rita **got married** <u>during</u> the war.
    b) A few people always **faint** <u>during</u> the examination.
    c) The rains **will come** <u>during</u> the month of August.
    d) *I **lived** there <u>during</u> two months.

The principal difference between *during* and *for* is that *during* indicates a single time period or event whereas *for* indicates countable units of time. Sentence (d) shows a common error: the substitution of *during* for *for*.

The preposition *throughout* indicates "for the entire" or "at every moment of." *Throughout* has no tense restrictions and only occurs in a prepositional phrase. Look at the following examples:

    a) The boys **were** unhappy <u>throughout</u> the school year.
    b) The prisoner **has been treated** well <u>throughout</u> the interrogation.
    c) It **will be** warm in Malysia <u>throughout</u> the year.

The primary difference between *throughout* and *during* is that *throughout* emphasizes the moment-by-moment passage of the duration whereas *during* only indicates an event (or events) that occur in the given time period. Surprisingly, *during* is more common in rules and regulations (e.g., *Door must be unlocked during business hours. No parking during performances.*), presumably because *throughout* is too insistent to be polite.

In summary, there are four ways that duration can be described:

1. in time units completed, e.g., He has worked here <u>for</u> twenty years.
2. in time units to be completed by a given point, e.g., He must retire <u>within</u> five years.
3. at some point in a given time period, e.g., He collected stamps <u>during</u> his imprisonment.
4. the entire time in a given time period, e.g., He collected stamps <u>throughout</u> his imprisonment.

ENDPOINT: ➞ ☐ BY

The preposition *by* indicates the point at which something must end. *By* is not restricted as to tense[2] and only occurs in a prepositional phrase. Look at the following examples:

a) <u>By</u> the end of the storm, 30,000 people **had lost** their homes.
a) The dress **was** not ready <u>by</u> Friday.
b) The grain **will be planted** <u>by</u> the time the rain comes.

The object of *by* is always the name of a time, just as it is for *since*. In fact, *since* and *by* are a natural pair, *since* showing the name of a starting point of a situation and *by* showing the name of a required end point.

The constraints on the prepositions of time are summarized in Table 13.1.

Table 13.1 Constraints on the Prepositions of Time

CATEGORY	PREPOSITION	TENSE RESTRICTIONS	ADVERBIAL RESTRICTIONS
Range	**from-to**	None	Prep. phrase only
	from-until	No pres. perf. w/clause	Prep. phrase or adverbial clause
	from-through	No present perfect	Prep. phrase only
	between...and	No present perfect	Prep. phrase only
Starting Point	**since**	Only past or pres. perf.	Prep. phrase or adverbial clause
	not...until	No present perfect	Prep. phrase or adverbial clause
Duration	**for**	None	Prep. phrase only
	within (in)	None	Prep. phrase only
	during	No present perfect	Prep. phrase only
	throughout	None	Prep. phrase only
Endpoint	**by**	None, but modal likely	Prep. phrase only

---

[2] *By* occurs with the present perfect tense only in an adverbial clause, e.g., *If he <u>has</u> not <u>appeared</u> by ten o'clock, I'm calling the police.*

EXERCISE 13.2

Directions: Fill the blanks with an appropriate preposition of time from Table 13.1.

1. Gofredo has been a taxi driver _____ he came to New York in 1974.

2. Nigeria has been independent _____ more than a quarter of a century.

3. The farmers ploughed the fields _____ dawn _____ dusk.

4. The dam must be completed _____ the end of September, well before the rains begin.

5. The eclipse of the sun will not be visible _____ 4:07 P.M.

6. The shop was open every day _____ 10 A.M. _____ all the bagels had been sold.

7. Donated organs must be transplanted _____ hours of their removal.

8. The squeaking of the piano pedals was audible _____ the entire recital.

9. The life span of a horse is _____ twenty _____ twenty-five years.

10. The stores are only open _____ 3 P.M. _____ 7 or 8 in the evening.

11. The best time to visit the Butchart Gardens is _____ the month of April.

12. Rented videotapes must be returned _____ forty-eight hours.

13. Leticia had not seen her grandfather _____ her brother's baptism in Oaxaca.

14. Women should not drink or smoke _____ pregnancy.

15. The reduced plane fares are only valid _____ New Year's Day _____ March 15.

Prepositions of Place

The prepositions of place include those that describe relative position (stationary) and those that describe passage or direction (moving).[3]

RELATIVE POSITION

Prepositions of relative position vary according to whether they show a horizontal relation, a vertical relation, or a volumetric relation.

Horizontal Relation

Horizontal relations are described by prepositions indicating 1) position in a line or group, or 2) proximity.

---

[3] Abstractions of prepositions of place are used to show measurement:
   The temperature fluctuated *between* 90 and 100 degrees Centigrade.
   The meteor weighed *in the neighborhood of* four kilograms.

POSITION

a. in a line: *behind, between, in front of, along*

	Example Sentences
A is behind B.	The barn is <u>behind</u> the house.
B is between A and C.	The Persian Gulf lies <u>between</u> Iran and Saudi Arabia.
C is in front of B.	There is a fountain <u>in front of</u> the White House.
A, B, and C are along the same line.	Garbage was strewn <u>along</u> the railroad tracks.

b. in a group: *among, amid, surrounded by, around*

	Example Sentences
E is among A, B, C, and D.	The soldier is buried <u>among</u> his compatriots.
E is amid A, B, C, and D.	A small girl cried <u>amid</u> the remains of her home.
E is surrounded by A, B, C, and D.	The queen bee was <u>surrounded by</u> her drones.
A, B, C, and D are around E.	The city walls are <u>around</u> the old part of town.

PROXIMITY: *AGAINST, NEXT TO, BESIDE, BY, CLOSE TO, NEAR, NOT FAR FROM, IN THE NEIGHBORHOOD OF, FAR FROM, A GREAT DISTANCE FROM, NOWHERE NEAR*

		Example Sentences
AB	A is against B.	The plywood is leaning <u>against</u> the wall.
A–B	A is next to B.	The refrigerator is <u>next to</u> the stove.
	A is beside B.	Plant the marigolds <u>beside</u> the lettuce.
	A is by B.	Crabs live <u>by</u> the ocean.
A—B	A is close to B.	The school is <u>close to</u> the river.
	A is near B.	The light switch is <u>near</u> the door.
A——B		
	A is not far from B.	The airport is <u>not far from</u> the city.
	A is in the neighborhood of B.	The remains were found <u>in the neighborhood of</u> a glacier.

A━━━━━━━━━━━━━━━━━━━━━━━━━━━━━━━━B

A is far from B. The pyramids are <u>far from</u> the city center.

A is a great distance from B. The Sun is <u>a great distance from</u> the center of the galaxy.

A is nowhere near B. Bali is <u>nowhere near</u> Moscow.

EXERCISE 13.3

Directions: Add the appropriate preposition of horizontal relative position to the blanks. There is one sentence for each preposition in the list below.

a great distance from	around	close to	next to
against	behind	far from	not far from
along	beside	in front of	nowhere near
amid	between	in the neighborhood of	surrounded by
among	by	near	

1. An island is _____ water.

2. Portugal lies _____ Spain on the Iberian peninsula.

3. During an eclipse, the sun is positioned _____ the moon.

4. Reef diving is usually best _____ the shore.

5. The boy stood _____ his mother in the photograph.

6. The onlookers formed a circle _____ the wrestlers.

7. In most cars, the radiator is located _____ the engine.

8. The starving peasants had walked _____ their villages to get food and water.

9. Even though the captain had a map, the salvage boat was _____ the treasure.

10. The hammock was strung _____ two palm trees.

11. The mountain cabin is located _____ the pollution of cars and factories.

12. The prince was standing _____ his many relatives in the palace garden.

13. Don't stand too _____ the fire or you'll get singed.

14. A walk _____ the canal is fine on a summer evening.

15. The terrified cowboy pushed a couch _____ the door to bar entry.

16. The vegetables grown _____ the highway revealed a high lead content.

17. Put the package _____ the door if I'm not at home.

18. The balloon was lost _____ the ash and steam coming out of the volcano.

19. No one should live _____ a chemical dump site.

Vertical Relation

Vertical relations are described by prepositions indicating 1) contiguity (touching), or 2) noncontiguity (separated).

CONTIGUITY: *ON, ON TOP OF, UNDERNEATH, BENEATH, ALL OVER*

A is on B.

A is on top of B.

C is underneath B.

C is beneath B.

Example Sentences

There is water <u>on</u> the floor.

The new city is situated <u>on top of</u> the old one.

A tiny transmitter was discovered <u>underneath</u> the stamp.

A lurid face appeared just <u>beneath</u> the surface of the lake.

A is all over B.

The victim had bruises <u>all over</u> his body.

NONCONTIGUITY: *ABOVE, OFF, OVER, BELOW, UNDER, INSIDE, OUTSIDE, THROUGHOUT*

A is above B.

A is over B.

D is off C.

D is below B.

C is under B.

Example Sentences

The funnel cloud hovered <u>above</u> the plains.

You must stand directly <u>over</u> the well to see the bottom.

Natural gas was discovered <u>off</u> the coast of Scotland.

Uranium was found <u>below</u> the Indian reservation.

The plant should be kept <u>under</u> the light.

| A | B |

A is inside B.   The altar always lies <u>inside</u> the church.

| A | | B |

A is outside B.   The fields were located <u>outside</u> the city walls.

A	A
B	B
A	B

A is throughout B.   Cancer has spread <u>throughout</u> the lungs.

EXERCISE 13.4

Directions: Add the appropriate preposition of vertical relative position to the blanks. There is one sentence for each preposition in the list below.

above	inside	on top of	throughout
all over	off	outside	under
below	on	over	underneath
beneath			

1. Most plants will not grow _____ redwood trees.

2. They found a stash of money _____ the floorboards.

3. What's that cow doing _____ the roof of the barn?

4. In a second, the bees were _____ him, even inside his clothing.

5. My office is on the ground floor, while Linda's is three floors _____ mine.

6 Once the buffalo were _____ the corral, the boys went home.

7. _____ the paint, the restorers found a cherrywood mantelpiece.

8. Flying _____ the radar scanners requires considerable skill.

9. Hydrogen and helium exist _____ the universe.

10. The red light _____ the building warns aircraft to keep their distance.

11. No points were awarded if the arrow was _____ the target.

12. The dog had to stay _____ because he was all wet.

13. There was once a bridge _____ the Grand Canyon, but it no longer exists.

PASSAGE OR DIRECTION

Prepositions of passage or direction show movement in either two or three dimensions.

Movement in Two Dimensions

Movement in two dimensions can be either 1) vertical, 2) horizontal, or 3) planar (i.e., staying within or passing across a plane).

VERTICAL: *ABOVE, BELOW, DOWN, OFF, OVER, UNDER, UP*

	Example Sentences
above	The plane flew <u>above</u> the clouds.
below	The ship sank <u>below</u> the waves.
down	The bucket fell <u>down</u> the well.
off	Get the dog <u>off</u> the sofa!
over	The cat jumped <u>over</u> the fence.
under	A creek flowed <u>under</u> the parking lot.
up	The climbers moved <u>up</u> the side of the building.

HORIZONTAL: *ALONG, BY (PAST), BY (TO), DOWN (◄─►), FROM, ON, PAST, TO, TOWARD(S), UP (◄─►)*

	Example Sentences
along	The oil flowed <u>along</u> the roadway.
by (past)	Many people passed <u>by</u> the injured man without stopping.
by (to)	The doctor drove <u>by</u> the hospital to see his patient.
down (◄─►)	The children ran <u>down</u> to the water's edge.
from	Oil was oozing <u>from</u> the damaged tanker.
on	There were very few boats sailing <u>on</u> the bay that day.
past	The lane went <u>past</u> an old monastery.
to	Paul went <u>to</u> the supermarket.
toward(s)	The rocket sped <u>toward</u> the armored tank.
up (◄─►)	Violet drove <u>up</u> to Scotland for the weekend.

PLANAR: *ACROSS, (A)ROUND, BEYOND, THROUGH*

	Example Sentences
across	Two dogs raced <u>across</u> the field.
(a)round	Fred drove <u>around</u> the block three times to find a parking place.
beyond	No one is allowed <u>beyond</u> the barrier.
through	The truck crashed <u>through</u> a brick wall.

EXERCISE 13.5

Directions: Add the appropriate preposition of movement in two dimensions to the blanks. There is one sentence for each preposition in the list below.

above	by (past)	on	under
across	by (to)	over	up
along	down	past	up (◄──►)
(a)round	down (◄──►)	through	
below	from	to	
beyond	off	toward(s)	

1. The hovercraft moved just _____ the waves.

2. The snake slithered _____ a low branch and into the water.

3. Juliette went _____ the office to pick up her check.

4. No man has traveled _____ the limits of the Solar System.

5. Many people walked _____ the fruit stand, but no one bought anything.

6. The deer was unable to jump _____ the stone wall.

7. A coyote was trotting _____ the road, minding its own business.

8. Although you could not see it, lava was flowing _____ the surface.

9. The farmer's son ran _____ the street to warn the neighbors about the flood.

10. The water had flowed _____ the stairs to the basement.

11. The girls always walked _____ the park on the way to school.

12. Several times the crew walked _____ the stowaway, but no one saw him.

13. Many people are afraid to walk _____ a ladder.

14. The doctor wrapped a tourniquet _____ her patient's arm.

15. Salmon swim _____ the river of their birth to spawn.

16. The first solo flight _____ the Atlantic was made by Lindbergh in 1927.

17. The thirsty troops crawled hopelessly _____ the oasis.

18. Winter tires are required for driving _____ snowy or icy roads.

19. The escaped parrot flew straight _____ to the highest branches.

20. These athletic shoes are _____ China.

21. Aren't you flying _____ Barcelona next summer?

Movement in Three Dimensions

Movement in three dimensions can be either 1) open (unrestricted) or 2) closed (contained).

OPEN: *ACROSS, AROUND, THROUGH*

	Example Sentences
across	The satellite moved <u>across</u> the night sky.
around	The hornets were buzzing madly <u>around</u> the hive.
through	The bullet passed <u>through</u> the body without causing injury.

CLOSED: *ALL OVER, AROUND, INTO, OUT OF, THROUGHOUT*

	Example Sentences
all over	Her company sells belts <u>all over</u> Europe.
around	You could hear people moving <u>around</u> the flat upstairs.
into	She poured the buttermilk <u>into</u> the bowl.
out of	The lobster practically jumped <u>out of</u> the pot.
throughout	The skateboard craze had taken hold <u>throughout</u> the land.

EXERCISE 13.6

Directions: Add the appropriate preposition of movement in three dimensions to the blanks. There is one sentence for each preposition in the list below.

across	around	out of	thoughout
all over	into	through	

1. How did the guinea pig get _____ its cage?

2. The smoke from the summer fires wafted gently _____ the mountains.

3. The Earth hurtles _____ space at a velocity of 18.5 miles per second.

4. Light moves at the same speed _____ the universe.

5. Sylvio put the money _____ his wallet before he left the automatic teller.

6. The victim sustained burns _____ her body.

7. The racquet ball bounced _____ the court like a wild thing.

Other Functions of Prepositions

Some of the other functions of prepositions include accompaniment, destination, means, possession, and relation.

ACCOMPANIMENT

The prepositions that show accompaniment are *with* and *without*.[4] *With* has the meaning of "accompanied by" and *without* has the meaning of "unaccompanied by." The object of the preposition can be either a person, an animal, or a thing. Look at the following examples:

    a) David went to a party <u>with</u> his friends.

    b) The lady upstairs always goes shopping <u>with</u> her dog.

    c) For supper, we had potatoes <u>with</u> gravy.

    a) A woman <u>without</u> a man is like a fish without a bicycle.

    b) <u>Without</u> his cat, Randal felt quite alone in the world.

    c) Hikers seldom travel <u>without</u> a pocket knife.

DESTINATION

The preposition that shows destination is *for*. The object of the preposition is usually a place, but it can also be a metaphorical destination (e.g., security), a purpose, or a beneficiary. Look at the following examples:

    a) The bus is leaving <u>for</u> Montreal in ten minutes.

    b) When it began to rain, the shoppers ran <u>for</u> shelter.

    c) The company is only in it <u>for</u> profit.

    d) The young soldier died <u>for</u> his country.

    e) The pole vaulting team was going <u>for</u> the gold.

    f) Bill paid the rent <u>for</u> his ailing father.

MEANS

Means includes the subsidiary functions of manner, instrument, and agent. They generally answer the question *How?* The prepositions that show means include *with*, *without*, and *by*.

Manner

Manner shows the way in which something is done. The prepositions that show manner are *with* and *without*. The object of these prepositions is usually an abstract noun. Look at the following examples:

    a) The official spoke to the young offender <u>with</u> sympathy.

    b) The famous chef diced the vegetables <u>with</u> practiced ease.

    c) Politeness <u>without</u> kindness is often felt as rudeness.

    d) The two tribes managed to speak <u>without</u> anger.

---

[4] A variation of accompanying *with/without* occurs in recipes:
    This pasta is made <u>with</u> eggs.
    This bread is made <u>without</u> yeast.
With, which shows only an ingredient, can be contrasted with *of* and *out of*, which show the material of which something is made in its entirety:
    This pen is made <u>of</u> plastic.
    The model was made <u>out of</u> chicken wire.

Instrument

Instrument shows the device, machine, method, substance, tool, etc., through which something is accomplished. It makes use of the prepositions *by*, *with*, and *without*.

THE PREPOSITION *BY*

The preposition *by* requires an object that is 1) a noun phrase containing the zero article plus a singular count noun (i.e., a machine, a device) or a noncount noun (e.g., a substance), or 2) a VERB$_{ing}$ structure with a method. Look at the following examples:

    a) The package was delivered <u>by</u> taxi.

    b) This calculator operates <u>by</u> solar power.

    c) The doctor eased the patient's pain <u>by</u> injecting him with morphine.

    d) The grease is removed <u>by</u> drawing it off the top with a baster.

THE PREPOSITIONS *WITH* AND *WITHOUT*

The preposition *with* and its opposite *without* is used with devices, machines, subtances, and tools. In contrast to *by*, they can never occur with the zero article and a singular count noun. Look at the following examples:

    a) The stability of the craft is maintained <u>with</u> a gyroscopic device.

    b) The foundation was reinforced <u>with</u> cement.

    c) The window cannot be opened <u>without</u> a screwdriver.

    d) The body could not digest food <u>without</u> enzymes.

Agent

An agent is the person, animal, or thing that initiates an action and is shown by the preposition *by*. This is the same *by* that shows the active subject in a passive sentence. Agentive *by* answers the question *By what?* or *By whom?* to indicate that an action was initiated by someone or something. The verb that the *by*-phrase modifies must be in the passive voice and the *by*-phrase must be in sentence-final position. This is not the same as the instrumental form of *by*, which answers the question *How?* to indicate purpose, intent, or a desired goal and can occur in either voice. Look at the following examples, which show the verbs in boldface:

    a) *Hamlet* **was written** <u>by</u> Shakespeare.

    b) The Titanic **had been sunk** <u>by</u> an iceberg.

    c) The postman **is being chased** <u>by</u> a dog.

    d) The kidnap victims **will be manipulated** <u>by</u> their own fear.

    e) The chief **was killed** <u>by</u> a rock.

Sentences (a-e) are in the passive voice (*be* + VERB$_{ed_2}$) and all show an agent in the *by*-phrase. Sentence (e) shows that a rock killed the chief and the implication is that this occurred by accident (e.g., a rock falling off a cliff). It can be contrasted with instrumental *with* (i.e., *The chief was killed <u>with</u> a rock*), which shows that the chief was intentionally killed.

POSSESSION AND RELATION

The functions of possession and relation may be signalled by the preposition *of*, the most frequent preposition in the English language. The possessive function is also referred to as genitive *of*. Prepositional phrases with genitive *of* modify nouns as part of a noun phrase.

They do not have an adverbial function. Look at the following examples, which show the determiners in boldface:

a) **The** atmosphere <u>of</u> Venus consists mostly of carbon dioxide.

b) Rome is **the** capital <u>of</u> Italy.

c) It was heartrending to witness **the** poverty <u>of</u> the women.

d) Tony was **the** brother <u>of</u> my fiancee's friend.

e) **The** rear tires <u>of</u> the truck were both completely flat.

In Sentences (a–e), the head noun with its modifying *of*-phrase can be reversed to make a possessive *-'s* structure. Such a reversal is generally only possible when the determiner before the head noun of the *of*-phrase is an identifying (e.g., *the, my, this*) rather than a classifying (e.g., *a, Ø, every*) determiner.

a) <u>Venus**'s** atmosphere</u> consists mostly of carbon dioxide.

b) Rome is <u>Italy**'s** capital</u>.

c) It was heartrending to witness <u>the women**'s** poverty</u>.

d) Tony was <u>my fiancee's friend**'s** brother</u>.

e) <u>The truck**'s** rear tires</u> were both completely flat.

"Relation" is a general term that describes the many uses of nonpossessive *of*. It simply indicates that there is one of a variety of relationships between the head noun and the object of the preposition *of*. Look at the following examples:

a) a quart of milk[5]   [partitive]
   a piece of chocolate

b) a work of art   [equative]
   a nation of sheep

c) the city of brotherly love [representative]
   the god of war

d) women of integrity   [associative]
   men of means

A partitive relation indicates that the head noun is the "part" and the object of *of* is a non-count noun which is divided into those parts. An equative relation indicates that the head noun and the object of *of* are "equal" in status. A representative relation indicates that the head noun represents the object of *of*. An associative relation indicates that the head noun has earned or is associated with the object of *of*.

EXERCISE 13.7

Directions: Fill the blanks with one of the following prepositions: *by, for, of, with, without.*

1. Acrobats rarely perform _____ a net.

2. Would you like bread _____ your salad?

3. The story describes a character who pays a million dollars _____ the murder of his wife.

---

[5] A classifying determiner before the head noun of the *of*-phrase (e.g., *a height of two meters,* ***every*** *bottle of wine,* *[Ø]pieces of cheese*) cannot usually be reversed into a possessive -'s structure (e.g., *two meter's height,* *wine's every bottle,* *cheese's pieces*).

4. The musician played the piano _____ grace and style.

5. Public speakers have to learn how to address an audience _____ nervousness.

6. The group traveled down to the bottom of the Grand Canyon _____ donkey.

7. The campers made the tent waterproof _____ throwing a piece of plastic over it.

8. The lumberjack first removed the branches _____ a chain saw.

9. Viruses cannot be seen _____ a microscope.

10. The rising river was held back _____ sandbags and determination.

11. The tail _____ the plane had been struck _____ lightning.

12. Let me tell you the story _____ my family's emigration to America.

13. After the first siren sounded, the citizens ran _____ cover.

14. Has your guide ever been rescued _____ helicopter?

15. _____ adding chlorine to the water supply, officials hope to meet the national water safety standards.

EXERCISE 13.8

Directions: Underline the prepositions in the following passage and classify them according to the categories used in the chapter.

    Example: David never works on Saturdays.

    Solution: David never works <u>on</u> Saturdays. [Time: day]

Schindler's Poland[6]

On September 1, 1939, Nazi troops invaded Poland. Oskar Schindler followed in their wake, settling in Krakow with the intention of making a profit on the war. He lost no time. Within three months of the invasion, he had established a factory that produced mess kits and kitchenware for the German army. He was quick with a bribe, he dealt in the black market, and made his money by exploiting the Reich's offer of cheap Jewish labor.

Schindler rescued 1,300 Jews, most of whom worked in his factory, from the Reich's death camps, which efficiently executed millions of people during the course of the war. He achieved this largely by bribing Nazi officials, draining his fortune and risking his life in the process.

In the years since the end of World War II, the stage on which Schindler acted has not been drastically altered. Krakow survived the war largely intact, the only major city in Poland to do so, and today it is easy to see why the young entrepreneur was taken with the place. Krakow is a beautiful

---

[6] John Conroy, Universal Press Syndicate, "Schindler's Poland," *The Fresno Bee* 144,26089: H1 and H4, July 17, 1994.

medieval city with a central square that ranks among the finest in Europe. In the middle of the square in the old city hall is the Sukiennice (The Cloth Hall), in which handicrafts and jewelry are sold from individual stalls. In Schindler's day, a black market flourished there.

On the eastern side of the square is the magnificent Kosciol Mariacki (St. Mary's Church), finished in the 15th century, from whose tallest spire a trumpeter performs on the hour, ending his brief performance on the note at which an ancient predecessor was shot through the throat by an invader's arrow. It was here Schindler met a group of black market operators in the rear pews of the church.

You cannot help but marvel at the enthusiastically corrupt young German who put his life on the line for 1,300 strangers at a moment in history when it would have been far safer to see them packed in cattle cars on their way to becoming cigarette cases, textiles, or ashes fertilizing the Polish countryside.

Problem Solving with the Preposition System

In the problems below, it is possible to get the following right:

> a. correct FUNCTION (time, place, accompaniment, destination, means, possession, and relation)
>
> b. correct STRUCTURE OF PP (preposition + NP, clause marker + adverbial clause)
>
> c. correct POSITION OF PP (after head noun within NP, in adverbial slot)
>
> d. correct CATEGORY OF OBJECT (e.g., device with *with*, V$_{ing}$ with *by*)
>
> e. correct VERB TENSE (e.g., pres/past perfect with *since*, all tenses with *for*)

These elements reflect what students are likely to do wrong in using a preposition: a) select the incorrect prepositional function, b) use an incorrect grammatical structure, c) put the grammatical structure in the wrong sentence position, d) use an incorrect category of object after the preposition, or (e) use an incorrect verb tense with the preposition.

EXERCISE 13.9

Directions: In the following sentences, a student made a single error in using a preposition. Your job is to address the error in three stages:

> a) bracket the error to focus your attention
>
> b) list what the student got right about the bracketed error (in this case, the error is the preposition) and show this in parentheses
>
> c) compare the original erroneous sentence to the correct sentence and explain what mistake the student made

Example: *Joseph has studied music since fifteen years

> [The star (*) indicates that the sentence contains an error.]

Solution:

> a) Bracket the error (some aspect of the preposition):
>   *Joseph has studied music [since] fifteen years.
>
> b) Show what is right about the preposition:
>   correct function (time)
>   correct PP structure (*since* + NP)
>   correct PP position (in adverbial slot)
>   correct verb tense (present perfect)

    c) Compare the erroneous sentence to the correct form and explain the mistake:
        *Joseph has studied music [since] fifteen years.
        Joseph has studied music for   fifteen years.

   Explanation: Duration in units of time is shown with *for*, not *since* (which shows starting point only).

1. *In twenty minutes, the boat will leave to New Orleans.

2. *The trolls dwell the bridge under.

3. *My daughter must by 11 P.M. be home.

4. *The hotel is open from April to the last guest departs.

5. *The factory has manufactured automobiles during the crisis.

6. *The mayor from the town owns a beauty shop in Salina, Kansas.

7. *Rosemarie is afraid to travel by a plane.

8. *By termites, the foundation of the house was destroyed.

9. *The health food store is located in 2224 Fulton Avenue.

10. *The wolves have not been noticed until a sheep was missing from the flock.

PARTICLES

The particles are words that look like prepositions but which are linked to the verbs they follow rather than to the noun phrase that follows them in a prepositional phrase. The function of the particles is to provide verbs with nuances of meaning that are not expressed by the verb alone. Such verbs are referred to as 1) phrasal verbs or 2) prepositional verbs, depending on whether the verb or the particle receives phonological emphasis.

Particles and Phrasal Verbs

Phrasal verbs are characterized by phonological emphasis (stress) on the particle. For example, the phrasal verb *look af´ter* has stress on the particle (*after*). Look at the following examples of phrasal verbs based on the verb *look*:

Example	Meaning
a) The nurse <u>looked after</u> her patients very well.	took care of
b) The detective <u>looked into</u> the matter.	investigated
c) The passengers <u>looked on</u> as the old woman was robbed.	watched without taking action
d) The lawyer <u>looked over</u> the contract.	carefully examined
e) Customers <u>looked through</u> the half-price merchandise.	casually examined
f) Sammy <u>looked up</u> the number in the phone book.	find in an ordered set

The underlined verbs in the sentences are often called *two-word verbs* because each verb consists of a verb plus a single particle.

SEPARABLE AND NONSEPARABLE PHRASAL VERBS

Phrasal verbs may be divided into two catagories 1) those that may be "pulled apart" or separated under certain conditions and 2) those that may not be separated under any conditions.

Separable Phrasal Verbs

A separable phrasal verb is one that must be separated when the direct object of the verb is a pronoun. Look at the following examples from Sentences (d) and (f) in the list above:

    a) The lawyer <u>looked over</u> **the contract**.

    b) *The lawyer <u>looked over</u> **it**.

    c) The lawyer <u>looked</u> **the contract** <u>over</u>.

    d) The lawyer <u>looked</u> **it** <u>over</u>.

    e) Sammy <u>looked up</u> **the number** in the phone book.

    f) *Sammy <u>looked up</u> **it** in the phone book.

    g) Sammy <u>looked</u> **the number** <u>up</u> in the phone book.

    h) Sammy <u>looked</u> **it** <u>up</u> in the phone book.

Sentences (a) and (e) show the unseparated state of these separable phrasal verbs. Sentences (c) and (g) show that the phrasal verbs may be separated by their direct object. Sentences (d) and (h) show that the phrasal verbs may also be separated by the pronoun form of their direct objects. However, Sentences (b) and (f) show that it is not possible for separable phrasal verbs to remain unseparated when the direct object is in its pronoun form.

Nonseparable Phrasal Verbs

A nonseparable phrasal verb is one that cannot be separated by its object under any circumstances. Look at the following examples from Sentences (b) and (e) in the list above:

    a) The detective <u>looked into</u> **the matter**.

    b) The detective <u>looked into</u> **it**.

    c) *The detective <u>looked</u> **the matter** <u>into</u>.

    d) *The detective <u>looked</u> **it** <u>into</u>.

    e) Customers <u>looked through</u> **the half-price merchandise**.

    f) Customers <u>looked through</u> **it**.

    g) *Customers <u>looked</u> **the half-price merchandise** <u>through</u>.

    h) *Customers <u>looked</u> **it** <u>through</u> .

Sentences (a) and (e) show the unseparated state of these phrasal verbs. Sentences (b) and (f) show that these phrasal verbs remain unseparated even when their direct objects are in their pronoun forms. Sentences (c) and (g) show that the phrasal verbs cannot be separated by their direct objects. Sentences (d) and (h) show that they cannot be separated by the pronoun forms of their direct objects. In other words, for nonseparable phrasal verbs, the two unseparated forms are allowable while the two separated forms are not; hence, the name *nonseparable*.

EXERCISE 13.10

Directions: Underline the phrasal verbs in the following sentences and identify them as separable (S) or nonseparable (N).

1. ____The heavyweight boxing champion gave up the fight after the second round.

2. ____ Harold was brought up in the country by his grandmother.

3. ____ Theresa came across an old trunk in the attic.

4. ____ It took several days for Raymond to get over his cold.

5. ____ Who crossed out my name on the list of winners?

6. ____ The professor was reluctant to go over the exam a third time.

7. ____ The police cannot figure out how the thief left the house.

8. ____ The children will be picked up at 4:30.

9. ____ William didn't know how to turn off the dishwasher.

10. ____ If you keep on walking in that direction, you'll find the cafe.

Particles and Prepositional Verbs

Prepositional verbs are characterized by phonological emphasis (stress) on the verb. For example, the prepositional verb *lóok at* has stress on the verb (*look*). Look at the following examples based on the verb *look*:

Examples	Meaning
a) The children <u>looked at</u> the old photographs of their parents.	examined
b) The caretaker <u>looked for</u> the key to the front door.	tried to find
c) Jamie's cousin <u>looks like</u> Groucho Marx.	resembles
d) The citizens <u>looked to</u> their president for leadership.	depend on

The underlined verbs in the sentences are often called *verbs with allied particles* to distinguish them from phrasal verbs.[7] Prepositional verbs are always nonseparable.

---

[7] There is also a substantial number of verb + particle structures that have obligatory objects, e.g., *blame sb. for st.* (*sb.* = somebody; *st.* = something), *introduce sb. to sb.*, *remind sb. of. st. or sb.*, *subtract st. from st.* There are also several adjectives with allied particles, e.g., *afraid of, different from, disappointed in, familiar with, famous for, surprised at.*

EXERCISE 13.11

Directions: Determine if the underlined phrase is a prepositional verb (PPV) or a phrasal verb (PhV). Then provide a brief definition of the meaning of the phrase.

1. _____ Someone has to <u>pay for</u> this broken window.

2. _____ When is he going to <u>hand in</u> his resignation?

3. _____ The secretary will <u>call up</u> all the members of the committee.

4. _____ I'm not sure that the warring factions will <u>consent to</u> the treaty.

5. _____ Lisa doesn't <u>believe in</u> Santa Claus any more.

6. _____ The food you have ordered <u>comes to</u> twelve dollars.

7. _____ Would you <u>drop off</u> this letter at the post office for me?

8. _____ My husband will <u>pick up</u> the dry cleaning on the way home from work.

9. _____ The game had to be <u>put off</u> because of the rain.

10. _____ If you don't know who it is, <u>hang up</u>.

Particles and Phrasal-Prepositional Verbs

Several verbs consist of a combination of both a phrasal and a prepositional verb. The first particle has phonological emphasis (e.g., *look dówn on*) and all phrasal-prepositional verbs are nonseparable. Look at the following examples based on *look*:

Examples	Meaning
a) The heiress <u>looked down on</u> all her suitors.	regarded as inferior
b) The students <u>looked forward to</u> their field trip.	anticipated with pleasure
c) The doctor <u>looked in on</u> a patient before he went home.	briefly visited and checked
d) Drivers were urged to <u>look out for</u> deer on the highway.	be aware of
e) Children <u>look up to</u> their teachers as models of behavior.	regard as superior

The underlined phrasal-prepositional verbs in the example sentences are often called *three-word verbs* since they consist of a verb followed by a particle and a preposition.

EXERCISE 13.12

Directions: Underline the phrasal-prepositional verbs in the following sentences. Then provide a brief definition of the meaning of the phrase.

1.   Grant knew that he wouldn't get through with his work until after midnight.

2.   Paula is getting behind in her assignments.

3.   Sirenia always talks back to her mother.

4.   It's not always easy to keep up with your older siblings.

5.   Please drop in on your ailing father some time.

6.   Guests are asked to check out of the hotel by noon.

7.   How can you put up with a roommate like that?

8.   We ran out of gas on the Bay Bridge.

9.   Amanda always gets along with animals very well.

10.   I have to catch up on my homework or I'm going to flunk out.

Problem Solving with the Particle System

In the problems below it is possible to get the following right:

      a. correct PARTICLE(S) (*in, on, over, up to*, etc.)

      b. correct SEPARABILITY (separable or nonseparable, when applicable)

      c. correct TYPE OF OBJECT (something or somebody)

      d. correct OBJECT (e.g., check out of *a hotel*; get over *an illness/surprise/loss*)

      e. correct STRUCTURE (verb + particle(s) + object, VERB_{ing}, no object, etc.)

      f. correct POSSIBLE FORM (the structure exists in English but is not correct in this instance)

These elements reflect what students are likely to do wrong in using a particle: a) select the incorrect particle, b) fail to apply the correct separability rules, when applicable, c) use the incorrect type (animate or inanimate) of object, (d) be unaware of the specific object noun phrases that are associated with a specific phrasal or prepositional verb, (e) use an incorrect grammatical structure, or (f) use a form that exists in English but is not correct in this sentence.

EXERCISE 13.13

Directions: In the following sentences, a student made a single error in using a phrasal or prepositional verb. Your job is to address the error in three stages:

      a) bracket the error to focus your attention

      b) list what the student got right about the bracketed error (in this case, the error concerns the phrasal verb) and show this in parentheses

      c) compare the original erroneous sentence to the correct sentence and explain what mistake the student made

Example: *The teacher always calls at the stronger students.
　　　　[The star (*) indicates that the sentence contains an error.]

Solution:
　　a) Bracket the error (some aspect of the phrasal verb):
　　　 *The teacher always calls [at] the stronger students.
　　b) Show what is right about the phrasal verb:
　　　 correct separability (object outside phrasal verb)
　　　 correct type of object (somebody)
　　　 correct object (*students*)
　　c) Compare the erroneous sentence to the correct form and explain
　　　 the mistake:
　　　 *The teacher always calls [at] the stronger students.
　　　 The teacher always calls on　the stronger students.

Explanation: The correct particle associated with the verb *call* to describe a
　　teacher's asking an individual student to respond is *on*, not *at*.

1.　*The room was so warm that Rob took out his sweater.

2.　*Mrs. Couret has looked her mother after since she became ill.

3.　*Several people dropped in on the museum last week.

4.　*The artist crossed out the large cupboard from her tiny studio.

5.　*Could you please help me to pick at a new hat?

6.　*My cousin looks for to coming to the wedding.

7.　*Before you buy that car, you had better check out it carefully.

8.　*The employer had to think her over before he gave Ms. Green the job.

9.　*The store detective handed the shoplifter in and then returned to the floor.

10.　*We are simply not interested on buying any more insurance.

Unit V: Sentence Combining

Chapter 14

THE COORDINATION AND SUBORDINATION SYSTEMS

The coordination and subordination systems allow us to combine sentences (i.e., clauses) in different ways to achieve different effects. All grammatical structures can be coordinated, but only clauses can be subordinated. Therefore, the focus in this chapter will be on coordination and subordination at the clause level.

When two clauses are coordinated in a sentence, the information in each clause is understood to have equal weight and importance in the mind of the speaker or writer. This is because the information in each clause is believed to be new to the listener or reader. When one clause is subordinated to another, on the other hand, the two clauses are not equal in weight and importance. This is because the information in the subordinated clause is presumed to be known to the listener whereas the information in the main clause is not. Look at the following examples:

    a) Joseph had a cold.

    +b) He went to the beach.

    c) Joseph had a cold **but** he went to the beach.

    d) **Although** Joseph had a cold, he went to the beach.

Clauses (a) and (b) have been combined using a coordinator (*but*) in Sentence (c) and combined using a subordinator (*although*) in Sentence (d). As a result, Sentence (c) shows that Clauses (a) and (b) were equally important in the mind of the speaker, i.e., it was presumed that the listener knew neither that Joseph had a cold nor that he went to the beach. A response to this sentence might be, "What a silly thing to do!" Sentence (d), on the other hand, shows that Clause (a) was less important in the mind of the speaker than Clause (b) because it was known to the listener that Joseph had a cold but not that he went to the beach. A response to this sentence might be, "What a fool Joseph is!"

In formal academic writing, subordination tends to occur more frequently than coordination, but if the amount of coordination exceeds the amount of subordination, the writing appears childlike and unsophisticated. This is demonstrated in the following passages, in which coordination markers are underlined with a single line and subordination markers with a double line. The first passage is from a children's book called *I Hate English!* by Ellen Levine,[1] the second from *The Silent Language* by Edward T. Hall.[2]

---

[1] Excerpted from Ellen Levine, *I Hate English!* (New York: Scholastic Inc.,1989), 5-7. Used with permission.

[2] From *The Silent Language* by Edward T. Hall. Copyright © 1959, 1981 by Edward T. Hall. Used by permission of Doubleday, a division of Bantam Doubleday Dell Publishing Group, Inc.

Mei Mei loved Chinese. Especially writing. Fast strokes, short strokes, long strokes— the brush, the pen, the pencil— all seemed <u>to</u> fly in her hand. <u>But</u> that was Chinese. Mei Mei wouldn't speak in school. Most of the time she understood <u>what</u> her teacher said. <u>But</u> everything was in English, <u>and</u> Mei Mei wouldn't speak English.

One day her cousin Bing took her to the Chinatown Learning Center. Students brought their homework for help. <u>But</u> not Mei Mei. She wouldn't work in English. Tutors helped the older ones with their English. Mei Mei helped the little ones with arithmetic. Numbers weren't English or Chinese. They were just numbers. Mei Mei loved the Center. She talked and listened and explained and argued. She did everything in Chinese.

Coordination = 4 Subordination = 2

<u>Though</u> the United States has spent billions of dollars on foreign aid programs, it has captured neither the affection nor esteem of the rest of the world. In many countries today, Americans are cordially disliked, in others, merely tolerated. The reasons for this sad state of affairs are many and varied, <u>and</u> some of them are beyond the control of anything [<u>that</u>] this country might try <u>to</u> do <u>to</u> correct them. <u>But</u> harsh <u>as</u> it may seem to the ordinary citizen, filled <u>as</u> he is with good intensions and natural generosity, much of the foreigners' animosity has been generated by the way <u>that</u> Americans behave.

As a country we are apt <u>to</u> be guilty of great ethnocentrism. In many of our foreign aid programs we employ a heavy-handed technique in <u>dealing</u> with local nationals. We insist <u>that</u> everyone else do things our way. <u>Consequently,</u> we manage <u>to</u> convey the impression <u>that</u> we simply regard foreign nationals as "underdeveloped Americans." Most of our behavior does not spring from malice but from ignorance, <u>which</u> is <u>as grievous</u> a sin in international relations. We are <u>not only</u> almost totally ignorant of <u>what</u> is expected in other countries, we are equally ignorant of <u>what</u> we are communicating to other people by our own normal behavior.

Coordination = 4 Subordination = 16

The passages show that the excerpt from a children's book has more coordination than subordination, while the excerpt from an adult nonfiction book has much more subordination than coordination.

The terms *coordination* and *subordination* may seem difficult, but in fact we have seen these systems operating before. Coordination is simply the use of coordinating conjunctions such as *and* and *but*, and conjunctive adverbs such as *in addition* and *however*. Subordination is the use of adverbial clauses with their clause markers such as *when* and *although*, adjective clauses with their clause markers such as *who* and *that*, and noun clauses with their clause markers such as *what* and *that*. Clauses with other markers are discussed in Chapter 15. Look at the following examples:

a) **The clouds gathered,** <u>but</u> **they did not bring rain**.
b) **The clouds gathered;** <u>however</u>, **they did not bring rain**.
c) **The clouds** <u>that</u> gathered **did not bring rain**.
d) <u>Although</u> the clouds gathered, **they did not bring rain.**

Sentences (a) and (b) show a coordinate relationship. Two independent clauses (in bold-face) are conjoined by the conjunction *but* in (a) and the conjunctive adverb *however* in (b). The comma in Sentence (a) is optional and usually reserved for longer clauses than these. The punctuation in Sentence (b) is required for conjunctive adverbs.[3] If a comma is mistakenly used in place of the semicolon, the result is a **run-on sentence** (a sentence that "runs on" beyond the sentence boundary). This error is also known as a comma splice. Semicolons are used between independent clauses except when a coordinating conjunction (e.g., *and*, *but*, *so*, or *or*) is present.

Sentences (c) and (d) show a subordinate relationship. The independent clauses (in bold-face) are attached to dependent clauses that begin with a clause marker, i.e., the adjective clause marker *that* in (c) and the adverbial clause marker *although* in (d). Notice the punctuation in (d). If a semicolon is used in place of the comma, the result is a **fragment** (a dependent clause with no attachment to an independent clause).

EXERCISE 14.1

Directions: Underline the sentence coordinators in the following passage with a single line and the subordinators with a double line.

The rattlesnake belongs to the family of pit vipers, *Crotilidae*, and it is one of the four poisonous snakes in North America. There is a deep pit on each side of the face, between the eye and the nostril. The pit contains a heat-sensitive membrane that helps the rattlesnake find its warm-blooded prey. Although the rattlesnake is a reptile, the female bears live young, so the eggs hatch inside the mother's body. The rattle from which the snake's name is derived consists of a series of rings that strike together when the snake is excited.[4]

While coordinators and subordinators are concerned with relationships between clauses, it is also possible to show a "subordinate" relationship between a clause and a noun phrase. This is accomplished by means of complex prepositions, which are related to the subordinators in meaning but not in function. The difference between the two is that subordinators indicate what is and what is not presumed to be known to the hearer while complex prepositions do not. Look at the following examples:

a) <u>In spite of the fact that</u> } there was a drought, the lawns were watered.
<u>Despite the fact that</u>

b) The lawns were watered { <u>in spite of</u> } the drought.
{ <u>despite</u> }

---

[3] Conjunctive adverbs may also be capitalized after a period, e.g., The clouds gathered. <u>However</u>, they did not bring rain.

[4] Adapted from "Rattlesnake," in Compton's Pictured Encyclopedia, © 1964 by Compton's Learning Company. Used with permission.

Sentence (a) is constructed with subordinators while Sentence (b) is constructed with complex prepositions that are related to the subordinators. In both sentences, the underlined structure indicates that what follows is contrary to the first part of the sentence. However, Sentence (a) also suggests that the hearer knew that there was a drought but not that the lawns were watered. Sentence (b) makes no such distinction.

There are two major types of coordinators and subordinators: the logical and the chronological. The logical coordinators and subordinators show basic logical relationships such as more information (*and*), contrary information (*but*), and causes and effects (*so*). The chronological coordinators and subordinators show time sequence relationships. The complex prepositions related to the subordinators will be indicated in each subsection.[5]

LOGICAL COORDINATORS AND SUBORDINATORS

Logical coordinators and subordinators can be divided into three major categories based on the relationships that exist between the two clauses: 1) those that show an AND relationship, 2) those that show a BUT relationship, and 3) those that show a SO relationship. These categories parallel the meanings of the coordinating conjunctions *and*, *but* and *so*.

The AND Relationship

The coordinators and subordinators that show the AND relationship indicate that more information of a similar nature will be supplied in the following clause. They include the categories of addition, explanation, condition, exemplification, choice, and summation.

ADDITION

Addition words indicate 1) more information, 2) surprising or unexpected information, or 3) a general or specific statement about a previous clause.

More Information

More information may come in the form of a) a different idea or b) a similar idea.

A DIFFERENT IDEA

A different additional idea is indicated with the following coordinators and subordinators:

a. <u>Coordinators</u>   b. <u>Subordinators</u>
   in addition   *in addition to the fact that*
   also
   moreover
   furthermore

Examples:

a) The skier broke his leg; { <u>in addition</u>, <u>also</u>, <u>moreover</u>, <u>furthermore</u>, } he sprained his elbow.

---

[5] The name *complex preposition* describes the function rather than the word class of the components. Some complex prepositions contain no prepositions at all.

b) The skier broke his leg <u>in addition to the fact that</u> he sprained his elbow.

A different additional idea may also be indicated with the following complex prepositions:

c. <u>Complex Prepositions</u>
   in addition to
   as well as

Example:

c) The skier hurt his leg $\left\{\begin{array}{c}\underline{\text{in addition to}}\\\underline{\text{as well as}}\end{array}\right\}$ his elbow.

A SIMILAR IDEA

A similar idea is indicated with the following coordinators and subordinators:

a. <u>Coordinators</u>   b. <u>Subordinators</u>
   similarly   *in the same way as*
   likewise   *much as*
   in the same way

Examples:

a) Amoebas engulf their food; $\left\{\begin{array}{c}\underline{\text{similarly,}}\\\underline{\text{likewise,}}\\\underline{\text{in the same way,}}\end{array}\right\}$ white blood cells engulf bacteria.

b) Amoebas engulf their food $\left\{\begin{array}{c}\underline{\text{in the same way as}}\\\underline{\text{much as}}\end{array}\right\}$ white blood cells engulf bacteria.

Surprising or Unexpected Information

Surprising or unexpected information that is additional, not contrary, to the information in another clause may be expressed in both a formal and an informal manner.

FORMAL

Surprising or unexpected information is indicated formally with the following coordinators and subordinators:

a. <u>Coordinators</u>   b. <u>Subordinators</u>
   furthermore   *not to mention the fact that*
   moreover
   in fact

Examples:

a) Electric trains are efficient; $\left\{\begin{array}{c}\underline{\text{furthermore,}}\\\underline{\text{moreover,}}\\\underline{\text{in fact,}}\end{array}\right\}$ they produce less pollution than trucks.

b) Electric trains are efficient, <u>not to mention the fact that</u> they produce less pollution than trucks.

Formal surprising or unexpected information may also be indicated with the following complex preposition:

    c. <u>Complex Prepositions</u>
       not to mention

Example:

    c) Electric trains are efficient, <u>not to mention</u> less polluting.

INFORMAL

Surprising or unexpected information is indicated informally with the following coordinators and subordinators:

    a. <u>Coordinators</u>   b. <u>Subordinators</u>
      besides   *not to mention that*
      what is more
      not only that

Examples:

    a) Jill's boyfriend is unfriendly; { <u>besides,</u> / <u>what is more,</u> / <u>not only that,</u> } he drinks too much alcohol.

    b) Jill's boyfriend is unfriendly, <u>not to mention that</u> he drinks too much alcohol.

General or Specific Information About the Previous Clause

Information about the previous clause may be general or specific.

GENERAL

General information about the previous clause is indicated with the following coordinators and subordinators:

    a. <u>Coordinators</u>   b. <u>Subordinators</u>
      in fact   *[none]*
      indeed
      as a matter of fact

Example:

    a) The schools are in trouble; { <u>in fact,</u> / <u>indeed,</u> / <u>as a matter of fact,</u> } the whole economy is in decline.

SPECIFIC

Specific information about the previous clause is indicated with the following coordinators and subordinators:

    a. <u>Coordinators</u>   b. <u>Subordinators</u>
      in fact   *[none]*
      indeed

as a matter of fact
to be specific

Example:

a) Acid rain hurts
    the environment;
$\left\{\begin{array}{l}\underline{\text{in fact,}}\\ \underline{\text{indeed,}}\\ \underline{\text{as a matter of fact,}}\\ \underline{\text{to be specific,}}\end{array}\right\}$
many mountain
lakes are dying.

EXPLANATION

Explanation words indicate that the information in the first clause will be made clearer in the second clause. It is indicated with the following coordinators and subordinators:

a. <u>Coordinators</u>
   in other words
   that is to say
   that is
   i.e. [from Latin *id est* "that is"]
   to be precise

b. <u>Subordinators</u>
   by which I mean that
   by which is meant that
   meaning that

Examples:

a) The manager was
    indiscrete;
$\left\{\begin{array}{l}\underline{\text{in other words,}}\\ \underline{\text{that is to say,}}\\ \underline{\text{that is,}}\\ \underline{\text{i.e.,}}\\ \underline{\text{to be precise,}}\end{array}\right\}$
he spoke to the
media.

b) The manager was
    indiscrete,
$\left\{\begin{array}{l}\underline{\text{by which I mean that}}\\ \underline{\text{by which is meant that}}\\ \underline{\text{meaning that}}\end{array}\right\}$
he spoke to
the media.

CONDITION

Condition words indicate that a situation described in one clause will occur (positive) or will not occur (negative) if the information in the other clause is true.

Positive

Positive conditions are indicated with the following coordinators and subordinators:

a. <u>Coordinators</u>
   in that case
   in this case
   in other words

b. <u>Subordinators</u>
   if
   in the event that
   provided (that)
   as long as

Examples:

a) The grapes are
    irradiated;
$\left\{\begin{array}{l}\underline{\text{in that case,}}\\ \underline{\text{in this case,}}\\ \underline{\text{in other words,}}\end{array}\right\}$
they may be brought
into the country.

b) $\left\{ \begin{array}{c} \underline{\text{In the event that}} \\ \underline{\text{If}}^6 \\ \underline{\text{Provided (that)}} \\ \underline{\text{As long as}} \end{array} \right\}$ the grapes are irradiated, they may be brought into the country.

Positive conditions may also be indicated with the following complex preposition:

c. <u>Complex Prepositions</u>
   in the event of

Example:

c) <u>In the event of</u> faulty irradiation, the grapes will be returned to the grower.

Negative

Negative conditions are indicated with the following coordinators and subordinators:

a. <u>Coordinators</u>   b. <u>Subordinators</u>
   otherwise   *unless*
   if not

Examples:

a) These eggs must be cooked for ten minutes; $\left\{ \begin{array}{c} \underline{\text{if not,}} \\ \underline{\text{otherwise,}} \end{array} \right\}$ they cannot be eaten.

b) <u>Unless</u> these eggs are cooked for ten minutes, they cannot be eaten.

Negative conditions may also be indicated with the the following complex preposition:

c. <u>Complex Prepositions</u>
   barring

Example:

c) <u>Barring</u> being undercooked, the eggs may be eaten without fear of food poisoning.

---

[6] Conditional sentences with *if* most commonly take one of the three following forms: 1) the real, 2) the present unreal, and 3) the past unreal conditional. The real conditional describes a non-hypothetical situation. It indicates either a) a single time or b) general time:

  a) a single time: <u>if</u> + VERB$_{simple\ present}$, VERB$_{will}$
      If it <u>rains</u> tomorrow, I <u>will take</u> an umbrella.

  b) general time: <u>if</u> + VERB$_{simple\ present}$, VERB$_{simple\ present}$
      If it <u>rains</u>, I <u>take</u> my umbrella.

The present unreal conditional describes a hypothetical condition in the present:

  <u>if</u> + VERB$_{simple\ past}$, VERB$_{would}$
      If it <u>rained</u> today, I <u>would take</u> my umbrella.

The past unreal conditional describes a hypothetical condition in the past:

  <u>if</u> + VERB$_{past\ perfect}$, VERB$_{would\ have}$
      If it <u>had rained</u> yesterday, I <u>would have taken</u> my umbrella.

EXEMPLIFICATION

Exemplification words precede a series of words or sentences that support a point or give examples. Exemplification is indicated with the following coordinators only:

    a. <u>Coordinators</u>   b. <u>Subordinators</u>
       first (second, third, etc.)   *[none]*
      in the first (second, etc.)
        place
      for example
      e.g. [from Latin *exempli gratia* "free example"]

Example:

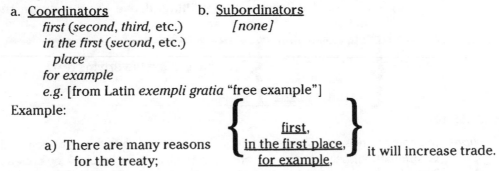

a) There are many reasons for the treaty; { first, in the first place, for example, } it will increase trade.

Exemplification may also be indicated with the the following complex prepositions:

    c. <u>Complex Prepositions</u>
      such as
      e.g.
      for example

Example:

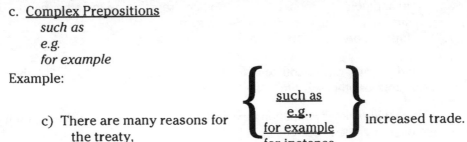

c) There are many reasons for the treaty, { such as e.g., for example for instance } increased trade.

CHOICE

Choice words have the same meaning as the coordinating conjunction *or*. They indicate that the information in one clause can be replaced by the information in another clause. Choice is indicated with the following coordinators only:

    a. <u>Coordinators</u>   b. <u>Subordinators</u>
      on the other hand   *[none]*
      alternatively

Example:

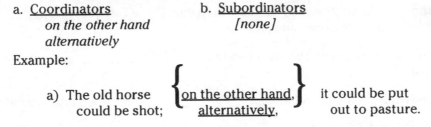

a) The old horse could be shot; { on the other hand, alternatively, } it could be put out to pasture.

SUMMATION

Summation words indicate that the final clause in a series summarizes the information in previous clause(s). Summation is indicated with the following coordinators only:

    a. <u>Coordinators</u>   b. <u>Subordinators</u>
      in conclusion   *[none]*
      in summary

> *in short*
> *in other words*

Example:

a) You turned left without signalling, drove too slowly on the freeway, and almost hit a pedestrian;

{
in conclusion,
in summary,
in short,
in other words,
} you have failed the driving test.

EXERCISE 14.2

Directions: Indicate the relationship (i.e., addition, explanation, condition, exemplification, choice, or summation) between the first and second clauses in the blank before each sentence. Then fill the remaining blanks with coordinators from the AND group below. There is one sentence for each coordinator.

in addition	in fact	otherwise	on the other hand
similarly	in other words	in summary	
furthermore	in that case	for example	

1. ____ Children must have a source of love and support; _____ , they will turn to street gangs or other substitute "families."

2. ____ There will be an examination next Friday; _____ , it will count for fifty percent of your grade in this course.

3. ____ People who fear flying can take the train from New York to San Francisco; _____, they can go by ship via the Panama Canal.

4. ____ That film has a weak story, mediocre acting, and uninspired photography; _____, it has little chance of being nominated for an Academy Award.

5. ____ The Suez Canal shortened the route from the Middle East to Europe; _____, it brought Egypt money and prestige.

6. ____ The elevators cannot be used when there is a fire; _____, you must use the stairs.

7. ____ The earth moves around the sun; _____, the moon orbits round the earth.

8. ____ English is the *lingua franca* of international business; _____, it is the language with which most international business-people communicate.

9. ____ John's grandfather would do anything for a bottle of whiskey; _____, he once gave someone his deed to a silver mine for a case of Johnnie Walker Red.

10. ____ Travel increases our understanding of other peoples; _____, my brother went to India last year, and ever since he's been volunteering at the Refugee Center.

EXERCISE 14.3

Directions: Choose five of the sentences from Exercise 14.2 and rewrite each one with a subordinator from the list below. Note that not all coordinators have corresponding subordinators.

in addition to the fact that	in the same way as	if
not to mention the fact that	unless	

Example: The king owns a yacht. <u>In addition</u>, he has a house in Paris.

Solution: The king owns a yacht <u>in addition to the fact that</u> he has a house in Paris.

EXERCISE 14.4

Directions: Rewrite the sentences from Exercise 14.2 with a complex preposition from the list below (where possible).

in addition to	in the event of	such as
not to mention		barring

Example: The king owns a yacht <u>in addition to the fact that</u> he has a house in Paris.

Solution: The king owns a yacht <u>in addition to</u> a house in Paris.

The BUT Relationship

The coordinators and subordinators that show the BUT relationship indicate that information of a contrary nature will be supplied in the following clause. They include the categories of contrast and rebuttal.

CONTRAST

Contrast words indicate that the information in one clause is in contrast with the information in another. Contrast may be specified or generalized.

Specified Contrast

Specified contrast indicates a direct contrast in a specific category, which is often completely opposite to the information in the other clause. Specified contrast is shown with the following coordinators and subordinators:

a. <u>Coordinators</u>
   in contrast
   by comparison
   conversely
   on the other hand

b. <u>Subordinators</u>
   whereas
   while
   where

Examples:

a) Switzerland is a mountainous country; { <u>in contrast,</u> <u>by comparison,</u> <u>conversely,</u> <u>on the other hand,</u> } Holland is flat.

b) { <u>Whereas</u> <u>While</u> <u>Where</u> } Switzerland is a mountainous country, Holland is flat.

Specified contrast may also be indicated with the the following complex prepositions:

    c. <u>Complex Prepositions</u>
       in contrast with
       compared with

Example:

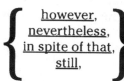

c) {<u>In contrast with</u> / <u>Compared with</u>} Holland, Switzerland is a mountainous country.

Generalized Contrast

Generalized contrast words indicate that the information in one clause contrasts in some manner with the information in another and that the information is usually surprising or unexpected. Generalized contrast is indicated with the following coordinators and subordinators:

  a. <u>Coordinators</u>   b. <u>Subordinators</u>
    however   *although*
    nevertheless   *even though*
    in spite of that   *in spite of the fact that*
    still   *even if*

Examples:

a) Helen thinks Vern is a wonderful artist; {<u>however,</u> <u>nevertheless,</u> <u>in spite of that,</u> <u>still,</u>} she doesn't trust him.

b) {<u>Although</u> <u>Even though</u> <u>In spite of the fact that</u> <u>Even if</u>} Helen thinks Vern is a wonderful artist, she doesn't trust him.

Generalized contrast may also be indicated with the the following complex prepositions:

    c. <u>Complex Prepositions</u>
       in spite of
       despite
       notwithstanding

Example:

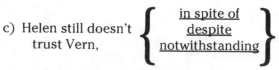

c) Helen still doesn't trust Vern, {<u>in spite of</u> <u>despite</u> <u>notwithstanding</u>} his artistic talents.

REBUTTAL

Rebuttal words indicate that the information in the first clause is not a true or correct opinion, whereas the information in the second clause is true or correct. Rebuttal is indicated with the following coordinators and subordinators:

a. <u>Coordinators</u>
  in fact
  as a matter of fact
  actually
  in reality

b. <u>Subordinators</u>
  when in fact
  when in reality

Examples:

a) The magazine proclaimed that Smith was dead; { in fact, as a matter of fact, actually, in reality, } he was living in Rio.

b) The magazine proclaimed that Smith was dead { when in fact when in reality } he was living in Rio.

Rebuttal may also be indicated with the the following complex preposition:

c. <u>Complex Prepositions</u>
  instead of

Example:

c) The magazine proclaimed that Smith was dead <u>instead of</u> living in Rio.

EXERCISE 14.5

Directions: Indicate the relationship (i.e., specified contrast, generalized contrast, or rebuttal) between the first and second clauses in the blank before each sentence. Then fill the remaining blanks with a coordinator from the BUT group below.

in contrast   however   in fact

1. _____ Your dog looks quite healthy; _____, it is not a good idea to feed a pet table scraps.

2. _____ The oil was supposed to have come from Saudi Arabia; _____, it came from Iraq.

3. _____ The color white is the presence of all the colors of light; _____, the color black is the absence of all the colors of light.

4. _____ The planet Saturn was once thought to have six rings; _____, it has more than a thousand and possibly as many as a hundred thousand rings.

5. _____ High-heeled shoes may be very stylish and attractive; _____, they can be quite harmful to the feet.

EXERCISE 14.6

Directions: Rewrite the sentences from Exercise 14.5 with a subordinator from the list below.

whereas   although   when in fact

  Example: The painting has been damaged; <u>however</u>, it is still worth a lot of money.

  Solution: <u>Although</u> the painting has been damaged, it is still worth a lot of money.

EXERCISE 14.7

Directions: Rewrite the sentences from Exercise 14.5 with a complex preposition from the list below (where possible).

in contrast with   in spite of   instead of

  Example: <u>Although</u> the painting has been damaged, it is still worth a lot of money.

  Solution: <u>In spite of</u> the damage, the painting is still worth a lot of money.

The SO Relationship

The coordinators and subordinators that show the SO relationship indicate that information showing cause or effect is supplied in another clause. They include the categories of cause, effect, and purpose.

CAUSE

Cause words indicate that the information in one clause will show why the information in another clause occurs or exists. Cause is indicated with the following coordinators and subordinators:

a. <u>Coordinators</u>
  the reason is [informal]

b. <u>Subordinators</u>
  because
  since
  as
  due to the fact that

Examples:

a) The sun rises in the east; <u>the reason is</u>, the earth rotates in a clockwise direction.

b) The sun rises in the east $\left\{ \begin{array}{c} \underline{because} \\ \underline{since} \\ \underline{as} \\ \underline{due\ to\ the\ fact\ that} \end{array} \right\}$ the earth rotates in a clockwise direction.

Cause may also be indicated with the following complex prepositions:

c. <u>Complex Prepositions</u>
  because of
  due to (used only after a linking verb such as *be*)

Example:

c) The sun rises in the east <u>because of</u> the earth's clockwise rotation.
   The sun's rising in the east is <u>due to</u> the earth's clockwise rotation.

EFFECT

Effect words indicate that the information in one clause is the result of the information in another. Effect is indicated with the following coordinators and subordinators:

a. <u>Coordinators</u>
therefore
as a result
thus
for this reason
consequently

b. <u>Subordinators</u>
because
so...(adjective or adverb)...that
such...(noun phrase)...that

Examples:

a) The patient was afraid of dentists; { <u>therefore,</u> <u>as a result,</u> <u>thus,</u> <u>for this reason,</u> <u>consequently,</u> } he refused to have his teeth examined.

b) The patient refused to have his teeth examined <u>because</u> he was afraid of dentists.

The patient { was <u>so</u> afraid / had <u>such</u> a fear } of dentists that he refused to have his teeth examined.

PURPOSE

Purpose words indicate that the information in one clause shows the desire for or the possibility of a result arising from the information in another clause. Purpose is indicated with the following coordinators and subordinators:

a. <u>Coordinators</u>
for this reason
[often paired
with clauses that have
verbs like *want* or *need*
to show desire]

b. <u>Subordinators</u>
so that
[the subordinate clause verb
often occurs with a modal
to show possibility]

Examples:

a) The company **needs** to reduce costs; <u>for this reason</u>, the factory will be moved to Asia.

b) The factory will be moved to Asia <u>so that</u> the company **can** reduce costs.

Purpose may also be indicated with the complex preposition *in order to*, which is often reduced to *to*. Either form must be followed by VERB$_{base}$.

c. <u>Complex Preposition</u>
(in order) to

Example:

c) The factory will be moved to Asia <u>(in order) to</u> reduce costs.

EXERCISE 14.8

Directions: Indicate the relationship (cause, effect, or purpose) between the first and second clauses in the blank before each sentence. Then fill the remaining blanks with a coordinator from the SO group below.

         the reason is   therefore   for this reason

1. _____ The child could not stop coughing; _____ , the doctor gave him some cough medicine.

2. _____ The tablecloth still has wine and coffee stains on it; _____ , the laundry forgot to use bleach.

3. _____ The train was moving very fast; _____ , it could not stop in time to avoid hitting the car on the railroad crossing.

4. _____ The car had a lock on the steering wheel; _____ , car thieves ignored it.

5. _____ The Mississippi River flooded in 1993; _____ , there was a heavy winter snow layer in the mountains.

EXERCISE 14.9

Directions: Choose three of the sentences from Exercise 14.8 and rewrite each one with a subordinator from the list below.

        because   so/such...that   so that

    Example: The politician had run a negative campaign; <u>therefore,</u> he lost the election.

    Solution: The politician lost the election <u>because</u> he had run a negative campaign.

EXERCISE 14.10

Directions: Find the sentence(s) in Exercise 14.8 that may be rewritten with the complex preposition and/or the complex subordinator below.

        because of   (in order) to

    Example: The politician lost the election <u>because</u> he had run a negative campaign.

    Solution: The politician lost the election <u>because of</u> his negative campaign.

Table 14.1 summarizes the primary logical coordinators, subordinators, and complex prepositions.

Table 14.1 Logical Coordinators, Subordinators, and Complex Prepositions

TYPE	CATEGORY	SUBCATEGORY	COORDINATOR	SUBORDINATOR	COMPLEX PREPOSITION
AND	Addition	Different Info.	in addition	in addition to the fact that	in addition to
		Similar info.	similarly	in the same way as	—
		Unexpected info.	furthermore	not to mention the fact that	not to mention
		Gen./Specif. info.	in fact	—	—
	Explanation		in other words	by which I mean that	—
	Condition	Positive	in that case	if	in the event of
		Negative	otherwise	unless	barring
	Exemplification		for example	—	such as
	Choice		on the other hand	—	—
	Summation		in summary	—	—
BUT	Contrast	Specified	in contrast	whereas	in contrast with
		Generalized	however	although	in spite of
	Rebuttal		in fact	when in fact	instead of
SO	Cause		the reason is	because	because of
	Effect		therefore	because/so [ADJ] that	—
	Purpose		for this reason	so that	—

EXERCISE 14.11

Directions: Choose the letter of the clause on the right that logically completes the clause on the left and write it in the blank.

A. The river was polluted

1. ; in addition, _____ .
2. ; in contrast, ___ .
3. ; in fact, ___ .
4. ; in other words, ___ .
5. whereas ___ .
6. , for example ___ .
7. , not to mention the fact that ___ .
8. ; however, ___ .
9. in addition to ___ .
10. by which I mean that ___ .
11. , e.g., ___ .
12. ; in short, ___ .
13. ; on the other hand, ___ .
14. in spite of ___ .
15. although ___ .

a. the other problems of the nation
b. it contained poisonous substances
c. factories were dumping chemicals in pits
d. nobody was protecting the environment
e. the Rebus River contained high dioxin levels
f. laws designed to protect the environment
g. the air was quite clean

B. Howard was a doctor and a researcher

1. ; in addition, _____ .
2. ; in contrast, ___ .
3. ; in fact, ___ .
4. ; in other words, ___ .
5. whereas ___ .
6. , for example ___ .
7. , not to mention the fact that ___ .
8. ; however, ___ .

a. he taught at the university medical school
b. he had quite a busy life
c. he had seven children
d. his physical disability
e. his wife was a waitress
f. having a wife and seven children
g. he saw about fifteen patients and worked in his laboratory four times a week

9. in addition to ___ .

10. , by which I mean that ___ .

11. , e.g., ___ .

12. ; in short, ___ .

13. ; on the other hand, ___ .

14. in spite of ___ .

15. although ___ .

CHRONOLOGICAL COORDINATORS AND SUBORDINATORS

The coordinators and subordinators that show a chronological relationship indicate that one clause took place at a different time than or at the same time as another clause. These words differ from the logical coordinators and subordinators in that they are not synonyms of each other but rather represent different time relationships. They include the categories of sequence and simultaneity. [Note: The associated prepositions are not indicated since they were discussed in Chapter 13.]

Sequence

Sequence words indicate that the information in one clause took place before or after the information in another clause. Sequence is indicated with the following coordinators and subordinators:

a. <u>Coordinators</u>
before that, previously
until then, up to then
after that, afterwards, then
since then
by then

b. <u>Subordinators</u>
before
until
after
since
by the time that

Notice that, with the exception of *by the time that*, the subordinators in this list are identical to certain prepositions of time. The difference is that subordinators are followed by an independent clause, whereas prepositions are followed by a noun phrase.

Examples:

a)
Julia bought a new car; {
<u>before that</u>, she had only a bicycle.
<u>until then</u>, she had had only a bicycle.
<u>after that</u>, she found a new job.
<u>since then</u>, she has found a new job.
<u>by then</u>, she had grown tired of her bicycle.
}

b) <u>Before</u> Julia bought a new car, she had only a bicycle.
<u>Until</u> Julia bought a new car, she had had only a bicycle.
<u>After</u> Julia bought a new car, she found a new job.
<u>Since</u> Julia bought a new car, she has found a new job.
<u>By the time that</u> Julia bought a new car, she had grown tired of her bicycle.

Other sequence coordinators with no parallel subordinators include the words *first* (*of all*), *at first, initially, subsequently, eventually, at last, finally,* and *in the end.*

Simultaneity

Simultaneity words indicate that the information in one clause took place at the same time as the information in another clause. Simultaneity is indicated with the following coordinators and subordinators:

a. <u>Coordinators</u>
  at this/that time
  during this/that time
  meanwhile, in the meantime
  at the same time, simultaneously

b. <u>Subordinators</u>
  when
  while
  as

Examples:

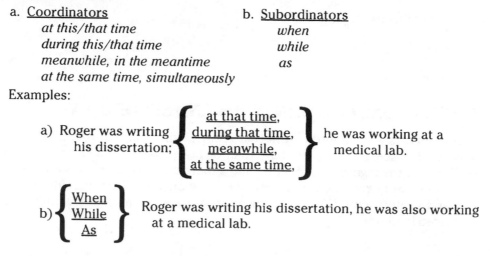

a) Roger was writing his dissertation; { at that time, during that time, meanwhile, at the same time, } he was working at a medical lab.

b) { When While As } Roger was writing his dissertation, he was also working at a medical lab.

Table 14.2 summarizes the primary chronological coordinators and subordinators.

Table 14. 2 Chronological Coordinators and Subordinators

CATEGORY	COORDINATOR	SUBORDINATOR
Sequence	before that	before
	until then	until
	after that	after
	since then	since
	by then	by the time that
Simultaneity	at that time	when

EXERCISE 14.12

Directions: Indicate the relationship (i.e., sequence or simultaneity) between the first and second clauses in the blank before each sentence. Then fill the remaining blanks with coordinators from the chronological group below.

before that   after that   by then
until then   since then   at that time

1. _____ The patient was conscious for a few minutes; _____ , she went into a coma and died.

2. _____ Mr. Packwood was asked to produce his personal diary; _____ , such a request had never been made of a senator.

3. _____ Dinosaurs roamed the earth during the Jurassic and Cretaceous periods; _____ , most of the earth was warmer than it is now.

4. _____ A few pieces of the satellite fell into the ocean; _____ , most of it had burned up in the earth's atmosphere.

5. _____ The sun will eclipse again in 1999; _____ , there will have been a number of lunar eclipses.

6. _____ The country became independent in 1960; _____ , it has experienced economic stagnation.

EXERCISE 14.13

Directions: Rewrite the sentences in Exercise 14.12 with a subordinator from the list below.

before   after   by the time that
until   since   when

Example: George became an actor. Before that, he was a musician.

Solution: Before George became an actor, he was a musician.

PROBLEM SOLVING WITH THE COORDINATION AND SUBORDINATION SYSTEMS

In the problems below it is possible to get the following right:

a. correct CHOICE OF COORDINATOR OR SUBORDINATOR (e.g., coordinator)

b. correct CATEGORY OF COORDINATOR/SUBORDINATOR (e.g., the AND group)

c. correct POSSIBLE FORM OF COORDINATOR/SUBORDINATOR (e.g. *however, although*)

d. correct POSITION OF COORDINATOR/SUBORDINATOR (e.g., before main clause)

e. correct PUNCTUATION (e.g., semicolon before coordinator)

These elements reflect what students are likely to do wrong in using coordination or subordination: a) choose a coordinator when the sentence structure requires a subordinator, and vice versa, b) use a coordinator/subordinator from the wrong category, c) use an incorrect coordinator/subordinator structure, d) put the coordinator/subordinator in the wrong place, or (e) use incorrect punctuation with the coordinator/subordinator.

EXERCISE 14.14

Directions: In the following sentences, a student made a single error in using cordination and subordination. Your job is to address the error in three stages:

    a) bracket the error to focus your attention

    b) list what the student got right about the bracketed error (in this case, the error concerns coordination/subordination) and show this in parentheses

    c) compare the original erroneous sentence to the correct sentence and explain what mistake the student made

    Example: *The student did not study; because, he failed the exam.

            [The star (*) indicates that the sentence contains an error.]

    Solution:

      a) Bracket the error (some aspect of coordination/subordination):

        *The student did not study; [because], he failed the exam.

      b) Show what is right about the coordinator/subordinator:

        correct category of coordinator/subordinator (the SO group)

        correct form of coordinator/subordinator (*because*)

        correct position of coordinator/subordinator (before second clause)

        correct punctuation (semicolon before a coordinator; comma after a coordinator)

      c) Compare the erroneous sentence to the correct form and explain the mistake:

        *The student did not study; [because], he failed the exam.

        The student did not study; therefore, he failed the exam.

    Explanation: The logic, sentence structure, and punctuation require a coordinator, not a subordinator.

1. *The plant survived eventhough it had had no water for months.

2. *The reward was not given; until, the criminal had been captured.

3. *In that case you have a question, please see the professor during her office hours.

4. *There is snow on the ground, the trees have no leaves, and it is very cold. It must be, in short, winter.

5. *First, the class designed the boat. Then, it built the boat. Nevertheless, it tested the boat in the swimming pool.

6. *The pump circulates the cooling water the heart circulates blood much as.

7. *The glass got so hot; that, it burned Janie's fingers.

8. *Imelda has fifty dresses; on the contrary, she has a hundred pairs of shoes.

9. *The old man collected some wood for this reason he could start a fire.

10. *Pluto is a small planet; in deed, it is the smallest planet in the Solar System.

COORDINATION AND SUBORDINATION IN DISCOURSE

Coordination and subordination is used sparingly in longer stretches of discourse. Although the exercises in this chapter suggest that any two logically or chronologically related sentences may be joined by means of coordinators and subordinators, these words occur only at pivotal points in discourse. For example, in the paragraph from *I Hate English!* at the beginning of this chapter, the coordinator *but* has one purpose: to contrast Mei Mei's use of English and Chinese. In the segment from *The Silent Language*, the twenty coordinators and subordinators set up complex relationships, some of which are shown in the following discourse map of that segment:

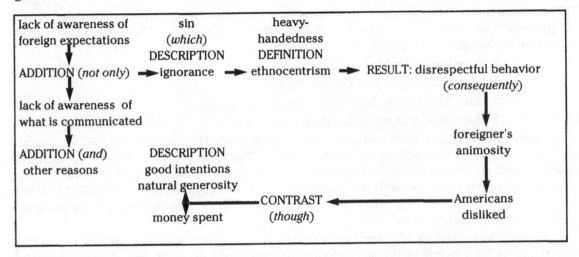

The discourse map shows that the coordinators and subordinators (in italics) signal essential relationships in the discourse propositions, but they do not occur between every sentence. For this reason, after we have taught students how to link sentences, we must be careful to show them how coordinators and subordinators are used in extended discourse.

Chapter 15

THE COMPLEMENT SYSTEM

The complement system allows us to embed a clause inside a sentence in order to complete or "complement" the sentence slot to which it was added. The major forms of complementation are shown in the following examples:

a) Mary knows **that** John left.

b) Mary wants John **to** mow the lawn.

c) Mary appreciates John's wash**ing** the windows.

d) Mary makes more money **than** John does.

All embedded clauses have a clause marker to indicate that embedding has taken place, and they are always subordinate to the main clause. The clause markers for complements are called **complementizers**. Sentence (a) is a *that*-clause with the complementizer *that*. Sentence (b) is an infinitive structure with the complementizer *to*. Sentence (c) is a VERB$_{ing}$ structure with the complementizer *-ing* (and the associated possessive). Sentence (d) is a comparison with the complementizer *than*.

The example sentences all have complements in the object slot. Depending on the type, complements also occur in the subject slot, the predicate noun phrase slot, the predicate adjective slot, the adverbial slot, and after certain prepositions and particles. Since *that*-clauses, the most common form of complementation, were covered in Chapter 8, we will concentrate here on the other major types of complements: infinitive structures, VERB$_{ing}$ structures, and comparisons.

INFINITIVE STRUCTURES

The requirement that a verb agree with its subject is one of the ways that subjects control verbs. Whenever a verb is controlled by a subject, that verb is said to be finite (e.g., VERB$_s$, VERB$_\emptyset$, and VERB$_{ed_1}$ are all finite verb forms that must be preceded by a subject, even if that subject is understood to be *you*, as in command forms). Look at the following examples:

a) The sun <u>shines</u>.

b) The trees <u>grow</u>.

c) The man <u>drowned</u>.

The underlined verbs in Sentences (a), (b) and (c) are all finite. However, when a verb is no longer controlled by a subject, it becomes unlimited or infinite, hence the term *infinitive*. Look at the following examples:

a) Sally hates <u>to drive</u>.

b) Rob seems <u>to want to meet</u> his pretty classmate.

c) <u>To live in Italy</u> would be marvelous.

In Sentences (a) and (b), the subject is separated from the infinitive by a finite verb which prevents the subject from controlling the infinitive verb. In Sentence (c), there is no subject before the infinitive verb. The lack of a subject in infinitive verbs has the effect of generalizing the sense of the verb. Thus, Sentence (c) can be understood to mean "For anyone to live in Italy would be marvelous." Infinitive structures have two forms: with *to* (the standard form) and without *to* (sometimes called the "bare infinitive").

Infinitive Structures with *To*

Infinitive structures are the result of a clause embedding process in which a repeated subject is removed, leaving the verb in its infinitive form. The most common form of the infinitive is *to* plus the base form of the verb. Infinitive structures may occur as an object complement (i.e., in the object slot), as a subject complement, as a predicate noun phrase complement, or as a predicate adjective complement.

INFINITIVE STRUCTURES AS OBJECT COMPLEMENTS

Infinitive structures most commonly occur as object complements. There are two possible infinitive structures, depending on whether the subjects of the main and the subordinate clauses are the same or different.

Same Subject

Object complements with the same subject as the main clause simply delete the subject of the subordinate clause. Look at the following example:

SUBJECT	VERB	OBJECT

The nurse plans X.

X_1= ~~The nurse~~ works in a hospital in Kenya.
X_2=   to work in a hospital in Kenya

The nurse plans to work in a hospital in Kenya.

In the example sentence, the subordinate clause to be embedded (X_1) has the same subject as the main clause (*the nurse*). Such repeated noun phrases are removed from the subordinate clause in the clause embedding process. Once the verb has lost its subject, it immediately reverts to the infinitive form in X_2. The infinitive structure is then ready to be embedded in the main clause.

EXERCISE 15.1

Directions: Combine the two clauses using an infinitive structure as an object complement.

1. The police promised X. X = The police found the boy who had been kidnapped.

2. Roger has refused X. X = Roger accepts a scholarship at a religious college.

3. Maria agreed X. X = Maria paid back the money she borrowed.

4. The wounded fox was trying X. X = The wounded fox hid in the corner of the garden.

5. Scientists are attempting X. X = Scientists map the entire human genome, or genetic blueprint.

Different Subject

Object complements with a different subject from that in the main clause retain the subject of the infinitive clause. Look at the following example:

SUBJECT	VERB	OBJECT

The party wanted X.

X_1= He   ran for President.
X_2= him to run for President

The party wanted him to run for President.

In the example sentence, the subordinate clause (X_1) has a different subject (*he*) from that of the main clause (*the party*). In such a sentence, the subject of the subordinate clause is "raised" in status to the object of the main clause, changing the subject pronoun (*he*) to the object pronoun (*him*) and causing the clause verb (*ran*) to lose its subject, which reverts to the infinitive form in X_2. The infinitive structure is then ready to be embedded in the main clause.

EXERCISE 15.2

Directions: Underline the main subject and the clause subject. Then combine the two clauses using an infinitive structure as an object complement.

1. The native peoples believed X. X = Their village was the center of the World.

2. Alicia's grandfather advised X. X = She accepted the offer of marriage from the diplomat.

3. The judges determined X. X = The man from Korea is the winner of the wrestling match.

4. The miners expected X. X = The tunnel was repaired by the next morning.

5. The children's teacher told X. X = They take the frog back to the pond.

The main verbs that may be followed by an infinitive structure no matter what the subject are limited to those which suggest unfulfilled possibilities (e.g., *expect, hope, plan, wish*) rather than real experienced events (e.g., *admit, enjoy, finish, resist*).[1] The most common "possibility" verbs are shown in the following list:

agree	dare	hope	prefer	tend
arrange	decide	intend	prepare	try
attempt	demand	learn	promise	want
choose	determine	need	refuse	wish
claim	expect	offer	resolve	
consent	fail	plan	seem	

---

[1] This contrast was described by D. Bolinger (1968), "Entailment and the Meaning of Structures," *Glossa* 2,2:119-127 and cited in M. Celce-Murcia and D. Larsen-Freeman, *The Grammar Book* (Cambridge, MA: Newbury House Publishers, 1983), 434.

INFINITIVE STRUCTURES AS SUBJECT COMPLEMENTS

Infinitive structures also occur as subject complements. There are two possible infinitive structures depending on whether the subject of the infinitive clause is generalized or particular.

Generalized Subject

If the subject of the infinitive clause is generalized, it is deleted. Look at the following example:

SUBJECT	VERB	PNP/PADJ/OBJECT
X	is	a wonderful feeling.
X_1 = ~~Somebody~~ is in love.		
X_2 = to be in love		

To be in love is a wonderful feeling.

In the subordinate clause (X_1), the generalized subject (*somebody*) is removed and the verb reverts to the infinitive form in X_2. The infinitive structure is then ready to be embedded in the main clause.

IT-FOCUS

It is quite common for sentences containing infinitive subject complements to take an alternate form with *it* as the subject. This allows the infinitive structure to have primary focus, as new information is expected to come at the end of a sentence. Look at the following example:

    a) <u>To be in love</u> is a wonderful feeling.

    b) **It** is a wonderful feeling <u>to be in love</u>.

Sentence (a) would logically follow a statement such as "Valerie is in love," where the instance of being in love is already known to the hearer. Sentence (b) would serve as the opening sentence of a conversation in which the idea of being in love is presented as new information. In Sentence (b), the infinitive structure has been moved to the end of the sentence, leaving the verb without a subject. The subject slot must then be filled with the "dummy subject" *it*; otherwise, we would be left with the sentence **Is a wonderful feeling to be in love*, which is not grammatical in English since every clause must have a subject. We will call this process "*it*-focus," although its formal linguistic name is a cleft sentence.

EXERCISE 15.3

Directions: Combine the two clauses using an infinitive structure as a subject complement. Then change the sentence into a form containing *it* as the subject. Which of the two forms sounds better to you?

1. X is too late. X = Somebody takes the bus.

2. X would require a great deal of money. X = Somebody is a member of Parliament.

3. X was a dangerous and courageous act. X = Somebody became a member of the resistance.

4. X is quite prestigious. X = Somebody owns a Mercedes Benz.

5. X is not something we look forward to. X = Somebody lives in an old people's home.

Particular Subject

If the subject of the infinitive clause is particular, it is retained as the object of the preposition (and complementizer) *for*. Look at the following example:

SUBJECT	VERB	PNP/PADJ/OBJECT
X	was	a tragic event.

X_1 =   The Titanic sank on its maiden voyage.
X_2 =   **for** the Titanic to sink on its maiden voyage

For the Titanic to sink on its maiden voyage was a tragic event.

In the subordinate clause (X_1), *for* is inserted in front of the particular subject (*the Titanic*). This process separates the subject from its verb (making it the object of the preposition *for*), and the verb reverts to the infinitive form. The infinitive structure is then ready to be embedded in the main clause.

As with generalized subjects, sentences containing infinitive subject complements often take the alternate form with *it* as the subject (*it*-focus). Look at the following example:

    a) <u>For the Titanic to sink on its maiden voyage</u> was a tragic event.

    b) **It** was a tragic event <u>for the Titanic to sink on its maiden voyage</u>.

In Sentence (b), the infinitive structure has been moved to the end of the sentence, and the subject slot is filled with the "dummy subject" *it*. *It*-focus is even more common with predicate adjectives, as in the following example:

    a) It is <u>essential</u> for small children to have a stable source of love.

EXERCISE 15.4

Directions: Combine the two clauses using an infinitive structure as a subject complement. Then change the sentence into a form containing *it* as the subject. Which of the two forms sounds better to you?

1. X is important. X = ESL teachers are well trained.

2. X was a logical step. X = Hawaii became the fiftieth state.

3. X would anger the members of the board. X = John accepts another position.

4. X was odd. X = Mary was gone for so long.

5. X was appropriate. X = Clara got a scholarship at the music conservatory.

INFINITIVE STRUCTURES AS PREDICATE NOUN PHRASE COMPLEMENTS

Infinitive structures sometimes occur as predicate noun phrase complements. The subject of the subordinate clause must be the same as the subject of the main clause. Look at the following example:

SUBJECT	VERB	PREDICATE NOUN PHRASE
The hiker	was	a fool X.

X_1 = ~~The hiker~~ left   the campfire burning.
X_2 =   to leave   the campfire burning

The hiker was a fool to leave the campfire burning.

In the example sentence, the subordinate clause (X_1) has the same subject as the main clause (*the hiker*). The repeated subject is removed and the verb reverts to the infinitive form in X_2. The infinitive structure is then ready to be embedded in the main clause.

EXERCISE 15.5

Directions: Combine the two clauses using an infinitive structure as a predicate noun phrase complement.

1. That nurse was an angel X. X = That nurse brought my father a chocolate milkshake.

2. The wooden duck was a decoy X. X = The wooden duck attracted females.

3. The counselor was a genius X. X = The counselor suggested a horse-riding camp for the homeless children.

4. The investors were idiots X. X = The investors thought they could make a profit in six months.

5. The covered pit was a trap X. X = The trap caught tigers.

INFINITIVE STRUCTURES AS PREDICATE ADJECTIVE COMPLEMENTS

Infinitive structures also occur as predicate adjective complements. There are two possible infinitive structures depending on whether the subjects of the main and the subordinate clause are the same or different.

Same Subject

Predicate adjective complements with the same subject as the main clause simply delete the subject of the subordinate clause. Look at the following example:

SUBJECT	VERB	PREDICATE ADJECTIVE
David	was	afraid X.

X_1 = ~~David~~ was alone in the house.
X_2 =   to be alone in the house

David was afraid to be alone in the house.

In the example sentence, the subordinate clause (X_1) has the same subject as the main clause (*David*). The repeated subject is removed and the verb reverts to the infinitive form in X_2. The infinitive structure is then ready to be embedded in the main clause.

EXERCISE 15.6

Directions: Combine the two clauses using an infinitive structure as a predicate adjective complement.

1. The Olympic athletes were anxious X. X = The Olympic athletes began the trials.

2. The refugees were happy X. X = The refugees found shelter in a neighboring country.

3. The district attorney was furious X. X = The district attorney learned that the prisoners had escaped.

4. The old actress was delighted X. X = The old actress was nominated for an Academy Award.

5. We were sad X. X = We heard that your puppy was killed.

Different Subject

Predicate adjective complements with a different subject from the main clause insert the complementizer *for* in front of the subject of the infinitive clause, and the verb reverts to the infinitive form. There are only a few adjectives in English, all expressing emotions of some kind, that allow this structure. Look at the following example:

SUBJECT	VERB	PREDICATE ADJECTIVE

Mr. Song   would be   unhappy X.

X_1 = His daughter will   fail the exam.
X_2 = **for** his daughter to fail the exam

Mr. Song would be unhappy for his daughter to fail the exam.

In the example sentence, the subordinate clause (X_1) has a different subject (*his daughter*) from the main clause (*Mr. Song*). *For* is inserted before the subordinate clause subject and the verb is changed into the infinitive form in X_2. The infinitive structure is then ready to be embedded in the main clause.

EXERCISE 15.7

Directions: Underline the main subject and the clause subject. Then combine the two clauses using an infinitive structure as a predicate adjective complement.

1. The mother would be afraid X. X = Her young children walk to school by themselves.

2. The professor would be happy X. X = The student writes the paper again.

3. The artist was anxious X. X = The beautiful model poses for him.

4. The author would be delighted X. X = Her book is awarded a Pulitzer Prize.

5. The general would be proud X. X = His son joins the air force.

Infinitive Structures Without *To*

Infinitive structures without *to* are produced in the same manner as the infinitive structures with *to*. However, such structures occur only as object complements. Look at the following example:

SUBJECT	VERB	OBJECT

The man   saw   X.

X_1 = ~~She~~ fell off the chair.
X_2 =   fall off the chair

The man saw her fall off the chair.

In the example sentence, the subordinate clause (X_1) has a different subject (*she*) from that of the main clause (*the man*). As we saw before, the subject of the subordinate clause is "raised" in status to the object of the main clause, changing the subject pronoun (*she*) to the object pronoun (*her*) and causing the clause verb (*fell*) to lose its subject and revert to the infinitive form in X_2. With a perception verb like *see*, however, the infinitive structure has no *to*.

Infinitive structures without *to* occur as the object complements of certain causative verbs and verbs of perception.

INFINITIVE STRUCTURES WITH THE CAUSATIVE VERBS *LET*, *MAKE*, AND *HAVE*

The causative verbs *let*, *make*, and *have* do not allow *to* in the infinitive structure. *Let* as a causative verb means "to allow, to make it possible for something to happen." *Make* as a causative verb means "to force, to cause, to act upon with considerable pressure." *Have* as a causative verb means "to get somebody to do something because of an accepted condition (e.g., authority, money, personal relationship)." [Note: Be careful not to confuse the modal equivalent *have to* (= "must") with the causative verb *have*.] Look at the following examples:

    a) The zoo <u>lets</u> the children **touch** certain animals.
        The zoo <u>allows</u> the children **to touch** certain animals.

    b) The policeman <u>made</u> the drunk driver **sign** the ticket.
        The policeman <u>forced</u> the drunk driver **to sign** the ticket.

    c) Larry <u>had</u> the barber **trim** his beard.
        Larry <u>got</u> the barber **to trim** his beard.

The example sentences show that it is only the causative verbs in the first sentence of each pair that require an infinitive structure without *to*. Other verbs require an infinitive with *to*.

INFINITIVE STRUCTURES WITH PERCEPTION VERBS

The perception verbs include *see*, *watch*, *notice*, *hear*, *feel* and *observe*. Look at the following examples:

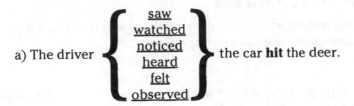

    b) The driver <u>expected</u> the car **to hit** the deer.

Sentence (a) shows that it is only the perception verbs that require an infinitive structure without *to*. Most verbs, such as *expect* in Sentence (b), require an infinitive structure with *to*. Perception verbs differ from the causative verbs in that perception verbs also allow complementation with VERB$_{ing}$ structures, whereas causative verbs do not. VERB$_{ing}$ structures will be discussed in the next section.

EXERCISE 15.8

Directions: Combine the two clauses using an infinitive structure without *to* as an object
complement.

1. The babysitter had X. X = The children cleaned their teeth before they went to bed.

2. The astronomer watched X. X = The supernova expanded to ten times its original size.

3. The dictator made X. X = The intelligentsia worked in the countryside.

4. The old man felt X. X = The earthquake rolled up the valley.

5. The people in the stands heard X. X = The plane broke the sound barrier.

VERB$_{ING}$ STRUCTURES

A VERB$_{ing}$ structure is a form that contains a verb with the *ing*-ending. In Chapter 4, we discussed the role of VERB$_{ing}$ forms in the verb tenses, specifically in relation to the continuous
aspect, e.g., *Joseph is living in Malaysia*. In Chapter 11, we discussed the role of VERB$_{ing}$ forms
as adjectives. In this chapter, we are concerned with VERB$_{ing}$ structures that function as complements. VERB$_{ing}$ structures that function as noun phrases or clauses are known as gerund
structures. VERB$_{ing}$ structures that function as modifiers are known as ING-participle structures.

Gerund Structures

Gerund structures are the result of a clause embedding process in which a repeated subject
is removed or transformed while the verb is transformed into its VERB$_{ing}$ form. A gerund
structure may occur as an object complement, a subject complement, a predicate noun
phrase complement, and after certain prepositions and particles.

GERUND STRUCTURES AS OBJECT COMPLEMENTS

There are two possible gerund structures depending on whether the subjects of the main
clause and the subordinate clause are the same or different.

Same Subject

Object complements with the same subject as the main clause delete the subject of the subordinate clause. Look at the following example:

SUBJECT	VERB	OBJECT
Students	enjoy	X.

$X_1 = $ ~~Students~~ take field trips.

$X_2 = $ taking field trips

Students enjoy taking field trips.

In the example sentence, the subordinate clause (X_1) has the same subject as the main
clause (*students*). As with the infinitive structures, repeated noun phrases are removed in the
clause embedding process. However, a fulfilled main verb such as *enjoy* requires that any verb

following it be a gerund. The verb in X_1 is therefore transformed into the gerund form in X_2. The gerund structure is then ready to be embedded in the main clause.

EXERCISE 15.9

Directions: Combine the two clauses using a gerund structure as an object complement.

1. Victoria cannot stand X. X = Victoria is with people who smoke cigarettes.

2. The reporter mentioned X. X = The reporter saw a gun in the victim's bedroom.

3. I could understand X. X = I desire to work in a friendly environment.

4. The therapist denied X. X = The therapist has too many patients.

5. The woman could not imagine X. X = The woman lives with other elderly people.

Different Subject

Object complements with a different subject from that in the main clause must retain the subject of the subordinate clause. Look at the following example:

SUBJECT	VERB	OBJECT

Sally   resents   X.
X_1 = He forgot   her birthday.
X_2 = **his** forgetting her birthday

a. Sally resents <u>his</u> forgetting her birthday.

In the example sentence, the subordinate clause (X_1) has a different subject (*he*) from that of the main clause (*Sally*). Fulfilled verbs such as *resent* require a verb that follows to be a gerund. The verb in X_1 (*forget*) is therefore transformed into the gerund form in X_2. However, since the subject is different in this case, it cannot be deleted. Instead, it is transformed into a possessive determiner (*his*). The gerund structure is then ready to be embedded in the main clause.

There are several situations, however, in which an object pronoun is used in place of the possessive determiner, as in the following example:

b. Sally resents <u>him</u> forgetting her birthday.

In general, the nonpossessive form is more likely to be used:[2]

1) when the situation is informal, e.g., *I understand <u>them</u> being angry.*

2) when a pronoun has no possessive form, e.g., *The judge cannot imagine <u>this</u> requiring a trial.*

3) when the subject of the gerund structure is inanimate, e.g., *Julia appreciates <u>the jewelry</u> being returned.*

4) when the subject of the gerund structure is a long proper name, e.g., *Many people resented <u>the Honorable Senator Joseph McCarthy</u> accusing innocent people of treason.*

---

[2] These limitations on the use of the possessive are described in M. Celce-Murcia and D. Larsen-Freeman, *The Grammar Book* (Cambridge, MA: Newbury House Publishers, 1983), 475.

The main verbs that may be followed by a gerund no matter what the subject are those which suggest real experienced events (e.g., *admit, enjoy, finish, resist*) rather than unfulfilled possibilities (e.g., *expect, hope, plan, wish*). However, gerunds generally occur much less frequently than infinitives. The most common "fulfilled" verbs are shown in the following list:

	admit	delay	finish	miss	resent
anticipate	appreciate	deny	imagine	postpone	resist
	avoid	detest	keep	practice	risk
	cannot stand	encourage	mention	recommend	suggest
	consider	enjoy	mind	report	understand

[Note: The underlined word can be replaced with other verbs, e.g., *endure, help, stop.*]

EXERCISE 15.10

Directions: Underline the main subject and the subordinate clause subject. Then combine the two clauses using a gerund structure as an object complement, both with and without the possessive forms. Which sounds better to you?

1.   The widow misses X. X = Her husband kissed her every morning.

2.   The Dean's Office recommended X. X = The student was put on probation.

3.   President Ronald Reagan denied X. X = Vice President George Walker Bush knew about the arms-for-hostages deal with Iran.

4.   The coach urged X. X = The team should try out for the Olympic Games.

5.   The newspaper admitted X. X = Those were unconfirmed reports.

GERUND STRUCTURES AS SUBJECT COMPLEMENTS

Gerund structures also occur as subject complements. They occur either with or without a possessive word, depending on the degree of generality required.

Generalized Subject

A gerund structure functioning as a subject complement has the same general sense that an infinitive structure in subject position has. Look at the following examples:

   a)   To live in Italy would be marvelous.
   b)   Living in Italy is marvelous.

The subject of Sentence (a) is an infinitive structure that has a generalized scope (i.e., it could apply to anyone) with the "unfulfilled possibility" sense that most infinitive structures imply. That is why it occurs with the modal *would*. The subject of Sentence (b) is a gerund structure that has a generalized scope with the "real experienced event" sense that most gerund structures imply. Facts are typically reported with the simple present tense, in this case *is*.

Gerund structures with a general subject have no possessive form. Look at the following example:

SUBJECT	VERB	PREDICATE NP/ADJECTIVE or OBJECT

X   is   a wonderful feeling.

X_1 = ~~Anyone~~ is in love.

X_2 =   being in love

Being in love is a wonderful feeling.

In the subordinate clause (X_1), the subject (*anyone*) is irrelevant. It is therefore removed and the verb is transformed into the gerund form in X_2. The gerund structure is then ready to be embedded in the main clause.

Particular Subject

Gerund structures that have a pronoun subject require a possessive form. Look at the following example:

SUBJECT	VERB	OBJECT

X   changed the course of European history.

X_1 = He was   defeated.

X_2 = **his** being defeated

a. <u>His</u> being defeated changed the course of European history.

In the example sentence, the subject of the subordinate clause (*he*) is transformed into a possessive determiner (*his*), while the verb (*was*) is transformed into the gerund form (*being*). The gerund structure is then ready to be embedded in the main clause. Gerund structures functioning as subject complements must use the possessive determiner if the subject of the gerund structure is a pronoun. The object pronoun is ungrammatical in this position:

b. *<u>Him</u> being defeated changed the course of European history.

Gerund structures with non-pronoun subjects need not be possessive, especially if they are lengthy:

c. <u>Napoleon Bonaparte's</u> being defeated changed the course of European history.

d. <u>Napoleon Bonaparte</u> being defeated changed the course of European history.

EXERCISE 15.11

Directions: Combine the two clauses using a gerund structure as a subject complement.

1. X cannot compensate for life's troubles. X = Anyone is famous.

2. X was a great idea. X = He suggested this hotel in the Dolomites.

3. X should stimulate the ecconomy. X = The government practices fiscal restraint.

4. X is less important than the process of getting there. X = Anyone reaches a goal.

5. X caused more harm than good. X = *The New York Times* printed the victim's name.

GERUND STRUCTURES AS PREDICATE NOUN PHRASE COMPLEMENTS

Gerund structures also occur as predicate noun phrase complements. However, they only occur in sentences with certain abstract subjects. Look at the following example:

SUBJECT	VERB	PREDICATE NOUN PHRASE
The main problem	is	X.

X_1 = They don't finish   high school.
X_2 = their not finishing high school

a. The main problem is <u>their</u> not finishing high school.
b. The main problem is <u>them</u> not finishing high school.

In the example sentence, the subject of the subordinate clause (*they*) is transformed into a possessive determiner (*their*) or object pronoun (*them*) while the verb (*don't finish*) is transformed into the gerund form (*not finishing*). The gerund structure is then ready to be embedded in the main clause. Sentence (a) shows the more specific **formal** gerund structure (*their not finishing high school*), which only applies to the subject (*they*) and is used in formal speaking and writing. Sentence (b) shows the more specific **informal** gerund structure (*them not finishing high school*), which again only applies to the subject (*they*) but is more likely to occur in informal speech or letter writing.

EXERCISE 15.12

Directions: Combine the two clauses using a gerund structure as a predicate noun phrase complement with and without the possessive forms when appropriate. Which sounds better to you?

1. The biggest difficulty is X. X = Someone got the peasants to register to vote.

2. The motive appeared to be X. X = He wanted to punish his former employer.

3. The advantage will be X. X = The company has control over the production facilities.

4. The problem was X. X = The former Union of Soviet Socialist Republics dissolved before the infrastructure was complete.

5. The alternative was X. X = Someone could do some kind of community service.

GERUND STRUCTURES WITH PARTICLES OR ALLIED PREPOSITIONS

Gerund structures occur after certain prepositions or particles, particularly after phrasal verbs (e.g., two word verbs), phrasal verbs with prepositions (three word verbs), or predicate adjectives with allied prepositions.

Phrasal Verbs

Some phrasal verbs require that the subject of the verb be the same as the subject of the subordinate clause. Others allow a different subject.

SAME SUBJECT

When the subject of the main clause is the same as the subject of the subordinate clause, the subject of the subordinate clause is deleted. Look at the following example:

SUBJECT	VERB	OBJECT

Sam   gave up X

X_1 = ~~Sam~~ tried to change her mind.

X_2 =   trying to change her mind.

Sam gave up trying to change her mind.

In the subordinate clause (X_1), the subject (*Sam*) is deleted because the same subject occurs in the main clause. The verb is transformed into the gerund form in X_2. The gerund structure is then ready to be embedded in the main clause.

DIFFERENT SUBJECT

When the subject of the main clause is different from the subject of the subordinate clause, the subject of the subordinate clause is retained in its possessive form. Look at the following example:

SUBJECT	VERB	OBJECT

Jane   insisted on X.

X_1 = He came   to her graduation ceremony.

X_2 = his coming to her graduation ceremony

a. Jane insisted on <u>his</u> coming to her graduation ceremony.

b. Jane insisted on <u>him</u> coming to her graduation ceremony .

In the subordinate clause (X_1), the subject (*he*) is transformed into a possessive determiner (or an object pronoun). Sentence (a) is formal while Sentence (b) is informal.

Phrasal Verbs with Allied Prepositions

Phrasal verbs with allied prepositions usually require a possessive determiner (and do not allow an object pronoun) even if the main subjects and the subject of the subordinate clause are the same. Look at the following example:

SUBJECT	VERB	OBJECT

The patient cut down on X.

X_1 = The patient smokes.

X_2 = his   smoking

The patient cut down on his smoking.

In the subordinate clause (X_1), the subject (*the patient*) is transformed into the appropriate possessive determiner (*his*) and the verb is transformed into a gerund (*smoking*). Examples of other phrasal verbs with allied prepositions that function in this way are shown below:

check up on	give in to	look down on	pick up on
get back to	go in for	look forward to	put up with
get through with	keep up with	look out for	stand up for

Predicate Adjectives with Allied Prepositions

Predicate adjectives with allied prepositions are frequently followed by gerund structures. The subjects of the main and subordinate clauses may be the same or different.

SAME SUBJECT

When the subject of the main clause is the same as the subject of the subordinate clause, the subject of the subordinate clause is deleted. Look at the following example:

SUBJECT	VERB	PREDICATE ADJECTIVE

Ann   is   famous for X.

X_1 = ~~Ann~~ paints   portraits
X_2 =   painting portraits

Ann is famous for painting portraits.

DIFFERENT SUBJECT

When the subject of the main clause is different from the subject of the subordinate clause, the subject of the subordinate clause is retained in its possessive form (or as an object pronoun). Look at the following example:

SUBJECT	VERB	PREDICATE ADJECTIVE

The bank   was   interested in X.

X_1 = He found good investment opportunities.
X_2 = his finding good investment opportunities

  a. The bank was interested in <u>his</u> finding good investment opportunities.
  b. The bank was interested in <u>him</u> finding good investment opportunities.

Sentence (a) is formal while Sentence (b) is informal.

Some examples of other predicate adjectives with allied prepositions that function in this way are shown below:

afraid of	familiar with	relevant to
aware of	fond of	satisfied with
certain of	frightened by	sensitive to
delighted with	happy with	surprised at
different from	known for	thankful for
disappointed in	opposed to	thrilled with

EXERCISE 15.13

Directions: Combine the two clauses using a gerund structure after the preposition or particle both with and without the possessive. Which sounds better to you?

1. The cat is no longer frightened by X. X = The dog barks at the mailman.

2. The soldier's children were not certain of X. X = The soldier's children still have a father.

3. The princess was thankful for X. X = The knight saved her from the local dragon.

4. The government is opposed to X. X = The church wants prayer in the public schools.

5. The athlete was disappointed at X. X = The athlete did not make his last high jump.

ING-Participle Structures

ING-participle structures are the result of a clause embedding process in which the subordinate clause subject is removed or transformed while the verb is transformed into its VERB$_{ing}$ form. They are different from gerunds in that the transformed subject may not be in a possessive form. ING-participle structures occur as object complements with perception verbs and as adverbial complements.

ING-PARTICIPLE STRUCTURES AS OBJECT COMPLEMENTS WITH PERCEPTION VERBS

Perception verbs (unlike causative *let, make,* and *have*) have the option of taking an ING-participle in place of the bare infinitive as an object complement. Look at the following example:

SUBJECT	VERB	OBJECT

The engineer watched the bridge X.

$X_1 = $ ~~The bridge~~ collapsed   into the river.

$X_2 = $ collapsing into the river

The engineer watched the bridge collapsing into the river.

The difference in meaning between the bare infinitive and the ING-participle is that the bare infinitive emphasizes the completion of the event whereas the ING-participle emphasizes the process. The same kind of complementation occurs with the perception verbs *feel, hear, notice, observe, see,* and *witness,* and other verbs such as *spend, find,* and *remember.*

EXERCISE 15.14

Directions: Combine the two clauses using an ING-participle structure as an object complement.

1. The doctor heard the old man's heart X. X = The old man's heart beat feebly.

2. Marianne noticed a spider X. X = A spider crawled up her leg.

3. The lawyer witnessed a taxi X. X = A taxi picked up one of the suspects.

4. The campers felt the hot tea X. X = The hot tea warmed their insides.

5. Several astronauts observed small asteroids X. X = Small asteroids flew past the shuttle.

ING-PARTICIPLE STRUCTURES AS ADVERBIAL COMPLEMENTS

ING-participle structures function primarily as adverbial complements. There are two possible ING-participle structures depending on whether the subjects of the main clause and the ING-participle clause are the same or different.[3]

---

[3] Adverbial complements may be constructed in almost the same way with ED$_2$-participles (e.g., *spoken, helped, exhausted*). The difference is that the passive *be* must also be removed before the clause is embedded, and the adverbial is almost always fronted. Look at the following examples:

    a) <u>Stolen from the museum</u>, the painting was badly scratched.

    b) <u>His body covered with scars</u>, the boxer stepped into the ring.

Sentence (a) shows an ED$_2$-participle structure with the same subject as the main clause. It is constructed from the following: <u>The painting</u> was badly scratched X. X = <u>The painting</u> was stolen from the museum. Sentence (b) shows an ED$_2$-participle with a different subject from the main clause. It is constructed from the following: <u>The boxer</u> stepped into the ring X. X = <u>His body</u> was covered with scars.

Same Subject

Adverbial complements with the same subject as the main clause delete the subject of the subordinate clause (X_1). Look at the following example:

SUBJECT	VERB	OBJ/PNP/PADJ	ADVERBIAL
Marisela	has	a lot of homework X.	

$$X_1 = \text{~~Marisela~~ is   a student.}$$
$$X_2 = \text{being a student}$$

a. Marisela has a lot of homework, <u>being a student</u>.

b. <u>Being a student</u>, Marisela has a lot of homework.

In the example sentence, the subordinate clause (X_1) has the same subject as the main clause (*Marisela*). As with the infinitive and gerund structures, repeated noun phrases are removed in the clause embedding process, while the verb in X_1 is transformed into the ING-participle form in X_2. The ING-participle structure is then ready to be embedded in the main clause. Sentence (a) shows the adverbial complement in the normal adverbial position. Sentence (b) shows the adverbial complement in the fronted position, which is much more common for these structures.

Adverbial complements with the same subject as the main clause also occur after certain prepositions, especially *before*, *after*, and *by*. Look at the following examples:

a) Grace went back to college **after** <u>leaving her husband</u>.
After <u>leaving her husband</u>, Grace went back to college.

b) Tim cleaned his teeth carefully **before** <u>going to the dentist</u>.
Before <u>going to the dentist</u>, Tim cleaned his teeth carefully.

c) The new employee made a good impression **by** <u>arriving early</u>.
By <u>arriving early</u>, the new employee made a good impression.

Different Subject

Adverbial complements with a different subject from the main clause, which occur much less often than the first type, retain the subject of the ING-participle clause (X_1) in its original state. Look at the following example:

SUBJECT	VERB	OBJ/PNP/PADJ	ADVERBIAL
Virgil	had	an inferiority complex X.	

$$X_1 = \text{His father was   a famous author.}$$
$$X_2 = \text{his father being a famous author}$$

a. Virgil had an inferiority complex, <u>his father being a famous author</u>.

b. <u>His father being a famous author</u>, Virgil had an inferiority complex.

In the example sentence, the subordinate clause (X_1) has a different subject (*his father*) from the main clause (*Virgil*). In ING-participle structures, the subject of the subordinate clause keeps the same structure when it is retained (i.e., no possessive form is allowed) while the verb in X_1 is transformed into the ING-participle in X_2. The ING-participle structure is then ready to be embedded in the main clause.

EXERCISE 15.15

Directions: Underline the subject of the main clause and the adverbial complement. Then combine the two clauses twice using an ING-participle structure, first placing the complement at the beginning and then at the end of the sentence. Which sounds better to you?

1. The Carltons could afford a three-week vacation in Hawaii X. X = The Carltons earned over $80,000 a year.

2. Mrs. Gooch was always worried about mining accidents X. X = Her husband worked for a nearby coal company.

3. The marathon runner felt an unexpected burst of energy after X. X = The marathon runner refused to give up.

4. The captain ordered the passengers into the lifeboats X. X = The ferry sank rapidly.

5. The rock star walked boldly into the theater X. X = The rock star wore nothing but a fly swatter.

DANGLING MODIFIERS

A common error that many English speakers make is to create a same-subject ING-participle structure when the subjects are different. The result is what is known as a *dangling modifier* because the ING-participle "dangles" rather than sharing the subject of the sentence. The reason native speakers make this error is that the listener usually understands perfectly well what the speaker means to say despite the error. Look at the following examples:

    a) *<u>Running for the train</u>, a banana skin caused John to slip and sprain his ankle.

    b) *<u>Smoking a cigarette</u>, the photograph made Sheila look very mature.

In Sentence (a), the subject of *running* has been deleted. As this is only possible when the subject of the complement is the same as the subject of the main clause, that subject must have been *a banana skin*, which means that the original subordinate clause must have been *A banana skin ran for the train*. This error can be repaired in two ways, as shown in the following examples:

    1) Running for the train, John slipped on a banana skin and sprained his ankle.

    2) When John was running for the train, a banana skin caused him to slip and sprain his ankle.

In Sentence (b), the subject of *smoking* has been deleted, which means that the original subordinate clause must have been *The photograph smoked a cigarette*. This sentence can be repaired as shown in the following examples:

    1) Smoking a cigarette, Sheila looked very mature in the photograph.

    2) Because Sheila was smoking a cigarette, the photograph made her look very mature.

In both cases, the lengthier repair in Sentence (2) uses the adverbial clause markers *when* and *because* along with the subordinate clause verb in the past continuous tense to make the statement grammatical.

EXERCISE 15.16

Directions: Repair the following sentences when necessary.

1.   Being a careful person, the error really upset Janine.

2.   The dam overflowing with the winter rains, the village below was in great danger.

3.   Bursting with pride, the gold cup was accepted by the captain of the winning team.

4.   Freezing in the icy winds, the dogs huddled together and waited for their master.

5.   Moving slowly westward, the dry mountains were soon ravaged by the raging brush fire.

SEQUENTIAL COMPLEMENTS

The infinitive and VERB_{ing} complements that we have studied have all been of the "simultaneous" type. That is to say, the action or state indicated by the complement takes place at more or less the same time as the main verb. It is also possible in English to indicate that the complement took place prior to the main verb. This is done with the auxiliary *have*.

Sequential Infinitive Structures

The hypothetical nature of infinitives makes it likely that they would appear either at the same time or somewhat later than the main verb. Look at the following examples:

  a) Paul **plans** to study medicine.

  b) To conquer the world **was** the desire of all the great kings.

In both sentences, the main verb (in boldface) occurs at the same time or somewhat before the time suggested by the infinitive structure. In Sentence (a), Paul plans now to study at some time between the present and the hypothetical future. In Sentence (b), conquering the world would take place between the time of the desire and the actual or hypothetical realization of that desire. Nevertheless, we will consider these to be examples of simultaneous complements.

Sequential infinitive structures use the auxiliary *have* to indicate that the complement took place before the main verb. Look at the following examples:

  a) Doris **is** glad to have studied medicine.

  b) Alexander the Great **was** happy to have conquered the world.

In both sentences, the main verb (in boldface) takes place after the time indicated by the infinitive structure. In Sentence (a), Doris is glad that she studied medicine prior to the moment of speaking (perhaps she has just saved somebody's life). In Sentence (b), Alexander the Great was happy that he conquered the world prior to the moment of speaking (perhaps he was on his deathbed).

When the subject of the infinitive clause is different from that of the main clause, the subject of the infinitive clause is preceded by the complementizer *for* and placed in front of the infinitive verb. Look at the following example:

  David is delighted for his nephew to have found a good job.

EXERCISE 15.17

Directions: Combine the following clauses using a sequential infinitive complement.

1. The country expected X by now. X = The country increased its exports to Russia.

2. X was a shock to the male scientists. X= Marie Curie discovered radium.

3. X is something only an orphan understands. X = Somebody lost a parent at a young age.

4. The contractor agreed X . X = The contractor completed the renovation within three months.

5. Rosa was not happy X. X = Her father declared bankruptcy.

Sequential VERB$_{ing}$ Structures

Sequential VERB$_{ing}$ structures also use the auxiliary *have* to indicate that the complement took place before the main verb. The structure is more complicated, however, as it requires shifting the *ing*-ending onto the auxiliary *have*, while the verb is transformed into its VERB$_{ed2}$ form.[4] This can be shown as a formula:

$$\text{VERB}_{ing} \rightarrow having + \text{VERB}_{ed2}$$

The event signalled by *having* + VERB$_{ed2}$ always occurs prior to the main verb of the sentence, showing a clear sequence of events. Look at the following examples:

a) Having washed the dishes, Flora **vacuumed** the living room.

b) The priest having performed the ceremony, the guests **will move** to the reception hall.

In both sentences, the main verb (in boldface) takes place after the time indicated by the VERB$_{ing}$ structure. In Sentence (a), Flora vacuumed the living room after she (same subject) washed the dishes. In Sentence (b), the guests will move to the reception hall after the priest (different subject) performs the ceremony.

In contrast to sequential infinitive structures, sequential VERB$_{ing}$ structures often suggest that they **caused** the main verb to take place. Look at the following examples:

a) Mrs. White **appreciates** her son's having washed the windows.

b) Having lost the election, the senator never **ran** for office again.

In both sentences, the main verb (in boldface) takes place after the time indicated by the VERB$_{ing}$ structure. In Sentence (a), Mrs. White appreciates the fact that her son (different subject) washed the windows before the moment of speaking, but his washing the windows also caused her appreciation. In Sentence (b), the senator lost the election prior to the moment of speaking, but did the loss cause or merely precede his (same subject) never running for office again? Sequential VERB$_{ing}$ structures are sometimes ambiguous as to whether they merely preceded or actually caused the event shown by the main verb.

---

[4] This constitutes the fourth possible combination of auxiliary + main verb mentioned in Chapter 4b. It is actually a modification of that possibility since *have* + VERB$_{ing}$ (e.g., *They *have studying medicine*) is not a possible structure in English.

EXERCISE 15.18

Directions: Combine the following clauses with a sequential VERB$_{ing}$ complement. Does the resulting sentence suggest a chronological or a causal sequence, or is it ambiguous?

1. Brian knows what poverty means X. X = Brian traveled widely in India.

2. Clothilde remembered X. X = Clothilde lived in a chateau when she was a girl.

3. The prisoners proceeded with their escape plans X. X = The guard turned out the light.

4. Barbara was happy with X. X = Her brother found a woman he could love.

5. X was a major discovery. X = The dinosaurs probably evolved into birds.

THE INTERCHANGEABILITY OF COMPLEMENT STRUCTURES

You may have noticed in doing some of the exercises in this chapter that you found your-self wanting to use an infinitive in place of a gerund structure or a *that*-complement in place of an ING-participle structure. The reason for this is that *that*-complements, *for*-infinitive comple-ments, gerund complements, and ING-participle complements are often interchangeable with a slight grammatical adjustment. We will consider this interchangeability in relation to simulta-neous and sequential complements. The following sentences provide examples of comple-ments first in the subject slot and then in the object slot (except ING-participles).

Simultaneous Complements

In simultaneous complements, the subordinate clause occurs at the same time as or some-what later than the main clause in real time. Sequential complements may have the same or different subjects.

SAME-SUBJECT COMPLEMENTS

In same-subject complements, the subject of the subordinate clause is the same as the sub-ject of the main clause (same-subject complements include the generalized subjects that occur with gerunds and infinitives).

Complement in the Subject Slot

THAT-COMP	a) <u>That one get a good education</u> is essential.
It-focus	b) It is essential <u>that one get[5] a good education</u>.
INFINITIVE-COMP	c) <u>To get a good education</u> is essential.
It-focus	d) It is essential <u>to get a good education</u>.
GERUND-COMP	e) <u>Getting a good education</u> is essential.

---

[5] Adjectives like *essential* (e.g., *necessary, required, mandatory*) include the modal meaning of "must" or "should" (i.e., one <u>should</u> get a good education), which is deleted in the subordinate clause in formal use. Verbs like *suggest* and *require* have the same effect, as shown in the following examples:

    a) The doctor <u>suggests </u>that your husband ~~should~~ take a vacation.

    b) The university <u>requires</u> that a student ~~must~~ pass English 1.

This grammatical process, which appears at first sight to break the rules of agreement, results in what is known as **the subjunctive mood.**

| ING-PARTICIPLE-COMP | f) | The students were happy to work hard in their classes, <u>knowing they were getting a good education</u>. |
| Fronted | g) | <u>Knowing they were getting a good education</u>, the students were happy to work hard in their classes. |

The second sentence in each pair (i.e., Sentences b, d, and g) probably sounds more natural to you as it occurs far more frequently than the first. With the exception of the passive structures, which are somewhat rare, this will be true in all subsequent example sentences.

Complement in the Object Slot

THAT-COMP	a)	Mary plans <u>that she will marry John</u>.
It-focus/passive	b)	It is planned by Mary <u>that she will marry John</u>.
INFINITIVE-COMP	c)	Mary plans <u>to marry John</u>.
It-focus/passive	d)	It is planned by Mary <u>to marry John</u>.
GERUND-COMP	e)	Mary plans on <u>marrying John</u>.
ING-PARTICIPLE-COMP	f)	Mary hopes for a happy life, <u>marrying John</u>.
Fronted	g)	<u>Marrying John</u>, Mary hopes for a happy life.

DIFFERENT-SUBJECT COMPLEMENTS

In different-subject complements, the subject of the subordinate clause is not the same as the subject of the main clause. Look at the following examples:

Complement in the Subject Slot

THAT-COMP	a)	<u>That John get a good education</u> is essential.
It-focus	b)	It is essential <u>that John get a good education</u>.
INFINITIVE-COMP	c)	<u>For John to get a good education</u> is essential.
It-focus	d)	It is essential <u>for John to get a good education</u>.
GERUND-COMP	e)	<u>John's getting a good education</u> is essential.
Without possessive	f)	<u>John getting a good education</u> is essential.
ING-PARTICIPLE-COMP	g)	There was no money left for his sisters, <u>with John getting a good education</u>.
Fronted	h)	<u>With John getting a good education</u>, there was no money left for his sisters.

Complement in the Object Slot

THAT-COMP	a)	Mary plans <u>that her sister will marry John</u>.
It-focus/passive	b)	It is planned by Mary <u>that her sister will marry John</u>.
INFINITIVE-COMP	c)	Mary plans <u>for her sister to marry John</u>.
It-focus/passive	d)	It is planned by Mary <u>for her sister to marry John</u>.
GERUND-COMP	e)	Mary plans on <u>her sister's marrying John</u>.
Without possessive	f)	Mary plans on <u>her sister marrying John</u>.
ING-PARTICIPLE-COMP	g)	Mary has carried out her mother's dying wish <u>by her sister marrying John</u>.
Fronted	h)	<u>By her sister marrying John</u>, Mary has carried out her mother's dying wish.

Sequential Complements

In sequential complements, the subordinate clause occurs before the main clause in real time. Sequential complements may also have the same or different subjects.

SAME-SUBJECT COMPLEMENTS

In same-subject complements, the subject of the subordinate clause is the same as the subject of the main clause. Look at the following examples:

Complement in the Subject Slot

THAT-COMP	a) <u>That one has gotten a good education</u> is essential.
It-focus	b) It is essential <u>that one has gotten a good education</u>.
INFINITIVE-COMP	c) <u>To have gotten a good education</u> is essential.
It-focus	d) It is essential <u>to have gotten a good education</u>.
GERUND-COMP	e) <u>Having gotten a good education</u> is essential.
ING-PARTICIPLE-COMP	f) The students easily found jobs, <u>having gotten a good education</u>.
Fronted	g) <u>Having gotten a good education</u>, the students easily found jobs.

Complement in the Object Slot

THAT-COMP	a) Mary plans <u>that she will have married John by next year</u>.
It-focus/passive	b) It is planned by Mary <u>that that she will have married John by next year.</u>
INFINITIVE-COMP	c) Mary plans <u>to have married John by next year</u>.
It-focus/passive	d) It is planned by Mary <u>to have married John by next year</u>.
GERUND-COMP	e) Mary plans on <u>having married John by next year</u>.
ING-PARTICIPLE-COMP	f) Mary can now concentrate on her garden, <u>having married John</u>.
Fronted	g) <u>Having married John</u>, Mary can now concentrate on her garden.

DIFFERENT-SUBJECT COMPLEMENTS

In sequential different-subject complements, the subject of the subordinate clause is different from the subject of the main clause and the subordinate clause occurs in some sequential relationship to the main clause. Look at the following examples:

Complement in the Subject Slot

THAT-COMP	a) <u>That John has gotten a good education</u> is essential.
It-focus	b) It is essential <u>that John has gotten a good education</u>.
INFINITIVE-COMP	c) <u>For John to have gotten a good education</u> is essential.
It-focus	d) It is essential <u>for John to have gotten a good education</u>.

GERUND-COMP	e) <u>John's having gotten a good education</u> is essential.
Without possessive	f) <u>John having gotten a good education</u> is essential.
ING-PARTICIPLE-COMP	g) It was now time for his sisters to get a good education, <u>John having gotten the same</u>.
Fronted	h) <u>John having gotten a good education</u>, it was now time for his sisters to get the same.

Complement in the Object Slot

THAT-COMP	a) Mary plans <u>that her sister will have married John by next year</u>.
It-focus/passive	b) It is planned by Mary <u>that her sister will have married John by next year</u>.
INFINITIVE-COMP	c) Mary plans for her sister <u>to have married John by next year</u>.
It-focus/passive	d) It is planned by Mary for her sister <u>to have married John by next year</u>.
GERUND-COMP	e) Mary plans on her sister's <u>having married John by next year</u>.
Without possessive	f) Mary plans on her sister <u>having married John by next year</u>.
ING-PARTICIPLE-COMP	g) Mary will be able to concentrate on her own life, <u>her sister having married John</u>.
Fronted	h) <u>Her sister having married John</u>, Mary will be able to concentrate on her own life.

EXERCISE 15.19

Directions: Combine the following clauses using as many of the complement structures (i.e., *that*-complement, infinitive-complement, gerund-complement, and *ing*-participle complement) or their variations (simultaneous, sequential, *it*-focus, fronted) as possible.

1. The instructor expects X. X = They will pass English 1.

2. X is very important. X = We vote.

3. The old woman had no desire to live X. X = The old woman lost her husband.

4. X is the greatest gift. X = One is healthy.

5. Elizabeth hates the fact X. X = He snores.

PROBLEM SOLVING WITH *THAT*-CLAUSE, INFINITIVE, AND VERB$_{ING}$ COMPLEMENTS

In the problems below it is possible to get the following right:

      a. correct TYPE OF COMPLEMENT (e.g., *that*-clause, ING-participle structure)

      b. correct COMPLEMENTIZER (*that, for/ to*, poss/ *-ing*)
      _{possible}

      c. correct COMPLEMENT FORM (e.g., *to* + VERB$_{base}$, Poss + VERB$_{ing}$)

      d. correct POSITION OF COMPLEMENT (e.g., subject slot, object slot, after PREP)

      e. correct *IT*-FOCUS STRUCTURE (*it* + verb + PNP/PADJ/OBJ + complement)

These elements reflect what students are likely to do wrong in using *that*-clause, infinitive, and VERB$_{ing}$ complements: a) choose the wrong type of complement, b) use the wrong complementizer, c) use a correct complement structure in the wrong context, d) put the complement structure in the wrong place, or e) use the wrong *it*-focus structure.

EXERCISE 15.20

Directions: In the following sentences, a student made a single error in using a complement. However, since complements are quite complicated, the use of a single incorrect complement structure may involve several sub-errors. Your job is to address the error in three stages:

    a) bracket the error to focus your attention

    b) list what the student got right about the bracketed error (in this case, the error is in the complement) and show this in parentheses

    c) compare the original erroneous sentence to the correct sentence and explain what mistake the student made

Example: *Ralph enjoys to sing in the shower.
        [The star (*) indicates that the sentence contains an error.]

Solution:

    a) Bracket the error (some aspect of the complement):
       *Ralph enjoys [to sing] in the shower.

    b) Show what is right about the complement:
       correct position of complement

    c) Compare the erroneous sentence to the correct form and explain the mistake:
       *Ralph enjoys [to sing] in the shower.
       Ralph enjoys singing   in the shower.

    Explanation: A "fulfilled" verb such as *enjoy* requires a gerund complement, not an infinitive complement.

1.   *Harriet wanted that you buy some ice cream.

2.   *The generator is, having worked for three consecutive weeks, broken again.

3.   *Is lucky that your sister found an apartment.

4.   *The mayor insisted on to give the hero a parade.

5.   *Them planting a redwood tree inspired other lumberjacks.

6.   *The company made the manager to resign.

7.   *To have reigned for six weeks, the young king was murdered.

8. *It hard for a young single woman to be a good parent.

9. *The boys saw the teacher's kissing the principal.

10. *It is for his wife to go with him necessary.

COMPARISONS

Comparisons indicate whether a main clause is similar to or different from a subordinate clause (the complement) and the degree to which this is so. Comparisons are the result of a clause embedding process in which the element being compared is marked with a comparison marker in the main clause, while repeated words are removed from the subordinate clause. The comparison markers and complementizers are shown in Table 15.1.

Table 15.1. Comparison Markers and Complementizers in Comparisons

	SIMILARITY	DIFFERENCE
Comparison Marker		
With ADJ/ADV	as	-er (more) less
With NOUN	as much/many	more less/fewer
Complementizer	as	than

A comparison may occur as an object complement and as a predicate noun phrase or predicate adjective complement, but not as a subject or adverbial complement.

Object Complements

Comparisons requiring object complements are usually comparisons of quantity. The main verb must be a Type I verb (i.e., non-linking) and the complements may show either similarity or difference.

SIMILARITY

Similarity may be expressed as an abbreviated or a full comparison.[6] A full comparison presumes the hearer does not know what is being compared. An abbreviated comparison presumes the hearer does know what is being compared, either because it is obvious or because of earlier discourse.

Full Comparison

A full comparison is concerned with specific units or quantities. It requires the selection of the comparison markers *as many* or *as much*, the choice determined by the countability of the noun it precedes (*as many* for count nouns, *as much* for noncount nouns). An alternative expression requires the selection of the noun *number* or *amount* (*number* for count nouns, *amount* for

---

[6] The terms *abbreviated* and *full* reflect the same relationship that occurs between the broad and narrow forms of WH-question words (e.g., *What* versus *What language*)

noncount nouns). Full comparisons require object complements. Look at the following example based on two clauses that show similarity:

Eileen wrote two essays. Joseph wrote two essays.

SUBJECT	VERB	OBJECT
Eileen	wrote	~~two~~ essays.
a. Eileen	wrote	**as many** essays X.
b. Eileen	wrote	the same number of essays X.

$$X_1 = \text{Joseph } \text{\sout{wrote two essays}}.$$
$$X_2 = \textbf{as } \text{Joseph did}$$

a. Eileen wrote <u>as many essays</u> as Joseph did.

b. Eileen wrote <u>the same number of essays</u> as Joseph did.

In the example sentence, only the quantifier of the object of the main clause is replaced with either (a) the comparison marker *as* and the postdeterminer *many* (because *essay* is count) or (b) the noun phrase *the same number of* (because *essay* is count), preparing it for the embedding of the subordinate clause at X. The subordinate clause is marked with the complementizer *as*, the clause verb is changed into the appropriate form of the auxiliary *do*, and the object is deleted. The resulting sentence emphasizes the action (the verb). It is also possible to emphasize the performers of the action (the subjects) by deleting the auxiliary *do*:

a. Eileen wrote <u>as many essays</u> as Joseph.

b. Eileen wrote <u>the same number of essays</u> as Joseph.

Abbreviated Comparison

An abbreviated comparison is not concerned with specific numbers or amounts. Abbreviated comparisons require object complements. Look at the following example:

Eileen wrote two essays. Joseph wrote two essays.

SUBJECT	VERB	OBJECT
Eileen	wrote	~~two essays~~.
Eileen	wrote	**as much** X.

$$X_1 = \text{Joseph } \text{\sout{wrote two essays}}.$$
$$X_2 = \textbf{as } \text{Joseph did}$$

Eileen wrote as much as Joseph did.

In the example sentence, the object of the main clause provides information about the nature of the complement (i.e., whether it should show similarity or difference) but plays no role in the structure of the sentence. Since the comparison shows similarity, the comparison marker *as much* is inserted after the main clause verb, preparing it for the embedding of the subordinate clause at X. The subordinate clause is marked with the complementizer *as*, the clause verb is changed into the appropriate form of the auxiliary *do*, and the object is deleted. The performers of the action may be emphasized by deleting the auxiliary *do*:

Eileen wrote as much as Joseph.

The same comparison can be expressed by replacing the comparison marker *as much* with the noun phrase *the same amount*.

Eileen wrote the same amount as Joseph.

DIFFERENCE

Difference can be shown with a positive comparison or with a negative comparison.

Positive Comparison

Positive comparisons may be either full or abbreviated.

FULL COMPARISON

A full comparison is concerned with specific numbers or amounts and requires an object complement. Look at the following example based on two clauses that show difference: The athlete runs ten miles. The student runs three miles.

SUBJECT	VERB	OBJECT
The athlete	runs	~~ten~~ miles.
The athlete	runs	**more** miles X.

X_1 = The student ~~runs three miles~~.
X_2 = **than** the student does

The athlete runs more miles than the student does.

In the example sentence, only the quantifier of the object of the main clause is replaced with the comparison marker *more*. The subordinate clause is marked with the complementizer *than*, the clause verb is changed into the appropriate form of the auxiliary *do*, and the object is deleted. These sentences emphasize the action. It is also possible to emphasize the performers of the action by deleting the auxiliary *do*:

The athlete runs more miles than the student.

ABBREVIATED COMPARISON

An abbreviated comparison is not concerned with specific numbers or amounts. Look at the following example:

The athlete runs ten miles. The student runs three miles.

SUBJECT	VERB	OBJECT
The athlete	runs	~~ten miles~~.
The athlete	runs	**more** X.

X_1 = The student ~~runs three miles~~
X_2 = **than** the student does

The athlete runs more than the student does.

In the example sentence, the object of the main clause serves only to determine if the comparison is similar or different. Since the comparison shows difference, the comparison marker *more* is inserted after the main verb. The subordinate clause is marked with the complementizer *than*, the clause verb is changed into the appropriate form of the auxiliary *do*, and the object is deleted. It is possible to emphasize the performers of the action by deleting the auxiliary *do*:

The athlete runs more than the student.

EXERCISE 15.21

Directions: Combine the clauses to show similarity or difference. Show the full and the abbreviated comparison in each case.

1. Mrs. Smith has four children. Mrs. Jones has four children.

2. Farmer Dan grew 500 pumpkins. Farmer Dave grew 400 pumpkins.

3. The ABC Company has fifty toxic-waste sites. The XYZ Company has thirty-seven toxic-waste sites.

4. The Hoover Dam reservoir holds 36,703 million cubic feet of water. The Shasta Dam reservoir holds 5615 million cubic feet of water.

5. In 1987, Louisiana executed eight prisoners. In 1987, Texas executed six prisoners.

Negative Comparison

Negative comparisons may be expressed by negating the main verb in a comparison that would otherwise show similarity. Look at the following example:

> The black pig ate 20 apples. The yellow pig ate 40 apples.
>
> FULL: The black pig **did not eat** <u>as many apples</u> as the yellow pig.
>
> ABBREVIATED: The black pig **did not eat** <u>as much as</u> the yellow pig.
>
>   The black pig **did not eat** <u>the same amount as</u> the yellow pig.

Negative comparisons are also indicated with the comparison markers *less* and *fewer* for nouns (*less* is for noncount nouns, *fewer* for count nouns[7]) and *less* for adjectives. Negative comparisons can be full or abbreviated.

FULL COMPARISON

Look at the following example based on the same two clauses:

SUBJECT	VERB	OBJECT
The black pig	ate	20 apples.
The black pig	ate	**fewer** apples X.

> X_1 = The yellow pig ~~ate 40 apples~~.
> X_2 = **than** the yellow pig did

The black pig ate fewer apples than the yellow pig did.

In the example sentence, only the quantifier of the object of the main clause is replaced with the comparison marker *fewer*. The subordinate clause is marked with the complementizer *than*, the clause verb is changed into the appropriate form of the auxiliary *do*, and the object is deleted. These sentences emphasize the verb. The subjects of the verb may be emphasized by deleting the auxiliary *do*:

> The black pig ate fewer apples than the yellow pig.

---

[7] The comparison marker *less* is used increasingly in spoken English with both count and noncount nouns, e.g., *There were less accidents this week.*

ABBREVIATED COMPARISON

Look at the following example based on the same two clauses:

The black pig ate 20 apples. The yellow pig ate 40 apples.

SUBJECT	VERB	OBJECT
The black pig	ate	~~20 apples~~.
The black pig	ate	**less** X.

$$X_1 = \text{The yellow pig } \sout{\text{ate 40 apples}}.$$
$$X_2 = \textbf{than} \text{ the yellow pig did}$$

The black pig ate less than the yellow pig did.

In the example sentence, the object of the main clause is replaced with the comparison marker *less*. The subordinate clause is marked with the complementizer *than*, the clause verb is changed into the appropriate form of the auxiliary *do*, and the object is deleted. The subjects of the verb may be emphasized by deleting the auxiliary *do*:

The black pig ate less than the yellow pig.

EXERCISE 15.22

Directions: Combine the clauses to make a negative comparison. Show both the full and abbreviated forms.

1. Joan suffers two migraine headaches a week. Diane suffers four migraine headaches a week.

2. The youngster knows the capitals of fifteen countries. His grandfather knows the capitals of twenty-five countries.

3. Richard enjoys himself at two parties a month. Ronald enjoys himself at five parties a month.

4. *Newsweek* costs $2.95. *Vanity Fair* costs $3.00.

5. Susie learned three words a day. Mandy learned ten words a day.

Predicate Noun Phrase and Predicate Adjective Complements

Comparisons requiring predicate noun phrase or predicate adjective complements are usually comparisons of degree. The main verb must be a Type II verb (i.e., linking). The complements show either similarity or difference.

SIMILARITY

Similarity expressed with predicate noun phrase or adjective complements may be full or abbreviated.

Full Comparison

A full comparison requires a predicate noun phrase complement. Look at the following example:

Inkjet is a ten-pound cat. Whiteout is a ten-pound cat.

SUBJECT	VERB	PREDICATE NOUN PHRASE
Inkjet	is	a ~~ten-pound~~ cat.
Inkjet	is	**as heavy** a cat X.
		X_1 = Whiteout is ~~a ten-pound cat~~.
		X_2 = **as** Whiteout is

Inkjet is as heavy a cat as Whiteout is.

In full comparisons, the modifier in the predicate noun phrase in the main clause provides information about the adjective to be used in the comparison but plays no role in the structure of the sentence. In this case, *ten pounds* is a weight and the adjective that describes weight is *heavy*.[8] Since the comparison shows similarity, the comparison marker *as* and the selected adjective (*heavy*) are inserted after the main clause verb, preparing it for the embedding of the subordinate clause at X. The subordinate clause is marked with the complementizer *as* and the predicate noun phrase is deleted. These sentences emphasize the predicate (being *heavy*). It is also possible to highlight the subjects of the comparison (the cats) by deleting the linking verb:

Inkjet is as heavy a cat as Whiteout.

Abbreviated Comparison

An abbreviated comparison requires a predicate adjective complement. Look at the following example based on the same two clauses:

Inkjet is a ten-pound cat. Whiteout is a ten-pound cat.

SUBJECT	VERB	PREDICATE ADJECTIVE
Inkjet	is	~~a ten-pound cat~~.
Inkjet	is	**as heavy** X.
		X_1 = Whiteout is ~~a ten-pound cat~~.
		X_2 = **as** Whiteout is

Inkjet is as heavy as Whiteout is.

In abbreviated comparisons, the entire predicate noun phrase in the main clause provides information about the adjective to be used in the comparison but plays no role in the structure of the sentence. Since the comparison shows similarity, the comparison marker *as* and the selected adjective (*heavy*) are inserted after the main clause verb, preparing it for the embedding of the subordinate clause at X. The subordinate clause is marked with the complementizer *as* and the predicate noun phrase is deleted. These sentences emphasize the predicate (being *heavy*). The subjects of the comparison (the cats) can be highlighted by deleting the linking verb:

Inkjet is as heavy as Whiteout.

---

[8] *Light*, the opposite of *heavy*, is also an adjective that describes weight. However, when such pairs exist we usually choose the greater rather than the lesser adjective in comparisons (e.g., *old* vs. *young*, *deep* vs. *shallow*, *long* vs. *short*).

DIFFERENCE

Difference expressed with predicate noun phrase or adjective complements may be positive or negative. Difference is expressed through the use of the comparison markers *-er, more,* and *less.* The *er*-ending is attached to all one-syllable adjectives and certain two-syllable adjectives. *More* is used before most two-syllable adjectives and all adjectives of three or more syllables. A few adjectives may take either form. Some examples are shown in Table 15.2.

Table 15.2 Adjectives (and Adverbs) with Comparison Markers

Adjectives with *-er*		Adjectives with *-er/more*	Adjectives with *more*	
one syllable	two syllable	two syllables	two syllables	three+ syllables
brighter	dirtier	cleverer/more clever	more common	more complicated
faster	heavier	friendlier/more friendly	more distant	more delectable
larger	nobler	handsomer/more handsome	more distinct	more elegant
longer	prettier	quieter/more quiet	more exact	more horrifying
taller	simpler	stupider/more stupid	more haunting	more political

Positive Comparison

Comparisons of positive difference expressed with predicate noun phrase or adjective complements are either full or abbreviated.

FULL COMPARISON

A full comparison requires a predicate noun phrase complement. Look at the following example:

The Mekong is a 4000 km. river. The Orinoco is a 2000 km. river.

SUBJECT	VERB	PREDICATE NOUN PHRASE

The Mekong   is   a ~~4000 km.~~ river.
The Mekong   is   **a longer** river X.
X_1 = The Orinoco is ~~a 2000 km. river~~.
X_2 = **than** the Orinoco is

The Mekong is a longer river than the Orinoco is.

In full comparisons, the modifier in the predicate noun phrase in the main clause again provides information about the adjective to be used in the comparison but plays no role in the structure of the sentence. In this case, *4000 km.* is a length and the adjective that describes length is *long.* Since the comparison shows difference and the adjective has one syllable, the comparison marker *-er* is attached to the adjective (*long*) which replaces the modifer (*4000 km.*) in the predicate noun phrase. The subordinate clause is marked with the complementizer *than* and the predicate noun phrase is deleted. These sentences emphasize the predicate (being *long*). It is also possible to highlight the subjects of the comparison (the rivers) by deleting the linking verb:

The Mekong is a longer river than the Orinoco.

ABBREVIATED COMPARISON

An abbreviated comparison requires a predicate adjective complement. Look at the following example: The Mekong is a 4000 km. river. The Orinoco is a 2000 km. river.

SUBJECT	VERB	PREDICATE ADJECTIVE
The Mekong	is	a 4000 km. river.
The Mekong	is	**longer** X.
		X₁= The Orinoco is a 2000 km. river.
		X₂= **than** the Orinoco is

The Mekong is longer than the Orinoco is.

In abbreviated comparisons, the entire predicate noun phrase in the main clause again provides information about the adjective to be used in the comparison but plays no role in the structure of the sentence. Since the comparison shows difference and the adjective has one syllable, the comparison marker *-er* is attached to the appropriate adjective (*long*) which replaces the modifier (*4000 km.*) in the predicate noun phrase. The subordinate clause is marked with the complementizer *than* and the predicate noun phrase is deleted. This sentence emphasizes the predicate (being *long*). It is also possible to highlight the subjects of the comparison (the rivers) by deleting the linking verb:

The Mekong is longer than the Orinoco.

EXERCISE 15.23

Directions: Combine the clauses to show similarity or difference. Show the full and the abbreviated comparison in each case. Which sounds better to you?

1. Polonium is a very rare element. Tellurium is a very rare element.

2. Cuba is a 44,000-square-mile island. Ireland is a 33,000-square-mile island.

3. The Williamsburg is a 1600-foot bridge. The Newport is a 1600-foot bridge.

4. The Suez is a 197-foot-wide canal. The Panama is a 110-foot-wide canal.

5. The St. Gotthard is a 118-year-old tunnel. The Mt. Blanc is a 30-year-old tunnel.

Negative Comparison

Negative comparisons utilizing predicate noun phrase or predicate adjective complements may be expressed by negating the main verb in a comparison that would otherwise show similarity. Look at the following example:

An opal is a $400 gem. A ruby is a $4000 gem.

FULL: An opal **is not** as expensive a gem as a ruby is.

ABBREVIATED: An opal **is not** as expensive as a ruby.

Negative comparisons may also be indicated with the comparison marker *less*. *Less* is used with all adjectives (or adverbs). Negative comparisons can be full or abbreviated.

FULL COMPARISON

Look at the following example based on the same two clauses:

An opal is a $400 gem. A ruby is a $4000 gem.

SUBJECT	VERB	PREDICATE NOUN PHRASE
An opal	is	a $~~$400$~~ gem.
An opal	is	a **less expensive** gem X.
		X$_1$= A ruby is ~~a $4000 gem~~.
		X$_2$= **than** a ruby is

An opal is a less expensive gem than a ruby is.

In full comparisons, the modifier in the predicate noun phrase in the main clause again provides information about the adjective to be used in the comparison but plays no role in the structure of the sentence. In this case, *$400* is an expense and the adjective that describes expense is *expensive*. Since the comparison shows difference, the comparison marker *less* is inserted before the adjective (*expensive*), replacing the modifer (*$400*) in the predicate noun phrase. The subordinate clause is marked with the complementizer *than* and the predicate noun phrase is deleted. These sentences emphasize the predicate (being *less expensive*). It is also possible to highlight the subjects of the comparison (the gems) by deleting the linking verb:

An opal is a less expensive gem than a ruby.

ABBREVIATED COMPARISON

Look at the following example based on the same two clauses:

An opal is a $400 gem. A ruby is a $4000 gem.

SUBJECT	VERB	PREDICATE ADJECTIVE
An opal	is	~~a $400~~ gem.
An opal	is	**less expensive**. X.
		X$_1$= A ruby is ~~a $4000 gem~~.
		X$_2$= **than** a ruby is

An opal is less expensive than a ruby is.

In abbreviated comparisons, the entire predicate noun phrase in the main clause again provides information about the adjective to be used in the comparison but plays no role in the structure of the sentence. Since the comparison shows difference, the comparison marker *less* is inserted before the appropriate adjective (*expensive*), which replaces the entire predicate noun phrase (*a $400 gem*). The subordinate clause is marked with the complementizer *than* and the predicate noun phrase is deleted. This sentence emphasizes the predicate (being *less expensive*). It is also possible to highlight the subjects of the comparison (the gems) by deleting the linking verb:

An opal is less expensive than a ruby.

EXERCISE 15.24

Directions: Combine the sentences to make a negative comparison. Show both the full and abbreviated forms. Which sounds better to you?

1. Rodney is moderately intelligent. William is very intelligent.

2. Mt. McKinley is 20,000 feet tall. Mt. Everest is 29,000 feet tall.

3. The Kalahari Desert is 120,000 square miles. The Sahara is 3,500,000 square miles.

4. The wing span of a B-52 bomber is 185 feet. The wing span of a C-5A transport is 222 feet.

5. Mercury is 332°F at the surface. Venus is 854°F at the surface.

Problem Solving with Comparisons

In the problems below it is possible to get the following right:

 a. correct COMPARISON MARKER (*as, as many, as much, more, less, fewer, -er*)

 b. correct COMPLEMENTIZER (*as, than*)

 c. correct COMPLEMENT STRUCTURE (complementizer + subordinate clause subject + optional AUX or linking verb)

 d. correct POSITION OF COMPLEMENT (e.g., verb slot, object slot, pred NP slot)

These elements reflect what students are likely to do wrong in using a comparison: a) choose the wrong comparison marker, b) use the wrong complementizer, c) use an incorrect complement structure, or d) put the comparison complement in the wrong place.

EXERCISE 15.25

Directions: In the following sentences, a student made a single error in using a comparison. However, since comparisons are quite complicated, the use of a single incorrect comparison structure may involve several sub-errors. Your job is to address the error in three stages:

 a) bracket the error to focus your attention

 b) list what the student got right about the bracketed error (in this case, the error is in the comparison) and show this in parentheses

 c) compare the original erroneous sentence to the correct sentence and explain what mistake the student made

Example: San Francisco is smaller as Los Angeles.

 [The star (*) indicates that the sentence contains an error.]

Solution:

 a) Bracket the error (some aspect of the comparison):
    *San Francisco is smaller [as] Los Angeles.

 b) Show what is right about the comparison:
    correct comparison marker (*-er*)
    correct complement structure (COMP + subordinate clause subject)
    correct position of complement (PREDICATE ADJECTIVE slot)

c) Compare the erroneous sentence to the correct form and explain the mistake:

*San Francisco is smaller [as] Los Angeles.

San Francisco is smaller than Los Angeles.

Explanation: Comparisons that show difference always require the complementizer *than*.

1. *An elephant eats more food than a monkey is.

2. *An apple has as much calories as an egg.

3. *Linda as Roberta is as good a skier.

4. *Donald's brother has the same car like his sister.

5. *A topographical map is exacter than a tourist map.

6. *A truck weighs than a locomotive less.

7. *The Mississippi is more longer than the Rio Grande.

8. *Germany has fewer nuclear reactors than Japan has them.

9. *Sandy weighs as much than Lee.

10. *The diplomats drank fewer wine than the politicians.

APPENDIXES

ANSWER KEY TO EXERCISES

1.1

train CW	surprise CW	under FW
every FW	gargle CW	weak CW
or FW	them FW	democracy CW
really CW	has FW/CW	dull CW
antiquated CW	and FW	near FW
did FW	bee CW	charge CW
blipped CW	purple CW	the FW

1.2

fast<u>est</u> IM	John<u>'s</u> IM	violin<u>ist</u> DM
<u>co</u>operate DM	hugg<u>ing</u> IM/DM	attract<u>ive</u> DM
friend<u>lier</u> IM	<u>pro</u>ven IM	<u>pro</u>long DM
king<u>dom</u> DM	<u>tri</u>athalon DM	develope<u>d</u> IM
tremendous<u>ly</u> DM	provoke<u>s</u> IM	train<u>ee</u> DM
watermelon<u>s</u> IM	<u>sub</u>category DM	rac<u>ist</u> DM
<u>anti</u>biotic DM	fanci<u>ful</u> DM	<u>ir</u>relevant DM

1.3

      DM   IM   DM   IM
1. Numer<u>ous</u> satel<u>lites</u> in the night sky are busi<u>ly</u> send<u>ing</u> data to the Earth.
    CW   CW FWFW CW CW FW CW   CW   CW FWFW CW

                IM   IM   DM/IM   IM   DM   DM
2. Even the industry<u>'s</u> strong<u>est</u> warn<u>ing</u> <u>s</u> were not tak<u>en</u> serious<u>ly</u> by the govern<u>ment</u>.
  CW FW   CW   CW   CW   FW FW CW   CW   FWFW   CW

                M   DMDM   DM
3. If the plane land<u>ed</u> on water, the fuselage is probab<u>ly</u> <u>re</u>cover<u>able</u>.
 FWFW CW   CW FW CW FW   CW FW CW   CW

        IM DM   DM   IM   DM   DM
4. A short<u>er</u> <u>des</u>crip<u>tion</u> appear<u>s</u> on the next page of this offic<u>ial</u> docu<u>ment</u>.
  FW CW   CW   CW FW FW CW CW FWFW CW   CW

              IM
5. Magellan cir<u>cled</u> the globe between 1519 and 1522.
    CW   CW   FW CW   FW   CW FW CW

1.4 (five sentences from newspaper)

1.5

            C   C   C
1. The annual <u>growth</u> of a <u>tree</u> is shown in its <u>rings</u>.
           abs   con   con

       C   P   C
2. The <u>brown bear</u>, which is native to <u>Tibet</u>, is an endangered <u>species</u>.
   con   abs/con   abs/con

     P   C   P
3. <u>Alexander Fleming</u> discovered <u>penicillin</u> before the <u>Second World War</u>.
      con   con   abs

        C   P   C   C
4. The <u>government</u> of <u>Italy</u> is speaking for a new <u>openness</u> in <u>public affairs</u>.
       abs   abs/con   abs   abs

       C   P   C   P   P
5. The <u>idea</u> that <u>Neptune</u> has several <u>moons</u> was confirmed by <u>Voyager 2</u> on <u>September 2</u>.
    abs   con   con   con   abs

1.6

1. An <u>iron</u> is made of <u>iron</u>, a <u>glass</u> is made of <u>glass</u>, but a <u>light</u> is not made of <u>light</u>.
      C   NC   C   NC   C   NC

2. That <u>guy</u> is not very careful with his <u>money</u>. He gave me two <u>quarters</u>, threee <u>nickels</u>, and a <u>penny</u> in <u>change</u>.

3. Don't buy a <u>paper</u>; it uses too much <u>paper</u>.

4. In <u>space</u>, the <u>spaces</u> between <u>galaxies</u> are almost inconceivable <u>distances</u>.

5. The <u>students</u> found a lot of <u>literature</u> about <u>air pollution</u> but only a single <u>article</u> on <u>noise pollution</u> in American <u>cities</u>.

1.7

1. The students <u>are working</u> in pairs. [dyn]
2. My uncle <u>dislikes</u> his neighbors. [stat]
3. The spaghetti sauce <u>smelled</u> wonderful. [stat]
4. The sunflowers <u>had grown</u> to a height of six feet. [dyn]
5. The pelican <u>died</u> from contamination by pesticides. [dyn]

1.8

1. The <u>little</u> <u>old</u> lady raced to her <u>favorite</u> supermarket in her <u>maroon</u> Cadillac.
2. It was a <u>tempestuous</u> day, a day of <u>racing</u> clouds and <u>roaring</u> wind.
3. It was <u>impossible</u> to imagine that a <u>simple</u> peasant could be so <u>beautiful</u>.
4. The <u>woolly</u> mammoth, a <u>hairy</u>, <u>elephant-like</u> creature, roamed the earth until 10,000 B.C.
5. A waiter should be <u>attentive</u>, <u>cordial</u>, <u>careful</u>, and <u>unobtrusive</u>.

1.9

1. <u>Gracefully</u>, the ballerina leaped across the stage.
2. The secretary wasn't <u>very</u> happy <u>yesterday</u>.
3. Ducks <u>seldom</u> take new mates.
4. Nobody can exchange any money <u>there</u>.
5. Pharmacists must work <u>fast</u> to fill their prescriptions.

1.10

1. <u>We</u> met <u>him</u> at the airport in my station wagon.
2. <u>She</u> didn't give <u>herself</u> enough time to get the name of <u>everybody</u> in the room.
3. Some countries are developed, <u>some</u> are not. <u>This</u> is the basis of the north-south dialog.
4. *To <u>each</u> his own* means that each person has the right to decide what <u>he</u> or <u>she</u> likes.
5. Has <u>anyone</u> seen the coffee? <u>It</u> must be <u>somewhere</u> in these cupboards.

1.11

1. Water <u>is</u> coming under the door.
2. That actor <u>has</u> starred in many films.
3. People <u>should</u> help the children in poor countries.
4. The fine is one hundred dollars. [*is* = main verb]
5. My brother has an old Chevrolet. [*has* = main verb]
6. The government <u>will</u> free the hostages next month.
7. The records <u>ought to</u> reveal the mistake.
8. Her grandparents do odd jobs for the community. [*do* = main verb]
9. The students <u>were</u> showing the photographs to their friends when the teacher came in.
10. His father <u>had to</u> have an operation last year.

1.12

1. <u>After</u> class, Alice has a cup <u>of</u> tea <u>in</u> a restaurant <u>before</u> she goes <u>to</u> the library so that she can study <u>for</u> the evening.
2. An ape is <u>like</u> a monkey <u>with</u> no tail.
3. Frogs covered the highway <u>from</u> one side <u>to</u> the other.
4. The ambulance arrived <u>in</u> five minutes <u>by</u> traveling <u>through</u> the park.
5. The ship sailed <u>out of</u> the harbor, <u>under</u> the bridge, <u>around</u> a small island, and then <u>out</u> <u>into</u> the open ocean.

1.13

1. Jupiter is <u>the</u> largest planet in <u>the</u> Solar System.
2. <u>Every</u> story has <u>a</u> good guy and <u>a few</u> bad guys.
3. <u>Sally's</u> parents asked <u>her</u> sister to take her and <u>her</u> brother to <u>another</u> doctor.
4. <u>A lot of</u> time was spent on revising <u>three</u> chapters in <u>the</u> <u>second</u> edition.
5. Almost <u>all of the</u> people in <u>this</u> country have <u>a little</u> trouble with <u>their</u> income taxes.

1.14

1. The king <u>and</u> the queen are not at home, <u>so</u> please come back on Tuesday.
2. A bacteria, <u>but</u> not a virus, can be killed by antibiotics.
3. You must pay the fee <u>or</u> face the consequences.
4. Those boys have lived <u>and</u> worked in Calcutta all their lives.
5. Whether beautiful <u>or</u> disfigured, intelligent <u>or</u> retarded, every human being has the right to a happy life.

1.15 (see 2.19)

Chapter 2

2.1

1. <u>A</u> ^{DET} <u>long</u> ^{ADJ} <u>green</u> ^{ADJ} <u>snake</u> ^N slithered across <u>my</u> ^{DET} <u>foot</u> ^N.

    DET ADJ ADJ N   DET N
1. <u>A long green snake</u> slithered across <u>my foot</u>.

    DET ADJ N   DET ADJ N
2. <u>[Ø] Hot coffee</u> is great on <u>a cold morning</u>.

    DET   N   DET N   DET N   DET N PREP DET N
3. <u>[Ø] Kennedy</u> wanted to send <u>a man</u> to <u>the moon</u> by <u>the end of the sixties</u>.

    DET N   PREP DET N   DET   N   PREP DET N
4. <u>[Ø] Life without [Ø] water</u> is impossible for <u>most creatures on this planet</u>.

    DET   N   DET   N   PREP DET ADJ   N
5. <u>Two policemen</u> examined <u>the fingerprints on the broken window</u>.

2.2

                 PREP DET   N
1. The Pacific Ocean is the largest ocean <u>in the world</u>.

       PREP DET N   N
2. The fluid <u>in the brain cavity</u> must be removed.

           PREP DET   N   PREP DET   N   PREP DET   N
3. The starship came <u>from the Pleiades</u> <u>with a message for [Ø] mankind</u>.

       PREP DET ADJ   N   PREP DET N
4. The apartment <u>on the top floor</u> has a fantastic view <u>over the city</u>.

               PREP DET N   PREP N
5. The inmates dug a tunnel <u>under the wall</u> and escaped <u>to freedom</u>.

2.3

1. We <u>drove along the river to the county fair</u>.
2. The doctor <u>cured the patient with an herbal tea</u>.
3. Light <u>travels at 186,000 miles per second</u>.
4. The hungry, growling beast in the dungeon <u>clawed at the damp walls</u>.
5. Snowflakes <u>drifted gently to the ground</u>.

2.4

1. The capital of the largest country in the world <u>is the city of Moscow</u>.
2. Stars <u>are gigantic balls of superheated gas</u>.
3. My sister <u>has been successful in her chosen profession of nursing</u>.
4. The mouse <u>was at the bottom of the cookie jar in a state of restful repose</u>.
5. Tuesday <u>is the day of the week with the best conditions for working at home</u>.

2.5

1. Sophia is a <u>dark, spirited Italian</u> horse.
2. The new manager is <u>intelligent, extremely organized, and diplomatic</u>.
3. The <u>entire deciduous</u> forest was <u>red-yellow-orange-brown</u> in its <u>autumnal</u> dress.
4. The mechanic removed the <u>small egg-shaped</u> device near the fuel pump.
5. <u>Tired, hungry, thirsty, and weak</u>, the soldier limped into the <u>completely deserted</u> village.

2.6

1. The gun was found <u>precisely here</u>.
2. <u>Too often</u>, the rich get richer while the poor get poorer.
3. The teacher <u>patiently and thoroughly</u> corrected her students' essays.
4. I want an answer <u>now</u>.
5. The bolt must be tightened <u>very carefully</u>.

2.7

1. [NP   ][VP [NP][AdvP   ]]
   This building uses heat too inefficiently.
2. [NP [PP[NP   ]]] [VP[AdjP   ]]
   The story in that magazine is very well written.
3. [NP][VP [AdvP   ][PP[NP]]]
   The river flows very quickly at this spot.
4. [AdvP   ][NP   ][VP [PP[NP]]]
   Unfortunately, the baseball team will move to another city
5. [NP   ][VP [AdjP   [PP[NP]]]]
   The old monk's skin was yellow and darkened with age.

2.8 (see 2.19)

2.9

[NP][VP [PP [NP   ]] [PP [NP   ]]] [NP][VP [AdjP][AdvP]] [NP

David lived in the country in his childhood. He was very happy there. His

][VP [NP   ]] [PP[NP   ]] [NP][VP [NP   ][PP[NP

grandfather had an organic vegetable farm. In the morning, he helped his grandfather in the

] [NP   ]] [NP][VP [PP[NP   ]][NP   ][PP [NP

garden and fed the chickens. He played in the fields and woods every afternoon until dinner

]]] [NP   ][VP [NP][AdvP]] [AdvP][NP][VP [NP][PP[ ]

time. The closest village was six miles away. Sometimes, David rode his bicycle to the

NP] [NP][VP[AdvP]   [NP]] [NP   ][VP[AdjP][AdvP]] [NP][VP [NP

village, but he usually   took the bus. David's grandfather is dead now and David owns the

]]

farm.

2.10

1. Bruce eats cereal in the morning <u>because it energizes him</u>.
2. <u>Although I never wear a watch</u>, I am rarely late.
3. Monica had a haircut <u>while she was waiting for her boyfriend</u>.
4. The tree grew <u>despite the fact that nobody ever watered it</u>.
5. <u>As the plane was landing</u>, a bird flew into one of the jet engines.

2.11

1. The stream <u>which we followed</u> came from a small cave.
2. The man <u>whose leg is broken</u> is in Room 242.
3. My dog refuses to eat food <u>that comes from a can</u>.
4. A person <u>who is rich</u> is not necessarily happy.
5. The official <u>whom we spoke with</u> could not give us any details.

2.12

1. She didn't know <u>why he was angry</u>.
2. <u>How much it costs</u> is of little importance.
3. Can you see <u>what time it is</u>?
4. I understand <u>that you are looking for an apartment</u>.
5. <u>What the university requires</u> is a complete transcript of all the courses that you have taken.

2.13

1. <u>What I want to know</u> (NCl) is the name of the person <u>who told you about the meeting</u> (AdjCl).
2. The forest <u>that they knew</u> (AdjCl) <u>when they were children</u> (AdvCl) has disappeared.
3. She doesn't care <u>how long it takes</u> (NCl); she just wants a portrait <u>that she can be proud of</u> (AdjCl).
4. <u>Because most of the gold is in the river</u> (AdvCl), prospectors are always present.
5. The earthquake did not frighten us <u>although it did wake us up</u> (AdvCl).

2.14

1. <u>The largest city in Turkey</u> is Istanbul.
2. Before he came to the United States, <u>Van's father</u> had had many horrifying experiences.
3. <u>The weather for the northern part of the Central Valley</u> will be cloudy and cool tomorrow.
4. <u>The new bridge that connects the two islands</u> has improved business opportunities.
5. Unfortunately, <u>the damaged space probe</u> is not sending data back to the earth.

2.15

1. Marianne <u>lives</u> in Scandinavia.
2. We <u>usually take</u> our dog when we go into the mountains.
3. The cliff <u>suddenly and violently collapsed</u> after the rainstorm.
4. During the operation, the doctor <u>will carefully remove</u> the appendix.
5. Antibiotics <u>are only</u> effective for the treatment of bacterial infections.

2.16

1. The hurricane devastated <u>the city</u> in a few hours. <u>vt</u>.
2. Adele's father works for the government in Belo Horizonte, Brazil. <u>vi</u>.
3. Few animals kill for no reason. <u>vi</u>.
4. This thermometer measures <u>temperature</u> in degrees Centigrade. <u>vt</u>.
5. The artist painted until he could paint no more. <u>vi</u>.
6. Her aunt died in Toronto. <u>vi</u>.
7. My office needs <u>a person who can type 100 words per minute</u>. <u>vt</u>.
8. The plumber complained about his assistant's work. <u>vi</u>.
9. The stapler fell into the wastebasket. <u>vi</u>.
10. Help <u>that poor child</u>! <u>vt</u>.

2.17

1. Trains are <u>always late</u> (P ADJ) in this country.
2. The chairman was really <u>a remarkably gifted man in many ways</u> (P NP).

3. An analysis of the characters in this novel would be <u>quite interesting</u>.
P ADJ

4. The sari is <u>a dress that is worn by many Indian women</u>.
P NP

5. The opera is <u>a tale of revenge and a commentary on the mores of the time</u>.
P NP

2.18

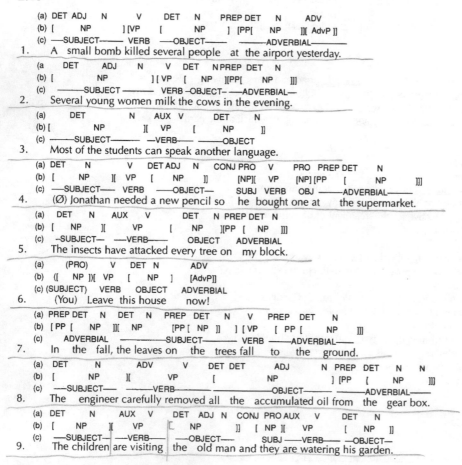

	Clause Marker	Clause SUBJECT	Clause VERB	Clause ADVERBIAL
1.	Vincent taught English <u>when	he	lived	in Bangkok</u>

	Clause Marker	Clause SUBJECT	Clause VERB	Clause P NP
2.	<u>Although	she	was only	a girl</u> , Sarah was the mother of the house.

	Clause Marker	Clause SUBJECT	Clause VERB	Clause OBJECT
3.	The patient went <u>to the beach even though	his doctor	warned	against it</u>.

	Clause Marker	Clause SUBJECT	Clause VERB	Clause P NP	Clause ADVERBIAL
4.	<u>If	there	is	a major earthquake	in Los Angeles</u>, many people will die.

	Clause Marker	Clause SUBJECT	Clause VERB	Clause P NP
5.	<u>Since	he	is	an actor</u>, he will probably be a good politician.

2.19

(a)	DET ADJ	N	V	DET	N	PREP DET	N	ADV	
(b)	[NP	] [VP	[	NP	]	[PP[	NP	]][AdvP]]	
(c)	—SUBJECT——	VERB	—OBJECT——			—————ADVERBIAL———			
1.	A small bomb	killed	several people			at the airport		yesterday.	

(a	DET	ADJ	N	V	DET	N PREP DET	N	
(b)	[	NP		] [VP	[NP	][PP[	NP	]]]
(c)	———SUBJECT———			VERB	–OBJECT–	——ADVERBIAL—		
2.	Several young women			milk	the cows	in the evening.		

(a)	DET	N	AUX V	DET	N	
(b)	[	NP	][VP	[NP	]]	
(c)	———SUBJECT———		—VERB——	———OBJECT		
3.	Most of the students		can speak	another language.		

(a)	DET	N	V	DET ADJ	N	CONJ PRO	V	PRO PREP DET	N
(b)	[	NP	][VP	[NP	]	[NP][VP	[NP] [PP	[	NP]]]
(c)	—SUBJECT—		VERB	——OBJECT—		SUBJ VERB	OBJ	——ADVERBIAL———	
4.	(∅) Jonathan	needed	a new pencil	so	he	bought one	at	the supermarket.	

(a)	DET	N	AUX	V	DET	N PREP DET	N
(b)	[NP	][	VP	[	NP	][PP [NP	]]
(c)	–SUBJECT–		——VERB——		OBJECT	ADVERBIAL	
5.	The insects		have attacked		every tree	on my block.	

(a)	(PRO)	V	DET N	ADV	
(b)	([NP])[	VP	[NP]	[AdvP]]	
(c)	(SUBJECT)	VERB	OBJECT	ADVERBIAL	
6.	(You)	Leave	this house	now!	

(a)	PREP DET	N	DET	N	PREP DET	N	V	PREP DET	N	
(b)	[PP [	NP	][	NP	[PP[NP	]]	] [VP	[PP [	NP	]]]
(c)	ADVERBIAL		———SUBJECT———				VERB	——ADVERBIAL———		
7.	In the fall,		the leaves	on	the trees		fall	to the	ground.	

(a)	DET	N	ADV	V	DET DET	ADJ	N PREP DET	N	N	
(b)	[	NP	][	VP	[	NP	] [PP [	NP	]]]	
(c)	—SUBJECT—		———VERB———			—————OBJECT———		———ADVERBIAL———		
8.	The engineer		carefully	removed	all the	accumulated oil	from	the	gear box.	

(a)	DET	N	AUX V	DET ADJ N	CONJ PRO AUX	V	DET	N	
(b)	[NP	][	VP	[NP	]]	[NP][VP	[NP	]]	
(c)	—SUBJECT—		—VERB—	——OBJECT—		SUBJ —VERB——	—OBJECT—		
9.	The children	are visiting		the old man	and they	are watering	his garden.		

(a) DET   N   AUX   V   DET N PREP DET   N
(b) [NP   ][VP   [NP   ][PP [NP   ]]]
(c) SUBJECT ——VERB—— OBJECT   ADVERBIAL

10.   (Ø)Elsie doesn't take (Ø)cream in her coffee.

2.20 [Note: The clause markers have been underlined.]

(a) [NP   ] [VP [AdjP]   [NP] [VP [NP   ]]]
(b)   [AdvCl   ]
(c) [Independent Clause   [++++++Dependent Clause++++++]]
(d)   SUBJECT   VERB PR ADJ ——————ADVERBIAL——————

1.   President Lincoln is   famous <u>because</u> he freed the slaves.

(a)   [NP   ][VP   [PP [NP   ]]] [NP] [VP [PP [NP   ]]]
(b) [AdvCl   ]
(c) [[++++++++++++++++Dependent Clause ++++++++++++++++]   Independent Clause   ]
(d) ————————————————ADVERBIAL———————————— SUBJ VERB   ADVERBIAL

2.   <u>As</u> the flight attendant was walking to   the   plane, she slipped on an oil spot.

(a) [NP   [NP] [VP   ][VP   [PP[NP]] [PP[NP   ]]]
(b)   [AdjCl   ]
(c) [[+++Dependent Clause+++]   Independent Clause   ]
(d) ————SUBJECT———————— VERB   ———————ADVERBIAL————

3.   The children <u>who</u> live in Managua must return to the bus at five o'clock.

(a) [NP   ][VP [AdjP]   [NP] [VP [AdjP]]]
(b)   [AdvCl   ]
(c) [Independent Clause   [+++++Dependent Clause+++++]]
(d)   SUBJECT VERB PR ADJ ——————ADVERBIAL——————

4.   The dinner was delicious <u>even though</u> it   was cold.

(a) [NP][VP   [PP[NP   ]]   [NP] [VP [PP [NP   ]]]]
(b)   [AdvCl   ]
(c) [Independent Clause   [+++++++Dependent Clause+++++++]]
(d)   SUBJ   VERB ———————————————ADVERBIAL———————————————

5.   A spy was hiding in the cupboard <u>when</u> Yoli came into the room.

(a) [NP   [NP] [VP   ]][VP [AdjP] [NP   ]]
(b)   [AdjCl   ]
(c) [[+++++Dependent Clause+++++]   Independent Clause   ]
(d) ——————————SUBJECT——————————— VERB PR ADJ   ADVERBIAL

6.   The class <u>which</u> they took last year is not available this semester.

(a) [NP   ][VP   [NP][VP   [PP[NP   ]][PP [NP]]]
(b)   [AdvCl   ]
(c) [Independent Clause   [++++++++++++++++++++++Dependent Clause++++++++++++++++++++++]]
(d)   SUBJECT   VERB ———————————————————ADVERBIAL———————————————————

7.   The volcano erupted <u>since</u> pressure had accumulated in the magma chamber below it.

(a)   [NP][VP][VP   [NP   ][VP]]
(b) [NCl   ]   [NCl   ]
(c) [[++++Dependent Clause++++] Independent Clause [++++Dependent Clause+++]]
(d) ————SUBJECT———————   VERB   ————————OBJECT————————

8.   <u>Where</u> a person works usually determines <u>where</u> he or she lives.

(a) [PP[NP   ]][NP   ][VP   [NP [NP][VP   [NP   ]]]]
(b)   [AdjCl   ]
(c) [Independent Clause   [+++++++++++Dependent Clause++++++++]]
(d) ———ADVERBIAL—————— SUBJECT   VERB   ———————————OBJECT———————————

9.   By tomorrow morning, a bulldozer will have removed the soil <u>that</u> is blocking the stream.

(a) [NP   ][VP   [NP   ][VP [NP   ]]]
(b)   [NCl   ]
(c) [Independent Clause   [+++++++++++Dependent Clause+++++++++++]]
(d) ————SUBJECT———————   VERB   ————————OBJECT————————

10.   The chemistry instructor cannot explain <u>why</u> forty-five students failed the exam.

Chapter 3

3.1

1. Plur/Past: The <u>Cantors</u> *were* living in Madison when I saw them.
2. "I"/Pres: <u>I</u> *am* taking several classes this semester.
3. Plur/Pres: The hostage slipped the reporter a note, which said, "Help us! <u>We</u> *are* being tortured."
4. Sing/Past: After the terrible fire, the little <u>boy</u> *was* told never to play with matches again.
5. Plur/Past: The <u>passengers</u> on the plane *were* asked to remain calm after the pilot described the storm ahead.

3.2

1. Sing/Pres: The <u>Ajax Company</u> *has* employed over 200 new workers in the last three weeks.
2. Sing/Past: Before coming back to the U.S., <u>Brian</u> *had* taught English in Spain for many years.
3. "I"/Pres: <u>I</u> *have* increased my knowledge of the Solar System.
4. Plur/Past: The lifeboats sank when <u>they</u> *had* taken on too much water.
5. Plur/Pres: Tiny <u>hearing aids</u> with no visible wires or batteries *have* done much to improve the lives of the hearing impaired.

3.3

1. Plur/Pres: Where *do* <u>mosquitoes</u> come from?
2. Sing/Past: *Did* <u>Eleanor</u> pay the rent yesterday?
3. "I"/Pres: <u>I</u> *do* have a master's degree! If you think I'm lying, ask my mother.
4. Plur/Pres: Many <u>people</u> in the southern hemisphere *do* not have enough to eat.
5. Sing/Pres: *Does inflammable* mean "burns easily" or "does not burn easily"?

3.4

1. When <u>will</u> you finish your master's degree?
2. Our office needs a person who <u>can</u> speak fluent Brazilian Portuguese.
3. <u>Can/Will</u> you please help me to move this piano?
4. Our office needs a person who <u>will</u> not be late.
5. <u>Can/Will</u> paper burn in a weightless environment?

3.5

1. The important papers were not taken from the safe but the jewelry was ~~taken from the safe~~.
2. The women are singing in the fall concert and some of the men are ~~singing in the fall concert~~, too.
3. Jaqueline does not like eggplant, and neither does Jack ~~like eggplant~~.
4. My brother had never seen a badger, but I had ~~seen a badger~~.
5. Some people cannot eat food prepared with MSG. Can you ~~eat food prepared with MSG~~?

3.6

1. a) *The marathon runner [have] won two gold medals so far.
   b) correct time of AUX (present)
      correct category of AUX (*have*)
   c) *The marathon runner [have] won two gold medals so far.
      The marathon runner has   won two gold medals so far.
      Explanation: The subject (*runner*) is singular so the auxiliary should also be singular (*has*), not plural (*have*), to make the subject and AUX agree.

2. a) *What [had] your girlfriend say to you last night?
   b) correct time of AUX (past)
   c) *What [had] your girlfriend say to you last night?
      What did   your girlfriend say to you last night?
      Explanation: The AUX used in question formation must always be *do* if there is no AUX in the statement form of the question (e.g., My girlfriend said "No!" last night.)

3. a) *I [was] working for a computer company at present.
   b) correct SUBJ-AUX agreement (*I was*)
      correct category of AUX (*be*)
   c) *I [was] working for a computer company at present.
      I am   working for a computer company at present.
      Explanation: The adverbial *at present* requires the present form of the AUX (*am*), not the past form (*was*)

4. a) *The prime minister [wills] speak to the parliament tomorrow afternoon.
   b) correct time (present)
      correct category of AUX (modal)
   c) *The prime minister [wills] speak to the parliament tomorrow afternoon.
      The prime minister will   speak to the parliament tomorrow afternoon.
      Explanation: Modals do not require agreement. [Note: the exceptions are the modal equivalents *be going to* and *have to*.]

5. a) *When the thieves entered the bank, they [did] already disconnected the alarm system.
   b) correct time of AUX (past)
   c) *When the thieves entered the bank, they [did] already disconnected the alarm system.
      When the thieves entered the bank, they had   already disconnected the alarm system.
      Explanation: The AUX *have* is required with VERB$_{ed_2}$ forms (*disconnected*), not *do*. [Note: The exception is in passive forms, which we will study in Ch. 4]

6. a) *[Will] you prefer chicken or fish for dinner, sir?
   b) correct time (present)
   c) *[Will] you prefer chicken or fish for dinner, sir?.
      Do   you prefer chicken or fish for dinner, sir?
      Explanation: The AUX used in question formation must always be *do* if there is no AUX in the statement form of the question (e.g., I prefer fish for dinner). [Note: This answer presumes that the customer is ordering the present meal and not a future one.]

7. a) *A bouquet of flowers [are] delivered every Friday morning.
   b) correct time (present)
      correct category of AUX (*be*)
   c) *A bouquet of flowers [are] delivered every Friday morning.
      A bouquet of flowers is   delivered every Friday morning.
      Explanation: The bare subject *bouquet* requires singular agreement (*is*), not plural (*are*).

8. a) *When [does] Alexander Graham Bell invent the telephone?
   b) correct SUBJ-AUX agreement (*Alexander Graham Bell does*)
      correct category of AUX (*do*)
   c) *When [does] Alexander Graham Bell invent the telephone?
      When did   Alexander Graham Bell invent the telephone?
      Explanation: Even though the time is not stated, we know that the telephone was invented in in the past. The AUX must therefore be in the past form (*did*), not the present (*does*).

9. a) *Susan [had] been very involved with this case since she joined the law firm earlier this month.
   b) correct category of AUX (*have*)
   c) *Susan [had] been very involved with this case since she joined the law firm earlier this month.
      Susan has   been very involved with this case since she joined the law firm earlier this month.
      Explanation: The adverbial *this month* requires the present form of the AUX (*has*), not the past form (*had*).

10. a) *Every other day, I [is] taken to the hospital for a dialysis treatment.
    b) correct time (present)
       correct category of AUX (*be*)
    c) *Every other day, I [is] taken to the hospital for a dialysis treatment.
       Every other day, I am taken to the hospital for a dialysis treatment.
       Explanation: "I" requires its own form of agreement (*am*), even though it is a singular subject.

3.7

1. 4 NPs
2. #7: *the people of Quebec*
3. intransitive; *prefer* = vt.
4. #10: *every other day*
5. #5 and #9; both are adverbial clauses

Chapter 4

4.1

Watching the Rain

I watch[Ø] quietly as the rain comes down. It has flooded the depressions in the field that the tractor carved as it was coming home last night. When the rain stops, those tiny lakes reflect[Ø] the light of the evening clouds like television screens that are recording the passage of the day. Now the sky is darkening again, and the light in the puddles disappears. Great torrents of rain strike[Ø] my window. The thunder roars. The lightning flashes. And I am happy to be safe and warm in my Navajo blanket.

4.2 (answers in text)

4.3

1. Uncle Ralph goes to church every Sunday.
2. Lionesses usually defend their cubs from predators. [fact]
3. The moon circles the Earth every 28 days.
4. My friends and I like to go dancing once in a while.
5. The capital city of Malaysia is Kuala Lumpur. [fact]
6. During the winter season, Doris usually rents an apartment on the Côte d'Azur.
7. Two hundred and thirty-one cubic inches of water equals one gallon. [fact] (quantities are treated as single entities)
8. Bats are rarely visible in the daytime.
9. Winds in a low-pressure area whirl counterclockwise in the northern hemisphere, clockwise in the southern. [fact]
10. The government announces the unemployment statistics once a month.

4.4 (answers in text)

4.5

1. The Second World War began in 1939.
2. The handle of the cup broke when it fell on the floor.
3. In the old days, his grandmother collected the harvest by herself.
4. Dinosaurs roamed the earth until the end of the Cretaceous period.
5. The Minoan civilization on the Greek island of Crete invented the flush toilet in about 2000 B.C.
6. The principal called you less than two minutes ago.
7. As the surgeon was performing the operation, he cut his thumb.
8. When she was a girl, Iliana took ballet lessons from a famous teacher.
9. In 1893, Edison showed the first motion picture.
10. David lost his home in the hurricane of 1992.

4.6 (answers in text)

4.7

1. The meeting will begin at eight o'clock tonight.
2. The Simpsons will return from their vacation a week from tomorrow.
3. I will remind my sister of her appointment with you this afternoon.
4. In a few minutes, Rhonda's husband will jump from the top of a cliff wearing a parachute.

5. The cook and her staff will need ten gallons of milk per day <u>when the students return to school</u>.
6. The free trade agreement will open the borders between the participant countries <u>three years from now</u>.
7. The school will pay for the drinks at party <u>at the end of the semester</u>.
8. Control of the island will revert to the native inhabitants <u>in five years</u>.
9. <u>On August 11, 1999,</u> a solar eclipse will be visible from Europe.
10. <u>After you take this medicine</u>, you will feel somewhat sleepy.

4.8

1. simple past
2. simple future
3. simple past
4. simple present

5. simple future
6. simple past
7. simple past
8. simple present

9. simple present
10. simple future

4.9 (answers in text)

4.10

1. The <u>plane</u> is moving down the runway <u>at this very moment</u>.
2. All the <u>members</u> of the basketball team are playing very well <u>right now</u>.
3. <u>Now,</u> I am descending into the mouth of the volcano.
4. <u>We</u> are living in Baltimore <u>for the time being</u>, but we soon hope to move to Washington, D.C.
5. <u>At present,</u> the <u>company</u> is having a very difficult time because of the recession.
6. My <u>son</u> is being silly <u>right now</u> because you are here, but he's not normally like this.
7. <u>Right at this precise second</u>, the <u>comet</u> is passing closest to the sun.
8. <u>For the time being</u>, I am using a rental car, but I will be happy to have my own car again when it's repaired.
9. The <u>woman</u> with the sunglasses is <u>now</u> telling the tourists to meet back at the hotel.
10. <u>At the moment</u>, I am working for a software company.

4.11 (answers in text)

4.12

1. When we <u>left</u> home, it was snowing.
2. The war <u>began</u> when David was working in Zagreb.
3. As the children were crossing the street, a drunk driver <u>missed</u> them by an inch.
4. My dog was walking through the park when a giant Siamese cat <u>ambushed</u> him.
5. When the guitarists were traveling in Mexico, one of them <u>lost</u> his instrument.
6. I <u>saw</u> them when they were eating at the neighborhood Chinese restaurant.
7. Julio's uncle <u>got</u> sick when he was driving to Alaska.
8. The young woman <u>slipped</u> as she was getting into a taxi.
9. While we were having lunch, there <u>was</u> a bomb scare.
10. The moon was shining brightly as we <u>rowed</u> across the lake.

4.13

1. The wind <u>blew</u> several trees over during the hurricane. I <u>was getting</u> off the bus when the wind <u>blew</u> my hat off. It <u>was</u> really <u>blowing</u> hard by the time I got home.
2. Mr. Laroche <u>drove</u> from Paris to Frankfurt last year. He <u>was driving</u> through Reims when he <u>got</u> a flat tire. He finally <u>drove</u> into Frankfurt as the sun <u>was going</u> down.
3. Jane <u>read</u> an entire issue of the *New York Times* yesterday. She <u>was reading</u> the last page when her friend Steve <u>came</u> over. Then he <u>read</u> the paper while she <u>was preparing</u> dinner.
4. The children <u>played</u> a lot of games yesterday because it <u>rained</u> all day. When they <u>were playing</u> Scrabble, Sally, the youngest, <u>spilled</u> her lemonade all over the game board. While Sally <u>was cleaning up</u> the sticky mess, the children <u>played</u> another game. Then they all <u>played</u> together for the rest of the day.
5. When World War II <u>started</u>, Jaime <u>was living and working</u> in Japan. He <u>lived</u> there for a total of six years and then he <u>returned</u> to Argentina. He <u>worked</u> at a language school while his wife Anna <u>was studying</u> Japanese at the university, but as soon as she <u>got</u> her certificate, he <u>began</u> his own studies. The war <u>changed</u> all that.

4.14 (answers in text)

4.15

1. By the time the letter <u>gets</u> here, Joan will be flying over the Atlantic Ocean.
2. My neighbors will be living in Honolulu when the baby <u>comes</u>.

3. When the emergency plan takes effect, the dockers will be working twelve-hour shifts until the situation <u>changes</u>.
4. If he gets the night job, Sarah will usually be sleeping when her husband <u>goes</u> to work.
5. Her mother will probably be hoping for a grandchild until the day she <u>dies</u>.
6. I will be watering the garden when you <u>arrive</u>, so please come around to the back.
7. At the time the merger <u>is</u> complete, the companies will still be producing films separately, but they are planning a joint venture for early next year.
8. Please don't <u>come</u> over on Saturday because I will be painting the floor.
9. By the time the volunteers <u>bring</u> the sandbags, the water will be rising more than three inches an hour.
10. The plane will be traveling 1088 feet per second when it <u>breaks</u> the sound barrier.

4.16

[Note: verbs with dotted underline cannot be made continuous]

1. The squirrel was running across the road <u>when a car hit it</u>. past cont.
2. <u>Right now</u>, everybody <u>loves</u> that actress. Let's see what happens in a couple of months. s. pres.
3. <u>The moment they discover the loss</u>, the thief will be carrying the jewels into Luxembourg. fut. cont.
4. The vice president of that company is <u>presently</u> taking a leave without pay because of the budget crunch. pres. cont.
5. Mrs. Gompias <u>had</u> four horses <u>when she lived in Ireland</u>. s. past
6. No one was watching the dial <u>when the reactor began to overheat</u>. past. cont.
7. <u>By the time you get this letter</u>, I will be cutting timber in the pine forests of the Northwest. fut. cont.
8. The children are sleeping <u>just now</u>. Can you come back later? pres. cont.
9. The coach yelled, "You will be sitting on the bench during the entire football season <u>unless you work that fat off</u>!" fut. cont.
10. <u>At the moment</u>, Barbara <u>thinks</u> she likes her neighbor, but tomorrow, she may not. s. pres.

4.17 (answers in text)

4.18

1. Mrs. Bumphries has been the mayor of this town <u>for six years</u>.
2. The boys have visited Mexico City <u>many times</u>.
3. Nancy has read five Victorian novels <u>this year</u>.
4. The Svensons have smoked salmon <u>for many generations</u>. It's the best.
5. Rats and mice have existed on this planet <u>since the Oligcene period 40 million years ago</u>.
6. <u>So far</u>, the soccer team has lost three times and won four.
7. George has learned to conjugate ten Russian verbs <u>since he started studying</u>.
8. That heart patient and his wife have had very bad luck <u>up to now</u>.
9. We have tried that seafood restaurant <u>several times</u>, but the fish is always too greasy.
10. My father has worked hard <u>all of his life</u>, so he's ready to retire now.

4.19 (answers in text)

4.20

1. When Mrs. Gooch had done the dishes, she <u>went</u> to bed.
2. The candidate <u>gave</u> a rousing speech, but we suspect that someone had written it for him.
3. The bus driver suddenly <u>realized</u> that he had taken the wrong road.
4. The miners <u>said</u> they had searched for years before they <u>found</u> any gold.
5. After Mary had signed the back of the check, the bank <u>cashed</u> it for her.
6. When she <u>got</u> home, Linda found that a thief had broken into her house.
7. Farmer Brown <u>sowed</u> his fields with alfalfa after his eldest son had plowed them up.
8. When I <u>invited</u> him to lunch, he said that he had had lunch, thank you.
9. The children <u>had</u> permission to watch television after they had finished their homework.
10. George Eliot <u>wrote</u> *Middlemarch* in 1872. She had written several other novels in earlier years.

4.21

1. The victim <u>was</u> sure that she <u>had seen</u> the man before.
2. At the trial, the lawyer <u>asked</u> the oil company executive whom he <u>had told</u> about the Alaska oil spill.

3. The professor's assistant <u>corrected</u> the papers that the students <u>had written</u> in class the hour before.
4. It <u>was</u> quite clear that the telephone operator <u>had given</u> us the wrong number.
5. The anguished mother <u>wanted</u> to know what <u>had happened</u> to her daughter during the hurricane.
6. The host <u>asked</u> his wife why the Johnsons <u>had left</u> so early.
7. As soon as the painter <u>had applied</u> the first coat of paint, it <u>was</u> obvious that the color <u>clashed</u> with the wallpaper.
8. The Coast Guard <u>had captured</u> the smugglers long before the FBI <u>heard</u> about the case.
9. When the musician <u>had composed</u> four symphonies, she <u>sent</u> one to a famous conductor for evaluation.
10. In 1553, after he <u>had divorced</u> Catherine of Aragon, Henry VIII <u>married</u> Anne Boleyn, who <u>gave</u> birth to Queen Elizabeth I.

4.22 (answers in text)

4.23

1. If Shirley <u>passes</u> Anatomy 1, she will have taken all the courses necessary to graduate.
2. By the time this building <u>is</u> complete, it will have cost the taxpayers ten million dollars.
3. When he <u>retires</u>, my grandfather <u>says</u> he will have accomplished everything he set out to do.
4. If our top salesman <u>gets</u> his brother to buy a car at this dealership, he will have sold over one hundred automobiles this year.
5. The logging company will have removed every old-growth redwood in this region by the time the court-ordered injunction to cease <u>arrives</u>.
6. The firefighters will have crossed every mountain range in the state when the fire season <u>ends</u> in October.
7. When she <u>finishes</u> Mr. Noon, Heather will have read every novel that D.H. Lawrence wrote.
8. If the gymnastics team from China <u>gets</u> a bronze medal for the next floor exercise, it will have won medals in every category.
9. If Ram <u>has</u> the opportunity to speak with the representative from the old Soviet Union, he will have met every member of the U.N. Security Council.
10. By this time tomorrow morning, the hot-air balloon will have crossed the Atlantic Ocean.

4.24

1. <u>When the bicyclists finally arrived in Vienna</u>, they had traveled over 1000 kilometers. <u>past perf.</u>
2. <u>By the time the boat docks at Southampton</u>, the passengers will have been at sea for nearly a week. <u>fut. perf.</u>
3. Chanel No. 5 is the only perfume that Roberta has worn <u>so far this season</u>. <u>pres. perf.</u>
4. <u>Since 1066</u>, over ten thousand words of French have entered the English language. <u>pres. perf.</u>
5. <u>When I started to get pains in my chest</u>, I knew that I had had enough exercise. <u>past perf.</u>
6. Tom did not believe the story until he had seen the evidence for himself. <u>past perf.</u>
7. Senator Ross will have delivered more speeches on this subject than anyone in the Senate when <u>he finishes this talk on the economy. fut. perf.</u>
8. After he had conquered Austria, Napoleon moved on to Italy. <u>past perf.</u>
9. After she has prepared her lesson plans, Sally usually reads for the rest of the evening. <u>pres. perf.</u>
10. My grandmother has done many exciting and wonderful things in her life. <u>pres. perf.</u>

4.25 (answers in text)

4.26

1. The faucet has been leaking continuously <u>for 24 hours</u>. Don't you think we should call a plumber? (irr)
2. It has been raining steadily <u>since we arrived here</u>, and all my clothes are damp and sticky. (irr)
3. Mr. and Mrs. Walton-Smith have been contributing to the AIDS hospice on a regular basis <u>since their son died two years ago</u>. (emph)
4. The artist has been working on the portrait without interruption <u>for two weeks</u>, but it still doesn't look very much like his model. (irr)
5. The telephone has been ringing continuously <u>since you left</u>! I am not your secretary! (irr)
6. Julia has been studying philosophy <u>for six years now</u> and she hopes to complete her doctoral degree by next June. (emph)
7. Your brother has been talking non-stop <u>since he got back from India</u>. He used to be such a shy fellow. (irr)
8. David has been having problems with his car <u>this week</u>, but that's nothing new. He insists on buying old cars. (emph)

9. The children have been swimming <u>since 3 o'clock</u>. Don't you think they should come out of the pool for a little while? (irr/emph)
10. John has been playing the piano <u>since he was a boy</u>, but he's never taken any lessons. (emph)

4.27 (answers in text)

4.28

1. The prospectors had been looking for the gold mine without pause since they <u>found</u> the old claim map in an attic.
2. It was easy to see that Fiona had been crying, because her eyes <u>were</u> all red.
3. The hurricane victims had been living on bottled water for several days as they <u>could not trust</u> the water supply.
4. It became clear that the witness had been lying the whole time when the attorney <u>confronted</u> him with the new evidence.
5. The victim had been bleeding for more than thirty minutes by the time the rescue team <u>got</u> to her.
6. You could tell that the boys had been swimming because their hair <u>was</u> still wet.
7. Julia had been driving for eight hours straight when the deer <u>ran</u> in front of her and she drove off the road.
8. The dam had been generating 1807 megawatts of electricity per day until the turbine <u>malfunctioned</u>.
9. The nurse had been helping hundreds of people each week until she <u>became</u> sick herself.
10. It turned out that the bank clerk had been taking money from the first moment he <u>began</u> working at the new branch.

4.29 (answers in text)

4.30

1. <u>When Ms. Dahl retires next year</u>, she will have been teaching science <u>for forty years</u> without a sabbatical leave.
2. If the couple from Georgia can last <u>until midnight</u>, they will have been dancing <u>for a total of sixty-five hours non-stop</u>, a new world record.
3. The top female marathon runner will have been averaging a speed of twelve miles per hour <u>if she passes this point within the next thirty-five seconds</u>.
4. <u>By the time he finishes his PhD</u>, Bruce will have studying without interruption <u>for twenty-four years</u>.
5. The mountaineers will have been climbing <u>for ten hours straight</u> <u>by the time they reach the summit</u>.
6. If my old Volkswagen can survive <u>until next month</u>, it will have been running without major repairs <u>for two decades</u>.
7. <u>By the time the tunnel construction crews meet each other deep beneath the Gotthard Pass</u>, they will have been digging continuously <u>for ten years</u>.
8. <u>When the boy finally has the first operation to remove the tumor in his brain</u>, he will have been suffering from intense nighttime headaches <u>for nearly two solid years</u>.
9. Senator Jarelewski will have been serving in the Senate <u>for eight years</u> <u>when he comes up for re-election next fall</u>.
10. If we do indeed reach Teheran <u>by nightfall</u>, we will have been driving <u>for six hours</u> without a decent meal.

4.31

1. <u>When we got to the ranch</u>, the cowboys had been rounding up the cattle <u>since six o'clock that morning</u>. past perf. cont.
2. My grandparents have been living in this house continuously <u>for fifty years</u>. pres. perf. cont.
3. <u>By the time they reach the White House</u>, the marchers will have been singing peace songs one after the other <u>for three hours</u>. fut. perf. cont.
4. My father has been watering his vegetable garden <u>since this afternoon</u>. pres. perf. cont.
5. Humans will have been inhabiting this planet <u>for more than five million years</u> <u>by the time the sun expands into a red giant</u>. fut. perf. cont.
6. <u>When Jane received the letter</u>, her boyfriend had been dating the other woman <u>for three months</u>. past perf. cont.
7. If Roger keeps it up <u>past next payday</u>, he will have been working here <u>longer than any other person in his family</u>. fut. perf. cont.
8. Julia had been taking photographs <u>for many years</u> <u>when she was asked to participate in an exposition of her work</u>. past perf. cont.
9. <u>By nine o'clock tonight</u>, my wife will have been having contractions <u>for three hours</u>. fut. perf.
10. The government has been printing that magazine every month <u>since the war started in 1983</u>. pres. perf. cont.

4.32

1. a) *Sally [took] a shower when the phone rang.
   b) correct time (past)
      correct possible form (*took*)
   c) *Sally [took]   a shower when the phone rang.
      Sally was taking a shower when the phone rang
      Explanation: When two verbs are present and one is in the past (and the intent is to show simultaneous
      actions), the other verb must be in the past continuous form.

2. a) *John [works] for IBM since 1982, so he knows a lot about computers.
   b) correct subj-verb agreement (*John works*)
      correct time (present)
      correct possible form (*works*)
   c) *John [works]   for IBM since 1982, so he knows a lot about computers.
      John has worked for IBM since 1982, so he knows a lot about computers.
      Explanation: Since always requires a perfect tense

3. a) *My aunt [are waiting] for me in the parking lot right now.
   b) correct time (present)
      correct aspect (continuous)
      correct form (*are waiting*)
   c) *My aunt [are] waiting for me in the parking lot right now.
      My aunt is   waiting for me in the parking lot right now.
      Explanation: The subject (*aunt*) is singular and therefore requires singular agreement (is)

4. a) *Janet was crossing the bridge last night when the earthquake [strikes].
   b) correct subj-verb agreement (*earthquake strikes*)
      correct aspect (simple)
      correct possible form (*strikes*)
   c) *Janet was crossing the bridge last night when the earthquake [strikes].
      Janet was crossing the bridge last night when the earthquake struck.
      Explanation: The past continuous tense requires a reference verb in the simple past.

5. a) *When Steven [had complete] his term paper, he put it in the instructor's mailbox.
   b) correct time (past)
   c) *When Steven [had complete] his term paper, he put it in the instructor's mailbox.
      When Steven had completed his term paper, he put it in the instructor's mailbox.
      Explanation: The past perfect tense requires that the main verb be in the VERB$_{ed_2}$ form.

6. a) *The university [have helped] migrant students for many years.
   b) correct time (present)
      correct aspect (perfect)
      correct possible form (*have helped*)
   c) *The university [have helped] migrant students for many years.
      The university has helped   migrant students for many years.
      Explanation: In AmE, *university* is singular and therefore requires singular agreement.

7. a) *My grandmother [is knowing] a lot about English grammar.
   b) correct subj-AUX agreement (*grandmother is*)
      correct time (present)
   c) *My grandmother [is knowing] a lot about English grammar.
      My grandmother knows   a lot about English grammar.
      Explanation: Verbs of cognition like *know* must be in the simple present and cannot occur in the present
      continuous tense.

8. a) *The plane [arrived] at 2 o'clock tomorrow morning.
    b) correct aspect (simple)
       correct possible form (*arrived*)
    c) *The plane [arrived]   at 2 o'clock tomorrow morning.
       The plane will arrive at 2 o'clock tomorrow morning.
       Explanation: The time phrase (*tomorrow morning*) requires the simple future tense.

9. a) *The tree [falled] on the roof of the house last night.
    b) correct time (past)
       correct aspect (simple)
    c) *The tree [falled] on the roof of the house last night.
       The tree fell   on the roof of the house last night.
       Explanation: Fall is an irregular verb whose past form is *fell*.

10. a) *Susan [writes] three letters so far this morning.
    b) correct subj-verb agreement (*Susan writes*)
       correct time (present)
       correct possible form (*writes*)
    c) *Susan [writes]   three letters so far this morning.
       Susan has written three letters so far this morning.
       Explanation: The time phrase (*so far this morning*) requires the present perfect tense.

4.33

1. a) *The patient's arm [bled] for three hours without stopping when he finally arrived at the
           emergency room.
    b) correct time (past)
       correct possible form (*bled*)
    c) *The patient's arm [bled]   for three hours without stopping when he finally arrived at the
           emergency room.
       The patient's arm had been bleeding for three hours without stopping when he finally arrived at the
           emergency room.
       Explanation: The bleeding had begun before arriving at the emergency room, not after, and the
               continuousness of that bleeding is implied by the PP (*without stopping*). Continuous
               sequence in the past requires the past perfect continuous tense.

2. a) *By the time the shuttle returns to the launching pad, it [will circle] the earth twenty-one times.
    b) correct time (future)
       correct possible form (*will circle*)
    c) *By the time the shuttle returns to the launching pad, it [will circle]   the earth twenty-one times.
       By the time the shuttle returns to the launching pad, it will have circled the earth twenty-one times.
       Explanation: The shuttle must circle the earth before it returns, not after. The prior event in a future
               sequence is shown with the future perfect tense.

3. a) *Up to now, only one of the students [have received] a scholarship.
    b) correct time (present)
       correct aspect (perfect)
       correct possible form (*have received*)
    c) *Up to now, only one of the students [have received] a scholarship.
       Up to now, only one of the students has received   a scholarship.
       Explanation: The bare subject of the sentence is singular (*one*). Auxiliary *have* must also be singular for
               the subject and AUX to agree.

4. a) *Every evening, the cat [is chasing] the dog around the garden.
    b) correct subj-AUX agreement (*cat is*)
       correct time (present)
       correct possible form (*is chasing*)
    c) *Every evening, the cat [is chasing] the dog around the garden.
       Every evening, the cat chases   the dog around the garden.
       Explanation: The time phrase (*every evening*) shows a habitual event and therefore requires the simple
               aspect (*chases*), not the continuous aspect (*is chasing*).

5. a) *My family [has been living] in this house for 100 years at this time next autumn.

b) correct subject-AUX agreement (*family has*)
correct aspect (perfect continuous)
correct possible form (*has been living*)

c) *My family [has been living]   in this house for 100 years at this time next autumn.
My family will have been living in this house for 100 years at this time next autumn.
Explanation: The time phrase (*at this time next autumn*) requires the future perfect continuous, not the present perfect continuous tense.

6. a) *That old drunk [has been given] his money away for the last fifteen minutes.

b) correct subj-AUX agreement (*drunk has*)
correct time (present)
correct possible form (*has been given*)

c) *That old drunk [has been given] his money away for the last fifteen minutes.
That old drunk has been giving   his money away for the last fifteen minutes.
Explanation: *For the last fifteen minutes* requires the present perfect continuous tense, which consists of the AUX *have/has been* (which is correctly used) + VERB$_{ing}$ (*giving*).

7. a) *The carpenter [was stepping] on a nail when he was walking across the lumber yard.

b) correct subj-AUX agreement (*carpenter was*)
correct time (past)
correct possible form (*was stepping*)

c) *The carpenter [was stepping] on a nail when he was walking across the lumber yard.
The carpenter stepped   on a nail when he was walking across the lumber yard.
Explanation: The past continuous verb (*was walking*) requires a reference verb in the simple past tense (*stepped*), not the past continuous tense. Furthermore, because the action (stepping on a nail) is an instantaneous event, not one that occurs over time, it does not logically occur in a continuous tense.

8. a) *By this time next year, Celia is [going to sailing] across the Atlantic by herself.

b) correct subj-AUX agreement (*Celia is*)
correct time (future)
correct aspect (continuous)

c) *By this time next year, Celia is [going to sailing]   across the Atlantic by herself.
By this time next year, Celia is going to be sailing across the Atlantic by herself.
Explanation: The future continuous structure requires a modal (or equivalent) + *be* + VERB$_{ing}$, not modal + VERB$_{ing}$.

9. a) *After the banker [has written] the check, he sent it to his lawyer.

b) correct subj-AUX agreement (*banker has*)
correct aspect (perfect)
correct possible form (*has written*)

c) *After the banker [has written] the check, he sent it to his lawyer.
After the banker had written   the check, he sent it to his lawyer.
Explanation: Since the purpose of this sentence is to show sequential events and a reference verb in the simple past (*sent*) is present, the verb needs to be in the past perfect, not the present perfect tense.

10. a) *I [am seeing] the rings of Saturn at the moment.

b) correct subj-AUX agreement (*I am*)
correct time (present)
correct possible form (*am seeing*; e.g., I am seeing my doctor this afternoon)

c) *I [am seeing] the rings of Saturn at the moment.
I see   the rings of Saturn at the moment.
Explanation: Perception verbs like *see* cannot occur in the present continuous tense.

4.34 (Analysis of the example paragraph from *The Magician*)

Of the 12 verbs underlined, 9 are in the past tense (7 simple past, 1 past continuous, 1 past perfect) and 3 are in the present tense (2 present perfect, 1 simple present). The dominant time is thus the past, but the three present tenses do not intrude. The reason for this is that the author is comparing aspects of the scene to characters that do not exist only in the past. In the first use of a present tense in the "sea" of past tenses (line 4), the author describes his character's perception as being the same as that of the many painters, past and present, who have tried to paint the Luxembourg gardens. In the second two uses of present tenses (line 9), the author compares the garden to a faded beauty who, like many faded beauties in the past and the present (i.e., timeless) tries to pretend that she is still beautiful. All timeless attributes are, like facts, reported in the present tense.

The discourse effects of the tenses may be described as follows: The past perfect tense (line 1) "repairs" the chronological sequence of events by telling us that the two characters had lunched before they went for a walk in the gardens. The past continous tense (line 2) is contrasted with an adverbial (*now*) rather than a verb in the simple past tense, although it could have been contrasted with a clause such as "…as they <u>observed</u> the gardens." The two uses of the present perfect show the experience of the subject in different ways. The first case (line 4), ("painters …have sought…to express their sense of beauty") shows the artistic experience of the painters in trying to express themselves through their work. The second case ("the hurrying years have rendered [fascination] vain") shows the personified experience of age (*the hurrying years*) that makes attempts to appear youthful vain in an older person.

This paragraph by Maugham skillfully combines a past narrative with timeless (present) observations that deeply enrich the storyline.

4.35 (many other verbs possible)

1. The truck hit a deer.
2. The doctor examined a patient.
3. The professor wrote a book.
4. A thermometer measures temperature.
5. Shakespeare wrote *Hamlet*.
6. Poison killed the ants.
7. The arrow hit the target.
8. The astronomer observed the moons of Saturn.
9. A thief robbed the woman who lives next door.
10. An earthquake with a magnitude of 7.0 on the Richter scale destroyed a small village in Columbia.

4.36

1. Someone built the bridges in 1945.
   1. someone built the bridges
   2. ———built the bridges
   3. the bridges built
   4. built = simple past
   5. s. past *be* = *was* (sing.), *were* (plur.)
   6. the bridges = plural
   7. the bridges were
   8. the bridges were built
   9. The bridges were built in 1945.
2. Somebody produces aluminum from bauxite.
   1. somebody produces aluminum
   2. ———produces aluminum
   3. aluminum produces
   4. produces = simple present
   5. s. pres. *be* = *is* (sing.), *are* (plur.), *am* ("I")
   6. aluminum = singular
   7. aluminum is
   8. aluminum is produced
   9. Aluminum is produced from bauxite.
3. Something formed the planet billions of years ago.
   1. something formed the planet
   2. ——— formed the planet
   3. the planet formed
   4. formed = simple past
   5. s. past *be* = *was* (sing.), *were* (plur.)
   6. the planet = singular
   7. the planet was
   8. the planet was formed
   9. The planet was formed billions of years ago.

4. People grow peanuts in Georgia.
   1. people grow peanuts
   2. —— grow peanuts
   3. peanuts grow
   4. grow = simple present
   5. s. pres. *be* = *is* (sing.), *are* (plur.), *am* ("I")

   6. peanuts = plural
   7. peanuts are
   8. peanuts are grown
   9. Peanuts are grown in Georgia

5. Something hit me in the eye.
   1. something hit me
   2. ——— hit me
   3. I hit
   4. hit = simple past
   5. s. past *be* = *was* (sing.), *were* (plur.)

   6. "I" = singular (in past tenses)
   7. I was
   8. I was hit
   9. I was hit in the eye.

4.37

1. Steel <u>is</u> produced from iron, carbon, and other trace elements.
2. The first locomotives <u>were</u> powered by steam.
3. Hundreds of people <u>have been</u> killed because of storms this year.
4. A lot of coffee <u>is</u> grown in South America.
5. The solar system <u>was</u> formed approximately 4.5 billion years ago.
6. My street <u>is being</u> repaired at the moment. There's dust everywhere.
7. The next space module <u>will be</u> sent to Venus.
8. The pores in a leaf <u>are</u> called stomata.
9. Microcomputers <u>will be</u> used more and more in the future.
10. A pound of potatoes <u>is</u> needed for this experiment.
11. The brain chemical that regulates growth <u>has been</u> recently synthesized.
12. The dissidents were sure the house <u>was being</u> watched night and day.
13. The check <u>had been</u> signed by a clever forger when it was deposited in the account.
14. At that very moment, the people of the nation <u>were being</u> told to prepare for a missile attack.
15. The national debt <u>has been</u> (or <u>is</u>) calculated to be over three hundred billion dollars.

4.38

1. The letters <u>were mailed</u> yesterday morning.
2. Relief supplies <u>are being distributed</u> at this very moment.
3. The doctor <u>has examined</u> hundreds of patients so far.
4. When the treaty <u>was signed</u>, trade increased significantly between the two countries.
5. By 2020, electric automobiles <u>will be required</u> in all major cities.
6. The treatment of Gandhi in his early life <u>dismayed</u> the school children.
7. The ship was attacked while it <u>was being loaded</u> with hidden weapons.
8. By the time we reach Lisbon, this plane <u>will have flown</u> eighteen hours nonstop.
9. Every day I <u>am carried</u> to the palace in my rickshaw.
10. Your husband <u>will be being operated</u> on at the time you arrive, so you will have to wait in the lounge until the procedure is finished.

4.39

Sentences 2, 4, 5, 7, and 10 have intransitive main verbs. They cannot be passive.

4.40

1. a) *Many snakes [are lived] in dry desert regions.
   b) correct subj-AUX agreement (*snakes are*)
      correct time (present)
      correct aspect (simple)
      correct possible form (*are lived*, but only for vt. meanings, e.g., *Lives are lived alone.*)
   c) *Many snakes [are lived] in dry desert regions.
      Many snakes live   in dry desert regions.
      Explanation: Live is intransitive, so it cannot be in the passive voice.

2. a) *When she [had been finished] the dishes, Sarah went to bed.
   b) correct time (past)
      correct aspect (perfect)
      correct possible form (*had been finished*)
   c) *When she [had been finished] the dishes, Sarah went to bed.
      When she had finished   the dishes, Sarah went to bed.
      Explanation: The subject *she* (i.e., *Sarah*) is performing, not receiving the action, so the active, not the passive, voice must be used.

3. a) *A box of old photographs [were found] in the attic.
   b) correct time (past)
      correct aspect (simple)
      correct possible form (*were found*)
      correct voice (passive)
   c) *A box of old photographs [were found] in the attic.
      A box of old photographs was found   in the attic.
      Explanation: The bare subject of the sentence (*box*) is singular, which requires singular agreement (*was*, not *were*).

4. a) *Mahler's Fourth Symphony [will be perform] on campus tomorrow night.
   b) correct time (future)
      correct aspect (simple)
      [partially correct voice](passive: *will be* + VERB)
   c) *Mahler's Fourth Symphony [will be perform]   on campus tomorrow night.
      Mahler's Fourth Symphony will   be performed on campus tomorrow night.
      Explanation: The subject (*symphony*) receives the action, so the passive voice is required. The simple future passive has the form *will be* + VERB$_{ed_2}$, not *will be* + VERB$_{base}$.

5. a) *My grandfather [has been grown] a long white beard this year.
   b) correct subj-AUX agreement (*grandfather has*)
      correct time (present)
      correct aspect (perfect)
      correct possible form (*has been grown*)
   c) *My grandfather [has been grown] a long white beard this year.
      My grandfather has grown   a long white beard this year.
      Explanation: The subject (*grandfather*) is performing the action, not receiving it, so the active voice is required.

6. a) *The school cafeteria [is renovated] right now.
   b) correct subj-AUX agreement (*cafeteria is*)
      correct time (present)
      correct possible form (*is renovated*)
      correct voice (passive)
   c) *The school cafeteria [is renovated]   right now.
      The school cafeteria is being renovated right now.
      Explanation: Right now triggers the present continuous tense, not the simple present.

7. a) *I came home and found that my apartment [has been robbed].
   b) correct subj-AUX agreement (*apartment has*)
      correct aspect (perfect)
      correct possible form (*has been robbed*)
      correct voice (passive)

    c) *I came home and found that my apartment [has been robbed].

      I came home and found that my apartment had been robbed.

      Explanation: The simple past reference verbs (*came/found*) would only occur with a past tense (past perfect or past continuous), not a present one.

8. a) *Ralph's brother had an accident when the road [was been repaired].

    b) correct subj-AUX agreement (*road was*)

      correct time (past)

      [partial correct voice] (passive: *was…repaired*)

    c) *Ralph's brother had an accident when the road [was been repaired].

      Ralph's brother had an accident when the road was being repaired.

      Explanation: The simple past reference verb (*had*) requires a past continuous verb in this case as the actions occurred simultaneously. The subject (*road*) is receiving the action, so the voice must be passive. Past continuous passive consists of *be* +*being*+VERB$_{ed2}$.

9. a) *Thousands of people [were died] during the Black Death.

    b) correct subj-AUX agreement (*people were*)

      correct time (past)

      correct aspect (simple)

    c) *Thousands of people [were died] during the Black Death..

      Thousands of people died   during the Black Death.

      Explanation: Die is intransitive and therefore cannot be in the passive voice.

10. a) *Next year, the automobile company [introduced] an electric car.

    b) correct aspect (simple)

      correct possible form (*introduced*)

      correct voice (active)

    c) *Next year, the automobile company [introduced]   an electric car.

      Next year, the automobile company will introduce an electric car.

      Explanation: The time phrase (*next year*) requires the simple future, not simple past, tense.

4.41

1. a) *We [are being bombarding] with cosmic rays even at this very moment.

    b) correct subj-AUX agreement (*we are*)

      correct time (present)

      correct aspect (continuous) [Note: Aspect is "carried by" *be* in passive structures]

    c) *We [are being bombarding] with cosmic rays even at this very moment.

      We are being bombarded   with cosmic rays even at this very moment.

      Explanation: The subject (*we*) is receiving the action, so the voice must be passive. Passive structures require *be* + VERB$_{ed2}$, not *be* + VERB$_{ing}$.

2. a) *English [taught] in many countries in the world.

    b) correct aspect (simple)

      correct possible form (*taught*)

    c) *English [taught]   in many countries in the world.

      English is taught in many countries in the world.

      Explanation: The subject (*English*) receives the action, so the voice must be passive. Passive structures always require auxiliary *be*.

3. a) *Herbal remedies [have used] by the Chinese for thousands of years.

    b) correct subj-AUX agreement (*remedies have*)

      correct time (present)

      correct aspect (perfect)

      correct possible form (*have used*)

    c) *Herbal remedies [have used]   by the Chinese for thousands of years.

      Herbal remedies have been used by the Chinese for thousands of years.

      Explanation: The subject (*remedies*) receives the action, so the voice must be passive.

4. a) *As the cake [has being taken] out of the oven, the cook slipped and dropped it on the floor.

    b) correct subj-AUX agreement (*cake has*)

    c) *As the cake [has being taken] out of the oven, the cook slipped and dropped it on the floor.

      As the cake was being taken out of the oven, the cook slipped and dropped it on the floor.

      Explanation: The subject (*cake*) is receiving the action, so the voice must be passive. Since the action was occurring when something else happened, the past continuous tense is required. The past continuous passive form is *was being* VERB$_{ed2}$.

5. a) *By the time we get home, the sun [will have been gone] down.
   b) correct time (future)
      correct aspect (perfect)
      correct possible form (*will have been gone*) [e.g., *The details will have been gone into.*]
   c) *By the time we get home, the sun [will have been gone] down
      By the time we get home, the sun will have gone   down.
      Explanation: The meaning of *go* in this sentence is vi. and therefore cannot be passive.

6. a) *In 1492, Columbus [discover] America.
   b) correct aspect (simple)
      correct possible form (*discover*)
      correct voice (active)
   c) *In 1492, Columbus [discover] America.
      In 1492, Columbus discovered America..
      Explanation: The simple past active form is $VERB_{ed_1}$, not $VERB_{\emptyset}$ (or $VERB_{base}$)

7. a) *A tree [will be planting] in his honor at a ceremony next week.
   b) correct time (future)
      correct possible form (*will be planting*)
   c) *A tree [will be planting] in his honor at a ceremony next week.
      A tree will be planted   in his honor at a ceremony next week.
      Explanation: The subject (*tree*) is receiving the action so the verb must be passive. Passive verb forms always require $VERB_{ed_2}$ as the last element of the verb.

8. a) *My young son [is been being] grouchy all day.
   b) correct subj-AUX agreement (*son is*)
      correct time (present)
   c) *My young son [is been being] grouchy all day.
      My young son has been being grouchy all day.
      Explanation: The present perfect continuous form of *be* (which can never be passive and is justified by the time phrase *all day*) is *have + been + being*. [Note: This sentence sounds more acceptable in contracted form (*My young son's been being grouchy all day*) but sounds best when the verb is not continuous (*My young son's been grouchy all day*).]

9. a) *When the end of the next century arrives, perhaps spaceships [will be being send] through black holes.
   b) correct time (future)
      correct aspect (continuous)
   c) *When the end of the next century arrives, perhaps spaceships [will be being send] through black holes.
      When the end of the next century arrives, perhaps spaceships will be being sent   through black holes.
      Explanation: The subject (*spaceships*) is receiving the action, so the passive voice is required. The future continuous passive form is justified by the reference verb (*arrives*). Passive forms require $VERB_{ed_2}$ as the final element.

10. a) *The students were not allowed to leave until they [will have paid] their phone bills.
    b) correct aspect (perfect)
       correct possible form (*will have paid*)
       correct voice (active)
    c) *The students were not allowed to leave until they [will have paid] their phone bills.
       The students were not allowed to leave until they had paid   their phone bills.
       Explanation: The reference verb (*were not allowed*) requires a past perfect, not a future perfect verb form.

4.42

Some Uses of Plants

<u>A plant</u> is a living organism. The plant is made up of <u>different parts, each with particular purposes or functions.</u> <u>Some parts of the plant</u> may be removed without harming it. Plants such as beets, carrots, and potatoes store <u>food</u> in the roots. <u>Other plants</u> are able to take nitrogen from the air and add it to the soil. These plants are called legumes. If they are plowed under, <u>they</u> make the soil more fertile.

4.43

A Doctor's Consulation

Dr. Smith is a general practitioner in a small town in Kentucky. This morning, his first patient is Mrs. Green. First, he greets the patient. Then he asks the patient for details about the problem. Next he examines the patient. Then he prescribes treatment or medication. Finally, he arranges a follow-up visit for the patient.

A Medical Student's First Patient

Mr. Singh is a new medical student at a large urban hospital. He will be meeting his first patient in a few minutes, so he reviews what he has learned. First, the patient is greeted by the doctor. Then the patient is asked for details about the problem. Next the patient is examined. Then treatment or medication is prescribed. Finally, a follow-up visit is arranged for the patient.

Chapter 5

5.1

1. The children <u>aren't</u> feeling well today.
2. Roger <u>hasn't</u> visited Prague since he was a teenager.
3. John <u>can't</u> speak Swahili.
4. I <u>am not</u> putting that chair in the living room.
5. You <u>shouldn't</u> tell her what you think.
6. The tourists <u>won't</u> have a very good time with Henry.
7. I <u>hadn't</u> seen the Blue Grotto before.
8. The earth <u>isn't</u> flat as many people once thought.
9. Bill <u>wasn't</u> angry when his wife left him.
10. The Simpsons <u>weren't</u> very pleased with their new car.

5.2

1. Lions <u>don't</u> mate for life.
2. The eucalyptus tree <u>doesn't</u> grow in colder climates.
3. Astronauts <u>didn't</u> get to the moon in the first half of the twentieth century.
4. Rats <u>aren't</u> welcome in the basement.
5. I <u>don't</u> like the sweater that Janet is wearing.
6. The house <u>hadn't</u> been taken care of.
7. The professor who helped me most in my studies <u>didn't</u> retire when he was 65.
8. A computer <u>doesn't</u> always know how to solve problems.
9. We <u>weren't</u> wearing our seat belts when the accident occurred.
10. Please <u>don't</u> do your homework on the kitchen table.

5.3 [Note: There is more than one possible answer depending on the perceived truth value.]

1. Trees <u>rarely</u> grow well in low light.
2. Letters without ZIP codes <u>seldom</u> reach their destination on time.
3. In California, it <u>hardly ever</u> rains in the summertime.
4. A black hole <u>never</u> emits visible light.
5. Early intertribal battles <u>rarely</u> took prisoners of war.

5.4

1. <u>No</u> senator has a higher salary than the president.
2. The striking mine workers got <u>no</u> help from their colleagues.
3. The richer children will get preferential treatment under <u>no</u> circumstances.
4. <u>No</u> visitors are allowed beyond this point.
5. There is <u>no</u> chance that it will rain tomorrow.
6. A candidate with <u>no</u> education will have a hard time winning the election.
7. <u>No</u> African team has ever won the Americas Cup sailing competition.
8. The geologist said that <u>no</u> land plant was older than moss or algae.
9. <u>No</u> planet in the solar system has a greater equatorial diameter than the gas giant Jupiter.
10. When the trekkers reached the Dead Sea, they were told that <u>no</u> place on earth was lower in elevation.

5.5

1. The star Beta Centauri is <u>no</u> brighter than Betelgeuse.
2. Miss Hinkle <u>no</u> longer works for IBM.
3. Mars has <u>no</u> fewer satellites than Neptune.
4. The Union of Soviet Socialist Republics (USSR) <u>no</u> longer exists.
5. Mt. Kunyang Kish in India is <u>no</u> taller than Mt. Dakum in Nepal.

5.6

1. Harry's reasoning is very <u>il</u>logical.
2. In my view, that painter is <u>un</u>imaginative.
3. A-type personalities are very <u>im</u>patient.
4. Some government officials are <u>ir</u>responsible.
5. The methods that the committee suggested were (usually) <u>im</u>practical.
6. Aunt Hilda is <u>in</u>capable of keeping a houseplant alive.
7. The Vermeer painting that was stolen last night is simply <u>ir</u>replaceable.
8. The Christmas holidays were very <u>un</u>pleasant this year.
9. Medical suppies were <u>non</u>existent.
10. The students in this class are <u>il</u>literate in their first languages.

5.7 (answers may vary)

A Letter from School

Dear Alicia,

I am sorry I haven't written to you for such a long time, but it has been a busy semester for me. Despite my <u>light</u> work schedule, however, I <u>haven't</u> had <u>much</u> fun. Since I arrived, I <u>haven't</u> gone on a tour of this city and <u>haven't</u> visited <u>any</u> famous landmarks or tourist spots. I <u>haven't</u> taken <u>any</u> pictures, <u>either.</u> I <u>haven't</u> spent <u>any</u> money on magazines, books, or art reproductions.

My cousin lives about ten miles away, and he <u>hasn't</u> experienced <u>any</u> more than I. He <u>hasn't</u> tried river rafting. He <u>hasn't</u> climbed the mountains in this area. He <u>hasn't</u> even jumped off a bridge attached to a bungee cord. We also <u>haven't</u> done <u>anything</u> together. We <u>haven't</u> <u>even</u> swum in the Kanawha River.

<u>Still,</u> I <u>have</u> done <u>a lot of things</u> I wanted to do this year. I <u>have</u> <u>already</u> been to a symphony concert <u>and</u> to a ballet performance. I <u>have</u> seen <u>some</u> art galleries <u>and</u> museums, <u>too.</u> I <u>have</u> <u>also</u> made <u>some</u> new friends. Write soon.

Love, Helena

5.8

1. a) *Many wild animals [do'nt] like fire.
    b) correct negation type (auxiliary)
       correct position of negator (after first AUX)
    c) *Many wild animals [do'nt] like fire.
       Many wild animals don't   like fire.
       Explanation: Contractions require that the apostrophe be placed where letters are deleted.

2. a) *Mary says [never] "Hello!"
    b) correct negation type (adverbial)
       correct form of negator (*never*)
    c) *Mary says [never] "Hello!"
       Mary never says   "Hello!"
       Explanation: Adverbial negators are placed after the first AUX or before the main verb.

3. a) *People with low self-esteem are often [undecisive].
    b) correct negation type (morphological)
       correct position of negator (adjective prefix)
    c) *People with low self-esteem are often [undecisive].
       People with low self-esteem are often indecisive.
       Explanation: The adjective *decisive* is negated with the prefix *in-*, not *un-*.

4. a) *I [amn't] satisfied with my test results.
    b) correct negation type (auxiliary)
       correct position of negator (after first AUX)
       correct contraction (**amn't*) [Note: It correctly follows the steps for contracting AUX + *not.*]
    c) *I [amn't] satisfied with my test results.
       I am not satisfied with my test results.
       Explanation: The AUX *am* + *not* cannot be contracted.

5. a) *The photography team spoke with the native peoples [hardly ever].
    b) correct negation type (adverbial)
       correct form of negator (*hardly ever*)
    c) *The photography team   spoke with the native peoples [hardly ever].
       The photography team hardly ever spoke with the native peoples.
       Explanation: Adverbial negators are placed after the first AUX or before the main verb.

6. a) *The children [haven't] sleeping at the moment.
    b) correct negation type (auxiliary)
       correct position of negator (before the main verb)
       correct contraction (*haven't*)
    c) *The children [haven't] sleeping at the moment.
       The children aren't   sleeping at the moment.
       Explanation: The correct AUX for continuous tenses is *be*, not *have*.

7. a) *My older sister will eat absolutely [not] red meat.
    b) correct position of negator (as part of NP)
    c) *My older sister will eat absolutely [not] red meat
       My older sister will eat absolutely no   red meat.
       Explanation: Noun phrases are negated with the negator *no*, not *not*. [Note: Alternatively, the sentence could have been corrected to *My older sister will absolutely not eat red meat*, in which case the negation type and form would have been correct but not the position.]

8. a) *Computer hard disk drives are sometimes [irreliable].
    b) correct negation type (morphological)
       correct position of negator (as an adjective prefix)
    c) *Computer hard disk drives are sometimes [irreliable].
       Computer hard disk drives are sometimes unreliable.
       Explanation: The adjective *reliable* is negated with the prefix *un-*, not *ir-*.

9. a) *The astronomers [couldn't] see no rings around Saturn last night.
    b) correct form of negator (*n't*)
       correct position of negator (after first AUX)
       correct contraction (*couldn't*)

c) *The astronomers [couldn't] see no rings around Saturn last night.
The astronomers could   see no rings around Saturn last night.
[Note: We could also say *The astronomers couldn't see any rings around Saturn last night.*]
Explanation: Only one type of negation is allowed in a standard English sentence.

10. a) *Bonn is [not] longer the capital of Germany.
    b) correct position of negator (before adverb of comparison)
    c) *Bonn is [not]   longer the capital of Germany.
        Bonn is no   longer the capital of Germany.
        Explanation: Adverbs of comparison require the negator *no*, not *not*.

Chapter 6

6.1

1. Aluminum <u>should melt</u> at 660°C.
2. Some toys <u>can be</u> lethal for children.
3. The best student in the department <u>will get</u> the Dean's Medal.
4. The government announced that it <u>would allow</u> AIDS victims to enter the country.
5. The United Nations <u>must have</u> financial support from many countries.
6. Sunlight <u>may relieve</u> depression in a surprising number of people.
7. Windows <u>could shatter</u> in an earthquake and injure people in the streets below.
8. Daphne <u>might be</u> bringing her boyfriend to the party.
9. Dog owners <u>had better clean up</u> after their pets or they will be fined.
10. I <u>used to live</u> with my uncle when I was a child.

6.2

1. certainty	Female lions will defend their cubs from males.
2. conclusion	The plane must have mechanical problems.
3. obligation	Doctors should have a pleasant bedside manner.
4. possibility	Aluminum may be the cause of Alzheimer's disease.
5. suggestion	Alice's mother could increase her daily exercise.
6. requirement	Students must pass English 1 in order to graduate.
7. opportunity	Students at the university can take courses in the evening.
8. command	The soldiers will report to headquarters on Monday at 7 A.M.
9. chance	The volcano might errupt at any time in the next few days.
10. probability	An electron microscope should reveal the structure of the virus.

6.3

Dear College Applicant:

In order to be admitted to this program, you <u>must</u> submit an example of your written work. You <u>should</u> send it by certified mail. You <u>will</u> be informed about our decision in four weeks.

We wish you success in your endeavors.

    Yours sincerely,
    Admissions Office

6.4

Dear Employer:

I am writing the ask if you <u>would</u> consider my application for a teaching position in your institution. Since I'll be in Arizona next week, I <u>could</u> stop by your office to meet the director. I <u>could</u> visit your school on Tuesday morning. I <u>would</u> appreciate your letting me know if this is possible.

    Yours sincerely,
    Applicant

6.5

1. Female lions <u>are going to</u> defend their cubs from males.
2. The plane <u>has to</u> have mechanical problems.
3. Doctors <u>are supposed to</u> have a pleasant bedside manner.
4. Aluminum <u>is likely to</u> be the cause of Alzheimer's disease.
5. Alice's mother <u>is advised to</u> increase her daily exercise.
6. Students <u>have to</u> pass English 1 in order to graduate.
7. Students at the university <u>have the opportunity to</u> take courses in the evening.
8. The soldiers <u>are to</u> report to headquarters on Monday at 7 A.M.
9. The volcano <u>has the chance to</u> errupt at any time in the next few days.
10. An electron microscope <u>ought to</u> reveal the structure of the virus.

6.6

1. capability	Bamboo plants can grow several inches a day.
2. hypothetical situation	If it rained right now, there would be an avalanche.
3. possibility	May women ask for a divorce in your country?
4. threat	Small dogs had better stay away from mountain lions.
5. polite request	Would you mail this letter for me?
6. permission	Passengers with children may board the plane now.
7. repeated past action	Susan's father would read her a story in the evening.
8. polite request	May I have another cup of tea?
9. permission	Can the children go to the beach this afternoon?
10. suggestion	Could you live in a quieter neighborhood?

6.7

1. Students <u>must not (are required not to)</u> put their feet on the furniture.
2. Subjects <u>are to (are not to)</u> sit in the presence of the king.
3. Passengers <u>might not (are not advised to)</u> watch the in-flight movie. (change in equivalent)
4. Patients <u>may not (do not have the opportunity to)</u> be visited after 8 p.m.
5. Guests <u>cannot (do not have the opportunity to)</u> swim in the canal. (change in equivalent)
6. You <u>could not (are not advised to)</u> take your dog on the ship with you. (change in equivalent)
7. Hikers <u>should not (are not supposed to)</u> feed the animals in the forest.
8. The children <u>must not (are required not to)</u> be left alone.
9. The priest <u>might not (is not advised to)</u> have a large congregation. (change in equivalent)
10. Oil <u>should not (is not supposed to)</u> be dumped in the garbage.

6.8

1. A small amount of ultraviolet light <u>will not (is not going to)</u> harm the skin.
2. Chemotherapy <u>may not (is not likely to)</u> halt the spread of breast cancer. (change in equivalent)
3. Cold temperatures <u>must not (does not have to)</u> affect aquatic mammals. (change in equivalent)
4. Daffodil bulbs <u>might not (do not have the chance to)</u> bloom every year. (change in equivalent)
5. Air bags <u>could not (do not have the possibility to)</u> harm the driver or the passengers.
6. This medication <u>should not (ought not to)</u> decrease your blood pressure.
7. A motorcycle helmet <u>cannot (is not able to)</u> protect the rider from serious back injuries.
8. The United Nations <u>will not (is not going to)</u> send troops to this troubled region.
9. Gold <u>may not (is not likely to)</u> be found in the sunken galleon.
10. Divorce <u>must not (doesn't have to)</u> end in bitterness between the husband and wife. (change in modal)

6.9

1. All bicycles <u>had to</u> be registered last year.
2. Three weeks ago, whale watchers <u>had the opportunity to</u> observe migrations of gray whales from Point Reyes.
3. The gang members <u>were not to</u> return to that neighborhood until two years had passed. (change)
4. Last summer, farmers <u>were advised to</u> spray their crops to avoid fruit fly infestation. (change)
5. In the nineteenth century, children <u>were obliged to</u> take care of their parents in their old age.
6. We <u>had the opportunity to</u> visit the Statue of Liberty or the Empire State Building on our trip last year.
7. At the meeting yesterday, mothers <u>were advised to</u> disguise bad-tasting medications in a teaspoonful of jam.

8. After the old man died, the heirs to the family fortune <u>were to</u> share the money equally.
9. Tulip bulbs <u>did not have to</u> be planted until late fall last season.
10. The doctors <u>were not obliged to</u> operate on the accident victim at that moment.

6.10

1. By that time, Elizabeth <u>would have finished</u> her medical training.
2. The bomb <u>could have exploded</u> at any minute after it was dropped down the hospital chimney.
3. The passengers <u>must not have known</u> that the ship was on fire because nobody jumped into the water.
4. In regard to the patient released last week, barbiturates <u>could have caused</u> the rashes on his hands and feet.
5. A disaster <u>might have been</u> avoided last year with the installation of a safety net.
6. Ice on the wings <u>should have been</u> reason enough to ground the plane in the last major accident.
7. During the first emergency drill, engineers <u>may not have opened</u> the valves in time.
8. The students <u>would not have been</u> ready for such a difficult examination two months ago.
9. In the last famine, the starving women <u>must not have been</u> aware of international relief efforts.
10. The unsatisfied tenants <u>should not have paid</u> the rent last month.

6.11

1. a) *[OPPORTUNITY] Teachers [can influencing] their students in many ways.
   b) correct modal meaning (*can* = opportunity)
      correct modal features (present; positive)
   c) *[OPPORTUNITY] Teachers [can influencing] their students in many ways.
      [OPPORTUNITY] Teachers can influence   their students in many ways.
      Explanation: The verb after a present modal must be the VERB$_{base}$ form.
2. a) *[POSSIBILITY] People with bone problems [may not get] enough calcium in their youth.
   b) correct modal meaning (*may* = possibility)
      correct verb form after modal (VERB$_{base}$)
   c) *[POSSIBILITY] People with bone problems [may not get]   enough calcium in their youth.
      [POSSIBILITY] People with bone problems may not have gotten enough calcium in their youth.
      Explanation: The time phrase (*in their youth*) requires a past modal.
3. a) *[POLITE REQUEST] [Will] you [help] me with my homework?
   b) correct modal features (present; positive)
      correct verb form after modal (VERB$_{base}$)
   c) *[POLITE REQUEST] [Will] you [help] me with my homework?
      [POLITE REQUEST] Would you help   me with my homework?
      Explanation: The modal for polite requests is *would* (or *could*), not *will* (or *can*)
4. a) *[CONCLUSION] You [must have like] chocolate when you were a child.
   b) correct modal meaing (*must* = conclusion)
      correct modal features (past; positive) [Note: *Have* after the modal shows selection of past tense.]
   c) *[CONCLUSION] You [must have like] chocolate when you were a child.
      [CONCLUSION] You must have liked chocolate when you were a child.
      Explanation: The past modal showing conclusion requires *have* + VERB$_{ed_2}$.
5. a) *[SUGGESTION] The pharaoh's wife [was to remain] in the pyramid with her husband.
   b) correct equivalent features (past; positive)
      correct verb for after modal (VERB$_{base}$)
   c) *[SUGGESTION] The pharaoh's wife [was to remain]   in the pyramid with her husband.
      [SUGGESTION] The pharaoh's wife [was advised to remain] in the pyramid with her husband.
      Explanation: The correct modal equivalent for suggestion is *be advised to*, not *be to*.
6. a) *[THREAT] He['d better left] me alone!
   b) correct modal meaning (*'d better* = threat)
      correct modal features (present; positive)
      correct contraction (*he had = he'd*)
   c) *[THREAT] He['d better left] me alone!
      [THREAT] He'd better leave me alone!
      Explanation: The verb after a present modal must be the VERB$_{base}$ form.

7. a) *[PERMISSION] The children [ca'nt swim] anymore because it's getting late.
   b) correct modal meaning (*can't* = no permission)
      correct modal features (present; negative)
      correct verb form after modal (VERB$_{base}$)
   c) *[PERMISSION] The children [ca'nt swim] anymore because it's getting late.
      [PERMISSION] The children can't swim   anymore because it's getting late.
      Explanation: The contracted form of *can not* is *can't*, not *ca'nt*.

8. a) *HYPOTHETICAL SITUATION] A fire [wouldn't burns] if there was no oxygen.
   b) correct modal meaning (*would* = hypothetical situation)
      correct modal features (present; negative)
      correct contraction (*would not* = *wouldn't*)
   c) *[HYPOTHETICAL SITUATION] A fire [wouldn't burns] if there was no oxygen.
      [HYPOTHETICAL SITUATION] A fire wouldn't burn   if there was no oxygen.
      Explanation: The verb after a present modal must be the VERB$_{base}$ form

9. a) *[OBLIGATION] A government [would protect] its citizens from harm
   b) correct modal features (present; positive)
      correct verb form after modal (VERB$_{base}$)
   c) *[OBLIGATION] A government [would protect] its citizens from harm.
      [OBLIGATION] A government should protect its citizens from harm..
      Explanation: The modal for obligation is *should*, not *would*.

10. a) *a)*[REPEATED PAST ACTION] In his youth, Martin Luther King [use to be] a first-class wrestler.
    b) correct equivalent meaning (*used to* = repeated past action)
       correct modal features (past; positive) [Note: This form can only be used in the past.]
       correct verb form after modal (VERB$_{base}$)
    c) *[REPEATED PAST ACTION] In his youth, Martin Luther King [use to be] a first-class wrestler.
       [REPEATED PAST ACTION] In his youth, Martin Luther King used to be a first-class wrestler.
       Explanation: The correct form for the equivalent is *used* to, not *use to*.

11. a) *[CAPABILITY] Acid rain [could of reduced] the fish population in the early 1980s.
    b) correct modal meaning (*could* = capability)
       correct modal features (past; positive) [Note: *Could of* sounds like *could have* in spoken English.]
       correct partial verb form after modal (VERB$_{ed_2}$)
    c) *[CAPABILITY] Acid rain [could of reduced] the fish population in the early 1980s.
       [CAPABILITY] Acid rain could have reduced the fish population in the early 1980s.
       Explanation: Past modals are constructed with *have*, not *of*.

12. a) *[CERTAINTY] Tax rates [willn't be lowered] this year because of the budget crisis.
    b) correct modal meaning (*will* = certainty)
       correct modal features (present; negative)
       correct verb form after modal (VERB$_{base}$)
    c) *[CERTAINTY] Tax rates [willn't be lowered] this year because of the budget crisis.
       [CERTAINTY] Tax rates won't be lowered   this year because of the budget crisis.
       Explanation: The contraction of *will not* is *won't*, not *willn't*.

13. a) *[CHANCE] The AIDS virus [might could infect] certain monkey species.
    b) [partial correct modal meaning (*might* = chance, *could* = chance)]
       correct modal features (present; positive)
       correct verb form after modal (VERB$_{base}$)
    c) *[CHANCE] The AIDS virus [might could infect] certain monkey species.
       [CHANCE] The AIDS virus might infect   certain monkey species.
       Explanation: Only a single modal is allowed in standard English.

14. a) *[COMMAND] The sailors [were not leave] the ship until 7 o'clock that night.
    b) correct modal equivalent (*were to* = command)
       correct modal or equivalent features (past; negative)
       correct verb form after modal (VERB$_{base}$)
    c) *[COMMAND] The sailors [were not leave] the ship until 7 o'clock that night.
       [COMMAND] The sailors were not to leave the ship until 7 o'clock that night.
       Explanation: The modal equivalent for *will* is *be to*, not just *be*, which is usually the case for modal equivalents.

15. a) *[REQUIREMENT] Scientists [must to protect] the ozone layer that shields the earth from ultraviolet rays.

  b) correct modal meaning (*must* = requirement)
     correct modal features (present; positive)
     correct verb form after modal (VERB$_{base}$)

  c) *[REQUIREMENT] Scientists [must to protect] the ozone layer that shields the earth from ultraviolet rays.

     [REQUIREMENT] Scientists must protect   the ozone layer that shields the earth from ultraviolet rays.

     Explanation: True modals are never followed by *to*, only modal equivalents.

6.12

1. *people with bone problems; people; the ozone layer that shields the earth from ultraviolet rays*
2. Dependent Clauses: 4, 7, 8, and 15; AdvCl: 4, 7, and 8; AdjCl:15.
3. Passive verb forms: 12.
4. Pronoun as indep. clause subject: 3, 4, and 6; pronoun as dep. clause subject: 4, 7, 8, and 15.
5. Intransitive verbs: 5, 7, 8, and 10.

Chapter 7

7.1

1. Can Maria speak Swedish?
2. Is the alligator a reptile?
3. Should motorists pay a road tax?
4. Has my sister seen the Eiffel Tower?
5. Doesn't George like vegetables?

7.2

1. Is this disease contagious?
2. Were the children well-behaved?
3. Should Evelyn take the train?
4. Has the university applied for a patent?
5. Can John use the car tonight?
6. Could the ambassador be appointed to a new post?
7. Was the new program installed in the computer?
8. Doesn't the money reach the people who need it?
9. Shouldn't your parents be concerned about the children's health?
10. Hasn't Pierre told the immigration office that he wants to stay?

7.3

1. Does the plane make a stopover in New York?
2. Does the book cost more than two hundred dollars?
3. Does the president of the company work on Fridays?
4. Does this tomato plant need more direct sunlight?
5. Does Mary want to get a master's degree?

7.4

1. Did the janitor come to work last night?
2. Do whales migrate south during the winter?
3. Are the people unhappy with the government?
4. Does the drinking water contain impurities?
5. Could the pilot have saved the plane?
6. Did the person who committed the crime go to jail?
7. Have sales of tropical hardwoods increased this year?
8. Is the lawyer for the defense being overly cautious?
9. Do women with young children have problems with their careers?
10. Does the heiress have a yacht in Piraeus?

7.5

1. a) *Richard [does] work in the evenings?
   b) correct category of AUX (*do*)
      correct subject-AUX agreement (*Richard does*)
      correct tense of AUX (simple present)
      correct punctuation (?)
   c) *Richard [does] work in the evenings?
      Does Richard   work in the evenings?
      Explanation: The AUX in a yes/no question must be before the subject of the sentence.

2. a) *[Was] the dog eat your dinner last night?
   b) correct position of the AUX (before subject)
      correct subject-AUX agreement (*dog was*)
      correct tense of AUX (simple past)
      correct punctuation (?)
   c) *[Was] the dog eat yout dinner last night?
      Did   the dog eat your dinner last night?
      Explanation: If the AUX is not present in the original statement, a form of *do* must be used.

3. a) *[Has] your parents received their passports yet?
   b) correct position of the AUX (before subject)
      correct category of AUX (*have*)
      correct tense of AUX (present)
      correct punctuation (?)
   c) *[Has] your parents received their passports yet?
      Have your parents received their passports yet?
      Explanation: The AUX must agree with the subject (*parents*) and is therefore *have*, not *has*.

4. a) *[Do] you visit Scotland last year?
   b) correct position of the AUX (before subject)
      correct category of AUX (*do*)
      correct subject-AUX agreement (*you do*)
      correct punctuation (?)
   c) *[Do] you visit Scotland last year?
      Did   you visit Scotland last year?
      Explanation: The time phrase (*last year*) requires that the AUX be in the past tense. [Note: An alternative explanation is that the verb in the original statement would have been *visited* and the ending from this verb (*-ed$_1$*) must be transfered to *do*.]

5. a) *Did the plane arrive safely[.]
   b) correct position of the AUX (before subject)
      correct category of AUX (*do*)
      correct tense of AUX (past)
   c) *Did the plane arrive safely[.]
      Did the plane arrive safely?
      Explanation: Questions must have a question mark at the end.

.6

1. Michael Gorbachev: who/what person
2. the Univ. of Cal.: where/which univ
3. your briefcase: what/whose briefcase
4. on Tuesday: when/on what day
5. fifty floors:—-/how many floors
6. 100 k.: how far/how many k.
7. a girl on a horse: who/what girl
8. Beijing: where/what city
9. since...money: why/for what reason
10. a mosquito: what/—
11. because...job: why/for what reason
12. once a month: how often/how many times a month
13. in Paris: where/in what city
14. nineteen years old: how old/how many years old
15. green: what/what color
16. 20,000 dollars: how much/how many dollars
17. two and a half years: how long/how many years
18. the planet's surface: what/whose surface
19. the man wearing sunglasses: who/which man
20. at home: where/at which place

7.7

1. Who is knocking at the door?
2. What caused the accident?
3. What did John lose?
4. What (Whose sweater) did Mary shrink?
5. How much did the suit cost?
6. What caused the fire to spread quickly?
7. Who's that?
8. What (How much insurance) must doctors have?
9. Who closed the old people's home?
10. Why (For what reason) did the teacher leave her job?

7.8

1. Who wrote *The Return of the Native*?
2. What color usually causes people to relax?
3. Whose classes are in the morning?
4. How many students passed the exam?
5. What triggered the First World War?

7.9

1. What (What novel) did D. H. Lawrence write?
2. Who(m) has the movie star called three times?
3. When (At what time) are John and Cindy's classes?
4. What (How many roses) does Nancy usually order for the church?
5. Why do birds fly south in the winter?

7.10

1. P; Where will your nephew be?
2. P; Why did Alice leave?
3. S; What is doing most of the calculations?
4. P; Whose house was that?
5. P; How much champagne does the bride want for the reception?
6. P; When should you take the medicine?
7. P; How far is it to San Francisco?
8. S; Who travels by dogsled?
9. P; What kind of cigarettes do the soldiers prefer?
10. P; What does this word mean?

7.11

1. a) *[What] did they get a divorce?
   b) correct position of WH-question word (at the front of the main clause)
      correct position of AUX (after WH-question word)
      correct category of AUX (*do*)
      correct tense of AUX (past)
      correct punctuation (?)
   c) *[What]   did they get a divorce?
      Why/When/Where did they get a divorce?
      Explanation: One gets a divorce for a reason (*why*), at a time (*when*) or at a place (*where*), not for an object (*what*).
2. a) *Can you buy [where] this book?
   b) correct choice of WH-question word (*where*)

      correct category of AUX (modal)
      correct tense of AUX (present)
      correct punctuation (?)
   c) *Can you buy [where] this book?
      Where can you buy   this book?
      Explanation: The WH-question word must always be placed before the AUX in a WH-question.

3. a) *When [you did] arrive in Madrid?
   b) correct choice of WH-question word (*when*)
      correct position of WH-question word (at the front of the main clause)

      correct category of AUX (*do*)
      correct tense of AUX (past)
      correct punctuation (?)
   c) *When [you did] arrive in Madrid?
      When did you   arrive in Madrid?
      Explanation: The AUX must always come before the subject in a P-form WH-question.

4. a) *How much [is] this book cost?
   b) correct choice of WH-question word (*how much*)
      correct position of WH-question word (at the front of the main clause)
      correct position of the AUX (after WH-question word)
      correct subj-AUX agreement (*book is*)
      correct tense of AUX (present)
      correct punctuation (?)
   c) *How much [is]   this book cost?
      How much does this book cost?
      Explanation: The original statement would have been something like *This book costs $10.* If no AUX is
                     present, we use a form of *do*, not *be*.

5. a) *Whose story [does] the police believe?
   b) correct choice of WH-question word (*whose story*)
      correct position of WH-question word (at the front of the main clause)
      correct position of the AUX (after WH-question word)
      correct category of AUX (*do*)
      correct tense of AUX (present)
      correct punctuation (?)
   c) *Whose story [does] the police believe?
      Whose story do   the police believe?
      Explanation: The subject (*the police*) is plural and the AUX must agree with the subject.

6. a) *How [is] President Kennedy killed?
   b) correct choice of WH-question word (*how*)
      correct position of WH-question word (at the front of the main clause)
      correct position of the AUX (after WH-question word)
      correct category of AUX (*be*)
      correct subj-AUX agreement (*Kennedy is*)
      correct punctuation (?)
   c) *How [is] President Kennedy killed?
      How was President Kennedy killed?
      Explanation: Since President Kennedy was killed in 1963, the AUX must be in the past tense.

7. a) *Who wrote that story[.]
   b) correct choice of WH-question word (*who*)
      correct position of WH-question word (at the front of the main clause)
   c) *Who wrote that story[.]
      Who wrote that story?
      Explanation: Questions must be followed by a question mark.

8. a) *Who [are] coming with me?
   b) correct choice of WH-question word (*who*)
      correct position of WH-question word (at the front of the main clause)
      correct position of the AUX (after WH-question word)
      correct category of AUX (*be*)
      correct tense of AUX (present)
      correct punctuation (?)
   c) *Who [are] coming with me?
      Who is coming with me?
      Explanation: If the subject is unknown, the singular form of the AUX or verb is used.

9. a) *How [many] water will you need?
   b) correct position of WH-question word (at the front of the main clause)
      correct position of the AUX (after WH-question word)
      correct category of AUX (modal)
      correct tense of AUX (present) [Note: Even though *will need* is the simple future tense, the modal *will* is a present form.]
      correct punctuation (?)
   c) *How [many] water will you need?
      How much   water will you need?
      Explanation: The WH-question word for a noncount noun (*water*) is how much.
10. a) *What [did kill] the sheep?
    b) correct choice of WH-question word (*what*)
       correct position of WH-question word (at the front of the main clause)
       correct position of the AUX (after WH-question word)
       correct tense of AUX (past)
       correct punctuation (?)
    c) *What [did kill] the sheep?
       What killed   the sheep?
       Explanation: There is no need to dig up the AUX in an S-form WH-question.

7.12

1. You are a teacher, <u>aren't you</u>?
2. Edward isn't home today, <u>is he</u>?
3. Those children live in Austria, <u>don't they</u>?
4. Susan has taken her medicine, <u>hasn't she</u>?
5. The newspaper didn't tell the whole story, <u>did it</u>?

7.13

1. Acid rain is hurting the forest, isn't it?
2. Simon would never drink and drive, would he?
3. The insects are terrible there, aren't they?
4. There hasn't been much rain this year, has there?
5. The rabbits won't be harmed, will they?

7.14

1. Your uncle writes novels, doesn't he?
2. It isn't raining now, is it?
3. The plane arrived at 8 P.M., didn't it?
4. There weren't many people at the concert, were there?
5. This exam has been given before, hasn't it?
6. The guests had to leave early, didn't they?
7. Those houses cost quite a lot, didn't they? [OR: don't they?]
8. His girlfriend had a headache, didn't she?
9. You shouldn't be such a snob, should you?
10. The book will be returned next week, won't it?

7.15

1. a) *The boy works in a factory, [can't] he?
   b) correct tense of AUX (present)
      correct polarity of AUX (negative)
      correct position of AUX (before question tag pronoun)
      correct category of pronoun (subject)
      correct type of pronoun (human)
      correct gender of pronoun (male)
      correct agreement of pronoun (singular)
      correct position of pronoun for a tag question (at the end of the tag question)
      correct punctuation (?)

c) *The boy works in a factory, [can't] he?
The boy works in a factory, doesn't he?
Explanation: If no AUX is present in the main sentence, a form of *do* must be used.

2. a) *Mice live underground, [doesn't] they?
b) correct category of AUX (*do*)
correct tense of AUX (present)
correct the polarity of AUX (negative)
correct position of AUX (before question tag pronoun)
correct category of pronoun (subject)
correct agreement of pronoun (plural
correct position of pronoun for a tag question (at the end of the tag question)
correct punctuation (?)
c) *Mice live underground, doesn't they?
Mice live underground, don't   they?
Explanation: The AUX must agree with the subject and the tag pronoun.

3. a) *The dinner was expensive, [isn't] it?
b) correct category of AUX (*be*)
correct subject-AUX agreement (*dinner is*)
correct polarity of AUX (negative)
correct position of AUX (before question tag pronoun)
correct category of pronoun (subject)
correct type of pronoun (non-human)
correct agreement of pronoun (singular)
correct position of pronoun for a tag question (at the end of the tag question)
correct punctuation (?)
c) *The dinner was expensive, [isn't] it?
The dinner was expensive, wasn't it?
Explanation: The AUX must be in the same tense as the AUX or verb in the main sentence.

4. a) *You can't park here, [can't] you?
b) correct category of AUX (modal)
correct tense of AUX (present)
correct position of AUX (before question tag pronoun)
correct category of pronoun (subject)
correct agreement of pronoun (singular)
correct position of pronoun for a tag question (at the end of the tag question)
correct punctuation (?)
c) *You can't park here, [can't] you?
You can't park here, can   you?
Explanation: The AUX in the tag must be opposite in polarity to the AUX or verb in the main sentence.

5. a) *Norma hasn't finished her work, [she has]?
b) correct category of AUX (*have*)
correct subject-AUX agreement (*Norma has*)
correct tense of AUX (present)
correct polarity of AUX (positive)
correct category of pronoun (subject)
correct type of pronoun (human)
correct gender of pronoun (female)
correct agreement of pronoun (singular)
correct punctuation (?)
c) *Norma hasn't finished her work, [she has]?
Norma hasn't finished her work, has she?
Explanation: In a question tag, the pronoun always comes after the AUX.

6. a) *John likes to swim, doesn't [John]?
   b) correct category of AUX (*do*)
      correct subject-AUX agreement (*John does*)
      correct tense of AUX (present)
      correct polarity of AUX (negative)
      correct position of AUX (before question tag pronoun)
      correct punctuation (?)
   c) *John likes to swim, doesn't [John]?
      John likes to swim, doesn't he?
      Explanation: The second element of the tag must be a pronoun, not a noun.

7. a) *Mr. Gomez is a physician, isn't [him]?
   b) correct category of AUX (*be*)
      correct subject-AUX agreement (*Gomez is*)
      correct tense of AUX (present)
      correct polarity of AUX (negative)
      correct position of AUX (before question tag pronoun)
      correct type of pronoun (human)
      correct gender of pronoun (male)
      correct agreement of pronoun (singular)
      correct position of pronoun for a tag question (at the end of the tag question)
      correct punctuation (?)
   c) *Mr. Gomez is a physician, isn't [him]?
      Mr. Gomez is a physician, isn't he?
      Explanation: The pronoun in a tag question must always belong to the subject class.

8. a) *The policeman drove to the accident, didn't [it]?
   b) correct category of AUX (*do*)
      correct tense of AUX (past)
      correct polarity of AUX (negative)
      correct position of AUX (before question tag pronoun)
      correct category of pronoun (subject)
      correct agreement of pronoun (singular)
      correct position of pronoun for a tag question (at the end of the tag question)
      correct punctuation (?)
   c) *The policeman drove to the accident, didn't [it]?
      The policeman drove to the accident, didn't he?
      Explanation: A human noun (*policeman*) must be replaced by a human pronoun (*he*).

9. a) *The actress has lost a lot of weight, hasn't [he]?
   b) correct category of AUX (*have*)
      correct subject-AUX agreement (*actress has*)
      correct tense of AUX (present)
      correct polarity of AUX (negative)
      correct position of AUX (before question tag pronoun)
      correct category of pronoun (subject)
      correct type of pronoun (human)
      correct agreement of pronoun (singular)
      correct position of pronoun for a tag question (at the end of the tag question)
      correct punctuation (?)
   c) *The actress has lost a lot of weight, hasn't [he]?
      The actress has lost a lot of weight, hasn't she?
      Explanation: A female noun (*actress*) must be replaced by a female pronoun (*she*).

10. a) *The men hadn't received a paycheck, had [he]?
    b) correct category of AUX (*have*)
       correct tense of AUX (past)
       correct polarity of AUX (positive)
       correct position of AUX (before question tag pronoun)
       correct category of pronoun (subject)

    correct type of pronoun (human)
    correct gender of pronoun (male)
    correct position of pronoun for a tag question (at the end of the tag question)
    correct punctuation (?)

  c) *The men hadn't received a paycheck, had [he]?
    The men hadn't received a paycheck, had they?
    Explanation: The pronoun in the tag must agree in number with the subject of the sentence.

11. a) *Sally knows the rules, [she doesn't]?
   b) correct category of AUX (*do*)
    correct subject-AUX agreement (*Sally does*)
    correct tense of AUX (present)
    correct polarity of AUX (negative)
    correct category of pronoun (subject)
    correct type of pronoun (human)
    correct gender of pronoun (female)
    correct agreement of pronoun (singular)
    correct punctuation (?)
   c) *Sally knows the rules, [she doesn't]?
    Sally knows the rules, doesn't she?
    Explanation: In a question tag, the pronoun always comes after the AUX.

12. a) *There is a flag on the moon, isn't there[.]
   b) correct category of AUX (*be*)
    correct subject-AUX agreement (*moon is*)
    correct tense of AUX (present)
    correct polarity of AUX (negative)
    correct position of AUX (before question tag pronoun)
    correct position of pronoun for a tag question (at the end of the tag question)
   c) *There is a flag on the moon, isn't there[.]
    There is a flag on the moon, isn't there?
    Explanation: Tag questions must always have a question mark at the end.

7.16

1. Columbus discovered America in 1942?
2. The Hawaiian Islands are the tallest mountains in the world?
3. Bats usually sleep at night?
4. The computer costs twenty-five dollars?
5. Cows are meat-eaters?
6. The United Nations Building is located in New York City?
7. Shakespeare wrote "Ode on a Grecian Urn"?
8. The government has doubled the taxes for next year?
9. Big fish eat little fish?
10. Fleming invented the telephone?

7.17

1. A <u>what</u> landed in our back yard?
2. My sister married <u>who</u>?
3. The surgeon removed the <u>what</u>?
4. We had to make an emergency landing <u>where</u>?
5. A movie ticket costs <u>how much</u>?
6. I'll be in Europe <u>how long</u> (or <u>what</u>)?
7. This is <u>whose</u> book?
8. They can't eat pasta because <u>why</u> (or <u>what</u>)?
9. <u>What</u> is clogging the drain?
10. You can remove the stain <u>how</u>?

7.18

1. a) *a)[WH-echo] *Your suitcase weighs [how long]?
   b) correct position of WH-question word (object position)
      correct punctuation (?)
   c) [WH-echo] *Your suitcase weighs [how long]?
      [WH-echo] Your suitcase weighs how much?
      Explanation: Weight requires the question *how much*, not *how long* (which is for length).

2. a) *a)[regular echo] *The frog turned into a carriage[.]
   b) [nothing correct]
   c) [regular echo] *The frog turned into a carriage[.]
      [regular echo] The frog turned into a carriage?
      Explanation: All questions require a question mark at the end.

3. a) *a)[WH-echo] *Who kept you out all night[.]
   b) correct choice of WH-question word (*who*)
      correct position of WH-question word (subject position)
   c) [WH-echo] *Who kept you out all night[.]
      [WH-echo] Who kept you out all night?
      Explanation: All questions require a question mark at the end.

4. a) *a)[WH-echo] *You flew to [when]?
   b) correct position of WH-question word (adverbial position)
      correct punctuation (?)
   c) [WH-echo] *You flew to [when]?
      [WH-echo] You flew to what city? [Note: This could also be *what country, what place,* etc.]
      Explanation: One flies to a location (*what city,* etc.), not to a time (*when*).

5. a) *a)[regular echo] *[Did] the lawyer worked for free?
   b) correct punctuation (?)
   c) [regular echo] *[Did] the lawyer worked for free?
      [regular echo]   The lawyer worked for free?
      Explanation: A regular echo question does not require an auxiliary.

6. a) *a)[WH-echo] *She said what[.]
   b) correct choice of WH-question word (*what*)
      correct position of WH-question word (object position)
   c) [WH-echo] *She said what[.]
      [WH-echo] She said what?
      Explanation: All questions require a question mark at the end.

7. a) *[WH-echo] *The general is leaving [when] the country?
   b) correct choice of WH-question word (*when*)
      correct punctuation (?)
   c) [WH-echo] *The general is leaving [when] the country?
      [WH-echo] The general is leaving the country when?
      Explanation: The WH-word must be in the same position as the unknown/unheard element.

8. a) *a)[WH-echo] *Who [are] going to help you?
   b) correct choice of WH-question word (*who*)
      correct position of WH-question word (subject position)
      correct punctuation (?)
   c) [WH-echo] *Who [are] going to help you?
      [WH-echo] Who is   going to help you?
      Explanation: If the subject is the unknown/unheard element, the agreement must be singular.

9. a) *a)[regular echo] *[What] he failed the course?
   b) correct punctuation (?)
   c) [regular echo] *[What]   he failed the course?
      [regular echo]   He failed the course?
      Explanation: No WH-word is required in a regular echo question.

10. a) [WH-echo] *[Who] Diane met at the party?
    b) correct choice of WH-question word (*who*)
       correct punctuation (?)
    c) *[WH-echo] *[Who] Diane met at the party?
       [WH-echo]   Diane met who at the party?
       Explanation: The WH-word must be in the same position as the unknown/unheard element.

7.19

1. a. Yes/No: Did the train leave the station at 8 o'clock?
   b.   WH: When (At what time) did the train leave the station?
   c.   Tag: The train left the station at 8 o'clock, didn't it?
   d. WH-Echo: The train left the station when?
2. a. Yes/No: Is English taught all over the world?
   b.   WH: Where is English taught?
   c.   Tag   English is taught all over the world, isn't it?
   d. Reg. Echo: English is taught all over the world?
3. a. Yes/No: Will the children be living in Paris for a year?
   b.   WH: How long will the children be living in Paris?
   c.   Tag: The children will be living in Paris for a year, won't they?
   d. WH-Echo: The children will be living in Paris how long?
4. a. Yes/No: Does Sally clean the motel rooms thoroughly with soap and water?
   b.   WH: How does Sally clean the motel rooms?
   c.   Tag: Sally cleans the motel rooms thoroughly with soap and water, doesn't she?
   d. Reg. Echo: Sally cleans the motel rooms thoroughly with soap and water?
5. a. Yes/No: Have these computers been tested by the quality control department?
   b.   WH: What has been tested by the quality control department?
   c.   Tag: These computers have been tested by the quality control department, haven't they?
   d. WH-Echo: What has been tested by the quality control department?
6. a. Yes/No: Was Therese jilted by her lover several times?
   b.   WH: Who was jilted by her lover several times?
   c.   Tag: Therese was jilted by her lover several times, wasn't she?
   d. Reg. Echo: Therese was jilted by her lover several times?
7. a. Yes/No: Before he came to California, had John ever seen Yosemite National Park?
   b.   WH: Before he came to California, what had John never seen?
   c.   Tag: Before he came to California, John had never seen Yosemite National Park, had he?
   d. WH-Echo: Before he came to California, John had never seen what?
8. a. Yes/No: Are students afraid of grammar because they feel inadequate?
   b.   WH: Why are students afraid of grammar?
   c.   Tag: Students are afraid of grammar because they feel inadequate, aren't they?
   d. Reg. Echo: Students are afraid of grammar because they feel inadequate?
9. a. Yes/No: Do ants usually live in colonies?
   b.   WH: Where do ants usually live?
   c.   Tag: Ants usually live in colonies, don't they?
   d. WH-Echo: Ants usually live where?
10. a. Yes/No: Can't a foreign language be mastered in a few weeks?
    b.   WH: What cannot be mastered in a few weeks?
    c.   Tag: A foreign language cannot be mastered in a few weeks, can it?
    d. Reg. Echo: A foreign language cannot be mastered in a few weeks?

Chapter 8

8.1

1. Susan believes that she will get the job.
2. The dean told the angry students that the class had been cancelled.
3. The doctors hope that the patient will live for several years.
4. The weatherman said that the storm would continue for another three days.
5. The detectives discovered that the witness had been lying.

8.2

1. (The fact) That the famine would not end soon was of no interest to him.
2. (The fact) That he has had too much to drink is patently obvious.
3. (The idea) That money is the root of all evil has been known since the dawn of economics.
4. (The idea) That dentists do not like to cause pain is rarely what patients think about in the dentist's chair.
5. (The fact) That you'd rather be alone is written all over your face.

8.3

1. Would somebody please tell me who made this mess?
2. Ask Susan if her mother bought the house.
3. I have no idea why Paul hasn't finished his dinner.
4. They wonder if the moon is made of cheese.
5. The map shows how far it is to New Delhi.

8.4

1. P-form
2. S-form
3. P-form
4. S-form
5. P-form

8.5

1. Tomorrow they'll tell us when father can leave the hospital.
2. You know perfectly well why Pierre doesn't like American coffee.
3. She wants to know what color she should dye her hair.
4. Mrs. Fong had forgotten where the library was.
5. I can never remember how long the Mississippi River is.

8.6

1. Everyone is afraid to ask why the building collapsed.
2. The timetable shows what time the next train arrives.
3. The veterinarian wasn't sure how often dogs attack their masters.
4. The old map indicated where Columbus landed.
5. Students always conveniently forget what *tardy* means.

8.7

1. The police discovered who stole the car.
2. It was easy to see how much wine was left in the bottle.
3. No one knew what had killed the trees.
4. People are afraid to say which government official ordered the massacre.
5. The guests have to guess whose wallet contains a fifty-dollar bill.

8.8

1. Where swans go in winter is a mystery to me.
2. What the Queen will wear to the dinner is of vital importance to the fashion world.
3. Why Houdini died is the subject of a new book.
4. How John does on this test will determine his course grade.
5. Whom she should choose as a husband has completely preoccupied the media.

8.9

1. What causes the disease is the most troubling health question of the century.
2. Who should sound the alarm is explained in the handbook.
3. Whose work generated the most criticism will not be addressed in this lecture.
4. What color reduces violence has been the subject of continuous debate.
5. Whoever can find work deserves the nicest bedroom.

8.10

1. Does anyone know what ate the hunter?
2. The newspaper described what the hurricane had destroyed.
3. The insect collector wants to know when the moths come around.
4. The city has no idea why the fire started.
5. We can't work out how John learned about the surprise party.
6. It makes no difference who told him to cheat on the test.
7. Why does the newspaper want to know where I live?
8. The researchers are mystified as to what causes the lightning to flash.
9. Can someone please tell me whose notebook this is?
10. Joan has decided which house she will buy.

8.11 (effect of sequence of tenses underlined)

1. Mary suddenly remembered where she <u>had left</u> the keys.
2. Did they say when the plane <u>would land</u>?
3. I cannot forget who <u>helps</u> the poor in India.
4. Who told you why Sally <u>was</u> angry?
5. The police didn't know whose handerkerchief it <u>was</u>.

8.12

1. At first, the engineer wasn't sure where to find a job.
2. The abandoned child didn't know who(m) to trust.
3. The new employee had no idea what to do.
4. The laundry knows exactly how much to charge for cleaning a sweater.
5. The older boys don't know when to stop teasing.

8.13

1. The policewoman asked if there was blood on the knife.
2. She wants to know if she can have a room with a bath.
3. Can you tell us if there has been much rain this summer?
4. The critic wondered if the interpretation had to be so dramatic.
5. The skiers needed to find out if the passes were open.

8.14

1. The tourist asked the guide if the "M" bus went downtown.
2. She wants to know if the children cry at night.
3. Can you tell me if Harriet wants a divorce?
4. The director wondered if you liked the play.
5. The passengers wanted to find out if the conductor sold tickets.

8.15

1. Whether Jorge can speak French is not important for this job.
2. Whether all bears sleep in winter is not precisely known.
3. Whether new medical students should see patients is the focus of a Harvard study.
4. Whether Hitler kept a diary is the subject of a new television "docudrama."
5. Whether I will go to Europe this summer has still not been decided.

8.16

1. a) *I can't remember when [does] the plane [arrive].
   b) correct choice of WH-question word (*when*)
      correct position of WH-question word (at beginning of noun clause)
      correct punctuation mark (period)
      Derivation: I can't remember X. X = When does the plane arrive?
      $$X_1 = \text{the plane arrives } \underline{\text{at 6 o'clock}}$$
      $$X_2 = \text{the plane arrives when}$$
      $$X_3 = \text{when the plane arrives}$$
      I can't remember when the plane arrives.
   c) *I can't remember when [does] the plane [arrive]
      I can't remember when   the plane arrives.
      Explanation: The AUX *do* in a WH-question must be reburied in the embedded (noun clause) form.

2. a) *Does your mother know [who] to make bread?
   b) correct position of WH-question word (at beginning of noun clause)
      correct deletion of identical or generalized subject (*your mother*)
      correct infinitive form of verb (*to make*)
      correct punctuation mark (question mark)
      Derivation: Does your mother know X. X = How does your mother make bread?
      $$X_1 = \text{your mother makes bread } \underline{\text{by mixing flour}}\ldots$$
      $$X_2 = \text{your mother makes bread how}$$
      $$X_3 = \text{how your mother makes bread}$$
      $$X_4 = \text{how to make bread}$$
      Does your mother know how to make bread?
   c)*Does your mother know [who] to make bread?
      Does your mother know how   to make bread?
      Explanation: The correct WH-question word for a method is *how*, not *who*.

3. a) *We're not sure [it is how far] to Sacramento.
   b) correct choice of WH-question word (*how far*)
      correct punctuation mark (question mark)
      Derivation: We're not sure X. X = How far is it to Sacramento?
      $$X_1 = \text{it is } \underline{\text{90 miles}} \text{ to Sacramento}$$
      $$X_2 = \text{it is how far to Sacramento}$$
      $$X_3 = \text{how far it is to Sacramento}$$
      We're not sure how far it is to Sacramento.
   c)*We're not sure [it is how far] to Sacramento.
      We're not sure how far it is   to Sacramento.
      Explanation: The WH-question word must be moved to the front of the noun clause before it can be embedded.

4. a) *Please tell me who [are] in my office.
   b) correct choice of WH-question word (*who*)
      correct position of WH-question word (at beginning of noun clause)
      correct punctuation mark (period)
      Derivation: Please tell me X. X = Who is in my office?
      $$X_1 = \underline{\text{Jan}} \text{ is in my office.}$$
      $$X_2 = \text{who is in my office}$$
      Please tell me who is in my office.
   c) *Please tell me who [are] in my office.
      Please tell me who is   in my office.
      Explanation: If the subject of the embedded question is the unknown element, the verb that follows is always singular.

5. a) *Leandre knew how much beer his cousin [drinks] that night.
   b) correct reburying of AUX
      correct choice of WH-question word (*how much*)
      correct position of WH-question word (at beginning of noun clause)
      correct punctuation mark (period)
      Derivation: Leandre knew X. X = How much beer did his cousin drink that night?
      X_1 = his cousin drank <u>two cases of beer</u> that night
      X_2 = his cousin drank how much beer that night
      X_3 = how much beer his cousin drank that night
      Leandre knew how much beer his cousin drank that night.
   c) *Leandre knew how much beer his cousin [drinks] that night.
      Leandre knew how much beer his cousin drank   that night.
      Explanation: If the main verb is in the past tense (*knew*), then sequence of tenses requires that the clause verb also be in the past tense (*drank*, not *drinks*)

6. a) *Satoko always knows what [Satoko says] at a job interview.
   b) correct reburying of AUX
      correct choice of WH-question word (*what*)
      correct position of WH-question word (at beginning of noun clause)
      correct punctuation mark (period)
      Derivation: Satoko always knows X. X = What does Satoko say at a job interview?
      X_1 = Satoko says <u>the right thing</u> at a job interview
      X_2 = Satoko says what at a job interview
      X_3 = what Satoko says at a job interview
      X_4 = what to say at a job interview
      Satoko always knows what to say at a job interview.
   c) *Satoko always knows what [Satoko says] at a job interview
      Satoko always knows what to say   at a job interview.
      Explanation: If the subject of the main sentence is the same as the subject of the noun clause, the clause subject is deleted and the clause verb becomes infinitive.

7. a) *[] I am going to get the job is still not sure.
   b) correct punctuation mark (period))
      Derivation: X is still not sure. X = Am I going to get the job?
      X_1 = <u>I am going to get the job</u>
      X_2 = whether I am going to get the job
      Whether I am going to get the job is still not sure.
   c) *[]   I am going to get the job is still not sure.
      Whether I am going to get the job is still not sure.
      Explanation: Embedded yes/no questions about the subject require the noun clause marker *whether* at the beginning of the clause.

8. a) *The cook never forgets [add] a little salt.
   b) correct deletion of identical or generalized subject (*the cook*)
      correct punctuation mark (period)
      Derivation: The cook never forgets X. X = Does the cook add a little salt?
      X_1 = <u>the cook adds a little salt</u>

      X = to add a little salt
      The cook never forgets to add a little salt.
   c) *The cook never forgets [add]   a little salt.
      The cook never forgets to add a little salt.
      Explanation: The infinitive form always requires *to* after a verb like *forget.*

9. a) *I can never remember what day it is[?]
   b) correct choice of clause marker (*what day*)
      correct position of clause marker (at beginning of noun clause)
      Derivation: I can never remember X. X = What day is it?
      $$X_1 = \text{it is \underline{Tuesday}}$$
      $$X_2 = \text{it is what day}$$
      $$X_3 = \text{what day it is}$$
      I can never remember what day it is.
   c) *I can never remember what day it is[?]
      I can never remember what day it is.
      Explanation: If the main clause is a statement, a period (not a question mark) must come at the end of the sentence.

10. a) *She asked me [that] I spoke Finnish.
    b) correct punctuation mark (period)   correct position of NCl marker (beginning of clause)
       Derivation: She asked me X. X = Do I speak Finnish?   correct reburying of AUX
       $$X_1 = \text{\underline{I speak Finnish}}$$ correct sequence of tenses
       $$X_2 = \text{if I speak Finnish}$$
       $$X_3 = \text{if I spoke Finnish (sequence of tenses)}$$
       She asked me if I spoke Finnish.
    c) *She asked me [that] I spoke Finnish.
       She asked me if   I spoke Finnish.
       Explanation: An embedded yes/no question about the predicate requires the clause marker *if* (or *whether*) after a questioning verb like *ask*. *That* is only used with asserting verbs like *say* or *tell*.

8.17 (many answers possible)

1. The car hit a deer.
2. A van loaded with dynamite destroyed the World Trade Center.
3. Ultraviolet rays from the sun can cause skin cancer.
4. Picasso created *Guernica*.
5. Pigs eat truffles.

8.18

1. The daughter of the ambassador is studying engineering at the university.
2. The children buried the dog in the corner of the garden.
3. The geologists found a perfectly preserved fossil in a cliff at the beach.
4. The President of the United States has signed a new treaty.
5. The cheese is in the refrigerator on the top shelf behind the milk.
6. The dog barked at whoever was passing by.
7. Joseph's father had little awareness of what his son had accomplished.
8. The missile was guided to where the target was located.
9. Ralph was impressed by how well his fiancee could cook.
10. The defense counsel wasn't happy with why the accused wanted another lawyer.

8.19

1. Jerry threw his teammate the ball.
2. Could you pass me the salt?
3. The angry father denied his son his rightful inheritance.
4. The Tax Office sent the wrong person the rebate check.
5. The government owed a Caribbean bank a lot of money.
6. Have we shown our neighbors the slides from our last vacation yet?
7. The gallant suitor promised his lady love the earth.
8. The policeman offered the young prisoner some coffee.
9. Some reseachers have taught dolphins a sign system.
10. Would you read the children a story?

8.20

1. The coast guard refused the boat people any assistance.
2. The judge fined the drunk driver $500.
3. The investigation cost the senator a lot of prestige.
4. June's fortune cookie wished her good fortune.
5. Should parents allow their teenage offspring greater freedom?
6. The carpenter billed the roofing company $250.
7. The school charged the boy's parents $5000 for the damage from the pipe bomb.
8. A washing machine will cost a poor family a year's salary.
9. The captain allowed the crew one evening's shore leave.
10. The wicked stepmother wished her husband's daughter harm.

8.21

1. Alice repeated the question to the professor.
2. Sally introduced her boyfriend to the family.
3. The doctor never said "Good morning!" to his patients.
4. The senator announced his candidacy for re-election to his supporters.
5. The veteran treated his old comrade to a hot meal.
6. Don't mention that man's name to me!
7. The young nun confessed her sins to the Mother Superior.
8. The discovery proved the existence of a high Indian culture to the anthropologists.
9. The docent pointed out the details of the painting to the interested museum-goers.
10. How soon after her husband's death is it polite to propose marriage to a widowed acquaintance?

8.22

1. John's grandfather left his entire estate to him and his sister.
2. Mr. Porridge paid the rent for his poor and troubled friend.
3. Did you bring some magazines for her to read?
4. You should take this sweater to the dry cleaner.
5. When the professor was ill, a graduate student taught his seminar for him.
6. Alice read the speech for her brother, who could not be present at the ceremony.
7. Will the post office get this letter to the income tax office in time?
8. Could you please write down the address for me?
9. Ellen did the dishes for her sister while she was away.
10. The engineer sent the schematic diagram to the manufacturer.

8.23

1. The students brought the teacher an apple.
2. I'll leave your mother a key in the mailbox.
3. The maid prepared the exhausted cook a light dinner.
4. The disc jockey has never played his girlfriend a record on the air.
5. The employment office was unable to find the distraught waitress a job.
6. The secretary reserved his boss a seat on the midnight flight to Chicago.
7. Please save the birthday girl a piece of cake.
8. The fashion designer made the president's wife an evening gown.
9. Could you get me some milk?
10. The boys ordered their girlfriends milkshakes while they were in the ladies' room.

8.24

1. Could you please watch my luggage for me?
2. We have prepared a nice room over the garage for your mother-in-law.
3. I must thank you for the beautiful present you gave me.
4. The doctor prescribed an antibiotic for the child.
5. Gary refused to do the yardwork for his brother.
6. The TV shop repaired the faulty stereo for the customer free of charge.
7. I could not close the garage door for him because my hands were full.
8. The doctor wrote down the last will and testament for the dying patient.
9. Uncle Joe played the accordion for the wedding party.
10. The bank will only cash checks for people with accounts in that bank.

8.25

Yesterday, Sarah took get-well presents to Betty and Harriet, her good friends who had both been hurt in an auto accident. She brought Betty a murder mystery and Harriet an embroidery kit. However, when Sarah gave Betty the book, she didn't seem terribly interested. Sarah wondered to herself if she should perhaps have given the book to Harriet and the embroidery kit to Betty. But Harriet was delighted with the embroidery kit. The dilemma was resolved when Harriet suggested that they each share the wonderful presents that Sarah had brought. Later, Betty wrote Sarah a note thanking her for her thoughtfulness.

8.26

1. Grandmother will read it to the children.
2. Could you please hand them to Larry?
3. The agency was unable to find it for Mr. Lin.
4. We sold it to our neighbors.
5. Mrs. Grant always tells it to her friends.
6. The priest made it for the visitor.
7. That company has sold them to the government.
8. The politician sent it to the reporter.
9. Would you order it for me while I make a quick phone call?
10. The artist is painting it for his friend.

8.27

1. a) *The bank cashed [Jimmy] the check.
   b) correct possible sequence (I.O + D.O)
   c) *The bank cashed [Jimmy] the check.
      The bank cashed the check for Jimmy.
      Explanation: Verbs like *cash* (*open* -type) may only use the external form of the indirect object with *for*.
2. a) *My brother owed ten dollars [for] me.
   b) correct position of indirect object (in a PP))
      correct possible sequence (D.O. + Prep. + I.O.)
   c) *My brother owed ten dollars [for] me.
      My brother owed ten dollars to   me.
      Explanation: Verbs like *owe* (*give* -type) require the preposition *to* in the external form.
3. a) *The boy drove [the farmer] the tractor.
   b) correct possible sequence (I.O. + D.O.)
   c) *The boy drove [the farmer] the tractor.
      The boy drove the tractor for the farmer.
      Explanation: Verbs like *drive* (*open* -type) may only use the external form of the indirect object with *for*.
4. a) *The personnel manager refused an interview [to the applicant].
   b) correct possible sequence (D.O. + Prep. + I.O.)
   c) *The personnel manager refused an interview [to the applicant].
      The personnel manager refused the applicant an interview.
      Explanation: Verbs like *refuse* (*ask* -type) may only use the internal form of the indirect object.
5. a) *The drunk driver didn't report [the police] the accident.
   b) correct possible sequence (I.O. + D.O.)
   c) *The drunk driver didn't report [the police] the accident.
      The drunk driver didn't report the accident to the police.
      Explanation: Verbs like *report* (*explain* -type) may only use the external form of the indirect object with *to*.
6. a) *Could you pass [me] it, please?
   b) correct possible sequence (I.O. + D.O.)
   c) *Could you pass [me] it, please?
      Could you pass it to me, please?
      Explanation: If the direct object is a pronoun, only the external form of the indirect object is allowed.
7. a) *The pilot has saved a seat [to] his girlfriend.
   b) correct position of indirect object (in a PP)
      correct possible sequence (D.O. + Prep. + I.O.)
   c) *The pilot has saved a seat [to] his girlfriend.
      The pilot has saved a seat for his girlfriend.
      Explanation: Verbs like *save* (*buy* -type) require the preposition *for* in the external form.

8. a) *John will read [the class] them.
    b) correct possible sequence (I.O. + D.O.)
    c) *John will read [the class] them.
        John will read them to the class.
        Explanation: If the direct object is a pronoun, only the external form of the indirect object is allowed.

9. a) *The thief is confessing [the priest] her crime.
    b) correct possible sequence (I.O. + D.O.)
    c) *The thief is confessing [the priest] her crime.
        The thief is confessing her crime to the priest.
        Explanation: Verbs like *confess* (*explain* -type) may only use the external form of the indirect object with
        to.

10. a) *A local restaurant supplied [the picnic] the food.
    b) correct possible sequence (I.O. + D.O.)
    c) *A local restaurant supplied [the picnic] the food.
        A local restaurant supplied the food for the picnic.
        Explanation: Verbs like *supply* (*open* -type) may only use the external form of the indirect object with *for.*

Chapter 9

9.1

1. <u>Joan</u> (person: 3rd; fem; sing) <u>she</u>
2. <u>my computer</u> (3rd; neut; sing) <u>it</u>
3. <u>Mr. Robecon</u> (2nd; masc; sing) <u>you</u>
4. <u>The children</u> (3rd; masc/fem; plur) <u>they</u>
5. <u>I</u> (1st; masc/fem; sing) <u>I</u>
6. <u>students</u> (2nd; masc/fem; plur) <u>you</u>
7. <u>Mediterranean fruit flies</u> (3rd; neut; plur) <u>they</u>
8. <u>An emaciated old man with a long white beard</u> (3rd; masc; sing) <u>he</u>
9. <u>My wife and I</u> (1st; masc/fem; plur) <u>we</u>
10. <u>my poodle Rogér</u> (3rd; neut/masc; sing) <u>he</u>

9.2

1. <u>some interesting people</u> (3rd; masc/fem; plur) <u>them</u>
2. <u>Dr. Watanabe</u> (3rd; masc; sing) <u>him</u>
3. <u>I</u> (1st; masc/fem; sing) <u>me</u>
4. <u>Mrs. White</u> (3rd; fem; sing) <u>her</u>
5. <u>the lawn mower</u> (3rd; neut; sing) <u>it</u>
6. <u>My brother and I</u> (1st; masc/fem; plur) <u>us</u>
7. <u>The Titanic</u> (3rd; neut; sing) <u>it</u> [or (3rd; fem; sing) <u>her</u>]
8. <u>Robert</u> (3rd; masc; sing) <u>him</u>
9. <u>ladies and gentlemen</u> (2nd; fem/masc; plur) <u>you</u>
10. <u>these plants</u> (3rd; neut; plur) <u>them</u>

9.3

1. We will eat our junk food in the living room. The children can eat <u>theirs</u> in the kitchen.
2. My book has a picture on the front, my friend, but I can see that <u>yours</u> doesn't.
3. Our neighbors' house has four bedrooms, but <u>ours</u> has only three.
4. I have never lost my passport, but my uncle has lost <u>his</u> twice.
5. The older manufacturers check their safety devices once a year, but the newer manufacturers check <u>theirs</u> at least three times a year.
6. Students, I have an announcement. The tour guide is taking **his** luggage on the plane but <u>yours</u> has already been checked.
7. Rita's house is in the country while <u>mine/ours</u> is in the city near where I work.
8. My story is silly enough, but <u>yours</u> is utterly ridiculous, at least the way **you** tell it!
9. Joseph's grandfather lost all <u>his</u> money in building speculation while my grandfather lost his in gambling casinos.
10. Aunt Joan spends her holidays in Tenerife while Aunt Dorothy spends <u>hers</u> at home.

9.4

1. The oven turns <u>itself</u> off when the food is cooked.
2. The common conviction of minority rights activists is the statement, " If we don't help <u>ourselves</u>, nobody will."
3. I cut <u>myself</u> with a knife when I was making the salad.
4. The young actress found <u>herself</u> to be the object of intense media attention.
5. Several Buddhist monks have burned <u>themselves</u> as a protest against their governments' policies.
6. Even though he smiled at his colleagues, the man in his midlife crisis thought to <u>himself</u>, "What am I doing here? I don't even **like** these people."
7. "Driver, **you** are responsible. It is not enough to tell <u>yourself</u> that you are perfectly capable of driving after a few drinks. You put other people in danger."
8. Computer programs are now being designed that can teach <u>themselves</u> how to deal with unexpected events.
9. "Young people of the nation, you must educate <u>yourselves</u>. The government will do its best to help you, but ultimately, you have to take charge of your own lives."
10. The flea-ridden dog scratched <u>itself</u> to the point of bleeding. [Note: <u>himself/herself</u> for a pet]

9.5

1. The photograph of <u>him</u> and <u>his</u> brothers was taken while <u>they</u> were having a beer.
2. My grandmother and <u>I</u> are leaving for Rome tomorrow.
3. He doesn't trust <u>himself</u> to make the right decision.
4. Just between you and <u>me</u>, this project is a waste of time.
5. Jane was freezing, so <u>we</u> lent <u>her</u> <u>your</u> coat. Hope <u>you</u> don't mind.
6. We like to congratulate <u>ourselves</u> for being compassionate human beings.
7. I am not sure whether the fault is <u>hers</u> or <u>theirs</u>, but <u>it</u> must be addressed.
8. Every company has <u>its</u> own special interests.
9. If Steve doesn't have a bicycle, <u>he</u> can take <u>mine</u>.
10. The Smiths built <u>themselves</u> a new garage last spring.
11. The Americans are responsible for <u>their</u> problems and we are responsible for <u>ours</u>.
12. Sally is a good friend of <u>mine</u>.
13. Those children of <u>yours</u> are wonderfully behaved.
14. A snake cannot protect itself if <u>its</u> head is trapped.
15. If a student does not speak English as a native language, is it fair to put <u>him or her</u> into a class with native English speakers right from the beginning?

9.6

1. We like that painting at the back of the store. Is <u>that</u> the only landscape you have?
2. The lawyer holds up the knife that was found in the defendant's pocket. "Does <u>this</u> look familiar to you?" asks the lawyer coldly.
3. This afternoon, the women are playing in the symphony. After <u>that</u>, they plan to do a little sightseeing.
4. "What are you going to do with the chairs in the basement?" "<u>Those</u> are for my nephew. He'll come and pick them up tomorrow afternoon."
5. "What beautiful jewels you are wearing! What are they?" "Well, <u>these</u> are diamonds, while <u>these</u> around the edge are emeralds."
6. Columbus discovered America in 1492. <u>That</u> was a pivotal year in the history of both Europe and the Americas.
7. "Remember how we used to go dancing every Friday night?" "Ah, yes, <u>those</u> were the days!"
8. "How are you going to divide the marbles your uncle gave you?" "Easy! <u>Those</u> next to you are nothing special; they're for my brother. <u>These</u> here are neat; they're for me."
9. Once upon a time there was a princess who was going to be married. <u>That</u> was a big day for her because she would be leaving the house of her father.
10. You shouldn't put bleach in the water when you wash your tennis shoes because <u>that</u> will ruin the rubber.

9.7

1. These houses are all different. <u>Each</u> has its own unique floorplan.
2. The boss wants <u>everyone</u> on the job at 8 A.M. sharp, so don't be late!
3. After the fire, <u>all</u> was confusion and disarray.
4. After the storm, <u>everyone</u> was running around trying to find food for the starving cattle.
5. The pewter figurines show magical figures: dwarves, wizards, and dragons. <u>Each</u> has a price tag glued discreetly to the bottom.

9.8

1. The mother seal refused to let <u>anyone/anybody</u> touch her offspring.
2. There's plenty of wine. Would you like <u>some</u>?
3. Susan called the insurance office but <u>no one/nobody</u> answered.
4. Don't get so upset! <u>Anyone/anybody</u> can make a mistake!
5. <u>Nothing</u> makes her husband angrier than a bicycle in the driveway.
6. <u>Someone/somebody</u> broke into the warehouse and stole a few tools.
7. The police examined the freshly dug grave, but they didn't find <u>anything</u>.
8. There used to be three or four cafes in this neighborhood, but now there is <u>none</u>.
9. Is there <u>anything/something</u> on TV tonight that you'd like to watch?
10. There were lots of dinosaurs in North America. Were there <u>any/some</u> in Africa?

9.9

1. After the accident, the bridge was covered with oil. Did (much/~~many~~) spill into the river?
2. The economy is bad for small businesses, but the mayor is happy that (a few/~~few~~) were able to open earlier this month.
3. The doctors could do (~~much~~/little) to help the terminal cancer patient.
4. Sandra has a lot of friends, but she was sad when so (many/few) came to her graduation ceremony.
5. The water should be purified with chlorine bleach. Add (a little/~~little~~) to the container and let it sit for 15 minutes.
6. The candidate was besieged with telegrams, and (a lot/~~lots~~) came from the South.

9.10

1. Swahili and Urdu are both fascinating languages. I don't know <u>which</u> I should learn first.
2. *Hamlet* is a play <u>that</u> is known around the world.
3. There are two glasses here. <u>Whose</u> is this? It's Fredericka's!
4. <u>How</u> could the alchemists make lead into gold?
5. With <u>whom</u> do you wish to speak?
6. The woman <u>who</u> works in the office next to mine is the boss's wife.
7. Do you have any idea <u>when</u> the plane will arrive?
8. The people cannot understand <u>why</u> the government failed to act.
9. <u>Who</u> was supposed to take out the garbage?
10. I can't hear <u>what</u> the guide is saying.

9.11

1. <u>Those</u> boxers over there really dislike <u>each other/one another</u>, don't <u>they</u>?
2. <u>Nothing</u> is cosier than a warm fire on a stormy night.
3. Don't worry! <u>No one/Nobody</u> will harm <u>us</u>.
4. A thing like <u>that/this</u> can happen to <u>anyone/anybody</u>.
5. <u>No one/Nobody</u> should ever lose sight of <u>his or her</u> cultural roots.
6. These apples cost fifty cents <u>each</u>. Should <u>we</u> buy <u>all</u> of <u>them</u>?
7. Hello? Is <u>anyone/anybody</u> there? <u>Who</u>'s there?!

9.12

1. <u>Everybody</u> felt the earthquake. SUBJECT
2. Tell <u>her</u> she's late. OBJECT
3. I don't know <u>what</u> I want. INTERROGATIVE
4. He blames <u>himself</u> for the accident. REFLEXIVE
5. Shelly ate some bread but Bill didn't have <u>any</u>. INDEFINITE
6. The story <u>that</u> you heard is completely false. RELATIVE
7. <u>They</u> love to swim at night. SUBJECT
8. You went to school looking like <u>that</u>? DEMONSTRATIVE
9. Those guys hate <u>one another</u>. RECIPROCAL
10. I don't take from your plate, so please don't take from <u>mine</u>. POSSESSIVE

9.13

The Ex-President's Daughter

Interviewer: Since your father is no longer President, <u>what</u> would <u>you</u> say in retrospect is the most difficult part of being the President's daughter?

Davis: <u>I</u> was seeing <u>my</u> father make policies with <u>which</u> I disagreed so strongly and yet could do <u>nothing</u> about. Like Nicaragua. <u>He</u> would make statements about the war there <u>which/that</u> I knew were simply not true, and yet <u>he</u> could persuade the American people to accept <u>them</u>. For example, to place a trade embargo on a particular country, the President has to state that such a country poses a clear and present danger to the United States. Well, Nicaragua is a country of 3.5 million people, a large percentage of <u>whom</u> are children. To say that such people pose a danger to the United States is stretching the truth just a bit.

Interviewer: <u>I</u> know that <u>you</u> disagreed with <u>your</u> father on the Vietnam war, that <u>you</u> were very much against <u>it</u> and <u>he</u> was not. <u>You</u>'ve also supported the Equal Rights Amendment, gun control and <u>a lot</u> of other issues <u>he</u> opposes. But at <u>what</u> point did <u>you</u> decide <u>you</u> could no longer discuss politics with <u>him</u>?

Davis: <u>My</u> memory for dates is awful, but <u>I</u> think <u>it</u> was in 1982. <u>I</u> took Helen Caldicott [the Australian physician <u>who</u> then led the anti-nuclear coalition Physicians for Social Responsibility] to the White House, and the three of <u>us</u> met for over an hour. And after <u>that</u> meeting, <u>I</u> decided that <u>I</u>'d never again discuss politics with <u>my</u> father, because <u>it</u> was just too futile and too painful. <u>I</u> mean, <u>we</u> were so far apart. There were no grounds even for discussion. <u>I</u> felt like <u>I</u>'d been beating <u>my</u> head against the same wall for years, and <u>I</u> couldn't do <u>it</u> anymore.

Patti Davis is recognized as a professional author, currently busy plotting <u>her</u> third novel. Among <u>her</u> contemporaries, <u>she</u> is respected as a writer-activist of integrity, unafraid to disagree publicly with <u>her</u> conservative parents on the important problems of the day.

9.14

1. a) *[Sandra bought a new car.] She wants to keep [him] in the garage.
   b) correct pronoun category (object)
      correct person (third)
      correct number (singular)
      correct possible form (*him*)
   c) *[Sandra bought a new car.] She wants to keep [him] in the garage.
      [Sandra bought a new car.] She wants to keep it   in the garage.
      Explanation: A car usually has neutral gender (*it*) unless it has a personal status, in which case the pronoun is usually feminine, not masculine.

2. a) *All animals need to protect [theirselves] from the cold.
   b) correct pronoun category (reflexive)
      correct person (third)
      correct number (plural)
   c) *All animals need to protect [theirselves] from the cold.
      All animals need to protect themselves   from the cold.
      Explanation: The third person reflexive pronoun is made with the object pronoun and *-self/-selves*, not with the possessive determiner.

3. a) *The prince and the servant girl truly loved [each another].
   b) correct pronoun category (reciprocal)
   c) *The prince and the servant girl truly loved [each another].
      The prince and the servant girl truly loved each other.
      Explanation: The two possible forms of the reciprocal pronoun are *each other* or *one another*. There are no other forms.

4. a) *Jennifer wants to sit between you and [I] during the horror film.
   b) correct person (first)
      correct number (singular)
      correct possible form (*I*)

c) *Jennifer wants to sit between you and [I] during the horror film.
Jennifer wants to sit between you and me during the horror film.
Explanation: After a preposition (*between*), only the object pronoun may be used (a PP consists of a PREP + PREPOSITIONAL OBJECT), not a subject pronoun.

5. a) *[Where did the flowers come from?] [That]? They are for Hilda's birthday.

b) correct pronoun category (demonstrative)
correct recognition of grammatical environment (not nearby)
correct possible form (*that*)

c) *[Where did the flowers come from?] [That?]   They are for Hilda's birthday.
[Where did the flowers come from?] Those? They are for Hilda's birthday
Explanation: Demonstrative pronouns must agree with their antecedent. *The flowers* is plural and therefore requires *those*, not *that*.

6. a) *We made the last payment on our house today, so the house is really [theirs] now

b) correct pronoun category (possessive)
correct number (plural)
correct possible form (*theirs*)

c) *We made the last payment on our house today, so the house is really [theirs] now.
We made the last payment on our house today, so the house is really ours   now.
Explanation: The sentence suggests that the house belongs to the people speaking and should therefore be in first person (*ours*), not third person (*theirs*).

7. a) *[The actress accepted the Oscar.] [He] thanked the Academy with a few well-chosen words.

b) correct pronoun category (subject)
correct person (third)
correct number (singular)
correct possible form (he)

c) *[The actress accepted the Oscar.] [He] thanked the Academy with a few well-chosen words.
[The actress accepted the Oscar.] She thanked the Academy with a few well-chosen words.
Explanation: An actress is feminine and therefore requires the feminine subject pronoun *she*.

8. a) *The police rang the doorbell but [*anybody*] was home.

b) correct pronoun category (indefinite)
correct person (third)
correct number (singular)
correct possible form (*anybody*)

c) *The police rang the doorbell but [anybody] was home.
The police rang the doorbell but nobody   was home.
Explanation: A negative environment requires auxiliary negation with the indefinite pronoun *anybody* (e.g., *There wasn't anybody home*). A better solution is to use the negative indefinite pronoun *nobody*.

9. a) *The house is full of guests, but all [is] leaving tomorrow.

b) correct pronoun category (universal)
correct person (third)
correct possible form (all)

c) *The house is full of guests, but all [is] leaving tomorrow.
The house is full of guests, but all are leaving tomorrow.
Explanation: Since the antecedent is *guests*, the universal pronoun *all* requires plural rather than singular agreement.

10. a) *The doctor [which] operated on my father is quite famous.

b) correct pronoun category (WH/relative pronoun)
correct possible form (*which*)

c) *The doctor [which] operated on my father is quite famous.
The doctor who   operated on my father is quite famous.
Explanation: Since the antecedent is *the doctor*, the correct WH/relative pronoun is *who*. *Which* is the WH/relative pronoun for things.

11. a) *[The United Nations consists of 159 members]. Each [desire] peace in the world.
    b) correct pronoun category (universal)
       correct possible form (*each*)
    c) *[The United Nations consists of 159 members]. Each [desire] peace in the world.
       [The United Nations consists of 159 members]. Each desires peace in the world.
       Explanation: The universal pronoun *each* always requires singular agreement.

12. a) *[Mrs. Swambo lives in Berlin now]. [What] did she live before she moved to Berlin?
    b) correct pronoun category (WH-pronoun)
       [correct recognition of grammatical environment (interrogative)]
       correct possible form (*what*)
    c) *[Mrs. Swambo lives in Berlin now]. [What] did she live before she moved to Berlin?
       [Mrs. Swambo lives in Berlin now]. Where did she live before she moved to Berlin?
       Explanation: The antecedent of the WH-pronoun is a place, which requires *where*. *What* is for things.

13. a) *[Bread is offered] Would you like [any] with your mock turtle soup?
    b) correct pronoun category (indefinite)
       correct number (singular)
       correct possible form (*any*)
    c) *[Bread is offered] Would you like [any] with your mock turtle soup?
       [Bread is offered] Would you like some with your mock turtle soup?
       Explanation: Politeness requires the positive environment of *some*, which presumes a "yes" answer. *Any* is impolite (though strictly speaking grammatical) because it presumes a negative answer.

14. a) *Those silver bracelets did not cost more than $100 [any].
    b) [correct number (singular)]
       correct possible form (*any*)
       correct recognition of grammatical environment (negative)
    c) *Those silver bracelets did not cost more than $100 [any].
       Those silver bracelets did not cost more than $100 each.
       Explanation: If a group (in this case *those silver bracelets*) is established, a universal pronoun, not an indefinite pronoun, must be used.

15. a) *[How do you do, sir?] I am very happy to meet [me].
    b) correct pronoun category (object)
       correct possible form (*me*)
    c) *[How do you do, sir?] I am very happy to meet [me].
       [How do you do, sir?] I am very happy to meet you.
       Explanation: The polite expression *How do you do?* is used when introducing one person to another. The other person is addressed as *you* (second person), not *me*, which is first person. One does not usually introduce oneself to oneself.

Chapter 10

10.1

1. Get <u>that</u> cat off the table! (DET; DET)
2. Will <u>they</u> print <u>this</u>? (PRO; PRO)
3. <u>These</u> apples cost a dollar <u>each</u>. (DET; PRO)
4. <u>Every</u> house should have <u>one</u>. (DET; PRO)
5. <u>Some</u> people don't have <u>any</u>. (DET; PRO)
6. She can't tell <u>which</u> boy is <u>which</u>. (DET; PRO)
7. There are <u>no</u> fleas on <u>theirs</u>. (DET; PRO)
8. I want <u>all</u> power or <u>none</u>. (DET; PRO)
9. <u>Neither</u> person is <u>my</u> candidate. (DET; DET)
10. <u>What</u> are <u>you</u> talking about? (PRO; PRO)

10.2

1. class
2. class
3. class
4. iden
5. class
6. iden
7. iden
8. iden
9. iden
10. iden
11. iden
12. iden
13. iden
14. iden
15. iden
16. class
17. class
18. iden
19. class
20. iden
21. iden
22. iden
23. iden
24. iden
25. iden
26. iden
27. iden
28. iden
29. iden
30. iden
31. iden
32. iden
33. iden

10.3

Once upon a time, [1] an entrepreneurial mouse owned [2] a cheese shop in [3] a small western prairie town. [4] The mouse had risen to prominence due to his success, so he was ready to take on [5] a political position. Since [6] the town was fundamentally democratic, there had to be [7] an election, but each candidate had to supply his or her own ballots. In order to improve his chances, [8] the mouse had ballots printed on thin slices of cheese from the cheese shop. On [9] the day of [10] the election, [11] the mouse was quite confident of winning the post of Rodentia Prima. But when the ballot box was opened, not a single cheese ballot had been deposited. As a result, [12] the election went to [13] a hitherto unknown prairie dog, who had had his ballots printed on [14] Ø dried oleander leaves.

10.4

1. Do Ø leopards have Ø stripes or Ø spots?
2. Dolores's car had a green hood with Ø purple fenders.
3. A thermometer is an instrument that measures Ø temperature.
4. Ø dinosaurs were not Ø lizards but rather Ø gigantic bird-like creatures.
5. An isotope is an unstable variant of a chemical element.

10.5

1. A lawnmower (G) is a device (G) for cutting Ø grass (G).
2. Did the surgeon (S) remove the appendix (S) from the patient (S)?
3. The recipe (S) called for Ø wine (G) but he used a mixture (G) of Ø vinegar (G) and Ø apple juice (G) instead.
4. A car that gets at least forty miles per gallon (G) would be fine for the needs of your family (S).
5. We hiked in the mountains (S) last weekend. We learned that, when camping at Ø high elevations (G), Ø hikers (G) should be sure to carry Ø foood and water (G), Ø warm clothing (G), a suitable tent (G), and a reliable stove (G), not to mention a compass (G).

10.6

1. There has never been a deeper crisis in the world. (EXISTENTIAL)
2. There he is! Throw him a rope! (LOCATIVE)
3. Whenever there's an earthquake, the horses go crazy. (EXISTENTIAL)
4. The Waltons go to Sardinia every year. They love it there. (LOCATIVE)
5. Gertrude Stein is famous for having said about Oakland, California: "There's no there there." (EXISTENTIAL; LOCATIVE)

10.7

1. When mud is placed into a glass of water, the sediment sinks to the bottom of the liquid.

2. <u>Huge undersea ranges</u> divide the ocean floor. <u>The mountains</u> are sometimes high enough to break the surface and become islands.

3. <u>Adequate rain</u> is crucial to <u>local growers</u> of <u>vegetables</u>. <u>The farmers</u> depend on <u>the moisture</u> to nourish <u>the plants</u> that are <u>their</u> only source of income.

4. Last summer, we visited <u>a spectacular cave</u> in <u>a limestone quarry</u>. Water had dissolved <u>the rock</u> to create <u>the underground cavern</u>.

5. The entomologists watched two <u>praying mantisses</u> mate just before <u>dawn</u>. <u>The early morning light</u> prevents <u>the females</u> from devouring <u>the males</u> for breakfast because they couldn't see them.

10.8

Mount St. Helens began to issue steam and ash on March 27, 1980 in preparation for <u>the largest</u> [SUP] eruption in Washington in 123 years. <u>The last</u> [SEQ] time <u>the same</u> [UN] mountain had erupted was in 1827. <u>The first</u> [SEQ] indication that something was going to happen was a series of earthquakes that lasted almost a week. Then, on May 18 at 8:32 A.M., 1,300 feet of <u>the previously</u> [SEQ] 9,677-foot tall mountain, the entire north side, was blasted into the air leaving a huge, bowl-shaped depression. In <u>the next</u> [SEQ] few minutes, a cloud of ash and steam rose 11 to 15 miles, spreading fine ash up to 500 miles away. One hundred and fifty square miles of forest were laid flat. <u>The principal</u> [UN] dangers on the mountain were forest fires and flash floods, and over 400 loggers, forest rangers, and others were evacuated. <u>The only</u> [UN] reason that there were not catastrophic floods is that Spirit Lake at the base of the mountain became plugged at the outlet by a slide of dirt and volcanic rock. Government officials set <u>the lowest</u> [SUP] damage estimate at 1.5 billion dollars.

10.9

1. Take <u>the</u> Franklin Freeway to <u>the</u> bridge.
2. Cross <u>the</u> bridge.
3. Turn left at <u>the</u> Court House.
4. Turn right at <u>the</u> university.
5. Turn left at <u>the</u> gas station.
6. Drive around <u>the</u> park.
7. Turn right at <u>the</u> library.
8. Stop at <u>the</u> second green house.
9. Open <u>the</u> door (it's unlocked).
10. Turn on <u>the</u> light.
11. Go through <u>the</u> living room
12. Take the stairs down to <u>the</u> back garden.
13. Simon will be working in <u>the</u> garage.

10.10

1. <u>The giraffe</u> is the tallest living quadruped mammal.
2. Diseases of <u>the heart</u> are the number-one killer in the United States.
3. Frogs and turtles bury themselves in the mud below frozen streams, while snakes and toads sleep through <u>the winter</u> under logs and leaves.
4. The bomb that was dropped on Nagasaki was based on the principle of nuclear fission (division) whereas <u>the hydrogen bomb</u> is based on the principle of fusion.
5. <u>The paper clip</u> is one of the most widely used paper fasteners in the world.

10.11

1. a) *Joe has [a] same hairstyle as Margaret.
   b)
      correct countability (count)
      correct number (singular)
      correct initial sound (*a* + consonant sound)
   c) *Joe has [a]   same hairstyle as Margaret.
      Joe has the   same hairstyle as Margaret.
      Explanation: The word *same* is one of the unique ranking adjectives, which always requires *the*.

2. a) *[A] car that I bought from you last week is a piece of junk!
   b) correct countability (count)
      correct number (singular)
      correct initial sound (*a* + consonant sound)
      correct possible form (*a car*)
   c) *[A]   car that I bought from you last week is a piece of junk!
      The   car that I bought from you last week is a piece of junk!
      Explanation: The subject (*car*) is identified by the phrase *that I bought from you last week* and thus
                    requires *the*.

3. a) *[A] moon affects the ocean tides on our planet.
   b) correct countability (count)
      correct number (singular)
      correct initial sound (*a* + consonant sound)
      correct possible form (*a moon*)
   c) *[A] moon affects the ocean tides on our planet.
      The moon affects the ocean tides on our planet.
      Explanation: Since in this case *moon* refers to our own satellite, shared knowledge identifies *moon*, which
                    thus requires *the*.

4. a) *The Sears Tower in Chicago is [a] tallest building in the United States.
   b) correct countability (count)
      correct number (singular)
      correct initial sound (*a* + consonant sound)
   c) *The Sears Tower in Chicago is [a] tallest building in the United States.
      The Sears Tower in Chicago is the tallest building in the United States.
      Explanation: Tallest is a superlative ranking adjective, which always requires *the*.

5. a) *[Definition] A plumber is [the] person who fixes leaking pipes and clogged drains.
   b) correct number (singular)
      correct possible form (*the person*)
   c) *[Definition] A plumber is [the] person who fixes leaking pipes and clogged drains.
      [Definition] A plumber is a   person who fixes leaking pipes and clogged drains.
      Explanation: A definition has the formula "An A is a B that C." Definitions classify nouns. With *the*, the
                    sentence would be a description, not a definition.

6. a) *This castle has a tower that is made completely of [a] stone.
   b) correct class/iden (*a(n)/Ø* for classification)
      correct number (singular)
      correct initial sound (*a* + consonant sound)
      correct possible form (*a stone*)
   c) *This castle has a tower that is made completely of [a] stone.
      This castle has a tower that is made completely of Ø   stone.
      Explanation: This sentence requires the noncount use of *stone* as a material. Classified noncount nouns
                    require Ø, not *a*.

7. a) *[Ring! Ring!] Could you answer [a] telephone for me?
   b) correct countability (count)
      correct number (singular)
      correct initial sound (*a* + consonant sound)
      correct possible form (*a telephone*)

c) *[Ring! Ring!] Could you answer [a] telephone for me
[Ring! Ring!] Could you answer the telephone for me?
Explanation: This sentence presumes that the telephone is part of the listener's shared knowledge and therefore requires *the*.

8. a) *I don't think there is [the] bookshop in this town.
   b) correct possible form (*the bookshop*)
   c) *I don't think there is [the] bookshop in this town.
   I don't think there is a   bookshop in this town.
   Explanation: Existential *there* always classifies a noun, which thus requires *a* for count nouns like *bookshop*.

9. a) *Would you like to go to [an] ocean with us this weekend?
   b) correct countability (count)
   correct number (singular)
   correct initial sound (*an* + vowel sound)
   correct possible form (*an ocean*)
   c) *Would you like to go to [an] ocean with us this weekend?
   Would you like to go to the ocean with us this weekend?
   Explanation: This sentence presumes that the ocean is shared knowledge, which always requires *the*.

10. a) *[An old man was walking down a dusty road with a boy.] The man was tired, the road was long, and [a] boy was hungry.
    b) correct countability (count)
    correct number (singular)
    correct initial sound (*a* + consonant sound)
    correct possible form (*a boy*)
    c) *[An old man was walking down a dusty road with a boy.] The man was tired, the road was long and [a] boy was hungry.
    [An old man was walking down a dusty road with a boy.] The man was tired, the road was long and the boy was hungry.
    Explanation: The subsequent mention of the same noun (*boy*) identifies it and thus requires *the*.

10.12

1. The Sears Tower in the city of Chicago is one of the tallest buildings in Ø North America.
2. The Suez Canal connects Ø Port Said on the Mediterranean Sea and Ø Port Taufiq on the Gulf of Suez in the Red Sea.
3. The Little Colorado River begins at the Zuni Reservoir in Ø Arizona, just south of the Petrified Forest, an extensive exhibit of petrified wood. It flows north of the city of Flagstaff and empties into the Colorado River, which passes through Ø Grand Canyon National Park.
4. Ø Mt. Kilimanjaro (19,340 ft.) is situated in Ø northern Tanzania between Ø Lake Victoria and the Indian Ocean. Ø Serengeti National Park lies to the west of it, the Masai Steppe to the south, and the Yatta Plateau to the northeast.
5. Ø LeConte Hall houses the Physics Department at the University of California at Ø Berkeley.
6. Bones from the largest known mammal, the baluchitherium, were found in the Gobi Desert in the People's Republic of Mongolia. This desert is southeast of the Khangai Mountains.
7. The Library of Congress, the Air and Space Museum, Ø NASA (the National Air and Space Administration) and the Department of Agriculture are all located on Ø Independence Avenue in Ø Washington D.C.
8. The largest of the Hawaiian Islands is Ø Hawaii. Ø Kilauea, one of the world's most active volcanoes, is located there.
9. When sailing from the city of Vancouver, one passes through the San Juan Islands to Ø Victoria, the capital of Ø British Columbia on Ø Vancouver Island. The Pacific Ocean lies to the west.
10. The Apple Computer Company, situated in the "Silicon Valley" near Ø Stanford University, competes with Ø IBM and other companies concerned with microelectronics.

10.13

1. [He owns a fishing boat.] His boat is docked at a marina on the Columbia River
2. [Saturn has over 1000 rings.] Saturn's rings are made mostly of ice.
3. [I possess a stainless steel watch.] My watch is powered by a battery.

4. [They have fences everywhere.] Their fences are all electrified.
5. [You own a boa constrictor.] Your boa constrictor is over 10 feet long.
6. [The schools have problems.] The schools' problems concern drugs, gangs, and firearms.
7. [We possess a gold mine.] Our gold mine is in Amazonia.
8. [She had a beautiful daughter.] Her daughter was only sixteen when she died.
9. [It has a varnished surface.] Its surface has been badly scratched.
10. [This model has a 68000 central processor.] Its processor is not as fast as newer versions.

10.14

1. In those days, people used to throw garbage into the street!
2. If you want to stay in this house, you will follow the house rules.
3. Do you see that building in the distance? I used to live there.
4. Do these glasses suit my personality, do you think?
5. Sheila has worked over fifty hours this week.

10.15

1. There are some apples in the refrigerator.
2. Would you like some tea?
3. The earth was inhabited by dinosaurs in the Jurassic period.
4. Sóme snakes bear live young while others lay eggs.
5. The voting material should be readable by ány person with a high-school education.
6. We haven't had ány tornadoes, hurricanes, or tropical storms this year.
7. Aspirin is a common pain-reliever.
8. Did any insects survive the atomic bomb tests that took place in the South Pacific?
9. No human being has the right to hurt any other human being.
10. Some people called to see if you wanted to buy a condo in Florida.

10.16

1. The advisor had no further comments.
2. No tree was standing after the forest fire.
3. What would you do if you were stranded in a foreign country with no money?
4. Julia's grandfather will allow no cats in the house.
5. I had no idea that you were in town!

10.17

1. What color would you like your house to be painted?
2. Astronomers know the position and magnitude of every star in the night sky.
3. Janet has been to Malawi and Joel has been to Zimbabwe, but stay-at-home Paula has been to neither country.
4. Whose dishes are those in the sink? They certainly aren't mine!
5. The two parties each nominate one person, but many voters don't care for either candidate.
6. The hospital orderlies bathe each patient on the ward on a daily basis.
7. The starving people didn't care what food they received as long as they got something to eat.
8. Jack's mother likes old houses but his father likes new ones. Which kind does your wife prefer?
9. Every book that is published has an ISBN number.
10. The thieves didn't know whose car they had stolen, but they knew that the owner would try to find them.

10.18

1. a) *[There is a book on the table in the kitchen.] Bring me [this] book please.
   b) correct determiner category (demonstrative)
      correct number (singular)
      correct possible form (*this book*)
   c) *[There is a book on the table in the kitchen.] Bring me [this] book please.
      [There is a book on the table in the kitchen.] Bring me that   book please.
      Explanation: On the table in the kitchen suggests "not nearby," which requires *that*, not this.

2. a) *Mr. Smith, don't forget [yours] credit card.
   b) correct number (singular)
   c) *Mr. Smith, don't forget [yours] credit card.
   Mr. Smith, don't forget your   credit card.
   Explanation: If a noun (*credit card*) is present, the determiner (*your*), not the pronoun (*yours*), is required.

3. a) *[All] child deserves a good education.
   b) correct environment (unlimited)
   c) *[All]   child deserves a good education
   Every child deserves a good education.
   Explanation: A singular countable noun (*child*) cannot occur with *all*. The universal determiner *every* is preferred because the noun set is unlimited.

4. a) *[This soldier will have to be carried.] She cannot use [neither] leg.
   b) correct number (singular)   correct determiner category (dual)
   correct environment (dual)
   correct possible form (*neither leg*)
   c) *[This soldier will have to be carried.] She cannot use [neither] leg.
   [This soldier will have to be carried.] She cannot use either   leg.
   Explanation: Double negatives are not grammatical in Standard English. Therefore, the assertive dual (*either*) rather than the negative dual (*neither*) determiner is required.

5. a) *[Which] time does the plane arrive?
   b) correct determiner category (WH-determiner)
   correct number (singular)
   correct possible form (*which time*)
   c) *[Which] time does the plane arrive?
   What   time does the plane arrive?
   Explanation: The normal question for asking the time is *What time?* because the answer is unknown and therefore unlimited. *Which* is only appropriate if a limited set of times has already been mentioned.

6. a) *Last semester, students couldn't get [some] money, not even a student loan.
   b) correct determiner category (assertive/nonassertive)
   correct number (singular)
   correct possible form (*some money*)
   c) *Last semester, students couldn't get [some] money, not even a student loan.
   Last semester, students couldn't get any   money, not even a student loan.
   Explanation: In a negative environment, the nonassertive determiner *any* is required as long as auxiliary negation (*couldn't*) is also present.

7. a) *We have had absolutely [not] problem with this machine.
   b) correct number (singular)
   correct environment (negative)
   c) *We have had absolutely [not] problem with this machine.
   We have had absolutely no   problem with this machine.
   Explanation: A determiner (*no*) is required before a noun, not an auxiliary negator (*not*).

8. a) *[One   company wants to reduce worker salaries. The other wants to move to a developing country.]
   [Either] company is being very fair to its workers.
   b) correct determiner category (dual)
   correct number (singular)
   correct environment (negative)
   correct possible form (*either company*)
   c) *[One company wants to reduce worker salaries. The other wants to move to a developing country.]
   [Either] company is being very fair to its workers.
   [One company wants to reduce worker salaries. The other wants to move to a developing country.]
   Neither company is being very fair to its workers.
   Explanation: Since both companies are being unfair, the limited set is negative, which requires *neither*.

9. a) *How many stereos have you sold [that] week?
   b) correct determiner category (demonstrative)
      correct number (singular)
      correct possible form (*that week*)
   c) *How many stereos have you sold [that] week?
      How many stereos have you sold this   week?
      Explanation: The present perfect tense (*have sold*) concerns the present, which requires the demonstrative determiner *this*. *That* refers to the past or future.

10. a) *[Every] person could have contaminated the milk container.
    b) correct number (singular)
       correct possible form (*every person*)
    c) *[Every] person could have contaminated the milk container.
       Any   person could have contaminated the milk container.
       Explanation: Since the perpetrator is unknown, the sentence requires the nonassertive determiner *any* rather than the universal determiner *every*.

10.19

1. <u>All</u> my relatives came to the family reunion.
2. Sally should have some food before she leaves.
3. The patient had fluid in <u>both (of)</u> his lungs.
4. How can you throw away <u>all (of)</u> those old love letters?
5. Customers may use either elevator.

10.20

1. <u>Half (of)</u> the trees were knocked down in the hurricane.
2. More than <u>three quarters</u> of your native peoples died of influenza.
3. That guy would eat <u>a quarter</u> of a sheep if you let him.
4. His latest text is <u>one-third</u> story book and <u>two-thirds</u> style manual.
5. The Concorde will allow you to get to Paris in <u>half</u> the time.

10.21

1. The Prime Minister was always <u>such a</u> gentleman.
2. "What Ø nonsense!" screamed the witness.
3. San Francisco isn't <u>such a</u> large city.
4. The team only realized <u>what a</u> wonderful athlete Billie Jean was after she had left.
5. The audience had never heard <u>such Ø</u> beautiful music.

10.22

1. Stockholm was <u>the first</u> city to ban traffic in the city center.
2. There were over <u>two hundred</u> guests at the wedding.
3. Oxygen is <u>the eighth</u> element on the periodic table.
4. <u>The sixteen</u> moons of Jupiter include Ganymede, the largest moon in the Solar System.
5. Mars is <u>the fourth</u> planet from the sun.

10.23

1. The old woman kept a few cows to supply her family with milk.
2. A lot of children send letters to Santa Claus at Christmas time.
3. There are few problems that cannot be solved with a little patience.
4. Not much water is left in the local reservoir.
5. The mother wept with joy when the jury found little evidence that her boy was guilty.

10.24

1. Ralph would like <u>another</u> beer, please.
2. Pluto with one moon has fewer satellites than <u>any of the other</u> outer planets.
3. Some animals sleep in the daytime while <u>other</u> animals sleep at night.
4. If one side of the brain is damaged, <u>the other</u> side can compensate to some degree.
5. I'm terribly busy at the moment. Could you call <u>some other</u> day next week?

10.25

1. a) *It was [what a hot day] yesterday.
   b) correct noncentral determiner category (intensifying predeterminer)
      correct co-occurring central determiner (article *a*)
      correct class/iden (class)
      correct countability (countable)
      correct number (singular)
      correct possible form (*what a hot day*)
   c) *It was [what a hot day] yesterday.
      It was such   a hot day yesterday.
      Explanation: The intensifying predeterminer *what* can only occur as the inital word in a clause. Otherwise, *such* must be used.

2. a) *A chicken's top speed (9 mph) is [the quarter of] a rabbit's top speed (35 mph).
   b) correct noncentral determiner category (fraction)
      correct countability (countable)
      correct number (singular)
      correct possible form (*the quarter*)
   c) *A chicken's top speed (9 mph) is [the quarter of] a rabbit's top speed (35 mph).
      A chicken's top speed (9 mph) is a   quarter of a rabbit's top speed (35 mph).
      Explanation: Fractions usually occur with the classifying article *a*, especially when describing general characteristics.

3. a) *Humans often do not hear equally well with [both ear].
   b) correct noncentral determiner category (quantifying predeterminer)
      correct co-occurring central determiner (article Ø)
      correct class/iden of co-occurring central determiner (class)
      correct countability (countable)
   c) *Humans often do not hear equally well with [both ear].
      Humans often do not hear equally well with both ears.
      Explanation: The quantifying predeterminer *both* can only occur with plural nouns.

4. a) *Sean is writing [the six revision] of his term paper.
   b) correct noncentral determiner category (numeral)
      correct co-occurring central determiner (article *the*)
      correct class/iden of co-occurring central determiner (class)
      correct countability (countable)
      correct number (singular)
   c) *Sean is writing the [six revision] of his term paper.
      Sean is writing the sixth revision of his term paper.
      Explanation: A sequence requires an ordinal (*sixth*), not a cardinal (*six*) numeral.

5. a) *Half the fish in this lake died; [other half] got sick.
   b) correct noncentral determiner category (form of *other*)
      correct countability (countable)
      correct number (singular)
   c) *Half the fish in this lake died; [other   half] got sick.
      Half the fish in this lake died; the other half got sick.
      Explanation: The fish are limited to those in the lake. Limited sets require *the other*. Only unlimited sets occur with Ø *other*.

6. a) *In this house, [all of Ø] children go to bed at 9:00 P.M. sharp.
   b) correct noncentral determiner category (quantifying predeterminer))
      correct countability (countable)
      correct number (plural)
   c) *In this house, [all of Ø] children go to bed at 9:00 P.M. sharp.
      In this house, all of the children go to bed at 9:00 P.M. sharp.
      Explanation: The quantifying predeterminer *all of* **must** co-occur with *the*. The alternative would be *all children*, which does not fit the limited set of *children* implied.

7. a) *Daphne always goes dancing with [few friends] on Saturday night.
   b) correct noncentral determiner category (*many* and its relatives)
      correct class/iden (*a(n)/Ø* for classification)
      correct countability (count)
      correct number (plural)
      correct possible form (*few friends*)
   c) *Daphne always goes dancing with [few friends] on Saturday night.
      Daphne always goes dancing with a few friends on Saturday night.
      Explanation: Since the environment is positive, the correct form is *a few*. *Few* suggests a dissatisfaction
      with the number of friends, which is not logical in this sentence.

8. a) *Both of [that regions] were harmed by the 1987 drought.
   b) correct noncentral determiner category (quantifying predeterminer)
      correct co-occurring central determiner (demonstrative determiner)
   c) *Both of [that regions] were harmed by the 1987 drought.
      Both of those regions were harmed by the 1987 drought.
      Explanation: The quantifying predeterminer *both* always requires a plural demon. determiner and a plural
      noun (*regions*). The plural demonstrative determiner is *those*, not *that*.

9. a) *There is more acid rain today than at [some other] time in history.
   b) correct noncentral determiner category (form of *other*)
      correct co-occurring central determiner (assertive/nonassertive central determiner)
      correct number (singular)
      correct possible form (*some other time*)
   c) *There is more acid rain today than at [some other] time in history.
      There is more acid rain today than at any   other time in history.
      Explanation: The "one but not this" meaning is expressed with *any other*. *Some other* implies "not this but
      one from a defined group."

10. a) *It will take them several days to climb [such Ø high mountain].
    b) correct noncentral determiner category (intensifying predeterminer)
       correct class/iden of co-occurring central determiner (class)
    c) *It will take them several days to climb [such Ø   high mountain].
       It will take them several days to climb such a   high mountain.
       Explanation: With the intensifying predeterminers, Ø can only occur with plural countable or
       uncountable nouns. Since *mountain* is singular and countable, *a* is required.

Chapter 11

11.1

1. Paris is a very <u>beautiful</u> city.
2. The cancer patient made a <u>remarkable</u> recovery.
3. The <u>basic</u> problem with nuclear power is disposing of nuclear waste.
4. How Marilyn Monroe died is still very <u>mysterious</u>.
5. Young mammals are <u>dependent</u> on their parents during their early years.
6. The people in the midwestern section of the U.S. are often very <u>friendly</u>.
7. The <u>childless</u> couple were anxious to adopt a baby.
8. People who suffer from manic depression are often extremely <u>creative</u>.
9. It is <u>customary</u> in Japanese houses to remove your shoes at the door.
10. Brightly colored mushrooms are usually not <u>edible</u>.

11.2

1. The professor gave a really <u>interesting</u> lecture yesterday. [*<u>interested</u>, because a lecture has no cognitive ability, so
   it cannot be "interested" but rather caused interest]
2. Sickle cell anemia is an <u>inherited</u> condition. [*<u>inheriting</u>, because a condition cannot cause inheritance but is
   rather a product of inheritance]
3. The dancers slipped on the <u>polished</u> floor. [*<u>polishing</u>, because the floor received the polishing rather than initiat-
   ing it]

4. Many students complained about the <u>exhausting</u> registration process. [*<u>exhausted</u>, because the process causes exhaustion rather than, like the students, being the recipient of it.]

5. The <u>stolen</u> jewelry was found in a garbage can. [*<u>stealing</u>, because the jewelry was not the thief but the object of the theft]

6. A <u>demanding</u> career can have a negative effect on personal relationships. [*<u>demanded</u>, because the career makes demands on the person rather than being in demand itself]

7. The <u>damaged</u> buildings would have to be rebuilt within a year. [*<u>damaging</u>, because the buildings received rather than caused the damage]

8. The animal pound is full of <u>neglected</u> pets. [*<u>neglecting</u>, because the pets receive neglect rather than cause neglect]

9. Roger built a <u>working</u> model of a steam locomotive. [*<u>worked</u>, because the sense of this sentence is that the model acts by itself rather than receiving the work]

10. The <u>ruling</u> classes make up the aristocracy. [*<u>ruled</u>, because the classes initiate the action of ruling rather than being the recipients of ruling]

11.3

1. Greg bought a <u>heavy Russian</u> coat for the winter.
2. Margaret said that her neighbor was a <u>silly old</u> bat.
3. The valve stem is a <u>thin cylindrical</u> metal rod.
4. That couple found a <u>flawless burgundy</u> prayer rug at a small bazaar.
5. The <u>ugly square</u> room began to feel like a prison.

11.4

1. The ink is invisible.
2. *The sea is angry. (change in meaning)
3. The room is L-shaped.
4. *The world is whole. (change in meaning)
5. *The idiot is complete. (change in meaning)
6. *the awake baby (not possible)
7. the repulsive movie
8. *the sorry thief (change in meaning)
9. the dead whale
10. *the responsible thugs (change in meaning)

11.5

1. a) *This water is not [drinkible].
   b) correct placement of adjective (after a linking verb)
   c) *This water is not [drinkible].
      This water is not drinkable.
      Explanation: The suffix for transforming the verb *drink* into an adjective is *-able* , not *-ible*.

2. a) *My grandmother really misses her [little gray faithful] dog.
   b) correct possible adjective suffix (*faith + ful*)
      correct placement of adjective (in front of *dog*)
   c) *My grandmother really misses her [little gray faithful] dog]
      My grandmother really misses her faithful little gray dog.
      Explanation: Adjectives must have the order opinion (*faithful*)->size (*little*)->color (*gray*), not size->color->opinion.

3. a) *A [stream narrow glacial] meandered across the alpine meadow.
   b) correct possible adjective suffix (*glacier + al*)
      correct sequence of adjectives (color before origin)
   c) *A [stream narrow glacial] meandered across the alpine meadow.
      A narrow glacial stream   meandered across the alpine meadow.
      Explanation: Attributive adjectives must come before the noun they modify, not after it.

4. a) *Hilda thought that her boyfriend's embarrassment was quite [amused].
   b) correct possible adjective suffix (*amuse + ed*)
      correct placement of adjective (after a linking verb)
   c) *Hilda thought that her boyfriend's embarrassment was quite [amused].
      Hilda thought that her boyfriend's embarrassment was quite amusing.
      Explanation: The embarrassment causes amusement, and is not caused by it. Therefore, the adjective must have the ING- , not the ED_2-form.

5. a) *Nathan had heard that the local people were warm and [friendish].
    b) correct placement of adjective (after a linking verb)
    c) *Nathan had heard that the local people were warm and [friendish].
       Nathan had heard that the local people were warm and friendly.
       Explanation: The suffix for transforming the noun *friend* into an adjective is *-ly*, not *-ish*.

6. a) *The snake ingested several [alive] mice.
    b) correct placement of adjective (in front of *mice*)
    c) *The snake ingested several [alive] mice.
       The snake ingested several live   mice.
       Explanation: Alive is a predicate adjective only (e.g., *The mice are alive*). The attributive adjective is *live*.

7. a) *Sheila bought a [Persian antique priceless] carpet.
    b) correct possible adjective suffix (*Persia + an* ; *price + less*)
       correct placement of adjective (in front of *carpet*)
    c) *Sheila bought a [Persian antique priceless] carpet.
       Sheila bought a priceless antique Persian   carpet.
       Explanation: Adjectives must have the order opinion (*priceless*)->age (*antique*)->origin (*Persian*), not
       origin->age->opinion.

8. a) *The night sky was filled with [fireworks colorful].
    b) correct possible adjective suffix (*color + ful*)
    c) *The night sky was filled with [fireworks colorful].
       The night sky was filled with colorful fireworks.
       Explanation: Attributive adjectives must come before the noun they modify, not after it (unless poetic
       license is invoked)

9. a) *The [frightening] kitten hid beneath the bed.
    b) correct possible adjective suffix (*frighten + ing*)
       correct placement of adjective (in front of *kitten*)
    c) *The [frightening] kitten hid beneath the bed.
       The frightened   kitten hid beneath the bed.
       Explanation: The kitten is receiving the fright, not causing it. Therefore, the ED_2 adjective must be used.

10. a) *This friend of mine is very [old] [*old* = "friends for a long time"].
    b) correct placement of adjective (after a linking verb)
    c) *This friend of mine is very [old].
       This is a very old friend of mine.
       Explanation: The adjective *old* only means "friends for a long time" as an attributive adjective. As a
       predicate adjective, it can only mean "aged." The sentence must therefore be changed to
       retain the intended meaning.

11.6

1. A young man who was wearing a gray jogging suit stole the beautiful new bicycle that I just bought.
2. The modern electric train which Germany has just developed went through a long dark tunnel that comes out on
    the Italian side of the Alps.
3. The old Persian cat that we have had for many years caught a tiny frightened mouse with beady red eyes.
4. My friend George, who is very careful with his money, had forgotten the black leather wallet which his mother had
    given him for his birthday.
5. The new President of the U.S., who is very popular now, has signed a treaty that will improve the economic rela-
    tions between our two countries.
6. That tall man who is walking up the stairs with the folded newspaper looks like my father.
7. The fascinating film at the Paramount Theater is about a crazy guy who falls in love with a girl who used to be his
    secretary.
8. The thing that I want most is a gold watch with a calendar.
9. Pharmaceutical experts at various medical schools disagree with the Polish scientist who invented the compound.
10. My classmate Mohammad, who comes from Saudi Arabia, is studying electrical engineering, an important subject.

11.7

1. The actor <u>who</u> played Dracula has had trouble finding other roles.
2. The thing <u>that</u> I like about June is her sense of humor.
3. The person with <u>whom</u> you should talk is the vice president.
4. The state <u>whose</u> economy was most affected by the storm was Florida.
5. The city <u>that/which</u> we really enjoyed was Sarajevo.
6. My uncle works with a woman <u>who</u> spent seven years in Zimbabwe.
7. It would be impossible to live on a planet <u>whose</u> atmosphere had no oxygen.
8. This wine was prepared by a method <u>that/which</u> has been used for centuries.
9. That doctor is not a man in <u>whom</u> I have a great deal of confidence.
10. Heloise had to sell the ring <u>that/which</u> her mother had given her.

11.8

1. The boy <u>who delivers the paper</u> is only ten years old.
2. The dog <u>that bit the mailman</u> was taken to the pound.
3. The plane <u>that/which crashed</u> was trying to land at JFK Airport.
4. The bank <u>that/which gave us a loan</u> was robbed last night.
5. The girl <u>who lost her mother last week</u> will live with her older sister.

11.9

1. The <u>airline</u> offered the <u>passengers</u> **that had waited the longest** a free <u>ticket</u>.
2. <u>People</u> **who smoke cigarettes** can cause <u>nonsmokers</u> to get <u>cancer</u>.
3. The <u>hotel</u> gave the irate <u>guests</u> a <u>room</u> **which had no bathroom**.
4. The <u>dog</u> was lying next to a <u>bird</u> **whose feathers were saturated with oil**.
5. The <u>play</u> **that disturbed me the most** was about a <u>man</u> and his <u>father</u> in a <u>prison camp</u>.

11.10

1. The student <u>whose grades improve the most</u> will win a trip to Disneyland.
2. The trees <u>whose roots have reached the water table</u> will not suffer during the drought.
3. The woman <u>whose friend was bitten by a poisonous snake</u> ran to the next village for help.
4. A truck <u>whose brakes fail on this hill</u> should use the runaway truck ramp.
5. A neighbor <u>whose dog barks all night</u> is not a good neighbor.

11.11

1. The lady <u>whose dress Betty made</u> was not satisfied.
2. The planet <u>whose surface mankind first landed on</u> is the moon.
3. A fawn <u>whose mother a hunter has killed</u> has little chance of survival.
4. The virus <u>whose structure the computer engineers were searching for</u> continued to destroy programs.
5. People <u>whose lives a government cannot protect</u> deserve a new government.

11.12

1. The classes <u>which we took last semester</u> were really interesting.
2. Some of the astronauts<u> whom the U.S. sent to the moon</u> became public figures.
3. The film <u>which Helen most enjoyed</u> is *Europa, Europa*.
4. The villagers <u>whom/that the army tortured</u> can hardly be expected to support the government.
5. The volcano <u>whose eruption scientists had predicted</u> spewed hot ashes up to 25 miles away.

11.13

1. The <u>agreement</u> **which the government made** allowed loaded <u>trucks</u> to be carried on <u>trains</u>.
2. The <u>babysitter</u> told the <u>children</u> **whom she was preparing for bed** a <u>story</u>.
3. The <u>president</u> nominated a <u>woman</u> **whose accomplishments the nation admired**.
4. The <u>journalist</u> found several <u>errors</u> in the <u>article</u> **that the editor had rejected**.
5. The <u>bicycle</u> **whose tires we replaced** should only be ridden on smooth <u>roads</u>.

11.14

1. The country <u>on which the UN depends for the largest proportion of its operating expenses</u> is the United States.
2. Midnight was the time <u>at which Cinderella's carriage turned back into a pumpkin</u>.
3. This is a situation <u>in which you should not interfere</u>.
4. The printer is the device <u>with which the company has had the most problems</u>.
5. Romania is the central European nation <u>about which Monica knows a great deal</u>.

11.15 (many possible answers)

1. The <u>woman</u> **whom I met on the train** had very little money.
2. A stranger bought the <u>person</u> **who was begging in the street** a loaf of bread.
3. Some boys torture <u>insects</u> **that cannot possibly harm them**.
4. Joy's grandfather left her a cottage in a <u>village</u> **that is situated right by the sea**.
5. The doctor was taking a nap when the <u>nurse</u> **who had been his constant companion** called him.

11.16

1. The person whom my cousin married was from a poor family. [IMP: The persons that other relatives married were from richer families.]
2. Margaret Thatcher, who used to be the Prime Minister of Great Britain, was the first woman to hold that office.
3. Buses, which usually have no dining facilities, are an uncomfortable way to travel long distances.
4. The planets which have rings orbit in the outer Solar System. [IMP: Only some, not all, of the planets have rings.]
5. Few creatures are stronger than the ant, which can carry many times its body weight.
6. The European Common Market, which unites most of the countries of Europe into a single economic block, has had a variety of difficulties to overcome.
7. Flying saucers, for which there has never been any material evidence, still excite the imaginations of modern earth-lings.
8. Many people do not eat sufficient dietary fiber, which is thought to reduce the risk of colon cancer.
9. The Maya, whose settlements date back to 9000 B.C., first appeared on the shores of Belize.
10. The energy which fires the Sun is being harnessed in the laboratory as fusion power. [IMP: Only the Sun's energy, not the energy from other sources, is meant, so it must be defined.]

11.17

1. The magazine <u>Jacob is reading</u> contains a story about his sister.
2. A vegetable **that** has seeds is technically a fruit. [EXP: not a P-form adjective clause]
3. The young couple did not like the house <u>the realtors showed them</u>.
4. The political appointees <u>to **whom** the President</u> referred are becoming increasingly nervous. [EXP: cannot reduce an adjective clause with a fronted preposition]
5. One species **whose** <u>existence is seriously threatened</u> is the cheetah. [EXP: cannot reduce any adjective clause with *whose*]
6. The ferry, **which** <u>is always on time</u>, runs between Naples and Palermo. [EXP: not a P-form adjective clause]
7. A television station gave a man <u>I work with</u> a free ticket to Hawaii.
8. Some men are intimidated by a woman **who** <u>knows her own strength</u>. [EXP: not a P-form adjective clause]
9. The room <u>the guest complained about</u> was directly above the kitchen.
10. John's grandmother, <u>whom he loved with all his heart</u>, came from an aristocratic family. [EXP: cannot reduce P-form nondefining adjective clauses]

11.18

1. The person <u>teaching this ESL class</u> is a graduate student in Applied Linguistics.
2. We have learned more about the planets <u>in the Solar System</u> than in any other decade in history.
3. Children **who** <u>are overweight</u> are often ostracized. [EXP: cannot reduce an S-form adjective clause unless it is followed by $VERB_{ed_2}$, $VERB_{ing}$ or a preposition]
4. Cats <u>spayed at six months of age</u> appear to be least harmed by the process.
5. Type A personalities are associated with men and women **who** <u>are very competitive</u>. [EXP: cannot reduce an S-form adjective clause unless it is followed by $VERB_{ed_2}$, $VERB_{ing}$ or a preposition]

11.19

1. a. He was a <u>ruined man</u>, an individual whose life would be forever changed.
   b. Yesterday, he was a <u>man ruined</u>. Today, he's on top of the world.
2. a. After the explosion, the <u>gas expelled</u> will be collected and analyzed.
   b. <u>Expelled students</u> are not allowed to register for new classes.
3. a. The <u>courses listed</u> in the Spring schedule are subject to change.
   b. The <u>listed ingredients</u> in this can of peaches include sugar and water.
4. a. Venus is one of the <u>visible planets</u> in the night sky.
   b. Venus was the only <u>planet visible</u> that cloudy night.
5. a. All substances melt at a <u>given temperature</u>.
   b. The only <u>information given</u> was that a tornado might touch down sometime during the night.

11.20

1. Dr. R.D. Smith, <u>an Associate Professor of Biology</u>, introduced his new graduate assistant.
2. Berlin, <u>the new capital of Germany</u>, is 1078 air miles brom Instanbul.
3. The magma, <u>a body of molten rock</u>, is forced up through the vent to the volcanic crater.
4. Rudolf Nureyev, <u>the first Russian ballet dancer to defect to the West</u>, never danced with Mikhail Baryshnikov.
5. Ruth Bader Ginsburg, <u>the second woman on the U.S. Supreme Court</u>, has joined Sandra Day O'Connor on the bench.

11.21

1. Gerald cannot stand his uncle, **who** <u>is well-meaning but selfish</u>. [EXP: cannot reduce an S-form adjective clause unless it is followed by $VERB_{ed_2}$, $VERB_{ing}$ or a preposition]
2. The clouds, <u>moving in from the west</u>, will bring us much-needed rain.
3. The shaman, **whose** <u>advice was taken very seriously by every member of the community</u>, could not prevent the oil companies from drilling on tribal land. [EXP: cannot reduce any adjective clause with *whose*]
4. The old bull, <u>in a field by himself</u>, is not particularly friendly to humans.
5. Deciduous trees, **which** <u>require abundant water,</u> lose their autumn leaves early in times of drought. [EXP: cannot reduce an S-form adjective clause unless it contains a form of *be*]

11.22

1. The book <u>I am currently reading</u> takes place in South Africa.
2. Dr. Smith, <u>a physician at Valley Medical Center,</u> was nominated for a Nobel Prize.
3. A house **which** <u>is painted</u> is more valuable than one **which** <u>is not</u>. [EXP: only $VERB_{ed_2}$ forms allow reduction, not $VERB_{ed_2}$-derived adjectives, and we cannot reduce an S-form adjective clause unless it is followed by $VERB_{ed_2}$, $VERB_{ing}$ or a preposition]
4. Tomatoes <u>grown in Fresno</u> are larger than those grown in Oakland.
5. The box <u>in the garage</u> needs to be taken to the dump.
6. The physics professor, **whom** <u>Michael cannot stand</u>, required a thirty-page research report. [EXP: cannot reduce P-form nondefining adjective clauses]
7. The high density of stars in the Milky Way, **which** <u>can be seen as a faint path across the sky</u>, results from looking along the plane of the galaxy. [EXP: reduction not allowed if a modal is present]
8. The telephone, <u>invented by Alexander Graham Bell</u>, has brought the world together.
9. Stars **which** <u>are red</u> are older than stars **which** <u>are blue</u>. [EXP: cannot reduce an S-form adjective clause unless it is followed by $VERB_{ed_2}$, $VERB_{ing}$, or a preposition]
10. A turtle, <u>found dead on the beach</u>, was covered with sticky oil.

11.23

1. a) *John doesn't like [the whom he met girl].
   b) correct category of relative pronoun (whom = person)
   correct grammatical form of relative pronoun (whom = P-form)
   correct defining/nondefining punctuation (defining + no commas)
   Derivation: John doesn't like the girl. + He met the girl.
           he met <u>whom</u>
           <u>whom</u> he met
       John doesn't like the girl <u>whom he met</u>.
   c) *John doesn't like [the whom he met girl].
   John doesn't like the girl whom he met.
   Explanation: An adjective clause must be placed directly after the head noun it modifies.

2. a) *The man [whom] told you that story is a liar.
   b) correct category of relative pronoun (*whom* = person)
      correct placement of adjective clause (directly after the head noun *man*)
      correct defining/nondefining punctuation (defining + no commas)
      Derivation: The man is a liar. + The man told you that story.
                                who told you that story
      The man who told you that story is a liar.
   c) *The man [whom] told you that story is a liar.
      The man who told you that story is a liar.
      Explanation: An S-form adjective clause requires *who*, not *whom*.

3 a) *John rides a motorcycle [, who lives in Los Angeles].
   b) correct category of relative pronoun (*who* = person)
      correct grammatical form of relative pronoun (*who* = S-form)
      correct defining/nondefining punctuation (nondefining + commas)
      Derivation: John rides a motorcycle. + John lives in Los Angeles.
                                      who lives in Los Angeles
      John, who lives in Los Angeles, rides a motorcycle.
   c) *John rides a motorcycle [, who lives in Los Angeles]
      John, who lives in Los Angeles, rides a motorcycle.
      Explanation: An adjective clause must be placed directly after the head noun it modifies.

4. a) *Mary can't find the room in [that] she stayed.
   b) correct category of relative pronoun (*that*= thing)
      correct placement of adjective clause (after the head noun *room)*
      correct placement of preposition (in front of WH-relative pronoun in formal contexts)
      correct defining/nondefining punctuation (defining + no commas)
      Derivation: Mary can't find the room. + She stayed in the room.
                              she stayed in which
                              which she stayed in
                              in which she stayed
      Mary can't find the room in which she stayed.
   c) *Mary can't find the room in [that] she stayed.
      Mary can't find the room in which she stayed.
      Explanation: Fronted prepositions always require a WH-relative pronoun, never *that*.

5. a) *The books, [they bought at a library sale], are all paperbacks.
   b) correct placement of adjective clause (directly after the head noun *books)*
      correct possible reduction form (remove relative pronoun in P-form reduction)
      correct defining/nondefining punctuation (nondefining + commas)
      Derivation: The books are all paperbacks. + They bought the books at a library sale.
                                    they bought which at a library sale
                                    which they bought at a library sale
      The books, which they bought at a library sale, are all paperbacks.
   c) *The books, [they bought at a library sale],   are all paperbacks.
      The books, which they bought at a library sale, are all paperbacks.
      Explanation: A P-form nondefining adjective clause cannot be reduced.

6. a) *The CIA, [that] has its headquarters in Washington D.C., is feared by many people.
   b) correct placement of adjective clause (directly after the head noun *CIA)*
      correct defining/nondefining punctuation (nondefining + commas)
      Derivation: The CIA is feared by many people. + The CIA has its headquarters in Washington D.C.
                                          which has its headquarters in Washington D.C.
      The CIA, which has its headquarters in Washington D.C., is feared by many people.
   c) *The CIA, [that] has its headquarters in Washington D.C., is feared by many people.
      The CIA, which has its headquarters in Washington D.C., is feared by many people.
      Explanation: A nondefining adjective clause always requires a WH-relative pronoun.

7. a) *The man with [who] I travelled to Atlanta was an old friend.
   b) correct relative pronoun (*who* = person)
      correct placement of adjective clause (directly after the head noun *man*)
      correct placement of preposition (in front of WH-relative pronoun in formal contexts)
      correct defining/nondefining punctuation (defining + no commas)
      Derivation: The man was an old friend. + I travelled to Atlanta with an old friend.

      I travelled to Atlanta with <u>whom</u>
      <u>whom</u> I travelled to Atlanta with
      <u>with</u> whom I travelled to Atlanta
      The man with whom I travelled to Atlanta was an old friend.
   c) *The man with [who] I travelled to Atlanta was an old friend.
      The man with whom I travelled to Atlanta was an old friend.
      Explanation: The P-form WH-relative pronoun is always required after a preposition.

8. a) *Jan's mother who was born in Detroit came to California in 1941.
   b) correct category of relative pronoun (*who* = person)
      correct grammatical form of relative pronoun (*who* = S-form)
      correct placement of adjective clause (directly after the head noun *mother*)
      correct defining/nondefining punctuation (defining + no commas)
      Derivation: Jan's mother came to California in 1941. + Jan's mother was born in Detroit.

      <u>who</u> was born in Detroit
      Jan's mother, <u>who was born in Detroit</u>, came to California in 1941.
   c) *Jan's mother who was born in Detroit came to California in 1941.
      Jan's mother, who was born in Detroit, came to California in 1941.

      Explanation: A single individual (*Jan's mother*) requires a nondefining adjective clause.

9. a) *The student [is sitting in your office] wants to talk to you.
   b) correct placement of adjective clause (directly after the head noun *student*)
      correct defining/nondefining punctuation (defining + no commas)
      Derivation: The student wants to talk to you. + The student is sitting in your office.

      <u>who</u> is sitting in your office
      sitting in your office
      The student <u>sitting in your office</u> wants to talk to you.
   c) *The student [is sitting in your office] wants to talk to you.
      The student sitting in your office wants to talk to you.
      Explanation: S-form reduction requires the removal of *be* as well as the relative pronoun.

10. a) *John's girlfriend, [he plans to marry someday], has a Mercedes.
    b) correct placement of adjective clause (directly after the head noun *girlfriend*)
       correct possible reduction form (remove relative pronoun in P-form reduction)
       correct defining/nondefining punctuation (nondefining + commas)
       Derivation: John's girlfriend has a Mercedes.+ He plans to marry John's girlfriend someday.

       he plans to marry <u>whom</u> someday
       <u>whom</u> he plans to marry someday
       John's girlfriend, <u>whom he plans to marry someday</u>, has a Mercedes.
    c) *John's girlfriend,   [he plans to marry someday], has a Mercedes.
       John's girlfriend, whom he plans to marry someday,   has a Mercedes.
       Explanation: A nondefining P-form adjective clause cannot be reduced.

11. a) *The computer George wants [it] costs over $2000.
    b) correct placement of adjective clause (directly after the head noun *computer*)
       correct reduction form (remove relative pronoun in P-form reduction)
       correct defining/nondefining punctuation (defining + no commas)
       Derivation: The computer costs over $2000. + George wants the computer.

       George wants <u>which</u>
       <u>which</u> George wants
       George wants
       The computer <u>George wants</u> costs over $2000.
    c) *The computer George wants [it] costs over $2000.
       The computer George wants   costs over $2000.
       Explanation: The pronoun *it* was the NP that was replaced by the relative pronoun *that* in constructing the adjective clause. Such so-called "resumptive pronouns" are not correct in English, though they are required in certain languages, e.g., Arabic.

12. a) *A man [, who is wealthy,] is not neccessarily happy.
    b) correct category of relative pronoun *(who* = person)
       correct grammatical form of relative pronoun *(who* = S-form)
       correct placement of adjective clause (directly after the head noun *man*)
       Derivation: A man is not neccessarily happy. + A man is wealthy.
                                    <u>who</u> is wealthy
                       A man <u>who is wealthy</u> is not neccessarily happy.
    c) *A man [, who is wealthy,] is not neccessarily happy.
       A man who is wealthy   is not neccessarily happy.
       Explanation: The head noun *man* requires a defining adjective clause in this case to differentiate him
                    from other men. Therefore, no commas are required.

13. a) *The class [Alice really likes which] is philosophy.
    b) correct category of relative pronoun *(which* = thing)
       correct placement of adjective clause (directly after the head noun *class*)
       correct defining/nondefining punctuation (defining + no commas)
       Derivation: The class is philosophy. + Alice really likes the class.
                                    Alice really likes <u>which</u>
                                    <u>which</u> Alice really likes
                   The class <u>which Alice really likes</u> is philosophy.

    c) *The class [Alice really likes which] is philosophy.
       The class which Alice really likes   is philosophy.
       Explanation: In constructing a P-form adjective clause, the relative pronoun must always be moved to
                    the front of the clause before it is inserted in the main sentence. (The clause could also
                    haved been reduced to *Alice really likes.*)

14. a) *The student [helped me to correct the exams] receives financial aid.
    b) correct placement of adjective clause (directly after the head noun *student*)
       correct defining/nondefining punctuation (defining + no commas)

       Derivation: The student receives financial aid. + The student helped me to correct the exams.
                                    <u>who</u> helped me to correct the exams
                       The student <u>who helped me to correct the exams</u> receives financial aid.
    c) *The student [helped me to correct the exams]   receives financial aid.
       The student who helped me to correct the exams receives financial aid.
       Explanation: S-form adjective clauses can only be reduced if a form of *be* is present. (Or: P-form
                    reduction cannot be applied to an S-form adjective clause.)

15. a) *The boy stole a sandwich [who lives next door].
    b) correct category of relative pronoun *(who* = person)
       correct grammatical form of relative pronoun *(who* = S-form)
       correct defining/nondefining punctuation (defining + no commas)
       Derivation: The boy stole a sandwich. + The boy lives next door.
                                    <u>who</u> lives next door
                       The boy <u>who lives next door</u> stole a sandwich.

    c) *The boy stole a sandwich [who lives next door].
       The boy who lives next door stole a sandwich.
       Explanation: An adjective clause must be placed directly after the head noun it modifies.

Chapter 12

12.1

1. Leontyne Price sang the part of Aida <u>beautifully</u>.
2. The satellite signal was finally directed <u>earthwards</u> by the computers at Mission Control.
3. Ralph doesn't have much experience <u>educationwise</u>, but he's a wizard at fixing electronic instruments.
4. Rosetta answered the telephone somewhat <u>guardedly</u> for several weeks after the man who had been harassing her
   was apprehended.
5. The trend has always been for people to move to the west, but now they seem to be heading <u>eastwards</u> again.

12.2

1. [ways and means] Jake was treated <u>abusively</u> as a child.
2. [point of view] <u>Technically</u>, Washburn won the match.
3. [intensification] The room must be cleaned <u>thoroughly</u> before you leave.
4. [ways and means] The stage can be raised <u>hydraulically</u>.
5. [intensification] The army <u>nearly</u> forced me to quit.
6. [ways and means] The parachute opens <u>automatically</u>.
7. [intensification] <u>Frankly</u>, I don't care where you go.
8. [point of view/ways and means] The northern part of the city is <u>ethnically</u> quite varied.
9. [ways and means] Robin has always dressed rather <u>carelessly</u>.
10. [point of view/ways and means] These two plays differ <u>stylistically</u>.

12.3

1. [point in time] The hospital was ordered to close <u>immediately</u>.
2. [duration] The bridge has been closed <u>permanently</u>.
3. [frequency] We watch the news <u>nightly</u>.
4. [point in time] <u>Previously</u>, Alice had been married to a lawyer.
5. [duration] The children are hungry <u>constantly</u>.
6. [point in time] The wine cellar is <u>presently</u> taking orders for next year's vintage.
7. [duration] The President spoke <u>briefly</u> with reporters.
8. [frequency] This bus is <u>invariably</u> late.
9. [frequency] My uncle comes to visit us <u>occasionally</u>.
10. [point in time] Alfreda <u>recently</u> lost her glasses.

12.4

1. Although the storm was <u>very</u> frightening, the house was not harmed.
2. The satellite failed to communicate because the signal wasn't strong <u>enough</u>.
3. The Charleston was <u>quite</u> popular in the 1920s.
4. Dr. Evans is <u>amazingly</u> calm under pressure, isn't he?
5. Algebra isn't <u>that</u> difficult if you put your mind to it.

12.5

1. <u>Almost</u> three quarters of the planet's fresh water lies in the Antarctic Icecap.
2. The weight was <u>well</u> within the tolerance limit of the elevator.
3. The Riyadh Airport is <u>quite</u> a piece of architecture.
4. The rent on the coast is <u>over</u> twice the rent in the interior.
5. Ruth lives <u>just</u> outside the city limits.

12.6

1. [ways and means] The sidewinder rattlesnake moves <u>in a curious fashion</u>.
2. [point of view] The ending of the film is unconvincing <u>from a psychological point of view</u>.
3. [intensification] <u>Of course</u>, the boy will be expelled from school.
4. [ways and means] It's over twenty miles <u>by road</u> to the next hostel.
5. [ways and means] The thieves broke into the bank <u>by means of a laser gun</u>.
6. [intensification] The sister is better than the brother <u>in all respects</u>.
7. [point of view] The family has little influence <u>with respect to education</u>.
8. [ways and means] Susan wrote <u>like a Victorian novelist</u>.
9. [point of view] <u>As to politics</u>, my husband never tells me a thing.
10. [intensification] The two countries still disagree <u>to some extent</u>.

12.7

1a. [location] The patio is <u>behind the house</u>.
  b. [direction] The sun moved <u>behind a cloud</u>.
2a. [direction] The little girl wandered <u>through the park</u>.
  b. [location] The tunnel was built <u>through the mountains</u>.

3a. [location] There's a hole <u>in your sweater</u>.
  b. [direction] Put the cat <u>in the garage</u>.
4a. [direction] The pelican flew <u>above the water</u>.
  b. [location] The Jimsons live in the apartment <u>above the manager</u>.
5a. [location] The oil derrick is situated <u>off the coast</u>.
  b. [direction] The boat drifted <u>off course</u>.

12.8

1. [point in time] A juggler can keep several rings, clubs and hoops in the air <u>at the same time</u>.
2. [frequency] I like a pizza <u>from time to time</u>.
3. [duration] Karen's grandfather slept <u>during the performance</u>.
4. [frequency] The mail is only delivered <u>on Fridays</u>.
5. [point in time] World War II ended <u>in 1945</u>.
6. [duration] The strange stones had been there <u>since time immemorial</u>.
7. [point in time] Rita didn't like the novel very much <u>at the beginning</u>.
8. [duration] The storm lasted <u>for several hours</u>.
9. [frequency] The rent is to be paid <u>by the week</u>.
10. [point in time] <u>Before you move in</u>, we have to establish a few ground rules.

12.9

1. Nancy prefers to vacation <u>where</u> the rich and famous congregate.
2. The young chess player wasn't very clever <u>as</u> far as psychology was concerned.
3. The people in this religious order live <u>wherever</u> the archbishop tells them to live.
4. <u>If</u> you ask the local residents, there'll be no peace until that dam is removed.
5. The Red Cross goes <u>wherever</u> people are suffering.

12.10 (sometimes several possible answers; preferred answer in boldface)

1. <u>After/**as**/before/once/until/when/whenever</u> the flag was raised into the air, the fireworks lit the sky behind it.
2. The shuttle will not be launched <u>before/**until**</u> all the safety systems are in good working order.
3. Steven lived in Los Angeles <u>when</u> he was a boy.
4. Dimitri hasn't been back to Russia <u>since</u> his parents left in 1948.
5. Ants come into the house <u>once/when/**whenever**</u> there is too little water outside.
6. President Kennedy was shot <u>before</u> he completed his Dallas motorcade.
7. <u>After/**once**/when/whenever</u> the pipeline was repaired, the danger of explosion diminished.
8. The second earthquake occurred <u>as/when/**while**</u> the people were clearing the rubble from the first.
9. The hostilities began <u>**after**/before/once/when</u> the nations had declared independence.
10. Jill's father works <u>until</u> 10 or 11 P.M. every night.

12.11

1. [ways and means] Cynthia would like to cook <u>the way her mother did</u>.
2. [intensification] It is a good idea to walk <u>a little bit</u> after a meal.
3. [point of view] <u>The way the workers see it</u>, this is only a temporary abode.
4. [intensification] Tina used to date <u>a great deal</u> before she met her husband.
5. [ways and means] If you don't send the package <u>air mail</u>, it will never get there in time.

12.12

1. [frequency] The moon is full <u>twelve times a year</u>.
2. [duration] Jackie's father was miserable <u>the whole evening</u>.
3. [duration] The lumber mill is open <u>Monday to Friday</u>.
4. [point in time] Charlie's birthday will be celebrated <u>tomorrow</u>.
5. [frequency] The restaurant is closed <u>every other Monday</u>.
6. [point in time] Oil was discovered <u>the following year</u>.
7. [duration] The pilot has only been flying <u>a short time</u>.
8. [point in time] There have been two robberies on my block <u>this week</u>.
9. [frequency] Sam has climbed this rock face <u>many times</u>.
10. [point in time] The taxi was here just <u>a minute ago</u>.

12.13

1. a) *[On occasionally], the ladies like to play bingo at the local church.
   b) correct function (time)
       correct sentence position (initial)
   c) *[On occasionally], the ladies like to play bingo at the local church.
       On occasion,   the ladies like to play bingo at the local church.
       Occasionally,   the ladies like to play bingo at the local church.
       Explanation: The time prepositional phrase is *on occasion*; the time adverbial is *occasionally*. The student has apparently confused the two expressions and created a prepositional phrase that does not exist in English.

2. a) *The students put the puppy [at 3 o'clock].
   b) correct adverbial type (prepositional phrase)
       correct sentence position (final)
       correct possible form (*at 3 o'clock*)
   c) *The students put the puppy [at 3 o'clock].
       The students put the puppy in the house. [or any other place prepositional phrase]
       Explanation: A verb like *put* requires a place prepositional phrase, not a time prepositional phrase.

3. a) *This country [needs really] an ocean port.
   b) correct adverbial type (adverb)
       correct function (manner)
       correct possible form (*really*)
   c) *This country [needs really] an ocean port.
       This country really needs   an ocean port.
       Explanation: Manner adverbs must precede the main verb, not follow it.

4. a) *Weather[wards], the temperatures will drop by tomorrow evening.
   b) correct adverbial type (adverb)
       correct function (manner)
       correct sentence position (initial)
   c) *Weather[wards], the temperatures will drop by tomorrow evening.
       Weatherwise,   the temperatures will drop by tomorrow evening.
       Explanation: The derivational suffix for changing nouns into adverbs is *-wise*. The suffix *-wards* is only for prepositions or prepositional noun phrases.

5. a) *In the summertime, the sheep are allowed to wander [to] wherever they like.
   b) correct function (place)
       correct sentence position (final)
   c) *In the summertime, the sheep are allowed to wander [to] wherever they like.
       In the summertime, the sheep are allowed to wander   wherever they like.
       Explanation: Adverbial clauses cannot be preceded with a preposition. Furthermore, the word *where* always implies a preposition of place.

6. a) *[Monthly], the magazine is delivered to his doorstep.
   b) correct adverbial type (time)
       correct function (time)
       correct possible form (*monthly*)
   c) *[Monthly], the magazine is delivered to his doorstep.
               The magazine is delivered to his doorstep monthly.
       Explanation: A time frequency adverb like *monthly* can only take sentence-final position.

7. a) *The children didn't sleep very well [at] last night.
   b) correct function (time)
       correct sentence position (final)
   c) *The children didn't sleep very well [at] last night.
       The children didn't sleep very well   last night.
       Explanation: Prepositional noun phrases do not require a preposition.

8. a) *[A great deal], the keeper has a tendency to tease the animals.
   b) correct adverbial type (prepositional noun phrase)
       correct function (manner)
       correct possible form (*a great deal*)

c) *[A great deal], the keeper has a tendency to tease the animals.
    The keeper has a tendency to tease the animals a great deal.
    Explanation: Intensifying manner prepositional noun phrases can only be sentence-final.

9. a) *The beaver cut down [with its teeth] a few trees.
   b) correct function (time)
      correct sentence position (initial)
   c) *The beaver cut down [with its teeth] a few trees.
      The beaver cut down   a few trees with its teeth.
      Explanation: Ways and means manner prepositional phrases must be either sentence-initial or sentence-final.

10. a) *Hortensia likes to dress [an aristocratic manner].
    b) correct function (manner)
       correct sentence position (final)
    c) *Hortensia likes to dress [an aristocratic manner].
       Hortensia likes to dress in an aristocratic manner.
       Explanation: The object of the preposition (*manner*) has not evolved into a prepositional noun phrase. Therefore, it requires a preposition.

Chapter 13

13.1

1. The plane leaves <u>at</u> 2:45 P.M.
2. What street does the President live <u>on</u>?
3. The pot-bellied pig is asleep <u>in</u> father's favorite armchair.
4. I want you to finish every drop of soup <u>in</u> your bowl.
5. When you said you wanted to try a new manufacturing process, did you have anything specific <u>in</u> mind?
6. Cinderella's carriage turned back into a pumpkin <u>at</u> midnight.
7. World War II ended <u>in</u> 1945.
8. There was a strange woman <u>on</u> the bus yesterday.
9. The Robertson family is going to have a picnic <u>on</u> July 4.
10. Cathy's purse was stolen while she was <u>at</u> the post office.
11. What does your baby have <u>in</u> his mouth?
12. Who spilled coffee <u>on</u> the couch?
13. This restaurant is closed <u>on</u> Mondays.
14. Two million gallons of crude oil is now floating <u>on</u> the Indian Ocean.
15. Who left a bicycle <u>in</u> the driveway?
16. Don't ask me now! I have a lot of things <u>on</u> my mind!
17. Please look up these words <u>in</u> the dictionary.
18. What did you do <u>at</u> school on Friday?
19. Travelers can rent a car <u>at</u> the airport.
20. How many professors are there <u>on</u> the faculty <u>in</u> your department?
21. We have a beautiful house <u>in</u> the country.
22. It rarely snows here <u>in</u> winter.
23. Her husband always goes to Italy <u>in</u> September.
24. Since it will be very cold tonight, you should put an extra blanket <u>on</u> your bed.
25. Susie couldn't have any dessert until she had finished everything <u>on</u> her plate.
26. There's a hole <u>in</u> his sweater!
27. A bird <u>in</u> the hand is worth two in the bush.
28. How many people live <u>in</u> Calcutta?
29. We met a really interesting woman <u>on</u> the plane from Paris.
30. My brother lives <u>at</u> 450 Sutter Street in San Francisco.
31. He doesn't know how many countries there are <u>in</u> the Western Hemisphere.
32. The service station is <u>at/on</u> the corner of Main Street and Columbus Avenue.
33. Do cats get lonely <u>at</u> night?
34. That plant would look pretty <u>in</u> the corner of the dining room.
35. The words <u>on</u> this page are a little difficult to read.

36. She's an expert <u>in</u> biochemistry.
37. Alex always rides <u>on</u> the roller coasters at amusement parks.
38. The bookseller took great joy <u>in</u> leafing through ancient volumes.
39. There was a lot of blood <u>on</u> the road after the accident.
40. How many people are living <u>in/at</u> your house now?
41. The teacher never let the students write <u>on</u> the blackboard.
42. The old shaman lived <u>at</u> the top of the hill.
43. What's <u>on</u> the menu today?
44. What's <u>on</u> T.V. tonight?
45. Why are you <u>in</u> such a bad mood?
46. Cuba is slightly larger than New Zealand <u>in</u> area.
47. She planted a lot of daffodils <u>in</u> her garden.
48. If you don't want it, throw it <u>in/on</u> the fire (<u>in</u> a fireplace; <u>on</u> a bonfire)
49. The duchess is leaving <u>at</u> midnight.
50. He was a good leader <u>in</u> many ways.

13.2

1. Gofredo has been a taxi driver <u>since</u> he came to New York in 1974.
2. Nigeria has been independent <u>for</u> more than a quarter of a century.
3. The farmers ploughed the fields <u>from</u> dawn <u>to/until</u> dusk.
4. The dam must be completed <u>by</u> the end of September, well before the rains begin.
5. The eclipse of the sun will not be visible <u>until</u> 4:07 P.M.
6. The shop was open every day <u>from</u> 10 A.M. <u>until</u> all the bagels had been sold.
7. Donated organs must be transplanted <u>within</u> hours of their removal.
8. The squeaking of the piano pedals was audible <u>throughout</u> the entire recital.
9. The life span of a horse is <u>between/from</u> twenty <u>and/to</u> twenty-five years.
10. The stores are only open <u>from/between</u> 3 P.M. <u>to/and</u> 7 or 8 in the evening.
11. The best time to visit the Butchart Gardens is <u>during</u> the month of April.
12. Rented videotapes must be returned <u>within</u> forty-eight hours.
13. Leticia had not seen her grandfather <u>since</u> her brother's baptism in Oaxaca.
14. Women should not drink or smoke <u>during</u> pregnancy.
15. The reduced plane fares are only valid <u>between/from</u> New Year's Day <u>and/to</u> March 15.

13.3 (alternative answers are possible for prepositions that are similar in meaning)

1. An island is <u>surrounded by</u> water.
2. Portugal lies <u>next to</u> Spain on the Iberian peninsula.
3. During an eclipse, the sun is positioned <u>behind</u> the moon.
4. Reef diving is usually best <u>near/not far from</u> the shore.
5. The boy stood <u>beside</u> his mother in the photograph.
6. The onlookers formed a circle <u>around</u> the wrestlers.
7. In most cars, the radiator is located <u>in front of</u> the engine.
8. The starving peasants had walked <u>a great distance from</u> their villages to get food and water.
9. Even though the captain had a map, the salvage boat was <u>nowhere near</u> the treasure.
10. The hammock was strung <u>between</u> two palm trees.
11. The mountain cabin is located <u>far from</u> the pollution of cars and factories.
12. The prince was standing <u>among</u> his many relatives in the palace garden.
13. Don't stand too <u>close to</u> the fire or you'll get singed.
14. A walk <u>along</u> the canal is fine on a summer evening.
15. The terrified cowboy pushed a couch <u>against</u> the door to bar entry.
16. The vegetables grown <u>not far from</u> the highway revealed a high lead content.
17. Put the package <u>by</u> the door if I'm not at home.
18. The balloon was lost <u>amid</u> the ash and steam coming out of the volcano.
19. No one should live <u>in the neighborhood of</u> a chemical dump site.

13.4

1. Most plants will not grow <u>beneath</u> redwood trees.
2. They found a stash of money <u>under</u> the floorboards.
3. What's that cow doing <u>on</u> the roof of the barn?
4. In a second, the bees were <u>all over</u> him, even inside his clothing.
5. My office is on the ground floor, while Linda's is three floors <u>above</u> mine.
6. Once the buffalo were <u>inside</u> the corral, the boys went home.
7. <u>Underneath</u> the paint, the restorers found a cherrywood mantelpiece.
8. Flying <u>below</u> the radar scanners requires considerable skill.
9. Hydrogen and helium exist <u>throughout</u> the universe.
10. The red light <u>on top of</u> the building warns aircraft to keep their distance.
11. No points were awarded if the arrow was <u>off</u> the target.
12. The dog had to stay <u>outside</u> because he was all wet.
13. There was once a bridge <u>over</u> the Grand Canyon, but it no longer exists.

13.5

1. The hovercraft moved just <u>above</u> the waves.
2. The snake slithered <u>off</u> a low branch and into the water.
3. Juliette went <u>by</u> the office to pick up her check.
4. No man has traveled <u>beyond</u> the limits of the Solar System.
5. Many people walked <u>by</u> the fruit stand, but no one bought anything.
6. The deer was unable to jump <u>over</u> the stone wall.
7. A coyote was trotting <u>along</u> the road, minding its own business.
8. Although you could not see it, lava was flowing <u>below</u> the surface.
9. The farmer's son ran <u>down</u> (◄━━►) the street to warn the neighbors about the flood.
10. The water had flowed <u>down</u> the stairs to the basement.
11. The girls always walked <u>through</u> the park on the way to school.
12. Several times the crew walked <u>past</u> the stowaway, but no one saw him.
13. Many people are afraid to walk <u>under</u> a ladder.
14. The doctor wrapped a tourniquet <u>(a)round</u> her patient's arm.
15. Salmon swim <u>up</u> (◄━━►) the river of their birth to spawn.
16. The first solo flight <u>across</u> the Atlantic was made by Lindbergh in 1927.
17. The thirsty troops crawled hopelessly <u>toward(s)</u> the oasis.
18. Winter tires are required for driving <u>on</u> snowy or icy roads.
19. The escaped parrot flew straight <u>up</u> to the highest branches.
20. These athletic shoes are <u>from</u> China.
21. Aren't you flying <u>to</u> Barcelona next summer?

13.6

1. How did the guinea pig get <u>out of</u> its cage?
2. The smoke from the summer fires wafted gently <u>across</u> the mountains.
3. The Earth hurtles <u>through</u> space at a velocity of 18.5 miles per second.
4. Light moves at the same speed <u>thoughout</u> the universe.
5. Sylvio put the money <u>into</u> his wallet before he left the automatic teller.
6. The victim sustained burns <u>all over</u> her body.
7. The racquet ball bounced <u>around</u> the court like a wild thing.

13.7

1. Acrobats rarely perform <u>without</u> a net.
2. Would you like bread <u>with</u> your salad?
3. The story describes a character who pays a million dollars <u>for</u> the murder of his wife.
4. The musician played the piano <u>with</u> grace and style.
5. Public speakers have to learn how to address an audience <u>without</u> nervousness.
6. The group traveled down to the bottom of the Grand Canyon <u>by</u> donkey.
7. The campers made the tent waterproof <u>by</u> throwing a piece of plastic over it.
8. The lumberjack first removed the branches <u>with</u> a chain saw.

9. Viruses cannot be seen <u>without</u> a microscope.
10. The rising river was held back <u>with/by</u> sandbags and determination.
11. The tail <u>of</u> the plane had been struck <u>by</u> lightning.
12. Let me tell you the story <u>of</u> my family's emigration to America.
13. After the first siren sounded, the citizens ran <u>for</u> cover.
14. Has your guide ever been rescued <u>by</u> helicopter?
15. <u>By</u> adding chlorine to the water supply, officials hope to meet the national water safety standards.

13.8

Schindler's Poland

a)   <u>On</u> September 1, 1939, Nazi troops invaded Poland. Oskar Schindler followed <u>in</u> their wake,
b)   settling <u>in</u> Krakow <u>with</u> the intention <u>of</u> making a profit <u>on</u> the war. He lost no time. <u>Within</u> three
c)   months <u>of</u> the invasion, he had established a factory that produced mess kits and kitchenware <u>for</u> the
d)   German army. He was quick <u>with</u> a bribe, he dealt <u>in</u> the black market, and made his money <u>by</u>
e)   exploiting the Reich's offer <u>of</u> cheap Jewish labor.

f)   Schindler rescued 1,300 Jews, most <u>of</u> whom worked <u>in</u> his factory, <u>from</u> the Reich's death camps,
g)   which efficiently executed millions <u>of</u> people <u>during</u> the course <u>of</u> the war. He achieved this largely <u>by</u>
h)   bribing Nazi officials, draining his fortune and risking his life <u>in</u> the process.

i)   <u>In</u> the years <u>since</u> the end <u>of</u> World War II, the stage <u>on</u> which Schindler acted has not been
j)   drastically altered. Krakow survived the war largely intact, the only major city <u>in</u> Poland to do so, and
k)   today it is easy to see why the young entrepreneur was taken <u>with</u> the place. Krakow is a beautiful
l)   medieval city <u>with</u> a central square that ranks <u>among</u> the finest <u>in</u> Europe. <u>In</u> the middle <u>of</u> the square
m) <u>in</u> the old city hall is the Sukiennice (The Cloth Hall), <u>in</u> which handicrafts and jewelry are sold <u>from</u>
n)   individual stalls. <u>In</u> Schindler's day, a black market flourished there.

o)   <u>On</u> the eastern side <u>of</u> the square is the magnificent Kosciol Mariacki (St. Mary's Church), finished
p)   <u>in</u> the 15th century, <u>from</u> whose tallest spire a trumpeter performs <u>on</u> the hour, ending his brief
q)   performance <u>on</u> the note <u>at</u> which an ancient predecessor was shot <u>through</u> the throat <u>by</u> an invader's
r)   arrow. It was here Schindler met a group <u>of</u> black market operators <u>in</u> the rear pews <u>of</u> the church.

s)   You cannot help but marvel <u>at</u> the enthusiastically corrupt young German who put his life <u>on</u> the
t)   line <u>for</u> 1,300 strangers <u>at</u> a moment <u>in</u> history when it would have been far safer to see them packed
u)   <u>in</u> cattle cars <u>on</u> their way <u>to</u> becoming cigarette cases, textiles, or ashes fertilizing the Polish
v)   countryside.

a) *on* [Time: date]; *in* [Containment]
b) *in* [Place: city]; *with* [Accompaniment]; *of* [Relation]; *on* [Allied preposition: NOT COVERED]; *within X* of [Time: dura-
      tion]
c) *of* [see *within X of,* line (b)]; *for* [Destination: beneficiary]
d) *with* [*be quick with* = quick to offer: NOT COVERED]; *in* [Containment: metaphorical space]; *by* [Means: instrument]
e) *of* [Relation]
f) *of* [Relation]; *in* [Containment]; *from* [Place: Movement in 2-D (horizontal)]
g) *of* [Relation]; *during* [Time: duration]; *of* [Relation]; *by* [Means: instrument]
h) *in* [Mode]
i) *in* [Time: year]; *since* [Time: starting point]; *of* [Possession]; *on* [Surface]
j) *in* [Place: city]
k) *with* [Allied preposition: NOT COVERED]
l) *with* [accompaniment]; *among* [Place: Horizontal Relation (position)]; *in* [Place: continent]; *in* [Containment]; *of*
      [Possession]
m) *in* [Containment]; *in* [Containment]; *from* [Place: Movement in 2-D (horizontal)]
n) *in* [Time: *day* = time period NOT COVERED]

o) *on* [Surface]; *of* [Possession]

p) *in* [Time: century]; *from* [Place: Movement in 2-D (horizontal)]; *on* [Time: *on the hour* = each hour NOT COVERED]

q) *on* [Place: line (*note* = metaphorical extension of a sound)]; *at* [Time: time (moment)]; *through* [Place: Movement in 3-D (open)]; *by* [Means: agent]

r) *of* [Relation]; *in* [Containment]; *of* [Possession]

s) *at* [Allied preposition: NOT COVERED]; *on* [Line]

t) *for* [Destination: beneficiary]; *at* [Time: time (moment)]; *in* [Containment]

u) *in* [Containment]; *on* [Line]; *to* [Place: Movement in 2-D (horizontal)]

13.9

1. a) *In twenty minutes, the boat will leave [to] New Orleans.
   b) correct PP structure (*to New Orleans*)
      correct PP position (in adverbial slot)
      correct category of object (destination with *New Orleans*)
      correct verb tense (*to* + all tenses)
   c) *In twenty minutes, the boat will leave [to] New Orleans.
      In twenty minutes, the boat will leave for New Orleans.
      Explanation: Destination is shown with *leave* + *for*, not *leave* + *to*.

2. a) *The trolls dwell [the bridge under].
   b) correct function (place)
      correct PP position (in adverbial slot)
      correct category of object (place with *the bridge*)
      correct verb tense (*under* + all tenses)
   c) *The trolls dwell [the bridge under].
      The trolls dwell under the bridge.
      Explanation: A preposition always comes before its object in a prepositional phrase.
      [Note: This is why it is called a <u>pre</u>position.]

3. a) *My daughter must [by 11 P.M. be home].
   b) correct function (time)
      correct PP structure (*by 11 P.M.*)
      correct category of object (time with *11 P.M.*)
      correct verb tense (*by* + modal)
   c) *My daughter must [by 11 P.M. be home].
      My daughter must be home by 11 P.M.
      Explanation: First, an adverbial structure always follows the verb (*be*). Second, the order of adverbials is generally manner-place-time. Thus, time should follow place (*home*).

4. a) *The hotel is open from April [to] the last guest departs.
   b) correct function (time)
      correct PP position (in adverbial slot)
      correct verb tense (*from...to* + no tense restrictions)
   c) *The hotel is open from April [to] the last guest departs.
      The hotel is open from April until the last guest departs.
      Explanation: An adverbial clause showing range requires the preposition *until*, not *to*, which requires a noun phrase.

5. a) *The factory [has manufactured] automobiles during the crisis.
   b) correct function (time)
      correct PP structure (*during the crisis*)
      correct PP position (in adverbial slot)
      correct category of object (duration with *the crisis*)
   c) *The factory [has manufactured] automobiles during the crisis.
      The factory manufactured   automobiles during the crisis.
      Explanation: *During* may not be used with a present perfect verb tense.

6. a) *The mayor [from] the town owns a beauty shop in Salina, Kansas.
   b) correct PP structure (*from the town*)
      correct PP position (after the head noun *mayor* within the NP)
      correct category of object (place   with *the town*)

    c) *The mayor [from] the town owns a beauty shop in Salina, Kansas.
       The mayor of   the town owns a beauty shop in Salina, Kansas.
       Explanation: Possession is shown with the preposition *of*, not *from*. [Note: Tense is irrelevant in a
          prepositional phrase modifying a head noun.]

7. a) *Rosemarie is afraid to travel by [a] plane.
    b) correct function (means)
       correct PP position (in adverbial slot)
       correct category of object (means with *plane*)
       correct verb tense (means *by* + no tense restriction)
    c) *Rosemarie is afraid to travel by [a] plane.
       Rosemarie is afraid to travel by   plane.
       Explanation: Means shown by the preposition *by* requires a single countable noun with the zero article
          (Ø), not *a*.

8. a) *[By termites], the foundation of the house was destroyed.
    b) correct function (means)
       correct PP structure (*by termites*)
       correct category of object (agent with *termites*)
       correct verb tense (agent *by* + passive voice)
    c) *[By termites], the foundation of the house was destroyed.
             The foundation of the house was destroyed by termites.
       Explanation: Agentive *by*-phrases do not normally occur in front of the subject.

9. a) *The health food store is located [in] 2224 Fulton Avenue.
    b) correct function (place)
       correct PP structure (*in* + NP)
       correct PP position (in adverbial slot)
       correct verb tense (place *in* + no tense restrictions)
    c) *The health food store is located [in] 2224 Fulton Avenue.
       The health food store is located at 2224 Fulton Avenue.
       Explanation: A specific building in an address requires the preposition *at*, not *in*, which is for the city or
          country.

10. a) *The wolves [have not been noticed] until a sheep was missing from the flock.
    b) correct function (time)
       correct PP structure (*until* + adverbial clause)
       correct PP position (in adverbial slot)
       correct category of object (starting point with *a sheep was missing from the flock*)
    c) *The wolves [have not been noticed] until a sheep was missing from the flock.
       The wolves were not noticed   until a sheep was missing from the flock.
       Explanation: Not...until as a starting point cannot occur in the present perfect tense.

13.10

1. **S** The heavy weight boxing champion <u>gave up</u> the fight after the second round.
2. **S** Harold was <u>brought up</u> in the country by his grandmother.
3. **N** Theresa <u>came across</u> an old trunk in the attic.
4. **N** It took several days for Raymond to <u>get over</u> his cold.
5. **S** Who <u>crossed out</u> my name on the list of winners?
6. **N** The professor was reluctant to <u>go over</u> the exam a third time.
7. **S** The police cannot <u>figure out</u> how the thief left the house.
8. **S** The children will be <u>picked up</u> at 4:30.
9. **S** William didn't know how to <u>turn off</u> the dishwasher.
10. **N** If you <u>keep on</u> walking in that direction, you'll find the cafe.

13.11

1. **PPV** Someone has to <u>pay for</u> this broken window. [DEF: provide money]
2. **PhV** When is he going to <u>hand in</u> his resignation? [DEF: officially submit]
3. **PhV** The secretary will <u>call up</u> all the members of the committee. [DEF: telephone]
4. **PPV** I'm not sure that the warring factions will <u>consent to</u> the treaty. [DEF: agree to sign]
5. **PPV** Lisa doesn't <u>believe in</u> Santa Claus any more. [DEF: hold as a belief]
6. **PPV** The food you have ordered <u>comes to</u> twelve dollars. [DEF: has a total cost of]
7. **PhV** Would you <u>drop off</u> this letter at the post office for me? [DEF: deliver]
8. **PhV** My husband will <u>pick up</u> the dry cleaning on the way home from work. [DEF: collect]
9. **PhV** The game had to be <u>put off</u> because of the rain. [DEF: postponed]
10. **PhV** If you don't know who it is, <u>hang up</u>. [DEF: put the telephone receiver back on the hook]

13.12

1. Grant knew that he wouldn't <u>get through with</u> his work until after midnight. [DEF: finish]
2. Paula is <u>getting behind in</u> her assignments. [DEF: not keeping up with]
3. Sirenia always <u>talks back to</u> her mother. [DEF: responds flippantly]
4. It's not always easy to <u>keep up with</u> your older siblings. [DEF: maintain the same pace as]
5. Please <u>drop in on</u> your ailing father some time. [DEF: visit]
6. Guests are asked to <u>check out of</u> the hotel by noon. [DEF: pay the bill and leave]
7. How can you <u>put up with</u> a roommate like that? [DEF: tolerate]
8. We <u>ran out of</u> gas on the Bay Bridge. [DEF: used up all of]
9. Amanda always <u>gets along with</u> animals very well. [DEF: has a harmonious relationship with]
10. I have to <u>catch up on</u> my homework or I'm going to flunk out. [DEF: complete unfinished work]

13.13

1. a) *The room was so warm that Rob took [out] his sweater.
   b) correct type of object (something)
      correct object (took out *his sweater*)
      correct structure (verb + particle + object)
      correct possible form (took out *his sweater*)
   c) *The room was so warm that Rob took [out] his sweater.
      The room was so warm that Rob took off   his sweater.
      Explanation: The context of the sentence is that the temperature is high. Therefore, it is more likely that Rob would remove (*take off*) his sweater than take it out to wear.

2. a) *Mrs. Couret has [looked her mother after] since she became ill.
   b) correct particle (*after*)
      correct type of object (somebody)
      correct object (look after *her mother*)
   c) *Mrs. Couret has [looked her mother after] since she became ill.
      Mrs. Couret has looked after her mother   since she became ill.
      Explanation: The phrasal verb *look after* is not separable.

3. a) *Several people dropped in on [the museum] last week.
   b) correct particles (*in on*)   correct separability (nonseparable)
      correct structure (verb + particles + object)
   c) *Several people dropped in on [the museum]   last week.
      Several people dropped in on the museum director last week.
      Explanation: One drops in on a person, not a thing.

4. a) *The artist [crossed out] the large cupboard from her tiny studio.
   b) correct particle (*cross + out*)
      correct type of object (something)
      correct structure (verb + particle + object)
   c) *The artist [crossed out] the large cupboard from her tiny studio.
      The artist removed   the large cupboard from her tiny studio.
      Explanation: The phrasal verb *cross out* has the sense of "remove" but it is limited to removing words or pictures from a page by drawing a line through them and not to removing pieces of furniture.

5. a) *Could you please help me to pick [at] a new hat?
   b) correct type of object (something)   correct structure (verb + particle + object)
      correct possible form (*pick at a new hat*)
   c) *Could you please help me to pick [at] a new hat?
      Could you please help me to pick out a new hat?
      Explanation: Pick at means to pull apart into small pieces. It is more likely that one would select (*pick out*) a hat than destroy it.

6. a) *My cousin looks [for] to coming to the wedding.
   b) correct type of object (something)   correct separability (nonseparable)
      correct object (look forward to *coming to a wedding*)
      correct structure (verb + particle   VERB$_{ing}$)
   c) *My cousin looks [for]   to coming to the wedding.
      My cousin looks forward to coming to the wedding.
      Explanation: The student has confused the prepositional verb *look for* with the phrasal-prepositional verb *look forward to*. One is more likely to look forward to a wedding than to look for one.

7. a) *Before you buy that car, you had better [check out it] carefully.
   b) correct particle (*check + out*)
      correct type of object (something)
      correct object (check out *that car*)
   c) *Before you buy that car, you had better [check out it] carefully.
      Before you buy that car, you had better check it out carefully.
      Explanation: Check out is a separable phrasal verb. Therefore, the pronoun form of the object (*it*) must come between the verb and the particle.

8. a) *The employer had to think [her] over before he gave Ms. Green the job.
   b) correct particle (*think + over*)
      correct separability (*think over* is separable))
   c) *The employer had to think [her] over before he gave Ms. Green the job.
      The employer had to think it   over before he gave Ms. Green the job.
      Explanation: Think over requires an inanimate object, not an animate one.

9. a) *The store detective [handed the shoplifter in] and then returned to the floor.
   b) correct particle (*hand in*)
      correct structure (verb + NP + particle with a separable phrasal verb)
   c) *The store detective [handed the shoplifter in] and then returned to the floor.
      The store detective turned the shoplifter in   and then returned to the floor.
      Explanation: One hands in a homework assignment or a project, not a person. In this case, the student probably meant *turn in*, which is the appropriate phrasal verb for an apprehended lawbreaker.

10. a) *We are simply not interested [on] buying any more insurance.
    b) correct type of object (something)   correct separability (nonseparable)
       correct object (interested in *buying insurance*)
       correct structure (adjective + particle + VERB$_{ing}$)
    c) *We are simply not interested [on] buying any more insurance.
       We are simply not interested in   buying any more insurance.
       Explanation: The adjective *interested* requires the particle *in*, not *on*.

Chapter 14

14.1

The rattlesnake belongs to the family of pit vipers, *Crotilidae,* <u>and</u> it is one of the four poisonous snakes in North America. There is a deep pit on each side of the face, between the eye and the nostril. The pit contains a heat-sensitive membrane <u>that</u> helps the rattlesnake find its warm-blooded prey. <u>Although</u> the rattlesnake is a reptile, the female bears live young, <u>so</u> the eggs hatch inside the mother's body. The rattle from <u>which</u> the snake's name is derived consists of a series of rings <u>that</u> strike together <u>when</u> the snake is excited.

14.2

1. [condition] Children must have a source of love and support; <u>otherwise</u>, they will turn to street gangs or other substitute "families."
2. [addition] There will be an examination next Friday; <u>furthermore</u>, it will count for fifty percent of your grade in this course.
3. [choice] People who fear flying can take the train from New York to San Francisco; <u>on the other hand</u>, they can go by ship via the Panama Canal.
4. [summation] That film has a weak story, mediocre acting, and uninspired photography; <u>in summary</u>, it has little chance of being nominated for an Academy Award.
5. [addition] The Suez Canal shortened the route from the Middle East to Europe; <u>in addition</u>, it brought Egypt money and prestige.
6. [condition] The elevators can be used unless there is a fire; <u>in that case</u>, you must use the stairs.
7. [addition] The earth moves around the sun; <u>similarly</u>, the moon orbits round the earth.
8. [explanation] English is the *lingua franca* of the international business community; <u>in other words</u>, it is the language with which most international business people communicate.
9. [exemplification] John's grandfather would do anything for a bottle of whiskey; <u>for example</u>, he once gave someone his deed to a silver mine for a case of Johnnie Walker Red.
10. [addition] Travel increases our understanding of other peoples; <u>in fact</u>, my brother went to India last year, and ever since he's been volunteering at the Refugee Center.

14.3

1. <u>Unless</u> children have a source of love and support, they will turn to street gangs or other substitute "families."
2. There will be an examination next Friday, <u>not to mention the fact that</u> it will count for fifty percent of your grade in this course.
3. (no equivalent)
4. (no equivalent)
5. The Suez Canal shortened the route from the Middle East to Europe, <u>in addition to the fact that</u> it brought Egypt money and prestige.
6. <u>If</u> there is a fire, the elevators cannot be used and you must use the stairs.
7. The earth moves around the sun <u>in the same way as</u> the moon orbits round the earth.
8. (no equivalent)
9. (no equivalent)
10. (no equivalent)

14.4

1. <u>Barring</u> a lack of love and support, children will not turn to street gangs or other substitute "families."
2. There will be an examination next Friday, <u>not to mention</u> the fifty percent of your grade in the course that it will count for.
3. (no equivalent)
4. (no equivalent)
5. The Suez Canal shortened the route from the Middle East to Europe, <u>in addition to</u> bringing Egypt money and prestige.
6. <u>In the event of</u> a fire, the elevators cannot be used and you must use the stairs.
7. (no equivalent)
8. (no equivalent)
9. John's grandfather would do anything for a bottle of whiskey, <u>such as</u> the time he once gave someone his deed to a silver mine for a case of Johnnie Walker Red.
10. (no equivalent)

14.5

1. [g. contrast] Your dog looks quite healthy; <u>however</u>, it is not a good idea to feed a pet table scraps.
2. [rebuttal] The oil was supposed to have come from Saudi Arabia; <u>in fact</u>, it came from Iraq.
3. [s. contrast] The color white is the presence of all the colors of light; <u>in contrast</u>, the color black is the absence of all the colors of light.
4. [rebuttal] The planet Saturn was once thought to have six rings; <u>in fact</u>, it has more than a thousand and possibly as many as a hundred thousand rings.
5. [g. contrast] High-heeled shoes may be very stylish and attractive; <u>however</u>, they can be quite harmful to the feet.

14.6

1. <u>Although</u> your dog looks quite healthy, it is not a good idea to feed a pet table scraps.
2. The oil was supposed to have come from Saudi Arabia <u>when in fact it</u> came from Iraq.
3. <u>Whereas</u> the color white is the presence of all the colors of light, the color black is the absence of all the colors of light.
4. The planet Saturn was once thought to have six rings <u>when in fact</u> it has more than a thousand and possibly as many as a hundred thousand rings.
5. <u>Although</u> high-heeled shoes may be very stylish and attractive, they can be quite harmful to the feet.

14.7

1. <u>In spite of</u> your dog's good health, it is not a good idea to feed a pet table scraps.
2. The oil was supposed to have come from Saudi Arabia <u>instead of</u> Iraq.
3. <u>In contrast with</u> the color white, which is the presence of all the colors of light, the color black is the absence of all the colors of light.
4. The planet Saturn was once thought to have six rings <u>instead of</u> more than a thousand and possibly as many as a hundred thousand rings.
5. <u>In spite of</u> the stylishness and attractiveness of high-heeled shoes, they can be quite harmful to the feet.

14.8

1. [purpose] The child could not stop coughing; <u>for this reason</u>, the doctor gave him some cough medicine.
2. [cause] The tablecloth still has wine and coffee stains on it; <u>the reason is</u>, the laundry forgot to use bleach.
3. [effect] The train was moving very fast; <u>therefore</u>, it could not stop in time to avoid hitting the car on the railroad crossing.
4. [effect] The car had a lock on the steering wheel; <u>therefore</u>, car thieves ignored it.
5. [cause] The Mississippi River flooded in 1993; <u>the reason is</u>, there was a heavy winter snow layer in the mountains.

14.9

1. The doctor gave the child some cough medicine <u>so that</u> he would stop coughing.
2. The tablecloth still has wine and coffee stains on it <u>because</u> the laundry forgot to use bleach.
3. The train was moving <u>so</u> fast <u>that</u> it could not stop in time to avoid hitting the car on the railroad crossing.
4. The car had <u>such</u> a good lock on the steering wheel <u>that</u> car thieves ignored it.
5. The Mississippi River flooded in 1993 <u>because</u> there was a heavy winter snow layer in the mountains.

14.10

1. The doctor gave the child some cough medicine <u>because of</u> his cough./The doctor gave the child some cough medicine <u>(in order) to</u> stop his cough.
2. The tablecloth still has wine and coffee stains on it <u>because of</u> the laundry's failure to use bleach./The laundry failed to use bleach <u>(in order) to</u> remove the wine and coffee stains.
3. <u>Because of</u> its speed, the train could not stop in time to avoid hitting the car on the railroad crossing.
4. Car thieves ignored the car <u>because of</u> the lock on the steering wheel.
5. The Mississippi River flooded in 1993 <u>because of</u> a heavy winter snow layer in the mountains.

14.11

A. The river was polluted
1. ; in addition, **c.**
2. ; in contrast, **g.**
3. ; in fact, **e.**
4. ; in other words, **b.**
5. , whereas **g.**
6. , for example, **e.**
7. , not to mention the fact that **c.**
8. ; however, **g.**
9. in addition to **a.**
10. , by which I mean that **b.**
11. , e.g., **e.**
12. ; in short, **d.**
13. ; on the other hand, **g.**
14. in spite of **f.**
15. although **g.**

B. Howard was a doctor and a researcher
1. ; in addition, **a.**
2. ; in contrast, **e.**
3. ; in fact, **b.**
9. in addition to **f.**
10. , by which I mean that **b/g.**
11. , e.g., **g.**

4. ; in other words, **b.**   12. ; in short, **b.**
5. , whereas **e.**   13. ; on the other hand, **e.**
6. ; for example, **g.**   14. in spite of **d.**
7. , not to mention the fact that **c.**15. although **e.**
8. ; however, **e.**

14.12

1. [sequence] The patient was conscious for a few minutes; <u>after that</u>, she went into a coma and   died.
2. [sequence] Mr. Packwood was asked to produce his personal diary; <u>until then</u>, such a request had never been made of a senator.
3. [simultaneity] Dinosaurs roamed the earth during the Jurassic and Cretaceous periods; <u>at that time</u>, the earth was generally warmer than it is now.
4. [sequence] A few pieces of the satellite fell into the ocean; <u>before that</u>, most of it had burned up in the earth's atmosphere.
5. [sequence] The sun will eclipse again in 1999; <u>by then</u>, there will have been a number of lunar eclipses.
6. [sequence] The country became independent in 1960; <u>since then</u>, it has experienced economic stagnation.

14.13

1. <u>After</u> the patient was conscious for a few minutes, she went into a coma and died.
2. <u>Until</u> Mr. Packwood was asked to produce his personal diary, such a request had never been made of a senator.
3. <u>When</u> dinosaurs roamed the earth during the Jurassic and Cretaceous periods, the earth was generally warmer than it is now.
4. Most of the satellite had burned up in the earth's atmosphere <u>before</u> a few pieces of it fell into the ocean.
5. <u>By the time that</u> the sun eclipses again in 1999, there will have been a number of lunar eclipses.
6. <u>Since</u> the country became independent in 1960, it has experienced economic stagnation.

14.14

1. a) *The plant survived [eventhough] it had had no water for months.
   b) correct choice of coordinator or subordinator (subordinator)
       correct category of coordinator/subordinator (the BUT group)
       correct position of coordinator/subordinator (at the front of the dependent clause)
       correct punctuation (none)
   c) *The plant survived [eventhough] it had had no water for months.
       The plant survived even though   it had had no water for months.
       Explanation: Even though is two separate words, not one like *although*.

2. a) *The reward was not given[; until,] the criminal had been captured.
   b) correct choice of coordinator or subordinator (subordinator)
       correct category of coordinator/subordinator (the chronological group)
       correct form of coordinator/subordinator (*until*)
       correct position of coordinator/subordinator (at the front of the dependent clause)
   c) *The reward was not given[; until,] the criminal had been captured
       The reward was not given until   the criminal had been captured.
       Explanation: Chronological subordinate clauses in the adverbial slot do not require punctuation. In this case, the student has used punctuation suitable for a coordinator (conjunctive adverb), not for a subordinator.

3. a) *[In that case] you have a question, please see the professor during her office hours.
   b) correct category of coordinator/subordinator (the AND group)
       correct form of coordinator or subordinator (*in that case*)
       correct position of coordinator/subordinator (at the front of the dependent clause)
       correct punctuation (comma after fronted dependent clause)
   c) *[In that case] you have a question, please see the professor during her office hours.
       If   you have a question, please see the professor during her office hours.
       Explanation: When the sentence combining device is placed at the beginning of a sentence, the combined sentence is set up for a subordinator, not a coordinator.

4. a) *There is snow on the ground, the trees have no leaves, and it is very cold. It must be [, in short] winter.
   b) correct choice of coordinator or subordinator (coordinator)
      correct category of coordinator/subordinator (the AND group)
      correct form of coordinator/subordinator (*in short*) [possible]
      correct punctuation (commas surrounding coordinator in sentence-medial position)
   c) *There is snow…and it is very cold. It must be [, in short,] winter.
      There is snow…and it is very cold. In short, it must be winter.
      Explanation: A coordinator cannot be placed between the main verb and a predicate NP. Coordinators of summation usually come at the beginning of an independent clause.

5. a) *First, the class designed the boat. Then, it built the boat. [Nevertheless], it tested the boat in the swimming pool.
   b) correct choice of coordinator or subordinator (coordinator)
      correct form of coordinator/subordinator (*nevertheless*) [possible]
      correct position of coordinator/subordinator (at the front of the independent clause)
      correct punctuation (period before coordinator; comma after coordinator)
   c) *First, the class…built the boat. [Nevertheless], it tested the boat in the swimming pool.
      First, the class…built the boat. Finally,   it tested the boat in the swimming pool.
      Explanation: This sentence calls for a chronological coordinator, not a logical coordinator.

6. a) *The pump circulates the cooling water the heart circulates blood [much as] .
   b) correct choice of coordinator or subordinator (subordinator)
      correct category of coordinator/subordinator (the AND group)
      correct form of coordinator/subordinator (*much as*) [possible]
      correct punctuation (none)
   c) *The pump circulates the cooling water the heart circulates blood [much as].
      The pump circulates the cooling water much as the heart circulates blood.
      Explanation: A subordinator always occurs at the front of the dependent clause.

7. a) *The glass got so hot[; that,] it burned Janie's fingers.
   b) correct choice of coordinator or subordinator (subordinator)
      correct category of coordinator/subordinator (the SO group)
      correct form of coordinator/subordinator (*so…ADJ…that*) [possible]
      correct position of coordinator/subordinator (*so* before ADJ; *that* after ADJ)
   c) *The glass got so hot[; that,] it burned Janie's fingers.
      The glass got so hot that   it burned Janie's fingers.
      Explanation: The subordinator *so…that* requires no punctuation. The student has punctuated *that* as if it were a coordinator.

8. a) *Imelda has fifty dresses; [on the contrary], she has a hundred pairs of shoes.
   b) correct choice of coordinator or subordinator (coordinator)
      correct form of coordinator/subordinator (*on the contrary*) [possible]
      correct position of coordinator/subordinator (at the front of the independent clause)
      correct punctuation (semicolon before coordinator; comma after coordinator)
   c) *Imelda has fifty dresses; [on the contrary], she has a hundred pairs of shoes.
      Imelda has fifty dresses; in addition,   she has a hundred pairs of shoes.
      Explanation: The second sentence has an AND relationship to the first, not a BUT relationship.

9. a) *The old man collected some wood [for this reason] he could start a fire.
   b) correct category of coordinator/subordinator (the SO group)
      correct form of coordinator/subordinator (*for this reason*) [possible]
      correct position of coordinator/subordinator (at the front of the dependent clause)
      correct punctuation (none)
   c) *The old man collected some wood [for this reason] he could start a fire.
      The old man collected some wood so that   he could start a fire.
      Explanation: The punctuation and the modal *could* requires that the second sentence have a subordinate rather than a coordinate relationship to the first.

10. a) *Pluto is a small planet; [in deed], it is the smallest planet in the Solar System.
    b) correct choice of coordinator or subordinator (coordinator)
       correct category of coordinator/subordinator (the AND group)
       correct position of coordinator/subordinator (at the front of the independent clause)

correct punctuation (semicolon before coordinator; comma after coordinator)
c) *Pluto is a small planet; [in deed], it is the smallest planet in the Solar System.
Pluto is a small planet; indeed,   it is the smallest planet in the Solar System.
Explanation: The coordinator *indeed* is written as a single word, not as two words.

Chapter 15

15.1

1. The police promised to find the boy who had been kidnapped.
2. Roger has refused to accept a scholarship at a religious college.
3. Maria agreed to pay back the money she borrowed.
4. The wounded fox was trying to hide in the corner of the garden.
5. Scientists are attempting to map the entire human genome, or genetic blueprint.

15.2

1. The native peoples believed their village to be the center of the World.
2. Alicia's grandfather advised her to accept the offer of marriage from the diplomat.
3. The judges determined the man from Korea to be the winner of the wrestling match.
4. The miners expected the tunnel to be repaired by the next morning.
5. The children's teacher told them to take the frog back to the pond.

15.3

1. To take the bus is too late.
   It is too late to take the bus.
2. To be a member of Parliament would require a great deal of money.
   It would require a great deal of money to be a member of Parliament.
3. To become a member of the resistance was a dangerous and courageous act.
   It was a dangerous and courageous act to become a member of the resistance.
4. To own a Mercedes Benz is quite prestigious.
   It is quite prestigious to own a Mercedes Benz.
5. To live in an old people's home is not something we look forward to.
   It is not something we look forward to to live in an old people's home.

15.4

1. For ESL teachers to be well trained is important.
   It is important for ESL teachers to be well trained.
2. For Hawaii to become the fiftieth state was a logical step.
   It was a logical step for Hawaii to become the fiftieth state.
3. For John to accept another position would anger the members of the board.
   It would anger the members of the board for John to accept another position.
4. For Mary to be gone for so long was odd.
   It was odd for Mary to be gone for so long.
5. For Clara to get a scholarship at the music conservatory was appropriate.
   It was appropriate for Clara to get a scholarship at the music conservatory.

15.5

1. That nurse was an angel to bring my father a chocolate milkshake.
2. The wooden duck was a decoy to attract females.
3. The counselor was a genius to suggest a horse-riding camp for the homeless children.
4. The investors were idiots to think they could make a profit in six months.
5. The covered pit was a trap to catch tigers.

15.6

1. The Olympic athletes were anxious to begin the trials.
2. The refugees were happy to find shelter in a neighboring country.
3. The district attorney was furious to learn that the prisoners had escaped.
4. The old actress was delighted to be nominated for an Academy Award.
5. We were sad to hear that your puppy was killed.

15.7

1. <u>The mother</u> would be afraid for <u>her young children</u> to walk to school by themselves.
2. <u>The professor</u> would be happy for <u>the student</u> to write the paper again.
3. <u>The artist</u> was anxious for <u>the beautiful model</u> to pose for him.
4. <u>The author</u> would be delighted for <u>her book</u> to be awarded a Pulitzer Prize.
5. <u>The general</u> would be proud for <u>his son</u> to join the air force.

15.8

1. The babysitter had the children clean their teeth before they went to bed.
2. The astronomer watched the supernova expand to ten times its original size.
3. The dictator made the intelligentsia work in the countryside.
4. The old man felt the earthquake roll up the valley.
5. The people in the stands heard the plane break the sound barrier.

15.9

1. Victoria cannot stand being with people who smoke cigarettes.
2. The reporter mentioned seeing a gun in the victim's bedroom.
3. I could understand desiring to work in a friendly environment.
4. The therapist denied having too many patients.
5. The woman could not imagine living with other elderly people.

15.10

1. The widow misses her husband's kissing her every morning.
   The widow misses her husband kissing her every morning.
2. The Dean's Office recommended the student's being put on probation.
   The Dean's Office recommended the student being put on probation.
3. President Ronald Reagan denied Vice President George Walker Bush's knowing about the arms-for-hostages deal
   with Iran.
   President Ronald Reagan denied Vice President George Walker Bush knowing about the arms-for-hostages deal
   with Iran.
4. The coach urged the team's trying out for the Olympic Games.
   The coach urged the team trying out for the Olympic Games.
5. *The newspaper admitted those's being unconfirmed reports. [Note: *Those* has no possessive form.]
   The newspaper admitted those being unconfirmed reports.

15.11

1. Being famous cannot compensate for life's troubles.
2. His suggesting this hotel in the Dolomites was a great idea.
3. The government's practicing fiscal restraint should stimulate the ecconomy.
4. Reaching a goal is less important than the process of getting there.
5. *The New York Times/Times'* printing the victim's name caused more harm than good.

15.12

1. The biggest difficulty is getting the peasants to register to vote.
2. The motive appeared to be his wanting to punish his former employer.
   The motive appeared to be him wanting to punish his former employer.
3. The advantage will be the company's having control over the production facilities.
   The advantage will be the company having control over the production facilities.
4. The problem was the former Union of Soviet Socialist Republics' dissolving before the infrastructure was complete.
   The problem was the former Union of Soviet Socialist Republics dissolving before the infrastructure was complete.
5. The alternative was doing some kind of community service. [Note: Inconsequential subjects such as *someone* are
   commonly deleted in this structure.]

15.13

1. The cat is no longer frightened by the dog's barking at the mailman.
   The cat is no longer frightened by the dog barking at the mailman.
2. The soldier's children were not certain of still having a father.
3. The princess was thankful for the knight's saving her from the local dragon.
   The princess was thankful for the knight saving her from the local dragon.
4. The government is opposed to the church's wanting prayer in the public schools.
   The government is opposed to the church wanting prayer in the public schools.
5. The athlete was disappointed at not making his last high jump.

15.14

1. The doctor heard the old man's heart beating feebly.
2. Marianne noticed a spider crawling up her leg.
3. The lawyer witnessed a taxi picking up one of the suspects.
4. The campers felt the hot tea warming their insides.
5. Several astronauts observed small asteroids flying past the shuttle.

15.15

1. Earning over $80,000 a year, the Carltons could afford a three-week vacation in Hawaii.
   The Carltons could afford a three-week vacation in Hawaii, earning over $80,000 a year.
2. Her husband working for a nearby coal company, Mrs. Gooch was always worried about mining accidents.
   Mrs. Gooch was always worried about mining accidents, her husband working for a nearby coal company.
3. After refusing to give up, the marathon runner felt an unexpected burst of energy.
   The marathon runner felt an unexpected burst of energy after refusing to give up.
4. The ferry sinking rapidly, the captain ordered the passengers into the lifeboats.
   The captain ordered the passengers into the lifeboats, the ferry sinking rapidly.
5. Wearing nothing but a fly swatter, the rock star walked boldly into the theater.
   The rock star walked boldly into the theater, wearing nothing but a fly swatter.

15.16

1. Being a careful person, Janine was really upset by the error.
2. Correct. The dam overflowing with the winter rains, the village below was in great danger.
3. Bursting with pride, the captain of the winning team accepted the gold cup.
4. Correct. Freezing in the icy winds, the dogs huddled together and waited for their master.
5. Moving slowly westward, the raging brush fire soon ravaged the dry mountains.

15.17

1. The country expected to have increased its exports to Russia by now.
2. For Marie Curie to have discovered radium was a shock to the male scientists.
3. To have lost a parent at a young age is something only an orphan understands.
4. The contractor agreed to have completed the renovation within three months.
5. Rosa was not happy for her father to have declared bankruptcy.

15.18

1. Brian knows what poverty means, having traveled widely in India. [causal]
   Having traveled widely in India, Brian knows what poverty means.
2. Clothilde remembered having lived in a chateau when she was a girl. [chronological]
3. The prisoners proceeded with their escape plans, the guard having turned out the light. [ambiguous]
4. Barbara was happy with her brother's having found a woman he could love. [causal]
5. The dinosaurs' probably having evolved into birds was a major discovery. [chronological]

15.19

1. a) <u>That they will pass English 1</u> is expected by the instructor.
   b) <u>It is expected by the instructor</u> that they will pass English 1.
   c) <u>For them to pass English 1</u> is expected by the instructor.
   d) It is expected by the instructor <u>for them to pass English 1</u>.
   e) <u>Their passing English 1</u> is expected by the instructor.

2. a) <u>That we vote</u> is very important.
   b) It is very important <u>that we vote</u>.
   c) <u>For us to vote</u> is very important.
   d) It is very important <u>for us to vote</u>.
   e) <u>Our voting</u> is very important.

3. a) The old woman had no desire to live, <u>having lost her husband</u>.
   b) <u>Having lost her husband</u>, the old woman had no desire to live.

4. a) <u>That one is healthy</u> is the greatest gift.
   b) It is the greatest gift <u>that one is healthy</u>.
   c) <u>To be healthy</u> is the greatest gift.
   d) It is the greatest gift <u>to be healthy</u>.
   e) <u>Being healthy</u> is the greatest gift.

5. a) <u>The fact that he snores</u> is hated by Elizabeth.
   b) Elizabeth hates <u>the fact that he snores</u>.
   c) <u>For him to snore</u> is hated by Elizabeth.
   d) Elizabeth hates <u>for him to snore</u>.
   e) Elizabeth hates <u>his snoring</u>.

15.20

1. a) *Harriet wanted [that you buy] some ice cream.
   b) correct complement form (*that* + independent clause) ^{possible}
      correct position of complement (object slot)
   c) *Harriet wanted [that you buy] some ice cream.
      Harriet wanted you to buy   some ice cream.
      Explanation: The hypothetical nature of the verb *want* requires that it have an infinitive rather than a *that*-clause or VERB$_{ing}$ complement.

2. a) *The generator is [, having worked for three consecutive weeks,] broken again.
   b) correct type of complement (sequential ING-participle)
      correct complementizer (*-ing*)
      correct complement form (*having* + VERB$_{ed_2}$) ^{possible}
   c) *The generator is [, having worked for three consecutive weeks,] broken again.
      Having worked for three consecutive weeks, the generator is broken again.
      The generator is broken again, having worked for three consecutive weeks.
      Explanation: ING-participle complements that do not contain perception verbs can only occur in the adverbial slot.

3. a) *[ ] Is lucky that your sister found an apartment.
   b) correct type of complement (*that*-clause)
      correct complementizer (*that*)
      correct complement form (*that* + independent clause) ^{possible}
      correct position of complement (predicate adjective slot)
   c) *[ ] Is lucky that your sister found an apartment.
      It is lucky that your sister found an apartment.
      Explanation: It-focus requires that the dummy subject *it* fill the subject slot.

4. a) *The mayor insisted on [to give] the hero a parade.
   b) correct complement form (*to* + VERB$_{base}$) ^{possible}
      correct position of complement (object slot)
   c) *The mayor insisted on [to give] the hero a parade.
      The mayor insisted on giving   the hero a parade.
      Explanation: Allied particles or prepositions can only be followed by gerund complements.

5. a) *[Them] planting a redwood tree inspired other lumberjacks.
    b) correct type of complement (gerund)
       correct position of complement (subject slot)
    c) *[Them] planting a redwood tree inspired other lumberjacks.
       Their   planting a redwood tree inspired other lumberjacks.
       Explanation: When a gerund structure has a specific pronoun subject and occurs as a subject
                      complement, the pronoun must be transformed into a possessive determiner.

6. a) *The company made the manager [to resign].
    b) correct type of complement (infinitive)
       correct possible complement form (*to* + VERB$_{base}$)
       correct position of complement (object slot)
    c) *The company made the manager [to resign].
       The company made the manager resign.
       Explanation: Causative *make* requires that an infinitive complement have no *to*-complementizer.

7. a) *[To have reigned] for six weeks, the young king was murdered.
    b) correct possible complement form (*to* + *have* + VERB$_{ed_2}$)
       correct position of complement (fronted adverbial slot)
    c) *[To have reigned] for six weeks, the young king was murdered.
       Having reigned   for six weeks, the young king was murdered.
       Explanation: Adverbial complements must be ING-participle complements; they cannot be infinitive
                      complements.

8. a) *It [ ] hard for a young single woman to be a good parent.
    b) correct type of complement (infinitive)
       correct complementizer (*for, to*)
       correct possible complement form (*to* + VERB$_{base}$)
       correct position of complement (predicate adjective slot)
    c) *It [ ] hard for a young single woman to be a good parent.
       It is hard for a young single woman to be a good parent.
       Explanation: An *it*-focus structure requires *it* as a dummy subject for the main verb. The main verb,
                      therefore, cannot be deleted.

9. a) *The boys saw the [teacher's] kissing the principal.
    b) correct type of complement (ING-participle structure)
       correct possible complement form (simultaneous ING-participle)
       correct position of complement (object slot)
    c) *The boys saw the [teacher's] kissing the principal.
       The boys saw the teacher   kissing the principal.
       Explanation: ING-participle structures may not be possessive.

10. a) *It is [for his wife to go with him] necessary.
    b) correct type of complement (infinitive)
       correct complementizer (*for/to*)
       correct possible complement form (*for* + NP, *to* + VERB$_{base}$)
    c) *It is [for his wife] necessary to go with him.
       It is necessary for his wife to go with him.
       Explanation: Infinitive structures as predicate adjective complements must follow the predicate
                      adjective, not precede it.

15.21 (a = full; b = abbreviated)

1a. Mrs. Smith has as many children as Mrs. Jones (does).
 b. Mrs. Smith has as much as Mrs. Jones (does).
2a. Farmer Dan grew more pumpkins than Farmer Dave (did).
 b. Farmer Dan grew more than Farmer Dave (did).
3a. The ABC Company has more toxic-waste sites than the XYZ Company (does).
 b. The ABC Company has more than the XYZ Company (does).
4a. The Hoover Dam reservoir holds more water (or more cubic feet of water) than the Shasta Dam reservoir
    (does).
 b. The Hoover Dam reservoir holds more than the Shasta Dam reservoir (does).
5a. In 1987, Louisiana executed more prisoners than Texas (did).
 b. In 1987, Louisiana executed more (often) than Texas (did).

15.22 (a = full; b = abbreviated)

1a. Joan suffers fewer migraine headaches a week than Diane (does).
 b. Joan suffers less than Diane (does).
2a. The youngster knows the capitals of fewer countries than his grandfather (does).
 b. The youngster knows less than his grandfather (does).
3a. Richard enjoys himself at fewer parties a month than Ronald (does).
 b. Richard enjoys himself less than Ronald (does).
4a. *Newsweek* costs fewer dollars than *Vanity Fair* (does).
 b. *Newsweek* costs less than *Vanity Fair* (does).
5a. Susie learned fewer words a day than Mandy (did).
 b. Susie learned less than Mandy (did).

15.23 (a= full; b = abbreviated)

1a. Polonium is as rare an element as tellurium (is).
 b. Polonium is as rare as tellurium (is).
2a. Cuba is a larger island than Ireland (is).
 b. Cuba is larger than Ireland (is).
3a. The Williamsburg is as long a bridge as the Newport (is).
 b. The Williamsburg is as long as the Newport (is).
 [Alternative: The Williamsburg Bridge is as long as the Newport Bridge (is).]
4a. The Suez is a wider canal than the Panama (is).
 b. The Suez is wider than the Panama (is).
 [Alternative: The Suez Canal is wider than the Panama Canal (is).]
5a. The St. Gotthard is an older tunnel than the Mt. Blanc (is).
 b. The St. Gotthard is older than the Mt. Blanc (is).
 [Alternative: The St. Gotthard Tunnel is older than the Mt. Blanc Tunnel (is).]

15.24

1a. Rodney is a less intelligent person than William (is).
 b. Rodney is less intelligent than William (is).
2a. Mt. McKinley is a lower mountain than Mt. Everest (is).
 b. Mt. McKinley is lower than Mt. Everest (is).
3a. The Kalahari Desert is a smaller desert than the Sahara Desert (is).
 b. The Kalahari Desert is smaller than the Sahara Desert (is).
4a. The wing span of a B-52 bomber is fewer feet than the wing span of a C-5A transport (is).
 b. The wing span of a B-52 bomber is less than the wing span of a C-5A transport (is).
 [Alternative: The wing span of a B-52 bomber is less that that of a C-5A transport. (is)]
5a. Mercury is a cooler planet at the surface than Venus (is).
 b. Mercury is cooler at the surface than Venus (is).

15.25

1. a) *An elephant eats more food than a monkey [is].
 b) correct comparison marker (*more*)
 correct complementizer (*than*)
 correct position of complement (object slot)
 c) *An elephant eats more food than a monkey [is].
 An elephant eats more food than a monkey does.
 Explanation: If a non-linking (Type I) verb in the complement is retained in a comparison, it must be in the form of auxiliary *do.*

2. a) *An apple has as [much] calories as an egg.
 b) correct complementizer (*as*)
 correct complement structure (complementizer + subordinate clause subject)
 correct position of complement (object slot)
 c) *An apple has as [much] calories as an egg.
 An apple has as many   calories as an egg.
 Explanation: Calories is a countable noun and therefore requires the comparison marker *as many.*

3. a) *Linda [as Roberta] is as good a skier.
   b) correct comparison marker (*as*)
      correct complementizer (*as*)
      correct complement structure (complementizer + subordinate clause subject)
   c) *Linda [as Roberta] is as good a skier.
      Linda is as good a skier as Roberta.
      Explanation: A comparison complement cannot be a subject complement.

4. a) *Donald's brother has the same car [like] his sister.
   b) correct comparison marker (*the same*)
      correct complement structure (complementizer + subordinate clause subject)
      correct position of complement (object slot)
   c) *Donald's brother has the same car [like] his sister.
      Donald's brother has the same car as   his sister.
      Explanation: Similarity requires the complementizer *as*. *Like* is not a complementizer.

5. a) *A topographical map is [exacter] than a tourist map.
   b) correct comparison marker (*-er*)
      correct complementizer (*than*)
      correct complement structure (complementizer + subordinate clause subject)
      correct position of complement (predicate adjective slot)
   c) *A topographical map is [exacter]   than a tourist map.
      A topographical map is more exact than a tourist map.
      Explanation: The two syllable adjective *exact* is one of those that requires the comparison marker *more* rather than *-er*.

6. a) *A truck weighs [than a locomotive] less.
   b) correct comparison marker (*less*)
      correct complementizer (*than*)
      correct complement structure (complementizer + subordinate clause subject)
   c) *A truck weighs [than a locomotive] less.
      A truck weighs less than a locomotive.
      Explanation: Comparison complements always come after the comparison marker, not before.

7. a) *The Mississippi is [more longer] than the Rio Grande.
   b) correct complementizer (*than*)
      correct complement structure (complementizer + subordinate clause subject)
      correct position of complement (predicate adjective slot)
   c) *The Mississippi is [more longer] than the Rio Grande.
      The Mississippi is longer   than the Rio Grande.
      Explanation: Single syllable adjectives require the *-er* comparison marker. Two comparison markers are not allowed.

8. a) *Germany has fewer nuclear reactors than Japan [has them].
   b) correct comparison marker (*fewer*)
      correct complementizer (*than*)
      correct position of complement (object slot)
   c) *Germany has fewer nuclear reactors than Japan [has them].
      Germany has fewer nuclear reactors than Japan does.
      Explanation: If a verb phrase follows the subject of the complement subordinate clause, it must be in the form of an auxiliary verb (or the linking verb *be*).

9. a) *Sandy weighs as much [than] Lee.
   b) correct comparison marker (*as much*)
      correct complementizer structure (complementizer + subordinate clause subject)
      correct position of complement (verb slot)
   c) *Sandy weighs as much [than] Lee.
      Sandy weighs as much as   Lee.
      Explanation: The complementizer for similarity is *as*, not *than*.

10. a) *The diplomats drank [fewer] wine than the politicians.
    b) correct complementizer (*than*)
       correct complementizer structure (complementizer + subordinate clause subject)
       correct position of complement (object slot)
    c) *The diplomats drank [fewer] wine than the politicians.
       The diplomats drank less   wine than the politicians.
       Explanation: In a negative comparison, the comparison marker for an uncountable noun must be *less*.

IRREGULAR VERBS

arise	arose	arisen	mean	meant	meant
awake	awoke	awakened	meet	met	met
be	was	been	pay	paid	paid
bear	bore	borne	put	put	put
beat	beat	beaten	read	read	read
become	became	become	rid	rid	rid
begin	began	begun	ride	rode	ridden
bend	bent	bent	rise	rose	risen
bid (offer)	bid	bid	ring	rang	rung
bind	bound	bound	run	ran	run
bite	bit	bitten	say	said	said
bleed	bled	bled	see	saw	seen
blow	blew	blown	seek	sought	sought
break	broke	broken	sell	sold	sold
breed	bred	bred	send	sent	sent
build	built	built	set	set	set
burst	burst	burst	shake	shook	shaken
buy	bought	bought	shed	shed	shed
cast	cast	cast	shine	shone	shone
catch	caught	caught	shoot	shot	shot
choose	chose	chosen	show	showed	shown
cling	clung	clung	shrink	shrank	shrunk
come	came	come	shut	shut	shut
cost	cost	cost	sing	sang	sung
cut	cut	cut	sink	sank	sunk
deal	dealt	dealt	sit	sat	sat
dig	dug	dug	sleep	slept	slept
do	did	done	slide	slid	slid
draw	drew	drawn	sling	slung	slung
drink	drank	drunk	slit	slit	slit
drive	drove	driven	speak	spoke	spoken
eat	ate	eaten	spend	spent	spent
fall	fell	fallen	spin	spun	spun
feed	fed	fed	spit	spat	spat
feel	felt	felt	split	split	split
fight	fought	fought	spread	spread	spread
find	found	found	spring	sprang	sprung
flee	fled	fled	stand	stood	stood
fling	flung	flung	steal	stole	stolen
fly	flew	flown	stick	stuck	stuck
forbid	forbade	forbidden	sting	stung	stung
forget	forgot	forgotten	stink	stank	stunk
forsake	forsook	forsaken	strike	struck	struck
freeze	froze	frozen	string	strung	strung
get	got	gotten	sweep	swept	swept
give	gave	given	swear	swore	sworn
go	went	gone	swim	swam	swum
grind	ground	ground	swing	swung	swung
grow	grew	grown	take	took	taken
have	had	had	teach	taught	taught
hear	heard	heard	tear	tore	torn
hide	hid	hidden	tell	told	told
hit	hit	hit	think	thought	thought
hold	held	held	throw	threw	thrown
hurt	hurt	hurt	thrust	thrust	thrust
keep	kept	kept	tread	trod	trodden
kneel	knelt	knelt	understand	understood	understood
know	knew	known	undertake	undertook	undertaken
lay (v.t.)	laid	laid	wake	woke	woken
lead	led	led	wear	wore	worn
leave	left	left	weave	wove	woven
lend	lent	lent	win	won	won
let	let	let	wind	wound	wound
lie (v.i.)	lay	lain	withdraw	withdrew	withdrawn
lose	lost	lost	wring	wrung	wrung
make	made	made	write	wrote	written

SEPARABLE AND NONSEPARABLE

SEPARABLE		NONSEPARABLE	
ask out	name for	ask for	look forward to
bring about	pass out [distribute]	become of	look up to
bring back	pass up [not take]	call for	pass away [die]
bring on	pay back	call on	pick on [annoy]
bring out [reveal]	pick out	catch on [fashion]	put up with
bring up	pick up	catch up (with)	run into [meet]
call back	point out	check in [a hotel]	run across
call down [scold]	put across [explain]	check into [a hotel]	run out (of)
call in	put away	check out (of)	see about
call off	put back	check up (on)	show up [appear]
call up	put off	come across [meet]	sit down
carry out	put on	come along	stand up [rise]
check off	put out [extinguish]	come up [arise]	take after
check out	run down [criticize]	come to [total]	talk back (to)
cheer up	run over [hit by car]	drop by [visit]	turn out [happen]
clean up	save up	drop in (on)	turn up [appear]
cross off	take back	drop out (of) [leave]	wait on
cross out	take off	do without	
cut out	take on	get along (with)	
do over	take out	get behind (in)	
drop off	take over	get in [board]	
figure out	take up [begin]	get into	
fill out	talk over	get off [deboard]	
find out	tear down	get on [board]	
get back (from)	tear up	get out (of)	
give back	think over	get over	
give up	think through	get through (with)	
give out	think up	get up	
hand in	throw away	go over	
hand down	throw out	go through	
hang up	throw up [vomit]	go with [harmonize]	
have on [wear]	try on	grow up	
hold up	try out	keep off [stay away]	
hold down	turn down	keep on [continue]	
keep out (of)	turn in [submit]	keep up (with)	
kick out (of)	turn off	lie down	
look over	turn on	look after	
look up	turn out [a light]	look down on	
make out [under-stand]	turn over	look for	
make up [invent]	turn up	look in (on)	
name after	wake up	look into	
		look out (for)	

INDEX

CPSIA information can be obtained
at www.ICGtesting.com
Printed in the USA
FSHW01n1942290818
51883FS